AIRLINES OF LATIN AMERICA
SINCE 1919

A typical South American air transport scene during the pioneering days—SCADTA's Junkers-F 13 seaplane C-26 *Nariño* moored to the bank of the Magdalena River in Colombia. This F 13 has the modified tail unit introduced in 1926. (*AVIANCA*)

AIRLINES
OF
LATIN AMERICA
SINCE 1919

R. E. G. DAVIES

SMITHSONIAN INSTITUTION PRESS
WASHINGTON, D.C.

BY THE SAME AUTHOR

A History of the World's Airlines
Airlines of the United States since 1914

HE
9815.5
.A3
D38
1984

#10184078

$10.11.85

Library of Congress Cataloging in Publication Data

Davies, R. E. G. (Ronald Edward George)
Airlines of Latin America since 1919.

Originally published: London: Putnam, 1983.
Bibliography: p.
Includes index.
1. Air lines—Latin America—History. I. Title.
HE9815.5.A3D38 1984   387.7'065'8   83–600341
ISBN 0–87474–358–3

CONTENTS

601273

Foreword

Airlines of Latin America since 1919 is the third volume of a series of books which have been acclaimed by scholars, reviewers and those most caustic critics of all, fellow writers. This book covers the social, economic, and technical relationships of a wildly adventuresome period in aviation, one in which the value of air transportation as a unifying force was proven beyond all doubt.

Like R. E. G. Davies's earlier books, *A History of the World's Airlines* and *Airlines of the United States since 1914*, this one can be read cover to cover, novel fashion, or can be dipped into like an anthology to savor the succinct anecdotal morsels which bring it alive e.g., the slogan of Aeronaves Nacionales, *'Con Dos Motores, No Hay Tremores'* ('With two engines there are no fears'), a most sanguine estimate of the Curtiss Kingbirds being flown. Another glimmering bit of insight reveals that the Wright Brothers started *Linhas Aereas Wright* in Brazil. It was, however, Francisco 'Chico' Ribeiro Wright and his brothers, rather than Orville and Wilbur. Ron Davies suggests that to expect 'that the Wright brothers could succeed in the land of Alberto Santos Dumont was challenging national sensitivity just a little too far'. Such light-hearted asides apart, this is of course a premier reference work, one from which authors will cull facts and check sources for the next twenty years.

Airlines of Latin America was a much more difficult work to undertake than the previous volumes, for there was far more airline activity in this area, relative to the total population and wealth, than there was in either Europe or the United States. The reason for this is the challenging geography, with its combination of tropical jungles, arid plains, vast mountain ranges and, for the trans-Atlantic lines, long over-water distances. Communities were and still are scattered, often not distant in terms of straight-line miles, but almost inaccessible by any other mode of transportation. There were far fewer records to draw on, for the history of the area is also one of vast political turmoil and much of the information was gained by a long series of personal interviews with the principals.

Davies approaches the monumental task by reviewing the history of the many airlines in a 'north to south' geographical manner as a start; he then follows the development of the multiplicity of airlines as a chronological narrative. The amount of information handled is enormous, for airlines were founded, merged, disbanded or expanded on a continuous basis over the more than six decades the book covers. Davies supplements the text with information-loaded tables and appendices and meticulously drawn maps.

Before I knew Ron Davies, I often wondered how he could create such vast stores of information, much less translate them into highly readable text. Then he was selected to become the Lindbergh Professor, the prestigious Chair at the National Air and Space Museum of the Smithsonian Institution, and the secrets of his success became clear. He works with tremendous energy and speed, and has a retentive memory, upon which he is far too systematic to rely. Instead he files

vi

away information with beaver-like diligence and computer capacity, in the filing cabinets which line his office; he has the capability to retrieve from this treasure trove on demand.

Perhaps more surprising, we found that he was once an expert in jazz music, having made a series of important pioneering recordings in England; he is a student of early cartography, and a moderately successful artist. I mention these facets not only to explain his productivity, but also to account for the breadth and scope of this book.

Far from giving a bare recital of dates, events and types, Davies breathes life into the people who created the airlines and what a brave and, sometimes rowdy, group they were. His intuitive thinking casts new light on what might ordinarily be considered familiar ground, e.g., Pan American Airways' buccaneering mode of operation, but it is especially valuable in revealing the true relative importance of French and German contributions to aviation in the area. More important, he stresses the work and development of the indigenous airlines which pulled themselves up by their bootstraps to evolve into a truly Latin American airline industry.

The time he covers is a tumultuous one, as varied in its effect as the wild territories over which the airlines flew. Airlines came and went amidst poverty, prosperity, revolutions, wars, and, always, radical changes in equipment. This book details the history, the personalities, the aircraft and the times; it is, however, far more than a look at the past, for the lessons to be learned from it have great application in the emerging countries of Africa and Asia.

As an invaluable bonus, *Airlines of Latin America since 1919* provides an understanding of the complex geography of the Americas, taking into account the physical dimensions and the twentieth-century political scene. It could be fairly said that it is as much a textbook of geography as of the airline business.

Perhaps the greatest compliment that can be paid to this volume is that it is not only a worthy successor to its predecessors, it improves on them.

Walter J. Boyne
Director
National Air and Space Museum
Smithsonian Institution

Washington, D.C.
June 12, 1983

Author's Preface

Many good books have been written about airlines and commercial aviation in several countries of Latin America, and especially in Brazil, Argentina, Mexico, and Colombia. But these have been in Portuguese or Spanish, and have not been given a wide distribution outside the country of publication. In the English language, which is accepted internationally by the airline world, only one book has previously been written about the airlines of Latin America as a whole. William Burden's *The Struggle for Airlines in Latin America*, published in 1944, was, moreover, dedicated to explore a particular aspect of airline development of special concern to the United States.

More than a third of a century has passed since then, and a whole continent, an entire community of nations, has undergone a social and economic metamorphosis. A heterogeneous collection of under-developed republics has been transformed into a powerful group of modern nations, at least two of which are classified as world industrial leaders.

Much of this transformation can be credited to the airlines. Many people in Latin America flew before they had ever ridden in a motor car, some even before they had ever *seen* a bicycle. Nowhere else in the world can such a revolution in social behaviour be attributed to a single factor: the progress of airline development. Before the transport aeroplane, the fastest way to travel from Bogotá to Leticia, or from Lima to Iquitos, city pairs in Colombia and Peru respectively, was by boat, including a two-thousand-mile journey up the Amazon.

This book about Latin America is at the same time a companion volume to *Airlines of the United States since 1914* (Putnam, 1972, and Smithsonian Institution Press, 1982). The narrative often contains more drama than any fiction writer could have invented. Nevertheless, the objective is to trace systematically the progress of the airline industry, country by country, resisting the temptation to fill the pages with countless anecdotes—though making room for them when a salient point is to be made. I hope that it will take its place in the libraries of students of modern Latin American geography, in which transport is such a key element.

Latin America is here defined as all countries south of the Rio Grande, and includes the islands of the Caribbean, not excepting the Bahamas and other territories of non-Latin settlement. To provide some kind of logical order, the countries are reviewed more or less from north to south, with some of them grouped, for example, in Central America, the Caribbean and the Guianas (see map).

The eternal problem of 'What is an airline?' (as opposed to an air taxi or irregular charter operator) has been decided mainly by the requirement for inclusion that regular, publicly-available services had to be flown over a substantial period, according to a published timetable. In the earlier years, this definition was allowed a certain flexibility, bearing in mind the pioneering nature of the first airline endeavours.

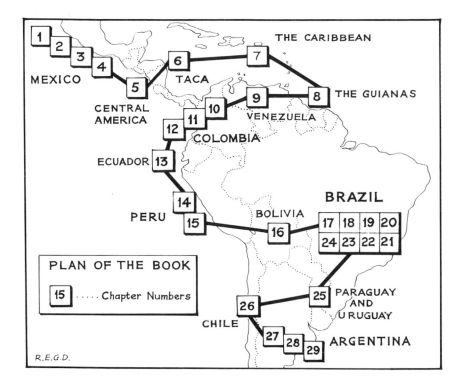

MEXICO
THE CARIBBEAN
TACA
CENTRAL
AMERICA
VENEZUELA
THE GUIANAS
COLOMBIA
ECUADOR
BRAZIL
PERU
BOLIVIA

PLAN OF THE BOOK

15 ..... Chapter Numbers

CHILE
PARAGUAY
AND
URUGUAY
ARGENTINA

R.E.G.D.

A common question about airlines, as in many other fields of study and research, is 'Who was first?'. Again, as with so many problems of this kind, precise definitions are of prime importance, and my answer, contained in the small table at the end of this preface, recognizes various criteria for selection and historical precedence. Incidentally, this table reveals that, contrary to widely-held opinion, much of the earliest pioneering work was accomplished with French technical sponsorship, not by Germany, although the latter was more successful in the later developmental years before the Second World War.

In addition to nearly 500 photographs and other exhibits which illustrate the entire period, the book contains almost 100 maps and diagrams. These are essential to portray in true perspective the astonishing growth of the Latin American airlines, at the same time underlining the critical importance of route structures. A successful airline depends upon good finance, good management, good aircraft, and good routes. Failure to maintain high standards in any one of these four categories invariably leads to peril, if not failure. And whereas shortcomings in the first three are normally within the control of the airline itself, and can be rectified, the route network is often decided by governments, and therefore beyond direct control.

In Brazil, Mexico, Argentina, and elsewhere, the fate of an aspiring airline has—as in the United States—more often than not rested entirely upon the existence of a good route network, and the ability of the company to serve those routes adequately and to extend them. In Latin America particularly, the unravelling of the complex tangle of route development has been a fascinating, if

ix

at times perplexing, task. The chronicle of such development goes a long way towards explaining how the indigenous airlines gained their commercial airline independence from once-dominant European or United States interests.

Airlines of Latin America since 1919 could never have been written without the generous help of a small volunteer army of indefatigable researchers. Substantial credit must go, therefore, to this happy band of enthusiasts, who are amateurs and connoisseurs in the true sense of those terms, and in particular to: Carlos Dufriche, Mario B. de M. Vinagre, Denir Lima de Camargo, Abel Leite, Nelson de Barros Pereira, João Lorenz and Paulo Fernando Laux, of Brazil; Francisco Halbritter, of Argentina; José Villela, Manuel Sosa de la Vega, Manuel Gómez-Méndez, Ing Perez y Bouras, Carlos Ramos, Henry Filsinger, Santiago Smith-Cumacho, and Herculano Sarabia, of Mexico; Klaus Vomhof and Günter Endres, from the United Kingdom; John Davis, Gary Kuhn, Terry Waddington, and Dan Hagedorn, from the United States; Col E. Petit, V. Ferry, and G. de Bure, from France; and Werner Bittner, Horst Burgsmüller, and Franz Preuschoff, of Germany. Additionally, of course, the aviation editors of Putnam Books, John and Patricia Stroud, have been towers of strength, contributing their extensive knowledge, experience, and judgement to ensure that the material content is well balanced and the traditional Putnam standards of accuracy maintained.

I hope this book will provide as much enjoyment for its readers as I have derived from writing it. I have tried to compile an historical reference book, but not a catalogue. Apart from the anecdotes which punctuate the pages, the complete airline narratives are fascinating in themselves. They also trace the development of the commercial aircraft up to the wide-bodied jets which carry the flags across the oceans today, a far cry from the primitive machines which first ventured into Latin American skies. For the specialists, the Fleet Lists which form the comprehensive Appendix should prove invaluable for detailed research. Above all, this is the story of thousands of Latin American airline hands, young and old. They include grease-monkeys, counter clerks, adventurous barn-stormers, and great organizers of operations and men, some of them outstanding personalities in the world of airlines. They have all played their parts in developing this dynamic business, and must collectively be given the substantial credit for creating an industry which has helped to launch Latin America into the Twentieth Century.

R. E. G. Davies
Washington, D. C.
1983

The First Airlines in Latin America

First Service	Country	Airline	Founded	Route	Aircraft	Regular	Sustained 1 Year	2 Years	Permanent	International
12 Oct. 1919	French Guiana	T.A.G.	7 June. 1919	St Laurent–Cayenne	Lévy-Lepen	(Irregular flights only, 1919–20)				
22 Feb. 1920	Colombia	C.C.N.A.	15 Sept. 1919	Barranquilla–Cartagena	Farman F.40	(Irregular flights only, early 1920)				—
7 Oct. 1920	French Guiana	T.A.G.	(see above)	St Laurent–Inini	Lévy-Lepen	✓	✓	✓	—	—
30 Oct. 1920	Cuba	Cia Aérea Cubana	October 1919	Havana–Cienfuegos	Farman F.60	✓	(Service for 3 months only)		—	—
12 July. 1921	Mexico	CMTA	1 July 1921	Mexico City–Tampico	Lincoln Standard L.S.5	✓	✓	—	—	—
19 Sept. 1921	Colombia	SCADTA	5 Dec 1919	Barranquilla–Girardot	Junkers-F 13	✓	✓	✓	✓	—
17 Dec. 1921	Argentina–Uruguay	Cia Rio Platense	1 Aug. 1919*	San Isidro–Villa Colón	D.H.16	✓	✓	✓	—	✓

*Date of foundation of River Plate Aviation Company which merged with Cia France-Argentina de Transportes on 21 September, 1921, to form Compañia Rio Platense.

The Oldest Surviving Airlines in Latin America

First Service	Country	Airline	First Regular Service	Route	
19 Sept. 1921	Colombia	SCADTA	19 Sept. 1921	Barranquilla–Girardot	See above. Changed name to AVIANCA in 1940. Continuous operation since 1919
5 Aug. 1925*	Bolivia	LAB	24 Dec. 1925	Cochabamba–Santa Cruz	Founded 15 September, 1925
12 July. 1921	Mexico	Mexicana	9 Dec. 1921	Mexico City–Tuxpan–Tampico	See above. Founded 24 Aug. 1924, and acquired assets of CMTA (see above)
22 June. 1927	Brazil	VARIG	22 June. 1927	Porto Alegre–Rio Grande	Took over route operated by German Condor Syndikat since 3 February, 1927

*Special demonstration flight.

Latin America

There are certain misconceptions concerning the geography of the American continent, so that a few definitions seem appropriate, together with a statistical abstract of the countries covered in this book.

Latin America refers to those parts originally colonized by European peoples who speak languages derived from Latin. Effectively this means all countries of the mainland south of the United States-Mexican frontier, plus all the islands of the Caribbean, originally colonized by the Spanish, but later annexed by others.

South America is the continental land mass separated from North America at the Isthmus of Panama. The seven small countries between Mexico and Colombia are commonly combined under the term Central America. All the islands of the Caribbean, sometimes called the West Indies, are normally included for statistical purposes as part of South America. Geographically the larger of the Caribbean islands, the Greater Antilles—Cuba, Hispaniola, Puerto Rico, and Jamaica— belong more naturally to North America.

Partly because of the terrain and vegetation, human settlement in Latin America has been characterized by vast areas which are still almost devoid of population, but are punctuated by relatively isolated urban concentrations. The Amazon jungles, the Andes mountains, and the arid deserts of the Atacama and the Bolivian *altiplano* combine to resist colonization throughout the entire interior of South America. Bolivia and Paraguay, sparsely populated, are the only countries without a coastline. Almost everywhere, high population growth rates are endemic.

The mushrooming urban concentrations have constituted a demographic phenomenon, their uncontrolled expansion creating social distress and economic pressures. Governments seem helpless in stemming the tide of rural families seeking employment in the cities. And what cities! There are now about 15 million people in Mexico City, which is confidently forecast to be the largest urban centre in the world within the next decade. São Paulo, with perhaps 12 million inhabitants in the greater urban area, is the largest—and the richest—in the southern hemisphere, a city where, it is said, a new skyscraper is completed every day. Buenos Aires is not far behind the Brazilian metropolis in population or wealth but its growth rate has declined in recent years.

While these are the largest single conurbations, large cities abound throughout Latin America. Brazil has no less than nine with more than a million inhabitants each; Mexico and Colombia have three each. The national capitals, as shown in the accompanying table, are places of substance, often of a size disproportionate to their countries. Yet this trend seems to be inescapable even if, as in the case of Uruguay, the capital city and its environs contain about 40 per cent of the country's total population.

Such a population distribution comprises a ready-made foundation for air transport, especially as—for the same reasons which deterred settlement— surface communications have seldom been developed to inter-city standards. The arena was ideal for the world's first airliners to demonstrate their capabilities, and their prowess changed the momentum and direction of the economic progress of the whole of Latin America.

The Countries of Latin America
Mexico and Central America

Country	Area (sq km)	Estimated or actual Population in 1980	Largest Urban Areas (with 1980 population)
Belize*	23,000	150,000	Belize (40,000)
Costa Rica	51,000	2·4 mn	San José (0·3 mn)
El Salvador	21,000	4·4 mn	San Salvador (0·9 mn)
Guatemala	109,000	7·1 mn	Guatemala City (1·5 mn)
Honduras	112,000	3·7 mn	Tegucigalpa (0·4 mn)
Mexico	1,967,000	70 mn	Mexico City (15 mn)
			Guadalajara (2·8 mn)
			Monterrey (1·5 mn)
Nicaragua	148,000	2·6 mn	Managua (0·6 mn)
Panama	77,000	1·9 mn	Panamá (0·8 mn)

The Caribbean Islands

Country	Area (sq km)	Estimated or actual Population in 1980	Largest Urban Areas (with 1980 population)
Bahamas*	14,000	250,000	Nassau (150,000)
Barbados*	430	270,000	Bridgetown (90,000)
British Virgin Is*	130	11,500	Road Town (3,500)
Cuba	115,000	9 mn	La Habaña (2 mn)
Dominica*	728	85,000	Roseau (18,000)
Dominican Republic	48,000	5·9 mn	Santo Domingo (1·1 mn)
Grenada*	344	125,000	St George (30,000)
Guadeloupe†	1,780	350,000	Point-à-Pitre (75,000)
Haiti	28,000	5 mn	Port-au-Prince (0·5 mn)
Jamaica*	11,000	2 mn	Kingston (0·6 mn)
Martinique†	1,079	308,000	Fort-de-France (0.1 mn)
Netherlands Antilles	993	260,000	Willemstad (55,000)
Puerto Rico‡	8,891	3·2 mn	San Juan (450,000)
St Lucia*	616	113,000	Castries (45,000)
St Vincent and The Grenadines*	389	120,000	Kingstown (25,000)
Trinidad and Tobago*	5,128	1 mn	Port of Spain (65,000)
Turks and Cocos Is*	430	7,200	Grand Turk (3,000)
US Virgin Is‡	212	120,000	Charlotte Amalie (15,000)
West Indies Associated States*:			
Antigua	440	75,000	St John's (25,000)
St Kitts-Nevis	262	45,000	Basseterre (15,000)
Anguilla	56	6,500	

South America

Argentina	2,778,000	25 mn	Buenos Aires (10 mn)
Bolivia	1,099,000	5 mn	La Paz (0·7 mn)
Brazil	8,512,000	123 mn	São Paulo (12 mn)
			Rio de Janeiro (8·5 mn)
			Belo Horizonte (2·5 mn)
Chile	752,000	11 mn	Santiago (4·5 mn)
Colombia	1,139,000	27·5 mn	Bogotá (4·2 mn)
			Medellín (2 mn)
			Cali (1·5 mn)
Ecuador	455,000	7·9 mn	Guayaquil (1·2 mn)
French Guiana†	91,000	65,000	Cayenne (36,000)
Guyana*	210,000	0·8 mn	Georgetown (0·2 mn)
Paraguay	406,000	3 mn	Asunción (0·5 mn)
Peru	1,285,000	17·8 mn	Lima (4·5 mn)
Surinam	163,000	0·4 mn	Paramaribo (0·1 mn)
Uruguay	187,000	2·9 mn	Montevideo (1·3 mn)
Venezuela	912,000	14·5 mn	Caracas (2·8 mn)

* Members of the British Commonwealth
† Departments of France
‡ Territories of the United States.

VARIG's Boeing 747-2L5B PP-VNA. (*VARIG archives, via Mário B. de M. Vinagre*)

One of the open cockpit Lincoln Standard biplanes which operated the first sustained Mexican air services. (*Mexicana*)

CHAPTER ONE

The First Mexican Airlines

The First Pioneer

Mexico entered the decade of the 1920s after a truly turbulent political period. A long era of almost uninterrupted autocracy by the flamboyant Porfirio Díaz had been succeeded in 1911 by nine years of near-chaos, during which time there were five presidents. The country had been ravaged by various revolutionary forces, led by unorthodox characters such as Pancho Villa and Emiliano Zapata. The normal way of terminating a presidency had been by assassination, so that the rule of Alvaro Obregón, which was to last for four years, was the beginning of a new age for Mexico, a political climate of comparative tranquillity. During this period, commercial aviation gained its first footing.

The main credit for establishing an airline industry must go to Ing Juan Guillermo Villasana who, in 1920, was working in the Air Force maintenance shops as assistant to Francisco Santarina. Mexico was ahead of most Latin American nations in the matter of flying aeroplanes, as in 1915 President Carranza, a benevolent dictator, encouraged productive undertakings on a national scale and had created the Mexican Air Force. Villasana put forward the idea of a civil aviation department, and President Obregón, who had succeeded Carranza, ordered the Ministry of Communications and Public Works (SCOP) to study this idea. On 11 October, 1920, Villasana took over a desk—and very little else—called the Mesa de Navegación Aérea. This later became the Sección Técnica de Navegación Aérea, which for a time came under the jurisdiction of the Directorate of Railroads before becoming a department of SCOP. Under Villasana's supervision, it then became the equivalent of the United States Civil

1

Aeronautics Board, and all air route concessions and contracts were its responsibility.

Early in 1921, the **Compañía Mexicana de Transportación, S.A. (CMTA)** was founded in Mexico City by L.A. Winship and Harry J. Lawson, two United States citizens resident in Mexico. Its aim was to carry passengers, mail, and freight, and for this purpose it purchased two Lincoln Standard biplanes from the factory in Lincoln, Nebraska, and flew them to Mexico City via El Paso, Chihuahua, Torreón, and the cities of central Mexico which were to become a kind of *camino real* for subsequent airline enterprises.

The company was awarded Concession Number 1 (Contract Number 1) on 12 July, 1921, by the Secretariat of Communications and Public Works, to operate routes from the capital to Tampico and Matamoros; and to San Luis Potosi, Saltillo, Monterrey, and Nuevo Laredo. Lawson and Winship quickly discovered that the main demand for air service came from the Gulf Coast region around Tampico, where the Mexican oilfields were booming. During the first year of operation, CMTA made 39 round trips between Mexico City and Tampico, and 68 round trips between Tampico and Tuxpan, plus many exhibition and survey flights to other cities. Much other work was done in the oilfield region, which accounted for 896 out of the total of 1,956 hours flown by the company; 312 hours were reported to have been flown on regular services, and 212 on inter-city—presumably charter—work. During this year of pioneer operations by Mexico's first airline, 1,248 passengers were carried, of whom 289 were on regular and inter-city flights. The first paying passenger was Humberto Jimenez.

During the last few months of 1921, CMTA is reported to have started a postal service, but this was suspended because of insufficient business. Nevertheless, although nothing more was heard of regular services, the company continued to fly charters and to perform aerial taxi work, mainly in the oilfield district, during 1922 and 1923. In the beginning, CMTA had no competition. The only other applicant for an airline concession was Mario Bulnes, who intended to use Farman biplanes on the Mexico–Tampico route. Concession Number 2, however, awarded on 2 August, 1921, was never used.

The Beginning of Mexicana

More effective were the applications of two more US citizens, at first acting independently, in 1924. On 11 July of that year, William 'Slim' Mallory was awarded Concession Number 3 (Contract 3) for the same potentially lucrative route: Mexico City–Tampico. Shortly afterwards, on 16 August, this concession was transferred to **Compañía Mexicana de Aviación, S.A., (CMA)** organized by George Rihl. The Contract was amended, as Number 4, to include Mexico–Tuxpan and Tampico–Matamoros.

Rihl clearly had his sights set on a trunk route to the United States border, but for some years activity was confined to the oil region. The team of Mallory, himself a pilot, and Rihl, a businessman, combined to make a success of a unique operation. To avoid the hazards of carrying payrolls on roads and tracks, where the chances of their safe arrival were slim because of local banditry, CMA became a specialist payroll delivery service. Sacks of currency were dropped at the oilfields, using the precision bomb-dropping techniques of the day, that is, for the co-pilot to take aim, guess the drift and speed, and throw out the sack. The sacks, incidentally, were specially made of strong canvas, with one inside the other, to avoid the shock and abuse of the impact. There is a story of one sack-dropper,

2

Juan Guillermo Villasana (*left*) the 'father' of Mexican commercial aviation, organized the first agency to regulate civil flying in 1920, under the Secretaría de Comunicaciones y Obras Públicas (SCOP). George Rihl (*centre*) was active during the early 1920s in oil-well drilling and joined with a pilot, William 'Slim' Mallory, in 1924 to fly payrolls to inaccessible mining camps in the Tampico area. Lic Gustavo Espinosa Mireles (*right*) was the first president of Rihl's airline, Compañía Mexicana de Aviación (CMA)—the Mexicana of today.
(*José Villela and Mexicana*)

later to become a respected vice-president of Pan American Airways, who missed the target. The sack fell into the jungle, and was never seen again. The sack-dropper lost his job.

On 24 August, 1924, Compañía Mexicana de Aviación was registered at the Public Notary office. Rihl and Mallory had interested R. G. Piper and Carl V. Schlaet to put up some money to form a company of substance. The capital was 50,000 pesos, then worth $25,000, and the first president was Lic Gustavo Espinosa Mireles.

While Rihl and Mallory were thus establishing themselves, the little airline of Lawson and Winship was struggling. Although further Lincoln Standards had been added, CMTA apparently had lost either the energy or the competence to continue. In September 1924 CMA purchased the assets, which by this time had dwindled to a fleet of three Lincoln Standards, from a reported maximum of ten.

CMA then began to make cautious but steady progress towards establishing credibility and acquiring operating experience. In 1925 considerable help came from a prominent industrialist from the United States. Sherman Fairchild, owner of the company which had made itself the world's leader in aerial photography, purchased a 20 per cent interest in CMA for 12,500 pesos. Henceforth, Fairchild would supply all equipment at cost and support all the company's aerial survey work. Fairchild and CMA represented each other mutually on an exclusive basis.

On 16 August, 1926, CMA signed a ten-year contract with the Secretariat of Communications and Public Works to carry mail between Mexico City and Tampico, via Tuxpan. The rail journey took two days for the 200 miles, so the air mail was an obvious improvement, even though, at one peso per kilometre, it was not exactly cheap. Reaching further afield, and keeping to the terms of the original contract, CMA made a survey flight on 9 December, 1926, with a Lincoln Standard, from Mexico City to Matamoros, stopping only at Tampico. The pilot, M. A. Nimenin, covered the distance of 1,213 km in 6 hr 5 min. It was the first direct flight from the capital to the United States frontier.

3

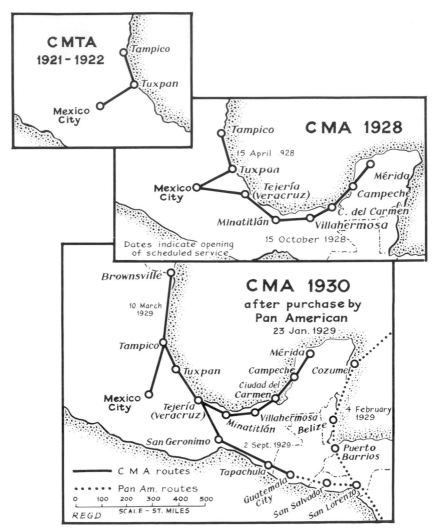

1. The First Mexican Air Routes, 1921–1930. Beginning with an air route between Mexico City and the Tampico oilfields, partly inherited from a previous operator, CMA became a vital link in the chain connecting Pan American Airways' routes from Texas and Florida to Central America.

During 1927, CMA was kept busy, and upgraded its flying equipment by introducing the Fairchild FC-1A and the Fairchild 71, products of its prominent shareholder's expanding business empire. The capital was increased to 150,000 pesos, with Fairchild maintaining his 20 per cent. SCOP granted permission to CMA to use the airfield installations at Tampico. Airline activities during this year, however, were completely overshadowed by an event which had caught the public imagination more than almost any other in the whole history of aviation since the Wright brothers. Charles Lindbergh had made the first solo flight across

4

CMA's Fairchild 71 X-ABCI, at Tuxpan (shown as TUXPAM on the corrugated canopy of the building). X-ABCI was the fourth Fairchild 71, it passed to Aerovías Centrales as X-ABEF and, as NC9727, was still flying in the mid-1970s. (*Mexicana*)

the Atlantic, and at the request of the United States Government he subsequently made a goodwill tour of Central America and the Caribbean, landing at Mexico City on 14 December, 1927. Here he was welcomed by the Mexican Government, much to the satisfaction of the US Ambassador, Dwight Morrow, whose daughter, Anne, was to become Mrs Lindbergh soon afterwards.

The next year was one of great achievement for CMA. On 28 February, 1928, the Government signed a new and more substantial contract with the company to carry the mails, this time on a scheduled basis. On 15 April, air mail and passenger scheduled service was inaugurated on the Mexico City–Tuxpan–Tampico route, using the Fairchild FC-2W *Ciudad de México*. The distance of 393 km was flown three times per week.

Outclassing this event, a longer route was started on 15 October, from the capital to Mérida, the capital of Yucatán. The distance of 853 km was flown by two

CMA began its scheduled mail and passenger service over the Mexico City–Tuxpan–Tampico route on 15 April, 1928, using a Fairchild FC-2W. This photograph was taken on that occasion, probably at Mexico City. (*Mexicana*)

5

Fairchild FC-2Ws, M-SCOZ *Ciudad de Mérida* and M-SCOY *Ciudad de Veracruz* via Minatitlán, Villahermosa, Cuidad del Carmen, and Campeche. All other communication between Mexico City and the Yucatán peninsula at the time was very slow, involving both land and sea journeys. Construction of a railway to Mérida was still several years off. CMA's operation was based at Veracruz, with a connecting flight to Tampico. Afternoon flights out of Mexico City during the rainy season were hazardous, so flights had to arrive at or depart from the capital by noon at the latest. Illustrative of the operating conditions at the time was a terse report that casualties for the year totalled six: one broken arm sustained by a passenger, two employees killed by propellers, and three spectators injured.

Pan American Takes Over

CMA had no rivals in Mexico at this time. **Secretaría de Comunicaciones y Obras Públicas (SCOP)–The Ministry of Communications and Public Works** had established its own commercial air route on 1 September, 1928, with a fleet of six Stinson Detroiter six-seat monoplanes. But they flew these between Mexico City and Nueva Laredo, on the Texas border, only until the next year, when General Escobar's revolution in the north disrupted activities, and SCOP handed over its aircraft to the Mexican Air Force.

Oddly enough, the event which was to change the whole course of commercial aviation history in Mexico took place in Washington, D.C. On 2 January, 1929, the United States Post Office advertised for bids on Foreign Air Mail Route (FAM) No.8: Brownsville–Tampico–Mexico City. There were seven bids for the contract, which carried the maximum rate of $2 per mile, including those of Walter Varney, an aviation entrepreneur from the western United States, Consolidated Aircraft Corporation, and Pan American Airways. Whether or not George Rihl foresaw this development when he obtained his original concession is unknown. His projected route to Matamoros terminated just across the frontier from Brownsville, certainly a happy coincidence.

On 23 January, 1929, Pan American Airways, under the determined and single-minded leadership of Juan Trippe, bought the entire stock of Compañía Mexicana de Aviación for 300,000 pesos ($150,000). Trippe had personally inspected the route, flying over the Sierra Madre, and perceived it as the key to the expansion potential of his airline. By controlling the route across Mexico, he not only forged an essential link in the chain of routes spanning Central America and the Caribbean (see Map on page 10) but also, by securing the rights at the Mexican end too, through Rihl's contracts, he protected his interests almost to monopoly status.

Because Pan American was short of cash, the acquisition was accomplished by an exchange of stock between CMA and the Aviation Corporation of the Americas (Pan American's parent corporation). 16,666 Aviation Corporation shares were exchanged for all the stock of CMA, with Aviation Corporation stock being valued at $15 per share, or $250,000 nominal value. Thus, Sherman Fairchild acquired $26,825 share worth of Aviation Corporation stock, plus 4,000 warrants to buy at $15. By the time the stock was actually exchanged in March, Aviation Corporation stock had soared to $40. George Rihl, meanwhile, had been offered $1,000,000 for CMA.

On 16 February, 1929, Pan American was awarded FAM-8 at the highest rate, on the grounds that it already owned CMA and therefore enjoyed the goodwill of the Mexican authorities, of which the mail contract was a substantial part. On 10

6

Col Charles Lindbergh at the controls of the Ford 5-AT-B NC9661 which inaugurated CMA's Brownsville–Mexico City service on 10 March, 1929. This Ford Tri-Motor was delivered to CMA in August 1929 and registered X-ABCO. (*Pan American World Airways*)

March, 1929, a Ford Tri-Motor, piloted by none other than Charles Lindbergh, flew the inaugural service from Brownsville, via Tampico and Tuxpan. The reciprocal flight was made by Mexican pilots. As a quaint postscript, some mail was left in the wing of Lindbergh's aircraft, which had a special compartment, unknown to the Mexican ground staff. The mail was not found until a month later.

Route expansion rapidly consolidated Pan American's grip on Mexican commercial aviation. On 15 May, 1929, a route opened from Tejería (serving Veracruz) to Tapachula, near the frontier of Guatemala; and this was extended to the Guatemalan capital on 9 October. This route was flown by Fairchild 71s, which also opened a link route on 1 September from Tampico to Veracruz. Progressively, however, Pan American moved to improve the airports, laying down paved runways so that the Ford Tri-Motor could operate in all weathers,

CMA's Ford 5-AT-B X-ABCC was handed over by Pan American Airways in May 1929 and used on the Brownsville–Mexico City route until late in 1937 when it went to Cubana. With numerous owners and under a range of identities this Tri-Motor was still working in the late 1950s. (*Mexicana*)

CMA provided a railcar service linking Tejería and Veracruz from 1928. This photograph of the tram-like vehicle gives no indication of the type of motive power. (*Mexicana*)

and introducing a special transit service between Tejería and Veracruz. The Fords replaced the Fairchilds to Guatemala on 16 September, 1930, and became standard equipment on all CMA routes by 1931.

On 9 September, 1929, CMA had entered into an intriguing agreement with two US airlines, Southern Air Transport and Universal Aviation Corporation, and two US railroads, the Missouri-Kansas-Texas, and the New York Central, to provide a rapid service between Mexico City and New York. Connecting at the frontier at Brownsville, and assuming that the five changes could be accomplished without mishap, the northbound schedule was advertised to take 49 hours.

Pickwick Airways

Simultaneously with Pan American's success in winning the mail contract for the Gulf Coast route to Mexico City, another aspiring airline pursued the goal of establishing one along or near the Pacific coast. **Pickwick Airways** had been founded in Los Angeles by Charles Wren, who began a service to San Diego on 29 March, 1929, using Bach trimotor cabin monoplanes, at a frequency of three per day. Apparently successful, service began to San Francisco in July.

Then, in September, Pickwick made the daring experiment of extending service to Mexico City, for which single-engined Fairchilds and five-seat Ryan Broughams were added to the fleet. In January 1930, the route was extended to San Salvador but this ambitious project was short-lived. Unable to obtain the vital mail contract, without which no airline could survive during this period, Pickwick ceased operations in June, having existed for little more than a year. Pan American influence with the US Post Office, and its indirect control of Mexican airline activity through its newly-acquired ownership of CMA, undoubtedly had something to do with Pickwick's demise. Such a fate was to befall many an airline which fell across Pan American's path. Pickwick's assets passed to G & G Airlines Company (operating as Gilpin Air Lines) in southern California on 8 December, 1930.

Abortive Challenge in the Gulf

Pan American did not always need to take action to subdue its rivals. One company's attempt to move into Juan Trippe's hallowed ground—or in this case water—never got under way. But it had the right ambition, reflected in its name, **Compañía de Transportes Aéreos México-Cuba, S.A.** The founders, Abel R. Pérez and Gonzalo Abaunza, acquired three Bellancas and two Italian Savoia Marchetti S.55 twin-hulled flying-boats in January 1931, and planned to start a service from Veracruz to Havana, via Frontera (Tabasco) and Progreso (Yucatán). Unfortunately, the flagship of this promising enterprise, *México*, came to grief on the inaugural flight on 19 June, 1931, and was towed to the shore with its 17-passenger load relieved that the engine fire had not been more distastrous. Apparently the company tried to remain afloat, metaphorically as well as literally, and issued a timetable in 1932 which included the novel idea of charging children under three years old by weight.

C.A.T., Varney, and Centrales

Although Pan American retained a firm grip on its political connections in Mexico as an insurance against officially-sponsored challenges, some enterprising individuals attempted to break its monopoly. Most memorable of these was an airline whose chronicles could easily be interpreted as fiction, were they not fact. **Corporación de Aeronáutica de Transportes (C.A.T.)** was founded early in 1929 by a Los Angeles banker and private pilot, Theodore Hull. A true aviation enthusiast who recognized the growth potential for mail and business flying from Texas to Mexico City, he conceived the idea of a trunk route to follow the traditional Aztec Trail from El Paso southwards.

C.A.T. started scheduled operations on 9 March, 1929, westwards from Brownsville (just across the border from Matamoros) to Monterrey, and this was

C.A.T.'s Lockheed Vega 5 X-ABHB about to carry silver ingots from Tayoltita.
(*John Underwood collection, courtesy of Langan Swent*)

9

soon extended across to the Pacific coast at Mazatlán, via Torreón, as soon as it was safe to do so. At the time, Mexico was experiencing a few minor revolutions of the kind which resulted in local interruptions of daily life and commerce, but which had little effect on the national political scene—a far cry from the days of Pancho Villa.

Theodore Hull had good aircraft, by the standards of the day: two Ryan Broughams to start with, then several Wasp-powered Lockheed Vegas, purchased for $18,500 each. He matched the aircraft with fine pilots, whose listing reads like a roll call of famous flyers: Paul Braniff (the same who founded the first airline in Oklahoma City); the famous Wiley Post (who obtained a Mexican

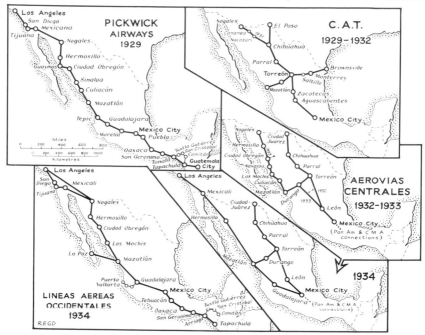

2. Pan American Airways Consolidation in Northern Mexico, 1929–1934. Several airlines, promoted by other US interests, tried to establish themselves in Mexico during the early 1930s, but Pan American Airways emerged with complete control of all routes to the United States frontier, through its subsidiary Aerovías Centrales.

commercial pilot's licence, even though he had only one eye); Lowell Yerex, who was to achieve fame as the creator of TACA; and Gordon Barry, who was to found LAMSA and make a significant contribution to the route network growth of Mexico. Under the general direction of Major Bernard Law, hired by Hull as operations manager, these pilots and aircraft built up an airline, based at Torreón, which became the centre of a classic cross-shaped network (see map) when the 1,104-mile El Paso (Ciudad Juárez)–Mexico City route opened on 11 August, 1929.

The adventures of C.A.T. would make a marvellous book in its own right. Seldom did a week go by without some bizarre incident. Passengers included on frequent occasions high-ranking members of the various Mexican armies which seemed to populate northern Mexico at the time. The airline was often ordered to

C.A.T.'s Bach 3-CT-6 Air Yacht at Tayoltita.
(*John Underwood collection, courtesy of Langan Swent*)

carry prisoners, alleged to be bandits—which they may have been, although their captors were probably no better. Strange cargoes included a live boa constrictor which escaped, with the pilot keeping it confined to the rear of the aircraft by climbing swiftly to 14,000 ft, at which altitude the reptile fortunately passed out.

Theodore Hull was not blessed by too much luck to match his enterprise. Trying to fly without the use of radio over the Sierra Madre was no picnic, and the Ryan Broughams paid the price when atrocious weather spelt disaster. In spite of crashes, however, the remainder of the operation was completed with remarkable

This view of the C.A.T.-operated Bellanca P-200 Airbus seen at Tayoltita, gives a good idea of the rugged terrain. (*John Underwood collection, courtesy of Langan Swent*)

11

Fokker F-10A X-ABEC, one of several supplied to Aerovías Centrales by Pan American Airways. X-ABEC was formerly NC396E. (*Mexicana*)

regularity—Major Law claimed a 98 per cent record. The stock-market crash of October 1929 did not help, but C.A.T. managed to carry 2,283 passengers in 1930 and more than double that number in the following year. However, when Hull crashed a new Bellanca in the Susquehanna River, Pennsylvania, on 25 November, 1931, and was killed, the heart went out of the airline, as no-one was left to fight for the coveted mail contract. The Mexican mail contract was simply not enough to cover expenses, and the Government was threatening to pass a law requiring that all pilots should be Mexican, a condition which was unacceptable to the United States financial backers who hitherto were prepared to share Hull's vision.

Although Law tried to keep the line going, services were suspended on 9 February, 1932. Pan American immediately founded **Aerovías Centrales, S.A.**, on 26 February, 1932, to take over the Aztec Trail route. Already controlling the main access point to Mexico at Brownsville, Pan American now controlled the important central route. It had no interest in linking Brownsville with Monterrey and Torreón, apparently, but did wish to reach the Pacific coast, and so retained the Torreón–Durango–Mazatlán link, putting Ford Tri-Motors on the route on 12 November, 1932. In March 1933, a coastal route was added to the Centrales network, as far as Ciudad Obregón, and this was extended to the border city of Nogales by the summer of that year.

The Consolidated Fleetster Model 20, with 575 hp Pratt & Whitney Hornet engine, was awarded its Type Certificate in May 1930. XA-BEK, illustrated, was operated by Aerovías Centrales. (*Gordon S. Williams*)

At first, Centrales used 'multi-motored' equipment—presumably Ford Tri-Motors; but began to meet competition from another entrepreneur following in the footsteps of Theodore Hull. Another man from the West, Walter Varney, had been involved in various air transport ventures since 1922; had formed one of the first air mail lines in the United States in 1926; and by the early 1930s was maintaining a healthy and competitive service between San Francisco and Los Angeles. His main sales pitch was Speed, which he backed with fast Lockheed passenger and mail aircraft. Early in 1934, possibly seeking new lands to conquer while the United States Post Office sorted out the massive scandal that had erupted, he moved his headquarters from Alameda, near San Francisco, to Burbank, near Los Angeles, and founded **Líneas Aéreas Occidentales, S.A. (L.A.O.)** (Western Air Lines—not to be confused with the US company of the same name). On 10 April, 1934, he inaugurated an ambitious line, flying a fleet of one Lockheed Orion and two Vegas all the way to Mexico City three times a week by a coastal route (see map). Thence he made a weekly connection to Tapachula, on the Guatemalan frontier, as well as providing a link with La Paz, Baja California, from Mazatlán. He possessed a mail contract of sorts from the Mexican Government, but he needed more than that to fight the mighty Pan American.

Lockheed Orion 9 X-ABHA, operated during 1934–35 by Líneas Aéreas Occidentales. Varney Speed Lines Inc appears in small letters on the fin and the inscription surrounding the Mexican flag on the engine cowling reads Correo Aéreo de México (Mexican Air Mail).
(*Lockheed*)

Early in January 1935, after only nine months of operation, the Mexican Government withdrew its 20-year contract. L.A.O. went out of business shortly thereafter, barely escaping with the aircraft before they were impounded. The next day, Pan American took over the route to Tapachula, while Varney, ever resourceful, used the remaining fleet to start what was to become Continental Airlines. Thus was a competitor eliminated. Pan American could probably have simply used its corporate strength. It had introduced its own Orions to match Varney's; and although the Northrop Delta, which would have outflown them all, crashed on its delivery flight, Pan American had always held a trump card by introducing the ten-seat Lockheed Electra in April of 1934 on a fast service to Los Angeles. The 4.30 a.m. departure from Los Angeles arrived at Mexico City at 6.15 p.m. local time, so that, for the first time, passengers from California could reach the Mexican capital within daylight hours on the same day, and vice versa. The coastal route, serving local communities, was dropped.

On 18 December, 1935, Aerovías Centrales itself was dissolved, mainly because Pan American refused to comply with the new Mexican law directing that all flying crew must be Mexican nationals. Already in charge of the Gulf coast route to Texas, with connections to the south, central, and eastern United States, the US carrier shrewdly judged that, whatever the romantic traditions of the Aztec Trail, the route to California was a better commercial proposition. Thus, the central route was dropped, to be rejuvenated under different management soon afterwards. Two decades later, this central route was to form part of an interesting sequel; but meanwhile, Pan American consolidated its position by controlling, indeed owning all the connections into Central America, via Mexico, from the border cities connecting with the main population centres of the USA.

Equipment Modernization

Except for the acquisition of Aerovías Centrales, Pan American and CMA made very few changes to the Mexican trunk network under their joint control during the next decade. As already noted, the central route to the north was abandoned, and the next one was not added until 5 September, 1941, when a direct service was opened to the important city of Monterrey. On 5 December of that year, this was extended to the US frontier at Nuevo Laredo, where a connection was made with Braniff Airways to the mid-western states of the USA. Other than this, only minor changes were made to stopping points in the south, and on 25 October, 1942, CMA was able to fly its aircraft through to Havana, to improve upon the arrangement whereby, since 1931, the Mexican airline had interchanged with Pan American at Mérida.

But Pan American was not interested in developing a network of routes as a Mexican national goal. Its main purpose was to serve the business communities, and especially US–Mexican business travel demand. There are few big countries of the world where commerce is concentrated so heavily in the capital; so that those cities receiving CMA service were simply the fortuitous beneficiaries of an operationally desirable itinerary. Nevertheless, by the time the United States entered the Second World War, an act which was profoundly to affect air service throughout the hemisphere, CMA served all the most important Mexican cities of large population, notably Guadalajara and Monterrey.

While CMA showed little interest in serving small communities, because these were unlikely to produce a profit, and the Mexican Government would not subsidize feeder routes, it could certainly not be criticized for lack of development work in other directions. The Mexican airline was a favourite son of its parent, Pan American, in this respect. Unwittingly or as a conscious policy, Pan American was, during the late 1930s, serving President Roosevelt's 'Good Neighbour' policy remarkably well, by ensuring that CMA always had the best aircraft available.

Thus, having taken over the west coast route to Los Angeles from the unfortunate Walter Varney and his Líneas Aéreas Occidentales, the fast Lockheed Electra had been introduced by the subsidiary, Aerovías Centrales, in May 1934. CMA took over the Electra fleet when it acquired the Centrales routes, and by 1936 had deployed it over most of its system. Successively, the Electras were superseded by Boeing 247Ds late in 1936, on the route to Los Angeles, and on 17 May, 1937, the first Douglas DC-2 fourteen-passenger airliner went into service. By the end of 1938, five DC-3s, each with twenty-one seats, had supplemented the DC-2s, and such was the traffic demand that the Mexico

14

Lockheed Model 10-C Electra XA-BEM was one of a small fleet employed by Aerovías Centrales. (*Gordon S. Williams*)

City–Brownsville service was increased to twice daily on 1 May, 1939.

Amazingly, the veteran Ford Tri-Motor continued to earn its keep. Not until February 1941, when it was retired from the branch line from Ciudad del Carmen to Campeche, did the old Tin Goose leave the service of CMA, and of course continued to serve Mexico for many more years.

Other innovations were made to support the new aircraft. On the Mexico City–Mérida route, for example, a system of Deferred Express (Expreso Diferido) was instituted, under which consignments were sent out only when capacity was available; but invariably a delayed despatch by air could still beat any form of surface transport, especially in the matter of security. On the prestige route to Los Angeles, the first illuminated airway was completed on 16 February, 1943, permitting overnight flights. New airports were built and owned by CMA, and several routes, hitherto operated under temporary certificates, were granted permanent status.

Thus, when, on 30 December, 1944, the capital structure of Compañía Mexicana de Aviación was changed, by the injection of 4,500,000 pesos to make a total of 12,500,000, the new Mexican shareholders found their investment to be fundamentally sound. With first-rate aircraft, most airports under its own control, a lighted airway, and healthy traffic demand, the premier Mexican airline was ready to move with postwar developments.

Mexicana's Boeing 247D XA-BFK was originally Varney's NC13356. It was for a time used by Pennsylvania-Central Airlines. (*Mexicana*)

15

CMA's Douglas DC-3A XA-FEG had been Pan American's NC30011. It passed to Servicios Aéreos Gómez Mendez. (*Mexicana*)

CHAPTER TWO

Mexican Airline Proliferation

A Law of Opportunity

During the 1920s, there had been a number of tentative efforts to start airlines either as competitors to, or to complement the well-established Compañía Mexicana de Aviación. George Rihl's airline had, with Pan American ownership, become the Establishment by the early 1930s. It served all the main cities and trunk routes, and there seemed to be little else but the crumbs from the Pan American master's table left over for other aspirants in the commercial aviation field.

Crumbs they may have been, but there were many of them, because Pan American's reason for acquiring CMA had been to secure a vital link in its international route system, serving at the same time only Mexico's important business centres. At first, it showed little interest in serving smaller communities other than those which happened to be on routes between main cities; and it even abandoned the central route to the north.

At the same time, the Department of Communications and Public Works which had jurisdiction over civil aviation was learning by experience and improving the regulations under which airlines could operate. During the 1920s, almost all the concessions had been for the same route: Mexico City to the oilfields, but none had succeeded in competition with CMA, already firmly in charge there. When, however, on 1 July, 1928, the Sección Técnica de Navegación Aérea, at Juan Villasana's instigation, became independent of the railways, it encouraged further applications for route franchises; and the new batch granted on 29 November, 1928, were notably for different routes.

On 29 August, 1932, the Law of General Lines of Communication issued by SCOP clarified the important provisions of air route concessions. The first step was to grant an experimental permit for a maximum of one year, with the requirement that operations start within 90 days, and that the service should operate at least twice a week. The holder of a permit could then apply for a permanent concession, which SCOP would then grant for a maximum of 30 years, after suitable investigation of the applicant's credentials. Guarantee bonds were required (though the amount does not seem to have been large, judging by the size of some of the successful applicants); tariffs were subject to SCOP approval; and during the first $7\frac{1}{2}$ years the airline was exempt from import duties on aircraft and materials. During the $7\frac{1}{2}$ years also, another provision was to have long-term importance of great significance to the way in which Mexican airlines developed: other airlines could not stop at points served by the concessionaire where competition would result, provided the incumbent continued to provide service.

This provision, in effect, gave monopoly status to the holder of a route concession. This meant that, once all routes of reasonable traffic potential throughout Mexico had been successfully applied for, a situation achieved by the late 1930s, the only way an airline could expand its network was by snapping up a concession if another airline failed to meet its obligations—by going out of business, for example, or, as became a feature of Mexican airline development, by amalgamation and mergers or outright purchase.

Thus, the early 1930s witnessed not only a flurry of new independent airlines in Mexico; but it brought to an end the sporadic activity of the late 1920s when nobody was quite sure what kind of permanency or security might be attached to a route concession, especially with the shadow of Pan American hanging over Mexican civil aviation operations wholly within Mexico. A Pickwick Airways map of 1929 shows a branch route from Tonalá to Tuxtla Gutíerrez and Comitán, in the state of Chiapas, suggesting that the brothers Sarabia were already active. Other than that, an attempt to start a service from the Yucatán peninsula to Cuba, by Werner Kaemmerer, a former director of SCADTA, Colombia, had been made in 1925. But this never came to fruition.

Francisco Sarabia

Undoubtedly the biggest name among the independents during the formative years of airlines with a purely Mexican identity was Francisco ('Pancho') Sarabia. Born in 1900, he went to the United States to learn to fly, to such good measure that he became a pilot for the US Postal Service. Returning to Mexico in 1928, he perceived that there was a great need for air freight transport in the southeastern part of Mexico, where the chicle (the gum of the sapodilla tree from which chewing gum is made) and coffee industries needed swift transport and where surface routes were almost non-existent.

By 1933, he and his brother Jesús were operating under the name of **Sarabia Hermanos** (Sarabia Brothers) in the states of Chiapas and Tabasco. No passengers were carried at first, but full service was offered from 1933 after the company's name had been changed to **Transportes Aéreos de Chiapas, S.A. (TACH)**, with the support of President Lázaro Cárdenas. The route concession for the former Pickwick branch route was obtained on 25 May, 1933, and for a few years TACH established itself in the region, flying Bellancas, Stinsons, and Travel Airs. For a short time in 1934, it provided a feeder connection to the Líneas Aéreas Occidentales trunk route.

By 1937, further miscellaneous aircraft had been added, including nine-seat Pilgrim 100s, and the operations of Aerovías de Quintana Roo, a small company

17

Francisco Sarabia (*left*), Mexico's aviation hero, started one of Mexico's first airlines, Transportes Aéreos de Chiapas, S.A. (TACSA), serving chicle camps in eastern Mexico. Gordon Barry (*right*) began as a pilot with the legendary CAT in 1929, then worked at the Tayoltita Mine before founding LAMSA in 1934. (*José Villela and John W. Underwood*)

from that Territory, were incorporated, with official concessions granted in 1939. This year, however, was to prove a tragic one for all concerned with the airline, or indeed aviation generally in Mexico. On 7 June, 1939, Francisco Sarabia, having completed a record-breaking flight from Mexico City to New York in his Gee Bee monoplane *Conquistador del Cielo*, (formerly the *Q.E.D.* originally built for Jacqueline Cochran to use in the England–Australia Air Race) crashed on take-off into the Potomac River in Washington on the return flight. A mechanic had left a piece of rag in the carburettor.

The ownership of the airline passed to his old chauffeur, Effego Cabrera, who married Sarabia's widow, Agripina Díaz. To honour the memory of one of the greatest of the Mexican aviation pioneers, the name of the Chiapas airline was changed to **Compañía Aeronáutica Francisco Sarabia, S.A.** In fact, the company lost its identity with the state of Chiapas, as the local routes were transferred to the Compañía Aeronáutica del Sur, and other feeder routes on the Gulf Coast were taken over by Francisco's brother, under the name **Líneas Aéreas Jesús Sarabia**. But Jesús survived Francisco by only three months, as he too was killed in the crash of a Spartan aircraft in Quintana Roo on 2 September, 1939.

The reorganized airline had ambitions beyond feeder services. It began operations from Tapachula to Mexico City, via Tuxtla Gutíerrez and Oaxaca, but CMA challenged the legality of this enterprise under the provisions of the law which effectively preserved monopoly rights. CMA's claim was apparently upheld, as, late in 1942, the Sarabia line stopped operating.

The local network in the state of Chiapas passed in due course to **Servicios Aéreos de Chiapas, S.A. de C.U. (SACSA)** a co-operative organization formed in the late 1940s, which also absorbed the operations of **Transportes Aéreos Yajalón, S.A. (TAYSA)**, based at Yajalón. SACSA served the coffee plantations with an assortment of small aircraft which included two Northrop trimotors, which however were too complex for the small airline to maintain. One crashed

XA-BJR, seen in Chiapas, was a Bellanca CH-300 Pacemaker operated by Francisco Sarabia. (*Courtesy Herculaneo Sarabia*)

A very rare aeroplane, the EMSCO (E. M. Smith Co) Model B-3-A used by Transportes Aéreos de Chiapas, possibly for the hauling of coffee beans. The B-3-A was powered by a 420 hp Pratt & Whitney Wasp engine and was certificated in February 1931. Only a few B-3-As were built. (*Courtesy José Villela*)

A Sarabia Pilgrim 100, XA-BJZ, about to load chicle from the growing area in Chiapas State. One of the loaded rail-borne trucks can be seen behind the figure on the right. (*Courtesy Herculano Sarabia*)

19

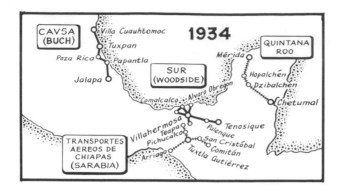

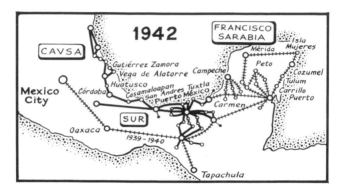

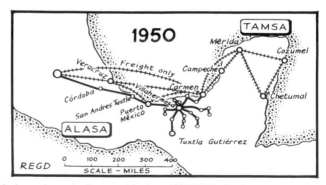

3. The Struggle for Independence in Eastern Mexico, 1934–1950. Surface transport in eastern and southern Mexico was always poor during the prewar years; but the small airlines were never able to do more than create local networks, because CMA and Pan American controlled the trunk routes.

20

tragically in the city of Tuxtla Gutíerrez, and by the mid-1950s, SACSA's fleet was reduced to a single Douglas B-18 bomber, before it finally passed into oblivion, overtaken by the march of surface transport. Between 1946 and 1957, a chicle producers' co-operative in the state of Campeche, **Los Chenes, S.C.L.** also performed a similar role to SACSA's.

Peck Woodside and Pancho Buch

Another worthy contributor to the spirit of independence was a US citizen, Garrett 'Peck' Woodside, a colourful entrepreneur and aviation believer who began air freighting work, similar to Sarabia's, from a base at Villahermosa, the state capital of Tabasco. He inherited a small network of lines started by **J. Hans Mattes** as early as 1930 (Concession No.28) thus laying claim to being the third oldest airline in Mexico, after CMA and C.A.T. Woodside's airline was called **Compañía Aeronáutica del Sur, S.A.**, and, with a fleet of Ryan Broughams, flourished to the extent that further route concessions were obtained in 1936, while in 1938 it took over the feeder services of Sarabia in the state of Chiapas.

A little further up the coast from Peck Woodside's 'territory', another pioneer had carved himself a special niche in the Mexican airline map. Francisco ('Pancho') Buch de Parada founded **Comunicaciónes Aéreas de Veracruz (CAVSA)** in Jalapa, capital of the state of Veracruz, in 1934. He was granted various route concessions, first within the state, then stretching as far as Puerto México (Coatzacoalcos), where he connected with Woodside's operation. Buch gained a certain notoriety because his first aircraft, a Fairchild 71, became known as *El Espinazo del Diablo (The Devil's Backbone)*, because of its red colour and an apparently symbolic design on the fuselage.

By 1940, Buch was operating a fleet of nine-seat Pilgrims, and had apparently acquired title to some of the Curtiss Condors which had been parked at Veracruz, awaiting a ship to deliver them to the Republican Government engaged in the Spanish Civil War. They were never delivered, and were later sold to small airlines such as CAVSA. Two of them are known to have ended their days with CNAC in China.

Buch was successful enough to be able to accept an offer, reported to be 575,000 pesos, for the assets of CAVSA in June 1943. It passed into the hands of William T. Churchill Morgan, whose first act was to acquire Woodside's

Travel Air 4000, Fleet No.34, of Cía Aeronáutica del Sur at Tuxtla Gutiérrez during the early 1930s.

21

Compañía Aeronáutica del Sur. Woodside was *hors de combat*, critically ill and in a US hospital at the time. Returning to Mexico to find his airline 'hijacked', he left it to found a shrimp business in Ciudad del Carmen. Peck Woodside, one of Mexico's true airline pioneers, died in 1973, by which time he had been raising turkeys in Tabasco.

Such was the pattern of airline development among the lower echelons of the Mexican airline industry in the Thirties and Forties. Almost every viable—or, for that matter, many a non-viable—route was held under concession by somebody; so that, with a one-airline-one-route policy imposed by SCOP, there was no alternative to purchasing companies outright, even if this sometimes imposed the obligation to acquire superfluous routes or aircraft, or to employ methods of doubtful ethics.

Garrett 'Peck' Woodside (*left*), a US citizen, founded Compañía Aeronáutica del Sur, one of Mexico's earliest airlines, in Villahermosa in 1934. Manuel Gonzales (*right*) headed a group of enterprising pilots in 1930, flying between Mexico City and the emerging resort city, Acapulco. They formed the nucleus of what was to become Aeronaves de México. (*Maxine Woodside and José Villela*)

In 1945, Morgan was operating Lockheed Electras and was negotiating for the coveted route connections to Mexico City. The name of the airline was changed to the more impressive **Aerovías Latino Americanas, S.A. (ALASA)** and an arrangement was made with ATSA for a co-operative operation, but this came to nothing. ALASA ceased operations in the late 1950s.

As for Peck Woodside's local routes based at Villahermosa, and the chicle contracts that accompanied the air service, these were acquired by Francisco Somoano, who formed **Compañía Tabasqueña de Aviación, S.A.** in the mid-1940s. Gradually, as roads were built, the character of the operation changed, and the chicle services were dropped in favour of a tourist connection from Villahermosa to the Mayan ruins at Palenque. Eventually, in 1970, the concession was transferred to Aeronaves Alimentadoras.

The First Airlines on the Pacific Coast

While the Sarabias were trying to provide a system of feeder routes in the eastern parts of Mexico, another group of individuals concentrated on trying to fill the commercial aviation gaps on the Pacific coast. During the early 1930s, there were no sizeable cities, except possibly the port of Acapulco, all the way from Mazatlán to the Guatemalan frontier. The states along the coast were almost cut off from the industrial heart of Mexico, with few roads or railways, and as yet the considerable attractions of the area as a tourist destination had not been realized. The airline pioneers of the region, therefore, began by providing a real community service, as the only form of transport, and few of them had any aspirations to making a large fortune from such slender resources of traffic potential.

Yet in a strange way, these small airlines were to play their part in providing the foundation of what was eventually to become Mexico's first national airline. One of the pioneers in this area was **Daniel P. Fort**, who began to operate a service from Guadalajara to Puerto Vallarta. The port was then little more than a village, and when Fort obtained Concession No.32 on 9 October, 1934, it was mainly to serve intermediate points in almost inaccessible mountain valleys.

Daniel Fort surrendered his Puerto Vallarta concession after only about two years' operation, for on 10 August, 1936, SCOP granted an experimental permit over the same route linking Guadalajara with the coast to General Roberto Fierro Villalobos and his brother Raul. Roberto, a former military air force chief, had founded **Transportes Aéreos de Jalisco, S.A. (TAJ or TAJSA)** and within less than a year found himself with a permanent route to what was to emerge, several decades later, as one of the world's most fashionable resorts. TAJ expanded its network modestly to some neighbouring communities in 1941, and linked Guadalajara with Tepic in 1943; but all operations ceased in 1945.

Fort had also operated across the neck of the Sea of Cortez to link Mazatlán with La Paz, but he sold or leased the Concession to a US citizen, **Ogden**, who operated his own Osprey on the route in the mid-1930s, to be followed by Noel Bullock. Gordon Barry took over with a Sikorsky S-38, but then the route came under Díaz Lombardo's control, giving **Aeronaves de México** its first foothold in the northwest of Mexico.

Lombardo also acquired at the same time **Transportes Aéreos del Pacífico**, owned by Mario Rivas Mercado and Joaquin Cortina Goribar. Formed on 31 May, 1935, it obtained Concession 33 for a route linking Acapulco with Oaxaca via intermediate points along the coast of Guerrero and Oaxaca. Its two Travel Airs were capably handled by reputable pilots such as Julio Zinzer, Cloyd Clavenger, and 'Pistol Pete' Baughan.

The two Zarate brothers, in an echo of the Sarabia family efforts, were active in these states. Enrique Zarate started **Servicios Aéreos Zarate** to vie with Taxis Aéreos Oaxaca for local routes around the state capital; while **Alfredo Zarate** began a route from Acapulco westwards along the coast, and then inland to Uruapan in Michoacán, using two Buhl sesquiplanes. Pistol Pete left Pacífico to operate a line from Mexico City to Oaxaca and Ixtepec, but could not obtain a permanent concession because he was not a Mexican citizen.

Taxi Aéreo Oaxaca was founded in 1938 by Capt **Luís Melgosa**, the concession being issued under his name. He started a circular route in the Oaxaca–Tehuacán–Mixteca region with one Stinson Detroiter, operating directionally on alternate days.

The service became known as **Taxi Aéreo de Oaxaca** and was the only form of transport in the area. As such it carried a high risk factor. On one occasion in 1940, at Jamiltepec, the pilot, Julio Zambrano, walked to the town to telephone for a new battery because he could not start the Stinson's engine. Walking back to the airstrip, accompanied by the Mayor of the town and the local agent, all three were shot by political enemies of the Mayor. When the relief aircraft arrived, the crew started the Stinson on its own battery.

Melgosa operated a cargo route to a gold mine near Juchatengo, for which purpose he acquired an ancient Boeing Model 40, and he also bought a Buhl sesquiplane besides more Stinsons. He conceded his concession to Aeronaves de México early in 1943, at which time the Stinsons were retired and the Travel Airs of Julio Zinzer's Transportes Aéreos del Pacífico used for all lines serving Oaxaca.

Eclipsing all these in its rapid growth and success, however, was the company which obtained the concession for the direct route from Mexico City to Acapulco. Originally, the idea of connecting these two points with a scheduled air service was conceived by **Francisco T. Mancilla**, who opened a service from Mérida to Payo Obispo (now called Chetumal) on 8 September, 1934, later extending to Belize to become one of Mexico's first international airlines. Mancilla cherished the visionary ambition of linking Mexico City with both Yucatán and Acapulco, both centres of expanding tourism. But Mancilla dropped out of contention and the Acapulco connection was operated experimentally by Ramon and Manuel Gonzalez, who, with the young Díaz Lombardo, nephew of the industrialist, and Leonardo Enriquez, used small Bellanca, Beech, Waco, Ryan, Verville, Fokker and Fairchild aircraft. An experimental permit was granted by SCOP on 15 May, 1934, by which time control of the fledgling company had passed to an enterprising industrialist and financier, Antonio Díaz Lombardo. He held the Mexican agency for Standard Oil of California and the largest Ford Agency in Mexico, controlled several Mexican bus lines, and was President of the Banco de Transportes. His holdings in **Aeronaves de México**—for this was the ambitious name dreamed up by the brothers Gonzalez—were through another holding company, Combustibles, Turismo y Transportes, S.A.

The Stinson Reliant XB-AJI which operated Aeronaves de México's first Mexico City–Acapulco service, on 14 September, 1934. The photograph was taken during the delivery flight from Detroit by Julio Zinzer. (*Courtesy José Villela*)

Díaz, together with Julio Zinzer (see Transportes Aéreos del Pacífico) flew to Kansas City and selected a better aircraft for what, with good foresight, he realized was a prestige route. The Stinson Reliant XB-AJI, brought from the USA by Julio Zinzer and now flown by Cloyd P. Clavenger, a well-known pilot, began the Mexico City–Acapulco service on 14 September, 1934. Aeronaves de México was formally incorporated on 7 November of that year, and a 30-year concession was obtained on 5 November, 1935.

During the next five years, the single route expanded in traffic volume, and the airline acquired more aircraft: Wacos, Curtiss Robins, Bellancas, Beechcraft, and Travel Airs. Of all the diminutive feeder airlines in Mexico, this one was clearly a winner; a circumstance which did not escape the attention of Pan American, which even in the late 1930s, was confident enough of its political strength to regard the Mexican airline industry as its own domain.

The First Expansion of Aeronaves de México

On 12 September, 1940, Pan American Airways entered into an agreement with Díaz Lombardo through the Combustibles company to acquire 40 per cent of the shareholding. This agreement was put into effect six days later, and the 120,000 pesos capital raised to 500,000. Pan American could nominate two of the five board members, one of whom, Wilbur Morrison (who had started in the Tampico oilfields dropping payrolls from Lincoln Standards) was to play an important part in the company's affairs in Mexico for many years to come. Carlos Ramos was appointed General Manager, with Luís Frías Carrillo as his assistant. Ramos eventually handed over to Jorge Pérez y Bouras. Frías Carrillo was still with the airline in 1981.

CMA's XA-DOJ, seen by the old terminal at Mexico City, had been the Wright R-1820 powered Douglas C-39. It was essentially a modified DC-2 with DC-3 fin and was referred to in Pan American Airways timetables as the DC-2½. (*Mexicana*)

As was customary when Pan American took over an airline, the fleet was immediately upgraded. Two ten-seat Boeing 247Ds augmented the Mexico City–Acapulco route to a daily service on 30 September, 1941, and the following year these aircraft were superseded by the Douglas C-39 version of the basic DC-2 type—sometimes referred to as the DC-2½. But the main development under the new management was to acquire almost every small airline operating on the Pacific seaboard, or in the Pacific states of Mexico. Thus, in 1941, Transportes

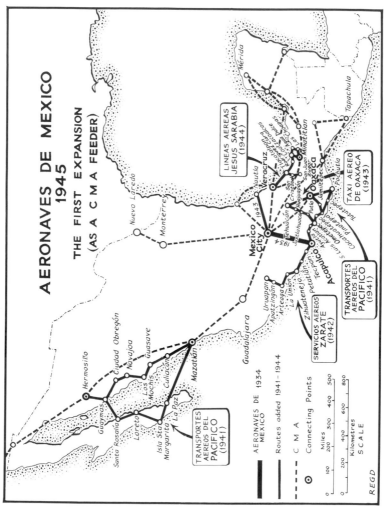

4. Aeronaves de México (The First Expansion) 1941–1945. Beginning with a single route, between Mexico City and Acapulco, Aeronaves de México, with Pan American backing, expanded considerably by the end of the Second World War. But CMA still controlled the main trunk air routes of Mexico at this time.

Aéreos del Pacífico—Julio Zinzer's airline—now operating a Sikorsky S-38 and some Stinsons—was acquired; to be followed the next year by taking over the concession of Servicios Aéreos Zarate, after Zarate himself was killed in a crash. The latter now became known as **Aeronaves de Michoacán**, operating first a Stinson, then Avro Ansons and a Boeing 247. Early in 1943, the routes of Taxi Aéreo de Oaxaca were added; an experimental service to the Gulf Coast was started from Mexico City to Nautla; and the routes of Líneas Aéreas Jesús Sarabia came under Aeronaves control.

Seen in the livery of Aeronaves de Michoacán is Boeing 247D XA-KAJ at Pie de la Cuesta Airport, Acapulco. (*José Villela*)

Pan American Airways explained its sudden devotion to the cause of feeder airlines in Mexico by stating (in a submission to the US Civil Aeronautics Board) that 'it would be healthier for the entire air transport industry in Mexico if a number of the smaller, under-financed airlines could be consolidated into one strong company'. This was substantially true, but could also be taken as a polite euphemism for 'eliminating possible future competition'. At any rate, the C.A.B. ruled on 9 December, 1943, that Pan American controlled Aeronaves, and rather than acquire more airlines (most of the feeder routes were progressively dropped during the next five years) the route network of Aeronaves was strengthened by linking Mazatlán with Mexico City, thus joining together the separate pieces of the network.

On 26 June, 1946, the authorized capital was raised to 2,250,000 pesos, and in September of that year, Aeronaves received its first Douglas DC-3, equipped with twenty-four seats. The extra capacity was needed to cope with the postwar demand on the Acapulco route by a new affluent society in the capital city, seeking relaxation on the beaches of the nearest place on the coast.

LAMSA

Early in 1932, Gordon Barry, one of the refugees from the late C.A.T. airline, began operating a short route between Mazatlán (a key point on C.A.T.'s former network) and the mining community of Tayoltita, 68 miles away. C.A.T. had originally started a service in mid-1931 under contract to the San Luís Mining Company, with a Ryan Brougham, after Lowell Yerex had made trial landings, first with a Ryan, then with a Vega at the Tayoltita airstrip, which most birds would inspect carefully before risking a landing. Barry salvaged a Bach trimotor from the debris of C.A.T. and signed a contract with the San Luís Mining Company, which had also bought a Bellanca Airbus. Barry connected with the operation of Walter Varney, whose short-lived Líneas Aéreas Occidentales passed through Mazatlán on its way from California to Mexico City. Occasionally, Barry would fly a Varney aircraft to California, to visit his home there. He incorporated **Líneas Aéreas Mineras, S.A.** (**LAMSA**) as a Mexican company on 27 August, 1934, under an agreement with the San Luís Mine, guaranteeing air service in exchange for a loan to establish the airline. The other applicant for the privilege of serving the mine was Charles Baughan, whose semi-military attire, complete with pistol slung on his belt, earned him his nickname Pistol Pete. Of course, all pilots in Mexico in those days carried arms as a sensible precaution against the hazards of a forced landing in the wild country of rural Mexico.

In spite of the tiny route, Barry built at first on a sound foundation. The company was capitalized at $25,000, and control was indirectly held by William Randolph Hearst, through the Mining company in which he held a majority interest. Obtaining an experimental permit for his single route on 24 September, 1934, this was converted into a 30-year concession (No.35) on 10 October, 1935. With a Waco biplane and a Bach trimotor he had expanded the network to La Paz and Durango on 3 September of that year, then obtained the experimental permit on 10 June, 1936, and received the route concession (No.45) on 29 March, 1937. In 1937, Barry appointed his capable wife, Judith, as President of LAMSA— probably the first woman in the Americas to hold such a position.

Barry took over the Mazatlán–La Paz route from Noel Bullock, who operated a Bach 'trimotor', with power reduced to a single engine (a 450 hp Wasp). That operation ended when the Bach crashed into the sea halfway across. A Pan American Ford Tri-Motor, piloted by Harold Gray (later to become President of Pan American) spotted the aircraft the next day and sent an S.O.S. to a Mexican patrol vessel. Bullock had been observed sitting on the tail of the Bach, brandishing a pistol. The five passengers were on the wing, still above the water. The search was called off after two days. Bullock had presumably shot the passengers, then himself, in preference to becoming shark-bait.

Barry realised that an opportunity existed for the north central route, as CMA did not appear to be interested. Accordingly, he started a Mexico City–Ciudad Juárez service, via Torreón and other stops, on 4 December, 1937, and duly received the 30-year concession (No.59) on 3 October, 1938. On 29 August, 1939, the link was made from Durango to Torreón (Concession No.69) and in March 1941 operations began to Nuevo Laredo. Thus, Gordon Barry had rebuilt LAMSA almost exactly on the pattern of C.A.T. (Maps 2 and 6 on pages 10 and 50) and there may have been some misgivings at CMA and Pan American that a prize fish had slipped through the net, even though Barry was gravely undercapitalized.

Minor changes were made to the LAMSA map. An experimental permit was obtained for a branch line northwest of Chihuahua to Nogales on 7 November, 1942. Barry withdrew from the Nuevo Laredo route after conceding that the combined strength of CMA and American Airlines—a newcomer into Mexico— was too much competition. But a month later, on 5 February, 1943, the Nogales route opened and a concession was awarded shortly afterwards. And this little border city (or cities—there was one on each side of the frontier) was to play a small part in the developing history of airline connections between Mexico and the USA.

For it was through Nogales that a new and powerful US airline, no less than United Air Lines, sought to gain entry into the Mexican market. On 6 October, 1942, United had granted a loan to Barry for $230,000 'to improve its financial and

28

technical position'. Barry used $50,000 of the money to buy six Lockheed Vegas. Then, in an important decision, on 17 September, 1943, the Civil Aeronautics Board approved the purchase by United of 75 per cent of LAMSA's shares, on condition that there was no route extension beyond the Mexican border. United had originally planned to buy the Mexico City–Tapachula route from Cía Aeronáutica Francisco Sarabia. But the latter withdrew from the route in 1943 and SCOP transferred the concession almost immediately to CMA, and the simultaneous attention given to Nogales, and United's take-over bid, was no coincidence.

Gordon Barry resigned from LAMSA on 28 October, 1943, having rejuvenated a network once thought to be a lost cause, but which now appeared as a key issue in a route battle between leading US airlines. But it had been a fearful struggle. Some idea of the difficulties overcome by Mexican independent airlines, without the solid backing of a corporation like Pan American behind them, can be gleaned from a United Air Lines report. Because of the impossibility of obtaining spare parts, improvization was a way of life with LAMSA. Most of the undercarriage fittings were made from old car frames. Piston rings were taken from tractor engines. Wheels were made by melting down old cylinder heads. Ignition cables were continuously spliced and patched instead of being renewed. Precision components such as valve guides and tappet bushings were home-made, while master-rod bearings were fashioned from salvaged propeller blades. It was a triumph of man over metal, and United's intervention must have come just in time to save LAMSA from an ignominious demise.

LAMSA's Boeing 247D XA-DIY *Estado de Chihuahua* in white, green and red livery. (*United Air Lines*)

Having acquired complete control on 1 October, 1943—increasing its shareholding to 80 per cent—United changed the name of the airline to **Líneas Aéreas Mexicanas, S.A.** (also **LAMSA**) on 9 February, 1944. The official concession (No.92) from Chihuahua to Nogales came through on 4 May, and United acted instantly to apply for an extension to Los Angeles and Phoenix, with the Mexican authorities on 13 May and with the US C.A.B. on 8 June, 1944. Shortly thereafter, United acquired complete ownership of LAMSA and on 8 October, 1944, transferred from its US fleet five ten-seat Boeing 247Ds. At the same time, money was allocated to improve station buildings, airports, and radio installations on LAMSA's network. The comparison with Barry's standards was dramatic; but the pioneer pilot had been trying to run a trunk airline without capital or resources, and it had been a minor miracle that in 1944 there was still an airline left for United to take over.

Immediately after the end of the war, United moved to consolidate its position in Mexico through LAMSA. On 6 September, 1943, it sold the irrelevant Mazatlán–Tayoltita line to Ing Adolfo García. At this time, it had just been upgraded from a Bach trimotor to a Lockheed Vega operation—hardly consistent with trunk-line standards in the postwar era. Further strategic route applications were made, Nogales to San Diego on 24 October, and Torreón to Houston and San Antonio, via Monterrey, on 19 August, 1945. A splendid new maintenance and overhaul base was completed at Torreón and six Douglas DC-3s added to the fleet during the first half of 1946. But United's enthusiasm was not reflected by a show of legislative momentum. The C.A.B., on 3 May, 1946, effectively delayed matters by amalgamating United's applications with those of other airlines in the Arizona–New Mexico Case. But this delay proved to be ineffective, as the United States and Mexico were unable to come to any bilateral agreement over postwar air routes and operators between the two countries. After interminable meetings, US President Harry Truman lost patience and ended the negotiations in 1952. This, incidentally, resulted in the odd circumstance in which the only direct service between New York and Mexico City was by Air France, and the issue was not resolved until President Eisenhower finally got things settled on 8 March, 1957.

LAMSA's Douglas DC-3A XA-JUT *Ciudad de Nuevas Casas Grandes*. This aircraft, which had a starboard passenger door, had been United Air Lines' NC25613 *Mainliner Washington D.C.* Later this DC-3 was Aeronaves de México's *Tizoc* and in the late 1970s it was in service with Aeronaves del Sureste. (*Gordon S. Williams*)

But United's problems in Mexico were not solely political. All kinds of factors served to make life difficult. In the summer of 1946, foot-and-mouth disease among Mexican cattle caused a severe interruption in business travel connected with the industry, much of which was centred on LAMSA's sphere of influence. Substantial devaluation of the Mexican peso stimulated tourist traffic from the USA, but LAMSA's network touched upon only one resort which was as yet little known. Because of its financial problems, Mexico imposed an economic embargo on consumer goods from the USA, many of which were normally carried by air.

LAMSA took certain prudent measures by reducing its route mileage over uneconomic routes. It tried to supplement revenue by offering special packages: sightseeing flights to Mount Popocatepetl, *Fishermen's Flights* to Guaymas, and a *Free Husbands* travel plan for full fare-paying wives. But to no avail. United became disillusioned with its Mexican operation, and moved to dispose of it. On

22 July, 1952, United sold LAMSA to a Mexican business group, Líneas Asociadas Mexicanas, S.A. (again LAMSA). This was a new name for Aerovías Continentales, which had been organized in 1946 as a contender for the Mexico City–New Orleans–New York route. In a strange kind of way, the LAMSA purchase was a means to that end.

United States Forays into Mexico

United Air Lines never did obtain a foothold in the Mexican market, mainly because of procrastination by the authorities north of the border. Its insecure tenure in LAMSA lasted from 17 September, 1943, when the US C.A.B. granted approval of its financial interest (acquired on 1 October), until 22 July, 1952, when in frustration United washed its hands of Mexico.

But it was not the only airline which reached southwards during the war years, when the exigencies of the time sometimes led to new directions of policy by the US authorities. American Airlines, in fact, had led the way by obtaining from SCOP a permit to serve Mexico City, via Monterrey, from Texas gateway cities, including El Paso and Laredo. The C.A.B. permit was forthcoming on 14 April, 1942—even in wartime, the C.A.B. moved at its own leisurely pace—and American opened its route on 5 September, 1942. Two DC-3s took off simultaneously from Fort Worth and El Paso to Monterrey and Mexico City. American Airlines was the first trunk airline from the United States to serve the interior of Mexico, as opposed to border station interline arrangements.

The other US airline which was defeated in its efforts to serve Mexico was Braniff Airways. In contrast with United's experience, however, Braniff's difficulties came from south of the border. Late in 1943, in the name of T. E. Braniff, it took over the experimental permits held by José Navarro Elizondo and changed the name of the temporary operation to **Aerovías Braniff**. On 4 April, 1945, a DC-3 route was opened from the frontier airport of Nuevo Laredo to Mexico City, via Ciudad Victoria, later extended to Puebla and Veracruz; and a Mexico City–Mérida route was opened on 1 July. Braniff was ordered to suspend the latter service but fought its case in the courts and continued to operate. On 22 May, 1946, the US C.A.B. granted T. E. Braniff permission to acquire Aerovías Braniff (but disapproved a similar application from Braniff Airways—a rose by another name, presumably. . .) but the action was irrelevant, as SCOP refused to convert the *Permiso* into a *Concesión*, with permanent authority, on 26 October of that year. Foiled at Mérida, where it was not even allowed to use the air terminal, Braniff tried to stay in the market by flying some charter services into Mexico during 1947 and 1948, and also unsuccessfully applied for a Mexico City–Balboa route on 10 September, 1947. But the invasion of United States airlines into Mexico on a grand scale had to await the signing of a comprehensive bilateral agreement, which was not forthcoming until 1957.

Panini and Reforma

Mexico has never lacked colourful characters as leaders of its airline industry. Another to join the ranks was Carlos Panini, an Italian immigrant who had settled in the state of Hidalgo, and had become successful in clay mining. He became interested in flying, became an amateur pilot (instructed by the veteran Julio Zinzer himself) and decided to go into the airline business. He founded **Servicios Aéreos Panini, S.A.** in 1934, and the following year he was awarded a concession

31

Julio Zinzer (*left*) one of Mexico's great pilots during the early 1930s, started air services on the west coast, which were later incorporated into Aeronaves de México. Francisco Buch de Parada (*centre*)—'Pancho' to his friends—started Comunicaciones Aéreas de Veracruz, S.A. (CAVSA) in 1934, which later became ALASA. Carlos Panini (*right*), was a colourful personality who fashioned an airline in 1934 which became part of Aerovías Reforma in 1948. Panini was killed in a car accident in 1951 while participating in the Pan American Car Race. (*José Villela*)

to link Mexico City with Morelia, state capital of Michoacán, by a circuitous route through the valley of the Río Balsas in northern Guerrero. Felipe Garcia made the initial flight in September 1936 in the Buhl sesquiplane XB-AAT over what became known as the *Ruta del Balsas*.

In those days the Río Balsas and its tributaries effectively barred the way between the cities of the high Mexican plateau and the Pacific coast for a considerable distance. There was no bridge for about 300 miles west of the Mexico City–Acapulco highway. This led to the odd circumstance of Panini operating an air ferry service across the Balsas, from Ciudad Altamırano to Coyuca de Catalán. The distance was one kilometre, the flight time was two minutes, and the fare was eight pesos over what was almost certainly the shortest air route in the world.

Panini was remarkably successful in discovering routes that nobody else had bothered about, or that had become available through default. Thus, during the next few years he built up a modest network which included Mexico's three largest cities. In 1939 his first route was extended to Colima and Guadalajara, and reached the coast at Manzanillo in July 1942. By this time Panini had four Buhls, had built a substantial base at Mexico City (later to become the headquarters of Aeronaves de México) and a secondary base at Morelia. In October 1942 he picked up the route from Mexico City to Durango, added one to Ometepec, in southeast Guerrero, and had replaced the Buhls in 1944 with three Boeing 247s, one of which had three-blade variable-pitch propellers, the other two having only two-blade propellers. In 1944 he reached Monterrey from Guadalajara, crossing the Durango route at Zacatecas. The next year, this was extended to the US frontier at Reynosa.

By July 1947 Panini was operating Douglas DC-2s and had received the important permanent concession for the Mexico City–Durango route; but the Guadalajara–Reynosa service was discontinued. Finally, the Durango route was

32

extended northwards to the state capital of Sinaloa, the prosperous city of Culiacán.

While Panini was establishing himself on the Mexican airline map, another company, **Aerovías Internacionales de México**, was organized in 1945, starting off in fine style with a small fleet of Douglas C-47s (DC-3s). It began operating from Ensenada, in the northern part of Baja California (and close to Tijuana) to Guadalajara. Early in 1946, its founder and chief stockholder, Ricardo 'Rico' Pani, owner of the Hotel Reforma in Mexico City, changed the name of the airline

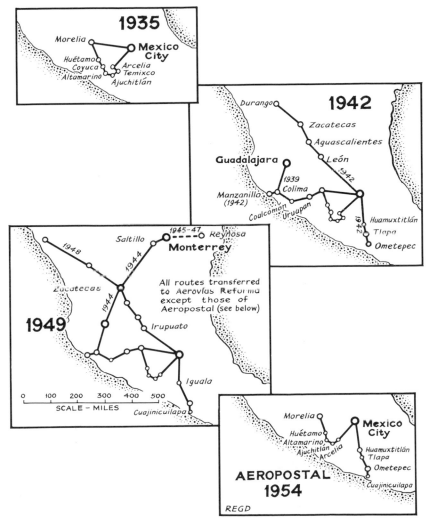

5. Rise and Fall of Panini, 1935–1954. Carlos Panini fashioned an airline network by linking together some minor routes which the larger companies did not want. These eventually passed to Aerovías Reforma, and thence to Aeronaves de México, where they provided the basis for further expansion.

Aerovías Reforma's Douglas C-47A XA-HUG (seen with single door).
(*Gordon S. Williams*)

to **Aerovías Reforma, S.A.** Although the line was extended to Tijuana in 1947, Pani was unable to support the enterprise, although he had, with considerable vision, made studies to show that an integrated Mexican airline was feasible. But he left it to others to put a formidable plan into effect.

In June 1945, another aspiring airline, **Golfo y Pacífico Aerotransportes, S.A. (GPA)** was founded by a group of investors, including Herculano Sarabia, brother of the famous Francisco. Later in the year, a service was opened from Veracruz, on the Gulf of Mexico, to Ixtepec, on the Pacific Ocean. But because of the conditions of Mexican law, the route was very circuitous, and GPA's Avro Anson could not pay its way.

In 1946, Carlos Oriani purchased control, and appointed Rubén Ruiz Alcántara as General Manager. Then, on 7 February, 1947, Oriani bought Aerovías Reforma from Rico Pani, who was experiencing problems with his hotel business. Then, in 1948, for a reputed 1,500,000 pesos, he acquired Servicios Aéreos Panini. GPA was liquidated, but Alcántara stayed on as General Manager of Reforma, with Raymundo Cano as his chief engineer. Cano was later to become President of Aeronaves and Alcántara was to form his own airline.

To Reforma's DC-3s, Oriani added a DC-2 and four Boeing 247Ds. But far more important, he acquired Panini's route certificates, which supplemented Reforma's own, to create a respectable-looking route map. This was the first systematic attempt to create a viable airline by amalgamating the route certificates of smaller companies. Individually, they were probably doomed to extinction, because of insufficient market base; but together they stood an outside chance of survival.

As for Panini, he bought a DC-3 with the proceeds of the sale, hired a pilot, and flew back to the land of his fathers to visit the family. His decision to sell was alleged to be partly because of a DC-2 crash; and the tragic sequel was that Panini himself should be killed, not in an aeroplane crash, but in a car accident, when he was participating in the Pan-American car race (Tapachula–Ciudad Juárez) between Oaxaca and Mexico City, driving an Alfa Romeo.

Another coast-to-coast aspirant was Miguel Anaya García, who founded **Servicio Aéreo Anaya** in Zitácuaro, in northern Michoacán, in 1942. Originally he operated a small route to Huétamo and Zirandoro, in the Río Balsas region, with a two-seat Aeronca Sedan and a small Cessna. He flew the aircraft himself, and his brother was the mechanic. Later in the 1950s, he transferred his base to Mexico City, and in the 1960s, now using Beech 18s, he extended his route to Zihuatanejo, on the Pacific. When, by a leasing arrangement with Manuel Gómez Méndez, Anaya added a Mexico City–Tuxpan route, he theoretically linked the Pacific with the Gulf; but the points served were insufficient to generate enough traffic. Anaya enjoyed a fine reputation for reliable service, but by the time Zihuatanejo began to emerge as a later-day Acapulco, in the early 1970s, Aeronaves Alimentadoras had engulfed all the small airlines.

T.A.T. and LAUSA

Among all the convoluted manoeuvres of the independent airlines to seek a place in the Mexican airline sun, one of the most bewildering was that of a group which underwent five or six distinct corporate changes within twenty years, each one of which produced a route network almost unrecognizable from the last—and all accomplished within the law which ordained that all routes should be monopolies.

In the beginning was a small airline operated by **Luís and Antonio Melgosa**, who managed to thread their way between Oaxaca and Mexico city without trespassing on anybody else's territory. This was in 1935 and the brothers Melgosa went quietly about their modest business for about fifteen years. Later than the Melgosas, and in another part of Mexico, Felipe Gutiérrez de Lara founded **Transportes Aéreos de Tampico (T.A.T)** in 1940 and obtained an experimental permit on 22 May of that year to operate a local service from Tampico to Huejutla. He started service with a Spartan biplane, and began full service, with a 30-year concession, on the *Ruta de las Huastecas* on 2 January, 1941.

This miniscule route did not seem to have much prospect of success, but it seems to have provided the foundation for growth, partly because Huejutla was strategically situated about half way to Mexico City, and in a direct line. After starting experimentally from Tampico to Monterrey, via Ciudad Victoria, on 15 October, 1942, T.A.T. abandoned this route the following year. Some time later, however, the Tampico airline turned its eyes southward and opened a service to Mexico City on 2 September, 1946. This was so successful that DC-3s were introduced in 1947. Then a Tampico–Poza Rica route was opened with Avro Ansons, with Cessna T-50s acting in a supporting role.

In 1950, by which time the Melgosa operation had become known as **Aeronaves Oaxaca**, under the direction of Tomás Calderón, Felipe Gutiérrez de Lara organized a merger with T.A.T., together with another small airline, **Servicios Aéreos Nacionales (SAN)**. The three-way amalgamation was named **Líneas Aéreas Unidas, S.A. (LAUSA)**, literally United Air Lines. Part of the network was the old Pacífico route of the early 1930s, taken over then by Aeronaves de México but later disposed of.

LAUSA sought permission in April 1953 to break out of the confines of local routes by applying to operate from both Acapulco and Tampico nonstop to Matamoros, using Lockheed Constellations. This never happened, but after a change of name to **LAUMSA** (by the insertion of **Mexicanas** to the former title) and a change of ownership, a connection was made from Tampico to Reynosa—close to Matamoros—in 1962. The airline then boasted a fleet of five four-engined Canadair DC-4M-2s.

While this was going on, another airline had been formed for the express purpose of evacuating deportees under a United States Government contract. **Servicios Aéreos Especiales, S.A. (SAESA)** was formed on 28 March, 1960, to operate between Reynosa and León, and later extended this flourishing trade to Matamoros and Ciudad Juárez. On 1 March, 1964, SAESA began a scheduled service on a Mexico City–Poza Rica–Reynosa route, and to do this appears to have come to an arrangement with LAUMSA (possibly in the form of a shotgun marriage) for the latter's routes and aircraft. In the fullness of time, SAESA took over the routes of **Aerolíneas Vega**, became a state-owned concern, and was eventually absorbed by Aeronaves de México, as an operating associate.

The First Air Freight Airlines in Mexico

Gordon Barry, like so many others of his breed, had the running of an airline so impregnated in his blood that his expulsion from LAMSA merely gave him the excuse to start another. Late in 1943, he founded **Red Aérea Mexicana, S.A. (RAMSA)** as a freight airline to operate from Mexico City to Oaxaca, Tuxtla Gutiérrez, and Tapachula in the south, and to Zihuatanejo, via Arcelia, north of Acapulco. Operating an old Curtiss Condor and a Lockheed Vega, RAMSA was the first all-freight airline in Mexico to operate over a trunk route paralleling that of a major company—in this case CMA. Concentration on air freight was probably the loophole in the law by which he was able to obtain a coveted route franchise. However, RAMSA did not survive the war for very long, and operations ceased in 1947.

Another of the early Mexican freight airlines was **Aerovías Azteca**, formed late in 1944 for operations down the west coast of Mexico, from Mexicali, and initially scheduling one round trip weekly as far as the capital, via all the main cities en route, including Guadalajara. The airline's ownership was 58 per cent US, and the fleet consisted of two Budd Conestogas, the same unusual type, built largely of stainless steel, which had been purchased by the Flying Tiger Line in the United States. Operations began in March 1945, but Azteca did not last for more than a few months.

The early promise of lucrative freight hauls did not materialize, once the brief postwar boom was over. As in other parts of the world, the new equipment added to the established airline fleets were able to handle the extra demands made for air freight; so that specialized air freight airlines quickly found the market too limited and the competition too tough from rivals who could cross-subsidize from passenger revenues. One area, however, which continued to attract airline speculators was Baja California, where, in the 1940s, the possibility of hauling fish to San Diego and southern California via the transit border station at Tijuana was beginning to look attractive. In 1947, Manuel Contreras, a Tijuana merchant in import-export, started **Aerovías Contreras**, at first on local passenger routes to Ensenada, Mexicali, and San Felipe, then branching out to La Paz, near the southern tip of the peninsula. Soon, the air freight volumes surpassed the

Aerovías Contreras Curtiss C-46A XA-GOT *Ensenada*. (*Gordon S. Williams*)

36

Unlike other Curtiss C-46s, the C-46E had a stepped windscreen. This example, XA-MEM, was operated by Aerocarga. (*Courtesy José Villela*)

passenger business, which was absorbed by Aeronaves de México but Contreras ceased to operate entirely in the mid-1950s.

To some extent, Contreras was usurped by **Aerocarga S.A. (ACSA)** which was formed in 1950 by Capt Carlos Cervantes Perez, concentrating, as its name implied, on the air cargo business. Its main commodity was fish, supplied to the California market via Tijuana from La Paz. It also operated a small passenger service to the Isla de Cedros and to Bahía Tortugas, and the *brazeros* service between Tijuana and León, on charter to the US Government after Tigres Voladores ceased operations in 1959. Operating mainly old Curtiss C-46s, Aerocarga also had a converted Douglas B-18 bomber and later acquired a Lockheed 188 Electra, with which it operated from Tijuana to Mérida. The airline ceased to operate in 1977, to be succeeded by **Transportes Aéreos de Carga, S.A.** (see Table 2 pages 11 17), after the proud achievement of having flown the longest route in Mexico.

Special mention should be made of a small airline which was pruned off the LAMSA trunk airline network when United Air Lines took over. The short route from Mazatlán to Tayoltita, site of the San Luís Mine and once the aerial domain of Gordon Barry, was taken over by **Transportes Aéreos Terrestres (T.A.T.)**, first under a temporary permit, later on a permanent basis. Operating at first, in the late 1940s, with a Stinson Station Wagon, T.A.T. acquired a Ford 5-AT-B Tri-Motor which had seen service with Pan American, CMA, Cubana, TACA, and other airlines in a long career which had started when it first flew in December 1928. T.A.T. bought it in Florida late in 1948 for $5,000. The mining company then spent $60,000 to modernize it. The old Ford kept going on this demanding route—the destination airfield was on a slope, was badly surfaced, and was hemmed in by inhospitable mountain slopes—until 1970 when it was sold to American Airlines and became known far and wide among the aviation fraternity for its longevity. T.A.T. replaced it with the first Twin Otter to fly in Mexico.

While not strictly an air freight operator, mention should perhaps be made of an airline in Mexico whose livelihood depended upon human cargo. **Tigres Voladores** (Flying Tigers) began a Mexicali–Mexico City route during the mid-1950s, calling at Guaymas, Durango, Aguascalientes, and León. Its passengers were Mexican illegal immigrants disparagingly known as *wetbacks*,

An unusual Ford Tri-Motor, XA-HIL, seen here at Tayoltita, was the 5-AT which had been delivered to Pan American Airways in January 1929 as NC9637. After long service in Latin America it was modified in 1948 and fitted with 450 hp Pratt & Whitney R-985 engines, cowlings and controllable-pitch propellers, from three Vultee BT-13 trainers. The Ford was then owned by the San Luís Mining Company and operated by Transportes Aéreos Terrestres (T.A.T.) on the Mazatlán–Tayoltita route. (*John W. Underwood*)

Curtiss C-46A XA-LEZ of Tigres Voladores was acquired in April 1955. (*Gordon S. Williams*)

because their entry into the United States was said to have been made by clandestinely swimming the Río Grande—and they were carried in Curtiss C-46s, that ex-wartime workhorse whose exploits have been the equal in adventure and incident of the more famous DC-3. Tigres Voladores managed to carry 82 deported passengers, sitting sideways on bench seats, in each C-46. One stewardess handed out box lunches, containing a selection of Mexican delicacies. The bottom layer was alleged to be a Greyhound bus ticket back to the US border, presumably in an effort to generate repeat business. Business stopped altogether, however, when a C-46 crashed in 1959.

Another airline which initiated a special freight operation was **Líneas Aéreas Guerrero-Oaxaca, S.A. (LAGOSA)**, founded in the summer of 1946 by Isidoro Linares and Anastasio Blanco Elola. Starting with a Ford Tri-Motor, then adding a Boeing 247, they carried livestock from the coastal towns of Guerrero and Oaxaca (La Costa Chica) to the important inland city of Puebla, and also to Huajuápan. Supplies of groceries and other domestic products to the coast made up the return-loads. Unable to keep the two aircraft airworthy, LAGOSA rented a Douglas C-39 from Aeronaves de México in December 1947, and hired a pilot, Manuel Gómez Méndez, to clear up the backlog. Gómez Méndez astutely bought the C-39 from Aeronaves, to start a brief but eventful career in Mexican aviation.

In February 1950, LAGOSA helped another pilot to buy a Lockheed C-60 (military Lodestar) to operate under contract. But on the first commercial flight (from Pinotepa), the cargo shifted to the rear, the aircraft stalled, and crashed, killing the crew. This was the end of LAGOSA.

A Proliferation of Small Airlines

In the labyrinthine ancestral history of the Mexican monopoly-route airline system, many marriages, alliances and divorces took place during the 1930s and 1940s. The foregoing sections of this chapter have narrated the activities of pioneers such as 'Peck' Woodside, 'Pancho' Buch, the Sarabia brothers, Gordon Barry, Carlos Panini, and others whose airline enterprises were, in the fullness of time, to become part of larger groups. In some cases their story was quite brief, while in others, their epilogue is recounted more appropriately in a later chapter.

In addition, however, there were many others whose existence, in an environment of constant flirtations, alliances, and marriages of convenience, could be described as celibate. Both their uncertain ancestry and ultimate fate have been lost in the mists of time, and their names have long since been erased from the official records, if indeed they were ever known at all outside their local spheres of influence. They represented the lowest stratum of an embryo industry. They operated semi-regular or on-demand services with diminutive single-engined types some thirty years before the term Third Level was coined.

They were part of a fraternity of aviation pioneers struggling to find an identity. Often the first to recognize the need for localized air transport in remote areas where no other form of communication existed, in their small way they broke new ground and were true innovators. Table 1 on page 40 may serve as a modest epitaph to their achievement.

TABLE 1

Small Local Airlines in Mexico, 1930–1960
other than those reviewed in the text
(in approximate order of service inauguration)

Period	Name	Base	Routes
1930–40	Law	Chihuahua	Western Chihuahua State, including Ciudad Juárez
	J. D. del Prato (La Sierra)	Parral	Parral–Guadalupe y Calvo, via Guancevi
	E. B. Sloan	Nogales	Nogales–Guaymas
	Carlos Mayse	Mexicali	Mexicali–Punta Rocosa
	Roberto L. Miranda	Ciudad Madero	Ciudad Madero– Huejutla
	Servicios Aéreos del Noroeste	Mazatlán	
	Cía de Aviación Aeroclub de Tampico	Tampico	
1940–50	Servicios Aéreos Cuauhtémoc	Villa Cuauhtémoc	Villa Cuauhtémoc– Ciudad Victoria–Ciudad de Valles–Mexico City
	Servicios Aéreos de Durango	Durango	Local routes, including Durango–Guancevi
	Aerotransportes de Sonora	Cananea	Naco–Cananea– Nacozari de García
	Cía Transportes Aéreos del Pacífico	Guadalajara	Guadalajara–Mazatlán
1950–60	Servicios Aéreas Salgado	Toluca	Local services in State of Mexico
	Líneas Aéreas del Sur	Toluca	Toluca–Huétamo; Toluca–Iguala
	Transportes Aéreos Rosalía	Santa Rosalía	Santa Rosalía– Guaymas
	Taxis Aéreos Nacionales	Mexico City	Mexico City–Huétamo– Zihuatanejo
	Aerotransportes de Ario	Morelia	Morelia–Ario de Rosáles–La Unión
	Luís A. Lopez	Mérida	Mérida–El Cuyo–Isla Mujeres
	Coatzacoalcos	Coatzacoalcos	Circular route, including Minatitlán
	Aeronaves de Balsas	Morelia	Balsas River region, linking Mexico City, Manzanillo
	Servicios Aéreos de la Laguna	Parral	Parral–Torreón
	Alberto Luís de la Pela	Chihuahua	Chihuahua–Guachochic

TABLE 2
Small Local Airlines in Mexico 1955–1970

(Aeronaves de México and Mexicana, together with Servicios Aéreos Especiales (S.A.E.), Aerovías Guest, Trans Mar de Cortes, and LAUMSA are dealt with in the text)

Period	Name	Base	Routes	Remarks
1950–1977	**Aerocarga S.A. (ACSA)**	Ensenada	Freight route from La Paz, supplying fish to California. USA. Passenger service to Bahia Tortugas	Carried almost 2,000 tonnes of fish in 1963
Mid-1960s	Aerolineas de Altamirano, S.A.	Iguala	Radial route through northern Guerrero to Morelia	
Latter 1960s	Aerolineas Continental, S.A.	Durango	Durango-Tayoltita: –Parral	Formerly operated by Manuel Morales Morales
Late 1960s	Aerolineas Anahuac, S.A.	Mexico City	Mexico City–Jalapa; Taxco–Acapulco; Puebla–Acapulco	Ceased operations in 1969
1961–1968	Aerolineas de la Frontera S.A. de C.V.	Ciudad Acuña, Coahuila	Local services in states of Puebla, Hidalgo, and Veracruz	Formerly Aerovias Hidalgo
12 Dec, 1962–1970	Aerolineas del Pacifico S.A.	La Paz	La Paz–Los Mochis	Also operated to Chihuahua
1958–1969	**Aerolíneas Vega, S.A.**	Puebla	Oaxaca–Acapulco; Mérida	Carried 30,000 passengers annually. (See text)

Continued on page 42

Late 1950s–1969	**Aerolíneas Fierro**	Tepic, Nayarit	Tepic–Puerto Vallarta, and local routes in Nayarit and Jalisco	
Late 1950s–1966	**Aeronaves de Guerrero, S.A.**	Chilpancingo, Guerrero	Local services, radiating from Chilpancingo, also to Puebla	Formerly operating as **Manuel Gómez Méndez**. Became part of Aeromaya (see text) in 1966
1962–1966	**Aero Safari, S.A.**	Cozumel	Cozumel–Isla Mujeres; Chetumal; Tulum	Merged with Gómez Méndez to form Aeromaya in 1966
Late 1950s–1970s	Aeroservicio del Norte, S.A.	Chihuahua	Chihuahua to mining communities in western Chihuahua State, and to Parral	
Late 1950s–1970s	Aeroservicio Pity, S.A.	Durango	Local services radiating from Durango and from Culiacán	
1962–	Aerotaxis, S.A.	Durango	Local routes from Durango	
1962–1969	Aerovías del Centro, S.A.	Izúcar de Matamoros, Puebla	Local routes to points in Oaxaca and Guerrero States; and to Puebla	
Late 1950s–1969	Aerovías del Sur, S.A.	Mexico City	Mexico–Morelia, Arcelia, Ciudad Altamirano	
Late 1950s–Mid 1960s	Aerovías del Noroeste, S.A.	Agua Prieta, Sonora	Local services in northern Sonora	
1955–1969	**Aerovías Rojas, S.A.**	Oaxaca	Oaxaca–Puerto Escondido and points in Guerrero. Mexico City–Pinotepa Nacional, Ometepec, Mexico City–Aguascalientes	Founded by Rojas family. Owner and son, and the Director of Civil Aviation killed in aircraft crash early in 1968

42

Late 1960s	Aerovías Omega, S.A.	Mexico City	Mexico City–Querétaro–Irapuato	
1963–1970	Aviones de Chihuahua, S.A.	Chihuahua	Local services in Chihuahua State	
1960–1970	Central Aeronáutica, S.A.	Chihuahua	Chihuahua–El Largo	
1951–early 1970s	Cía Impulsora de Aviación, S.A.	Tuxtla Gutiérrez, Chiapas	Local routes from Tuxtla Gutiérrez and Yajalón, including Palenque	Routes operated from 1951 until 1960 by Transportes Aéreos Yajalón, S.A. (TAYSA)
1948–1970	**Cía Tabasqueña de Aviación, S.A.**	Villahermosa	Local routes radiating from Villahermosa, including Palenque and Tuxtla Gutiérrez	Network based on routes formerly operated by ALASA
1960s	Comercial Aérea, S.A.	Ciudad Obregón	Local routes radiating from Ciudad Obregón	
Late 1960s	Fumigadora de Chiapas, S.A. de C.V.	Villahermosa	Local routes to installations of Mexo Fina in Tabasco	
Late 1950s–1970	Líneas Aéreas de la Sierra, S.A.	Culiacán	Local routes from Culiacán	
1956–1970	Líneas Aéreas Mixtecas, S.A.	Huajuápan, Oaxaca	Local services to points in Oaxaca and Guerrero	
1949–1969	**Líneas Aéreas Picho, S.A.**	Uruapan, Michoacán	Uruapan–Apatzingán–Playa Azul; –Colima–Manzanillo; and other points in Michoacán	Founded by José Lucino Loperana

Continued on page 44

43

1968–1969	Líneas Aéreas Turísticas	Acapulco	Acapulco–Técpan–Zihuatanejo	
Early 1960s	Rutas Aéreas Costeñas, S.A.	Puebla	Local services from Puebla	
1960s	Servicios Aéreos, S.A.	La Paz	Local services in southern Baja California	Formerly operated as Abelardo L. Rodríguez
Later 1950s–early 1970s	Servicio Aéreo Baja, S.A. de R.L.	Tijuana	Tijuana–Bahia de los Angeles–Guerrero Negro–Mulegé–Puerto Vallarta; –Mexicali; –Navojoa–Los Mochis	Routes operated at first under name of Francisco Muñoz Cebellos
1960s	Servicios Aéreos Castellanos, S.A.	Comitán, Chiapas	Comitán–Tuxtla Gutiérrez, Yajalón, and other points in Chiapas	
1962–1969	Servicios Aéreos Madero, S.A.	Chihuahua	Chihuahua–Nuevo Casas Grandes–Cananea–Nogales, and points in Chihuahua State	
Late 1950s–1969	Servicios Aéreos Solis, S.A.	Oaxaca	Oaxaca–Playa Vicente, and points in Oaxaca	
Mid-1960s	Servicios Aéreos Sud-Pacífico, S.A. de C.V.	Uruapan	Uruapan–Playa Azul–La Unión–Zihuatanejo–Petatlán	
Late 1950s–1966	**Servicio Aéreo Gómez Méndez, S.A.**	Mexico City	Mexico City–Uruapan–Apatzingán–Colima–Manzanillo–Guadalajara; Manzanillo–Puerto Vallarta; Mexico–Tuxpan; Mexico City–Manzanillo	Merged with Aero Safari to form Aeromaya in 1966 (see text)

Continued on page 46

1943–	**Servicio Aéreo Leo Lopez, S.A.**	Chihuahua	Chihuahua–Madera; –Ojinaga; –El Granero	(see text)
Early 1960s	Servicio Aéreo Toluca, S.A.	Toluca	Local services from Toluca	
1962	Servicios Aéreos de Veracruz, S.A.	Martinez de la Torre, Ver.	Local services in northern Veracruz State	
Late 1950s– 1969	Taxis Aéreos de la Huasteca	Huejutla, Hidalgo	Local services in Hidalgo	
Mid-1950s	**Taxis Aéreos de Sonora, S.A.**	Hermosillo	Local routes radiating from Hermosillo	
1960–	**Transportes Aéreos de Carga, S.A. de R.L.**	Ensenada	Ensenada–Tijuana, Ensenada– Isla Cedros–Punta Abreojos	Cargo only
Late 1960s	Transporte Aéreo de Tabasco, S. de C.L.	Villahermosa	Many multi-stop circular routes in State of Tabasco, based mainly at Villahermosa, but also at Zapata, Tenosique, and Palenque	
Late 1950s– 1969	Transportes Aéreos Ernesto Saenz, S.A.	Parral, Chihuahua	Local services from Parral	
Mid-1950s	**Transportes Aéreos de Nayarit, S.A.**	Tepic, Nayarit	Tepic–Puerto Vallarta; Guadalajara–Puente de Comotlán; several other local services in Nayarit and Jalisco	

45

1948–	**Transportes Aéreos Terrestres, S.A.**	Tayoltita	Tayoltita–Durango; Tayoltita–Mazatlán	Took over route discarded by LAMSA. Famous as one of last operators of Ford Tri-Motor (see text)
1942–1972	**Anaya García, Miguel**	Huétamo	Huétamo–Mexico City, and to points in Guerrero, including Zihuatanejo	Founded as Líneas Aéreas de Zitácuaro. Name changed to Aerovías Anaya in 1957
1962–1963	Bello Rojo, Ignacio	Jalacingo	Local routes in northern Veracruz	
1960s	Castillo Meza, Manuel	Guadalajara	Local routes from Guadalajara	
Late 1960s	Covarrubias Pérez, José	Ciudad Guzmán, Jalisco	Local routes from Ciudad Guzmán	
Late 1960s	Fernandez Gonzalez, José	Ciudad Juárez	Ciudad Juárez–Nuevo Casas Grandes	
1968	Fierro Felix, Roberto	Los Mochis	Los Mochis–Tohayana	
1968	Jarquin Sanchez, Hector	Oaxaca	Oaxaca–Alemania, Pochutla	
1968	Juárez Floriano, José	La Paz	Local service from La Paz	
1963–1968	Léon Eucario Reyes	Tehuacán, Puebla	Tehuacán–San Juan	
Late 1950s–1970	Lopez Orozco Mario	Guadalajara	Guadalajara–La Yesca; and local services from Magdalena, Nayarit	
Early 1960s	Esteva Davila, Sergio	Oaxaca	Oaxaca–Villa Hidalgo and Zacatepec	

Late 1960s	Lopez Romera, Librado	Tehuacán	Tehuacán–Huautla–Ayautla	
1960s	Lopez Tejeda, Francisco	Cuautla	Local services radiating from Cuautla	
1968	Marquez Romero, Ruben	Mazatlán	Mazatlán–San Blas	
Late 1950s–1970	**Molina Moreno, Francisco**	Jalapa, Veracruz	Local services from Jalapa to points in Veracruz and from Zacapoaxtla (Puebla). Also Teapa (Tabasco) to Simojovel (Chiapas)	Carried 16,000 passengers and 1,400 tonnes of freight in 1963
Late 1960s	Morales Pérez, Francisco	Santa Rosalía	Routes from Santa Rosalía and San Ignacio	
1968	Osorio Pastrana, Mario and Marco Antonio Camacho Culebro	Pichucalco, Chiapas	Routes from Pichucalco	
1968	Rodriguez Miguel, Angel	Toluca	Local route to Guerrero State	
Late 1960s	Valderrabano Parades, Saul	Poza Rica	Routes from Poza Rica to Cuetzalán, and from El Chote	
Late 1950s–1970	Varela Lazo, Desiderio and Alberto Ruiz de la Peña	Chihuahua	Chihuahua to mining areas in western Chihuahua State	

CHAPTER THREE

Two National Airlines for Mexico

The Big Merger

During the complex early history of Mexican airline development, there had been one or two mergers by individuals; or a hardy survivor had acquired route concessions from those who could not last the pace—typically the aircraft crashed or simply wore out, and there was no capital left to replace them. Pan American Airways had acquired Aeronaves de México in 1940 and had made some predatory moves by taking a few small lines under its wing. In 1952, however, an amalgamation of airlines took place which was to change the course of Mexican airline history, bring about a fundamental change in the balance of forces, and specifically to undermine Pan American's grip on the industry. The President of Mexico, Miguel Alemán, who had taken office in 1946, initiated the manoeuvres which were eventually to add a new name to the ranks of international airlines: **Aeronaves de México**. This second-level domestic operator underwent a complete transformation, to become an airline of substance and prestige, able to challenge CMA which had hitherto been a law unto itself.

Following an increase in share capital, Aeronaves acquired its first Douglas DC-3 (XA-GAU) in September 1946. During the next few years, the small feeder routes (which today would be called Third Level) in the States of Michoacán, Guerrero, Oaxaca, and on the Gulf coast, were suspended. On the other hand, the DC-3 fleet was augmented, while the routes from Mexico City to Acapulco and to Nogales, via Tepic and Pacific coastal cities, were consolidated. In November 1949, the first Douglas DC-4 (XA-JAV) made its appearance, to supplement eight DC-3s, and the next year permission was granted to add

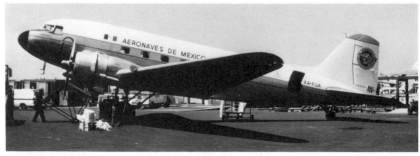

Aeronaves de México's Douglas DC-3A XA-FUA *Topiltzin* was delivered to United Air Lines in 1940 as NC25615 *Mainliner Medford*. It passed to LAMSA as XA-FUA *Ciudad de Torreón* in 1946 and to Aeronaves de México in 1952. (*Aeroméxico*)

48

CMA's Douglas DC-4 XA-GIK had been Pan American's NC88924 *Clipper Sunny South*. (*Mexicana*)

Guadalajara to the coastal network, with the important provision, however, that no local traffic was to be carried from the capital to Mexico's second largest city. This city pair was still CMA's territory.

On 22 July, 1952, a purchasing syndicate, headed by Miguel Alemán, bought Gordon Barry's old airline, LAMSA, from United Air Lines for $1,230,000. Its operations were immediately combined with those of Aeronaves de México, in which Mexican interests, again at Alemán's instigation, had acquired 60 per cent of the shareholding. Pan American's interest, now a minority, was further reduced to 21 per cent on 17 July, 1953, and the first stage of a great merger was complete. The veteran Carlos Ramos, who had worked for Walter Varney's Líneas Aéreas Occidentales, was selected by Alemán to manage the amalgamated airline.

The second stage was the acquisition of Aerovías Reforma, on 16 October, 1953. This added a substantial network in northwest Mexico to the newly-acquired north central routes of LAMSA, and the combined network of the three airlines, quickly consolidated into one organization, with a joint timetable, made an impressive showing on a redrawn map of Mexican air routes (see Map 6).

Alemán's worthy objective had been to create a national Mexican airline. It would have been called Aeronaves de México y Centro America, S.A., to operate both domestic and international services. Hitherto, the efforts of Mexicans to reach into the realms of foreign operation had been frustrated mainly by Pan American, whose subsidiary, CMA, served its masters in New York, and whose sphere of influence, therefore, was limited to that chosen by Juan Trippe. But Alemán's term of office (Mexican presidents serve a single six-year term) came to an end in 1952, the very year in which his ambitions began to materialize. The new government did not adopt the idea of a national—and nationalized—company; and the object for a grand intercontinental airline under the Mexican flag was shelved for a while. Operations of Aeronaves de México were confined to the domestic scene, with Convair CV-340s replacing the old DC-3s on all the main routes, at least providing a pressurized service to challenge the once omnipotent CMA.

CMA Fights a Rearguard Action

It was Alemán's administration which, by taking advantage of the postwar boom which swept the Americas, accelerated and intensified many commendable

49

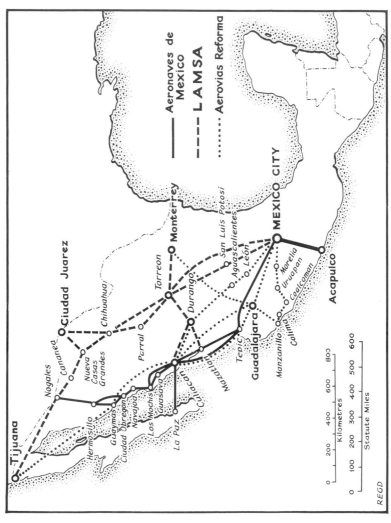

6. The Big Merger of Aeronaves de México, 1952. The merger of three airlines: Aeronaves de México, Aerovías Reforma, and LAMSA, created the first serious challenge to CMA's dominance of Mexican air routes since its foundation.

Two men who considerably influenced the development of the Mexican airlines during the post-Second World War development period were Walter Buchanan (*left*), Sub-Secretary of Public Works, 1952–1955, and Secretary of Communications and Transportation from 1958 to 1964; and Miguel Alemán (*right*) President of Mexico from 1946 to 1952, who inspired the expansion of Aeronaves de México, which became Mexico's national airline, rivalling the Pan-American-controlled Mexicana.

projects started by his predecessor, Avila Camacho. Under Alemán, paved roads in Mexico, for example, increased from less than 2,500 miles (4,000 kilometres) to more than 10,000 (17,000). Electricity production doubled, large irrigation schemes were undertaken, and the huge University City was completed as a suburb of the capital. The new roads, of course, were a factor leading to the demise of several small airlines which had literally taken Mexican transport straight from the mule-train to the aeroplane. Manuel Gómez Méndez, a veteran bush flyer who pioneered many small routes to small, isolated communities, commented 'the day that the first truck got through, we were dead'. But Alemán's sights were aligned to a greater vision: to tap the vast potential of Mexico's growing population and wealth, not least its oil resources, by creating a national airline industry.

While his long-term plan was to form a completely independent airline—and the big merger of Aeronaves de México already outlined was the materialization of this dream—steps were also taken to break Pan American's control of the only airline of substance, **Compañía Mexicana de Aviación, S.A. (CMA)**. Following the requirements of a new law, Pan American sold 13,750 CMA shares on 28 March, 1946, reducing its interest to 45 per cent. Although outright dominance was eroded, the US company continued to support its subsidiary in the manner to which it was accustomed. The latter, meanwhile, which was intensely Mexican in personnel and character, if not in control, continued its fine record of innovation, putting into service the best aircraft available.

On 6 June, 1946, a converted Douglas C-54 (XA-FIU) was delivered to Mexico City and named by the First Lady, Señora Soledad Orozco de Avila Camacho. The aircraft was one of three, purchased for $73,000 each, and converted to commercial DC-4s at an additional $120,000 each. Pan American may have been a restrictive influence on route expansion, but it believed in deploying the best

51

(*Left to right*) Elton 'Tubby' Silliman, General Manager of Compañía Mexicana de Aviación from 1944 to 1958; Lic Aaron Sáenz, Senior Director of Mexicana for many years; and Wilbur Morrison, from 1929 Pan American Airways' Manager, then Vice President of the Latin American Division from 1944 to 1966. These men guided the fortunes of Mexico's largest airline during the long period of Pan American control.

aircraft over the routes of its important subsidiaries. Introduction of the four-engined DC-4 into CMA service was only a few months after its debut in the United States.

Alemán's policy could have been interpreted as anti-Pan American—its shareholding in CMA was reduced further to 41 per cent on 5 August, 1946—but common sense and the realities of the airline business in Mexico ensured that the relationship was not wholly antagonistic. On 29 April, 1947, for example, a CMA DC-4 (XA-FIT) made a special flight to Washington with President Alemán and his delegation, making the journey nonstop in 9 hr 45 min. Demonstrating a determination not to surrender its leadership and dominance without a struggle, CMA then proceeded to make headline news. On 12 May, 1948, the first overhaul of a DC-4 in Mexico was completed by its maintenance department (on XA-FIT at 8,000 hours); on 14 July, 1949, a cargo division was created; and the following year a turning point was made by introducing four-engined pressurized equipment.

The first Douglas DC-6 arrived straight from Douglas on 6 November, 1950. This was a special version, fitted with Pratt & Whitney CV 16-17 engines, designed to perform well out of the 8,000-ft high airport at Mexico City. It turned out to be so well adapted to the stringent demands of Mexican operations that it outlasted the DC-6B, the first of which was delivered to CMA on 12 June, 1953. The two DC-6Bs were sold in 1954, but the four DC-6s remained in service.

Without matching Aeronaves de México's volume of acquisitons, CMA made some modest changes to its network. On 7 January, 1954, it took over the operations of **Transportes Aéreos de Jalisco (TAJ)**. This provided access to Puerto Vallarta, offsetting to some extent Aeronaves de México's Acapulco asset as a priceless tourist dollar-earner. TAJ had resumed operations in November 1945, and had survived precariously with its local services in the state of Jalisco. In

February 1950, it had been taken over by ATSA, which appointed Henry Filsinger as General Manager. Although TAJ had an old converted Douglas B-18 bomber, it depended mainly on two DC-3s, which opened up a new route from Guadalajara to San Martin de Bolaños. For this hazardous operation, the DC-3s had to use 'steps' cut into the side of a canyon, and each aircraft carried a spare mainwheel tyre and spare tailwheel, because, once landed, there would be no room for a second aircraft to land on the 'terrace' to bring a spare. The route became known as *La Ruta de los Porta-Aviones (Route of the Aircraft Carriers)* because of the strictly limited landing area available. Such were the complex local politics in the region that, at one stopping point, the village priest was appointed as the airline representative, to avoid internecine warfare.

CMA had also, at this time, signed an agreement (in 1951) with Cubana, for a co-ordinated service to Madrid, thus vicariously reaching across the Atlantic. In the same vein, an air mail service to Europe was organized in co-operation with the Scandinavian airline SAS via the latter's Polar Route, connecting at Los Angeles. But these could in no way be interpreted as international route extensions.

Aeronaves de México's Douglas DC-6 XA-NAII *Huitzilihuitl*, acquired in December 1959, was originally SAS's *Skjold Viking*. (*Aeroméxico*)

The Leftovers in Michoacán

When the Aeronaves de México-LAMSA-Aerovías Reforma merger took place, it aspired to become Mexico's national airline, or at least one of them. Accordingly, it took steps to dispose of some of the small feeder routes which did not fit into the pattern of an inter-city network.

In 1948, Carlos Cortez, assisted by Antonio Díaz Lombardo (nephew of the Aeronaves de México founder) took over the former Zarate routes which the emerging Aeronaves de México did not want. Cortez started his **Aerovías Michoacán-Guerrero** with Avro Ansons, then three Boeing 247Ds, changing the name to **Aeronaves de Michoacán**. According to one observer, one of the Boeings was painted brown, but was literally 'polished to death' in an effort to produce a bright aluminium finish. In October 1949, Cortez was killed in a car accident, just after signing the papers to buy a DC-3 from Aeronaves de México. His widow and brother continued to operate for a year or so but sold out to Líneas Aéreas Picho.

Aeronaves de México also disposed of the Mexico City–Morelia–Uruapan–Colima–Manzanillo route, originally started by Carlos Panini in 1936 and later acquired by Reforma. Late in 1953, Manuel Argüelles founded **Líneas Aéreas del Balsas** to take over this local service, using a Beechcraft C-45 and an AT-11, twin-engined light transports more suitable in size than the DC-3 for the traffic.

José Lucino Loperana had started a service between Uruapan and Playa Azul and Petatlán in 1949, using a Stinson Reliant to serve communities still not reached by the coastal road gradually being built from Acapulco westwards into the state of Michoacán. In 1955, Loperana, who had named his airline **Líneas Aéreas Picho**, took over the Argüelles concession, and renamed the operation **Servicios Aéreos de Michoacán**. In the bewildering line of succession, typical of Mexican feeder routes, Capt Bustos, who had founded **Aerolíneas Sud Pacífico** to link Acapulco and Petatlán (in spite of the road) inherited the Michoacán operation in 1960, and he, in turn, was succeeded in 1966 by Capt Manuel Cardenas, who introduced four new Piper Cherokee 6s. In the mid-1970s, however, two of these crashed, one killing Cardenas himself, and the Guerrero–Michoacán local air service link finally came to a halt.

Head-on Competition

By the mid-1950s, the rivalry between Aeronaves de México and CMA, now beginning to call itself Mexicana, intensified. There seems to have been a love-hate relationship, as at times the two companies jealously fought for or guarded precious operating rights, both domestically and internationally; while at other times they co-operated closely—albeit sometimes under pressure from the Mexican Government—to help each other in times of need, such as when there was a strike, or a shortage of aircraft.

In the matter of first-line equipment, for example, each airline was determined to assert its superiority. In February 1957, Mexicana took delivery of the first of four long-range Douglas DC-7Cs. Aeronaves de México promptly leased two Lockheed 049 Constellations for its service to Tijuana—the nearest it could reach, as yet, to Los Angeles. The early series Constellation may not have been a match for the DC-7C, but it was not in direct competition. Furthermore, Aeronaves dealt a trump card, placing an order on 31 May, 1957, for two 92-seat Bristol Britannia 302 four-engined propeller-turbine airliners from Britain. The Britannia had been produced originally as a medium/long range 'Empire' airliner for the British national airline BOAC, and had experienced frustrating delays because of icing problems in its Proteus engines. But these were finally put right, and because of late certification, quick delivery off the production line was possible. Aeronaves received its first Britannia (XA-MEC) on 4 November, 1957, and, having inaugurated Constellation service to New York on 16 December, put

Aeronaves de México Bristol Britannia 302 XA-MEC *Moctezuma* was delivered in November 1957, bore several names, and crashed at Tijuana on 9 July, 1965. (*Aeroméxico*)

the new turbine-powered type on this prestige route two days later, whereupon it immediately began to set records for the shortest journey times.

Compared with the Mexico City–New York route—which incidentally put an end to the odd situation in which the only direct service between these two great cities had been by Air France—Mexicana's expansion in the United States had been a little disappointing. Under the 1957 bilateral agreement between Mexico and the United States, President Eisenhower had approved Mexicana routes to Chicago and San Antonio, and confirmed the existing one to Los Angeles; but the coveted New York route, together with Washington, went to Aeronaves de México. Mexicana started DC-6 service from Mexico City to San Antonio, via Monterrey, on 10 September, 1957, and Mexico City–Chicago nonstop DC-7C service on 15 October of that year.

Fight for the Border Traffic

During the 1950s, a new source of traffic began to emerge in Mexico. Proximity to the prosperous United States led to the creation of a steady traffic flow of migrant workers from the relatively poor country south of the Río Grande. Mexico had one of the highest population growth rates in the world, and a chronic surplus of unemployed workers began to flock towards California and Texas, where there was a constant demand for low-paid agricultural labour. While the railways and bus lines carried the bulk of this traffic, the airlines also benefitted and one in particular provided a minor success story of its own.

Aerolíneas Mexicanas was formed by Rubén Ruiz Alcántara, with a capital of only US $2,000 (to buy the fuel), when Aerovías Reforma was taken over by Aeronaves de México in 1955. On the insistence of the Mexican Government, the little company was taken over by Aeronaves on 12 May, 1956, for the purpose of separating some of the unprofitable routes from the major network, and thus to isolate and simplify accounting procedures. Aerolíneas Mexicanas found itself with a fleet of two ex-Reforma DC-3s, ten Aeronaves pilots, and a government loan of 4.5 million pesos. Its first flight was to the tiny fishing village of Zihuatanejo, some 200 kilometres northwest of Acapulco, and still a quiet backwater. Then in December 1956 a route was opened to the United States border at Piedras Negras, in the State of Coahuila, right across the Río Grande from Eagle Pass, Texas, and only a short distance from San Antonio. This was basically the former Panini route via San Luis Potosí. This was followed on 28 April, 1958, by a new route direct to Matamoros, opposite Brownsville. Ruiz Alcántara inaugurated this DC-4 *Fiesta Flight* service in great style, and stirred up the competition.

CMA, which had operated in this territory since opening service to Nuevo Laredo in 1941, now moved to match its new competitor for the trans-border migrant traffic. In May 1958 a daily service began to Matamoros, via Monterrey, a far more important en route stop than Aerolíneas's San Luis Potosí. Early in 1960, the latter airline suspended service to Piedras Negras and concentrated on the Matamoros gateway. In September of that year, by which time the traffic demand had grown to justify a fleet of five DC-3s and a DC-4, Aeronaves bought Aerolíneas Mexicanas, which had now served its purpose of proving that profits could be made from low-fare no-frills services. The price paid was reported to be two million pesos, a substantial increment from Ruiz Alcántara's original 2,000 US dollars. Shortly before the takeover, Aerolíneas had completed the first 10,000 hour major DC-3 overhaul in Mexico—at half the USA contract price.

CMA also bought an airline, yet another Mexican company with a chequered history. Early in 1943, Líneas Transcontinentales de Aero-Transportes, S.A., usually known by its shortened form **Aero-Transportes, S.A.** (**ATSA**), was organized in Monterrey by a group of Mexican and United States businessmen. The capital of 1,000,000 pesos was equally divided between the two countries. On 21 October, 1943, the Mexican Government granted some route concessions, centred on San Luis Potosí, and operations began on 21 February, 1944. At first the fleet was a poor reflection of the airline's ambitious name, consisting of miscellaneous old Wacos, Vultees, and Stinsons. On 6 November, 1944, a certificate was issued to operate to Brownsville, and four Boeing 247Ds were acquired. But operations were sporadic, suffering from long suspensions between 1945 and 1947. Nevertheless, something was salvaged from the uncertainty, and by May 1948, two Douglas DC-3s had been added, some additional personnel hired from the defunct Aerovías Braniff, and the Mexican shareholding raised to 62 per cent, including investment by Romulo O'Farrell and Pedro Maus. A permit was again granted for service to Brownsville, the major gateway to Texas, and the goal of all operators trying to exploit the migrant worker traffic. ATSA began to recover, and by 1949 was possibly the third largest airline in Mexico.

By 1950, it was operating a respectable network, somewhat reminiscent of the old LAMSA, with one route linking Mexico City with two US border cities, together with a transcontinental network from Mazatlán to Tampico.

During 1951 and 1952, ATSA ventured into the dangerous waters of co-operative agreements, loosely aligning itself with Transportes Aéreos Jalisco (TAJ) and Aerovías Latino-Americanas (ALASA). The combined fleet, on paper, was 44 aircraft, but as these were of 20 different types, this motley fleet was not as impressive as it seemed. Many of the 'aircraft' were heaps of spare parts in the back of a hangar.

The merger was unsuccessful, and the idea was dropped in September 1952. TAJ resumed its independence until acquired by Mexicana. ALASA continued to operate between Mexico City and Villahermosa; and ATSA itself continued on a restricted network, dropping its coast-to-coast route, and drawing support from Mexicana, which took over the operating and maintenance functions and ticket agencies. This was effectively to adopt the status of a Mexicana affiliate, in which role ATSA found itself designated for duty on the Monterrey–Brownsville segment. Then the inevitable sequel to such manoeuvres occurred in 1959 when ATSA was completely absorbed by the big airline.

Confidence and Crisis—Jet Service and Industrial Strife

While the trans-border activity constituted an important category of traffic for both major Mexican airlines, the drama of development and the publicity associated with innovation still belonged to the traditional trunk routes. But the pathways were anything but smooth. There were minor crises involving route rights, leasing of aircraft, labour and pilots' contracts, as well as the question of Pan American's investment in both airlines.

As mentioned before, Aeronaves de México opened Britannia service to New York on 18 December, 1957. On 31 July, 1958, Max Healey succeeded Elton (Tubby) Silliman who had been General Manager of CMA since 1944. Among his first decisions was an attempt to upgrade service from California, using Acapulco as an intermediate point between Los Angeles and Mexico City, and deploying a Britannia hired from Aeronaves de México. There were again rumours of a

Mexicana's de Havilland Comet 4C XA-NAR *Golden Aztec* taking off from Mexico City.
(*Mexicana*)

merger between the two big airlines, but they came to nothing, and CMA/Mexicana was paralysed by strikes, forcing the Mexican Government to take over on 29 January, 1959. For a few days in September, the Aeronaves Britannias were also used on the nonstop Los Angeles–Mexico City route. This again led to some speculation about a merger, but this was quickly subdued by Mexicana's announcement on 27 October, 1959, that it had ordered three de Havilland Comet 4C four-engined jet airliners. Mexicana began Comet service to Los Angeles on 4 July, 1960, and to Chicago on 10 August that year. Comet services to Houston and San Antonio were added during 1960 and a new route, to Dallas, opened on 5 April, 1961.

Yet again, however, Mexicana was engulfed in a frustrating series of problems. Rumours were rampant once more that the three airlines Mexicana, Aeronaves, and Guest were to form 'Aeromex' with 60 per cent Government and 40 per cent private investment. Although Mexicana put the Comet on the Miami route on 8 November, 1961, its brave showing with the jet was tarnished by another strike during the first two weeks of April 1962. But worse was to come. In May 1962, de Havilland foreclosed on all outstanding payments on the three Comets, and obtained a $12 million lien on all Mexicana property and income. Somehow or other, Max Healey survived this crisis of confidence, and was able to announce in March 1963 some aggressive fares promotion, with single-class service on all international flights—a condition which has survived to this day—and 25 per cent discounts on domestic flights, together with other concessions.

Mexicana was not alone in its trials and tribulations. Riding on a wave of confidence after taking a dramatic technical lead with the long-range Britannia, Aeronaves became part of the international establishment by becoming a member of IATA (International Air Transport Association) in September 1957; and began negotiations to acquire Aerovías Guest in March 1958. As previously mentioned, there were strong moves to promote a merger with Mexicana, but these did not materialize. However, the Pan American interest was reduced to less than 11 per cent on 26 November, 1958, almost as a prelude to such a move; but this plan collapsed when the strike of January 1959 hit Aeronaves as it did Mexicana.

The Mexican Government immediately took control of Aeronaves de México. In April 1959, all the capital stock was purchased by Nacional Financiera, S.A.

and the Government took official ownership on 28 July. The remaining Pan American interest was formally withdrawn on 26 December. Walter Buchanan, Secretary of Transportation, nominated Ing Pérez y Bouras as Director General, charged with the responsibility of spending 100 million pesos of Government money which had been allocated for a rescue operation. Some of these funds were used to buy six 69-seat Douglas DC-6s from SAS to replace the Constellations, Convair-Liners, and DC-4s. The now profitable Aerolíneas Mexicanas was absorbed in September 1960, the month in which Pérez y Bouras was able to negotiate with the Douglas company and Eastern Air Lines an early position in the DC-8 jet delivery schedule.

The first 138-seat DC-8 was delivered on 15 November, 1960. Plans were immediately implemented to put Mexico firmly on the international jet map with DC-8 services to Washington and New York. Also Aeronaves took steps to acquire Aerovías Guest so as to expand its network to Europe. Once again high hopes were unceremoniously dashed when the DC-8 (XA-XAX) crashed on take-off from New York. Because of the loss, Aeronaves de México joined an equipment consortium with Mexicana and Guest in February 1961 and three more DC-6s were added in the following month. Ever resourceful, Aeronaves even began a service to Montreal in April 1962 with a Boeing 707 leased from SABENA.

Aerovías Guest and Trans Mar de Cortes

While Compañía Mexicana de Aviación and Aeronaves de México were fighting things out on the North American mainland, it was left to an airline whose name had no obvious Mexican connotation to begin service to Europe. **Aerovías Guest, S.A.** was founded on 25 June, 1946, with a capital of 5,000,000 pesos. 63 per cent was held by Mexican citizens, but the biggest single shareholder was the colourful US financier Winston Guest, a man of wealth and leisure who gave his name to the airline.

Service was inaugurated on the trans-Atlantic route on 8 January, 1948, using the unpressurized Douglas DC-4 on a route from Mexico City to Madrid, via Miami, Bermuda, the Azores, and Lisbon. Traffic rights were obtained to operate turnaround services to Miami, which were promoted as the *Route of the Sun*. But by late 1951 the Atlantic route was suspended and Guest concentrated on Miami.

Aerovías Guest Lockheed 749 Constellation XA-GOQ. Guest aircraft had the Mexican colours (green uppermost) on fuselage and tail unit, red company name and spinners, and the white condor's head was backed by a gold sun. (*Lockheed*)

The Fairchild Packet saw relatively little use by airlines but a small batch served with Mexican carriers and two examples are illustrated. The upper view shows Guest Aerovías México's C-82A XA-LIL and the lower picture CMA's C-82A XA LOJ after being fitted with dorsal fins to improve its yaw characteristics.

At a one-way fare of $77, this connection, cunningly presented in the timetables to provide the illusion of high frequency, was so successful that two ex-QANTAS Lockheed Constellations were substituted for the DC-4s on 10 November, 1955.

Guest clung to its slender Mexican foothold and even expanded during the 1950s. A direct service started to Panamá in October 1954 and this was extended to Caracas in April 1958. Other services were not sustained. One, to Windsor, Ontario, lasted from April 1956 until October 1957 and was interpreted by the United States authorities, ever watchful to detect evasions of their laws, as a thinly-disguised route to neighbouring Detroit. Another route, to Guatemala, hardly got started and was suspended on 13 September, 1957.

Aerovías Guest then became the subject of an experiment in international airline politics, serving as a case study—and perhaps as a warning—for other ventures of the same kind. Many European airlines had cast their eyes on selected foreign companies, more as a device to acquire operating rights—often otherwise denied—as much as a simple desire for aggrandisement. In this vein, Scandinavian Airlines System (SAS) bought control of Guest on 20 February, 1959, by acquiring 42 per cent of the stock. Douglas DC-6s were transferred to reinforce Guest's fleet of two Constellations and two Fairchild Packets, and the Atlantic routes reinstated on 18 April, 1959, with an important extension to Paris.

With vigorous support from SAS, Guest now began to put on a show. Lockheed Super Constellations were deployed on the Atlantic and Central American–Caribbean services in May 1960 at a frequency of thrice weekly on both routes; and there were eleven a week to Miami. After negotiating an agreement with

Mexicana to join forces on international routes, Comets were introduced on the route to Paris on 1 March, 1961. But this was the last gasp of a doomed airline. SAS checked its books, discovered an operating loss estimated at 70 million Norwegian kronor, and in May 1961 decided to pull out. Acting on behalf of Aeronaves de México, which inherited the entire Guest route system, Nacional Financiera bought 87.8 per cent of the Guest stock in August 1962. Things had got so bad that one rental on a Comet was reported to have been paid with a DC-6B.

On a more modest scale, covering the four northwestern states of Mexico, another Mexican airline tale unfolded during the same period that Guest's fortunes rose and fell. In 1947 **Trans Mar de Cortes** was founded by Mayo Obregón, son of former Mexican President Alvaro Obregón. In December 1948 scheduled services began over a network centred on Ciudad Obregón, the city in Sonora named after the President. In July 1952, Mayo Obregón bought **Líneas Aéreas del Pacífico, S.A. (LAPSA)**, a small airline operating between Tijuana and La Paz, in Baja California, and two years later was able to make an important connection to Ciudad Juárez.

Mayo Obregón was ahead of his time. Serving resorts such as Guaymas and La Paz from Tijuana (adjacent to San Diego and close to Los Angeles) and Ciudad Juárez (opposite El Paso) the tourist potential was substantial. Recognizing this, Obregón ordered a twin propeller-turbine Fokker Friendship in July 1958; but he was not to earn a just reward for such commendable enterprise. Twenty years later, his network would have become the proverbial goldmine. But Obregón was then struggling, and under somewhat doubtful circumstances was obliged to suspend service on 6 February, 1962, when the Mexican Government withdrew his certificate. The Friendship was sold to Ozark Airlines, and Aeronaves de México (who else?) took over the route network.

More Acquisitions and Route Consolidation

While the engulfing of smaller fry in the Mexican skies may not have been the only way to expand route networks or to consolidate territorial gains, the workings of the Mexican law, by which concessions for routes were made on a monopoly basis, made this procedure necessary. But by the latter 1950s, few of the original independent concessionaires were left. The last link with the prewar past was severed when, almost simultaneously with the acquisition of ATSA, which secured a better share of the trans-border traffic, Mexicana also took over **Transportes Aéreos Mexicanos, S.A. (TAMSA)**. By doing so, it strengthened its grasp on routes to the Yucatán peninsula, balancing in eastern Mexico the gains of Aeronaves de México in the north. It also thereby laid claim to a distant kinship with one of Mexico's most famous pioneers.

Francisco Sarabia's old airline, which had suspended operations in 1942, was purchased by a group of Mexican investors in June 1943. It was registered on 16 August, 1944, with a shareholding of 2,200,000 pesos, and given the new name TAMSA, to incorporate a form of national identity. It began a cargo service to Matamoros, and restricted service only to the larger cities of the Yucatán and neighbouring states. The chicle camp services were suspended, except on demand, although these were expanded in 1945 by the absorption of a local operator, Pedro Silviera y Sosios, based at Peto.

By March 1947, TAMSA's main services consisted of a triangular route linking Mérida, Cozumel, and Chetumal, with a small international service to Belize, British Honduras, and a route, mainly for freight, from Mérida to Mexico City, via Gulf cities (see Map 3). The aircraft fleet was, like those of other independents defying the inevitable, a collection of second-hand types which would not be out of place in the Smithsonian Institution in Washington: sundry Bellancas, Curtiss Robins, Spartans, Avro Ansons, the odd Ford Tri-Motor, even a Boeing 40B, and—the pride of the fleet—three DC-3s.

By the early 1950s only the DC-3s remained, and a few years later a Consolidated B-24 Liberator was added. This decision ended in tragedy. TAMSA's B-24 crashed at Mérida on 14 April, 1957, attracting much publicity because Pedro Infante, a popular singer, was killed in the crash. TAMSA then had to face a bitter pilots' strike, and its fate was sealed. In the summer of 1960, Mexicana bought the airline, whose assets by this time consisted of little more than a route certificate and a general manager named Manuel Sosa.

This was Mexicana's last airline takeover. For the next few years it concentrated on deploying its Comet fleet throughout the network. The first-generation British jet was an impressive performer, leaving the piston-engined propeller fleets almost contemptuously in its wake when climbing steeply out of high-elevation airports such as Mexico City and Guadalajara. But the Comet paid a heavy penalty for having been designed primarily for BOAC's 'hot and high' stations throughout the British Commonwealth, and thus, fortuitously, for Mexico. Its economics were questionable. With good revenue rates, with a first-class fare ingredient, the costs could be tolerated. But in Mexico the economic balance was precarious, and furthermore was exacerbated by repeated strikes.

During the mid-1960s, the only important route change was the direct link to Miami from the island of Cozumel, newly-discovered as another Mexican place in the sun for US tourists. By the same token, Puerta Vallarta received Comet service, a far cry from the stick-and-string aircraft of Daniel Fort thirty years previously.

Carlos Ramos (*left*) first worked for Walter Varney's Líneas Aéreas Occidentales, S.A. (LAOSA) in 1932 and was General Manager of Aeronaves de México from 1941 to 1959. His successor was Ing Jorge Perez y Bouras (*right*) appointed by the Government to steer the newly nationalized airline into the international field, a task which he accomplished successfully before retiring in 1971.

Mexicana did have one fundamental advantage over Aeronaves. Although the latter's big merger had been fashioned into a workable organization, Mexicana had all the best inter-city routes, inherited on what the United States C.A.B. would describe as a 'grandfather rights' basis. Thus, although Aeronaves de México served more places, its route density was thinner; and Mexicana's possession of the nonstop route rights between Mexico's three largest cities, and to the Yucatán peninsula (which was, in terms of surface transport, as isolated as an island) served as a major factor in maintaining its survival.

Meanwhile, Aeronaves de México, under the leadership of Jorge Pérez y Bouras, was growing from exuberant adolescence into stable, if still inexperienced, maturity. It set about digesting the acquisitions of Guest and Trans Mar de Cortes, at the same time adding further routes, aimed to build the airline into a corporate entity of the necessary strength to match the adult seniority of Mexicana.

On the domestic front, the importance of Tijuana both as a resort and as a US gateway was recognized. There had been much dispute between the two airlines about the west coast route, and the 1957 US bilateral agreement, confirming Mexicana's Los Angeles rights, blocked off Aeronaves ambitions in that direction. In June 1962, some compensation was obtained by the award of a direct Los Angeles–La Paz route, while in September of the same year, the Mexico City–Tijuana route was extended to the southern Californian metropolis. Thus, for the next fifteen years or so, there was tacit recognition that the nonstop Los Angeles–Mexico City rights belonged to Mexicana, while a permutation of stopping services, including one at Acapulco, was operated by Aeronaves de México.

Pérez y Bouras also looked across the US border for more gateway traffic. Tucson was added on 30 June, 1961, linking with the Aeronaves system at Hermosillo; San Antonio was given direct access to Mazatlán via Monterrey and Torreón on 27 July of the same year; and the Tucson route was extended to Phoenix on 6 May, 1966. The trans-border matter, however, became the subject of considerable dispute, and was finally settled by the Secretary of Communica-

The Douglas DC-8-63CF N4865T *Chiapas* was leased by Aeronaves de México from Trans International Airlines of Oakland in March 1971. (*Harold G. Martin*)

tions and Transport who, in a balanced judgement on 14 August, 1963, allocated San Antonio exclusively to Mexicana, and Tijuana to Aeronaves de México. Nonstop service to the latter point from Mexico City began on 14 August, 1964, with DC-8s allocated to the route on 15 October, 1966.

During the 1960s, the enormous potential of Acapulco as a traffic-generating point was manifest. Service frequency increased steadily until, on 3 May, 1965, by which time it was eleven a day, the Mexico City link metaphorically came of age with the establishment of a no-reservations *Puente Aéreo* (Air Bridge).

Internationally, Aeronaves de México integrated the Aerovías Guest network with its own routes to the USA. DC-8s were introduced on the Atlantic trunk service on 11 April, 1963, shortly after the Douglas jet transport had begun the medium-haul links to Panamá, Bogotá, Caracas, and Miami. Bogotá was soon omitted from Aeronaves's plans, as was Guatemala, inherited from Guest but never operated on a sustained basis. Far more important financially was the granting, in June 1964, of a permanent US certificate not only to include Miami as an intermediate stop on the Atlantic route, but also the all-important Fifth Freedom rights to be able to carry passengers between Miami and Europe. On 23 July of the same year, the Canadian Air Transport Board also confirmed the ex-Guest Windsor route, with an alternate terminus at Toronto. Aeronaves managed to have its cake and eat it. Not only did it operate to Toronto, but on 17 December started service direct to Detroit, permission having been granted by the C.A.B.

More for publicity and image-building purposes than anything else, Pérez y Bouras reserved two delivery positions for the projected US supersonic airliner on 23 April, 1964. More practically, the Madrid service gained a new extension, to Rome on 1 April, 1966, as an alternative to Paris. Exactly one year later, a pool agreement was signed with the Spanish airline Iberia under the terms of which a daily Mexico City–Madrid service was consolidated, thrice weekly flights being made by the Mexican partner, and four a week, via Santo Domingo, by Iberia. The Atlantic route was a big money-spinner, combining as it did the ethnic link between two great Spanish-speaking nations, with tourist and business traffic in both directions. The addition of a route to Rome should have provided a certain injection of religion-related traffic.

Demonstrating that a large route map was not the sole objective of Aeronaves de México's policy of expansion, service to Washington was suspended after only a year, on 1 January, 1967, and the same fate befell Panamá and Caracas on 20 March. Such was the strict budgetary control that even the Rome service was suspended on 1 July of that year, having lasted for little more than a year.

Aeronaves de México was not free from other problems which, to a certain extent, inhibited its ambitions for route expansion. The airline lost a Britannia in 1965, two DC-8s in 1966 and three other aircraft in 1967, but thanks to a combination of structural resilience, good emergency drill by crews, and perhaps luck, not a single passenger was killed. In compensation for these losses, Aeronaves embarked on a programme of aircraft replacement aimed at converting the entire fleet to jet propulsion. The DC-8s, allocated to all international and long-distance trunk routes, were supplemented by a fleet of short/medium-haul twin-jet Douglas DC-9s. These 85-seat aircraft were ordered on 20 November, 1965, and the first arrived at Tijuana on 29 May, 1967.

The DC-9 order was the result of a shrewd selection process. As previously discussed, one discernible difference between the two Mexican national carriers was that, in general, Mexicana had the better network of domestic trunk services between the largest cities, while Aeronaves de México tended to serve a multiplicity of secondary—and even tertiary—points. Thus, Mexicana had ordered, in October 1965, four Boeing 727-100 tri-jets for $20,000,000. These 116-seat aircraft were appropriate to the route density of such city pairs as Mexico City–Guadalajara and Mexico City–Monterrey. They were also ideal for the range requirement of the Mexico City–Los Angeles international route, easily the best profit-making service of all Mexican routes. Such an aircraft would, in terms

This view of Douglas DC-9-15 XA-SOJ *Oaxaca* shows Aeronaves de México's new red and black livery and Aeroméxico styling. (*Douglas Aircraft Company*)

of traffic volume, have been excellent for the Mexico City–Acapulco connection also. But this 300-kilometre route was too short for the tri-jet to operate at its most economic capability; and the smaller DC-9 was better not only from the operating cost viewpoint, but also for maintaining the higher frequency which was the key to successful non-reservation systems. Also, multi-sector flights to the State capitals needed a smaller and more versatile aircraft and the DC-9 proved to be as reliable and efficient a workhorse for Aeronaves as the Boeing 727 was to become for Mexicana, each one ideal for its vital role in the development of Mexican commercial aviation.

CHAPTER FOUR

A New Era in Mexico

Mexicana Nearly Goes Under

While the order for four Boeing 727s in 1965 might have provided the outward appearance of an airline confident of its future, discriminating analysts could find grave cause for concern for Mexicana's very survival. They might have deduced that the near-stagnation of route mileage was an indication that something was wrong. Since the acquisition of ATSA and TAMSA in 1960, the Mexicana map did not change for a decade, except for the addition of the Miami–Cozumel link. Strikes and high operating costs of the Comets eroded the basic strength of a fundamentally sound system, and when Miami–Cozumel and the Dallas extension of the San Antonio route were both discontinued in August 1967, this was only the prelude to a crisis.

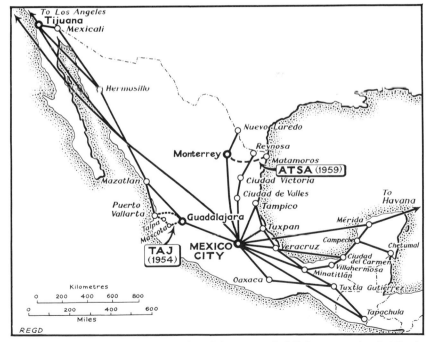

7. CMA, 1957. Reacting to the creation of Aeronaves de México as a national airline in 1952, CMA added a few routes. But in general it served the same areas and cities as in the late 1930s.

65

When the mid-year accounts were checked, a $4.6 million loss was revealed for the 12-month period. Outstanding debt was three times that amount. On 23 September, 1967, the stockholders met to decide the future of Mexicana. Debate on the cause of the operating losses revealed that intensified competition from US airlines and wage increases had accounted for much of the financial imbalance. The choice seemed to be frighteningly simple: bankruptcy or a massive injection of capital. A factor for serious consideration regarding the latter alternative was Pan American's shareholding, which still stood at 35 per cent. Increased Pan American investment—assuming that the New York airline wished to make this move—would have effectively converted Mexicana once again into a satellite airline, which was contrary to national aspirations.

A solution was found by going to the Mexican courts and asking for special dispensation, allowed under Mexican law, under which a company could make deferred payments to pay off accrued debt, subject to approval by the creditors. Action was quickly taken. The most important single event was the purchase of the outstanding Pan American stock by Señor Crescencio Ballesteros, a prominent Mexican industrialist in the construction business. This settled one issue. Mexicana was now a Mexican airline, pure and simple. Other actions were far-reaching and effective. Ten airports, an inheritance of the early days of CMA when an airline had to build its own, were sold to the Mexican Government, for cash. A vigorous publicity campaign and overhaul of the airline's top, middle, and lower management were put in hand to restore the fading image of the airline. Three Boeing 727s (the order had been reduced by one) were put into service to supplement the Comets.

Pan American's 35 per cent was transferred on 13 January, 1968, but the year 1968 was an uneasy one for Ballesteros, to put it mildly. After careful reflection, he eventually chose a successor to the Pan American appointee Max Healey as Director General. When Manuel Sosa de la Vega took over the office in

Crescencio Ballesteros (*left*) was a prominent Mexican industrialist who purchased the controlling interest of the ailing Mexicana in 1967. He appointed Manuel Sosa de la Vega (*right*) as Director General and the two men made the name Mexicana a synonym for reliability and good service, and, measured in passengers boarded, built the largest airline in Latin America. (*Mexicana*)

December, he faced a legion of problems. On 19 October, one 727 had been impounded at Dallas by the engine overhaul company, Dallas Airmotive, to hasten the settlement of an unpaid $200,000 bill. Two more 727s were seized by the Bank of America, on behalf of the group financing the purchase. The pilots were threatening to strike. The route network was in danger of severe pruning. Staff layoffs were imminent.

But Ballesteros and Sosa together managed to convince both the financial institutions and the troubled staff that Mexicana was basically sound, and it was a great tribute to their collective enthusiasm and integrity that they received support from the banks and from their own staff. On 28 January, 1969, the fourth Boeing 727 was ordered and a leasing arrangement worked out with PSA, the Californian intra-state airline. A shrewd deal was made with the rival Aeronaves de México, in which the first breach was made in the hitherto almost impregnable—and potentially harmful—route monopoly law. Aeronaves de México traded its exclusive rights to Acapulco, in exchange for certain rights from the capital to Guadalajara and Puerto Vallarta. This exchange of rights was the first positive move which was in due course to lead to a gradual easing of tension between the two airlines on issues which could be solved to their mutual advantage; and recognition that competition need not be a bad thing, if kept in sensible perspective.

One of Mexicana's JATO (Jet Assisted Take Off) equipped Boeing 727-264s seen during its flight-test programme. (*The Boeing Company*)

In 1969 Mexicana, under its new leadership, reached the most critical period in its existence. On the credit side, in a remarkable turnaround of fortunes, Ballesteros and Sosa were able to report a 1968 profit of $624,000—not extraordinary, but a great improvement on the $3.2 million loss of 1967. The drastic actions taken and the wise husbandry of assets were beginning to show results. Tragically, however, the success was marred by two fatal Boeing 727 crashes during the summer. Mexicana's reputation hung on a thread. Another crash would have drawn severe censure from the authorities, and probably made the airline vulnerable to a humiliating takeover.

But the management and staff weathered the storm of protest, and gradually began to rebuild morale and to improve standards of service. The Miami–Cozumel route was reinstated on 8 September, 1969; through flights were introduced from Chicago to Acapulco, via Mexico City (one result of the route trade with Aeronaves) on 4 December; and new routes were added: Mazatlán to Denver on 15 December, 1971, and Mérida–San Juan on 6 May, 1972. The

Boeing 727s were to become not only the backbone of the fleet, as the Comets were retired, but were contemplated as the basis of a single-type fleet. During the Spring of 1970 Mexicana ordered three of the stretched 200 series of the well-proved Boeing 727, with 155 all-economy seats. To carry the full load on the critical sectors out of Mexico City, these aircraft were equipped with JATO (Jet Assisted Take-Off) units, the largest aircraft in the world to be so equipped. Other Boeing 727s of the smaller 100 series were acquired on lease.

In spite of the investment in new equipment, and the cost of opening new routes, Mexicana had turned the financial corner. When in 1972, after five years' stewardship, the leadership of Ballesteros and Sosa was reviewed, the record stood for itself. Profits had averaged more than $2,000,000 per year; employment was steady; morale was good, the public image of Mexicana was excellent; the fleet and the traffic were growing healthily.

Final Acquisitions of Aeronaves de México

While Mexicana was going through an agonizing reappraisal of its entire policy and future aspirations, the other national Mexican airline continued to seek ways to invade Mexicana's sphere of influence, in spite of the handicap imposed by the monopoly route laws. Acting in parallel with Mexican Government policy, Pérez y Bouras pursued the device of buying other airlines, to obtain coveted route certificates—although there were precious few of any consequence still left. He also sought a rational solution to the problem of feeder routes to small communities, which could not be served by first-line jet aircraft because the traffic was not sufficient and the airports were inadequate.

The situation of feeder services in Mexico during the late 1960s can be visualized from a cursory inspection of the records of the time. In 1968 no less than 68 airlines were listed by the Ministry of Communications and Transport. Of these only 20 (including the two trunk airlines, Aeronaves de México and Mexicana) were authorized with a *Concesión*, that is, the exclusive and permanent right to operate defined, established routes. The rest were with *Permiso*, that is, temporary permission, subject to cancellation (even after only a year) but with the prospect of a permanent tenancy if a high enough standard of efficiency could be demonstrated.

The great majority of the airlines, especially those with *Permiso* only, were small, even diminutive in size. Excluding the two trunks, only five carried more than 10,000 passengers annually. Thirty-seven carried an average of fewer than ten passengers per day, sixteen fewer than 1,000 per year. Of the few freight airlines, only two carried more than 1,000 tonnes annually.

The heterogeneous collection of operators owned a motley collection of aircraft, mostly of the Piper, Cessna, Beech light-plane variety. But scattered amongst them were the remnants of a bygone age of earlier generations. These ranged from the veteran Douglas DC-3/C-47s, scattered everywhere, to the occasional Lockheed, Ryan, or Stinson, even a surviving Ford Tri-Motor. Sometimes the odd four-engined DC-4/C-54 was to be found, hauling cargo mostly. Only rarely did a Mexican feeder airline buy a new aircraft from the manufacturer. In the main the ancestry of the fleets was obscure and did not bear too much looking into.

The transitory nature of the existence of the small airlines, and the mushrooming growth which characterized the late 1950s and the 1960s, is shown by a comparison of the Table (page 84) in this chapter and a similar compilation

Aeronaves Alimentadoras de Havilland Canada Twin Otter Series 200 XA-BOQ. Fuselage flash and wingtips are red.

from the previous era (pages 41–47). Only a mere handful of companies are mentioned in both. For those who believed in a rational airline industry for Mexico, therefore, the unembellished facts alone seemed to speak for themselves. Some form of co-ordination and a reduction in the number of mostly tiny airlines appeared to be a reasonable solution.

On 28 October, 1968, Pérez y Bouras formed **Aeronaves Alimentadoras** as an

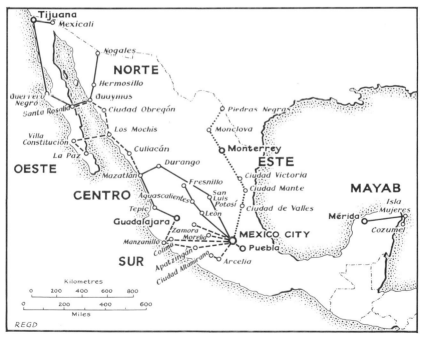

7a. Aeronaves Alimentadoras, 1970. Under the aegis of Aeronaves de México, an attempt was made to co-ordinate the feeder routes of Mexico into one system. The idea was sound but in practice was financially unsuccessful, partly because of the high maintenance costs of the small aircraft used.

69

Rubén Ruiz Alcántara (*left*) was one of the last of Mexico's postwar airline entrepreneurs, founding in 1956 Aerolíneas Mexicanas, which he ran profitably before selling to Aeronaves de México in 1960. Manuel Gómez Méndez (*centre*) started a small airline in the State of Guerrero in 1953 before merging with Aero Safari in 1966 to form Aeromaya. This eventful and colourful partnership was the last attempt to challenge Mexico's two-airline system. Leo Lopez (*right*) has been flying ever since 1929, first for the Mexican Army air service, Mexicana and Gordon Barry; then, from 1939, for his own company, Servicio Aéreo Leo Lopez. A true bush pilot, Lopez laid down more than 100 airstrips and organized an efficient emergency radio network throughout northern Mexico.

affiliate of Aeronaves de México, in co-operation with Pedro Maus, owner of Nacional Aérea, the Mexican Piper Aircraft distributor, each holding one-third of the shares, with the rest subscribed by local Mexican businessmen. The initial fleet consisted of eight Piper Navajos, able to carry seven passengers and with rapid-change interiors for cargo work; and two de Havilland Canada Twin Otters for the 'denser' routes, mainly Mexico City–Zihuatanejo. The ubiquitous and ageless Douglas DC-3 was allocated to the Baja California routes.

Aeronaves Alimentadoras—the name is Spanish for Feeder Airline—began operations on 19 November, 1968, and followed a pattern of taking over either the existing or dormant route authority of small airlines. These consisted of Aeronaves del Sur (formerly Aerovías del Sur, which had taken over from Aeromaya, formerly Gómez Méndez); Aeronaves del Oeste (formerly Aerolíneas del Pacífico); Aeronaves del Centro (former routes of the defunct Aerovías Rojas); and Aeronaves del Este (transfer of some of Aeronaves's own routes). Later, Aeronaves del Norte was hived off the Oeste network. The areas served by these divisions are shown on the map on page 69. All were under way by the end of 1969, and in February 1970 they were joined by Aeronaves del Mayab, operating in Yucatán. The last-named component had been split off a route structure which had probably been the last attempt to create an airline of substance in Mexico outside the control of one of the two established large companies.

The Aeromaya Interlude

Servicio Aéreo Gómez Méndez and Aero Safari and their fleeting appearance in the pages of Mexican airline history was an echo of the earlier cavalier days of rival factions.

Servicio Aéreo Gómez Méndez had been founded in March 1953 by Manuel Gómez Méndez to operate short local routes from Chilpancingo, Guerrero, using a Cessna 170. Over the next few years he added a few more routes, including one to Puebla, and upgraded his fleet to a Beech C-45 (military Beech 18). In 1962 he sold his small route concessions to Elias Naime (who maintained them until 1966) but kept the Beech. This was because he had obtained the more valuable concession from Mexico City to Apatzingán, Michoacán, on 6 March, 1962. In the same year he included Uruapan as an en route stop, extended it to Colima and Manzanillo, and bought a DC-3 from Mexicana. He was thus retracing the steps of notable pioneers such as Carlos Panini, of the late 1930s, and of individuals like Manuel Argüelles and José Lucino Loperana, who had kept the line going in the postwar years.

In 1963, Gómez Méndez made a move, the significance of which was not realized at the time. In March he extended operations at the western end to Guadalajara; and at the eastern end to Tuxpan, on the Gulf of Mexico. He thus boasted a coast-to-coast route, including Mexico's two largest cities, and purchased another DC-3, stationing one at each end of the line. In August 1964, he bought a third Douglas, from the ill-fated Aerovías Rojas, and added Puerto Vallarta, the latest fishing port to join the ranks of the sophisticated resorts on Mexico's Pacific Coast.

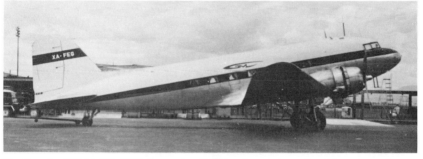

The Douglas DC-3A XA-FEG, formerly of CMA, after passing to Servicios Aéreos Gómez Mendez. (*Courtesy José Villela*)

In a quite unconnected development, far away in the Caribbean, Capt Roberto Fierro had founded **Aero Safari** in 1961, to begin local air taxi services from Isla Mujeres to Cozumel and to neighbouring points in Yucatán and Quintana Roo. To serve these places, also emerging as desirable tourist destinations, Fierro had a Beech Twin Bonanza and a Lockheed-Azcarate LASA-60 Santa Maria, a six-passenger, high-wing monoplane built in San Luis Potosí. In the same area, Fernando Barbachano, owner of a hotel chain and travel service based in Cozumel, had started **Aero Taxi, S.A.** Barbachano bought Fierro's operation in 1965 and on 24 October of that year put the operation on a scheduled basis.

In August 1966, Aero Safari obtained permission to fly from Mérida to Tuxpan. This was an apparently harmless route which Mexicana did not challenge, but in September of the same year, the Mexican Government gave permission for Aero Safari to interchange equipment and service at Tuxpan with Manuel Gómez Méndez. The former had already leased a Hawker Siddeley HS.748 from the Panamanian airline COPA, while the latter had formed himself into a corporation, late in 1965.

71

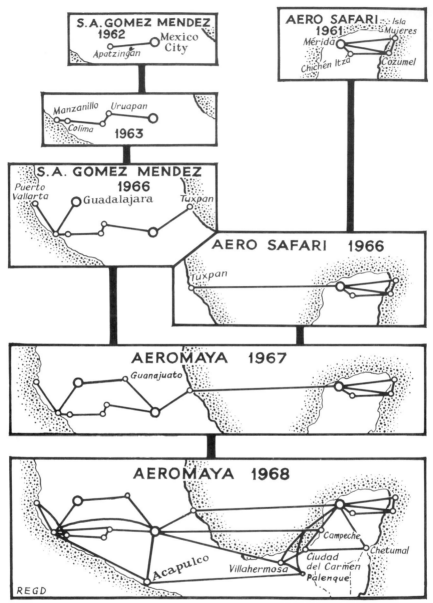

8. Aeromaya, 1961–1968. During the 1960s, only one serious challenge was made to the two-airline national system. By an ingenious linkage of two separate local airline networks, Manuel Gómez Méndez and Aero Safari came close to constructing a viable trunk pattern. This speculative venture collapsed, however, after a memorable period of 'snapping at the heels' of the incumbents.

On 1 November, 1966, the plot thickened, as the two companies merged to form **Aeromaya**. Barbachano was responsible for finance, promotion, and 'politics' while Gómez Méndez took care of all the operations. The combined fleet consisted of four DC-3s and two HS.748s, purchased new, during the negotiations for which Barbachano leased a suite of well-appointed offices in London, suggesting a flamboyant approach to the airline business.

In fact, when the first 748 service opened from Mexico City to Mérida, via Tuxpan, on 12 December, 1966, it was the talk of the Mexican air travel world. The competition was Mexicana's Comet, much faster, but also more expensive— 1,040 pesos round trip against Aeromaya's 799 pesos. Aeromaya offered excellent service: hotel-style catering (from Barbachano's resources) and 'educated' stewardesses. Surprisingly—or perhaps not so surprisingly to the airline clientèle—alleged bad weather and poor airport conditions at Tuxpan often forced the Aeromaya HS.748 to make the Mexico City—Mérida journey nonstop.

On 20 December, 1966, a DC-3 service from the Federal Capital to Guadalajara, via Guanajuato, was inaugurated in fine style. Two *Playboy* Bunnies assisted the stewardess with her duties. Then in May 1967, personal negotiations between Barbachano and Jorge Pérez y Bouras, head of Aeronaves de México (with Manuel Gómez Méndez acting as moderator) resulted in a route trade: Aeromaya gained access to Acapulco, while Aeronaves was granted a route to Mérida, an idea which was approved, even encouraged by the Government.

In this fight for the Mexican airline skies, there were no holds barred. On one occasion, Barbachano and his supporters who were shareholders of Mexicana forced their way into the annual stockholders' meeting and demanded to know the true financial position. This was at a time when Crescencio Ballesteros was trying to rescue Mexicana, and the headlines in the newspapers next day announcing that the airline was insolvent did not endear Aeromaya to its competitor. Then on 1 June, 1967, the trade unions called a strike on Aeromaya which lasted for four months. Service was finally resumed on 16 September over a network which stretched from Puerto Vallarta to the Caribbean.

During 1967 and 1968, Barbachano and Gómez Méndez, each working independently for the purpose of route applications, kept up the pressure to expand Aeromaya's network. Constantly 'snapping at Mexicana's heels' they neatly exploited what could be termed Domestic Sixth Freedom rights. Tuxpan was no great traffic generator, but was the key to linking desirable traffic points and circumventing Mexican airline regulations without actually breaking them.

All good things came to an end, however, and in 1969 the threat of Aeromaya to disturb the equanimity of the Mexican airline scene suddenly collapsed. Although Aeromaya had become a corporation in 1968, other forces cut short its ambitions. Early in 1969 all routes west of Mexico City—the former Gómez Méndez network except Mexico City–Tuxpan—were suspended, and taken over by the Aeronaves Alimentadoras, newly-formed associate of Aeronaves de México, to become its Aeronaves del Sur division. On 10 May, 1969, Aeromaya ceased operations completely. The aircraft were grounded by Government decree, and the eastern section of the network taken over by Servicios Aéreos Especiales (S.A.E.), another Aeronaves de México associate.

Servicios Aéreos Especiales (S.A.E.) had been formed as SAESA in 1960 for the purpose of evacuating deportees from Texas under US Government contract. In 1968 it had been threatened with suspension and the Mexican Government took

A Hawker Siddeley HS.748 of Servicios Aéreos Especiales at Tapachula.

over the airline and asked Pérez y Bouras to take it under his wing (The terminal S.A. was dropped as it lost its independent status). S.A.E. in turn took over most of the Aeromaya network on 22 May, 1969, thus gaining direct access on behalf of Aeronaves de México to the Yucatán peninsula, a goal which had long eluded Mexicana's rival. The HS.748s were allocated to S.A.E. which, in due course, surrendered the easternmost segments of its network to form **Aeromayab**, but continued to operate the 748s to eastern Mexico as far as Tapachula.

During 1969, as well as taking over Aeromaya, Aeronaves de México extended its mopping-up programme, at the same time fashioning two interesting routes to connect Los Angeles with the booming tourist resorts of Yucatán. The process began when, on 24 April, 1969, the northern border city of Tijuana was linked with Mérida via Ciudad Juárez and Monterrey. Then, after Aeronaves had acquired Aerolíneas Vega, direct service began on 5 August, 1969, from Los Angeles to Cozumel, via Acapulco, Oaxaca, and Mérida.

Aerolíneas Vega inherited the former concession of Líneas Aéreas Guerrero-Oaxaca, S.A. (LAGOSA) which had linked Puebla with the Pacific coast. Manuel Gómez Méndez (who seemed to have been a human catalyst to small airline activity at this time) took over the concession for about a year at the beginning of the 1950s, under a temporary permit, and this then passed to **Aerolíneas Vega** in 1952. This airline was named after its founder, Gustavo Rodriguez Vega, who obtained also, in 1953, the concession for a passenger route from Acapulco to Oaxaca, using C-39s and C-47s. Vega operated a nonstop

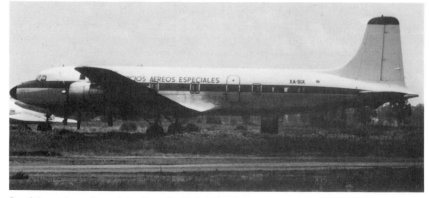

Servicios Aéreos Especiales Douglas DC-6 XA-SIX was originally delivered to American Airlines in April 1947 as N90709 *Flagship Virginia*. (*Douglas Aircraft Company*)

74

service to cater for the growing tourist trade (Oaxaca was close to the important archaeological site of Monte Alban) and a multi-stop service for the 'chicken route', so named because the local people were usually accompanied by their livestock.

In 1955, the Puebla–Oaxaca route was added, and Vega advertised *El Suriano* (*The Man from the South*) flights over the Golden Triangle. The airline changed its character during the next few years, adding two Douglas DC-6s, painted in eye-catching colours, for the Triangle, and adding a route from Oaxaca to Mérida, thus linking Acapulco with the growing resort area of Yucatán. The 'chicken route' was dropped when new road construction killed off the local air service. As Gómez Méndez succinctly put it, 'the first truck killed us'—but aircraft were still used in the rainy season, when the dirt roads were impassable.

In 1969, Aeronaves de México offered to buy the now attractive route network in an effort to expand east of Mexico City. Although Rodriguez Vega refused, he lost the concession anyway. Aeronaves not only gained the Triangle, by which the pleasures of the capital, ancient ruins, and sophisticated beaches, would be combined into one package; it was also a key link in its chain of route segments. After the Vega takeover, the northern circuit route from Tijuana was converted to international status by the substitution of Los Angeles as the northern terminal in April 1970.

In due course, Aeronaves de México took over S.A.E. completely, so that by 1970 Mexico was, to all intents and purposes, served only by two large airlines, although Aeronaves Alimentadoras survived as a subsidiary organization for a few years. In contrast with the intensive activity on the domestic scene, Aeronaves was circumspect in its expansion of long-range routes. Service was resumed to Panamá and Caracas on 31 March, 1969, in a pool arrangement with the Venezuelan airline, VIASA, under the terms of which passengers would find themselves boarding a VIASA aircraft at Los Angeles on an Aeronaves service. The Madrid route was extended to Paris two days later, restoring the European terminus to that pioneered by Guest, the ancestral airline. Late in 1970, Philadelphia was included on some New York flights, although this was not sustained.

During the period of consolidation of small routes and airlines, Aeronaves de México had progressively turned over its mainline domestic and regional routes to the Douglas DC-9. International routes were the responsibility of the DC-8. Traffic was healthy, and negotiations were completed in February 1971 to lease three 'stretched' DC-8s, the -63 version with 180 seats, to keep pace with traffic demand. On 1 August, 1971, the Mexico City–New York frequency was increased to twice daily.

But all was not well. While Mexicana had undergone its financial nightmare in 1967–68, the elements of a similar crisis were present in Aeronaves de México, although the danger was not apparent so quickly. Much of the true state of financial health had been obscured as the airline became involved with the nationalization policy of the Mexican Government in absorbing the small companies. Gradually a serious situation became evident, much of it laid at the door of Aeronaves Alimentadoras, which had been Jorge Pérez y Bouras's brainchild. The theory behind the idea of a state-supported system of feeder services serving the whole of Mexico was good; but the losses were much greater than had been forecast. The Director General was blamed for not having reorganized the complex miscellany of routes and companies more expeditiously, and he was obliged to resign on 7 September, 1971. One of the more colourful leaders of Mexican airlines, he was able to point to a record of having steered a fledgling international airline to a level of maturity which the world had recognized by electing him President of IATA in 1965. During the $12\frac{1}{2}$ years of his stewardship, Aeronaves de México never killed a passenger—though Jorge would be the first to admit that there had been a few near misses.

The Mexican Airlines Reach Maturity

The pendulum swung violently as first Mexicana, then Aeronaves de México, went through critical financial crises. Just as in the late 1960s Mexicana had had to watch its rival moving along confidently while it was putting its own house in order, so it was in reverse during the early 1970s. Jorge Pérez y Bouras was succeeded by Ing Raymundo Cano, the former Chief Engineer, whose first act was to change the entire image of Aeronaves de México. The paint scheme of the aircraft was enlivened; the Aztec warrior symbol was modernized; and most important, the trading name was changed to the shorter, easily remembered **Aeroméxico** on 28 January, 1972. In June of the same year, Cano placed an order with McDonnell Douglas for two wide-bodied DC-10-30s, each fitted with 255 seats, to upgrade the New York and trans-Atlantic routes. It was a reflection on the airline's basic weakness, however, that the Mexican Government, which owned the airline, refused permission for the purchase, recommending instead that it should order more DC-8s. Although the veto was eventually rescinded, the official action was a blow to the airline at a time when its rival was going from strength to strength.

President Nixon had granted two new US gateways for Mexicana, to St Louis and Kansas City, and services started on 28 June, 1973, and 1 December, 1974, respectively. Also, after a period of suspension, the Dallas service had been reinstated on 13 December, 1972. While the addition of new destinations was welcome after a period of limited network growth, the intensification of service on its premier route, to Los Angeles, was of greater importance in economic terms. By the end of 1974, Mexicana was offering 60 frequencies a week between the southern Californian metropolis and Mexico City. Twenty-two of these were nonstop; others were routed via Guadalajara, Puerto Vallarta, and Mazatlán, each an important destination in its own right. Against powerful wide-body competition from Western Airlines, it was nevertheless enjoying more than 30 per cent of the total business. To cope with the continuously growing traffic, Mexicana continued to order Boeing 727s, to make 19 by the end of 1974.

One of the more fascinating developments in Mexico which directly affected the progress of the airlines was the systematic creation of new vacation resorts. The energetic tourist authorities, partly inspired by private enterprise, partly by the Government, recognized with penetrating clarity that Mexico was a tourist paradise. What Spain had achieved in Europe—creating an extensive tourist industry which benefitted the nation as a whole—Mexico could do in America. Spain drew on the sun-seeking population of northern Europe, who poured money into the Spanish economy. Mexico was on the very doorstep of the USA. The cosmopolitan charm of the capital, the Spanish and pre-Columbian heritage, and the tropical beaches, all combined to provide an ideal tourist environment, capable of vast potential.

Already, the spectacular success of Acapulco had provided a clue to the enormous possibilities. But the Mexican authorities were determined that mistakes in the entrepreneurial, laissez-faire environment under which the old port had been transformed would not be repeated. Acapulco's smart seafront hotels and night clubs were only a stone's throw away from poor, overcrowded, unsanitary slums. Basic amenities such as water, electricity, and sewage lines had come after, not before the development.

In the late 1960s therefore, a new organization was established, called Infratur, later to be renamed Fonatur. It was responsible for the total planning, design, construction, and franchise allocation for new resort areas. The land was owned by the Government, Infratur made the master plan, private enterprise was invited to participate only after Infratur had prepared the infrastructure. The result was a carefully monitored programme of holiday resort development which could serve as a model for the world.

And so a new name was added to the airline maps of Mexico, even before it was included in the national ones. On 17 February, 1973, Mexicana began nonstop DC-6 service to Cancun, a narrow strip of beach on the shores of the Caribbean near the northeastern tip of the Yucatán peninsula. It was followed shortly after by Aeroméxico's stopping service with an HS.748. These aircraft had to be used temporarily while Cancun's new airport was rapidly being constructed. But this was not long delayed, and by July 1975 Mexicana was able to open Miami–Cancun service with its Boeing 727s. Aeroméxico followed with DC-9 service from Miami, Houston, and Mexico City (nonstop) in August of that year.

Other Infratur/Fonatur resorts began to emerge, like the magical blooming of cacti in the desert. The little fishing port of Zihuatanejo soon had an upstart neighbour, Ixtapa, carefully screened from the traditional village, a few kilometres up the coast. The airport was, quite logically, one of the first amenities to be built. The Twin Otters and HS.748s which had landed between the coconut palms at the old strip were replaced by jets at Ixtapa in 1975. Next on the list was San José del Cabo, on the southernmost tip of the Baja California peninsula, and hitherto reached only by private chartered aircraft from nearby La Paz, itself undergoing a transformation as 'The Baja' suddenly became a booming destination for US Californians. In July 1977, both airlines were providing direct services to the Cabo, and Manzanillo also joined the group of places in the sun.

A glance at the map reveals that the Mexican policy of developing tailor-made resorts served a variety of commendable purposes. Obviously, it drew more tourists, with their foreign currency, to Mexico. But more important, it decentralized the business to areas which needed new industry. The Mexican states selected for new resort sites were all the most impoverished. The influx of the tourist industry provided employment, federal support, and hope. Collectively, they are changing the face of the tourist industry of a large segment of North America, not to mention Europe—for enterprising airlines such as Air France and Lufthansa have already discovered Cancun.

New Aircraft, New Routes, A New Era

Aeroméxico set the pace in 1974 by introducing two new aircraft. First was the larger DC-9, the -30 version with 115 seats, revenue services with it beginning on 1 March. Soon after the upgrading of domestic equipment came the wide-body debut for Mexico in the international arena. The first DC-10-30, with 277 seats, took off for Madrid on 1 May, and went on the Acapulco–Mexico City–New York route on 1 June. Aeroméxico's route policy during the mid-1970s was, however, somewhat uncertain, a heady mixture of ambitious projects and experiments on the one hand, and cautious withdrawal or reluctance to open service on the other.

Aeroméxico's McDonnell Douglas DC-10-30 XA-DUG *Ciudad de México.*
(*Douglas Aircraft Company*)

In April 1975, for example, it applied for permission to fly DC-8s to Honolulu, but this service was never operated. In September of the same year, because of political differences between Mexico and Spain, during the twilight era of the despotic Franco Government, Aeroméxico withdrew its service to Madrid as a protest. The altruistic gesture was soon redundant, as Spain's political course made an abrupt change of direction. Service to Philadelphia was suspended in 1975, but the following year, Aeroméxico boldly extended its South American route to Buenos Aires, via Bogotá and Lima, although this venture, too, did not last long.

In Mexico, as with many other countries, a change of Government inevitably leads to a changing of the guard in the nationalized industries. Thus, Raymundo Cano gave way to Pedro Vasquez Colmenares, appointed by President López Portillo as Director General of Aeroméxico in January 1977. Some of the decisions made by the new management were surprising but necessary in the interests of strict economy. The DC-10 was withdrawn from New York and replaced with DC-8 service, with better departure times. The wide-body aircraft was redeployed on the busy domestic trunk services from Mexico City and Guadalajara to Tijuana. But by the summer of 1978, by which time there were five weekly DC-10 flights to Europe, the aircraft was reinstated to New York.

The nature of its corporate structure ensured that Aeroméxico was vulnerable to management changes. When the Mexican Government took over the airline in 1959, it was established that the Board of Directors should be appointed by the Government, and that they in turn would appoint the Director General. He would then select his top executives. But Aeroméxico was not part of the civil service, and retained its own legal identity. Nevertheless, changing top management now seems to be accepted as normal for a state airline. In contrast, the management of Mexicana continued unchanged as it rode on a wave of financial stability and commercial success.

By 1978 Mexicana was able to record ten years of continuous annual profits, and was dubbed the 'miracle airline' by the Mexican press, which remembered the desperate days before Ballesteros appointed Manuel Sosa de la Vega to make or break the company. The latter was able to announce with pride that the 1977

78

traffic figures made Mexicana the largest passenger airline in the whole of Latin America, measured by journeys flown (leading place in passenger-kilometres still being retained by the Brazilian airline VARIG). The Boeing 727 fleet numbered 31, and the money for the latest additional aircraft had been lent by the Bank of America without either government guarantees or Export-Import Bank financing, an unprecedented occurrence. Mexicana was carrying 40 per cent of all traffic between the United States and Mexico, in spite of powerful competition with eight US operators, including three large trunk carriers.

The conditions were ideal to expand further. On 28 April, 1978, the United States authorized no less than thirteen new points which could be served, and Mexicana lost no time in opening service in December of the same year to the long sought-after San Francisco gateway. Hitherto, Western Airlines had enjoyed a monopoly of service from the Bay Area; but now, with its aggressive promotion, Mexicana quickly established itself. Service to Harlingen, Texas, was also added at the same time as San Francisco; while on 1 December, 1979, Seattle became Mexicana's ninth US gateway (service to both St Louis and Kansas City had been suspended in July).

The airline policy of the Carter administration had overflowed generously in favour of the Mexican airlines, although Aeroméxico adopted the policy of intensifying service from existing gateways, rather than open new ones. But both airlines took advantage of a new attitude also by the Mexican aviation authorities. Possibly taking a leaf out of President Carter's book, the rigid domestic route concession system was relaxed, so that both airlines could compete on certain routes. Thus, towards the late 1970s, both Mexicana and Aeroméxico were able to fulfil long-cherished ambitions, with the former, for example, expanding service to Tijuana, and the latter widening its network to Yucatán, and particularly celebrating its newly found freedom of manoeuvre by starting, on

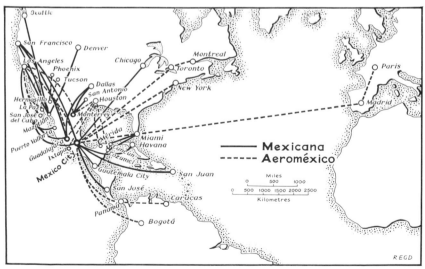

9. Mexican International Air Routes, 1980. The Mexican airlines provide extensive service to North American and Caribbean area countries. However, routes to Europe still seem inadequate and other trans-oceanic routes still await development.

Mexicana's McDonnell Douglas DC-10-15 *Azteca* flying as N19B.
(*McDonnell Douglas Corp*)

Christmas Day, 1979, its first nonstop service from Los Angeles to both Mexico City and Guadalajara.

The Mexican airline industry is probably the most underrated of any country in the world, partly because in Europe it is little known—both Mexican airlines have been inexplicably determined not to serve London or Frankfurt, and only recently, because of the more liberal route authority, have they served more than a few of the United States. But customers can testify to the excellent service. Aeroméxico's New York service started *Margarita* flights on 24 June, 1977, with free tequila, wine, and champagne to accompany an elegantly-served meal. Not to be outdone, Mexicana consistently offered the best fare bargains from Los Angeles, with *tecolote* (*night owl*) discount fares at $138 return. But the record bargain was Aeroméxico's $99 fare on the same route, Los Angeles–Mexico City, and $65 to Guadalajara, introduced on 2 January, 1980, for three months, to celebrate and to promote its newly-acquired nonstop authority.

The booming business brought with it more imposing statistics. In 1978 Mexicana became the first Latin American airline to carry 5 million passengers in a year; and within twelve months the figure was 6 million. Aeroméxico, meanwhile, increased its DC-10 trans-Atlantic services to six a week. Such expansion demanded additional equipment, and both airlines confirmed great confidence in the Douglas company, a traditional supplier of aircraft to Mexico since the days of the DC-2. On 24 September, 1979, Mexicana and Aeroméxico each ordered two McDonnell Douglas DC-10 wide-body jets. Equipped with 315 seats, they were of the -15 Series, a special version built to provide the best take-off performance out of Mexico City consistent with low operating costs.

Aeroméxico's McDonnell Douglas DC-9-82 *Torreón* operated as N1003X.
(*Douglas Aircraft Company*)

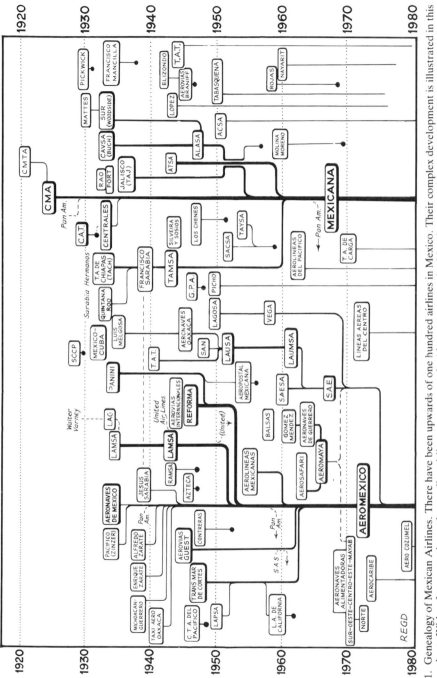

1. Genealogy of Mexican Airlines. There have been upwards of one hundred airlines in Mexico. Their complex development is illustrated in this chart. With a few exceptions, the smaller airlines were merged with, or were acquired by the two major companies which survive today.

Aeroméxico also ordered some of the new 155-seat DC-9 Super 80s for the shorter routes; Mexicana stayed with the Boeing 727 and early in 1980 purchased five more, raising its total to 39, then the largest single fleet of the record-selling type outside the United States.

In some respects the multi-million dollar investment in the DC-10-15 was a courageous decision. On 25 May, 1979, a DC-10 had crashed at Chicago in spectacular fashion. The engine had actually fallen off—giving a literal interpretation to the term 'losing an engine'. The Mexicans took note of the official judgement on the causes, which had decided that Douglas was not to blame, and went ahead with the order as planned.

By 1982, however, the Mexican airlines were feeling some effects from a deteriorating national economy. In spite of the abundant riches which should have flowed into the treasury as a direct result of one of the biggest oil booms in history, the country's budget went into a colossal deficit. The peso was devalued twice within a few months and currency transfers to the USA were halted by mid-summer. Because of a decline in earning power, and an increase in the equivalent costs of US equipment, Mexicana, for example, failed to make a profit for the first time in fifteen years. An order for six Boeing 727–200s was cancelled.

One of the last acts of the López Portillo government before it left office was to purchase, on 15 July, 1982, 40 per cent of the outstanding stock of Mexicana from Crescencio Ballesteros, making 54 per cent in total. At the next shareholders' meeting, on 29 July, the former Minister of Transport and Communications, Emilo Mujica Montoya, was elected Chairman, and Enrique M. Loaeza Tovar, President of Aeroméxico, succeeded Manuel Sosa de la Vega, who took a well earned retirement. After a few months, however, Sosa was recalled to take the helm once again, to guide Mexicana through a new round of problems.

A Fresh Start at the Third Level

When Aeronaves Alimentadoras came to a grinding halt in the early 1970s, there was a temporary hiatus in the lower echelons of Mexican commercial aviation affairs. Like the rebirth of vegetation in the desert after the breaking of a drought, new little airlines predictably emerged sporadically all over Mexico. But the mood was different. Mexican entrepreneurs, never slow to spot the opportunity to earn a fast peso, were alert as always, but things were never the same after the Alimentadoras experiment.

To begin with, the early 1970s witnessed a prohibitive increase in fuel costs, so that the old aircraft, which could previously have flown with poorly paid crews, minimum maintenance, and very little other cost, suddenly became expensive to fly. Also, Mexico was improving its road system everywhere, and the ramshackle old buses were no longer so common; in fact, Mexican long-distance coach travel, with air-conditioned comfort, and extremely low fares, ruled out any challenge from the air, at least on inter-city routes up to about 150 miles (250 km). Even in the mountain regions, where the battered old Stinson or ageless DC-3 was once the lifeline of an isolated mining community, a new competitor arrived on the scene: the four-wheel-drive truck, pickup, or Jeep, which could almost dispense with the luxury of a road.

Thus, instead of a headlong rush to start new airlines everywhere, a note of caution prevailed. Certainly, there was a rash of Servicios and Aeroservicios during the mid-1970s at key spots like La Paz, Hermosillo, and Durango; but most of these did not last long. Of the ones which have survived to the present day,

Aerocaribe Convair CV-340 *Kukul Kan*. Fuselage flash is green and lettering black. The tail badge shows a black aircraft against a red sun beneath which two bars represent sea and earth. (*T. R. Waddington collection*)

many took advantage of special traffic demand resulting from Mexico's booming tourist trade, especially in Yucatán and Baja California.

One of these little airlines was exceptional, in that its locale was not dependent upon the whims of tourists, or on the shifting sands of Mexican industry. Like an old-time prospector who refuses to move on after all the gold is panned out, one of the earliest of the gypsy operators of Mexico survives today.

Leo López Talamantes learned to fly in El Paso in 1927, and went to fly for the bush operators of Curtiss Jennies in the Tampico oilfields. He worked successively for Gordon Barry of LAMSA, and Pancho Buch of CAVSA, then flew with Harold Bromley for a British company, Wenmeco, at Parral, and worked for CMA before winding up at Chihuahua in 1940, where, with a Ryan B-5, he gained a reputation for flying into 'impossible' landing strips, many of which he surveyed himself as well as organizing the local labour force to build them.

In 1943, he founded **Servicio Aéreo Leo López T**. and began flying regularly to some of the gold-mining camps in the mountains of the state of Chihuahua. The small network changed from time to time as the mines shut down or opened, but one steady route, started in 1948, was from Chihuahua to Ojinaga, the nearest point on the US frontier. Interestingly, this survived the opening of the new railway in 1961, the Chihuahua-Pacific, which provided an outlet from Texas to the Pacific Ocean at Topalibampo; but it did not survive the competition from the trucks and buses when the new road from Ojinaga to Chihuahua was built in 1961.

As both the city and state of Chihuahua grew in prosperity, Leo López grew with it—he was a leading Cessna dealer. The new railway did not fulfil the purpose of rapid access to the coast, although providing a breathtaking scenic attraction for those with a day to spare. Thus on 26 March, 1980, a daily Cessna 402 round-trip began from Chihuahua to Los Mochis, to preserve the López name on the Mexican airline map.

A true bush pilot, Leo López was a link with an exciting past, from the earliest days of Mexican airline pioneering to modern times, doggedly maintaining the spirit of independence in a world of big business and government control. Some of this individualism is still to be found, in a country where private enterprise has a habit of flourishing, in circumstances which would be considered quite intolerable north of the border. These hardy survivors we listed in Table 3 on page 84.

TABLE 3

Mexican Local Service Airlines 1980

Airline	Base	Routes	Main Equipment	Remarks
Aerocaribe (Aerovías Caribe, S.A.)	Mexico City	Mexico City–Mérida–Cozumel, Isla Mujeres, Cancun, Tulum	CV-340/440	Founded mid-1970s
Aero Cozumel S.A.	Cozumel	Local services to Cancun, Chichen Itza, and points in Yucatán	Islander	Founded by Nassim Joaquin 5 January, 1979
Aerolíneas del Pacífico, S.A.	La Paz	La Paz–Los Mochis	DC-3	Founded 12 December, 1962
Aerotaxis, S.A.	Durango	Local services	Islander	
Líneas Aéreas del Centro, S.A.	Mexico City	Mexico City–Morelia–Apatzingán–Uruapan, Lázaro Cárdenas–Colima–Guadalajara	CV-440 DC-3 Twin Otter	Founded by Capt M. Arquelles. Took over routes formerly operated by Aeronaves del Sur (of Aeronaves Alimentadoras)
Líneas Aéreas Oaxaquenas, S.A.	Oaxaca	Local services	DC-3	
Líneas Aéreas Mexicanas, S.A. (LAMSA)	Chihuahua	Local services	Islander	
Transportes Aéreos Terrestres S.A. (TAT)	Tayoltita	Durango–Tayoltita–Mazatlán	Twin Otter Islander	(See text and other tables) Airline dates back to 1934
Aerocarga, S.A. (ACSA)	Ensenada	Tijuana–Ensenada–La Paz–Mérida, and points in Baja California	DC-6A	Founded 1950. Since 1967 operates freight services throughout Baja California and to Mérida
Comercial Aérea S.A.	Ciudad Obregón	Local services	Islander	
Transporte Aéreo de Carga, S.A.	Mexico City	Non-scheduled	DC-6	Freight services only

TACA Douglas DC-3A YS-70 at Tegucigalpa, Honduras. YS-70 was originally ordered by Pan American but went to the US Navy as an R4D-4. It passed to Transocean Airlines as N3980C and after service with TACA went to Iran as EP-ADI. On the left is another TACA DC-3.

CHAPTER FIVE

Airlines of Central America

Fragmented Arena for Airline Enterprise

During the early 1920s, the United States had shown little interest in developing commercial air routes or in establishing airlines. In Europe, on the other hand, airlines were founded in almost every country, and sustained by government subsidy, direct or indirect, in recognition of their value as a potentially fast transport mode, especially for the carriage of mail. Germany had been prevented from maintaining its military aviation industry by the provisions of the Treaty of Versailles, and had thus concentrated—more than any other European power—on air transport. By this circumstance, it transpired that Central America's first introduction to the full potential of air transport was inspired by German interests.

As will be narrated in the Colombian chapters of this book, a Colombian-German company had been established in Barranquilla as early as 1919, and had successfully pioneered air routes in Colombia. Realizing its opportunity—and in the absence of any apparent United States interest or opposition—this company, SCADTA, ventured into the international air, with the ambition to start a trans-Caribbean and Central American air service. As a prelude and necessary planning and negotiating step, SCADTA launched an historic survey flight in

1925. Two Dornier Wal flying-boats were assigned by the German Condor Syndikat for the purpose. *Atlántico* and *Pacífico* arrived in Havana on 19 September. The month-long journey took them through all seven Central American countries, as well as Mexico and Cuba. And although this bold sortie failed in its objectives the Germans had served notice that the era of the commercial aircraft was approaching.

On a more localized level, a Dr T. C. Pounds began an air mail service in 1923 in Honduras, where the capital, Tegucigalpa, almost alone among the world's capitals in being without a rail link to the outside world, offered a unique opportunity. Dr Pounds was to be usurped by Lowell Yerex, the New Zealander who founded TACA. This airline was to spread its wings so extensively throughout Central America and beyond that its exploits are dealt with later in a special chapter.

More than two years after the historic SCADTA flight sponsored by the German-Colombian pioneers, Charles Lindbergh made an equally historic—and far more publicised—goodwill tour, encircling the Central American and Caribbean region, leaving Mexico City on 14 December, 1927, and arriving in Miami on 7 February, 1928. Flying his famous Ryan *Spirit of St Louis* the trans-Atlantic aviator covered roughly the same route—in the reverse direction—as von Bauer and his colleagues in the Dornier Wals. One notable difference, however, was that whereas the German team had to keep to the coastline and convenient lakes, Lindbergh landed in spectacular fashion before adoring crowds at the capital cities which, with the exception of Panamá, were all inland.

Lindbergh's flight was not only a goodwill tour for the United States, but also a survey flight on behalf of Juan Trippe's Pan American Airways. Having established itself as a going concern, with the support of a generous Foreign Air Mail contract, Pan American quickly progressed from its Latin American springboard, a short route from Key West to Havana, started on 28 October, 1927. The first through mail service to reach the Panama Canal Zone, via the Central American capitals, left Miami on 4 February, 1929. During this period, the necessary traffic rights were usually easy to obtain. The small countries, lacking resources to start their own airlines, were pleased to be on the Pan American network. Nevertheless, there were some snags. The President of Costa Rica, for example, broke off negotiations on 31 January, 1929, because the planned mail tariffs between San José and Limón were too high. A firm mail contract was not signed until 27 August, 1929.

Many years were to pass before the Central American countries were to have either the technical expertise, the operational experience, or the necessary finance to found their own airlines. Indeed, most of the investment in railways and roads was by United States business interests throughout the region, particularly the United Fruit Company of Boston, which provided one of the earliest examples of what was later to become a familiar economic phenomenon: an international conglomerate whose strength was greater than that of many of the countries in which it conducted its business.

What the United Fruit Company was to the surface transport, Pan American was to the airways. Having started its inter-Central American mail service on 4 February, 1929, passenger service began on 22 May of the same year. Juan Trippe's company held a virtual monopoly of international air routes, from Mexico City to Panamá, for a whole decade. Its only real challenger was TACA, whose ambitions were confined mainly to local services during most of the 1930s. When Lowell Yerex also turned his eyes towards building an airline empire, the chronicle of airline history in Central America became inextricably interwoven with the industrial struggle between the promoters of those two foreign-owned corporations.

The First Independent Airlines in Central America

Honduras can claim to have opened the first air service in Central America. Early in 1923, **Dr T. C. Pounds**, an oculist from Brooklyn, New York, obtained a mail contract from the Honduran Government, and hired a pilot named Mayes to join him. Mayes supplied the aircraft, a 1918 model Lincoln Standard, but by the end of the year the partnership had broken up. Mayes took his Standard and joined Dean and Company, automobile dealers, in an air venture. Presumably Pounds's contract (to carry the mails from the coast to the capital, Tegucigalpa, in the absence of the railway that was never built) was inoperative by default, as **Empresa Dean's** work was undertaken mainly for the Tela Railroad, a subsidiary of the United Fruit Company.

Waco OEC, one of only three or four built, outside the Empresa Dean hangar at Tegucigalpa in about 1932. The man on the left is believed to be Norman Scholes, an Englishman who took over the Dean operation, but would never fly. Next to him is the Chief Pilot, C. N. Shelton, who taught the legendary Lowell Yerex instrument flying and later became the promoter of low fares in Central and South America as head of TAN and other associated airlines. The centre figure is R. C. Forsblade, who shared with Shelton the task of both flying and maintaining the Dean fleet. Shelton died in Miami in 1965.
(*Robert C. Forsblade*)

Revolution broke out in February 1924 and stopped commercial flying. But while Tegucigalpa was under seige, the Empresa Dean brought in supplies for the radio station and for foreigners marooned in the capital. Later, the successful revolutionaries commandeered the aircraft to use as an improvised bomber. The revolution no doubt put a stop to plans for a seaplane service along the north coast of Honduras and to Puerto Barrios, in Guatemala, and Belize, in British Honduras. A Curtiss HS-2L was flown 1,883 miles from Washington, to join the small fleet of the E. E. Huber Honduras Company. But there is no record of this company getting under way.

Dr Pounds emerged again in 1925, this time having persuaded a pilot named Morgan to contribute his Aeromarine flying-boat (possibly one of Huber's former fleet) to form an operation known as **Central American Air Lines**. From 28 April to 22 December of that year, C.A.A. flew the mails, initially from Puerto Cortés, on the Gulf of Honduras, to Tegucigalpa, a distance of about 200 kilometres, in about one and a half hours. Tegucigalpa was almost isolated from the rest of Honduras as there was no rail connection (neither is there one today) and the roads were so bad that much of the route was served by mule-trains. The mails consequently took more than a week to reach port. On 4 December, 1925, C.A.A. transferred its northern terminus to San Pedro Sula, headquarters of the United Fruit Company, which has remained as a key service point for the airlines of the area ever since. The partnership of Pounds and Morgan did not last long, and by 1927 the worthy doctor had only one airworthy aircraft, a Caudron of uncertain ancestry.

The **Tela Railroad Company** then seems to have taken affairs into its own hands, having bought two Lincoln Standards, amongst other aircraft; but finding life difficult, preferred to sub-contract with other flyers. It started its own service in 1927, but on 3 August, 1928, advised the authorities that it did not wish to renew its licence. Tela then changed its mind, and changed its airline title to **Compañía Aéreo Hondureño** (Honduran Air Company), operating a route from Tela to Tegucigalpa, via Puerto Castilla and San Pedro Sula.

Two other minor airlines in Honduras in the early airline days were **Líneas Aéreas de Sula**, founded by a German pilot who was killed in a crash near Santa Barbara; and **Empresa Sierke**, which operated a Waco which was sold to the Guardia Nacional in Nicaragua in 1932.

Once again Dr Pounds—described by one writer as 'a ruffled W. C. Fields in flying togs'—made his presence felt. On 26 August, 1931, he obtained permission to bring a Stinson Detroiter from the United States, and on 14 September of that year started **Transportes Aéreos Hondureños (T.A.H.)**. But Pounds fell out with his partners again and T.A.H. ended service on 30 December.

Dr Pounds's mail contract was renewed several times under the T.A.H. title until 20 February, 1932, but the flights were sporadic. The regular mule-trains could compete favourably except on those days when Pounds elected to fly. Tempted no doubt to divert capacity by the offer of lucrative charter flights in the region, he appeared to have lost the confidence of the Honduran Government. But the reason for his fall from grace was rather more fundamental. It involved the personality of that remarkable individual, Lowell Yerex, whose story would justify a book in its own right.

Yerex's airline, TACA, was to dominate all the Central American domestic airways. In Honduras, in fact, it absorbed the only other company that survived into the 1930s. Empresa Dean had been taken over by Roy Gordon, from the USA, and Norman Scholes, from Britain, in 1931. They operated a Fokker, a Bellanca, and a Waco for a while, but were taken over by TACA on 24 April, 1934.

The Tela Railroad handed over its operations to the pilot Morgan, the man who had parted company with Pounds in 1927. In a partnership with LANEP, of Nicaragua, he operated a Ford Tri-Motor and a Bellanca as **Morgan Airlines**. But both of his aircraft crashed in 1934 and Lowell Yerex took over Honduran commercial aviation for the next ten years, unchallenged until Pan American forced its way into the Central American domestic airline field towards the end of the war. Dr Pounds, who had started the whole thing in Honduras ten years earlier, started a new company **Vías Aéreos Nacionales, S.A. (VANSA)** but a succession of accidents put an end to his airline activities.

In nearby Guatemala the Government purchased three Ryan Broughams in 1927, in a wave of enthusiasm for commercial aviation, following Lindbergh's goodwill flight. A route to San Salvador was projected under the name of **Servicio Aéreo Militar Guatemalteca** but a crash curtailed this venture. The Servicio then began service to Flores, in the northern province of Petén, where chicle was gathered in the jungles and needed rapid transport.

On 4 June, 1930, a private company, **Compañía Nacional de Aviación (C.N.A.)**—also known as the Central American Aviation Corporation Ltd—got under way. It used Kreutzer trimotors and a Don Berlin designed Hodkinson trimotor sesquiplane, with name credit to the airline president, W. Hodkinson. C.N.A. operated to Petén, to Puerto Barrios, and to Retalhulen, via Quezaltenango, Guatemala's second city. Lowell Yerex purchased the airline and integrated it with his rapidly-growing consortium of Central American airlines. But TACA's presence in Guatemala lasted only five years. In 1940 a local butcher took over the TACA franchise when Yerex's flirtation with American Export Lines, a large United States shipping company, threatened Pan Am.

Next in chronological order among the airline countries of Central America was Panamá, represented by the unique **Isthmian Airways Inc**, founded by Ralph Sexton. This was in fact a United States company operating in the then perpetually-leased territory of the Panama Canal Zone. Starting service on 5 May, 1929, using Hamilton H-45 and H-47 floatplanes, it linked the cities at each end of the Canal, Cristobal and Balboa, a distance of 47 miles, and made the tongue-in-cheek claim that its 30-minute flight was the fastest transcontinental air route in the Americas. Isthmian's fleet constituted almost the entire Canal Zone civil aircraft register, but the service lasted only about three years, although Sexton himself continued to be active in aviation.

It was succeeded on the same route by **Panama Airways**, a wholly-owned subsidiary of Pan American, founded on 7 November, 1936. Panama Airways owned no equipment, and had no employees. It owed its existence to a request by the Panama Canal Zone authority, to discourage possible applications from foreign airlines. It began operations in December, with Ford Tri-Motors, and continued to provide this convenient link until dissolved on 30 April, 1941, by which time the frequency had grown from two a week to daily, but which was being duplicated not only by Pan American's own service, but also by the Douglas DC-3s of UMCA, the parent company's Colombia-based subsidiary.

Pan American's interest in Panama derived simply from the need for an important base and interchange station on its international route network throughout Latin America. If a Pan American airliner called at a Panamanian provincial port, this was only because it needed to refuel, not to provide a social service for the citizens of the Panamanian Republic. This responsibility was undertaken by local flyers, to whom much credit is due.

Compañía de Transportes Aéreos Gelabert was founded in 1935 by a former officer of the Air Corps, Capt Marcos A. Gelabert. Fourteen domestic points were served, including a thrice-weekly service from Panama City to David, Panama's second city, and Puerto Armuelles. The aircraft used were the usual assortment of types common to Central America then, as now, a Lockheed Vega, a Stinson, a Vultee, not to mention a Sikorsky S-38, a Bellanca, and a Hamilton, probably one of Isthmian's.

Simultaneously, under the name of **Aerovías Nacionales**, Enrique Malek flew over a similar network, from a base at David. Although Gelabert had tried to open a service to San José, Costa Rica, in 1938, both he and Malek were forced to close down with the approach of the war. In November 1939 Gelabert actually applied for permission to suspend operations, which were literally a family business—the Captain flew the aircraft along with two other pilots, his wife kept the books and sold the tickets. But apparently his father talked him into continuing, even though the $1,000 a month subsidy did not cover the costs. Gelabert did suspend service in December 1941 (when the United States entered the war and viewed with alarm any flying over the Canal Zone) and was killed in an aeroplane crash in 1952. His competitor Enrique Malek also closed down and went to Costa Rica, where he too was killed. Such was the regard held for the two pioneers by aviation authorities in Panama that two aerodromes are named after them.

Costa Rica was next, distinguishing itself by having two local airlines which began scheduled services within the tiny republic in 1934. First of the two, founded on 2 March, 1932, was **Empresa Nacional de Transportes Aéreos (ENTA)**. Promoted by an emigré United States citizen, William Schoenfeldt, it began irregular services to small communities, linking them with the capital, San José, and was granted a mail subsidy of 8,000 colones a year on 29 October, 1932.

While ENTA was gaining experience, and flying sightseers over San José, a Costa Rican citizen, Roman Macaya, was learning to fly in the United States, and flew home in his own Curtiss Robin, arriving to a big welcome on 5 October, 1933. On 20 January, 1934, he announced the formation of a new airline, **Aerovías Nacionales**, obtaining support from the province of Guanacaste. This prompted

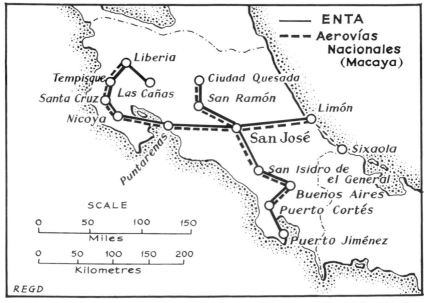

10. The First Airlines in Costa Rica, 1934. Whereas within most of Central America, Pan American and TACA developed the majority of the airline networks of substance, Costa Rica was unique in having a competitive system of its own as early as 1934.

The Aerovías Nacionales' Stinson Model U TI-34 had been NC12196 and was bought from William Randolph Hearst. (*Courtesy Dan Hagedorn*)

ENTA to put its services on a scheduled basis on 5 April of that year, using a single-engined Fokker aircraft. Although Macaya could not persuade the Government to give him a subsidy he also started regular flights, using Curtiss Kingbirds, on 3 July. Macaya's pride in his twin-engined aircraft was reflected in his marketing slogan 'Con dos motores, no hay temores' (With two engines, there are no fears). He was also to use several Travel Air 6000s, a Stinson U, three Ford Tri-Motors and a number of small aircraft. ENTA more than matched this competition by putting into service a Fokker trimotor, equipped with twelve seats, on 23 May, and during the next two years the rival airlines laid the foundations of a Costa Rican domestic airline system.

On 13 March, 1935, Bill Schoenfeldt retired from ENTA and a Scot, Eric Murray, replaced him. Shortly thereafter, on 30 May, Murray and Roman Macaya reached a gentleman's agreement to unify tariffs and avoid duplication of services. On 14 July, 1936, ENTA opened international routes to David, Panama; and to Managua in Nicaragua. He replaced his old single-engined Fokker with a Travel Air. It crashed in the mountains on 20 June, 1937, and was not found until 9 February, 1941, and the incident caused much debate in Costa Rican aviation circles, as ENTA was suspected of covering up evidence of the cause of the crash.

The Costa Rican aviation scene was complicated in the late 1930s by the launching, or attempts to launch, several small airlines. On 29 February, 1936, a group of Costa Ricans, headed by Guillermo Nunez, raised 50,000 colones to purchase some small aircraft with which to establish **Empresa de Aerotransportes**

Aerovías Nacionales' Curtiss Kingbird D-2 TI-16 at Liberia Airport in Costa Rica. (*Courtesy Gary Kuhn*)

Costarricenses (EDAC). The company also leased the *Espíritu Tico*, the Curtiss Robin which Roman Macaya had flown in from Oklahoma City in 1933, but crashed it on 7 September, 1936. EDAC ceased operations about two years later, after its sole aircraft, a Flamingo G-2W, was declared unsafe. Then, early in 1938, one of the EDAC promoters, Clarence Ross Bonilla, formed **Transportes Aéreos Costarricenses (TAC)** out of the ashes of the former company, and announced services to every part of the country. With some of his old partners, he also formed Líneas Aéreas Nacionales (LAN) in August 1938, but this never operated.

During the period of internal squabbling, the Honduran company TACA, under the forceful leadership of Lowell Yerex, was trying to spread its wings southward. After much litigation and dispute, TACA made its inaugural flight to San José on 20 October, 1939, using a Lockheed Model 14. Not long afterwards, on 16 January, 1940, Roman Macaya announced the merger of the former rivals ENTA and Aerovías Nacionales, as a preliminary step towards complete absorption by TACA. On 20 June of that year, the Government announced the cancellation of the contracts of both ENTA and Aerovías Nacionales. In its time, ENTA had operated three Fokkers, five Fords, five Travel Airs, and various other types, including a Boeing 40B-4. TAC also ceased to exist and was absorbed by TACA in January 1940.

While TACA appeared to have consolidated a strong foothold in Costa Rica, this was in fact quite precarious. Two crashes in October 1940 did its image no good, and on 2 June, 1941, the Government enacted new aviation legislation which included a clause requiring airlines to pay 10,000 colones indemnity per person in case of accidents (the old ENTA Travel Air had just been found, thus exacerbating the problem). On 26 July TACA threatened to withdraw its services, and after much dispute in the Costa Rican Congress, the law was rescinded on 24 September. A new contract was drawn up with Yerex on 14 August, 1942, which, among other clauses, demanded a 50 per cent discount for hospital patients.

In Nicaragua, the need for air transport was two-fold: to link Managua, the capital, with the east coast—like Honduras, there was no effective national railway system—and to supply the mines in the remote northeast region of the country. In about 1933, **Líneas Aéreas de Nicaragua, Empresa Vendetti (LANEV)** operated Ford Tri-Motors to the mines and a Curtiss Kingbird to link Managua with the coast. Control of this operation passed to the firm of Palazio & Co, which renamed the diminutive airline **Líneas Aéreas de Nicaragua, Empresa Palazios (LANEP)**. This latter company worked in association with the experienced pilot Morgan, from Honduras, but sold all its assets to TACA on 16 October, 1935.

There was another small company in Nicaragua called **Nicaraguan Atlantic Coast Airlines (NACA)**, owned by T. P. Fitzgerald. It operated two Fokker Super Universal floatplanes and carried on a disastrous rate war with LANEP. Later, TACA's contract in Nicaragua was cancelled, by some devious political manoeuvre, and Lowell Yerex was obliged to buy another Nicaraguan company for $20,000. This was called **Líneas Aéreas Nicaragüenses (LANIC)** and probably existed mainly for extracting protection money from Lowell Yerex.

In tiny El Salvador, which measured only about 150 miles (250 km) long, and boasted a railway along this length, there was little reason for a national airline. There is a report of **Transportes Aéreos Salvadoreños (TAS)** being organized in 1934 by a group of Salvadorian Air Force pilots, using a Bellanca and a Waco; but there is no record of sustained operations. On 25 August, 1939, TACA established its operating base in San Salvador.

British Honduras remained aloof from the coveted area, being geographically off the main channel of commerce. It was a poor country, and the British were inclined to see commercial aviation as a means of linking Belize not with Central America but with their own sphere of interest in Jamaica and the West Indies. Except for Pan American and TACA branch services from other Central American countries, the British colony did not have its own airline until after the war (see page 93).

TACA and Pan American

During the period from 1939 (when TACA made El Salvador its centre for the integration of all its local airlines) until 1970 (when Pan American began to sell its shareholdings in Honduras, Costa Rica, Panama, and Nicaragua) the airlines of Central America were controlled by, if not owned, by those two international adversaries. There were one or two exceptions, and one notable one; but the region had little national airline identity during those 30 years.

As will be related in the TACA chapter, Lowell Yerex and his later associates, including American Export Lines and TWA, fought for a place in the Central American sun until 1948. Then, except for a completely reconstituted airline which became the national carrier of El Salvador, Central America passed into Pan American control, and the badges of all the airlines incorporated the Pan American wings to underline the point. Their establishment is set out in Table 4 and illustrated in Chart 2.

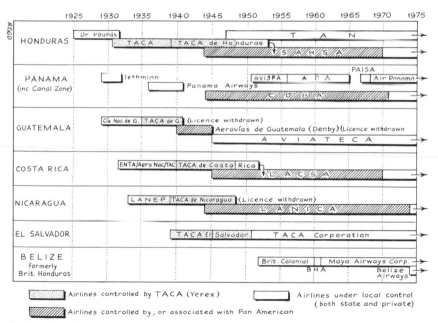

2. Changing Control of Airlines in Central America. The rival forces of TACA and Pan American Airways fought for control throughout Central America during the 1930s and 1940s. Eventually Pan American conceded its dominance to locally-based national companies.

Although Pan American's headlong entry was motivated by completely self-serving political and industrial reasons, the Central American republics also gained inestimable benefits. While Pan American was inclined to contribute its standard 40 per cent shareholding not so much in the form of limited technical expertise but by the supply of flying crews and handed-down equipment, these were still recognizably better than anything which TACA could produce. The sheer corporate strength of the United States international flag carrier was completely dominant; it raised the standard of commercial aviation in Central America by several degrees of magnitude. Eventually, it was to provide the essential framework and foundation for the national airlines that the Pan American associates were eventually to become.

National Flag Carriers for Central America

The standard formula for Pan American's sponsorship of the joint ventures was to take a 40 per cent interest for itself—often in the form of equipment supplied, rather than direct financial investment, and for the individual republic to take the remainder, split 20 per cent government, 40 per cent private. This was not invariably the case. The LANICA local share was all government and COPA's was all private; but in this part of the world, it was a fine distinction, as some governments were run almost as private fiefdoms. Pan American never invaded TACA's territory in El Salvador; while TACA never established an operating airline in Panama, but this balancing act was certainly not the result of any gentleman's agreement. In Honduras, TACA's influence remained even after Lowell Yerex had departed, and the Pan American affiliate was not allowed to operate international services for several years.

While Pan American provided the much-needed high level of expertise and experience which, in the fullness of time, was to give the republics the confidence and abilities necessary to stand on their own feet, some reference must be made to the first national airline in Central America. After the Guatemala Incident, in which Alfred Denby, acting for Pan American, emerged to usurp the local TACA airline, the new company, **Aerovías de Guatemala**, started services on 7 November, 1940, using at first a Lockheed and two Ford Tri-Motors. Later, in the summer of 1942, these were replaced by two Douglas DC-2s. After the overthrow of the dictator General Ubico, the new government appointed an intervenor to manage the airline, having instituted legal proceedings against Denby, who had wisely left the country.

Taking the view that Pan American was no improvement on TACA, the Government thereupon established a truly national airline, the **Compañía Guatemalteca de Aviación, S.A. (AVIATECA)** in which it held 30 per cent of the shares, with the remainder to be subscribed by private Guatemalan citizens. These were not forthcoming, and on 20 July, 1946, the Government acquired the entire stock. Scheduled international airline services began on 7 July, 1948, to San José, Costa Rica, and to Belize; but these were suspended, and AVIATECA concentrated for several years on domestic routes.

Political conditions in Guatemala were volatile during the postwar decades, and local enterprise in aviation was discouraged until January 1955, when the United States C.A.B. authorized AVIATECA to serve New Orleans, a city which, possibly because of traditional shipping connections, had some community of interest with the Central American republic. During the next ten years, AVIATECA gradually put itself on the airline map. New Orleans was followed

AVIATECA's Douglas C-47A TG-AKA at Tikal in Guatemala. The livery stripes are yellow and red. (*R. E. G. Davies*)

AVIATECA's Douglas DC-6B TG-ADA *Chichicastenango* at Guatemala City's La Aurora International Airport. This DC-6B was originally delivered to Pan American as N6531C *Clipper Viking* and was acquired by AVIATECA in August 1961.

AVIATECA's white, yellow and red Convair CV-340 *Quirigua* at Guatemala City. A second CV-340, TG-AJA *Tikal*, can be seen in the background. (*R. E. G. Davies*)

by Miami, the booming United States air gateway to the whole of Latin America; then in the mid-1960s Mexico City and San Salvador were added. Services began to Honduras, under a sensible arrangement by which AVIATECA provided the link to San Pedro Sula, the important Honduran city in the north, while the Honduran airline SAHSA provided the link with the Honduran capital, Tegucigalpa.

In September 1972, service began to Mérida, the Mexican provincial capital of the Yucatán region, and in June of 1973, this city was included as a stop on the New Orleans route. During this period, resulting from chronic bilateral problems with neighbouring states, service to Mexico City and San Salvador had been intermittent. Compensating for the lack of expansion in the international arena, however, was the development of a healthy domestic network. This not only served Puerto Barrios, Guatemala's Caribbean outlet, but the provincial chicle-producing city of Flores, and, growing annually in importance, the village of Tikal. This tiny community was the site of one of the finest Mayan ruins and its rise as a tourist resort gave AVIATECA a lucrative captive market.

AVIATECA had begun life with the familiar DC-3, and later added a heterogeneous collection of types, including a Northrop YC-125 Raider and Fairchild C-82 Packets. The airline moved into the jet age in March 1974 with the purchase of the British BAC One-Eleven, at the same time adding Convair CV-440 Metropolitans for local routes. Also, it changed its rather drab colour scheme to a handsome yellow and orange, which was applied to the Convairs, and to the surviving DC-3s which continued to serve the earthen strip at Tikal. By the paintwork alone, the DC-3s were given a new lease of life.

Having been the first national airline in Central America, AVIATECA took a further bold step in 1976 to extend the service of *The Route of the Mayans*. On 1 May of that year, with the co-operation of the Spanish airline Iberia, it became the first trans-Atlantic operator in the region by opening a Douglas DC-10 service to Madrid, via Santo Domingo. The aircraft and operation were Iberia's but flown under a joint flight number. It allowed the Spanish airline direct access to an ethnically-related society, at the same time giving credit to an airline whose name was unfamiliar outside the region. Indeed, AVIATECA's operating base, Guatemala City, is known mostly as the point where Pan American passengers change aircraft en route to points further south; and the Guatemalan airline's lack of progress, and even curtailment of operations during the late 1970s, have been a source of disappointment.

It was in Guatemala's neighbouring country, Honduras, that the first Pan American affiliate got under way when the US flag airline took vigorous and ruthless steps to eliminate the TACA organization from Central America during the mid-1940s. **Servicio Aéreo de Honduras, S.A. (SAHSA)**, formed on 10 November, 1944, began domestic services with a single Douglas DC-3 on 22 October, 1945. At first restricted to local routes, SAHSA ventured as far as San Salvador and Belize in March 1949. Four years later, it acquired all the stock of TACA de Honduras which, however, continued to operate as a separate entity for several years. In 1957, it also bought **Aerovías Nacionales de Honduras (ANHSA)**, a small private airline which had been founded in 1950, and whose main business had been derived from transporting the *aguardiente* (an alcoholic drink) of the government liquor monopoly.

During the mid-1960s, SAHSA began to expand, as it was in danger of being deposed by a rival, the privately-owned Honduras airline, TAN. By 1970, having obtained the necessary US permit in 1964, SAHSA was operating to New

SAHSA's Curtiss C-46A HR-SAN at Guatemala City. (*Gordon S. Williams*)

Orleans—paralleling AVIATECA—and was serving the capitals of all the Central American republics, as well as the Colombian island resort of San Andrés, en route to Panamá.

When, on 21 January, 1970, Pan American finally disposed of its last shareholding in SAHSA, it was sold to TAN. The size of the share, 38 per cent, was significant, in that the two airlines now operated as partners, with the internationally-experienced TAN giving added stature to SAHSA. Hitherto restricted to DC-3s, the Honduran airline modernized its fleet, first with propeller-turbine Lockheed Electras, then in October 1974 with a Boeing 737 twinjet, a move which, by comparison with the national airlines of its neighbours, was long overdue.

In 1980, the activities of ANHSA were revived. It had been dormant as a wholly-owned SAHSA subsidiary for about two decades, but now emerged as a domestic arm of its parent company, equipped moreover with one of the latest aircraft designed for short-field performance, the de Havilland Canada DHC 7.

SAHSA's blue and white Boeing 737-2K6 HR-SHA. (*The Boeing Company*)

97

While SAHSA's early development was inhibited by local political pressures, the tribulations of Pan American's Costa Rican affiliate were due to even more direct forms of restraint. **Líneas Aéreas Costarricenses (LACSA)**, founded on 17 October, 1945, made its first flight on 1 June, 1946, a short hop from San José to Parrita. This was more a display of intention, and to show off its DC-3. The only effect was to prompt TACA to introduce the same type. LACSA's DC-3 had been borrowed from COPA, and it crashed on 26 November, with a full load, a widely-publicised tragedy which dampened morale for a while. Understandably, subsequent efforts were somewhat muted, but during 1947 a joint service was undertaken to Managua, in co-operation with Nicaragua's LANICA, and, on 16 August of that year, flights were started to Panamá. LACSA used DC-3s, C-46s, and Beech 18s on internal services, the last-named being referred to as *picapiedras*, a word derived from the sound of stones striking the metal fuselage.

LACSA's Douglas C-47B TI-1051C, and Curtiss C-46D TI-1008C at San José. The C-46 was later reregistered TI-LRB and named *Chorotega*. Markings and lettering are traffic blue.
(*Courtesy John Kirschner*)

To add to LACSA's troubles, revolution broke out in Costa Rica on 12 March, 1948. TACA's three DC-3s were captured by the revolutionary forces of José Figueres, and the Costa Rican Government promptly requisitioned LACSA's three DC-3s. Figueres meanwhile sent his to Guatemala. The revolution succeeded on 24 April and the ousted government fled to Nicaragua in the three LACSA aircraft. These were later repatriated on payment of a fee but sold profitably in Miami because of a fortuitous price inflation resulting from the Korean War. TACA, meanwhile, was given a new lease of life when, on 19 May, Roberto Kruse and Robert Darmstedt bought the airline for $175,000.

During this period, the small airline **Transportes Aéreas Nacionales (TAN)**, founded by Manuel Guerra in June 1945 and which had grown to compete domestically with both LACSA and TACA, disappeared from the scene. LACSA struggled to its feet again, and by 1950 was able to start international services with Curtiss C-46s. On 12 March Panamá appeared on the LACSA map, and more ambitiously, on 2 June, Havana. By the end of the year Miami, Mexico City, and San Salvador were also added, and LACSA was firmly back in business.

Its fortunes further improved when, on 2 June, 1952, after much legal dispute, (related to the original insurance claims of the ENTA crash of 1937) TACA de Costa Rica was taken over by LACSA, the assets including four DC-3s. On 5

LACSA's Douglas DC-6A/B TI-1018C *Cariari* was previously Pan American's DC-6B
Clipper Pathfinder and *Clipper Frankfurt*. It is seen here at Lima in 1965.
(*Gordon S. Williams*)

LACSA's BAC One-Eleven 531FS TI-1084C seen while on lease to Cayman Airways.
(*Harold G. Martin*)

One of LACSA's Boeing 727-2Q6s. Markings are dark blue with red centre band on tail.
(*The Boeing Company*)

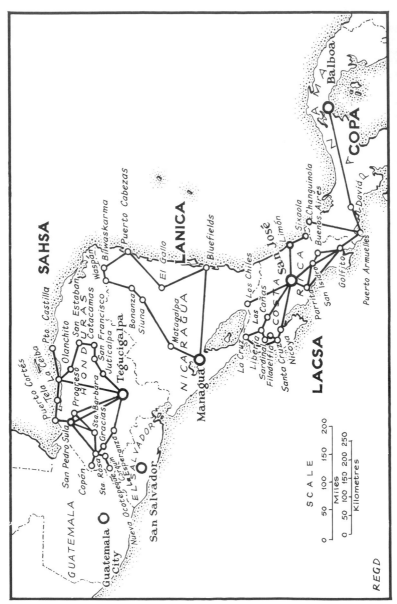

11. Pan American Airways' Affiliates, 1950. After a virtual blitzkrieg in Central America towards the end of the Second World War, Pan American Airways emerged with control of most of the local airlines, mainly at the expense of the TACA organization.

March, 1954, these were reinforced by two Convair CV-340s, the first pressurized airliners to fly in the colours of any Central American national airline.

There was an intriguing interlude in January 1955, when the exiled government of Calderon Guardia, supported by the Nicaraguan Somosa regime and others, attempted to invade Costa Rica to overthrow José Figueres. A few sorties were flown by both sides, whose 'air forces' both included the old faithful Douglas DC-3.

But from this time, comparative serenity reigned in Costa Rica, which began to develop a reputation as one of the more attractive places in the whole region for emigrant settlers. LACSA began to spread its wings with confidence. In February 1955, it even founded a subsidiary in the Cayman Islands. The British airline, BWIA, had run into difficulties and was anxious for assistance in its feeder operations. Accordingly, LACSA founded **Cayman Brac Airways** in February 1955, to link the smaller island with Grand Cayman, using a Cessna T-50.

Aerovías Cariari Douglas Hyper DC-3 TI-ACB *Ciudad de Guápiles*. This aircraft had been a USAF C-47 before going to AVIANCA as HK-102 and being converted to Hyper DC-3. It passed to SANSA as TI-SAA. The original Costa Rican registration was TI-1075C.

The British islands were directly en route between San José and both Havana and Miami, and United States permission was soon granted for LACSA to make a stop at Grand Cayman on its 'Super Convair' trans-Caribbean services. In February 1956 a connection with San Juan, in Puerto Rico, was started; but this was unsuccessful. Equipment improvements were made, Douglas DC-6Bs being introduced on the international routes in 1961, and then, on 14 May, 1967, the first jet service was inaugurated with a BAC One-Eleven. At first using the Series 400 on lease, these were superseded by the Series 500 in 1972. By this time, LACSA had become the truly national airline of Costa Rica, Pan American having sold its last remaining shareholding—to Lloyd International of London—on 14 September, 1970. LACSA promptly replaced the Pan American wings with a handsome new badge. On 1 June, 1976, a Lockheed Electra joined the DC-6Bs on the LACSA freight services which had been plying to and from the Miami gateway since the introduction of the Convair CV-340s in the mid-1950s had released the C-46s as maids-of-all-work.

101

The oft-maligned C-46s were popular in Costa Rica, one theory being that as they were larger than the DC-3 they were correspondingly safer. At any rate, they continued in service until 1978, when they were considered finally to be more than a calculated risk. **Ruta Aérea Nacional S.A. (RANSA)** was then organized as a stop-gap measure by Manuel E. Guerra (who had formerly started TAN), but his DC-3 operation did not receive permanent authority. Instead **Servicios Aéreos Nacionales S.A. (SANSA)** was organized as a joint-stock company between the Costa Rican Government (49 per cent) and a reluctant LACSA (51 per cent). SANSA began life with two DC-3s, and some small aircraft, including two new Spanish-built CASA 212 feeder airliners.

LANICA's Vickers-Armstrongs Viscount V.786 AN-AKQ *Ruben Dario* was built as Lloyd Aéreo Colombiano's HK-947 but not delivered. It was sold in the USA but appears to have gone direct to LANICA. Markings were dark blue. (*Vickers-Armstrongs*)

By Central American standards, the airline history of Nicaragua has been straightforward. It started with LANEV and LANEP which were purchased by TACA in 1935. Then on 17 November, 1944, **Líneas Aéreas de Nicaragua (LANICA)** was founded as the Pan American affiliate. Scheduled service by LANICA started in 1946, at first with Boeing 247Ds, then with DC-3s, an international connection to San José being added to the domestic service late in that year. In 1948 it took over the operations of TACA, whose contract was cancelled by the Nicaraguan Government, presumably as an expression of sympathy with the Costa Rican Government which had been deposed in the revolution whose forces included TACA aircraft.

LANICA took over a local airline **Flota Aérea Nicaraguense S.A. (FANSA)** in 1950, thereby controlling the lucrative Bonanza/Siuna goldmine traffic. But it made little progress until June 1956, when the United States C.A.B. recommended a permit to operate from Managua to Miami, for which route, started in December 1957, the Nicaraguan carrier ordered two Vickers Viscounts which went into service on 17 February, 1958. Deceived into over-confidence by the prestige and publicity which accrued from this big step, LANICA then opened a route to Guayaquil in Ecuador, and Lima, in Peru. Like a predecessor, **Aerovías Inca**, which made an attempt to link Nicaragua directly with South America in 1949–50, LANICA quickly ran into financial problems so acute that it had to suspend the route and sell the Viscounts.

102

An unidentified BAC One-Eleven with mixed livery of TAN and LANICA.
(T. R. Waddington collection)

As the national airline of Nicaragua, and enjoying a monopoly, LANICA was able to recover with an injection of further capital, and on 15 September, 1961, put a Douglas DC-6 on its Miami route, which also included San Salvador as a valuable source of Fifth Freedom traffic, an aspect of the operation not entirely to Pan American's liking. In 1965, LANICA leased a BAC One-Eleven from Aer Lingus, and thus became the first jet operator in Central America. On 1 November, 1967, it concluded an interesting pool agreement with the Honduran airline TAN for joint One-Eleven services, but these efforts at co-operation, like many other tentative experiments of that nature, were short-lived.

In March 1972, plans were announced whereby LANICA acquired two Convair CV-880 long-range jet aircraft from the United States industrialist, the legendary Howard Hughes, in exchange for a 25 per cent share of LANICA's stock, effective from 21 August. Pan American terminated its interest in Nicaragua in August 1974.

In 1977, LANICA leased a Boeing 727-100, but service was suspended in 1979 when a civil war in Nicaragua finally ejected the autocratic Somosa regime, which had long controlled the national airline and effectively guaranteed its success. The airline was reorganized and the Boeing 727 renamed after the Sandanista revolutionary party leader. It resumed international services with the Boeing, while DC-3s and C-46s maintained domestic flights.

LANICA suspended operations completely on 31 August, 1981, to be succeeded by **Aerolíneas Nicaraguenses, S.A. (Aeronica)** as the new flag airline

LANICA's Convair CV-880-22 AN-BIA. This aircraft was owned by the Hughes Tool Company, as N8495H, and had been leased to Northeast Airlines and TWA before it was leased to LANICA in July 1972. (*T. R. Waddington collection*)

owned and controlled by the Ministry of Transportation. Formed in November 1980, Aeronica began limited international services early in November 1981, using a Boeing 727–100 purchased from Eastern Air Lines. But this was severely damaged by a bomb explosion on the ground in Mexico City on 12 December, 1981. International services were resumed to Mexico on 30 December with another Boeing 727, and extended to San José and Panamá. The year 1982 opened encouragingly with US C.A.B. permission to fly from Managua to Miami. For this operation, a Boeing 720B was obtained from Olympic Airways.

Last of the Pan American affiliates to start service was **Cía Panameña de Aviación (COPA)**. This airline was formed on 21 June, 1944, by the Panamanian Government, and Pan American took its 40 per cent shareholding on 30 August. COPA did not start service until 5 May, 1947, and then only to Changuinola, on the Costa Rican frontier, using ex-military C-47s. Truth to tell, Pan American did not encourage ambition on the part of its offspring, and it took a long time for most of them to assert themselves.

COPA's Hawker Siddeley HS.748 HP-484. This aircraft returned to the United Kingdom and became the prototype Coastguarder. (*T. R. Waddington collection*)

But progress in COPA's route expansion was gradually made, to San José in January 1966, Managua in September 1969, Barranquilla in October of that year, and San Salvador in January 1971. On 5 August, 1966, COPA acquired its first propeller-turbine aircraft, a Hawker Siddeley 748, with which it was able to start a service to Medellín in Colombia. On 15 March, 1971, Pan American terminated its interest, but unlike its rival airlines in Central America, COPA did not signal its complete independence by joining the ranks of jet aircraft operators. Instead, it introduced Lockheed Electras in October 1971, since when, in a manner somewhat reminiscent of the tortoise-and-hare fable, COPA has established an enviable reputation as the reliable bus service of the region. While the BAC One-Elevens and their successors provided a little more glamour for LACSA, TACA, and others, the distances between the Central American capitals were so short that only a modest time-saving could be demonstrated over the Electras. Additionally, COPA was able to sell tickets at a discounted price for its slower service, and that made a big difference in an area where every dollar, colon, cordoba, or lempira had to be stretched to its limit.

A COPA Lockheed 188A Electra at San Salvador. (*R. E. G. Davies*)

While the Pan American affiliates in Guatemala, Honduras, Costa Rica, Nicaragua, and Panama progressively unburdened themselves of foreign control, the **TACA Corporation**, remnant of Lowell Yerex's once-proud Central American empire, underwent a metamorphosis in El Salvador, where Pan American was unable to put down local roots or routes. TACA had been kept alive during 1949 by a financial lifeline thrown by the Waterman Steamship Corporation, which bought TWA's 35 per cent shareholding. With shipping involvement technically illegal under US law, litigation ensued to determine the eligibility of the airline to qualify for a renewal of the route certificate between San Salvador and New Orleans, including service to Guatemala City and Belize. This was granted for a period of three years on 30 March, 1949.

On 24 May, 1951, the TACA Corporation was established as a US company, under Delaware law, with the issue of two million shares of 10¢ each. Waterman began to dispose of its control, mostly to its own shareholders, and the C.A.B. seemed satisfied. Nevertheless, the issue of control was raised again on 16 June, 1954, when the C.A.B. initiated hearings for a further extension of the permit to fly across the Gulf of Mexico. With the 1951 corporate change, the Panamanian base was closed down.

TACA International's Vickers-Armstrongs Viscount V.745 YS-28C was acquired from United Air Lines in February 1969. The aircraft in the background is a modified North American B-25.

In May 1955 McLean Industries acquired Waterman Airlines—the airline stock of Waterman Steamship Company employees—and then in January 1966 the Southern Industries Corporation purchased McLean's interest. At this time, the TACA International flagships were old, unpressurized Douglas DC-4s, and the new owners began to improve the company's image. In October 1957, a Vickers Viscount was leased from Philippine Air Lines and put into service on the New Orleans route on 2 December.

In 1960 the issue of control and legal qualification for a Foreign Air Carrier certificate again came before the C.A.B. To ease the problem, on 29 March the TACA Corporation transferred all its properties and assets to TACA International, its operating subsidiary in El Salvador, in exchange for two million shares of common stock. The Corporation was then liquidated, and El Salvador took the necessary steps under international law to facilitate the transfer of ownership and financing of its aircraft. The C.A.B. was apparently satisfied and renewed the permit for another three years, effective from April. Waterman appeared to be divesting itself of control; and Pan American, it was thought, could use a little competition.

A new era began for TACA International in 1964. In that year, Ricardo Kriete, a United States citizen who had arrived in El Salvador in 1921 to attend a friend's wedding but had stayed on, purchased 32 per cent of the company's shares. Thenceforward, although the remainder of the shares were in the hands of US nationals, TACA had a definite Salvadorian identity, and became so regarded by the US C.A.B. In April 1964 the coveted New Orleans route permit was renewed, and the Honduran city of San Pedro Sula added as an intermediate point.

Late in 1966 TACA introduced the BAC One-Eleven, the first to be owned by a Central American airline. Throughout the complications in corporate ownership, location of headquarters, financial crises, and management changes, TACA had somehow managed to maintain the integrity of the name for which its acronym stood: the Air Transport of Central America, serving as it did, with no measurable interruption, all the republic capitals from Mexico City to Panamá. To this network it added the important trans-Caribbean route to Miami in March 1969, although the elder Kriete did not live to see it, his son having succeeded him in 1968.

The record of continuity was eventually broken in July 1969, for an astonishing reason. Beginning with a World Cup football match between El Salvador and Honduras at which tempers were inflamed to riotous levels, the trouble escalated to a local war at the frontier. Although military action was limited, diplomatic activity resulted in the closing of the border and cessation of trade. Thus, because of a football match fracas, TACA lost its operating authority to Tegucigalpa, but was able to compensate for the loss by opening a service to Jamaica on 1 June, 1971. Routed via Belize, it also provided a link between two English-speaking territories. In October 1975, TACA also suffered from restrictions in Guatemala, but again made up for the loss by opening a route via Mérida in 1976. El Salvador and Honduras, incidentally, were persuaded in November 1980 by the Organization of American States to heal their diplomatic rift.

Last of the Central American countries to have its own airline was Belice (or Belize, a British protectorate and, until 1973, called British Honduras). There were several reasons for the delay. As a British colony, it had been disassociated from the politics or the commerce of Latin America, and was relatively free from United States influence, which permeated throughout the region. For the British, it had little strategic value, was sparsely populated, and possessed little natural wealth except hardwood timber. When air transport arrived, in 1930, it was through the trunk services of Pan American. Later on came connections with TACA and branch lines from neighbouring republics.

British Honduras eventually had its own little airline when **British Colonial Airlines (B.C.A.)**—a subsidiary of The Freiberg Mahogany Co—was founded on 1 March, 1952, to formalize a charter operation conducted by British timber interests. Scheduled service, with two Cessna 170s, began on 4 August of that year, to Stann Creek, Punta Gorda, and Corozal. There was also a thrice weekly service to Chetumal in Mexico. On 24 October, 1956, the assets were purchased by British West Indian Airways and the name changed to **British Honduras Airways**, at which time the fleet consisted of two Cessna 180s. However, scheduled services ceased in the summer of 1961, and the operation was confined to charter services once again. The equipment was taken over by the **Maya Airways Corporation**, with the backing of local businessmen, and modest expansion instigated. By the mid-1960s, a domestic network was again in operation, together with links to Mérida and San Pedro Sula, using a DC-3.

Belize Airways' Boeing 720-022 VP-HCO *Belize City* was acquired in April 1976 and had been United Air Lines' N7213U.

When Belize gained its independence, the new government sought wider horizons. **Belize Airways** was founded on 28 November, 1974, and ambitiously acquired a fleet of five Boeing 720s. Services were started sporadically to Central American points, and on 1 October, 1977, the airline became yet another to add to the long line of ticket desks at the international terminal at Miami Airport. On 17 January, 1980, however, Belize's daily Miami service was suspended, because of financial difficulties. Service was resumed in November of the same year, with a BAC One-Eleven leased from Cayman Airways.

Independent Airlines of Central America

If Lowell Yerex was the prewar cavalier who challenged the might of Pan American, his postwar successor and free spirit was C. N. Shelton, a United States citizen who was a constant thorn in the side not only of Juan Trippe but also of the Civil Aeronautics Board of the United States, the legal department of which must sometimes have wished that Shelton had never been born. In an historical and geographical echo of the formation of Yerex's TACA, in Honduras C. N. Shelton, in company with R. C. Forsblade, also from the USA, and a local ranch-owner Miguel Brooks, founded **Transportes Aéreos Nacionales, S.A.** (TAN) in August 1947. At first TAN did charter work to Miami, operating a Douglas B-18 and two Curtiss C-46 trips per week on behalf of the

Inter-American Affairs Institute, carrying medical supplies and food southwards, and timber and chilled beef northwards to Cuba. On 12 June, 1950, this became a scheduled operation with the award of a three-year C.A.B. permit.

TAN's initial expansion was correct enough: the addition of San Pedro Sula as a co-terminal in Honduras, with direct connections to Salvador and Guatemala; and a route to Managua. But in June 1954, taking advantage of Honduran legislation, Shelton opened a route through Managua to Guayaquil and Lima, vastly expanding his sphere of influence. The trouble was that he operated through-plane service from Miami to those places, which was completely against the spirit of the C.A.B. permit, and an evasion of the internationally-accepted Five Freedom agreements—though Shelton was by no means the only entrepreneur to do that.

TAN's Douglas DC-6A HR-TNO was originally Overseas National Airways N650NA *Lois W.* (*Harold G. Martin*)

When, in 1957, the C.A.B. renewed TAN's certificate, it expressly limited its authority to services terminating in Honduras. Shelton thereupon circumvented the law by establishing partner airlines in Ecuador and Peru, and established the TAN/CEA/APSA partnership which became notorious in the region's aviation circles as a fare- and rate-cutting competitor to Pan American and PANAGRA. The intricacies of this activity are discussed in the Peruvian and Ecuadorian chapters. In retrospect, the C.A.B.'s forebearance was remarkable, as TAN's certificate was renewed time after time. In March 1965, Shelton died, and his business was taken over by his widow. Gradually, the consortium broke up, and TAN became more respectable in the eyes of the C.A.B., especially when, by the purchase of Pan American's 38 per cent shareholding, it became identified with the Honduran national airline SAHSA. In fact, in April 1980, the C.A.B. granted full Fifth Freedom rights for a TAN air freight service to and through Belize.

Other than SAHSA and TAN, two small airlines are active in Honduras. **Aero Servicios** has been operating semi-scheduled services from Tegucigalpa, using small Piper and Cessna aircraft, since 1957. **Líneas Aéreas Nacionales (LANSA)**, founded in 1967 at La Ceiba, one of the small ports on Honduras's northern coast, specializes in flying to the offshore islands, using a fleet which includes four DC-3s, a Fairchild F-27J, and a DC-4, the last-named used for freight charter work.

In El Salvador, a small company **Aerolíneas El Salvador (AESA)** tried to launch a freight service in 1960, beginning C-46 cargo flights in August to Miami; but this

TAN's Curtiss C-46A XH-TNA was acquired in November 1954 and went to Peru in 1958.
(*Harold G. Martin*)

TAN's Boeing 737-2A3 HR-TNR was delivered in May 1974 and had earlier been
PLUNA's CX-BHM.

Aerolíneas El Salvador's Curtiss C-46A YS-012C at Miami in early 1965.
(*Gordon S. Williams*)

was never sustained, and the United States C.A.B. suspected that the airline was controlled by the Nicaraguan LANICA. Guatemala and Nicaragua permitted no rivals to AVIATECA and LANICA. After LACSA emerged as Costa Rica's only airline, private enterprise was restricted to a number of small third-level operators. These are listed in Table 5.

In contrast, Panama has had several international airlines whose stature rivalled or even surpassed that of COPA. Indeed, the situation today is that, unlike other Central American countries, Panama's airline flag has been carried overseas by several companies. First of these was **Aerovías Interamericanas de Panamá, S.A. (AVISPA)**, founded in November 1951 by Panamanians to operate international freight services—mainly carrying shrimp—with a C-46 leased from Colombia. Although designated by the Panama Government to operate to Miami in March 1952, it completed only a few flights under charter. After reorganization, it resumed scheduled service on 1 August, 1953, on a domestic route paralleling COPA's, but this too was not sustained.

AVISPA then managed to obtain US permission to fly to Miami, and late in 1954 came to an agreement with a US airline, Trans Caribbean Airways, to lease a Douglas DC-6 at $2.50 per mile. *El Panamá* flights began in the summer of 1955, and after terminating its agreement with TCA at the end of the year, the Panamanian airline, now named **Aerovías Panamá (A.P.A.)**, acquired a DC-4.

It then began to expand, and by 1957 had extended service to Guayaquil and Lima, to carry Sixth Freedom traffic from Miami to South America, at lower fares than the established competition could offer under the IATA structure. Inevitably, as it was operating almost in parallel with the similar route of TAN from Honduras, A.P.A. became associated with C. N. Shelton's consortium in 1959. But this was short-lived, and late in 1960 A.P.A. was associated with RAS (Rutas Aéreas de Colombia) on a route to Bogotá, with direct connection to Brazil.

Although during the early 1960s, A.P.A. seemed to be developing into an organization of some strength, with routes to Caracas, via Barranquilla and Maracaibo, as well as Bogotá, all activity was abruptly suspended on 19 January, 1965, because of serious financial problems. A.P.A. was at first succeeded by **Aerovías Panamá, S.A. (APASA)** which began service over the same routes, using four ex-United Air Lines DC-7s, but this airline lasted little more than a year.

Then came **Panameña de Aviación Internacional, S.A. (PAISA)**, which began service on 3 May, 1967. It was an affiliate of VIASA, the Venezuelan international airline which had close ties with the Dutch KLM. PAISA made a few flights with a DC-9 leased from VIASA, which in turn had leased some from AVENSA (also from Venezuela), and flew for PIASA with the markings of CDA (Santo Domingo) also visible. The network linked Caracas with Panamá, via Maracaibo, and on to San José, Costa Rica. The operation appeared to be a device for KLM to gain vicarious entry into Central America, but PAISA had disappeared by the autumn of 1969.

Far more permanent and substantial was **Air Panamá**. First founded in September 1966, it was reorganized on 27 April, 1967, supported by Iberia, the Spanish airline, which held 49 per cent of the shares. It started a DC-9 operation on 27 August, 1969, and the intention was to play a part in a loosely-knit consortium, by which Iberia could assert itself in a Spanish-speaking world, in company with established US and other foreign-based interests. While this objective was never realised in a clear-cut manner, Iberia undoubtedly raised its sights in Latin America during this period, and became an international airline force to be reckoned with.

A Boeing 727-81 of Air Panama.

Air Panamá lost no time in constructing a viable international network. Within two months, it was operating through services to Guayaquil and Lima, via Panamá (in the old A.P.A. tradition) from Miami, Mexico City, and Guatemala City. By October 1972, Bogotá was on the map, and Boeing 727-181s had been substituted for the DC-9. In 1975, the Mexico City route had been extended to Los Angeles, and the Miami route to both New York and Montreal. Montreal and Guatemala were dropped in favour of a new route to Caracas in January 1976. Iberia's presence faded in November 1978 when a private consortium took over Air Panamá, and signed a mutual assistance contract with British Airways in August 1979.

Other Panamanian airlines have crossed the scene in this small country, the main aerial crossways for inter-American routes between the North and South. **Panamá Aeronáutica**, founded on 3 October, 1960, made a tentative effort to enter the Miami market in March 1962 but never got under way, in spite of receiving C.A.B. permission. **Rutas Aéreas Panameñas, S.A. (RAPSA)** was incorporated on 23 December, 1944, and was particularly active between September 1958 and 1972. RAPSA gained a reputation in Panama for reliability and safety. For part of its existence, its fleet exceeded that of COPA, boasting a DC-4 as its flagship. It was one of the last airlines to operate a Boeing 247D on regular flights.

Internacional de Aviación, S.A. (Inair) has been one of the rare all-freight airlines to escape the usual fate of early bankruptcy. Formed as a charter company in January 1967, it began regular cargo services with Curtiss C-46s to points in Central and South America. In December 1969, it received the coveted

RAPSA's Douglas C-53 HP-309.

111

The white, orange and black Inair Convair CV-880-22 HP-821 was formerly Delta Air Lines' N8810E. (*Harold G. Martin*)

permission to serve Miami. It has expanded steadily, if not spectacularly, and by the late 1970s had a fleet of four Douglas DC-6Bs, plus a Boeing 720. Inair's aircraft are a familiar sight all through the Spanish-speaking Latin American world, from Miami to Santiago, and to Manaus in Brazil. Air Panamá, COPA, and Inair together ensure that Panama is able to maintain a share of both international passenger and freight markets out of proportion to the size of the country. On the home front, a few diminutive airlines compete for the domestic traffic which now includes a fair proportion of tourism (see Table 6).

Central America today is no longer the Pan American dominion it once used to be. In addition to its own commercial objectives, the United States flag carrier was formerly encouraged by its own State Department, both during the war and afterwards, to keep a grip on air transport affairs as a national defence measure. But such emphasis is irrelevant in a nuclear age. And any encroachment would now be regarded as heavy-handed interference. The Spanish airline enjoys some privileges, for example in its service to Guatemala, and in its interest in Air Panamá, but this is insignificant as a major influence. Fragmented though Central America may be, the sum of the parts amount to a fascinating, vigorously independent whole.

AeroPerlas de Havilland Canada Twin Otter Series 300 HP-730 *Isla Contadora*.

TABLE 4

Pan American Airways Participation in Central American Airlines

Airline	Date Founded	Pan American Initial Share Date	%	Changes in Pan Am Share Date	%	Date of Pan Am Sale	Remarks
Panama Airways, Inc.	7 Nov, 1936	(foundation)	100	—		—	Dissolved 30 April, 1941
Aerovías de Guatemala, S.A.	10 Oct, 1940	(foundation)	40	15 April, 1942	20	30 Nov, 1945	Airline acquired by AVIATECA
Cía Panameña de Aviación (COPA)	21 June, 1944	30 Aug, 1944	40	18 Sept, 1946 31 Dec, 1968	33 26	15 Mar, 1971	Pan Am stock sold to local interests
Servicio Aéreo de Honduras, S.A. (SAHSA)	16 Nov, 1944	(foundation)	40	5 April, 1957	38	21 Jan, 1970	Pan Am sold stock to TAN
Líneas Aéreas de Nicaragua (LANICA)	17 Nov, 1944	(foundation)	40	6 Sept, 1950 14 Oct, 1957 31 Dec, 1973	20 13 10	August 1974	Pan Am sold to local interests (with Hughes Tool participation)
Líneas Aéreas Costarricenses, S.A. (LACSA)	17 Oct, 1945	(foundation)	40	7 Aug, 1953 1 June, 1964	36 33	14 Sept, 1970	Pan Am sold to local interests

Note: Pan American had no associated airline in El Salvador (conversely, TACA had no operating airline in Panama).

113

TABLE 5

The Smaller Postwar Costa Rican Airlines

Airline	Date of Foundation	Routes	Fleet	Remarks
Aerovías Occidentales, S.A. (AVO)	24 July, 1947	San José–Osa Peninsula (Parrita, Puerto Jiménez)	2 Boeing 247D 1 Norseman	Owned by two US citizens. Ceased operations, 1951
Aerovías del Valle, Ltda (AVE)	Dec, 1951	Points in southeast, centred on San Isidro el General. Later, in the 1970s, flew to the west coast also	Various, including 3 Islanders	Operated domestic routes as LACSA withdrew from feeder services. Acquired ACASA in 1976. Ceased operations 1978
Aerovías Puntarenas, S.A. (APSA)	1961	Points in western Costa Rica, centred on Puntarenas, and to San José	1 DC-3 1 C-46 1 Electra	Ceased operations 1978, but continued existence as an agency. Routes taken over by SANSA
Aerolíneas del Pacífico, S.A. (ALPA)	1952	Domestic services, San José to Bijagual, Carate, Playa Hermosa	Piper PA-18A	Ceased operations during the latter 1950s
Expreso Aéreo Costarricenses, S.A. (EXACO)	1956	Based at Limón. Part of a transport organization combining road and air freight, serving all Costa Rica. Expanded internationally as Líneas Aéreas del Caribe, Ltda	Curtiss C-46 2 Beech 18 1 DC-3 1 DC-6	Originally founded as a small taxi operator in 1951 by Dr Francisco Vanolli. Ceased operations 1980
Transportes Aéreos de Integración, S.A. (TAISA)	1970	Services between Costa Rica and neighbouring countries	1 C-46 1 DC-6A	Created to relieve the transport congestion within the Central American Common Market, following the Honduras–El Salvador conflict in 1969
Aerovías Cariari (ACASA)	1968	Based at Limón. Operated to agricultural area of Guápiles and Río Frío	3 DC-3 2 Beech 18 1 CV-240	Merged with AVE (see above) about 1976

Other small airlines operated air taxi or semi-scheduled services with Piper and Cessna aircraft, but their operations were too limited to justify definition as airlines. Indeed, the qualifications of some of those included are marginal. For RANSA and SANSA (1978) see text.

TABLE 6

The Smaller Postwar Panamanian Domestic Airlines

Airline	Date of Foundation	Routes	Fleet 1979–80	Remarks
Transportes Aéreos Interioranos, S.A. (TAISA)	1948–49	(Not known)	—	Operated Stinson 108s and Cessna Bobcats. Ceased activities
Aviación General, S.A. (AGSA)	1948	Around Santiago, and along San Blas coast	—	Operated Piper aircraft. Transported Indian labourers from villages to Colón. Ceased operations in early 1960s
Cía Chitréana de Aviación, S.A. (Chitréana)	1952	Panamá–Chitré, Las Tablas	2 DC-3	Started operations with a Stinson V-77
Aviones de Panamá, S.A.	1964	Panamá–San Blas ⎫ Panamá–Darien ⎭provinces	4 Islanders 1 Beaver 1 Cessna 402	Charter work only.
Compañía de Turismo Aéreo, S.A. (TASA)	May 1955	Panamá–San Blas ⎫ Panamá–Darien ⎭provinces	1 Islander 1 Cessna 185	Also operated a Twin Otter and various Cessnas, etc.
Aerovías Darienitas, S.A. (ADSA)	1960	Fanamá–Darien Frovince	1 Islander 2 Cessnas	Taxi service only. Used to operate a DC-3
Aerolíneas Islas de las Perlas, S.A. (AeroPerlas)	1970	Panamá–Contadora, Bocas del Toro, David and other western points	3 Twin Otters 2 Islanders	Has operated a DC-3 and various Piper aircraft. Main business is to the Contadora island resort

Several other small airlines operated air taxi or semi-scheduled services with small Piper and Cessna aircraft, but their operations were very limited in scope.

Typical South and Central American transport before the arrival of the aeroplane.

CHAPTER SIX

TACA

The Incomparable Airline

There has never been an airline quite like TACA anywhere in the world. It was founded by the purest chance, launched on its way by a remarkable example of entrepreneurial opportunism, expanded to become an international consortium, attracted the covetous attentions of large corporations in the United States, came very close to becoming a giant airline in its own right, collapsed to a mere shadow of its former considerable stature, and finally revived, phoenix-like, to take its place in the airline world of Central America today.

Transportes Aéreos Centro-Americanos, or **TACA** as it was always known as a household word, from Mexico to Panama and beyond, throughout most of the 1930s and early 1940s, was the creation of one man, Lowell Yerex, who started operations in 1932 with one aeroplane and one route. He developed this modest enterprise to a fleet of more than fifty, and a route network which filled several pages of the airline guides of the early and mid-1940s. At its peak, TACA served 235 points on a scheduled basis alone, and many more on contract work and charters to sixteen countries, reaching from Miami to Rio de Janeiro.

Primarily a freight carrier, pioneering air transport in the most elemental meaning of the term, in the inhospitable environment of Central America in the mid-1930s, its formula of operation was so successful that it claimed, with supporting statistical evidence, that between 1937 and 1941 it carried more air freight than all the airlines of the United States put together. Only one other airline in the world came close—Guinea Airways, in far-off New Guinea; but compared with TACA, Guinea's was a relatively simple operation, concentrating on one small region and a limited number of fields.

Eventually, TACA's success may have been its own downfall, as it became the pawn in a game of international transport politics, attracting the attention of railway, steamship, and trunk airline interests, notably, in the last category, TWA, which may for a short while have cherished ambitions of using TACA as a stick with which to beat Pan American, its arch-rival. But this was much later than the time, late in 1931, in Honduras, when Lowell Yerex grasped his opportunity, realising perhaps, in a flash of subconscious inspiration, that Tegucigalpa was at that time one of the few capital cities in the world not served by a railway.

Yerex forms TACA

Air mail services in Honduras were, as related earlier, first started by Dr T. C. Pounds, a US citizen, who established the first air route in Central America in 1923, to begin a succession of short-lived and precarious operations in that small country. He and other rivals never managed to find the right combination of operational skill and political acumen which Yerex was able to bring to bear upon the local community. Furthermore, they did not have the added ingredient of luck in being at the right place at the right time.

Yerex was born in New Zealand, educated in the United States, at a University in Indiana, and received his first flying instruction when he joined the RFC (Canada) in 1917. In May 1918 he was shot down behind the German lines and became a prisoner of war. After the war he returned to Canada, thence to the United States, where he worked in a San Francisco shipyard to save enough

One of the obstacles to surface transport in Nicaraguan jungle areas.
(*Courtesy Esso Air World*)

117

money to buy a surplus military aircraft. With this he embarked on a short career as one of the colourful postwar barnstormers, stunting and joy-riding, before moving to Santa Fe, New Mexico, to sell automobiles, and incidentally to learn Spanish in that bilingual city. At the time of the Depression, he crossed the border to join the swashbuckling C.A.T. airline in Mexico. When that cavalier enterprise folded up, he found a job in October 1931 when a prospector named Henshaw needed a new pilot to take him from Mexico City to Tegucigalpa in a four-seat Stinson Junior biplane.

Henshaw and Pounds were associated in using the Stinson in any way they could to earn money, flying passengers and cargo as well as the mail, all on an *ad hoc* basis, and apparently Yerex the pilot did not get paid. Even though he solicited extra business for the owners, he still received no pay but took a half-interest in the Stinson in lieu of salary. Eventually, as the situation deteriorated further, Yerex became sole owner of the aircraft, in December 1931.

At the same time, he founded TACA and, with a demonstrated practical ability to fly and organize the transport of mail and cargo, even though the official owners of the government mail contract were unreliable, he applied for the mail contract to succeed Dr Pounds when the latter's contract expired on 20 February, 1932. This was duly granted by Decree 110 of 16 February, to come into effect one month later.

Yerex contracted to provide mail and cargo service from Tegucigalpa to many provincial points in Honduras, including La Ceiba, Trujillo, Juticalpa, and Catacamas. An unusual feature of the mail contract was that the payment (about 50¢ per kilogram of mail to the various points) should be made 'out of the proceeds from the sale of the stamps made for that purpose' and Yerex himself was allowed to sell the stamps and receive the normal governmental agency discount for the sale.

Reward for Services Rendered

Yerex showed great ingenuity in working out a system of reduced tariffs for deferred freight haulage, under which any packages delivered to the airport would leave on the first aircraft which departed with spare capacity, even though this might mean some delay when the warehouse had a backlog. However, the air freight was so superior to the primitive surface transport, mainly mule-train, that this proved to be satisfactory for the shippers. For his part Yerex had contrived a system under which 100 per cent load factors would be assured.

While this was wholly commendable as a commercial experiment, its success was overshadowed in the public eye by a dramatic incident in which Yerex's experience and instincts reinforced the lucky streak which seemed to be going his way. Late in 1932, only a few months after TACA was founded, Yerex was requested by the new Honduran Government under General Tiburcio Carias-Andino to make some reconnaissance flights over mountains where guerilla strongholds still supported the former regime of ex-President Colindres. Flying low to drop pamphlets, he was shot in the eye by a stray bullet, but he flew back to base, where a doctor found that, in addition to losing an eye, he had also fractured his skull. Such was the gratitude of the President for this valiant demonstration of support that he offered Yerex a cash reward. This was shrewdly declined in favour of continued guarantees of mail contracts (confirmed on 1 February, 1933) together with certain privileges such as being able to import materials, including aircraft, free of customs duty.

In the eyes of officialdom in Honduras, Lowell Yerex could do no wrong, and he made the most of his privileged position. He proceeded to consolidate his grandfather rights in Honduras, and expanded to neighbouring countries.

Early Expansion

During the 1930s, Central America was a happy hunting ground for itinerant flying adventurers who were prepared to accept almost any challenge to prove that an aeroplane could provide transport services under conditions which often defied credulity. Sometimes the mining or plantation supply activity was continuous enough to provide steady work, and casual services gave way to fairly regular flights, leading logically to the establishment of small airlines. But the operative word was 'small' and their existence was so precarious that it required an organizing ability of near-genius to provide any assurance of stability or permanence. Yerex supplied such ability, and systematically took over almost all the local operations throughout Central America south of the Mexican border as far as the Panama Canal.

Ox-carts provided the competition for TACA's freighters in Central America.
(*Courtesy Esso Air World*)

His first objective was to clean up the home front, by purchasing, in 1933, the only airline of any substance remaining in Honduras, **Empresa Dean**, formed by the Dean Company, an automobile dealer, which operated a Bellanca and a Fokker. During the same year, TACA opened its first international service, to San Salvador, a city which was later to figure largely in the history of the airline.

Lowell Yerex (*left*), a New Zealander, was one of the few airline promoters who became a legend in his own time. In 1931 he formed Transportes Aéreos Centro-Americanos (TACA). C. N. Shelton (*right*), (christened Cornell Newton but always known as 'C.N.' or just 'Shelton') first went to Honduras in the early 1930s and competed with Lowell Yerex's TACA while flying for Empresa Dean. After flying in the United States and for TWA in China during the war, he founded TAN in Honduras, and other associated airlines such as APA (Panama), CEA (Ecuador), and APSA (Peru). His low-fare policies were a constant thorn in the sides of Pan American and PANAGRA. He died on 15 March, 1965, with a clean record—airlines under his control never killed a passenger and were always profitable.
(*Right-hand picture Philip Schleit*)

The next step was to purchase, in 1935, the small Guatemalan airline, Compañía Nacional de Aviación, S.A., which was promptly renamed **Compañía Nacional TACA de Guatemala, S.A.** It immediately became part of the TACA system, Guatemala City having already been connected with Tegucigalpa by an extension to San Salvador in 1934.

Also in that year, TACA opened its second international route, to Managua, in Nicaragua, which paved the way for the almost inevitable purchase of the local airline, **Líneas Aéreas de Nicaragua, Empresa Palacios (LANEP)** on 16 October, 1935. This airline's local contract was rescinded in 1938, during which year, however, TACA aircraft made a noteworthy contribution to the Nicaraguan economy by an impressive airlift (see page 127). On 16 March, 1939, TACA once again resumed regular operations when the parent Honduran company purchased Líneas Aéreas Nicaraguenses, and renamed it **Compañía Nacional TACA de Nicaragua, S.A.**

Two more countries were added to the TACA collection during this period. Service started in 1936 to Belize in British Honduras, although in this instance Yerex did not go through the formality of establishing a local airline, probably because, with his ancestry, the local authorities accepted TACA's credentials as they stood.

On 14 July, 1936, **Empresa Nacional de Transportes Aéreos (ENTA)**, a small airline in Costa Rica started by Bill Schoenfeldt, had opened two short international routes. Schoenfeldt's mixed fleet of Fokker aircraft: a trimotor, a Universal, and an F-XIV, provided the connecting route from San José to the rest of the TACA system at Managua. ENTA became **Compañía de TACA de Costa Rica** on 16 January, 1940. Meanwhile, this southern end of the network was consolidated by the purchase of two other small Costa Rican airlines: **Aerovías Nacionales de Costa Rica** (associated with ENTA) and **Transportes Aéreos Costarricenses (TAC)**; and these were duly incorporated into **TACA de Costa Rica.**

An important change was made to the TACA organization on 25 August, 1939. **TACA, S.A.** was established in Panama City as a non-operating holding company of the TACA group, with an authorized capital of $4,000,000. TACA, however, did not operate to Panamá until four years later, when another reorganization took place. The Honduran company was incorporated as **TACA de Honduras**; while in El Salvador, another TACA subsidiary was established as the international division of the TACA system, operating between the Central American national capitals, with the individual companies in Honduras, Guatemala, Nicaragua, and Costa Rica providing local connecting services in their respective countries.

TACA Flies Anything Anywhere

Airline operators in Central America, as in most of Latin America or any other underdeveloped part of the world, usually had to build their own airfields, negotiating with local interests for assistance, according to local needs. Typically, Yerex would arrange to lease land from some local owners, often paying for the privilege by providing free flights for the owner and members of his family to other cities in Honduras. Much depended upon the co-operation of the local populace, both in providing labour to build the strips and a permanent staff of volunteers to chase cattle off the fields when an aircraft was expected.

Many of the strips were on flat land near the coast, but in Central America, many of the inland places were in hilly or mountainous country with hardly a level piece of ground available. In these circumstances, a careful balance had to be

Bellanca 31-50 Pacemaker XH-TAS sits on an unfinished jungle landing ground, probably in Honduras or Guatemala. Trees have been felled and burned and the stumps burned or dynamited. The site is seen ready for the Ford Tri-Motors to fly in the heavy grading equipment. (*Eichenberger photograph, courtesy Esso Air World*)

TABLE 7

Airfields of Honduras 1946

Airfield		Strip Length (ft)	Strip Width (ft)	Elevation AMSL (ft)	Distance from town (miles)
Agua Fria		2,200	300	3,500	2
Amapala		1,600	100	83	½
Catacamas		3,000	400	1,500	¼
Choluteca		2,200	400	150	¼
Cocolito		2,000	250	10	5
Comayagua		2,500	200	1,500	3
Corquin		3,000	170	2,870	1⅛
Esquias		3,070	200	2,500	5
Gracías		2,100	300	2,500	2
Jesús de Otoro		2,000	500	1,400	¼
Juticalpa		2,700	300	1,400	1
La Ceiba		2,100	200	25	½
La Esperanza		5,000	300	5,350	1
La Lima		2,600	400	85	Adjacent
La Paz		2,400	400	2,000	Adjacent
Marcala		2,400	100	4,000	½
Nacaome		1,800	300	200	½
Nueva Ocotepeque		1,800	200	2,500	1
Olanchito		2,100	200	500	1
Progreso		2,500	200	100	¼
Puerto Cortés		1,900	75	3	Adjacent
Ruinas de Copán		2,800	200	2,000	½
San Francisco de La Paz		3,000	180	1,500	1
San Ignacio		2,550	200	2,000	Adjacent
San Lorenzo		2,400	150	25	1½
San Marcos de Colón		2,910	180	2,900	4½
San Pedro Sula		2,200	300	100	¼
Santa Bárbara		3,000	200	900	1
Santa Rosa de Copán		2,736	180	3,500	1
Siguatepeque		3,000	150	3,700	Adjacent
Tegucigalpa	(E–W)	2,400	300	3,200	3
	(N–S)	3,280	300		
	(NE–SW)	3,160	300		
Tela	(N–S)	2,500	200	10	¾
	(NE–SW)	2,000	300		
Yorito		2,500	200	2,000	5½
Yoro		3,200	300	1,500	3

TACA's Ford Tri-Motor with Nicaraguan registration AN-TAX and Honduras-registered Bellanca Pacemaker at Siuna in Nicaragua. (*TACA*)

struck in judging the minimum tolerable distance of the strip from the community if it was to enjoy any air service at all. It was not unusual for the strips to terminate at the face of a mountainside, or at the edge of a ravine. Sometimes an aircraft would be out of sight when it landed, until it literally taxied up the hill and over the crest of the runway before reaching the air terminal. As for the surfaces, at least the mountain airfields, though short, usually had good drainage, in contrast with many of the coastal fields, where the pilots had to learn the location of the soft spots during the rainy season.

To illustrate the general standard in Latin America during the formative years of air transport, at the time when Lowell Yerex and TACA were providing the country with its first integrated transport system, the list of airfields in Honduras tells its own story (Table 7).

The flying equipment which Yerex deployed between these airfields throughout Central America during the period between 1932 and the early 1940s grew steadily in numbers. By 1934, he had fourteen aircraft—seven Stinsons, one Bellanca, two Fokkers, and four Ford Tri-Motors. By 1938, there were thirty aircraft in service, carrying a total of about 20,000 passengers and 4,000 tons of freight during the year. Early in 1940, the fleet totalled forty-six, of which no less than twenty-six were Ford Tri-Motors (almost all Model 5-ATs), thirteen

Two TACA Ford 5-AT Tri-Motors at Tegucigalpa in Honduras. LG-AAG, on the left, was Stout Air Service's NC9669 and it flew with National Air Transport and Pennsylvania Air Lines before going to Guatemala. LG-AAD, on the right, was also with NAT and Pennsylvania before going to TACA. (*Foto Serra*)

123

registered in Honduras, nine in Guatemala, and four in Costa Rica. Later that year, TACA acquired its first modern aircraft—following the reorganization noted above—a fleet of five Lockheed 14s.

But before upgrading its class of service to match the international standards of Pan American, the primarily-Ford fleet had accomplished great things. The statistics alone were noteworthy: 65,000 and 90,000 passengers, 12,500 and 14,000 tons of cargo, in 1940 and 1941, respectively. Curiously, for the forty-six aircraft, Yerex employed only twenty-eight pilots, but to compensate for the difficulty of having only one pilot for every two aeroplanes, he operated twenty-nine radio stations, sophistication indeed in those days.

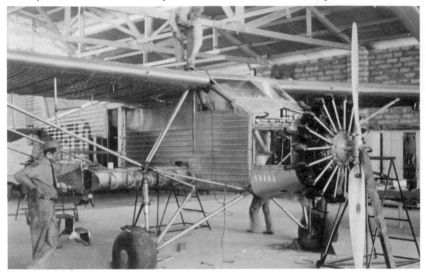

TACA engineers modifying a Metal Aircraft Corporation Flamingo for dusting operations. Unlike other Flamingos this one was provided with short stub-wings to increase lift and from which to spray to achieve maximum swath width. (*Courtesy Esso Air World*)

The Fantastic Fords

The Ford Tri-Motors were put to work in a way which its designer never dreamed of when he conceived the specification for the all-metal aeroplane; but he would no doubt have been proud to observe the lengths to which TACA was able to go to squeeze the utmost output from the long-suffering airframe; proud in the sense that the 'Tin Goose' endured what could be described as a form of operational torture.

The structural maltreatment started early in TACA's history. In 1934, a landing strip was built at the Agua Fria mine 3,500 feet (over 1,000 metres) up in the mountains of Honduras, 50 miles north of Tegucigalpa and about 75 miles from the coast. In September, the first Ford Tri-Motor flew in from the coastal base at San Lorenzo, over a 6,000-ft mountain range. During the next ten months, it then proceeded to carry into the mine all its equipment, machinery, food, and other essential supplies. This included a 50-ton flotation and cyanide mill, a 450-hp hydro-electric plant, two 320-ft compressors, a 150-hp diesel generator, and various shop equipment, piping, and other machinery.

The double loading doors of a TACA Ford Tri-Motor. The roll-up doors shown in another illustration were a later modification. (*Courtesy Esso Air World*)

Unloading aerodrome grading equipment from TACA's Ford 5-AT XH-TAZ somewhere in Honduras. XH-TAZ's upward-sliding cargo doors can be clearly seen. (*Courtesy Esso Air World*)

Loading a tractor into TACA's Ford 5-AT XH-TAZ via the widened doorway which was equipped with twin roll-up doors. The tractor was used to tow grading and surfacing equipment during the preparation of jungle landing grounds in Guatemala.
(*Courtesy Esso Air World*)

To accomplish this, TACA engineers cut a 4 ft by 6 ft hatch in the top of the fuselage, immediately over the door, for loading the supplies into the fuselage by hoist. Subsequently, TACA maintained a regular shuttle service, making the 20-minute journey as often as twenty-four times per day, until the Agua Fria mining company built a highway which permitted trucking operations in about six hours.

This would seem to have been a difficult act to follow. But in 1939 TACA found itself providing the lifeline, indeed the umbilical cord without which the La Luz gold mine in Nicaragua might never have survived. Located at Siuna, almost in the centre of the country, its nearest communications point was 50 miles away, at Alamicamba, a tiny port on the Prinzapolca River 60 miles from the coast. The new owners of La Luz decided that roads were too expensive, not only in construction, but also to maintain; and no doubt they considered also the severe risk of theft and pilferage if the ponderous surface modes were used.

During the next six years, about 30,000 tons of equipment and supplies were flown into the La Luz mine at Siuna. Formerly, an aging Curtiss Condor had carried some supplies, but riverboat and overland pack were mainly used. The Ford Tri-Motor added a new element to the economic calculations, because of its rugged adaptability. Again, the list of weights carried into La Luz by TACA (Table 8) is a staggering record of air freighting; but it is only part of the story of ingenuity displayed by this incomparable airline.

The Bucyrus shovel, weighing nearly 25 tons, for example, was disassembled: the track was cut into pieces, while the boom was cut in two and welded together again at the destination. Trucks were disassembled down to chassis, engine, wheels, and bodies, but the wide dumping bodies had to be cut in two and re-welded on arrival. The 12-ft (4-metre) gears for the grinding mills were cut in two and given the same welding treatment.

TABLE 8

The Airlift to the La Luz Mine
Weight of Major Equipment Flown in by the Ford Tri-Motor

Equipment	Total Weight (lb)
Dominion-Crossley diesel engine, including base	41,000
Generator for the Dominion-Crossley diesel	11,500
One 4¼-ft Symons cone core crusher	62,300
One main frame for crusher	10,800
Birdboro ore crusher, 36 in by 42 in	79,000
Two 3-ft Symons ore crushers	24,025
Three 8 ft by 8 ft ball grinding mills	52,325
Eleven water, solution, and other tanks	196,955
Three caterpillar D-6 tractors	90,134
Linings for the 8 ft by 8 ft grinders	35,000
One Dorr bowl classifier, plus six tanks	114,756
One 18 in by 24 in jaw crusher	40,760
Equipment for Merrill precipitation process	29,000
One drop bar grizzly for 30 in by 36 in mill	11,950
Bullion furnace and accessories	4,875
One 14 in by 11 in air compressor	6,700
Three trailers	8,640
One Bucyrus shovel, with 2 cu yd bucket	50,000
One Bucyrus shovel, with ¾ cu yd bucket	30,000
Six English diesel engines, including bases	90,000
Six 10-ton Autocars with dump bodies	211,608
Five 4-ton White dump trucks	75,000
One 4-ton White truck	10,000
Sixteen 2-ton ore cars	16,000
Four industrial locomotives	32,000
One generator shaft	6,500
One Sullivan scraper hoist	4,000

In addition may other major items were carried, the weights of which were not reported: other shovels and buckets, skip-hoist and cage, two saw mills, one shingle mill, belt conveyor and belt, gondola cars for railway, equipment for laundry, hospital, refrigeration, and miscellaneous supplies.

The Neptune Gold Mining Company's offices, hospital and stores at Bonanza, Nicaragua, are in the foreground. Most of the mining equipment was carried in TACA's Ford Tri-Motors. (*Courtesy Esso Air World*)

Such demands tested the load-carrying capability of the Ford Tri-Motor to the limit. Maximum payload of the 5-AT was specified at 2,500 lb, but TACA had found that 4,000 lb could be carried on short hauls. By further manipulation, such as calculating the fuel for the single journey and not a mile further, stripping every non-essential item from the aircraft, and dispensing with the co-pilot, TACA managed to increase the load-carrying capability so that the 5,300 lb (2½ metric tonnes) bases of some heavy English diesel engines could be flown into La Luz.

One aircraft, in typical TACA tradition, was modified with special cross-bracing and the floor strengthened, so as to accommodate a 600-gal fuselage tank, to fly supplies of diesel oil to the mine. TACA did the modification itself, of course, and thoughtfully provided a ladder so that the pilot could climb in through the top of the cockpit—the normal entrance being blocked by the fuel tank. The tank could be filled in eight minutes, and emptied in six; and TACA was thus able to haul 2,400 gallons a day between Alamicamba and Siuna.

While the Agua Fria and La Luz mines were outstanding examples of air transport's unique contribution to the economy of developing countries in Latin America, they were by no means the only cases. TACA was prepared to undertake any logistics task, and did so on frequent occasions, in many locations, not only with the venerable Ford, but with the equally adaptable Douglas C-47 or DC-3, which, with the twin-engined Lockheed, were to succeed the earlier generation of aircraft.

TACA was able to perform such transport miracles because it demonstrated convincingly that the task could be performed economically, not only in terms of time-value—although this alone would provide ample justification for calling upon Lowell Yerex and his team. Table 9 shows the emphatic time-saving advantages which the TACA aircraft could achieve, compared with the surface-bound pack mule, truck, or riverboat, or combinations of all three.

But this was not all. TACA could actually show that, time-saving aside, air transport was actually cheaper. The La Luz case was typical. The mining company tried buying its own mules and its own muleteers. But by the time it had paid the four men needed to handle a five-mule train, and fed the mules, the transport cost worked out at $2.70 per ton-mile. TACA could more than match this by a 76-cent per ton-mile charge for air express, and 54 cents for deferred freight.

TABLE 9
Comparison of Air and Surface Journey Times Central America 1940

From	To	Air Time (minutes)	Surface Time (hours)
Honduras			
Tegucigalpa	La Ceiba	45	24
	San Pedro	30	34
	Santa Rosa de Copán	50	48
	Nueva Ocotopeque	20	72
	Agua Fria	20	6
	Guayape	25	60–120
	Lamani	25	24–72
	Marcala	25	6–48
	Comayagua	18	5
Amapala	San Lorenzo	15	2
Costa Rica			
San José	Palmar	35	12
	Puntarenas	20	5
	Parrita	17	25
	San Marco de Terrazo	19	72
	Los Chiles	45	10 days
	Settento da Avril	20	24
	San Juanicito	20	5
Puntarenas	Altamira	50	5

Note: Surface journeys by pack mule, truck, or riverboat, singly or in combination.

In other cases, a combination of the time-value and cost factors combined to give TACA the advantage, as the products involved were perishable, such as coffee, beans, rice, tobacco, and fruit. Central America was the territory of the United Fruit Company, which had, in fact, built most of the few narrow-gauge railways which operated in the region, invariably in coastal areas. Water transport worked out at about 27 cents per ton-mile—only half of TACA's rates—but was agonisingly slow. The choice was a half-spoiled crop because of deterioration and damage during the many hours or days by surface, or the prompt delivery of profitable merchandise to the international port or airport by TACA.

Ore cars entering the ore bin shed of the Neptune Gold Mining Company. Most, if not all, of this equipment was carried to the site by TACA. (*Courtesy Esso Air World*)

End of an Era

After some eight years of sterling work in Central American jungles, swamps and mountains, performing feats which would have been dismissed as subject material for fiction-writers, Lowell Yerex and TACA underwent a change of life style. This was heralded by the foundation in 1939 of **TACA Airways**, as a holding company in Panama and the establishment of TACA, S.A. in El Salvador specifically as an international regional airline, rather than a parochially-centred local operator.

It was probably no coincidence that Yerex also founded, later in the same year, **British West Indian Airways (BWIA)** in Trinidad, and transferred his attentions from a US-dominated region to a colony of the British Empire. For, with the entry of TACA into the international arena, the airline which had become a household word throughout Central America discovered that there were other household words, such as Pan American.

TACA's first awareness that its privileges were not boundless came in 1940 in what became known in aviation circles at the time as the Guatemala Incident. The onset of war gave Yerex some cause for reflection in an area where British

130

interests were limited to the impoverished colony of British Honduras, a precarious foothold and under constant threat from Guatemala, which regarded the British as intruders. Thus Yerex decided to put himself, as it were, under the protective cloak of the United States, which enjoyed economic dominance over Central America, by selling the controlling interest of TACA to a United States corporation.

When the deed was done, it was no normal business enterprise, but one which directly threatened the incumbent US foreign operator in the area, the mighty Pan American. As long as TACA concentrated on carrying local freight (the passenger business accounted for only 40 per cent of TACA's revenues) Juan Trippe, Pan American's President, was inclined to brush off Yerex's outfit as a minor irritant. But when, on 1 October, 1940, American Export Lines, Inc, a US shipping company, announced that it had bought the controlling interest of TACA, Pan American acted decisively in defence of its sphere of interest.

Ten days later, on 11 October, 1940, a new airline was founded in Guatemala. **Aerovías de Guatemala** was financed by Pan American, and managed by Alfred Denby, a US citizen resident in Guatemala City, and owner of the largest meat business there. On 7 November, services started with Douglas DC-2 aircraft quickly supplied by the US carrier, which had been operating these fine 14-passenger airliners on its intercontinental links with South America. On 1 January, 1941, TACA de Guatemala's franchise was withdrawn by General Ubico, the dictator of Guatemala.

This was a bitter blow to Yerex, who had built up a fine commercial enterprise in Guatemala. Notably, besides establishing air routes from the capital to the hinterland, and installing radio stations, he had transported in 1939 the entire chicle crop from the Flores region in northern Guatemala (where he had built four small landing strips) to Puerto Barrios, the Guatemalan port on the Caribbean. While gold from the La Luz mine may have been more valuable, more than 1,000 tons of the raw material needed for chewing-gum was not bad business, either for Yerex or Guatemala. Nevertheless, Yerex was paid a paltry five cents in the dollar for his fixed assets, and the Pan American/Denby airline promptly moved in. Yerex took his aeroplanes elsewhere, mainly to Nicaragua.

American Export meanwhile found itself in a real fight, with no holds barred. Yet it was by no means an opportunist industrial enterprise trying to enter a money-making business, simply as an investment gamble. It had genuine ambitions to establish an intercontinental airline of substance and integrity, having started by trying to introduce an Atlantic operation. It obtained permission from the Civil Aeronautics Board on 15 July, 1940, to launch this route and was receiving both moral and practical support from Government agencies, including the Navy, which even gave up its place in the line for some new Vought-Sikorsky VS-44A flying-boats. A Senate Sub-committee, however, mysteriously turned down a $500,000 appropriation intended to subsidize and support the operation.

If this blow was not sufficient to impress upon American Export the danger of clashing with Juan Trippe, then the Guatemalan Incident was enough to underline the risks it was taking. By purchasing TACA for a reported $2,000,000, American Export must have felt that it was killing two birds with one stone: acquiring an airline as a going concern (and therefore overcoming objections to its participation in the airline world on the grounds that it was a shipping company); and starting a short-cut route from the United States to Panamá, from New Orleans rather than Brownsville, Texas, which was Pan American's traditional gateway. The Am Ex route would have saved a day's travelling, compared with Pan Am's route, and this could have been competitively decisive.

Interestingly, the choice of Guatemala as the battleground was no accident. Although several cities in that region of Central America could have qualified as a transit or distribution point in terms of distances from other important points, Guatemala City was the largest city between Mexico and Colombia, and thus justified service in its own right. Also, the airport at Tegucigalpa was unsuitable at that time for operation by the heavier modern aircraft, while Pan American shrewdly avoided challenging TACA at San Salvador, where Yerex had recently set up his international organization, presumably with excellent credentials with the El Salvador Government. As a matter of history, Guatemala City remains as Pan American's main air junction, including change of gauge of aircraft, for example Boeing 747 to Boeing 727, to this day.

American Export may have cherished ambitions of building up a worldwide airline network, what with having C.A.B. approval for the Atlantic, and buying an airline which would provide a launching pad for expansion throughout Latin America. But its hopes were ruthlessly dashed when Pan American took Am Ex through the courts on the basis that, under Section 408 of the Civil Aeronautics Act, it was unlawful for any common carrier to acquire control of any air carrier in any manner whatsoever. And so TACA changed hands again.

Inter-American Airways and TWA

Yerex was joined by other United States investors after American Export Lines was forced to withdraw. In 1942, the TACA system, having suffered a blow from the Guatemala Incident, began to change the general direction of its marketing thrust. Although the holding company was still registered in Panamá, and the head office still advertised as being in Tegucigalpa, emphasis began to be placed on the international service connecting the Central American capitals rather than on the local feeder services. The name of TACA, S.A., of Panama was changed to **Inter-American Airways, S.A.**, on 27 January, 1943, and the Inter-American Airways Agency was incorporated in New York, with a branch in Miami, to co-ordinate the promotion and selling of Yerex's two main enterprises: Transportes Aéreos Centro-Americanos (TACA) and the newly-founded (27 November, 1940) British West Indian Airways (BWIA).

An indication of the shape of things to come was the appearance of a new name in the group: **Empresa de Transportes Aerovias Brasil, S.A.**, which was founded by Yerex on 26 August, 1942. The shareholding was divided between Yerex (42 per cent), Charles E. Matthews, a Vice-President of TACA (18 per cent), and two Brazilians, the brothers Oscar and Roberto Taves (40 per cent). Operations were authorized by Brazilian Presidential Decree 11,160 on 29 December, 1942, by which time some *ad hoc* flights had already been made with two Lockheed 14s, carrying valuable air freight destined for critical use in the war effort from Rio de Janeiro to Miami. Thus, Yerex suddenly added a vast new dimension to his TACA empire, and was apparently poised to undertake considerable route and traffic expansion.

On 11 May, 1943, British West Indian Airways was incorporated as a limited company, but Yerex's personal stake was reduced soon afterwards, on 5 October, an important landmark in the eventful corporate history of TACA. On this day, Yerex sold stock to the value of $2,225,000 to various United States interests, including the Maryland Casualty Company, the Adams Express Company, Time

Inc, and—significantly—Transcontinental & Western Air Inc (TWA). The move to Americanize TACA was undoubtedly provoked by desperation on Yerex's part to comply with the necessary C.A.B. requirements to obtain a temporary

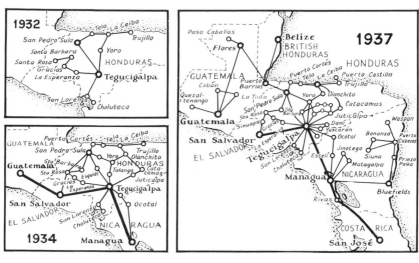

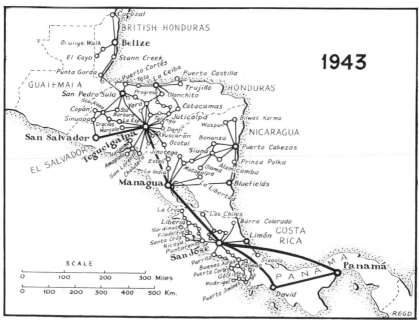

12. TACA 1932–1943 (The Years of Adventure). Beginning from a small base in Tegucigalpa in 1931, Lowell Yerex negotiated the purchase of several small airlines in Central America. At its peak, TACA claimed to serve 235 points, many on a scheduled basis as shown in the 1943 map.

foreign carrier permit to fly to Miami. Even though he had the unqualified support of the US Army, which was well pleased with TACA contract work, Yerex's British nationality was actively stressed by anti-TACA lobbyists in Washington.

Shortly afterwards, on 26 November, 1943, the name of Inter-American Airways was changed back to the more recognizable TACA Airways, S.A. The capital, already augmented in January to $5,000,000, was now doubled. Yerex retained 53.8 per cent and US interests the remainder of the approximately $3,500,000 issued. The Pennsylvania Railroad was one of the minor stockholders, but TWA's share was substantial.

It is interesting to speculate that American Export's unfortunate experience with Pan American as its adversary had served as a case study for Howard Hughes, who had become TWA's principal stockholder in April 1939. A record-breaking international flyer himself, Hughes's horizons began to spread beyond the frontiers of the United States during the war. Indeed, as already mentioned, within the space of less than a year, TWA bought a large interest in TACA (on 5 October, 1943); an interest in Hawaiian Airlines (in May 1944); and applied to the Civil Aeronautics Board for round-the-world routes (10 June, 1944). Uninhibited by any doubts as to whether TWA was an airline or not, Hughes seemed to be offering a direct challenge to Juan Trippe, czar of Pan American's worldwide empire, with TACA as the chosen instrument by which he hoped to perform the Latin American part of the operation.

A Lockheed Model 14 of TACA. On the nose can be seen TACA's red, blue and yellow parrot symbol, which was later used by Aerovias Brasil. (*Gary Kuhn*)

While TACA's operations had, at least until 1939, consisted of feeder routes in the Central American republics, and its aircraft fleet made up of miscellaneous second-hand aircraft, the image of TACA as a shoe-string operator would have been misleading. There may have been a time when Yerex's ground staff were authorized to start the engines by tying a rope around the propeller and pulling hard; but those days were long past. TACA was an airline of substance and integrity. Its repair and maintenance shops at Tegucigalpa* were probably as good as any south of the Rio Grande. It operated forty radio stations, and its staff throughout the network exhibited a high morale, feeling that they belonged to a

* Repair and maintenance shops were later established at San José.

respected institution and were members of an honourable profession. In 1939, when the holding company in Panama was established and Yerex had started to solicit US investment, five Lockheed 14s had been purchased, heralding the end of the romantic era and the entry of TACA into the world of Big Business.

TACA started to dispose of its older aircraft, including the extensive fleet of Ford Tri-Motors, most of which had been expertly rebuilt or modified in the TACA shops at Tegucigalpa, and were probably sold to subsequent owners in better condition than when they were received. And gradually a complete transformation took place, in some ways a repetition of the series of foreign acquisitions of the mid-1930s, but transferring the action beyond the confines of Central America.

Zenith of TACA's Ambition

While the TACA group of companies in Central America, the British West Indies, and Brazil ostensibly appeared to provide the basis for a continent-wide airline network, it was a rather loosely-knit assembly, and on the map there were many gaps between key points. To reinforce the framework, TACA's new owners started to patch up the holes, so as to present itself more plausibly to the airline world, and to the prospective passengers in particular. For TACA's network was transparently still a makeshift structure, and much consolidation work needed to be done.

The first move in this new round of expansion was to establish **TACA de México, S.A.** in 1944. This was simply a non-operating subsidiary of TACA which, however, enabled TACA El Salvador—the international division—to operate into Mexico, with locally-owned ground facilities.

In quick succession followed **Línea Aérea TACA de Venezuela**, formed jointly with Venezuelan interests on 18 August, 1944, the latter holding a guaranteed 55 per cent of the shares; and **Líneas Aéreas TACA de Colombia**, in which TACA held 22·5 per cent. On 2 January, 1945, in co-operation, the two companies began a nonstop service between Caracas and Bogotá, using Lockheed Model 10 Electras. Each airline flew its own equipment, and this may have been one of the world's first examples of an international pool agreement, in which, to simplify accounting, revenues were shared on a previously agreed basis, and tickets sold freely and interchangeably by both airlines.

Local services were also started to the major cities in both Colombia and Venezuela, and a connecting service provided from San José, Costa Rica, to Medellín and Bogotá, Colombia, by TACA El Salvador. At the peak of its international expansion, TACA was able to advertise flights connecting Mexico City with Bogotá, calling at all the Central American capitals; and from Caracas to Lima, linking with the Central American route at Bogotá, and thence via Cali, Quito, and Guayaquil to the Peruvian capital. Additionally, from Ciudad Trujillo, in the Dominican Republic, Aerovias Brasil flew to Brazil, via Trinidad and Dutch Guiana.

But it was a flimsy structure, a thing of shreds and patches. Although there were some wartime contract routes into Miami from connecting points at Ciudad Trujillo and Havana, TACA never operated a scheduled service into the United States during this period of its existence. The peak seems to have been reached with the extension to Lima in the summer of 1946, by which time also Aerovías Paraguayas, S.A. was established as a wholly-owned (except for 4 per cent) subsidiary, and an unsuccessful attempt was made to gain a foothold in

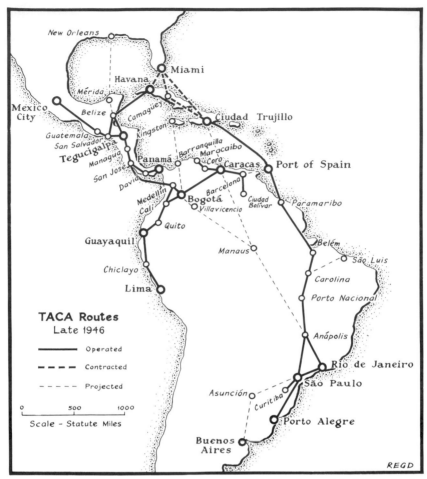

13. Furthest Extent of the TACA Network, late 1946 (The Years of Ambition). Under TWA's influence, TACA aspired to develop a route network which would encompass most of Latin America. But in spite of an impressive-looking timetable, there was little co-ordination or control beyond the well-established Central American area.

Argentina. But these planned southern route extensions, as well as a direct route from Florida to Colombia, and a short cut route across South America via Manaus, never materialized, and by the end of 1946, it became apparent that the TACA bubble was about to burst.

Collapse of an Airline Empire

If the TACA David had ever cherished any illusions of winning a fight with the Pan American Goliath, they were quickly and decisively shattered. Pan American Airways had already systematically plugged up the loopholes in what might have been a weakness in the defence of its supremacy in Latin America. In retrospect, there does not seem to have been a serious threat, as Pan Am was far too well established as the senior service throughout the continent; but Juan Trippe was not the kind of man to take chances.

At the time of the Guatemala Incident, when Pan American moved in quickly to stop American Export Lines from gaining a foothold, it also took a 40 per cent interest in Aeronaves de México, to reinforce its grip on Mexican commercial aviation, where CMA was an extension of the Pan American Airways system. Three years later, when under TWA's influence, TACA started to acquire more subsidiaries, Pan American took political action again. Within little more than twelve months, it took a controlling interest in five airlines around the periphery of the Caribbean Sea, which it regarded as its sphere of dominance by inherited right. It bought a share in AVENSA of Venezuela on 14 July, 1943, soon after its formation; bought a share of Bahamas Airways on 10 December, 1943; and helped to found Cía Dominicana de Aviación (CDA) on 26 April, 1944. This plugged up possible weaknesses on the eastern sector of Pan American's Caribbean routes.

Then, while TACA was founding its subsidiaries in Venezuela and Colombia, Pan American simultaneously made some shrewd moves in Central America, the heart of the TACA empire. Cía Panameña de Aviación (COPA), Líneas Aéreas Costarricenses (LACSA), Servicio Aéreo de Honduras (SAHSA), and Líneas Aéreas de Nicaragua (LANICA) were all founded within less than three months of 1944, on 30 August, 17 October, 16 November, and 17 November, respectively.

These airlines invariably enjoyed governmental support, either through direct State involvement in the capital shareholding, or in favouring the Pan American associate. The local route networks often ran parallel with those of the TACA competitors and, with Pan American's aid, usually flew superior equipment. Thus, while geographically TACA was stretching its complex and fragmented route system to the limits—the extension to Lima seems to have been the final gesture—the foundations were crumbling in the TACA heartland, much as the pyramids of the Mayan civilization had deteriorated during a previous era. Yerex apparently felt that he was not receiving whole-hearted support from the US interests that he had taken to his heart, and made some moves in Great Britain to buy out the Americans. This irritated the new TACA stockholders to the extent that they elected the Pennsylvania Railroad's Benjamin Pepper as Chairman of TACA, and bought out Yerex's contract as President in December 1945.

Enter Waterman

During 1947 and 1948, TWA manoeuvred to sustain TACA as a force in Latin American commercial aviation. The year 1947 started well when on 6 January the US Civil Aeronautics Board granted permission for TACA El Salvador, the international division responsible for the Central American trunk network, to operate to Miami, via Havana. But offsetting this gain was a loss: Yerex sold his interest in Aerovias Brasil on 11 January, and although TWA still retained a 9 per cent shareholding in the Brazilian affiliate, this was no more than a nominal echo of a former ambition; and TWA never actively pursued it. Aerovias Brasil had reported a loss of $900,000, but the situation in Colombia, once thought to be the potential hub of a South American TACA network, was even worse. It sustained a series of DC-3 accidents, was reported to have shown a financial loss of more than $4 million, and predictably ceased operations in May 1947.

137

During this period, TWA's shareholding in TACA was at its peak—48 per cent—with minority holdings by Royork & Company (19 per cent), the Pennsylvania Railroad (7 per cent), Hallgarten & Company (8 per cent) and other small United States interests. Lowell Yerex retained only 10 per cent, and was no longer influential in TACA's affairs. The TACA Airways Agency, a Delaware Corporation, acting as agent for the TACA system in the United States, had closed its New York office, and moved to Miami. Now, on 13 January, 1947, it obtained the assistance of the Waterman Steamship Corporation, which was appointed as general agent for the TACA Agency in the United States. The office in Miami was merged with those of the steamship company as an obvious economy measure, and it also agreed to represent TACA in all of its sixteen permanent selling outlets in the United States.

The TACA Agency, with Waterman backing, leased two Douglas DC-4s plus three more DC-3s to augment the TACA fleet, which was not exactly impressive. With the residual collection of antique aircraft still making only token flights in the small republics, the fleet of six Lockheed Model 18 Lodestars and nine DC-3s was inadequate to provide TACA with sufficient capacity of the right standards to match the competition in the booming airline industry of the postwar era. The additional aircraft simply prolonged the agony and put off the day when the awful truth had to be faced.

For the record, a token gesture was made in 1947 at the home base in Salvador when a small local concern, **Aerovías Latino-Americanos (ALA)** was incorporated into the TACA system by purchase of 51 per cent of the shareholding. But when Paul Richter, Executive Vice-President of TWA took over as Chairman of TACA on 15 September, 1947, it was simply to preside over the dissolution of an empire.

On 28 February, 1948, on the day when service to Miami was suspended, TACA de Honduras was sold to Messrs Augusto Rodriguez and James A. Jett for a mere $94,000—a sad commentary on the company which had once been an institution throughout Central America. Also on the same day, TACA sold its interests in TACA de Nicaragua. Then, on 12 March, only two weeks later, a revolution in Costa Rica abruptly terminated operations not only within the republic, but also from San José to Panamá, which had been TACA de Costa Rica's allocated franchise. The new Costa Rican government seized the fleet of three DC-3s, and on 19 May, the company was sold to two Costa Ricans, Robert Darmsted and Roberto Kruse, for $175,000.

With the exception of El Salvador, therefore, TACA's presence in Central America entirely evaporated during the Spring of 1948. Its companies in Brazil and Colombia had already disappeared; only the one in Venezuela was left on the South American continent, completely severed geographically and operationally with what was left of the TACA system.

All the time, Pan American grew from strength to strength, having brushed off the TACA threat to its Latin American supremacy almost with contempt. Nevertheless, taking a commercial course involving considerable risk, the Waterman Steamship Corporation expanded its interest in TACA from that of an agency to become an active stockholder, acquiring 35 per cent of the shares from TWA in February 1949. It then propped up the ailing airline in providing direct assistance by an injection of operating funds to the value of more than $600,000.

By 1950, it was apparent that TACA stood a chance of survival. Waterman's subsidy had saved it. The holdings in Venezuela were liquidated; the threads in Panama, and Mexico, and elsewhere, were broken. On 24 May, 1951, the company changed its status from that of a Panamanian corporation to become a

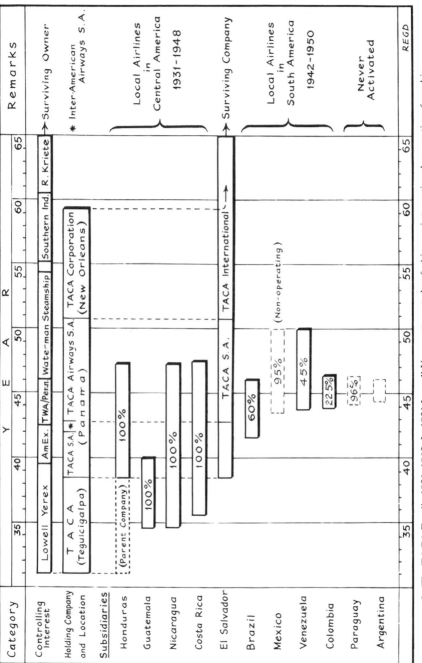

3. The TACA Family 1931–1965. In 1931 Lowell Yerex attempted to fashion an international consortium from his precarious base in Honduras. To some extent he succeeded but by 1950 little remained of his airline empire.

139

United States organization. All assets and liabilities were transferred to the new TACA Corporation, based in New Orleans, and organized under Delaware Law with a capital of $200,000. TACA International Airlines was named as the foreign subsidiary of the new US holding company.

Gradually, TACA struggled back towards reasonable health. Concentrating on a reduced network of international routes, without the burden of local networks, with their operational hazards and political complexities, TACA improved its finances, and Waterman was able to dispose of its interest by sale of the stock to its own shareholders. Nevertheless, the Civil Aeronautics Board still raised the issue of control in the summer of 1954, recalling no doubt the problem raised by American Export Lines, and regarding Waterman's involvement as a repetition of history and to be treated with the same critical examination.

At this point, the story of the old TACA gives way to that of the new, and is appropriately dealt with in the chapter on the modern airlines of Central America. The Latin American TACA lasted from late 1931 until 1951, twenty eventful years during which, for the majority of the time, the hand of its founder could be felt, always innovating, always reaching out to further the influence of his airline. TACA epitomized an age of adventure, romance, and the true pioneering spirit. Nobody who had any part in it, whether the dauntless pilots flying by the seat of their pants over impenetrable jungles, the mechanics at the Tegucigalpa base keeping the aircraft flying with spare parts made on the premises, or the agents taking on contracts which no other transport organization would look at; none of these, and least of all the privileged brotherhood of passengers who flew with Lowell Yerex's men, will ever forget the experience of helping to make history.

TABLE 10

TACA
Major Changes in Corporate Ownership, Capital Structure, and Interests in Subsidiary Companies

Date	Changes in Ownership or Capital Structure	Airlines established (E), Acquired (A), or Disposed of (D)	Country
Late 1931	**Transportes Aéreas Centro-Americanos (TACA)** founded by Lowell Yerex		Honduras
24 Apr, 1934		A **Empresa Dean**	Honduras
1935		A **Compañía Nacional de Aviacíon, S.A.** (became TACA de Guatemala)	Guatemala

140

16 Oct, 1935		A	**Líneas Aéreas de Nicaragua, Empresa Palacios (LANEP)** (became TACA de Nicaragua on 16 March, 1939)	Nicaragua
25 Aug, 1939	**TACA, S.A.** established as non-operating holding company in Panamá	E	**TACA de Honduras**	Honduras/ Panama
		E	**TACA El Salvador**	El Salvador
20 Oct, 1939		A	**Transportes Aéreos Costarricenses**	Costa Rica
		A	**Aérovias Nacionales de Costa Rica**	Costa Rica
16 Jan, 1940		A	**Empresa Nacional des Transportes Aéreos (ENTA)** (became TACA de Costa Rica)	Costa Rica
1 Mar, 1940	Merger of Costa Rican airlines to form TACA de Costa Rica			
1 Oct, 1940	American Export Lines bought control			USA
27 Nov, 1940		E	British West Indian Airways (BWIA). Not part of TACA system, but founded by Yerex	Trinidad
Jan 1941		D	TACA de Guatemala bought out by Guatemalan Govt	Guatemala
26 Aug, 1942		E	Empresa de Transportes **Aerovias Brasil, S.A.**	Brazil
27 Jan, 1943	Name of TACA, S.A., changed to **Inter-American Airways, S.A.** Branch offices in New York and Miami			Panama/ USA
5 Oct, 1943	TWA and Pennsylvania Railroad acquired substantial interest			USA

26 Nov, 1943	Name changed to **TACA Airways, S.A.**	E	**TACA, S.A.** (formerly TACA El Salvador)	Panama/ El Salvador
1944		E	**TACA de México, S.A.** (non-operating)	Mexico
18 Aug, 1944		E	**Línea Aérea TACA de Venezuela**	Venezuela
17 Nov, 1944		E	**Líneas Aéreas TACA de Colombia**	Colombia
1945		E	Aerovías Paraguayas, S.A. (never operated)	Paraguay
1945		E	Aerovías Argentinas (never incorporated)	Argentina
June 1946	Yerex disposed of all stock			
11 Jan, 1947		D	Aerovias Brasil	Brazil
13 Jan, 1947	Waterman Airlines bought large share			
May 1947		D	TACA de Colombia ceased operations	Colombia
1947		A	**Aerovías Latino- Americanos, S.A. (ALA)**	El Salvador
30 Sept, 1947			Yerex sold interest in BWIA	Trinidad
28 Feb, 1948		D	TACA de Honduras (continued under same name until bought by SAHSA in 1953)	Honduras
28 Feb, 1948		D	TACA de Nicaragua	Nicaragua
19 May, 1948		D	TACA de Costa Rica (continued under the same name until bought by LACSA, 1952)	Costa Rica

Date			
Feb 1949	Waterman Steamship Corporation acquired full control		USA
1950		D TACA de Venezuela (LAV took control in 1952)	Venezuela
24 May, 1951	**TACA Corporation** formed in New Orleans as a US company under Delaware Law		USA
		E **TACA International Airlines** (formerly TACA, S.A., El Salvador)	El Salvador
1962	Waterman Steamship Corp disposed of shares to its own stockholders		USA
May 1955	McLean Industries acquired stock		USA
Jan 1956	Southern Industries Corporation bought McLean's interest		USA
29 Mar, 1960	TACA Corporation transferred properties and assets to **TACA International**		El Salvador
April 1961	Ricardo H. Kriete bought control		El Salvador
1968		D TACA de México	Mexico

CHAPTER SEVEN

The Caribbean Islands

Pioneering in Cuba

One of the lesser known of the early airlines in Latin America was one founded towards the end of 1919 in Havana, Cuba, by a local industrialist, a Señor de Mesa. In October he established **Compañía Aérea Cubana**, and appointed Agustín Parlá as the general manager. Before the end of the year de Mesa and Parlá had ordered two Goliaths and four Type F.40s from the French Farman company, and requested technical and flying assistance. The aircraft were despatched by ship, via Dakar, together with a team of six, comprising two pilots, Lucien Coupet and Guy de Roig, and four mechanics, led by Coupet's brother Léon.

Arriving during the early part of 1920, the Frenchmen began zealously to popularize aviation. A flying school was established; sightseeing flights were made regularly over and around Havana, dispelling much apprehension about the hazards of flight; survey and demonstration flights were made to other cities in Cuba, and work was started on a programme of aerial photography to assist mapmaking. Most important, however, among these varied activities was the establishment of an airline operation.

Regular services began on 30 October, 1920, from Havana to Santiago de Cuba, via Cienfuegos, Santa Clara and Camagüey, using the Farman Goliaths. Some flights terminated at the intermediate points, and the timetable was probably intermittent. It was certainly short-lived. By January 1921, the Cuban sugar boom, which had encouraged the creation of the company in the first place, collapsed as the European sugar beet industry resumed production after the ravages of war. Compañía Aérea Cubana disappeared from the records as the first and, as far as is known, the only airline enterprise to be founded by local Caribbean interests until the 1940s.

During its brief operating existence, from February 1920 until January 1921, the company's record was impressive for its time. Covering all its operations, flying school, survey, sightseeing, and airline, it flew 60,000 km, carried 2,000 passengers, and completed 900 flights without notable incident.

West Indian Air Express

After the isolated experiment in Cuba, there was little incentive in the Caribbean area for local entrepreneurs to start airlines. The independent republics were quite poor and lacked the means. Thus, throughout the developing period of the 1930s—from 1928 to 1945 to be exact—the commercial airways were owned entirely by companies based overseas, in the USA, the Netherlands, and Great Britain. The Caribbean, of course, was traditionally Pan American Airways' sphere of influence, but this did not materialize until after bitter corporate struggles for coveted mail contracts in the United States. The story of the rise and fall of a great airline, NYRBA, is narrated in a later chapter of this book. Less known, perhaps, because it was diminutive by comparison, is another which also operated for less than a year, and was also swallowed by Pan American. And although initiated by United States citizens, it was founded as a Dominican company, with some local participation.

West Indian Aerial Express, C por A., (WIAX) was incorporated on 20 June, 1927. It had its origins in the fortuitous meeting of the two major elements necessary to justify a transport system: a market need and the equipment for the job. The market need was a supply route to the small city of Barahona, in the Dominican Republic, where a group of sugar planters were almost isolated because of the inadequate surface communications. When a barnstorming pilot arrived with two Waco 9 biplanes, exploring ways to supplement his precarious income, the idea for WIAX was born. The pilot, Basil Rowe, was later to become one of Pan American's most experienced crew members, with a remarkable record of sophisticated commercial flying. In 1927, however, he was one of a gallant band of simple but resourceful airmen who were the real pioneers of the airline business.

WIAX was promoted by H. L. Harper, with other local business men; Rowe was chief pilot, and his Wacos constituted the fleet. The capital was $50,000. An experimental flight was made from Barahona to Port-au-Prince, Haiti, on 14 July, 1927, and another on the next day, from Port-au-Prince to Santo Domingo. Then on 19 October occurred a strange event which set the course of history. On that date, a hired pilot named Cy Caldwell was delivering a Fairchild FC-2 floatplane, *La Niña*, from the factory at Amityville, New York, to WIAX in Barahona, and arrived at Miami. There he met an agent of the then embryo Pan American Airways which was in desperate straits, because the Fokker F.VII ordered by the company had not arrived in time to make a flight to Havana. This act was mandatory to demonstrate Pan Am's ability to operate and thus meet the requirements for obtaining the mail contract between the USA and Cuba. The agent paid Caldwell $145 to make Pan Am's flight. Had Caldwell not performed

This Fairchild FC-2 *La Niña* carried Pan American Airways' first mail from Key West to Havana on 19 October, 1927. The aircraft was chartered from West Indian Aerial Express for this single flight so as to qualify for a US Post Office mail contract. Ironically, WIAE was the unsuccessful bidder. (*Pan American World Airways*)

145

The Keystone Pathfinder 1612 *Santa Maria* was the flagship of West Indian Aerial Express's fleet. (*Pan American World Airways*)

the Good Samaritan act, Pan Am might have had some difficulty in upholding its case—although its influence with the Postmaster General was considerable. The first Fokker flight did not take place until 28 October.

At about the same time, Rowe delivered to Santo Domingo a Keystone Pathfinder, a large biplane, weighing 17,000 lb, with three Wright Whirlwind engines, and able to carry ten passengers. Furthermore, it could land in what Rowe termed 'dollar bill-sized airfields'. Named *Santa Maria*, this aircraft was formerly called *American Legion* and was originally intended to fly the Atlantic as a contender for the Orteig prize won by Charles Lindbergh.

West Indian Aerial Express began scheduled services on 1 December, 1927, from Santo Domingo to San Juan (three a week) and to Port-au-Prince (one a week). The company carried mail from 3 December, holding franchises from the Dominican Republic, Haiti and Cuba, for all types of load between all four of its landing points, except for the outward mail from San Juan, a United States territory. The passenger fares were $50 from San Juan to Santo Domingo, $85 to Port-au-Prince. Cargo was carried at 25¢ per pound, mail at $2·50 per pound. An interesting interlude occurred on 6/7 February, 1928, when Charles Lindbergh, passing through the area on his goodwill tour from Mexico City around the Caribbean to Miami, was persuaded to carry WIAX's mail through to Havana in the Ryan monoplane *Spirit of St Louis*, probably the only time that famous aircraft ever made a flight for commercial purposes.

On 20 February, West Indian extended its route at both ends, to Santiago de Cuba and to St Thomas and St Croix. Then, on 8 March, the US Foreign Air Mail Act was passed, and on 31 May bids were advertised for FAM-6, the strategically important Miami–San Juan route, amongst many others. Rowe and his colleagues were suddenly faced with the harsh realities, not of corporate strength—at the time Pan American was, if anything, smaller than WIAX—but of corporate influence in Washington. To comply with the imminent battle, West Indian Aerial Express Inc was formed as a United States holding company in June 1928, to comply even more fully with the law requiring that the majority of the shares of the successful bidder for a Foreign Mail Contract should be held by US citizens. This was probably so of WIAX, C por A, but could have been more easily

146

challenged. The new company's capital was $92,000, with additional investment by Sherman Fairchild (President) and Graham Grosvenor.

On 14 July the bids were opened. Both Pan American and West Indian bid the top rate possible: $2·00 per mile. The contract was awarded to Pan American 'because the company had already demonstrated on another route that it could perform service satisfactorily'. On the face of it, this seems to have been either the height of cynicism, or an example of blatant favouritism. Not only was West Indian practically an incumbent carrier. Pan American might never have obtained its Havana route were it not for the rival airline's inadvertent magnanimity on 19 October, 1927.

There was some delay following the first report on 7 August, 1928, that Pan American had agreed to purchase WIAX. Matters were complicated by a typhoon which hit San Domingo on 12 September. Apart from grounding the FC-2 it destroyed all WIAX's records. But the takeover was on its way. On 20 September the flagship *Santa Maria* was handed over to its new owners, and on 15 October, Basil Rowe flew the first mail from San Juan to Port-au-Prince, a mission he could not have undertaken without Trippe's mail contract. On 16 October, the shareholders of WIAX, C por A, agreed to sell its assets to WIAX Inc for $100,000, simultaneously transferring the title to Pan American. On 28 November, Pan American paid $75,000 for WIAX Inc, and on 22 December Basil Rowe's airline was finally dissolved.

The Second Cuban Airline

Pan American Airways expanded rapidly into the Caribbean, and its three mainline routes southwards from Miami all went across Cuba: through Havana en route to the Yucatán peninsula and Central America; through Cienfuegos en route to Kingston and Barranquilla; and via the eastern end of the island to the West Indies and beyond to Venezuela and Brazil. Within Cuba, another United States airline group had secured a foothold. North American Aviation, through a subsidiary, Intercontinental Aviation, had established, on 8 October, 1929, **Compañía Nacional Cubana de Aviación Curtiss, S.A.** The company started a

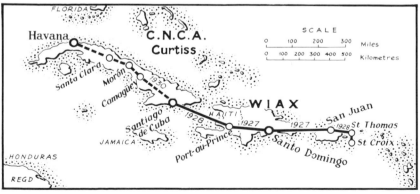

14. Early Pan American Airways' Ancestors in the Caribbean, 1927–1929. Pan American Airways made an important move in the Greater Antilles by buying West Indian Aerial Express in 1928 and the Curtiss airline in Cuba in 1929. These two companies provided key links in a planned route network which was soon to encircle the Caribbean.

147

Cuban domestic service, from Havana to Santiago, via intermediate points, on 30 October, 1930.

Juan Trippe bided his time, and when the Curtiss-Keys-North American empire got into difficulties, Pan American bought the airline on 6 May, 1932. The word Curtiss was dropped from the title, to allow the abbreviation **C.N.C.A.**, and Pan American Ford Tri-Motors replaced the small Travel Airs and Curtiss aircraft. On 29 July, 1935, Lockheed Model 10 Electras were introduced on the main route, the *Cuban Air Ltd* reducing the time from Havana to Santiago from $6\frac{1}{4}$ hr to $4\frac{1}{4}$. Fords were still used on the extensions past Santiago, including the *Oriente Flyer* to Baracoa. All Pan Am points in Cuba were now neatly integrated.

This service pattern continued for almost ten years, a commendable record of continuity, until in March 1945 two C-53s (military Douglas DC-3s) were introduced. By this time, the airline name had been further shortened to Cía Cubana de Aviación, in preparation for the entry of Cuban national interests on 31 December, 1945, when Pan American's shareholding was reduced to 52 per cent. On 15 May, 1946, Cubana introduced international service to Miami, under its own name, thus paralleling Pan American's original route, started almost twenty years previously.

Dutch Enterprise in the Caribbean

Although the Netherlands' colonies in the Caribbean were not as extensive as the British or French, they were certainly given more attention by the homeland in matters of commercial aviation. The Dutch airline, KLM, had demonstrated considerable élan in fashioning an efficient service across Asia to link the distant Netherlands East Indies (now Indonesia) with Amsterdam. During the mid-1930s, KLM took steps to make its presence known in the West Indies as well, even though commercial aircraft were not yet able to fly with a payload across even the shortest trans-Atlantic route, from West Africa to the northeastern tip of Brazil.

Accordingly, in December 1934, the Fokker F.XVIII *Snip* flew from Amsterdam to Curaçao, to celebrate 300 years of Dutch rule in the Lesser Antilles. The aircraft was fitted with eight extra fuel tanks for the ocean crossing. These were then removed and the aircraft became the flagship of the **KLM West Indies Division**, founded on 19 January, 1935. Joined by a second F.XVIII, *Oriol*, and the Fokker F.VIII *Duif*, the first service, made on the day of the establishment of the Division, was between the two Dutch islands, Curaçao and Aruba, but an international route was added to Maracaibo on 1 July, 1936.

A route to Caracas started on 19 January, 1937, but attempts to begin service to Miami, with possible extensions north and east towards Europe, were frustrated when the USA refused landing rights. KLM concentrated on improving the standard of its service along the northern coast of South America. On 16 May, 1938, a Lockheed 14, delivered in February by the famous KLM pilot Geysendorffer, opened a route to Barranquilla; and on 6 May, 1939, Port of Spain, Trinidad, and Barbados were added. This eastern section was extended to Paramaribo, Surinam, on 4 September of the same year, thus linking most of the Dutch colonies in the New World.

In May 1950, the West Indies Division of KLM became the first and, in a sense, the only commercial operator of the Douglas DC-5, a high-wing twin-engined aircraft, and the first modern aircraft to have a nosewheel undercarriage. Its stay at Curaçao was short, as it was transferred to the Netherlands East Indies

The Fokker F.XVIII PH-AIS *Snip* which made KLM's first trans-Atlantic flight, from Amsterdam to Curaçao, with Christmas mail in December 1934. The flying time was 55 hr 58 min. The crew are (*left to right*) radio operator Van der Molen, Captain Hondong, co-pilot Van Balkom and flight engineer Stolk. (*KLM*)

KLM's Lockheed 14-F62 PJ-AIT *Troepiaal* over Willemstad, Curaçao. (*KLM*)

KLM's Douglas DC-5 PJ-AIW *Wakago*. (*Douglas Aircraft Company*)

associate, KNILM, soon afterwards. However, with a fleet of four Lockheed 14s, three Lockheed 18 Lodestars, and the trusty F.XVIIIs, KLM made great strides. Service to Kingston began on 19 August, 1941, and in connection with the war effort, contract flying began to Miami in 1941. A temporary permit having been issued by the United States C.A.B. in 1943 to operate a public service on the route, via Jamaica, Haiti, and Cuba, scheduled service began on 17 August, 1943. Starting flights to Ciudad Trujillo (Santo Domingo) on 11 January and to the small Dutch colony of St Maarten on 27 July of the same year, the Dutch presence throughout the Caribbean was well established by the end of the war.

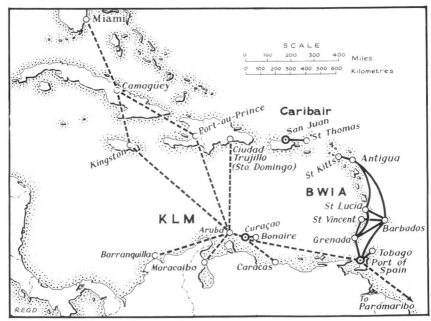

15. Caribbean Airlines, 1943. During the Second World War, two airlines were firmly based in the Caribbean as well as Pan American. KLM had set up an autonomous division in Curaçao, while Yerex, the promoter of the famous TACA, established BWIA in 1939.

150

British West Indian Airways

The first airline in a British colony in the Caribbean region was **Bahamas Airways, Ltd (BAL)** incorporated in 1936 by Sir Harry Oaks, and Hon H. G. Christie, who had started charter flights from Nassau to the outer Bahamas islands in 1933. In 1937, Christie obtained a contract from the colonial Government to fly passengers, mail, and freight on his routes, and the operation was good enough to attract the attention of Pan American, which bought a 45 per cent interest on 10 December, 1943. At first, Pan American depended on the old Consolidated Commodore flying-boats, once the proud flagships of the NYRBA Line, but these were supplemented by Consolidated Catalina PBY-5As in 1947.

On 27 May, 1947, the C.A.B. granted permission to Bahamas Airways to operate international routes from Nassau to Miami and West Palm Beach. Operations began the following February, using DC-3s, and an additional Bahamian terminal was added: West End, serving the new Butlin's Holiday Camp on Grand Bahama Island. Bahamas Airways returned to British hands when British South American Airways, performing a mopping-up exercise in the Caribbean, bought the airline on 23 October, 1948. At that time, the airline operated 761 miles of local routes, with an assortment of flying-boats: a Catalina, a Commodore, a Republic Seabee, and two Grumman Goose amphibians.

Bahamas Airways' Douglas C-47B VP-BBM. (*T. R. Waddington*)

But the Bahamas were, in British eyes, on the northern fringe of the Caribbean, and in political terms not even defined as West Indian. The centre of air operations for a British equivalent to the West Indies Division of KLM lay further south. Even so, in the late 1930s, when the initiative came to augment British airline activity in the area, it was from the New Zealander, Lowell Yerex, whose name was synonymous with the legendary TACA, which had expanded from tiny beginnings in Honduras into a Latin American airline consortium. The airline establishment in London, represented by Imperial Airways, remained aloof from Latin America, and the British colonies in the Caribbean were not on their list of priorities, especially as a European war seemed imminent.

Yerex founded **British West Indian Airways (BWIA)** in Trinidad on 27 November, 1939, and made the first scheduled flight under that name on 26 November, 1940, using a single Lockheed Lodestar, on a local route from Port of Spain to Tobago and Bridgetown, Barbados. This, however, was quickly augmented by several connections to the Leeward and Windward Islands, using a fleet of various twin-engined Lockheeds.

On 11 May, 1943, BWIA was incorporated as a limited company. One thousand shares were sold to the public, including 250 reserved for the employees; another thousand were subscribed by the Trinidad Government;

Vickers-Armstrongs 498 Viking VP-TAT *Trinidad* was one of BWIA's Viking fleet which initially had light blue fuselage flashes. The white flight-deck roof is unusual.

Lowell Yerex received 3,000 shares plus BW $113,000. He was appointed managing director but resigned shortly afterwards. On 5 October of the same year, his interest was reduced to 40 per cent, most of which was turned over to TACA Airways, which was still the main selling agent for BWIA in the USA. But the TACA influence was quickly receding, and this arrangement was terminated. The British state airline BOAC, meanwhile, was permitted to appoint a director, implying a direct interest through the Government shareholding.

Fulfilling the role of linking British possessions in the Caribbean, BWIA extended service to Kingston, Jamaica, on 16 December, 1944; Belize, British Honduras, on 4 March, 1945; and Georgetown, British Guiana, on 6 September, 1945. Later that year, Ciudad Trujillo was added to the Kingston route. Thus, together with the Dutch KLM network, the European influence in the Caribbean was quite evident (see Map 15)

After the war, the British Government had set up a third airline corporation, British South American Airways (BSAA). During 1947 the ownership of BWIA changed. On 11 January, the TACA interest was reduced to 28 per cent, then in August this was sold to the Trinidad Government. BSAA then acquired 47 per cent of the shares, while British West Indies colonists retained 25 per cent. Later, on 1 October, BSAA acquired all the remaining shares, through its wholly-owned subsidiary, **British International Airlines, Ltd (BIA)**, and for a short while, until June 1948, BWIA was officially known by that name.

A BWIA Lockheed Model 18 Lodestar at Antigua in 1952. This aircraft is in BOAC-type livery, with modified Speedbird. (*David West*)

Further routes were added: a link to Kingston, via Caracas, in February 1948, and Curaçao the following month. BWIA had long cherished the ambition of serving Miami, and made its formal application for permanent route authority on 14 March, 1949. The British influence was now strong, and five Vickers Viking twin-engined airliners, the same type that had been ordered in quantity by British European Airways, were introduced in preference to the more familiar DC-3. On 30 July, following deep misgivings about operating efficiency and, indeed, safety standards of BWIA's parent company BSAA, BOAC took over ownership.

In October of the same year, BOAC purchased **British Caribbean Airways (BCA)**. This company had been formed in Jamaica on 18 December, 1946, with 79 per cent local capital, the rest from the United States. Non-scheduled flights began in the following year to Miami, and a DC-3 scheduled route was opened in July 1948 from Kingston to Nassau, via Montego Bay. On 14 July, 1949, the United States C.A.B. granted permission to operate to Miami and scheduled service began shortly afterwards. BOAC acquired all the stock in October 1949, and replaced the DC-3s with Vikings as it merged the operations with those of BWIA. BCA ceased to trade on 31 March, 1950.

In 1952, under the BOAC reorganization plan for the Caribbean, BWIA took over the international services of Bahamas Airways. These linked Nassau with Miami, West Palm Beach, and Havana. Bahamas Airways' Grumman fleet continued to operate inter-island services, but the DC-3s were sold. Later, however, the DC-3 had to be re-introduced, proving to have greater longevity—as befitting an aircraft whose reputation in that sense is legendary—than the Vikings. Towards the late 1950s, BOAC formed an association with a British independent company, Skyways, promoted by Eric Rylands, to whom 80 per cent of the Bahamas Airways stock was sold in November 1958, in the name of the Skyways Bahamas Holding Coy Ltd. The new agreement was effective from 1 April, 1959, but was soon in trouble. The US C.A.B raised some bureaucratic obstacles over traffic rights, and the four-engined Handley Page Hermes 4 aircraft introduced on the Nassau–Florida routes were plainly unsuitable. By December 1960, BOAC had to repossess the operation and restored faith by replacing the old postwar interim type with modern propeller-turbine Vickers Viscounts.

In the western Caribbean, in the Cayman Islands, BWIA found it convenient to sublease the local service traffic rights to LACSA, the Costa Rican airline. LACSA took over Cayman Brac Airways in 1955, the twin-engined Cessnas of this company having started charter services in the islands when the company was founded by William Bigler a few years earlier. BWIA also took over the management of British Guiana Airways.

Independent Progress in Cuba

After the war, Pan American Airways surrendered its ownership of **Compañía Cubana de Aviación**, by offering 48,000 shares, or 48 per cent, to the Cuban public. This was increased to 52 per cent on 5 April, 1948, and Cuba began to assert its independence of the former parent company. The biggest single step towards this goal was to inaugurate trans-Atlantic service from Havana to Madrid, via the Azores, on 26 April, 1948, using, however, Douglas DC-4s leased from Pan Am. But route expansion was now under way, with Havana recognized as a traffic hub in its own right, rather than as a point on the Pan American Miami-based system.

A US air mail contract was obtained on 15 February, 1950, and DC-4s put on the Miami route. In May 1953, both Cubana and National Airlines were authorized to operate the reciprocal services between New York and Havana, a route which quickly gained in popularity as a direct vacation resort competitor with the long-established New York–Miami trunk line. Further routes were added in 1953, Miami–Varadero Beach on 23 January, Havana–Port-au-Prince on 28 November, and Mexico City, via Mérida, on 17 September. Three Lockheed 049 Constellations had been purchased for this last-named route, as Cubana tried to upgrade its equipment.

Pan American now pulled out of Cuba altogether. Its shareholding was reduced to 42 per cent on 31 March, 1951, then to 20 per cent on 7 April, 1953, and finally to zero on 23 July, 1954. For a while, the now independent Cubana, deprived of a sponsor, found itself in difficulty, because United States citizens, who comprised the majority of the clientèle, preferred to travel by US airlines. Steps were taken to create an attractive image. On 22 November, 1954, Model 1049E Super Constellations were introduced on the services to Madrid and Mexico City. These were supplemented on 14 March, 1956, by newer Model 1049Gs which also began a daily nonstop service to New York on 12 May, 1956. Using another technique, Cubana took some of the front seat rows out of its older aircraft, and staged a Cuban band and dancers on what it called *The Tropicana Express*—named after the night club which supplied the act.

Less colourfully, but with deeper implications, Cubana made some shrewd technical decisions. It ordered three Vickers Viscounts from Great Britain in December 1955, and put them into service on 25 May, 1956. The superiority of these aircraft, in competition with piston-engined types, was not lost on the public, and Cubana began to attract an enviable reputation for quality of service and reliability. The propeller-turbine, almost exclusively the result of British development, must have made a good impression in Havana, as Cubana followed the Viscount success by ordering two long-range Bristol Britannias in August 1958. This aircraft, which unfortunately arrived in production numbers too late to enjoy its superiority before the jets swept onto the scene, went into service on Cubana's Mexico City route on 22 December, 1958, and were deployed to New York shortly afterwards.

Just as Cubana was emerging as a potent airline force in the Caribbean, challenging the best which the United States could throw against it, political

Cubana's Lockheed 1049E Super Constellation CU-P573 was later Seaboard & Western Airlines' N1005C. (*Lockheed*)

Although Cubana operated four Bristol Britannias, the Series 300 aircraft G-ANCD, seen here in Cubana livery for publicity purposes, was not one of them.

events overshadowed the entire operation. On New Year's Day 1959, the revolution headed by Fidel Castro overthrew the hated Batista regime, and, following its declared socialist policy, took steps to nationalize Cubana as a state corporation in May 1959. At first, this had little effect. On 5 June the Britannia went on to the Madrid route, and the daily Havana–New York flight became all-Britannia operated. But by the time the fourth of these aircraft was delivered, on 25 August, Cubana was in deep financial straits. Under the Batista Government, the financing had come from generous loans from what has been described as 'arbitrarily established but ill-defined sources of revenue', including the illicit proceeds from Havana's thriving gambling industry. When Batista went, so did Cubana's funds.

The airline took immediate and creditable steps to meet the crisis. During 1960, it leased one Britannia to Eagle, and two Boeing 707s (still on order) to Western Airlines. It offered the fleet of five Viscounts and three Super Constellations for sale. But the situation deteriorated. On 20 September, Cubana suffered the indignity of having its aircraft impounded at New York and they were not released until November. By this time the Castro Government had established close ties with the Soviet Bloc. In February 1961, it signed an agreement with the Czechoslovak airline, ČSA, under which the latter operated the Britannias on a route from Havana to Prague, on Cubana's behalf, in ČSA's colours. The Madrid route was maintained, but the New York and Miami routes abruptly terminated as all communication and travel to and from the United States came to an end in a direct political confrontation.

Cubana changed its course completely. In October the USSR supplied five Ilyushin Il-14 piston-engined aircraft for domestic routes, and on 23 December, 1962—just four years after the Britannia—the four-engined Soviet equivalent of the Bristol airliner, the Ilyushin Il-18, went into service on the Havana–Mexico City route. Cubana acquired seven of these medium-range airliners, which were also placed on domestic routes.

Before the Castro coup, there had been other independent airlines in Cuba. First of these was **Expreso Aéreo Inter-Americano, S.A. (Expreso)**, organized on 4 August, 1942, with a capital of $100,000, mainly by Cubans. A US charter company had a 17½ per cent interest. Cargo operations began from Havana to Miami on 28 August, 1943, and services to Santa Fé, on the Isle of Pines, and other Cuban domestic points were added in 1945 and 1946. During the next few years Expreso sustained a precarious existence, with frequent interruptions of service, and there is no record of it after 1952.

Another independent and ambitious company was **Aerovías Cubanas Internacionales (Cuinair)**, founded in November 1946. Aircraft were chartered from Peninsular Air Transport, from Miami; and trans-Atlantic service operated sporadically until an accident in Spain in February 1947, after which flights were confined to a daily service from Havana to Nassau and suspended in 1948.

Somewhat more substantial was **Aerovías 'Q'**, organized on 13 October, 1945, with a capital of $1,000,000. Operations began in September 1946 from Havana to Varadero and later to Nueva Gerona. Then, after obtaining a US C.A.B. permit, scheduled flights started on 24 February, 1947, on an international route from Havana to Key West, to which point it also received the exclusive operating rights from Cuba. Additional routes were added: to Camagüey, Holguín and Port-au-Prince later in 1947, and a connection to Mexico (to Veracruz, via Mérida) on 1 July, 1949. This last-named was suspended after a few years, and Aerovías 'Q' contracted its operations to Key West, Miami, West Palm Beach, and Nassau.

One other small company was founded in Cuba in the postwar period: **Cuba Aeropostal, S.A.**, organized on 16 August, 1948, with a capital of $400,000, all Cuban. It started service from Havana to Nueva Gerona on 3 May, 1949, and made some contract flights to Miami. But this airline disappeared when at the end of 1960 the commercial airline operations of Cuba were nationalized. The only small company left to be absorbed by the new Cubana was Aerovías 'Q', whose timetable appeared under its own name for a while in Cubana's literature.

More Airlines in the Greater Antilles

The islands of the Caribbean are divided into two major groups, the Greater and the Lesser Antilles, to identify the larger and the smaller. The large comprise Cuba, Hispaniola, Puerto Rico, and Jamaica, of which the last two were, until recent years, dependencies of the United States and Great Britain, respectively. Puerto Rico now enjoys the status of a Commonwealth, and may one day become the 51st State of the Union. Jamaica has achieved its independence, as have other former British colonies in the Lesser Antilles. Hispaniola is divided into two countries, Haiti and Santo Domingo.

The first Antillean airline to be founded east of Cuba was in Puerto Rico. Its history was covered in the companion volume to this book, dealing with the United States, but is repeated here as the island is both geographically and ethnically part of Latin America, in spite of its close ties and political affiliation with the USA. In October 1938, **Powelson Air Service** began semi-scheduled flights between San Juan and Ponce, the second city. This operation was then acquired on 1 June, 1939, by Dionisio Trigo, who had founded **Caribbean-Atlantic Airlines (Caribair)** on 27 February of that year. Using ten-seat Stinson aircraft, Caribair extended its routes to the US Virgin Islands, and a C.A.B route certificate was issued on 23 July, 1942.

Caribair made gradual progress in route expansion and equipment upgrading. When a new route to Ciudad Trujillo (the renamed Santo Domingo) was added on 27 December, 1948, it introduced its first Douglas DC-3, supplementing the Lockheed Lodestars operated since 1945. Service to St Maarten, Netherlands West Indies, started on 15 January, 1958, and this was extended to Guadeloupe in 1961. Convair CV-340s, fitted with 54 seats plus JATO (Jet Assisted Take Off) rockets to cope with mountain-fringed airports like St Thomas, were used on the main routes from 1959; and the CV-640 from December 1965.

156

Caribair's turquoise and white McDonnell Douglas DC-9-31 'fiesta jet' N938PR.
(*Douglas Aircraft Company*)

Caribair became a jet operator when Douglas DC-9s entered service in December 1967, and the route network began to reflect the all-embracing airline name. Direct connections were added between San Juan and Port-au-Prince, Curaçao and Aruba, as well as a multi-stop feeder route calling at eleven points in the Leeward and Windward Islands (Lesser Antilles) as far as Port of Spain, Trinidad.

But by 1968, Caribair's spirits began to wane. Its founder seemed to have become disenchanted with the problem of maintaining profitable operations over a costly route structure in an era of sharply reduced assistance from the Federal Government in the shape of subsidy or mail payments. After a long period of uncertainty, the C.A.B. Examiner recommended a merger of Caribair with Eastern Air Lines, which had long cherished the ambition of flying into the Caribbean. The C.A.B. felt it was forestalling the bankruptcy of an airline that was needed to secure the US position in the feeder network of the Caribbean. But strong protests were made, supported by considerable political lobbying, by Pan American Airways, which felt that its grandfather rights throughout the Caribbean would be severely eroded by a trunk airline like Eastern, able through a merger to offer through service to many points in eastern USA. The argument dragged on for several years. In October 1972, President Nixon sent the case back to the C.A.B., supporting Pan American's case as a Foreign Policy decision. Eastern promptly withdrew its considerable financial support—it had pumped $5 million into Caribair in less than two years. On 30 October, 1972, the C.A.B. rejected the merger by a 3:2 decision, but the battle continued.

Caribair could point ruefully to the severe competition which had always eroded its revenue-earning potential. The postwar boom in aviation throughout the Caribbean was nowhere healthier than in Puerto Rico, which attracted the attention of many small operators which found legal ways of conducting scheduled service without the restrictions imposed by the C.A.B. At first operating as air-taxi services, and granted exemption to operate to a timetable, provided their aircraft did not weigh more than 12,500 lb, these airlines expanded throughout the United States with remarkable rapidity, both in number and in scope. In 1964, twelve such companies could be identified; by 1968 there were more than 200, and the story has become one of spectacular growth. Quickly dubbed Third Level airlines as a convenient term, they were recognized by the Civil Aeronautics Board as Commuter Air Carriers on 1 July, 1969.

Rising to the enviable position of being the largest traffic generator of the entire Third Level industry, a Puerto Rican airline has demonstrated that the most important formulae for success are to have specialized, well-selected equipment, to operate frequent services, and to be content with well-tried profitable routes rather than to seek prestige by route expansion. **Puerto Rico International Airlines (Prinair)** was originally founded on 4 July, 1964, as **Ponce Air**, changing its name in 1965 when it spread its wings to the Virgin Islands. Prinair's equipment choice was the de Havilland Heron, a little British 20-seat airliner with four piston engines, which for various reasons had never sold well. Re-engined with US Lycomings, the Herons proved just right for Prinair. Their size matched the traffic demand as—in contrast with Caribair—Prinair concentrated on high frequency for its shuttle services, achieving, for example, a 15-minute interval throughout most of the day on its route to St Thomas. At the latest count, Prinair had 26 Herons, which have managed to carry about 800,000 passengers every year, and although the temptation to expand the route network is considerable the Herons reach only as far as Santo Domingo in the west, and Guadeloupe in the east.

Prinair's Lycoming Heron N576PR at Harry S. Truman Airport, St Thomas, Virgin Islands. Fuselage band and tail colour on this aircraft was light beige.

Pre-dating Prinair by a few months, **Antilles Air Boats**, based at St Croix, echoed Prinair's specialization policy, choosing, however, the flying-boat, partly because of admitted sentiment by its founder, Charles Blair, a veteran Pan American captain. Founded on 23 October, 1963, Blair concentrated on the Grumman Goose for his frequent service between the Virgin islands, and is affectionately remembered for his commendable efforts to preserve old flying-boats. He resurrected a Vought-Sikorsky VS-44A in January 1968. This was the same aircraft which had once operated for American Export Airlines across the Atlantic during the war, and its longevity in the face of corrosion problems was remarkable. More recently, after the VS-44 had to be taken out of service, Antilles Air Boats acquired two old Short Sandringhams which Blair flew in splendid walk-around luxury on his routes and, in 1976, made a sentimental journey across the Atlantic to re-trace the steps he had once pioneered with American Export.

Three Vought Sikorsky VS-44A flying-boats were built for the North Atlantic services of American Export Airlines. One was lost but two continued in service until replaced by landplanes after the war. The last survivor, *Excambia*, was used by Antilles Air Boats in the Virgin Islands from 1969 until 1971. It was the last Sikorsky flying-boat in service. (*Fritz Henle*)

Antilles Air Boats' Grumman G-73 Mallard amphibian N26DF taxi-ing at St Thomas, Virgin Islands, on 25 February, 1980. (*Robert C. Mikesh*)

Antilles Air Boats' Short flying-boat *Excalibur VIII* seen here at Washington D.C., on 9 October, 1974, was a Sunderland of the Royal New Zealand Air Force which was acquired by Ansett Airways and converted to near Sandringham standard for use on the Sydney–Lord Howe Island service. With Antilles Air Boats *Excalibur III* was registered VP-LVF. (*Robert C. Mikesh*)

159

Charles Blair lost his life in a Grumman Goose accident at St Thomas in September 1978. Antilles Air Boats was sold to Resorts International in April 1979, and the flying-boat service ended temporarily on 10 September, 1981. It resumed again on 15 March, 1982, as a new company, **Virgin Islands Seaplane Shuttle Inc**, with a small fleet of Grumman Mallards, continuing a now well-established tradition. Flying-boats mean to St Croix and the Virgin Islands what cable cars mean to San Francisco.

This area is also one of the last retreats of the Douglas DC-3. In 1983, not only was **Aero Virgin Islands** operating five of these venerable aircraft, some pre-dating the Second World War, on the San Juan–St Thomas shuttle service; but **Air BVI** (see also Table 13) was also operating five more from San Juan to Tortola, British Virgin Islands, and onwards to Antigua.

Aero Virgin Islands' Douglas C-53 N331P taking off from Harry S. Truman Airport, St Thomas.

Many other entrepreneurs in Puerto Rico and the Virgin Islands have joined Prinair and Antilles. Taking advantage of the phenomenal opportunities provided by the growth of the region as a vacation resort, at the same time recognizing air transport as the only practicable means of travel, a dozen or so Third Level or Commuter airlines have joined the ranks. These are listed in Tables 11 and 12.

By comparison with the intensive activity in Puerto Rico and the prosperous Virgin Islands, indigenous air services in neighbouring Hispaniola have been modest. In Haiti, the **Corps d'Aviation de la Garde d'Haiti** started domestic air mail services on 31 May, 1943, and was authorized to carry passengers the following year. During the 1950s, Garde d'Haiti operated DC-3s and a Boeing 307 Stratoliner. In 1961, the name was changed to **Compagnie Haitienne de Transports Aériens (COHATA)** as the national airline of Haiti. The Boeing Stratoliner was replaced by a Curtiss C-46.

During the immediate postwar period, the only other airline in Haiti was **Quisqueya, Ltd**, founded in March 1948 by James O. Plinton, an American negro who had been a flying instructor, later working for TWA and Eastern Air Lines. Plinton operated an inter-island service for about three years, linking Port-au-Prince with all the neighbouring islands, and with Miami, using a Boeing 247D and a Lockheed Lodestar. Plinton was the first to provide an air service to the Turks and Caicos Islands.

Much later, in 1961, a private company, Air Haiti International obtained permission to start international routes, but, in a confused situation, the Government of Haiti intervened and the proceeding was dismissed in February

Air Haiti's Curtiss C-46A HH-AHC *La Crête à Pierrot*. (*Harold G. Martin*)

1962, the issue at question being that the majority shareholding should be Haitian.

In 1973 the Government established Haiti Air Transport, presumably as a successor to, or reorganization of COHATA. It provided domestic services under the name of **Haiti Air Inter**, with Britten-Norman Islanders, and local international flights as **Haiti Air International**.

Another airline, **Air Haiti** was founded in December 1969, to operate non-scheduled cargo flights with Curtiss C-46s and Douglas DC-6s. In 1981 it obtained a licence to operate scheduled international cargo flights to Miami, New York, and San Juan, for which it leased two Boeing 707-331Cs.

Not long after Haiti joined the list of air transport nations, its next-door neighbour, the Dominican Republic, followed suit. On 5 May, 1944, **Compañía Dominicana de Aviación (CDA)** was organized by Guillermo Santoni Calero in conjunction with Pan American Airways, on the same lines as a number of Central American airlines, that is, with Pan Am holding 40 per cent of the shares. Operations started on 5 July, 1944, on a short domestic route, using a Ford Tri-Motor leased from Cubana. After an experimental period of hauling chilled beef to San Juan, Puerto Rico, the C.A.B. granted a full scheduled service certificate for routes to that city and to Miami in February 1951, and this service started soon afterwards.

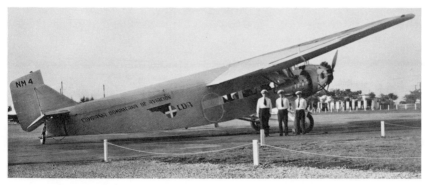

Compañía Dominicana de Aviación's Ford 4-AT-E Tri-Motor NM 4. The registration is Cuban and the true owner of this Ford may have been Pan American Airways'.

161

Dominicana's red, white and blue Boeing 727-2JI HI-242 *Duarte*. (*The Boeing Company*)

Pan American withdrew its interest on 26 July, 1957, and although discussions were held with other US companies, including Trans Caribbean Airways, CDA became wholly Dominican owned, through the Corporación Dominicana de Empresas Estatales (CORDE). Douglas DC-9s were acquired in 1970, followed by Boeing 727-100s in 1972, and route expansion was made to New York, Curaçao, and Caracas, the last in co-operation with the Venezuelan carrier VIASA.

Another airline whose aircraft were a familiar sight in the northern Caribbean area for several years was **Aerovías Nacionales Quisqueyana**, founded in 1962, and modifying its name to omit the 'Nacionales'—presumably at CDA's insistence—on 13 August, 1963. Although it acquired a Boeing 707-320 from Yugoslavia for a period during the late 1960s, Quisqueyana's mainline fleet consisted of Lockheed Constellations. When it finally ceased operations in 1980, the one still remaining, a Model 049, passed to Aerotours Dominicano, which continued to use it for freight charters around the Caribbean, supplementing two Model 1049C Super Constellations.

The Dominican Republic seems to have been the last happy hunting ground for the famous Lockheed airliner, as another company, **Argo, S.A.** was also still operating an 049 in 1980 on scheduled charter routes throughout the Antilles and to Miami, for which it had a C.A.B. permit from the USA. Argo had been founded on 13 February, 1971, and had used Curtiss C-46s and a Douglas DC-6A before obtaining its Constellation.

ARGO S.A.'s Lockheed 749A Constellation HI-328 was originally the USAF C-121A 48-615 and at one time General Vandenburg's *Dewdrop*. (*T. R. Waddington collection*)

Two Dominican domestic operators are of interest. **Alas del Caribe** was founded in 1967 and later acquired a fleet of Britten-Norman Islanders. One of the points served is Barahona, the birthplace of the Caribbean area's first airline, West Indian Aerial Express, way back in June 1927. Another company, **Aerolíneas Dominicanas, S.A.**, which started scheduled services in 1979 from Santo Domingo to San Juan, is one of the last remaining operators of the Martin 4-0-4.

A Reconstituted BWIA

Towards the latter 1950s, the whole question of British rule over the various colonies in the West Indies and Caribbean area generally came under scrutiny. While independence was recognized as inevitable and imminent, there was uncertainty as to the form it would take, and which parts of this scattered portion of the former British Empire would become fully independent. One idea which was widely canvassed at the time, and one which held out hopes for maintaining stability, was the possible formation of a West Indian Federation which could qualify for an honoured place at the Commonwealth Conference tables in London, should such a unit adopt Commonwealth status. Unfortunately, politics were a little more complex than the motivation for forming cricket teams, and as the various colonies chose to go their own ways rather than federate, the airline representing them, British West Indian Airways, found itself beset with many organizational problems, just at a time when it was poised for expansion.

The inclusion of Bahamas Airways' routes from Nassau to Florida and Havana in 1952 was a temporary expedient until BOAC linked these with its own services on the North Atlantic a few years later. BWIA concentrated on serving the West Indies, with connections to British Guiana, British Honduras, and Miami, via Jamaica. In co-operation with BOAC, a direct single-plane service to New York started from Antigua and San Juan, with BWIA controlling the segment as far as Bermuda. Vickers Viscounts were introduced in 1955 to improve the quality of service considerably. To cater for specialized air transport in the Leeward Islands, where most of the small islands possessed only short, often unpaved strips, BWIA helped to establish **Leeward Islands Air Transport Services (LIAT)** in 1956, providing 51 per cent of the capital, with the islands subscribing the remainder. A small Piper Apache paved the way for a developing air service network from Trinidad to the Virgin Islands. On 24 October, 1956, BWIA also purchased the assets of British Colonial Airlines and changed its name to **British Honduras Airways (BHA)** to consolidate its local position in that colony.

The outstanding event, however, during the last years of BOAC influence was to inaugurate a trans-Atlantic service to London. For this prestige operation, started on 29 April, 1960, BOAC leased a Britannia 312 to BWIA on one of its daily flights routed via New York. Additionally, the Britannia service from Port of Spain to New York was increased to a daily frequency on 11 December, and on 22 January, 1961, the same type served Miami. The following June, Boeing 707s replaced the Britannias to New York, so that BWIA could be said to be matching the best the competition could offer as preparations were made to change the controlling interest in the company.

On 1 November, 1961, the Trinidad Government paid BW$2,500,000 for 90 per cent of the stock of BWIA. BOAC retained four of the Viscount fleet and 10 per cent of the stock. Irrevocable differences between Trinidad and Jamaica prevented the latter country from participating in the new ownership, as the vision of West Indian Federation became submerged under the pressures of

This blue and white de Havilland Heron 2C was bought by BWIA in August 1965 and operated by Jamaica Air Services as 6Y-JED. (*T. R. Waddington*)

partisan and parochial ambitions. Also, for purely commercial reasons, Jamaica was not convinced that BWIA would do justice to the service demands between Kingston and Montego Bay and the lucrative US market. Jamaica, in short, preferred to go it alone. BWIA meanwhile sold British Honduras Airways to local businessmen, but to retain some interest in Jamaica, it formed **Jamaica Air Service Ltd** in May 1963, in association with local interests.

For many years, BWIA had to proceed cautiously, its finances limited. Nevertheless it did order three Boeing 727s in November 1963, the first one going on to the Miami route in January 1965. But with BOAC now out of the picture, the North Atlantic operation ceased. In September 1967, the Government of Trinidad and Tobago accepted in principle a proposal by a New York investment banking firm. for the reorganization, financing, and expansion of BWIA. On 14 December, 1968, a Boeing 707 was leased from QANTAS, and on 21 February, 1969, new financing was announced from a group of US investors, led by Allen & Co, a firm of brokers. On 3 May, 1969, service to Toronto began, after a licence was granted by the Canadian Government the previous day. During the next few years, charter services, including trans-Atlantic, were expanded, LIAT was sold to Court Line, a British independent operator. In April 1974, after the addition of further Boeing 707s, a scheduled service was resumed on the North Atlantic, direct from Trinidad and Barbados to London. After a difficult transition period, BWIA could thus be said to be back on its feet again.

This McDonnell Douglas DC-9-51, 9Y-TFF, was ordered by Finnair but delivery was delayed and it was leased by BWIA from July 1976 until July 1977 when it went to Finnair as OH-LYS. The main livery is gold and white, with a lower blue band and BWIA in red. The full title on the fuselage reads The Airline of Trinidad & Tobago BWIA International. (*McDonnell Douglas Corporation*)

164

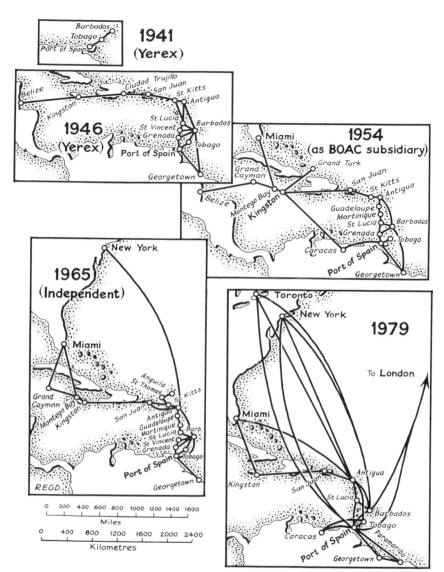

16. Development of BWIA, 1941–1979. Lowell Yerex's original route from Trinidad to Barbados first expanded to serve the British colonies in the West Indies. Later, as a BOAC subsidiary, it expanded to Florida. Then, becoming independent, it added long-distance routes, first to New York, then to Europe.

165

Air Jamaica

The British colony which did not come to the BWIA table, Jamaica, may be said to have been born on a wave of nationalism which regarded independence in its clearest terms. When, therefore, the first **Air Jamaica** was founded, on 27 August, 1963, BWIA's shareholding was only 16 per cent, while the Government of Jamaica had 51 per cent. BOAC, in association with its new partner, the Cunard shipping line, had 33 per cent. It was far from straightforward to start service to the United States, however, as the C.A.B was deeply suspicious of what might turn out to be a perfidious plot to circumvent the terms of the Bermuda Agreement between the United States and the United Kingdom. Eventually, after much delay while the C.A.B. ascertained the propriety of the wet-lease agreements signed with BOAC and BWIA, Air Jamaica started service to New York and Miami on 1 May, 1966.

During this adolescent period, all Jamaican BWIA employees were transferred to the new airline, while the foster parents still provided technical services, although they were now in competition. By 1967, the Jamaican Government decided that complete independence could be justified and looked for a partner to replace the illogical BOAC or BWIA. This action was also in line with C.A.B demands that Jamaica must have a national airline. Partly because of long-standing trading and cultural ties with Canada, the new **Air Jamaica (1968) Ltd** was founded in November 1968 with 40 per cent of $1,000,000 common stock subscribed by Air Canada. The first service under the new administration started on 1 April, 1969, the day after the old leasing agreements expired.

To help the new airline establish itself, two DC-9-30s were purchased, with the help of Canadian as well as Jamaican banks; and a DC-8-61 was leased from Air Canada. Late in 1968, the US Government committed a *faux pas* by announcing new Jamaican route awards to three US airlines, before a bilateral agreement had been signed; but the matter was straightened out, with Air Jamaica receiving generous reciprocity, and extensive route authority.

On 1 June, 1970, Air Jamaica began its steady programme of route expansion, aimed to tap the rich vacation-market potential in northern and eastern USA, by starting a service to Chicago, via Nassau, with full traffic rights at both points. Philadelphia was added on 1 December, 1971, Toronto on 1 March, 1972, and Detroit on 1 December, 1973. Trans-Atlantic service began direct to London on 1 April, 1974, and to Frankfurt on 26 October, 1975, using Douglas DC-8-62s.

An Air Jamaica Douglas DC-8. (*Harold G. Martin*)

ALM's McDonnell Douglas DC-9-15 PJ-DNA *Aruba* had been KLM's PH-DNE *Rome*.
(*Douglas Aircraft Company*)

The Jamaican airline demonstrated considerable marketing skill in providing a standard of on-board service which many larger airlines envied. In addition to the usual amenities, the Jamaican air hostesses—described as 'our rare tropical birds'—alternated between serving free Rum Bamboozles and giving in-flight fashion shows to the more-than-satisfied customers. And the novelty of the innovation was reflected in high load factors.

Dutch Transition

The West Indies Division of KLM maintained service continuously throughout the war. It preserved the great Dutch airline's distinguished record, and was in good shape to cope with postwar demands. The prewar ambition of starting a colonial service from Amsterdam to Curaçao was quickly realised. At first starting a series of weekly trial services via the Central Atlantic route via Dakar and Paramaribo on 10 April, 1946, this was suspended when the more direct link was made via New York on 4 June of that year. Paradoxically, this did not result in stimulating traffic for the West Indies Division, as the need for feeder services was reduced, especially as there were alternative ways to reach Europe.

Little expansion took place, therefore, and only a few new points were added to the network: Havana, via Ciudad Trujillo, Port-au-Prince, and Kingston, on 20 April, 1947, Panamá on 3 January, 1949, and Managua and San Salvador on 5 May, 1951. Douglas DC-3s and DC-4s were used during the immediate postwar period, but Convair CV-340s replaced the latter in 1954, the year in which the Netherlands West Indian colonies were given the status of full provinces of the Netherlands.

After ten uneventful years, on 1 August, 1964, the West Indies Division of KLM was converted into a wholly-owned subsidiary, **Antilliaanse Luchtvaart Maatschappij (ALM)**, at which time the Convair CV-340s were being supplemented by Convair CV-880 jets on lease. Finally, ALM became completely independent on 1 January, 1969. The President of the new airline was Ciro Yrausquin, who had throughout the transitional years promoted the idea of local autonomy, pointing out the advantages that would accrue in such matters as local traffic rights. He also urged that ALM should change its marketing thrust away from concentration on business traffic—mainly to serve the Royal Dutch Shell oil company—and develop the tourist trade.

Yrausquin replaced the CV-340s with two Fokker F.27-500s and two DC-9-32s, and then in April 1971 replaced the Fokkers with a third DC-9 to give ALM an all-jet fleet.

Cubana's Ilyushin Il-62M CU-T1215 in landing configuration. (*Harold G. Martin*)

Cubana Survives

When the Cuban revolutionary government emphatically cut off its political and commercial ties with the western world of which it was a geographical part, its economic problems were intensified, not least in the field of transport. As recorded earlier, most western sources of supply were severed, and for Cubana this constituted near-disaster. The communist world came to the rescue. The Soviet Union provided a fleet of seven Il-18s for mainline services and Il-14s for local routes. The Czechoslovak airline, ČSA, assisted in the operation of the three Britannias, which continued to operate to Prague and Madrid.

Cubana extended its route network to the south on 26 June, 1971, when a weekly service started to Santiago, via Lima. This action was motivated by the political affinities between the two capitals, now that Salvador Allende had come to power in Chile. The Santiago service was curtailed to Lima when Allende was assassinated on 11 September, 1973. Then on 24 April, 1972, Cubana's first jet, an Ilyushin Il-62, was introduced on the route to Madrid, via the Azores, and this aircraft replaced the Britannias to Prague, on 19 September, 1972, and—a new service—to Berlin on 3 April, 1973. Regionally, Il-18s began to serve Georgetown, Guyana, via Port of Spain and Bridgetown, on 3 October, 1973. Domestically, the Il-18s and the Antonov An-24s (which had supplemented the

Cubana leased this Douglas DC-8-43 from Air Canada in February 1976. The aircraft was reregistered CU-T1201 and painted in the Cubana livery introduced in 1970 – red fuselage stripes and rudder with very dark blue lettering and fin markings. (*T. R. Waddington*)

Il-14s since the late 1960s) were joined by some trijet Yak-40s each with 30 seats.

Still cut off from its neighbouring big power, the USA, by political barriers, air traffic between the two countries is limited mainly to regular flights for emigrants and refugees which are made under the joint auspices of the two governments, using chartered aircraft. For foreigners and the few US and Cuban citizens who wish to travel to Havana, the only practical air route is via Cubana's flights from Mexico City, where service has been continuous throughout all the upheavals on the political front.

Complexities in the Bahamas

During the difficult political atmosphere in the British West Indian colonies as the local communities strove to assert their independence, BWIA had endeavoured, as the agency of BOAC, to keep the air communications links going as an integrated system. Thus, from 1947 to 1963 various forms of association had been contrived: with British Guiana, through a management contract; the smaller islands, by the establishment of LIAT; a minority holding in the air activity in Jamaica; a loose link with the Bahamas through BOAC; and—uniquely in the British tradition—allowing a foreign airline (LACSA) to perform local services in the Cayman Islands.

During the latter 1960s, however, the tide of nationalism swept over the shores of British hegemony in the area, as each colony took its own road towards complete independence. BWIA's management contract with British Guiana Airways ended when Guyana Airways was formed in 1963. Its interest in Jamaica ended in 1968. In the same year, the Cayman Islands Government reorganized Cayman Brac Airways, originally operated on behalf of BWIA, and made a simpler arrangement with LACSA, to form **Cayman Airways**.

Elsewhere, BOAC seemed prepared to wash its hands of the whole local matter, preferring to concentrate on transocean routes to London. Almost inevitably, British entrepreneur airline personalities began to assess new opportunities for air transport enterprise, spurred by the successful promotion of vacation traffic in Europe. The Caribbean Islands seemed ready-made for airline investment.

One of the earliest of the swashbuckling private irritants to the British state airline near-monopoly had been Harold Bamberg, founder of the successful Eagle Airways. He had formed **Eagle Airways (Bermuda) Ltd** on 2 June, 1958, mainly to provide competitive services to New York; then, in the spring of 1959 **Eagle Airways (Bahamas) Ltd** had the same objective to Miami. Service started from Nassau, using Vickers Viscounts on 1 March, 1960, a notable improvement on Bahamas Airways' DC-3s. Bamberg completed a commercial coup in the same year by linking his British Eagle International Airways with the Cunard Steamship Company to form a formidable-looking **Cunard Eagle Airways**, which was awarded a British trans-Atlantic air route to serve Bermuda, Bahamas, and Miami. The first Britannia service opened on 15 October, 1960.

But Bamberg was cruelly rewarded for his enterprise. Within less than two years, the great Cunard company deserted him and formed an association with the state airline BOAC. The new airline, BOAC-Cunard, formed on 7 June 1962, took over as subsidiaries the two Eagle companies in Bermuda and Bahamas, which lost their separate identities. Bamberg lost his claim to retain ownership of the overseas companies, and sadly was forced out of the airline business by adverse decisions by the British Air Transport Licensing Board.

Bahamas Airways Ltd struggled on to maintain air service, as a subsidiary of BOAC. Its local flights to the outer islands were uneconomic, because of low traffic volumes, and the need to use small aircraft which lost money. Equally, the flights to Florida, conducted against heavy competition from several US operators, were on routes so short as to be economically marginal, at best. Curiously, BOAC never tried to establish the potentially lucrative route to New York for Bahamas Airways, convinced perhaps that some initiative should have come from the Bahamian Government itself. At all events, the latter, which had been prepared to help Eagle Airways and to issue a permit, did not see eye to eye with BOAC.

A bold effort was made to save Bahamas Airways in October 1968, when the British Swire Group, owners of Cathay Pacific Airways in Hong Kong, took a 60 per cent shareholding, installed a new management, and introduced BAC One-Elevens in an effort to revive the company's fortunes. But it was too late. Cathay could not turn the balance sheet around and decided to pull out, and Bahamas Airways ceased to exist early in 1973, forty years after its original foundation.

Coinciding with the attainment of independence for the Bahamas, a new company **Bahamasair**, stepped into the breech. It was founded on 18 June, 1973, as the national airline by amalgamating two existing small companies: **Out Island Airways**, which had operated Grumman Goose amphibians and other small types since the late 1960s; and **Flamingo Airways**, formed in March 1971, which had operated a variety of twin-engined Convairs and Martins, plus a BAC One-Eleven and a Lockheed Electra. The new company acquired a new fleet of two BAC One-Eleven 400s, two Fairchild Hiller FH-227Bs, and one Twin Otter, in an effort both to improve the service and to match the aircraft with the particular route requirements. But the inherent basic problems of air operations in the Bahamas prevailed, and Bahamasair also lost money heavily, forcing it to prune its staff and cut services in 1976. In fairness, the new airline started at a bad time: just as the price of aviation fuel suddenly increased because of the action of the OPEC oil producers' actions.

Bahamasair sought a solution to its problems by hiring Aer Lingus as management consultants in December 1977. The first step towards rejuvenation was to start additional service between Miami and Bahamian islands other than to Nassau and Grand Bahama; and to open direct service from Fort Lauderdale, at the same time intensifying frequencies on the busy Miami–Nassau sector.

Equipment changes were made. On 15 December, 1978, a 130-seat Boeing 737-200 was leased for the trunk route, thus releasing BAC One-Elevens for other routes. Four Hawker Siddeley HS.748s were acquired from BAC to replace the Fairchilds. On 13 December, 1979, a new route was added to the mainland, direct to Nassau from Atlanta, a pleasing departure from the overcrowded airways from Florida.

Trans-Atlantic Ambitions Realized

The Bahamas may have experienced frustration in the local and regional airways but had never lacked good connections with Great Britain. While BOAC may have neglected local route development in the Caribbean, it always provided good service to Nassau, either via New York, or Bermuda, or direct; and had demonstrated its determination to secure the area permanently when it usurped Eagle's neatly contrived foothold by siding with Cunard. BOAC, however, laid

Air Bahama's red and white Douglas DC-8-55F N802SW was leased from Seaboard World Airlines during the winter of 1969–70. (*T. R. Waddington*)

itself open to challenge by charging consistently higher fares than many private airlines felt were necessary. Accordingly, on 22 July, 1968, Norman Ricketts, an enterprising English financier, started Boeing 707 service from Nassau to Europe with a new company, **Air Bahama (International) Ltd**. To evade the traffic restrictions imposed by the British Government at the time, Ricketts had to fly to Luxembourg, but his fare undercut the lowest offered by BOAC so that the extra flight from London to Luxembourg was well worthwhile.

Ricketts sold his company to the Icelandic airline, Loftleidir, in August 1969. The Icelanders, pioneers of low-fares and past masters at exploiting Fifth or Sixth Freedom traffic opportunities, changed the name to **International Air Bahama**, integrated the service pattern with its own Luxembourg–New York (via Iceland) route, and deployed its own Douglas DC-8 aircraft to Nassau. In 1976, the airline became known simply as **Air Bahama**.

Norman Ricketts moved on to Barbados, where he repeated his success in the Bahamas. He founded **International Caribbean Airways (ICA)** in September 1970 and began flying to Luxembourg on 14 December, 1970, with service to London on 14 December, 1971. Laker Airways supplied the Boeing 707 for the operation. Later, when Laker Airways was awaiting permission to start its Skytrain service,

Laker Airways white, red and black Boeing 707-351B G-BFBZ on lease to International Caribbean Airways as *Bridgetown*.

171

the Douglas DC-10s ordered for the purpose were sometimes deployed on the ICA route.

In January 1975, ICA became the national airline of Barbados, which had joined the new independent nations of the Caribbean. The Barbados Government took the 51 per cent majority shareholding, with Laker the remaining 49 per cent.

In addition to the many European flag airlines providing trans-Atlantic service direct to the Caribbean, as well as Pan American, there were soon four new national participants from the area, Air Jamaica and BWIA joining Air Bahama and ICA in the market on 1 April and 6 April, 1974, respectively.

LIAT's Hawker Siddeley HS.748 Series 2 VP-LIK was delivered in May 1965.
(*British Aerospace*)

There might have been a fifth, if some ambitious plans of another British private group had come to fruition. BWIA, which had established LIAT to serve the special needs of the many small British islands in the Leewards and Windwards group, was becoming disenchanted with the responsibility of sustaining unprofitable routes for the social needs of communities which were no more inclined to align themselves politically with Trinidad than they were with Great Britain. Nevertheless, good service was maintained to 22 points, with a combination of HS.748s and Britten-Norman BN-2 Islanders, aircraft which, in the circumstances of the short-stage operations into small airstrips, were ideal for the purpose.

172

In November 1971, Court Line, which had experienced a meteoric rise to the front rank of British independent airlines, purchased BWIA's 75 per cent share of LIAT for $4 million. It saw an opportunity to turn LIAT into a regional airline in its own right, with services to the South American mainland and the USA, with ultimate connection to the United Kingdom and Court's other route system, for which it had ordered two Lockheed TriStars. But pride came before a plummeting fall. Although it added more HS.748s and two BAC One-Elevens, LIAT continued to incur losses. At first, on 8 June, 1973, Court tried to raise fares, but the island governments refused. It then cut service and some islands acquiesced to the new fares. Service to those that did not was suspended until they did, and altogether there was much acrimony between the parties. To add to the problem, this was the time of the fuel crisis, which forced the withdrawal of the new jet services, right at the height of the winter vacation season. Court Line's difficulties were not confined to the Caribbean; indeed they were even worse back in Britain, and in August 1974 it went into bankruptcy. LIAT was kept alive by emergency aid from Britain and the local governments, and the latter took action to preserve their vital air link by forming a new **Leeward Islands Air Transport (1974)**. The new ownership was shared between the governments of St Lucia, St Vincent, Dominica, Antigua, St Kitts-Nevis, and Granada, with funds provided from Venezuela and with Air Canada as consultants. After some precarious months, services were restored, and an agreement was reached with BWIA to avoid pointless competition.

The French and other Colonial Connections

During recent years, the remnants of some of the outposts of European colonial empires cast off their invisible chains and went their own independent way. Among the smaller islands of the West Indies which are part of the Lesser Antilles, and known also as the Leeward and Windward Island groups, the resultant fragmentation of sovereignty produced many problems of practical government and fluent commerce. Not least of the difficulties was the search for a co-ordinated inter-island airline system. The colonial rivalries still survived, with British, French, Dutch and American local administrations controlling their own little parishes. To these were added new republics, with Trinidad and Tobago, which had been one of the first to gain independence, joined by Barbados, Grenada, Dominica, and St Lucia. Some aspired to launch their own airlines, but the scale of traffic potential, dictated by the tiny populations of each, militated against airline viability.

A few managed to establish themselves and some achieved permanency. These delightful examples of the Third Level are listed and summarised in Table 13. Names like Arawak, Air Turks & Caicos, and Air Guadeloupe evoke the charm of the air equivalent to Caribbean beachcombing, in small twin-engined aircraft like the Britten-Norman Islander, open to any traveller who cares to wander off the beaten track from the sophisticated resorts of San Juan or Montego Bay. From San Juan to Port of Spain it is theoretically possible to travel through the territories of twelve different administrations, without once taking a jet, and with the distinct chance of surveying the Caribbean scene from a reasonably close viewpoint. The airlines of the Antilles may not be very large, but few can offer more pleasurable travel, not to mention a few curiosities such as the Dutch company based in what the British call the Leeward Islands but which calls itself by the older term now usually used only for the islands south of Guadeloupe.

TABLE 11

Commuter Airlines in Puerto Rico (and Vieques)
(in order of service inauguration date)

Date	Airline	Routes	Main Equipment	Remarks
June 1964	Trade Winds & Western Airways	San Juan–St Thomas, Culebra, and points in Puerto Rico	Twin Otter	Tradewinds Airways began irregular charters, 15 June, 1959. Tradewinds acquired Western Air Services in 1968. Started with Beech 18. Terminated in mid-1970s
4 July, 1964	**Puerto Rico International Airlines (Prinair)**	San Juan–Ponce, Mayagüez, Virgin Islands, Netherlands Antilles, Guadeloupe and Santo Domingo	Heron CV-580	One of the largest of all US-registered commuter airlines. Very high frequency to main points (see text)
21 Oct, 1964	North Cay Airways	San Juan–Virgin Islands	DC-3 BN-2	Operations ceased in 1967
Oct 1964	**Dorado Wings**	Dorado Beach and San Juan to St Thomas (for St John) and Virgin Gorda (BVI)	BN-2 Jetstream	Formed by Henry Wolf in 1958 as affiliate to the Rockresorts organization (Rockefeller interests) based at Dorado Beach. Changed name to **Crownair**, 2 November, 1981, under new ownership

Date	Airline	Aircraft	Routes	Notes
Sept 1967	**Air Indies**	Beech 18 Beech 99 Twin Otter DC-3	San Juan–St Thomas, St Croix, Ponce, Mayagüez	Formed originally to make scenic flights from Miami to Bahamas. Owned Colony Airlines, of Nassau. Ambitious schedule frequency, but operations terminated in 1973
May 1972	Vieques Air Link	BN-2A	Vieques–US Virgin Islands and to San Juan	Originally incorporated as air taxi operator in October 1965
15 Nov, 1975	Air Mont	Bonanza	Vieques–San Juan, Culebra, and other points in Puerto Rico	Founded by Capt Yves Dumont, 5 November, 1975
Dec 1975	Air Caribbean	DC-3	San Juan–Aguadilla (P.R.) ard US Virgin Islands	Owned by Old South Air Service, Inc. Ceased operations in 1979
1979	**Casair**	C-46	Scheduled air freight to Caribbean Islands	Originally Caribbean Air Services, St Croix (see Table 12)
8 Nov, 1979	**Oceanair**	F-27 CASA-200	San Juan–St Thomas, San Juan–St Croix	Purchased assets of Trans-Commuter Airlines, founded in 1973, operating irregularly with Queen Airs. Began service to Dominican Republic, 18 February, 1983

Note: During the late 1960s and early 1970s, several small airlines operated regular services between San Juan and St Thomas, invariably during the vacation season. Among these companies which specialized in the so-called 'booze run' to the duty-free emporia of St Thomas were Caribbean Executive, Air Best, Ponce Air, and St Thomas Air Taxi. The Beech 18 was the most commonly-used aircraft.

TABLE 12

Commuter Airlines in the US Virgin Islands
(in order of service inauguration date)

Date	Airline	Routes	Main Equipment	Remarks
Sept 1960	Tropical Flight Service	St Croix–Tortola, St Croix–Vieques–Humacao	Aero Commander	Founded by Bill Bohlke Sr, to carry British West Indian indentured labourers for periodic passport checking to comply with US regulations.
Late 1963	**Virgin Island Airways**	St Croix–St Thomas St Croix–San Juan	Beech 18 Dove Heron	Also founded by Bohlke. Routes and some aircraft sold to Prinair, early 1968
Autumn 1964	**Antilles Air Boats**	St Croix–St Thomas, other US Virgin Islands, and to San Juan	Goose	Founded 23 October, 1963, by Charles Blair, ex-Pan Am pilot. Operated a VS-44A, 1968, and later two Sandringhams and some Mallards. Ceased operations 10 September, 1981 (see text)
Early 1968	Caribbean Air Services (Casair)	St Croix–San Juan, and to neighbouring islands in Virgin group. C.A.B. certificated routes from Haiti to St Lucia (Freight only)	DC-3 Beech 18 C-46	Also founded by Bohlke. Purchased by Midland Capital, 1 May, 1974, and base transferred to San Juan, 1979 (see Table 11)

Date	Airline	Routes	Aircraft	Notes
1968	Inter-Island Airways	St Thomas–Tortola	Geronimo BN-2	Founded by Jack Chapman. Ceased operations, 19 March, 1980
1969	Caribbean Island Airways	St Thomas–San Juan	Beech 18	Ceased operations, mid-1970s
19 Dec, 1970	Virgin Air	St Thomas–St Barthélémy (French West Indies)	Apache Aztec	Founded by Paul and Margaret Wikander
March 1975	Eastern Caribbean Airways	St Croix–St Thomas, St Croix–Nevis	Beech 18, Pipers, Twin Otter	Founded by Bill Bohlke Jr and Ruth Bohlke in 1960 as Virgin Island Flight School. Route authority purchased by Coral Air, May 1980
Late 1975	Clipper Air International	St Croix– St Juan, St Croix–St Maarten, St Croix–Tortola	Beech 18	Founded by J. S. Jervis. Service terminated 1976
4 March, 1977	Aero Virgin Islands	St Thomas–San Juan, St Thomas–St Croix	DC-3	Founded by Joe Cranston
15 Feb, 1980	Coral Air	St Croix–St Thomas–San Juan, St Croix–Tortola	Twin Otter	Founded by J. S. Jervis, beginning service with five Australian Nomads. Under new ownership 6 August, 1982.
15 March, 1982	V. I. Seaplane Shuttle	St Croix–St Thomas, St John, and Tortola	Malllard	Replaced the Antilles Air Boats service (see text)
5 July, 1982	Sunaire	St Croix–St Thomas	Twin Otter	Founded by Stephen Milden, 1 April, 1981

TABLE 13

Commuter Airlines in the Caribbean (Other than US)

(in order of service inauguration date)

Territory	Airline	Date of First Service	Routes	Main Equipment	Remarks
French West Indies	Air Antilles	Jan 1957	Basse Terre–Marie Galante; Fort de France; St Barthélémy	DC-3 Apache BN-2 Beech 18	Formed as Antilles Air Service in 1954. Changed name to Air Antilles in 1964. Scheduled service to F de F and St B. on 26 July, 1977, but ceased operations in March 1978
	Air Guadeloupe	July 1970	Point-à-Pitre and Basse Terre to Marie Galante, St Barthélémy, St Martin, Dominica, Fort de France, and other small French islands	BN-2 DHC-6 DC-3 F.27	
	Air Martinique	1978	Fort de France–St Lucia, St Vincent, Grenada, and Dominica	BN-2 F-27	Began as charter operator in June 1974
Netherlands Antilles	Windward Islands Airways	5 Aug, 1962	St Maarten–Netherlands, British, French Leeward Islands	Twin Bonanza DHC-6 BN-2	
British Virgin Islands	**Air BVI**	Aug 1971	Tortola–British West Indies, and Puerto Rico	BN-2A DC-3 HS.748	Formed as Air British Virgin Islands in June 1971. Holds US Foreign Air Route Carrier permit

178

Location	Airline	Date	Routes	Aircraft	Remarks
Caicos Islands			Cap-Haïtien (Haiti)	DC-3	Formed by T & C Govt (30%), Trans-Jamaican Airlines (35%), and local interests to take over services previously flown by TIGAS (Turks and Caicos Islands) Government Air Services
Trinidad	Arawak Airlines, Ltd	June 1970	Port of Spain–Tobago	CV-440 Beech 99	Took over route from BWIA
	Trinidad & Tobago Air Services Ltd	June 1974	Port of Spain–Tobago	DC-6B HS.748	Took over from BWIA after Caribbean United Airlines ceased operations
Jamaica	Jamaica Air Services Ltd	June 1963	Montego Bay–Kingston, Port Antonio, Mandeville, Ocho Rios, Grand Turk	Heron	Subsidiary of BWIA. Ceased operations about 1969
	Trans-Jamaican Airlines Ltd	1975	As above	BN-2A DC-3	Formerly Jamaica Air Taxi, Ltd. Helped form Air Turks & Caicos in 1976
Anguilla. BWI	Valley Air Service	1977	Anguilla–other British and Netherlands Leeward Is, and to St Thomas	BN-2	Founded by Clayton Lloyd; ceased operations Dec 1979
Montserrat	Montserrat Airways	1979	Local services	BN-2A DHC-6	
St Vincent	St Vincent and The Grenadines Air Service	Mar 1976		Apache BN-2A	
	Mustique Airlines	Apr 1980		BN-2 Baron	

179

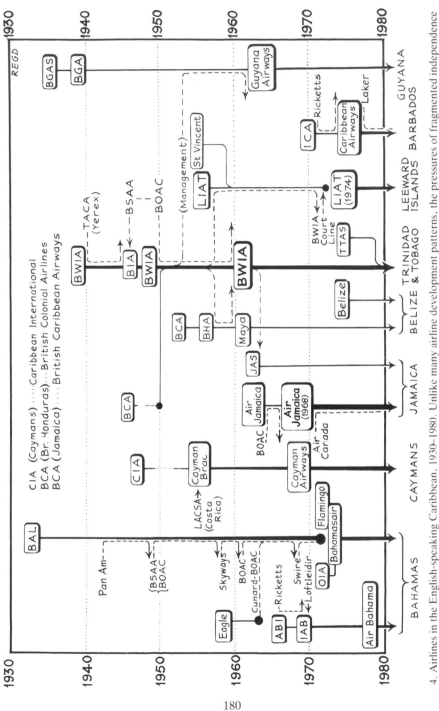

4. Airlines in the English-speaking Caribbean, 1930–1980. Unlike many airline development patterns, the pressures of fragmented independence movements in the Caribbean area have ensured that a federated airline system is as far from consummation as when BOAC cherished a hope of a BWIA which would act as an instrument of co-operation in 1950.

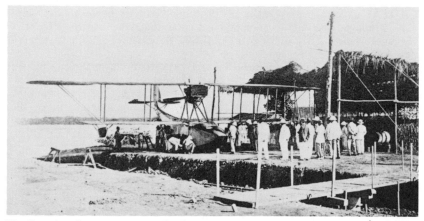

The first aircraft to operate sustained non-seasonal scheduled services anywhere in the Americas were the Lévy-Lepen single-engined flying-boats of Société des Transports Aériens Guyanais. These small flying-boats are believed to have been of the Type R. Photographs of the type are extremely rare but, although of poor quality, this is a genuine picture taken in French Guiana.

CHAPTER EIGHT

The Guianas

The First Scheduled Airline in Latin America

The three Guianas, British, French, and Dutch, survived as the only colonial possessions in South America after the Spanish and Portuguese colonies gained their independence in the early decades of the 19th Century. Immune from the pressures of Monroe Doctrine principles, the three colonies were seldom regarded as of much importance, as their agricultural production was small, their mineral resources confined to dreams of Eldorado gold, and their strategic importance negligible. They were in fact the poor relations of rich empires, and unfortunately best known during the 20th Century for the notorious French penal colony of Devil's Island.

To record a minor claim to fame, therefore, is a satisfactory contrast; for in French Guiana was born one of the world's first airlines. Debates about firstliness are considered by some to be irrelevant, and lead to problems about definition among those who care about such things. Let it be recorded, however, that the **Société des Transports Aériens Guyanais (T.A.G.)** was the first airline in the Americas founded to operate a sustained schedule service; and which went into operation, without seasonal interruption, for the transport of both passengers and freight. Earlier aspirants to the claim of being first do not fulfil all the qualifications as stated. The St Petersburg-Tampa Airboat Line of 1914 lasted only three months; the first Colombian airline, C.C.N.A., did not get under way until later in 1920, and its service was spasmodic, and was not sustained;

SCADTA made a survey flight in 1920 but did not begin service until 1921—although it has operated continuously under that name and as AVIANCA ever since. Other early services in the USA were either seasonal, suffered interruptions, or were for mail only.

On the other hand, the Société des Transports Aériens Guyanais was founded on 7 June, 1919, before any of the other claimants, began operations soon afterwards, and operated on a regular schedule from 12 October, 1920, until the company was disbanded two years later. With headquarters in Paris, the company's operating base was at Saint Laurent du Maroni, at the mouth of the Maroni River which divides French Guiana and Surinam—then known as Dutch Guiana. From this base, a flying-boat service linked Saint Laurent not only with Cayenne, capital of the colony, but also with Inini, a point some 250 km up the Moroni River. The aircraft type used was the Lévy-Lepen, of which type the Société obtained six during the summer of 1919, from war-surplus stocks. This little flying-boat carried two passengers and had a unique record: not only did it pioneer air services in America but also flew the first regular service in Africa south of the Sahara.

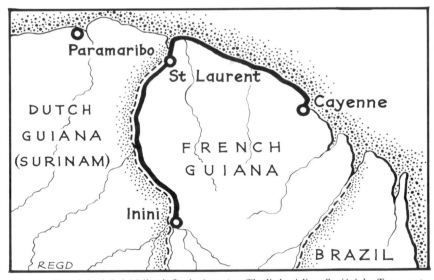

17. The First Scheduled Airline in Latin America. The little airline, Société des Transports Aériens Guyanais (TAG) can lay a legitimate claim to being the first regularly scheduled airline to operate on a sustained basis in the whole of the Americas. Beginning service in October 1920, its Lévy-Lepens and Breguet 14s maintained a vital air link in French Guiana until October 1922.

T.A.G. completed its first inter-city flight from Saint Laurent to Cayenne on 12 October, 1919, and subsequently made several demonstration flights along the coast and up the Maroni River. But there were some mishaps with the fragile aircraft and they were temporarily retired from service in April 1920.

The little Lévy-Lepen biplane had fabric wings and a wooden hull, which suffered badly from the climate or from the wildlife—the fabric either literally came unglued, or was eaten by insects, and the hulls were easily damaged. Four new aircraft were obtained from France, with aluminium cladding on the hull, and when these arrived, regular service was inaugurated from Saint Laurent to Inini, twice weekly, starting on 7 October, 1920. An additional service from Saint Laurent to Cayenne was added on 10 October.

Lignes de Guyane

MARDI & VENDREDI			MERCR. & SAMEDI
15.00	Inini		9.00
17.00	Saint-Laurent		7.00
LUNDI & JEUDI			MARDI & VENDREDI
15.30	Cayenne		9.00
17.15	Saint-Laurent		7.00

Correspondances.
à Cayenne avec tous les courriers de France.

Cie DES TRANSPORTS AERIENS GUYANAIS

A Paris :
A Paris : 13, rue Notre-Dame-des-Victoires. Tél. : Gutenberg 53-90.
A Cayenne :
A Saint-Laurent-du-Maroni.

APPAREILS
Levy le Pen — 300 chevaux — 2 passagers — 400 kgs.
Limousine Breguet — 300 chevaux — 3 passagers — 450 kgs.

TRANSPORT DES PASSAGERS

		Aller et retour
Tarifs.		
Saint-Laurent-du-Maroni à Cayenne ou vice-versa......Fr. 200		500
Saint-Laurent-du-Maroni à Inini ou vice-versa............ 500		800
Cayenne-Saint-Laurent-Inini ou vice-versa................ 650		1.000

Bagages.
15 kgs en franchise.

TRANSPORT DES MESSAGERIES

Cayenne-Saint-Laurent .... **2 fr.** le kilog avec minimum de **2 fr. 50**
Saint-Laurent-Inini................ .... **3 fr.** le kilog avec minimum de **5 fr.** »

SOCIÉTÉ des TRANSPORTS AÉRIENS GUYANAIS

Siège Social : 13, Rue Notre-Dame-des-Victoires — Tél. Gut. 53-90 — PARIS
Siège d'Exploitation Saint-Laurent du Maroni (Guyane Française)
PASSAGERS - MARCHANDISES - POSTE
SERVICE RÉGULIER ULTRA RAPIDE PAR HYDRO — LIMOUSINE entre :
SAINT-LAURENT : Cayenne en 2 heures — SAINT-LAURENT : Inini en 2 heures
Correspondance avec tous les courriers venant de France

— 33 —

Lignes de Guyane Timetable, 1922. This extract from *L'Indicateur Aérien* of June 1922 is one of the earliest known which relates to air transport in Latin America, and is of special interest as it shows the operation of the first non-seasonal sustained scheduled air service in all the Americas.

183

By March 1921, 13,754 km had been flown, and 64 passengers carried on forty flights. There were also several cancellations because of bad weather. An experiment was made with a steel hull on the Lévy-Lepen, but the solution to the problems was sought by introducing four Breguet 14Tbis Limousine three-seat seaplanes. The service ended on 30 October, 1922, and unfortunately few records remain of this isolated example of air enterprise, although the Exhibit reproduced recalls the nostalgia of long-forgotten standards of travel at the dawn of commercial air transport.

Air Connections

In 1927, an attempt was made to start air services in British Guiana by the British Guiana Air Transport Company, Ltd, which acquired two seaplanes from the Real Daylight Balata Estates, Ltd, with the intention of providing one or two local routes. The colonial government approved the payment of an annual £3,250 subsidy, for three years, but the plans failed to materialize through lack of capital. Later, in 1929, a company called Atlantic Airways Ltd proposed to operate a weekly service from Georgetown to Port of Spain, Trinidad, with ambitious ideas of extending this northwards to Canada, where discussions were held the following year. But nothing came of this scheme.

The Guianas were by this time being recognized for their strategic value in some intercontinental plans for air routes by some of the major powers. The visionary Aéropostale company planned a connection from Natal, Brazil, along the northeast coast of South America to connect the existing mail route from France to Brazil and Argentina with the French West Indian colonies, via the Guianas. Aéropostale actually established a subsidiary airline in Venezuela, as a link in this chain, but the company was forced into liquidation in 1931 and the French did not pursue the matter until after the war.

It was left to the United States to provide the first air links between the Guianas and the outside world. Pan American Airways, having been awarded all the mail contracts it wanted by an indulgent Postmaster General, extended its mail route from Port of Spain to Paramaribo, via Georgetown, using Sikorsky S-38 amphibians, on 23 September, 1929. This was to remain the southern terminus of

British Guiana Air Service's Fairchild 71 NC9108 *The Lotus*.

the US flag carrier until 27 November, 1930. On that date, the pioneering east coast route from Miami to Rio de Janeiro and Buenos Aires, which was started on 26 February, 1930, by the enterprising New York, Rio and Buenos Aires Line, was absorbed into Pan American's system. Pan Am was thus able to substitute the fine Consolidated Commodore flying-boats which had been developed especially for the route, under the direction of Capt Ralph O'Neill. These were subsequently replaced by the famous Sikorsky *Clipper* 'boats, the S-40 and the S-42, so that the Guianas enjoyed excellent service from the three colonial capitals northwards and southwards from that time.

The Dutch were next on the scene. The mid-1930s were great days for their national airline, KLM, which set records of achievement in intercontinental air service out of all proportion to the Netherlands' relative status as a world power. During 1934, KLM astonished the world by coming in second in the spectacular England–Australia Air Race. The feat was notable because a standard airliner, a Douglas DC-2, was used in competition with specially-designed racing types. KLM's noteworthy flight with the *Uiver* in that race in October 1934 was talked about in aviation circles for many months afterwards and could be said to have changed the course of airliner development the world over. It certainly overshadowed another achievement by KLM during the same year. For between 15 and 22 December—KLM liked to time its great flights for the festive season—the Fokker F.XVIII *Snip* flew from Amsterdam to Curaçao, Netherlands West Indies, via the South Atlantic route, calling at Paramaribo. The journey took eight days, but this was commercially less important than the positioning of the nucleus of an aircraft fleet in the area.

After carefully and methodically developing a route network in the Caribbean KLM opened service to Paramaribo, as an extension of its route from Curaçao to Port of Spain, on 4 September, 1939. By this time, the two F.XVIIIs of the West Indies fleet had been supplemented by four Lockheed 14s. To its great credit, KLM continued to operate its West Indian network, including the service to Paramaribo, throughout the war (which had broken out simultaneously with the service to Dutch Guiana). This service contributed substantially to the Allied war effort by supplementing Pan American and the TACA organization, which also operated through Paramaribo during the latter part of the war.

Local Services in Guiana Again

About the same time when KLM was making all the headlines in 1934, a US citizen, A. J. Williams, who had tried to start an air service in the Bahamas but had lost his aircraft in a hurricane, tried his luck again in British Guiana. He made some experimental flights with an Ireland amphibian, and did some useful work for the British Guiana-Brazil Boundary Commission—trying to settle one of the many sources of disagreement on the issue of national frontiers.

This led to his obtaining a contract with the colonial government on 30 January, 1939, to form **British Guiana Airways, Ltd (BGA)**, to operate on a state-assisted basis. Williams made some of the first experiments with what later became known as an Air Beef operation, whereby cattle in the grazing lands in the south and central parts of the colony were slaughtered there and the meat brought by air to Georgetown. This was a more economical way of bringing the product to the market, compared with driving the cattle through bad terrain for hundreds of kilometres. But the Air Beef idea was not put on a commercial footing until September 1948.

British Guiana Airways Grumman G.21A Goose VP-GAD on the Demerara River at Mackenzie (now Linden) in 1958. (*Courtesy Buzz Piggott*)

Meanwhile, in June 1944, Williams had started two regular air services for passengers, mail, and freight from Georgetown to Tumereng and the Rupunimi cattle district. Frequency was minimal, fortnightly to the former, and monthly to the latter; but it was a start, and at least provided valuable experience in mounting a regular service. This event occurred on 6 September, 1945, when British West Indian Airways (BWIA) opened a route from Port of Spain to Georgetown, and British Guiana Airways was subcontracted to provide a short feeder service between the bauxite town Mackenzie and the city of Georgetown, about 45 miles away. This was started with a single Grumman Goose amphibian, but BGA was able to augment this minimum capacity by adding a second Goose, plus two Douglas C-47s, in 1946.

Although the shuttle service became redundant soon afterwards, because the necessary highway improvements had been made, BGA's Goose amphibians were sub-contracted to operate a local service based at St Vincent in the Windward Islands, and connecting with BWIA's inter-island services. The amphibians were able to provide what would now be called Third Level service into small strips, where even the C-47s could not land.

An unidentified British Guiana Airways Douglas C-47 at Mackenzie International Airport, en route to Orinduik. (*Courtesy Buzz Piggott*)

British Guiana Airways was operating a commendable domestic service by 1948, reaching outlying points in the Colony, catering for gold shipments, maintaining the Air Beef operation (now going well), and providing charter flights for the more adventurous tourists to the Kaieteur Falls. However, the total volume of traffic was still quite small, annual passenger numbers reaching only about 7,500 by 1954.

In July 1955, the colonial government took control, buying A. J. Williams's shareholding for £170,000. BWIA was asked to take over the management of what was essentially a feeder operation to that airline's Caribbean network. The regional routes of BGA were then terminated. Late in 1963, as the colony moved towards independence (achieved in 1966) the name of the airline was changed to the **Guyana Airways Corporation**, since when the domestic network has been expanded, and the old equipment replaced by propeller-turbine aircraft, including the Twin Otter, Hawker Siddeley HS.748, and a Lockheed 188 Electra. Two DC-6As maintain a non-scheduled cargo service to Miami.

Guyana Airways' de Havilland DHC-4A Caribou 8R-GDO. Very few Caribou have seen commercial service but two were used by Guyana Airways in the early 1970s.
(*T. R. Waddington collection*)

Domestic air service in Dutch Guiana started about ten years after that of its British neighbour. Late in 1954, **Surinaamse Luchtvaart Maatschappij, N.V. (S.L.M.)** was founded by the Dutch colonial government and began to operate the following year on a small network along the coast in both directions from Paramaribo. Traffic was sparse, even though by this time Paramaribo was connected directly with Amsterdam, the southerly Central Atlantic route via Sal Island having been opened by KLM on 29 May, 1949, to provide service to the Dutch Caribbean without having to go through North America. The Dutch portion of the Guiana hinterland was not as productive as the British, and only small light aircraft were employed until 30 August, 1962, when the official name was registered and a DC-3 was added. Then in 1964 a joint service was started with ALM, with S.L.M. providing cabin crews. Later, asserting its status as a colony in its own right, rather than as an offshoot of the Netherlands Antilles, S.L.M. leased a Douglas DC-9 from ALM (formerly the West Indies Division of KLM) to start its own service to Curaçao, via Port of Spain.

On 27 November, 1975, Surinam gained its independence from the Netherlands, having already, on 2 November, celebrated its political freedom by

Guyana Airways' Boeing Advanced 737-2L9 OY-APR leased from Maersk Air of Denmark. Livery is yellow and dark green.

leasing a Douglas DC-8 from KLM and operating it to Amsterdam under S.L.M. colours. It thus became the first—and so far the only—airline in the Guianas to fly long-distance trunk air services. Additional routes were added during the late 1970s to Miami, Manaus, and Belém.

Further east, Cayenne had been connected directly with Paris, via Paramaribo and Fort-de-France, where Air France established a flying-boat base for its six-engined Latécoère 631s. These large trans-Atlantic airliners had originally been designed to specifications laid down in 1936 and, although making the first flight in 1942, did not enter service until 26 July, 1947. Their presence on the aviation scene was short-lived, as accidents forced the withdrawal of the type on 1 August, 1948. Possibly spurred by the experience of being directly connected

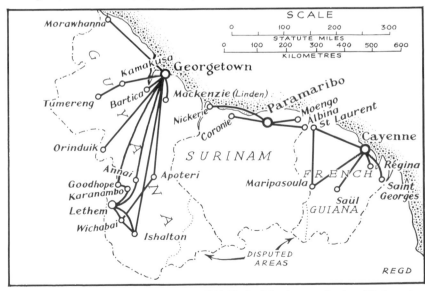

18. Domestic Air Routes in the Guianas, 1960. Each of the three territories of Guiana, two of them now independent states (Guyana and Surinam), has a small domestic network to serve its local needs.

188

This Douglas DC-8-55F was originally delivered to Philippine Air Lines in August 1965 as PI-C802. It became KLM's PH-DCW *Gerard Mercator*, spent further time with PAL and in this view bears Surinam Airways' yellow, orange and red livery and the name *Sabaku* but retains its Netherlands registration. (*Harold G. Martin*)

with the homeland, a small company was formed in Cayenne to handle the furthest outpost of the Air France Caribbean network.

This agency, the **Société Aérienne de Transports Guyane-Antilles (SATGA)**, eventually began to operate services of its own, rather similar to those of the neighbouring colonies; but traffic demand was also not substantial. French Guiana, unlike the British and Dutch colonies, remains politically a department of France, and the incentive to have an independent airline for regional operation has not been evident. SATGA appears to have been renamed **Guyane Air Transport (GAT)**, possibly to make identification with the colony easier and to avoid confusion with other acronyms.

It is perhaps a disappointing commentary on the lack of economic progress made in the French colony to reflect that the domestic air operation today differs only slightly from the one started sixty years ago. The aircraft are a little more modern, the network is a few kilometres longer, but the basic service rendered to the local populace is much the same. Perhaps there should be some consolation that the Britten-Norman Islanders of GAT did not need to be impregnated against termites.

Zanderij Airport, Paramaribo, Surinam. The date of the picture is not known. (*KLM*)

CHAPTER NINE

Venezuela

Aéropostale

Although Venezuela has its fair share of mountains, jungles, and other terrestrial barriers to communications, air transport did not enter the transport scene until much later than in most of the countries of South America. Venezuela's population is concentrated mainly along or near the coast. There are no large cities inland, and scattered short railway lines have always been able to provide the necessary links between populated areas and ports. Venezuela's major problem for passenger and freight transport used to be the formidable water barrier provided by the Orinoco River, which bisects the country into roughly equal parts. While not in the same league as the Amazon, this is a truly great river, with its 240 tributaries draining a large area affected by heavy rainfall, ensuring that the lower reaches of the main stream are wide and treacherous.

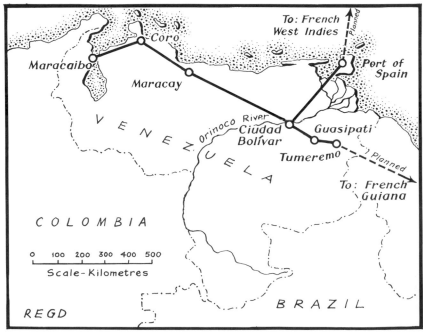

19. Aéropostale de Venezuela, 1930. The Venezuelan branch of Marcel Bouilloux-Lafont's Aéropostale empire was a strategic focal point of potential routes which were aimed to link Europe with North America via Brazil and the Caribbean Islands.

When, therefore, the French **Aéropostale** company, under the dynamic leadership of its owner, Marcel Bouilloux-Lafont, sought to extend its empire into Venezuela in 1929, it found receptive ears in Caracas. The area south of the Orinoco River, virtually cut off from the rest of the country, was rich in minerals, including gold (and was later to become the site of some massive discoveries of iron ore). The shipments were made from the Orinoco port of Ciudad Bolívar, situated 300 kilometres from the Atlantic Ocean, but convenient to the British port of Port of Spain, in Trinidad. The situation was somewhat parallel to that of the oil-producing region of Lake Maracaibo, whose product was taken to the neighbouring Dutch island of Curaçao for refining.

No.3 in Aviación Nacional Venezolana's Latécoère 28 fleet, the Laté 28-6 YV-ABI *General Urdaneta. (Air France)*

Thus, Aéropostale's ambition for an eventual link from the French islands of Guadeloupe and Martinique to Natal, Brazil, to connect with its trans-Atlantic service, coincided with Venezuela's desire for a trans-Orinoco air service. Accordingly, on 3 July, 1929, a contract was signed with Bouilloux-Lafont for the exclusive carriage of mail. On 23 December the Compagnie Générale Aéropostale was registered in Caracas, and the necessary Decree relating to internal air postage was issued on 30 January, 1930.

The route was surveyed and the company organized by Paul Vachet, who had been chief pilot of the Latécoère Mission in Brazil in 1924, had surveyed the Brazilian routes, and had been the nominal founder of Aeroposta Argentina. With other French pilots, including Gaston Chenu and Pierre Lemoigne, Aéropostale began a weekly scheduled service early in 1930. Two routes were operated from the airfield at Maracay, about 50 miles west of Caracas. One was to Maracaibo, to the west, the other to Ciudad Bolívar, Guasipati, and Tumeremo, to the east across the Orinoco. Effectively, Aéropostale provided air service from one end of Venezuela to the other, and on 9 January, 1931, a branch route was opened from Ciudad Bolívar to Trinidad.

The aircraft used were three Latécoère 28s, although the first flights were made with an older Latécoère 26. The Venezuelan service was operated under the title **Aviación Nacional Venezolana** after the Venezuelan Government bought the airline on 31 December, 1933. The sale was forced upon Bouilloux-Lafont when the French Government suddenly and inexplicably withdrew the subsidy on the strength of which he had invested heavily in Aéropostale. But the Venezuelan venture was locally owned and not subsidized by the French; and the sale enabled

191

him to recoup a small part of his once considerable fortune.

At first, Aviación Nacional continued with French management, headed by Robert Guérin, under Ministry of Labour and Communications control. But on 1 January, 1935, the operation became autonomous, under the name **Línea Aeropostal Venezolana (LAV)** under the command of Lt-Col Francisco Leonardi, with a capital of 1,160,000 bolívars.

Development of Airlines in Venezuela

On 21 May, 1937, Aeropostal's complete independence as a state-owned corporation was confirmed by Decree, the capital was increased, three Fairchild 71s replaced the Latécoère 28s, and a programme of route expansion began. This was accelerated in 1938 when the first of six Lockheed Model 10A Electras arrived. In 1939 the centre of operations was transferred to Maiquetía, on the coast near Caracas, and more convenient to the capital than Maracay. By 1942, the fleet included six Electras, two Lockheed 14s and a four-seat Howard. The route network now reached all the populated parts of Venezuela, and all the frontiers. The Second World War stimulated air activity in Venezuela. Its oil resources were vital for the Allied war efforts, while South America was an important supplier of raw materials of all kinds; and Venezuela lay athwart the

Línea Aeropostal Venezolana's Lockheed 10-A Electra YV-ACI was delivered in February 1937.

main supply route. Progress was not entirely without setbacks—there were several accidents—but traffic increased by leaps and bounds. LAV was reorganized in 1946, and, with the domestic network firmly established, it set about the task of putting Venezuela on the international map.

A service having been opened in July 1945 to Boa Vista, Brazil—connecting with the Brazilian network, and thus cementing a direct supply route from the Amazon basin—the first international service to the north was opened on 24 January, 1946, to Aruba, and another to Bogotá, via Cúcuta, in co-operation with the Colombian national airline, AVIANCA. DC-4s and Martin 2-0-2s were acquired. The DC-4s started to operate to the USA on a contract basis in November 1946 in preparation for direct scheduled service to New York.

Meanwhile, two other airlines had begun to operate domestic services within Venezuela, such was the increase in demand for air services. First of these was **Aerovías Venezolanas, S.A. (AVENSA)**, founded by Henry L. Boulton, who was granted permission to operate on 13 May, 1943. The original capital was 500,000 bolívars ($150,000), of which 30 per cent was subscribed by Pan American Airways. The first privately-owned airline in Venezuela, it started scheduled freight services in December 1943.

AVENSA's Douglas C-54A YV-C-EVB was originally the USAAF's 42-72303. It passed to California Eastern as N54305 and was acquired by AVENSA in 1952.

Early in 1944, the capital was raised to 600,000 bolívars, when LAV secured a 23 per cent interest. At that time, other stockholders included Henry Boulton (31 per cent) and the German Vegas group (23 per cent). Pan American's share was reduced to 23 per cent. Passenger services opened from Caracas (Maiquetía) to Ciudad Bolívar, using a fleet of old aircraft which included three Ford Tri-Motors, one Stinson, and a Lockheed 12. This fleet was inadequate to compete with LAV and a further reorganization took place in 1946 when Pan American increased its shareholding to 37 per cent as the capital increased to 2,000,000 bolívars. By the end of 1948, the fleet consisted of eleven Douglas DC-3/C-47 and two twin-engined Lockheeds.

The competition in the late 1940s stemmed not only from the recognized flag carrier, LAV, but also from another newcomer. On 18 August, 1944, **Línea Aérea TACA de Venezuela** was founded with a capital of 700,000 bolívars, 55 per cent of which were Venezuelan, and the remainder owned by the international consortium TACA Airways, S.A., now controlled by United States interests. The establishment of this company had been part of a grandiose scheme to set up subsidiary companies of TACA in all the countries of South America. Whether or not the idea was ultimately to challenge the Pan American empire—an ambition doomed to failure because of the US airline's deep-rooted foundations on the

LAV's Martin 2-0-2 YV-C-AMB *Rafael Urdaneta*. The main fuselage band was a medium blue with dark blue outline, the three centre lines were red and the Venezuelan colours of yellow, blue and red were carried on the tail and wingtips. (*The Glenn L. Martin Company*)

193

continent—TACA de Venezuela served its purpose during the short period when the parent company was testing the potential for market expansion.

On 2 January, 1945, in co-operation with a sister company, TACA de Colombia, TACA de Venezuela opened nonstop service from Caracas to Bogotá. Each airline flew its own equipment, and because of its common ownership, did not attempt to work on the basis of direct competition, preferring to co-ordinate schedules. This was possibly the first example of a pooled service in Latin

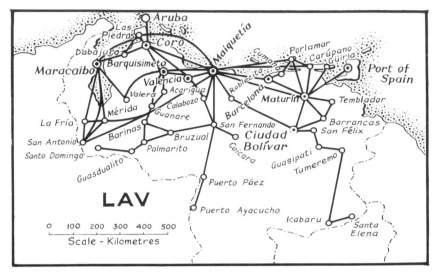

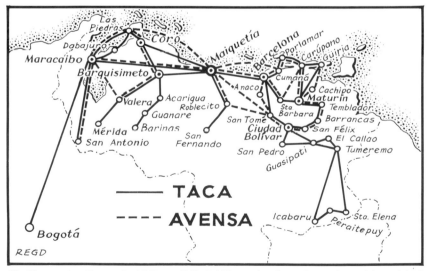

20. Venezuelan Domestic Airlines, 1949. LAV was the direct descendant of the original Aéropostale and is still known as Aeropostal. Of the two rival airlines, only AVENSA survives as a vigorous competitor.

194

America, a practice which in later years was to become common all over the world.

Other services quickly followed, to Ciudad Bolívar on 9 January, to San Antonio and Valera, via Maracaibo, on 7 March. Later in the year, on 1 October, as an expression of firm intentions, the capital was raised to 2,100,000 bolívars—a direct challenge to Pan American's AVENSA—and the service pattern expanded considerably, with Maracaibo, as well as Caracas, receiving direct service to Bogotá on 1 July, 1947. The success was short-lived. In 1950, as the TACA empire collapsed, the Venezuelan branch was liquidated and, early in 1952, LAV acquired full control, although the airline continued to operate under its own name for a further five years.

Inauguration of International Service

On 21 March, 1947, Línea Aeropostal Venezolana began its service to New York, using two new Lockheed Constellations. At the same time, a new international route was opened to Port of Spain, Trinidad, while the joint service with Colombia was transferred to a new Colombian partner, LANSA, TACA de Colombia having already preceded TACA de Venezuela in its demise. On 9 June a law was passed revising the regulations governing LAV. The capital was again increased, to 14.6 million bolívars ($4,375,000), permitting the purchase of two more Constellations and ten C-47s, but, more significantly, it permitted the formation of an international division, in which private capital would be able to subscribe up to 49 per cent of the total.

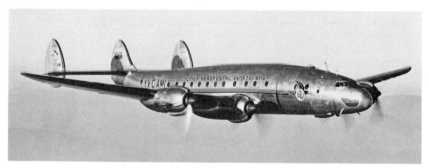

LAV's Lockheed 049 Constellation YV-C-AMI *Francisco Miranda*. Apart from red spinners and the Venezuelan colours on the nose and tail, all markings were black. (*Lockheed*)

The 1950s were eventful for LAV. There were successes and disappointments. As already mentioned, TACA de Venezuela came under its control, as it purchased all the outstanding stock of that company. On 1 July, 1947, the routes and schedules of TACA were completely integrated, so that the competition within Venezuela was reduced to a straight fight between LAV and AVENSA. This latter airline took delivery of its first modern aircraft, a Convair CV-340, in 1953 and in November 1954 obtained permission from the US C.A.B to start a route to Miami, via the Netherlands Antilles and Jamaica. The C.A.B. stipulated that the name of Pan American was not to be mentioned in any advertisement, to offset the danger of the US airline's imposing vicarious control over the route. The Miami service began in June 1955. During the latter 1950s, AVENSA made

195

Built as Convair CV-440-61 and owned by Trans America Aeronautical Corporation, YV-C-EVJ was delivered in 1957 and operated by AVENSA. It was converted to a CV-580 with Allison 501 propeller-turbines in 1969 and later reregistered YV-63C.
(*T. R. Waddington collection*)

steady progress, ordering five Fokker/Fairchild F-27 feederliners in 1957 and acquiring three Douglas DC-6Bs from Pan American in 1958. Then in February 1960 it ordered its first jet aircraft, a Convair CV-880, strengthening its claim to be fit and willing to operate internationally at the highest levels.

AVENSA's rise to near-equality in airline status with LAV was partly by the default of the national airline, which during the early 1950s had been riding high, having joined the privileged ranks of potential jet airliner operators long before many companies of world renown. It was one of the early customers for the Comet, ordering two Comet 2s in the summer of 1952. Sadly, this was before the 1954 crashes which caused the grounding and complete redesign of that aircraft; and LAV withdrew its interest. However, in November 1953, it was able to inaugurate its first trans-Atlantic flight, from Caracas to Rome, via Lisbon and Madrid, using Constellations. It also started to serve Panamá, but the New York route was terminated in favour of Miami, the dominant US gateway to the Caribbean, where no less than three Venezuelan airlines had been granted permission to operate by the United States C.A.B.

LAV, with seemingly inexhaustible resources—reflecting Venezuela's oil wealth—introduced three Vickers Viscounts in January 1956 and expanded its

Vickers-Armstrongs V.749 Viscount YV-C-AMX was the second of three delivered to LAV early in 1956. (*Vickers-Armstrongs*)

196

Constellation fleet by adding some Super Constellations. But for a time, it seemed that the airline was crashing aeroplanes as fast as they were arriving. Between June 1956 and October 1958 no fewer than three of these long-distance aircraft were lost, and although on 1 March, 1958, a Decree (No.65) declared that LAV was an Instituto Autonomo, and the European frequency was increased from one to two per week, there was a strong movement in Venezuela to change the framework of the airline business.

Formation of VIASA

Vías Internacionales Aéreas, S.A. (VIASA) was formed jointly by LAV and AVENSA on 21 November, 1960, with the objective of merging the international operations of both companies. The capital of 12,000,000 bolívars (about $3,000,000) was shared 55 per cent LAV and 45 per cent AVENSA. VIASA had the option to buy Pan American's 30 per cent remaining interest in AVENSA, and Pan American did eventually withdraw from Venezuela on 28 April, 1976. In February 1961, the new airline signed an agreement with KLM to act as its general agent in Europe and initially to operate a fleet of Douglas DC-8s on its behalf. This was a practice in which KLM was well-experienced, realising that the benefits of interlined ticketing could augment its own traffic and help it to gain footholds in markets which, under international bilateral arrangements, were sometimes difficult to obtain. Meanwhile, VIASA placed a firm order for two Convair CV-880s, to supersede the one placed by AVENSA a year earlier.

This Douglas DC-8-53 was delivered to KLM as PH-DCI in April 1961 and went to VIASA in November 1975 as YV-131C. The fuselage stripe and the word VENEZUELA were blue and the VIASA and fin and rudder orange.

On 1 April, 1961, VIASA inaugurated DC-8 service, with an aircraft wet-leased from KLM, from Caracas to Lisbon and Madrid; Paris, London, and Amsterdam; and Curaçao, Bogotá, and Lima. This replaced the LAV international network except the route to Rome, which was delayed pending a new agreement with Alitalia. If, however, the former airline had been regarded as unreliable because of its accident record, the new airline's start was hardly auspicious, as a DC-8 crashed at Lisbon less than two months after starting service. But VIASA got under way. Later in the year, after delivery of its own 102-seat Convair jets, services opened to New York on 8 August; to Miami on 1 October; and to New Orleans on 5 October, the last-named replacing AVENSA flights.

Progress thereafter was steady and systematic, adding extra frequencies and consolidating agreements with other countries, including a new pool agreement with Alitalia, signed on 1 May, 1964. Services opened to Santo Domingo and

Panamá in October 1962, and to Mexico City in June 1965. On 5 December of that year, the first VIASA-owned DC-8-53 started service to New York, replacing a leased Alitalia DC-8-40. In the fullness of time, VIASA's own DC-8s went on to the Atlantic route, on 6 October, 1966.

VIASA did not confine its partnerships to one airline. In the latter 1960s, it expanded its services on a broader base. In May 1967 it leased two of AVENSA's 80-seat Douglas DC-9-10s, which were then sub-leased to CDA, the Dominican airline, and to PAISA, a joint Venezuela–Panama venture formed earlier in the year. These aircraft, though smaller than the Convair CV-880s which they replaced, were adequate for the shorter VIASA routes and, with their two engines, certainly more economical, and were deployed on all the local Caribbean routes.

On 10 January, 1968, VIASA created a subsidiary, Transcarga, to cope with the heavy air cargo traffic to the USA; and on 20 April of that year a new European terminus, London, was added. New York was by now receiving daily service, so that VIASA was firmly balanced internationally. On 1 January, 1969, it introduced the stretched DC-8-63 to New York, and subsequently replaced all the standard DC-8s. Services began to Beirut on 15 May, 1970, and to Frankfurt on 1 June, 1971.

VIASA joined the ranks of wide-bodied jet operators when it ordered two Douglas DC-10-30s in April 1972. These aircraft had been purchased previously by KLM and the Venezuelan airline took an opportunity of securing early delivery when the Dutch airline cut back its order. The first DC-10, with 251 seats in mixed class, went into service on the Atlantic route on 30 April, 1974, VIASA having already claimed to be the first wide-bodied operator in South America by leasing a Boeing 747 from KLM a few months earlier.

AVENSA's McDonnell Douglas DC-9-14 YV-C-AVR was delivered in May 1967 and later reregistered as YC-57C. (*McDonnell Douglas Corporation*)

This McDonnell Douglas DC-10-30, seen with VIASA livery and the Netherlands registration PH-DTH, has served VIASA and KLM since April 1975. Its Venezuelan registration is YV-138C. (*McDonnell Douglas Corporation*)

Venezuelan Cargo Carriers

Throughout the history of Venezuelan air transport, airlines other than the state-owned company or the Pan American subsidiary have seldom been able to pick up more than a few crumbs from the traffic demand—and these have been in the nature of freight operations. The first of these, other than the TACA subsidiary already mentioned was **Rutas Aéreas Nacionales, S.A. (RANSA)**, founded as an all-cargo carrier in September 1948. The original capital was 500,000 bolívars, shared between a Venezuelan, Carlos Chávez, and a US citizen, Everett Jones.

Operating a fleet of three Curtiss C-46s and three Douglas DC-3s/C-47s, RANSA operated to Miami, either direct or via the Netherlands Antilles, on an irregular basis, and authorized by the United States as a non-common carrier. The permits were somewhat elastic, and RANSA's operations were successful enough to allow the flights to be scheduled so regularly that the question arose as to whether it was effectively acting as a common carrier. In 1952, the US C.A.B. instituted an investigation into the matter.

This was overtaken by subsequent events. In March 1953, the capital was increased to 2,500,000 bolívars ($750,000) of which Chávez (formerly the Operations Vice-President of LAV) held 85 per cent. In December of the same year, RANSA was granted a US foreign carrier permit to operate regular services, one of three Venezuelan airlines so nominated, and the investigation was thus irrelevant. RANSA began to augment its services, including domestic flights, and added more aircraft to its fleet. But although legally permitted to do so, it never opened passenger services to Miami, possibly because it was making a success out of its air freighting and was reluctant to risk jeopardizing a good thing.

RANSA's demise was dramatic, even melodramatic. In June 1960 the Venezuelan authorities ordered its services to be suspended, because it was suspected of having illegally carried arms into the country. Carlos Chávez was

The Canadian Car & Foundry Burnelli CBY-3 Loadmaster N17N in its final form and the livery of RANSA. (*Gordon S. Williams*)

arrested, charged with helping to plot the assassination of President Betancourt, fortunately unsuccessful. The company was placed under the control of the Government, which maintained the now daily service to Miami. The fleet by this time had grown to thirteen C-46s and two Douglas DC-6As were added.

In August 1963, RANSA bought five old Boeing Stratocruisers, to be modified as cargo aircraft and to be used on the lucrative Miami, Jamaica, and Antilles routes. But this was the last gesture of an airline doomed to destruction, and in 1964 it abruptly ceased operations.

By this time another all-cargo airline stood ready to usurp RANSA's inheritance. Early in 1958, **Línea Expresa Bolívar, C.A. (LEBCA)** was founded in Maracaibo with a capital of 500,000 bolívars ($167,000). Seventy-one per cent of the shareholding was held by Venezuelans, the rest by US citizens. On 18 August of the same year, LEBCA started contract operations to Miami, using the much-favoured Curtiss C-46s. Most of the traffic was southbound, and the contract lasted about a year. LEBCA was then awarded one of the three certificates to operate regular cargo services between Venezuela and the USA. Venezuelan authority was granted on 9 July, 1959, the US in the following December.

Armed with this increased franchise, LEBCA purchased three old Canadian-built DC-4M North Stars in January 1962 from Overseas Aviation, one of the transient products of the new charter airline explosion in the United Kingdom. With these, plus five C-46s and a couple of DC-3s, LEBCA flourished for about five years, before falling a victim to the political influences which decided the fate of all Venezuelan airlines from time to time.

On 14 September, 1967, it was assigned as the official cargo carrier of Venezuela by the Ministry of Communications. The Venezuelan flag airline VIASA acquired all the shares, and LEBCA was thereupon wound up, ceasing operations on 22 January, 1968. Simultaneously, **Transportes Aéreos de Carga, S.A. (Transcarga)** was incorporated by VIASA as a wholly-owned subsidiary on 10 January. On 24 April, all traffic rights were granted to Transcarga, which leased four Douglas DC-7Fs and began negotiations to buy a DC-8–55F from Seaboard World Airlines.

For several years Transcarga operated under VIASA's name, as it could not obtain a foreign carrier permit from the United States C.A.B., which no doubt looked askance at the 100 per cent VIASA ownership, suspecting that some plan was afoot to evade the intent, if not the letter of US commercial air law. The question of market share between the airlines of the two countries had always been a problem, and at one time had hindered the smooth achievement of a mutually agreed bilateral agreement. Presumably the USA wished to retain the stability that had been achieved, and eventually the Venezuelans appeared to have accepted the inevitable. Transcarga was integrated into VIASA in 1979, its passing almost undetected as it had been little more than a book-keeping entry in VIASA's accounts during its last years.

In recent years, a few small airlines have made a small contribution to Venezuelan commercial air transport. All have been cargo carriers. **Aero B** was founded in April 1978 by some ex-military pilots, who flew two Convair CV-340s and a Douglas DC-6A on contract work, including the burgeoning flower business from Colombia. **Latinamericana Aérea de Carga S.A. (Latin Carga)**, with four C-46s; and **Rutas Aéreas, C.A. (Rutaca)**, with two Convair CV-340s and seven DC-3s, also did similar work, including contracts with the mining companies, especially to Ciudad Bolívar, a fast-growing city where Rutaca is based.

The Aeropostal Hawker Siddeley HS.748 YV-C-AMC later became YV-08C.
(*British Aerospace*)

These companies, however, survive on the fringe of the mainstream. Unless there is a complete restructuring of the framework regulating the airline industry, the Government will continue to dominate both the domestic and the international scene. No doubt the Boulton family, by inherited right through the foundation of AVENSA, will continue to play their part and influence the course of events. Other than this, VIASA and its parent-associate LAV will call the tune. By accident, rather than design, they will also preserve for posterity the illustrious name of Aéropostale, the great French airline which failed to survive French political intrigue, but whose name lives today in Venezuela.

CHAPTER TEN

The Pioneer Days of SCADTA

A Geographical Challenge

To describe Colombia's terrain in dramatic terms, emphasizing the barriers to communication presented by the mountain ranges, is to incur the danger of perpetrating a cliché, if viewed in the general context of the South American continent. There is hardly a country south of the Caribbean which does not have its problems of topography. Bolivia, for example, used to rival Tibet as the world's most inaccessible country; Peru might well have been several countries, so arduous were the channels of surface travel from Lima; and the vast size of Brazil, and the lack of surface routes into its interior, virtually restricted all economic development to the coastal area until only a few decades ago.

Colombia's unique geographical problems stemmed almost entirely from the geological upheaval millions of years ago which split the Andes mountain chain into three parts. From an area near Pasco, near the southern frontier with Ecuador, the mountains to the north divide into three: the Cordillera Occidental,

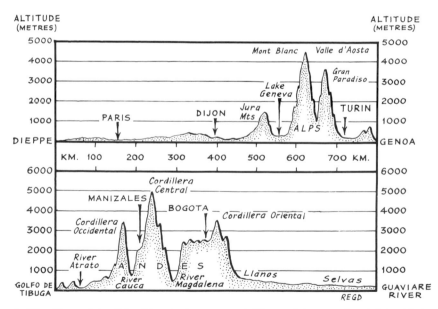

5. The Alps and the Colombian Andes compared. The special geography of Colombia is illustrated in this orographical map of that country, compared with one on the same scale across northwestern Europe. The subdivision of Colombia by the mountain ranges into several distinct regions is clearly shown.

Central, and Oriental. While not reaching the heights and extent of the Andes further south, they are formidable enough, with the peak of Tolima, in the central range, and the isolated volcano-shaped peak of Cristóbal Colón in the north, comfortably exceeding 5,000 metres in height.

21. The Main Physical Features of Colombia. Most of Colombia's inhabitants live in the western third of the country. This in turn is divided into three parts because of the natural barriers formed by the three cordillera into which the Andes are subdivided. Until the advent of air transport, the capital, Bogotá, was several days' journey (by riverboat and mule-train) from the other main cities.

203

The main effect of these parallel ridges is to split western Colombia into three parts, rather as if Europe was divided not by one range of Alps but by three. The precipitous slopes of the three cordillera have effectively barred surface access, so that all traffic routes were traditionally oriented north to south, mainly by turning the rivers into major highways, with the Magdalena River becoming the major transport lifeline of Colombia (see Map 21). During the age of railway construction, breaking through the western range, to link the Pacific port of Buenaventura with many of the commercial and administrative centres of the interior, was a major achievement. Nevertheless, the few railway lines which were built were totally inadequate to act as a spur to economic development. Some simply aimed to link cities with the Magdalena River, whence the riverboats—an echo of the Mississippi River activity in the USA—conveyed passengers and goods northward to the port of Barranquilla which was the gateway for Colombia to the Caribbean Sea and shipping routes to North America and Europe.

One special peculiarity of Colombia was the comparative isolation of Bogotá, the capital. Situated at an altitude of 8,700 ft above sea level (almost 3,000 metres) on a pleasantly green plateau ideal for concentrated cattle-farming, Bogotá was splendidly separated from the rest of Colombia for several centuries; and bearing in mind the difficulty of access, and recognizing the independent characteristics of the people of some of the provinces, the continued unity of Colombia during the decades of topographical separation has been a source of satisfaction, if not relief.

During the entire period of early transition into the modern industrial age, Colombia had no roads. Not until the early 1930s were any metalled highways constructed to link any of the major cities. The primary means of transport was by horseback for people and by mule for goods. Indeed mule-trains were responsible for most of Colombia's distribution of goods until well into the twentieth century. The journey from Bogotá to Medellín, for example, involved a horseback ride—or later a train—to a port on the Magdalena River, a boat trip down to the port for Medellín, and thence again overland to that city. Thus, to travel from Colombia's capital to the major industrial city was a matter of several days' arduous—and potentially hazardous—travel.

All these special problems, moreover, were restricted to only half of the area of Colombia, wherein the majority of the population lived. East of the Cordillera Oriental, the vast plains stretching to the Venezuelan, Brazilian, and Peruvian frontiers were inaccessible and largely unexplored territory. Still only penetrated in some parts even today, the vast stretches of the savannah region (the *llanos*) merging into the equally remote tropical forest (the *selva*), amounting to half of Colombia, were effectively, until about 1920, part of another world.

The First Experiment—C.C.N.A.

Into this environment, at once a challenge and an opportunity for the transport innovator, came the entrepreneurs of commercial aviation, anxious to demonstrate that the newly-invented aeroplane, proved by trial and error during the First World War, was capable of breaking the transport deadlock which had plagued Colombia for so many years.

The aeroplane was still a novelty when that war ended. Hundreds of pilots the world over were able to become instant heroes by demonstrating their skills at handling the new flying machines, and one United States flyer, William Knox-Martin, gained such fame in Colombia by his exploits. Cast in the mould of the barnstorming pilots who were stunting their way across the United States during the aftermath of war, Knox-Martin, to be fair, was more practical than most. In fact, he is credited with carrying the first air mail in Colombia, a claim stemming from his feat in carrying some letters from Barranquilla to Puerto Colombia on 18 June, 1919, using a single-engined Curtiss Standard, later named *Bolívar*.

The distance was less than twenty kilometres (about a dozen miles) and the city-centre time by horseback was arguably quicker than the aeroplane in this instance; but the effect on the transport development of Colombia was measured in terms of psychology rather than cold logic, and the potential of the aeroplane was recognized as a solution to the chronic communications problem. And so the scene shifted to the industrial centre of Colombia, Medellín.

Señor Alejandro Echaverria and a group of businessmen contributed an initial capital of 500,000 gold pesos to found, on 16 September, 1919, the **Compañía Colombiana de Navegación Aérea (C.C.N.A.)**. The parties included members of the Echavarría families, Vasquez Correa, Pedro Vasquez, Gonzalo Mejia, Pedro nel Ospina, and others. Guillermo Echavarría was nominated as general manager, assisted by Gonzalo Mejia, when the company was officially registered in Medellín, by Public Notary Advice 2448, on 28 September, 1919. This day has now been commemorated as the Colombian National Aviation Day, by Decree 1905 of 1979.

On 3 December, 1919, C.C.N.A. was granted exclusive rights by the Government to develop air mail services throughout Colombia. Meanwhile, arrangements were made to acquire three Farman F.40 aircraft from France, to be followed later by a larger F.60 Goliath. To provide the necessary flying expertise, three French pilots, veterans of the war, were invited to join C.C.N.A.

The senior member of the trio, René Bazin, made the first test flight with an F.40 at Cartagena on 14 February, 1920, and the aircraft was named *Cartagena*. On the next day, he made another demonstration flight, accompanied by Don Guillermo Echavarria, the manager, and Señorita Tulita Martínez, the Queen of Carnival. A few days later, on 22 February, Bazin made the first C.C.N.A. air mail flight, from Cartagena to Barranquilla, a distance of 140 kilometres, in a time of 1 hr 10 min. He returned on 4 March.

During March, various demonstrations and intermittent mail flights were made, some with passengers, between the two cities. Expansion of the network, an attempt to start service from Barranquilla to Santa Marta, was marred, however, by a forced landing on 17 March. Then, on 29 April, one of the pilots,

Compañía Colombiana de Navegación Aérea's Farman F.40 seaplane *Santa Marta* at Barranquilla on 6 June, 1920. (*Courtesy William Rojas*)

Jacques Jourdanet, was killed, together with passengers; and C.C.N.A. decided to convert the F.40s to floatplanes. The first flight with the modified F.40 was made on 3 June, the aircraft named *Santa Marta*, and the more or less regular flights between Cartagena and Barranquilla were resumed. But sadly, another pilot, P. Fratoni, was killed while landing at Cartagena, and C.C.N.A. paused in its activities to consider its future.

With grim determination, the company persevered. In August, the Farman Goliath was delivered, and Bazin made the first test flight on 26 September, 1920. In the Goliath *Barranquilla*, Bazin made a long flight of 5 hr 15 min on 30 September over mountainous country, and further sorties were made during October, carrying twelve passengers.

Colombiana's Salmson-powered Farman F.60 Goliath *Barranquilla*, photographed in 1920.
(*Courtesy William Rojas*)

Sensing perhaps that more was expected than to link two cities which were more accessible to each other than most, C.C.N.A. embarked on a more ambitious venture, to penetrate the hinterland of Barranquilla to the south, up the Magdalena River, in the general direction of Medellín and the capital. Bazin made a test flight in the F.40 *Medellín* on 22 November, 1920, and then, on 30 November, set off up the river, aiming to reach Puerto Berrío, which was the rail terminus on the Magdalena serving Medellin. Unfortunately, the aircraft was damaged at El Banco—roughly halfway to Puerto Berrío—and delayed until 7 December. Bazin eventually reached Medellín by canoe, pack-mule, and train, after having yet another misfortune, hitting a tree-trunk in the river at San Bartolomé. The Farman was towed to Puerto Berrío on 12 December.

This was effectively the end of C.C.N.A. It had lost three of its F.40s and two of its three pilots. Bazin was asked to resign, together with his mechanic who had been confronted with the unenviable task of keeping the fleet in the air. During the following year, the company enrolled the pilot Knox-Martin, of first Colombian air mail fame, to fly the Goliath, but he was unable to handle the large aircraft satisfactorily. An Italian pilot, Guiseppe Guiccardi, was invited to try his luck.

On 16 April, 1922, the *Barranquilla* left Barranquilla on what was to have been an inaugural flight to Medellín; but it was delayed at Montería until 29 April, and did not arrive at the capital of the Antioquian province until 24 July. Although the Farman Goliath made several demonstration flights there, all hopes of establishing C.C.N.A. were abandoned, as by this time another company was demonstrating a measure of success where the Medellín company had failed.

C.C.N.A's main claim to fame rests in the commemoration of its activities by the issue of an attractive series of postage stamps, the first of its kind to be issued in Latin America, and in great demand by philatelists. In full colour, the choice of subject material was not directly associated with the airline operations. This was perhaps not surprising, bearing in mind that their design was based on a series of Curtiss Aeroplane Company advertisements.

The Birth of SCADTA

Two days after the Colombian Government had awarded air mail rights to C.C.N.A., a second airline was founded in Colombia, on 5 December, 1919. This was the **Sociedad Colombo–Alemana de Transportes Aéreos (SCADTA)**, or the Colombian-German Air Transport Company. The group of eight founding fathers comprised five Colombian businessmen and three Germans resident in Colombia. The heaviest investment was by Gieseking and Company, which nominated the first chairman of the board, Alberto Tietjen. Prominent among the others were Ernesto Cortissoz, a Colombian banker, Cristóbal Restrepo, and Werner Kaemmerer, a German engineer who was largely responsible for assembling the group and inspiring it to invest in what might have been considered at the time to be an uncalculable risk. The capital was 100,000 pesos, equivalent at that time to about the same amount in United States dollars. All the original members were from Barranquilla, where the company was registered, by Public Notary Advice No.2374.

Bearing in mind that C.C.N.A. had been granted official governmental blessing, SCADTA's apparent chances for immediate success could not have been good. But the Colombian Government's guarantee to the earlier company was not entirely without safeguards. The exclusivity had been granted for only one year, and the assurance of continued air mail contracts for five years was given only if the airline could demonstrate its ability to fulfil its obligations for the safe and efficient transport of passengers and goods, including mail. The Government was also not very interested in a mail service between Barranquilla and Cartagena, and specified service to Bogotá and the important highly-populated provinces of Antioquia, Caldas, Cundinamarca, Tolima, and others.

A SCADTA fleet line-up at Girardot on the Magdalena River. From left to right the Junkers-F 13 floatplanes are A-4 *Bogotá*, A-8 *Magdalena* and A-10 *Caldas*. Built in 1921, *Magdalena* had flown 3,200 hr by 1933 when it was returned to Junkers for structural examination having worked all that time as a seaplane. *Caldas* has the original triangular fin but the others are seen with extended fins.

SCADTA considered that it stood a fair chance of demonstrating that it too could fulfil these obligations, and set out systematically to create the infrastructure, as well as the equipment, to carry out the task. While it waited for the arrival of the first aircraft, ordered from Germany, C.C.N.A. was in the process of learning the business in an agonizing way, alternately operating for a few weeks, then having to readjust its plans because of aircraft disasters. By the time the great day arrived, at the end of July 1920, for SCADTA to unload the first consignment of aircraft from the docks in Puerto Colombia, C.C.N.A. had already lost two-thirds of its fleet and crews.

The two trim little Junkers-F 13 floatplanes which were unloaded at the docks were no less important to the success of SCADTA's early efforts than the two men who accompanied the flying equipment, Fritz Hammer and Wilhelm Schnurbusch, who were destined to play significant roles in the development of commercial aviation, not only in Colombia, but in the whole continent. Hammer was a German ex-naval pilot who had shown a flair for commerce and marketing, and was the technical representative of the Junkers aircraft manufacturing company of Dessau. This was no light task, as the postwar Treaty of Versailles imposed severe restrictions on the manufacture of aircraft. The little F 13, in fact, was a minor triumph of ingenuity, achieving a creditable performance in range and load, with a low-powered engine, and at the same time using metal construction, thought by many to incur unnecessary penalties in weight.

His companion, Schnurbusch, also ex-navy, was an aircraft engineer, possessed of basic skills, while at the same time—as became necessary all too often—displaying an inventiveness which was often to mean the difference between success and failure. Because of the severe penalties for the slightest lapse in standards, Schnurbusch was to become a strict disciplinarian, and many were the staff—later to become veterans—who were to feel the lash of his tongue.

Shortly after the arrival of Hammer and Schnurbusch, another key member of the German contingent arrived: Hellmuth von Krohn, who was to become SCADTA's chief pilot. The airline was quickly to learn that it would take the many and varied resources of them all to turn an idea into a going concern. Although C.C.N.A. had had its problems, SCADTA's first attempts were even less auspicious. The F 13 floatplane refused to leave the water. The fuel was the wrong type for the engine, thus reducing the power below the minimum required; and the engine overheated in the tropical climate of the Caribbean, a somewhat different environment from the chilly Baltic. Schnurbusch solved the problem by adapting a car radiator to supplement and improve the engine cooling system.

The First Survey Flights up the Magdalena

Decree No.599, authorized by the Minister of War, Dr Jorge Roa, had, on 15 March, 1920, established the first Civil Aeronautics regulations. But the practical application and testing of these regulations through the control of regular flights was still elusive. The target level of performance implied by the Government's terms of its undertaking to C.C.N.A. was a service from the Caribbean (or Atlantic) coast to Bogotá and other inland cities. While regular service was not achieved by SCADTA during 1920, it at least made considerable progress in establishing the infrastructure which would make it possible.

On 12 September of that year, SCADTA made its first survey flight from Barranquilla to Puerto Berrío ('all change' for Medellín). The F 13 was forced to stop at Zambrano and El Banco for repairs, plus another delay at El Ciego. The

The river- and sea-port of Barranquilla (*top*) was the centre of Colombian commerce during the nineteenth and early twentieth centuries. Strategically placed at the mouth of the Magdalena River (*centre*), fleets of riverboats, reminiscent of Mississippi stern-wheelers, linked merchant shipping with the interior. During the 1920s there were only about 100 km of paved roads in Colombia, and the pioneering SCADTA was able to supersede the riverboats. Such was the airline's importance to Colombian commerce that it was permitted to organize its own air mail service, with its own postal offices (*bottom*) and its own stamps.

209

This view of SCADTA's Junkers-F 13 floatplane *Caldas* shows its features to advantage. The registration A-10 has not yet been applied. (*AVIANCA*)

pilot was Fritz Hammer, the mechanic the resourceful Wilhelm Schnurbusch, and the passenger a member of the SCADTA board, Stuart Hosie. The journey took two days, but the interruptions had been more irritating than fundamental.

Under an unusual arrangement with the postal authorities, SCADTA was allowed to sell its own stamps, at a surcharge over and above the regular rate. These were printed in Germany and show attractively an F 13 flying against the competition—a Magdalena riverboat. The first recorded issue was on 4 October, 1920, after Hammer's survey flight.

The second survey flight was more ambitious and more eventful. This time, the objective was the river port of Girardot, a bustling community 1,250 kilometres up the Magdalena from Barranquilla, and owing its importance partly to the fact that it was at the limit of practical navigation for the riverboats, and partly because it was the most convenient place to make the connection to Bogotá, linked by a railway which, since 1916, had been able to cross the Magdalena gorge by a suspension bridge, thus linking Bogotá with Ibagué, Tolima, and Huila Provinces, and thence westwards to the prosperous southwest part of Colombia.

Hellmuth von Krohn took off in SCADTA's flagship Junkers-F 13 *Colombia* on 19 October, 1920, and, by all accounts, enjoyed an uneventful flight, with the essential Schnurbusch as his companion, until arrival at Girardot. Here, the F 13 foundered in the river on alighting; von Krohn and three passengers escaped unharmed, but the mechanic, Schroeder by name, was drowned. The *Colombia* was severely damaged, and so a second aircraft was sent for. Fritz Hammer set off in another F 13, with a Colombian mechanic, Herrera. At Puerto Berrío, a critical decision was made: to exchange the mechanic for Alberto Tietjen, so that Hammer and Tietjen could travel to the city of Neiva, capital of Huila Province, to solicit further investment for the financially desperate SCADTA, now in need of spare parts and equipment. This commercial promotion was entirely successful. Hammer, Tietjen, and Schnurbusch returned to Girardot from Neiva with an additional 10,000 pesos.

The resourceful Schnurbusch also took the train to Bogotá, where he obtained two wheels from a Hudson car, judging these to be adaptable to the F 13. On the improvised landing field at Flandes, across the river from the city of Girardot, the undercarriage of the second aeroplane was converted from floats to wheels. This scene was to herald a sustained period of SCADTA activity in the Flandes/Girardot base, which was to be the hub of the scheduled operation for many years.

The SCADTA Junkers-F 13 *Bogotá* seen as a landplane. (*AVIANCA*)

On 14 November, Hellmuth von Krohn flew the converted F 13 landplane from Flandes to Bogotá, carrying with him a mechanic named Varsch. Two days after landing at the capital city, and being fêted by the entire community, the F 13 was named *Bogotá* amid great pomp and ceremony. But pride went before a fall, and this aircraft, too, was badly damaged when making a forced landing in the *sabana*—the lush countryside around Bogotá. Von Krohn had to endure the ignominy of being helped out by the railway company, which transported the fuselage and assorted pieces of the Junkers to a place where it could be repaired.

Meanwhile, the *Colombia* was being slowly put back together at Girardot/Flandes. Poor Schnurbusch went down with typhoid fever, but the help of an engineer from Bogotá resulted in the aircraft being able to return to Barranquilla early in March 1921. The round trip had taken five months.

Thus the early days of SCADTA were no less eventful than those of C.C.N.A. They had been a shade luckier, possibly learning a little from the latter's misfortunes. The choice of a floatplane, rather than a landplane, was at the time well-judged. But there was more than luck involved. The Junkers-F 13 was a superb little aircraft, with its metal structure the key to its tropical superiority over other types, the wooden structures of which could—literally—be eaten by termites. But in addition SCADTA was fortunate in having the right people to organize and operate an airline: the drive and élan of Hammer, the airmanship of von Krohn, and the ingenuity of Schnurbusch. They were soon to be joined by another essential ingredient for success: an organizing genius and a man of vision.

Peter Paul von Bauer

Dr Peter Paul von Bauer, an Austrian industrialist, was introduced to the SCADTA organization early in 1921, and he became so intrigued and enthusiastic with the prospects of the Colombian airline that he returned to Austria to sell some of his assets so as to invest in the enterprise. Armed with advice and instruction from Hammer and Schnurbusch, he visited the Junkers factory to order additional F 13s, with specification improvements to cope with the onerous operating conditions in the Colombian tropics. Arrangements were made to supply two more F 13s, with more to follow. Before his visit, the single-engined Junkers could carry only 150 kg, equivalent to little more than two passengers, without extra baggage. Now they would carry a better load, partly because of improved design of the floats.

Von Bauer established agencies in Paris, Berlin, and Hamburg, and also in New York, and distributed SCADTA literature to inform the world in general that Colombia had an airline and furthermore was intending to expand it. However, during this period, as throughout its later existence, the question of government subsidy did not arise, because there was none—in direct contrast with Europe, where all the airlines were dependent upon government subsidy, direct or indirect. In the United States, the only services were isolated mail routes, dependent upon a subsidy from the Post Office, and those airlines which had tried to survive without such assistance had failed or were about to when von Bauer began to take the reins in Barranquilla. On the other hand, SCADTA's postage stamp franchise was almost the equivalent of a subsidy. Its importance to the company was indicated by the requirement that all employees regardless of status should be available for stamping duty, if necessary.

Scheduled Services Begin

SCADTA began scheduled services, on a fixed timetable, between Barranquilla and Girardot, with an extension of some flights to Neiva, on 19 September, 1921. This date must be regarded as one of the most important dates in the whole calendar of events which comprises the history of commercial aviation in Latin America. The inauguration of scheduled services represents the culmination of preparation, planning, organization, and technical competence which is the actual symbol of achievement of any transport organization. Other airlines existed in South America before this date, in Argentina, in French Guiana, and in Colombia itself; but none reached the level of achievement whereby the public could depend on the availability of a service, on a regular, guaranteed, basis. Several years were to pass before such a claim could be made in the United States, although airlines meeting such criteria existed in many countries in Europe, and in Australia.

Hub of SCADTA's operations during the early 1920s was Girardot, the river port on the Magdalena which owed its importance partly to its proximity to the Colombian capital, Bogotá, and partly to the only railway bridge across the river along its navigable length. In this picture can be seen some of the stern-wheel riverboats from Barranquilla, 1,000 km distant, and, at the top to the right, the SCADTA floatplane and landplane base.

The SCADTA seaplane base at Girardot, with the adjacent airfield of Flandes shown in the air view (*top*). A closer view of the specially-constructed ramp and hangar (*bottom*).

The achievement was possible because, resulting from von Bauer's visit to Germany, the fleet of Junkers-F 13s was now increased to six, and modified to permit a load of 260 kg. This was equivalent to three passengers, plus about 40 kg of freight, including luggage and mail. If a passenger weighed more than 65 kg he was charged extra. The fare from Barranquilla to Girardot, one way, was 250 pesos (roughly the same in US dollars) or about 20¢ per kilometre by the river route. This was not cheap but, measured against the saving in time, had its attractions for the businessman or the politician/administrator. SCADTA's time was about seven or eight hours. This compared with 10–14 days by the stern-wheel, flat-bottomed riverboats.

Later, as the matter of price competition became more refined, the route provided an unusual example of directional fare imbalance. With more efficient aircraft permitting slightly lower fares, the charge from Barranquilla to Girardot was $200, but only $150 in the reverse direction, because the riverboats made much better time going downstream. The Girardot–Neiva route, on the other

213

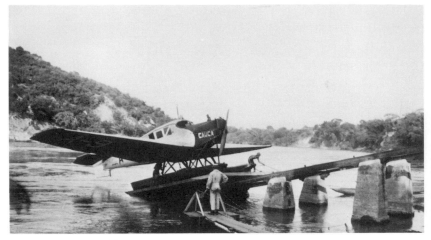

The SCADTA Junkers-F 13 *Cauca* (*top*) being hauled up the ramp at Girardot by the winding engine (*below*) installed by Wilhelm Schnurbusch, SCADTA's technical director. The metal-built floatplanes were relatively fragile and needed to be protected from weather and possible turbulence on the river, as well as for routine maintenance well above the highest water level.

hand, was consistently popular for many years because, until road and rail connections were built after the SCADTA service had got under way, the alternative was a four-day horseback ride.

The frequency achieved, incidentally, was commendable, especially in view of the operating conditions: twice a week as far as Girardot, with one flight going on to Neiva. A little later, services were opened from Barranquilla to Cartagena and Santa Marta, so that the six F 13s were kept busy, as were Schnurbusch and his team of mechanics and the brotherhood of pilots who pioneered the routes.

Consolidation of an Airline

Shortly after this scheduled service inauguration, Peter Paul von Bauer arrived back from his self-appointed mission to Europe. Accompanying him was Hermann Kuehl, an engineer who was appointed chief of a special branch of SCADTA, the Sección Científica, or Scientific Section. Its prime purpose was aerial photography, and the necessary equipment had been smuggled across the German-Dutch frontier, by night, because of the restrictions of the Allied Control Commission set up by the Treaty of Versailles, for consignment on a Dutch steamship destined for Puerto Colombia. Paradoxically, the very harshness of these restrictions seemed to inspire ingenuity, invention, and innovation in the German industry which might never have emerged, at least not as quickly, but for the imposition of dire necessity simply to survive.

On 28 July, 1922, Dr von Bauer was made a director of SCADTA, by buying the Gieseking investment for 100,000 pesos. Effectively, he controlled the company and its destiny from this time, owning as he did about four-fifths of the shares. Gieseking, incidentally, wanted to start his own company, using two Fokker aircraft, purchased from a Julius Berger. He hired a pilot named Roth, but the airline never operated.

Von Bauer set in motion an extensive programme of development, in addition to the establishment of the Scientific Section. This involved the survey of new routes, construction of an engineering and operational base on the banks of the Magdalena River at Veranillo (Barranquilla), and negotiations for a long-term contractual agreement with the Colombian postal authorities. The programme had a kind of balance: some activities were designed to produce supplementary revenue to supplement that from flying. Thus, revenues earned from the scientific department's aerial photography could be used to finance such luxuries as an engine testbed at Veranillo.

One of the first duties of the Scientific Section under Hermann Kuehl was to make a survey of the segment of the Colombia–Venezuela frontier in the area near Cúcuta. This had long been the subject of dispute between the two countries, but a decision had been made under international arbitration in March 1922, and SCADTA's assistance was sought to establish the precise delineation of the boundary in a region where accessibility by surface was difficult, if not impossible.

SCADTA's Junkers-F 13 C-25 *Boyacá* at the Barranquilla base. This is a later version of the F 13, with metal airscrew and the reshaped and balanced tail surfaces introduced in 1926. A riverboat can be seen on the left. (*AVIANCA*)

215

Towards the end of 1922, SCADTA consolidated its position, C.C.N.A. having abandoned its hopes and its plans, thus leaving the field clear for the German–Colombian company. Undoubtedly, when the President of Colombia, Pedro nel Ospina, made a flight on a SCADTA aircraft in September, SCADTA's star must have been in the ascendant. It was certainly a red-letter day for the airline, as it could probably claim to be the first airline ever to carry a Head of State.

On 5 December, the Council of Ministers of the Colombian Government authorized SCADTA to carry mail under contract, an arrangement which the President, possibly with the memory of his flight still fresh, approved on 16 December. Simultaneously, SCADTA celebrated its strengthening position by issuing its first official timetable.

The following year, 1923, was marked by an unusual success. On 19 July, SCADTA was able to help the Colombian Government in a crisis, when there was a run on the State Bank in Bogotá. The airline flew $3\frac{1}{2}$ million pesos, weighing $1\frac{1}{2}$ tons, from Medellín to Bogotá to save the situation.

The year 1924 was disappointing. A tragic accident on 8 June, when Hellmuth von Krohn was celebrating a holiday occasion in the city of Barranquilla by giving a small air show, resulted in the death of the crew, including von Krohn himself, Don Ernesto Cortissoz, SCADTA's President at the time, together with four passengers. The aircraft was the F 13 *Tolima*, and during the same year two Fokker C.II aircraft, *Cali* and *Manizales* of LIADCA were also lost, fortunately without casualties.

While the crashes were distressing, especially as four had occurred during a period of about a year, after two years of safe flying, another loss was one of talent rather than equipment. Late in 1924, Fritz Hammer, the driving force behind much of the Junkers bid for export markets in the postwar period, wrote to von Bauer from Germany, announcing that he had formed, on 5 May, the Condor Syndikat, in conjunction with an investment group consisting of Aero Lloyd, a German airline, and Schlubach Theimer, a German trading agency. Von Bauer, believing that this new company might in some way present a competitive threat to SCADTA, protected his position by taking a $20,000 share of Condor's $200,000 capital.

SCADTA's Dornier Merkur floatplane C-23 *Simón Bolívar*. (*AVIANCA*)

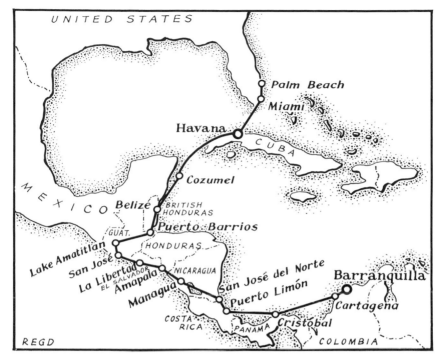

22. The SCADTA/Condor Flight to Florida, 1925. This map traces the route flown by the two Dornier Wal flying-boats leased to SCADTA by the Condor Syndikat. Stops were made in every country of Central America and in Cuba, en route to the USA. This remarkable survey, made two years before Pan American Airways began service from Key West to Havana, may have inspired the creation of the United States company.

The Trans-Caribbean Survey

During 1925, SCADTA pulled itself together after the disappointments of the previous year. On 8 April, it made the first survey flight on an international route, from Barranquilla to Curaçao and La Guaira, Venezuela; followed by one to Maracaibo, Venezuela, on 27 June. But these were only a modest hint to what von Bauer really had in mind.

On 18 August, 1925, two Dornier Wal twin-engined flying-boats, the *Atlántico* and the *Pacífico*, left Barranquilla under the command of Freiherr von Buddenbrock, with Dr von Bauer leading the delegation as chief diplomatic negotiator for an ambitious scheme of route expansion. The aircraft had been retained through the initiative of Don Ernesto (he who had been killed in June the previous year) and a young politician Dr Olaya Herrera, later to become the President of Colombia. Fritz Hammer had been sent to Germany to select the best aircraft to develop international services. These had to be superior to the Junkers-F 13s, as clearly these little single-engined craft were totally unsuited to long over-water journeys. The Wals were constructed in Italy and shipped to Curaçao for final assembly. They were owned by the Condor Syndikat, of Germany, and leased to SCADTA.

217

Permission being granted to alight in the Panama Canal Zone, the two Wals flew via Cartagena, Cristóbal, through Central America, thence from the Yucatán peninsula to Cuba (see Map 22). The two Wals, flying the Colombian flag, alighted in Havana harbour on 19 September.

Doctor von Bauer had developed plans to expand SCADTA's routes across the Caribbean to the United States, in collaboration with Condor, of which Hammer was now the marketing director. Von Bauer had approached the US Post Office on 1 April, 1925, and was at first well received. He had already registered a company in Delaware, Inter-American Airways. Had the negotiations been

The two Condor Syndikat Dornier Wals *Atlántico* and *Pacífico* made a Central America expedition during 1925. *Pacífico* (A-20) is seen in front view at Barranquilla, and the side view shows one of the Wals on Lake Amatitlan in Guatemala. (*Lufthansa*)

218

successful in signing a commercial agreement with Washington, SCADTA would probably have operated the trans-Caribbean service through a US associate, Compañía Aeromaritima de Colombia, which could have been backed by US interests in partnership with von Bauer, with the Condor Syndikat as a sleeping partner.

At first, the delegation could not obtain permission to take the two Wals to Florida, but through the intervention of Werner von Meister, representative of the German Zeppelin Company in the USA, von Bauer was able to take one aircraft, the *Pacífico*, to Palm Beach, via Miami. Hammer, meanwhile, went to New York, to try to win support among commercial and travel interests there. Von Bauer and Hammer had already taken the precaution of negotiating air agreements and mail contracts with some of the Central American states, albeit on a non-exclusive basis.

Discussions with the Postmaster General of the United States were far from encouraging. Equally, experts of the Strategic Military Command, perhaps with strong memories of German submarine action against US shipping in Caribbean waters only eight years earlier, were firmly against the idea. President Coolidge, with whom von Bauer was able to obtain an audience, saw no reason to advocate the cause of SCADTA/Condor against his experts' advice, even if von Bauer could claim the support of the Colombian Government. Only the Commerce Department was sympathetic.

While it was natural that the United States should regard the Colombian flag and SCADTA's house colours as a possible device by which German interests could gain a priceless entry into the field of United States commerce, there were other factors involved, not the least of which was one of pride and prestige. At this time, the airline industry in the USA was conspicuous by its almost complete absence, and certainly there was no recognizable international service. Indeed, such an enterprise as Pan American Airways was as yet only a figment of the imagination; so that, while quasi-military objections may have been the official reason for turning down the SCADTA-Condor initiative, the underlying reason may have been simply that the USA could not suffer the loss of face by watching a foreign power inaugurate a foreign air service before it was ready to embark on one under its own flag.

Frustrated, the crew of the *Pacífico* returned to Havana. The *Atlántico* was shipped back to Germany, and subsequently back to South America again, to Montevideo, whence it flew northwards to become Brazil's first airliner. The *Pacífico* was shipped to Curaçao, but it crashed in 1926 on a flight from Curaçao to Barranquilla, thus frustrating another of von Bauer's plans: to open an international route from Curaçao to Panamá, via Barranquilla, under the name Aero Maritima.

While the inspired venture by von Bauer and Hammer did not succeed, it was nevertheless a great achievement. It aroused great interest in the United States, underlining a current of opinion which was expressing dissatisfaction with the inertia being displayed at the time by the United States Government in its attitude towards the concept of air transport. Within weeks of von Bauer's US discussions, the US State Department called an interdepartmental aviation conference, on 8 January, 1926. Throughout 1926, there was intense activity in the USA, and the Air Commerce Act was passed on 20 May. The Wals' flight to Havana accelerated action to pass the Foreign Air Mail Act and spurred initiative in commercial circles towards the formation of internationally-oriented airlines. The flight certainly awakened US commercial interests to the idea of a trans-Caribbean air route, the direct outcome of which was the formation of Pan American Airways, with routes to the Canal Zone and the Caribbean as the first objective.

COSADA and LIADCA

With hopes of making a spectacular incursion into international air-space having been destroyed, von Bauer turned elsewhere, looking towards Colombia's neighbours to the south. Meanwhile, however, a domestic development arose in which the initiative came from another source. In the region of Santander, to the northeast of the country, on 4 May, 1920, a group of citizens in the city of Bucaramanga—aware no doubt of their isolation from the rest of the nation—had formed a committee to investigate and promote the possibility of air service. In due course, on 12 March, 1923, the **Compañía Santandereana de Aviación (COSADA)** was formed. Headed by a local banker, Dr Isaias Cepeda, and a businessman, Don Gustavo Lupinus, COSADA's capital amounted to 100,000 gold pesos, of which 10,000 were budgeted for the purpose of acquiring an aircraft through the good offices of SCADTA. COSADA was authorized, like SCADTA, to issue its own stamps.

After some initial problems—the first aircraft (a Dornier Komet) would not take off—the landplane operation got under way early in 1926. An airfield was opened at Puerto Wilches, on the Magdalena River, on 3 March, to enable connections to be made with the floatplanes of SCADTA en route from Barranquilla to Girardot. The first regular mail services from Bucaramanga to Puerto Wilches started on 24 March, with the Junkers-F 13 landplane *Cúcuta*.

COSADA also maintained an overland express service to neighbouring communities in the provinces of Santander and Norte de Santander. This resulted in the unique philatelic circumstance in which three different stamps could appear on one letter: those of Colombia, SCADTA, and COSADA.

The route was very short, only about 80 km, and existed simply because no other convenient transport service was available. However, in 1930 a railway was opened, and COSADA ceased operations.

Echoing the efforts at Santander were those of another group in western Colombia. **Líneas Aéreas de Cauca (LIADCA)** was formed in 1924 to operate between Medellín and Cali, along the valley of the Cauca River. However, the total fleet, two Fokker C.IIs, crashed in the same year, before operations were established.

SCADTA's Barranquilla base, showing entrance arch, terminal, offices, hangars and slipways. The aircraft on the hard standing are the Junkers-F 13 seaplanes C-24, C-25, C-35 and C-40, the Dornier Wal C-28 and the Dornier Merkur seaplanes C 23 and C-27. (*AVIANCA*)

CHAPTER ELEVEN

Airline Transition and Growth in Colombia

Linking the Atlantic and the Pacific Oceans

In 1924 one of the many German pilots who were invited to go to live in Colombia and work for SCADTA was Herbert Boy. His decision to emigrate had been prompted partly because his mother had sold the family property for what she thought was a good price, only to find the money worthless when the devastating currency inflation wiped out the value of the mark—on 15 November, 1923, the exchange rate against the dollar was 1½ US billion. Boy was to play a prominent part in SCADTA's fortunes in the years to come, and is remembered warmly by aviation people in Colombia as the author of a book of reminiscences which display a great sympathy, even partriotism, for his adopted country.

In 1927, von Bauer, foiled by United States intransigence in his efforts to start a route across the Caribbean or even to the Canal Zone, sought to go in the opposite direction. The first step, however, had to be to develop a domestic service to the Pacific coast. Attempts to break out from the narrow confines of the Magdalena River route by means of branch lines had been only moderately successful. In fact, only the connection from Puerto Wilches to Bucaramanga had been sustained as a regular service. Attempts to link the important cities of Medellín, Manizales, and Cali had resulted only in some survey flights in 1924 using Fokker biplanes, fitted with improvised long-range tanks. These were destined to bring local fame to the pilots, Feruccio Guicciardi and José Ignacio Forero, but no regular service for SCADTA.

The reason for the inability to establish what were apparently direct routes was essentially the topography, described at the beginning of the last chapter. SCADTA eventually adopted the policy of adapting itself to the geography, rather than trying to conquer it. In 1927, therefore, a completely new route was developed, with Herbert Boy as the prime mover, by flying southwest from Barranquilla along the coast of the Caribbean, then following the Atrato River southwards to its source, and then further on down the San Juan River to meet the Pacific coast at Buenaventura. The route avoided mountains throughout. In fact, the terrain was so low that the area has often been the subject of discussion as a possible alternative to the Panama Canal. However, the area was densely forested and suffered from one of the worst climates in the world, experiencing tropical rainfall for almost the whole year round.

SCADTA's Junkers-F 13 C-32 *Pacífico*, with 1926-type tail unit, in the Bay of Zarzurro. (*AVIANCA*)

Herbert Boy made a survey flight from Barranquilla to Buenaventura on 23 October, 1927, and others followed before the inaugural mail service began on 10 June, 1928, to Guayaquil, Ecuador. This was a new departure for SCADTA, the first time it had provided passenger and air mail service on an international route. On 30 July, regular services began, using the F 13 floatplane *Boyaca*.

Meanwhile, Pan American Airways had made its inaugural Miami–Key West flight on 28 October, 1927, and Peter Paul von Bauer had once again gone to Washington, at about the same time, desperately trying to obtain permission for SCADTA to fly to the Canal Zone, promoting Aeromaritima. But as before, he met only evasion and procrastination on the part of the US authorities.

SCADTA Timetable 1929. The Colombian airline managed to start a service from Panamá ▶ to Ecuador in 1929. But the Pan American Airways involvement in SCADTA resulted in the curtailment of the network to within Colombia's frontiers.

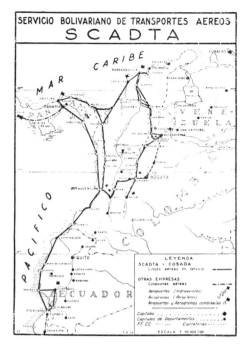

SERVICIO BOLIVARIANO DE TRANSPORTES AEREOS
S C A D T A

LEYENDA
SCADTA Y COSADA
Lineas aereas en servicio

OTRAS EMPRESAS
Conexiones aereas

Aeropuertos (hidroaviones)
Aeropuertos (Aeroplanos)
Aeropuertos y Aerodromos combinados

Capitales
Capitales de Departamentos
FF CC — Carreteras
ESCALA 1 10 000 000

S E R V I C I O
B O L I V A R I A N O
DE
T R A N S P O R T E S
A E R E O S

Colombia
Ecuador
Panamá

ITINERARIO
VIGENTE
DESDE DICIEMBRE 1º DE 1929

ITINERARIO

SUBIDA LINEA DEL MAGDALENA **BAJADA**

DOMINGO	LUNES	MARTES	MIERCOLES	JUEVES	VIERNES	SABADO	VUELO NUMERO	DOMINGO	LUNES	MARTES	MIERCOLES	JUEVES	VIERNES	SABADO
1	3	5	7	9	11	13	VUELO NUMERO	2	4	6	8	10	12	14
6-00	6-00	5-30	6-00	6-00	6-00	6-00	Barranquilla	14-30	14-00	14-30	14-00	14-30	14-30	14-30
		6-30		(6-30)	(6-30)	6-30	Calamar	13-30			13-30	13-30		
		7-30					Magangué							12-30
8-30	8-30	8-30	8-30	8-30	8-30	8-30	El Banco	11-30	11-30	12-00	11-30	11-30	11-30	11-30
				9-30			Gamarra	10-30						
		10-30		10-30		10-30	Pto. Wilches			10-15		10-15		10-15
		11-00			11-00	11-00	Bca. Bermeja	9-45		9-45	9-45		9-45	
12-30	12-30	12-30	12-30	12-30	12-30	12-30	Pto. Berrio	9-00	9-00	9-00	9-00	9-00	9-00	9-00
	13-30	13-30			13-30		La Dorada	7-30		7-30		7-30		7-30
15-00	15-00	15-00	15-00	15-00	15-00	15-00	Girardot	6-00	6-00	6-00	6-00	6-00	6-00	6-00

LINEA DEL ATLANTICO

			21				VUELO NUMERO					22		
		6-00					Barranquilla					15-00		
		7-30					Cartagena					14-00		
		12-00					Sautata					10-30		
		16-00					Cristóbal, C. Z.					6-00		

		31	33				VUELO NUMERO			32	34			
		6-00	6-00				Barranquilla			9-30	9-30			
		6-30	6-30				Ciénaga			9-00	9-00			

		21	41				VUELO NUMERO				42	22		
		6-00	6-00				Barranquilla				16-00	13-00		
		7-00	7-00				Cartagena				15-00	12-00		

LINEA INTEROCEANICA

			41				VUELO NUMERO				42			
			6-00				Barranquilla				16-00			
			7-30				Cartagena				15-00			
Vuelos de servicio según demanda			10-30				Sautata	Vuelos de servicio según demanda			12-00			
			13-00				Quibdó				9-30			
			14-00				Istmina				8-30			
			16-00				Buenaventura				6-00			

LINEA DEL PACIFICO

				51	57		VUELO NUMERO					52		58
					6-00		Cristobal							11-30
					7-00		Balboa, C. Z.							10-30
				6-30	11-30		Buenaventura					16-00		6-00
				9-40			Tumaco					13-00		
				11-15			Esmeraldas					11-00		
				13-15			Bahia de Car.					9-00		
				15-00			Salinas					7-00		
				16-00			Guayaquil					6-00		

LINEA DE SANTANDER

				61	63		65	VUELO NUMERO			62		64		66
				12-00	12-00		12-00	Puerto Wilches			16-30		16-30		16-30
				13-00	13-00		13-00	Bucaramanga			15-30		15-30		15-30

The Servicio Bolivariano

There followed a period when von Bauer made a subtle change in the promotion of SCADTA's image. Hitherto the accent had been strictly Colombian, but with Ecuador now on the route map, and with aspirations of expansion further south, the spirit of the great liberator Simón Bolívar was invoked by the adoption of his name, implying closer communication by air transport between the countries of the Spanish-speaking republics of South America.

On 22 October, 1928, Herbert Boy flew the F 13 *Atlántico* on a survey flight to Paita, in the extreme north of Peru. A second survey was made in the *Boyaca* on 22 January, 1929, and the aircraft returned without incident the next day. On 27 April, an agreement was signed with the Peruvian authorities permitting SCADTA aircraft to alight at Puerto Pizarro (or at Talara) en route to Paita, but without cabotage rights within Peru. However, the agreement was redundant, as SCADTA did not start regular services. The US State Department had exerted pressure on the Peruvian authorities to favour the Pan American-PANAGRA plans. This ruled out other US airlines. And although SCADTA had conducted exploratory talks with Faucett in Peru, Harold P. Grow, the US Naval Commander who had created the Peruvian Naval Air Service, had intervened to protect PANAGRA.

Possibly more important, had things turned out differently, another route was being developed. On 1 April, 1929, the Guayaquil–Buenaventura flight was extended along the Pacific coast to Panama City and Cristóbal, using the new Junkers-W 34 *Cundinamarca* from Buenaventura northwards. The same aircraft began the service between Cristóbal and Barranquilla two days later. Service to Panamá had been assiduously sought for many years. The fact that permission was not forthcoming until Pan American Airways inaugurated service from Miami on 3 February, 1929, did not go unnoticed in Colombia.

SCADTA's timetables took on a new look. In addition to the familiar SCADTA acronym and the well-known badge, the literature included a reference to the Servicio Bolivariano de Transportes Aéreos, even, in some cases, taking preference over the parent company's name. A Dornier Wal replaced the old single-engined Junkers as a more graceful flying symbol. The system was impressively broken down into routes with names such as Línea de Atlántico (Barranquilla–Cristóbal), Línea del Pacífico (Puerto Pizarro to Cristóbal) and the Línea Interoceánica (Barranquilla–Buenaventura), in addition to the traditional Línea del Magdalena and the Línea Santander (COSADA). The cartographers of the Scientific Section were kept busy. The route network had, within the period of little more than a year, doubled its area served and trebled its route mileage.

The Pan American Challenge

But pride came before a fall, and the fine ambitions were abruptly terminated. Pan American was gathering momentum, having already caught the headlines by selecting Charles Lindbergh himself as pilot for the inaugural Sikorsky S-38 flight to Panamá. SCADTA was beset by financial problems—the Wall Street 'Black Tuesday' occurred on 29 October, 1929. Simultaneously, Pan American Airways and its partner the W. R. Grace shipping line, with whom it had struck up an alliance to form PANAGRA, were beginning to move decisively to start services down the entire length of the South American Pacific Coast. The inaugural Pan American-PANAGRA joint service from Miami to Peru was accomplished during May 1929 and by the time SCADTA was deploying its W 34 to Guayaquil

224

and Panamá, PANAGRA was firmly in the ascendant with the superior Sikorsky S-38s and Ford Tri-Motors.

Also there was a measure of political apprehension in the United States over the strategic position of Colombia with regard to the Canal Zone. Although the subject was delicately avoided in international discussions or negotiations, the USA's direct recognition of Panama as an independent state in 1903 was the death knell of any hopes of retaining the Peninsula as part of Colombian territory. It was generally conceded that, the decision having been decisively made (and settled by a reparations payment to Colombia by the United States in 1903) Colombia was relieved of a chronic source of political unrest. But the issue was still an irritant.

Some United States strategists were anxious to isolate air routes from the USA to the Canal Zone, or the Republic of Panama, unless these could be kept strictly under the control of the USA. The prospect of a Colombian airline, backed by a German partner (the Condor Syndikat lurking somewhere in the background) was therefore not exactly welcome in Washington.

The Gentleman's Agreement

A bilateral air agreement was finally signed between Colombia and the USA on 23 February, 1929, the first, incidentally, between the USA and a foreign country. Pan American was going from strength to strength, consolidating air mail and passenger service throughout the Caribbean region. In a major development, a so-called 'gentleman's agreement' was reached between Peter Paul von Bauer, representing SCADTA, and Juan Trippe, President of Pan American Airways. In truth, van Bauer must have had his back to the wall; but neither side was willing to expose the terms of the agreement to the full glare of public scrutiny. Juan Trippe, a veritable Machiavelli guiding Pan American, did not make public the existence of a skeleton organization, La Sociedad Anomina Colombo-Americana de Aviación.

Juan Trippe (*left*) controlled the destiny of Pan American Airways from its formation in 1927 until his retirement on 7 May, 1968. Much of his early success could be attributed to the technical and operational advice given by Charles Lindbergh (*right*) who flew nonstop from New York to Paris in 1927. He made a notable series of survey flights for Pan American, including a Goodwill Tour of Central America and the Caribbean in 1927–1928.

This SCADTA Ford 5-AT-DS C-60 *Barranquilla*, with additional port-side door, was the 5-AT-D NC9657 which was previously used as a landplane by National Air Transport, Pacific Air Transport and United Air Lines. It was powered by 420 hp Pratt & Whitney Wasps and mounted on Edo floats. (*AVIANCA*)

Briefly, in exchange for the surrender of control of SCADTA to Pan American (which undertook to provide a new infusion of capital to a financially-troubled company), the Colombian airline agreed to withdraw from international routes and confine itself to domestic services within Colombia. SCADTA effectively would become part of the rapidly-growing Pan American system, soon to envelop the whole of Latin America. It began to show Pan American connections on its route maps and timetables; Pan American reciprocated in like manner.

Von Bauer resigned from the Presidency, and a Colombian nominee took his place—actually only two United States citizens were added to the SCADTA board of directors, thus obscuring the real change of control. And for the next ten years, evidence of Pan American control was everywhere, notably by the arrival of Sikorsky S-38s, Ford Tri-Motors and other aircraft. SCADTA schedules were included in Pan American's timetables, and the association was mentioned in that company's annual report. But the agreement was never publicly announced. To describe it as secret, however, would overstate the case. People simply did not talk or write about it.

For the record, Pan American Airways acquired 84·4 per cent of the stock of SCADTA between 10 February, 1930, and 10 April, 1931, a percentage which underwent only minor changes until the formation of AVIANCA in 1940. The formal agreement was signed on 15 February, 1930, and SCADTA operated without Pan American participation until 3 March, 1931. Service to Guayaquil ceased in December 1930 and to Panamá in June 1931.

New Directions

Although the short-lived Servicio Bolivariano and the Pan American acquisition were the major events affecting SCADTA's existence as the twentieth century moved into its fourth decade, many routine activities still had to be taken care of by the airline's operational and administrative departments, simply to keep the wheels turning, whatever might be the political outcome. Thus some new aircraft appeared on the SCADTA register, even before Pan American began to transfer used aircraft from the United States to Colombia. The Pan American aircraft, broken into service though they might have been, proved to be, in general, superior to the German types; and if Pan American seemed to have regarded SCADTA simply as a junior division of its continent-wide network, a glance at the map, putting SCADTA's network in perspective, shows this to be no less than the case, and to Colombia's advantage.

Nevertheless, some other aircraft types, from three different countries, had already been added to the SCADTA inventory. Before the full implications of the deteriorating financial situation had confronted von Bauer, arrangements had been made with Junkers to supply improved versions of the single-engined F 13 which had borne the brunt of the pioneering efforts. From 1929, SCADTA acquired five of these, of which one was a W 33, with a Junkers water-cooled engine, and the remainder W 34s, with Pratt & Whitney Hornet air-cooled radials. The *Cundinamarca*, which opened the service to Panamá, was probably the first to be delivered.

SCADTA also acquired a Dornier Wal, *Colombia*, which figured in all its publicity, and was the flagship of the fleet for several years, although it was unable to operate up the Magdalena River, still SCADTA's busiest route by a considerable margin.

In the late 1920s, five de Havilland Moth aircraft were purchased from England. These *avionetas*—the charming Spanish word for a diminutive aeroplane—were used for survey work, air photography, mail and special flights, and appear to have been the favourite type of Herbert Boy, even though the casualty rate was high. To complete the cosmopolitan fleet content, two Fokker Super Universals were used sporadically, mainly as part of the desire to find a larger landplane suitable for Colombian airfield conditions.

SCADTA's Junkers-W 33 C-33 *Cundinamarca* at Girardot on the Magdalena River. The then new bridge and a number of riverboats can be seen in the background. (*AVIANCA*)

SCADTA's C-28 *Colombia* was an early version of the Dornier Wal flying-boat. The passenger steps for boarding at the water's edge are of interest. (*AVIANCA*)

SCADTA's de Havilland 60 Gipsy Moth C-43 *Halieto* as a floatplane. (*AVIANCA*)

With the multiplicity of types, SCADTA began slowly to expand its domestic system, not so much in adding more route mileage, but to provide direct connections, and particularly to avoid having to ask passengers to complete their journeys to their final destinations by some other means of transport. Most important of these was the landplane connection from the airfield at Flandes (adjacent to the Girardot floatplane base on the Magdalena River) to Bogotá, the first flight in the F 13 *Garcia Rovira* taking place in December 1930. Also a landplane connection was made to Ibagué at the same time, coinciding almost symbolically with the withdrawal of service to Ecuador on 13 December, thus fulfilling the obligations of SCADTA to Pan American under the 'gentleman's agreement.'

A new President of Colombia had been installed on 7 August, bringing some new impetus to transport development within Colombia. Dr Olaya Herrera, who had been a source of continual support for von Bauer during the 1920s, not only sought to uplift Colombia's surface communications out of the pack-mule era; but gave encouragement for the expansion of the major existing inter-city mode, namely SCADTA. This policy fitted neatly with Pan American's added support, so that SCADTA began to take on a new life. On 16 July, 1931, a joint air mail service was inaugurated between Bogotá and New York, a direct result of co-operation with the new majority stockholder.

ADELCA

An important development was the formation of the Administración del Correo Aéreo de Colombia (ADELCA), under which SCADTA became, in effect, the official air mail agency. Under a contract with the Colombian Government signed on 1 December, 1931, the airline was permitted to retain 98 per cent of all air mail charges through the sale of air mail stamps, which were valid to pay the air mail fee only. Coming into force on 1 January, 1932, SCADTA sold the stamps, issued money orders, and maintained a corps of 300 letter carriers—air mail postmen. It was a unique system, and was created out of necessity in a country where surface transport was still so poor that the carriage of letters or packages from one city to another was time-consuming and, because of the many changes of transport carrier, subject to both pilferage and damage.

UMCA

One of the oddest sequels to the Pan American take-over, giving practical support to the idea that protectionist policy over the Panama Canal was an important consideration, was the formation of the mysterious airline with the strange-sounding name. **Urabá, Medellín and Central Airways (UMCA)** was originally the nucleus of a visionary idea by Gonzalo Mejia, none other than one of the former Antioquians who had formed C.C.N.A. in Medellín in 1919. Subsequently he became part of the SCADTA commercial organization, and made many visits to New York, in which city he was for some time the SCADTA agent.

Mejia's vision was for a transcontinental South American route from Panamá to Buenos Aires, overland through Colombia, calling at points such as Turbo, at the southernmost point on the Caribbean shore, thence through Medellín, Bogotá, Villavicencio (the gateway to the llanos), Leticia, Porto Velho (Brazil), and Asunción (Paraguay). On 14 January, 1931, the Colombian Government granted a 15-year concession for a route from Medellín to Turbo, on the Gulf of

Sikorsky S-38 *Marichu* is seen on its first arrival at Medellín, inaugurating the route of Urabá, Medellín, and Central Airways (UMCA). UMCA was a legal creation of Pan American Airways, to prevent SCADTA, predominantly staffed by technicians and pilots of German origin, from approaching the Panama Canal. UMCA never owned aircraft of its own, nor had any distinctive markings. (*Pan American World Airways*)

Urabá—hence the airline name. The law promulgating this concession required an international connection with a North American transport company, of which there was only one. Accordingly, Mejia went to the United States to meet Juan Trippe, and UMCA was incorporated under the laws of the State of Delaware on 24 August, 1931.

The Aviation Corporation of the Americas, alias Pan American, acquired a 54 per cent interest in UMCA on 13 April, 1932, and the first service was flown on 12 July of that year, at a frequency of twice a week, passengers only. Mail service began on 20 June, 1933, when the Colombian Government approved a contract for UMCA to carry mail between Medellín and Turbo at about $1·00 US per lb.

Throughout its entire history, UMCA never owned any aircraft, or employed any staff. It was simply a device to permit Pan American to make a connection with Colombia at a key point (Medellín was right in the middle of the domestic route network) at the same time keeping SCADTA—with its undertones of German influence—away from Panamá. UMCA served the purpose well. Starting with Sikorsky S-38 amphibians, and moving through a succession of superior aircraft: S-43, DC-2, DC-3, and finally Convair CV-240, it provided steady, reliable, and mainly unpublicised service—although the schedule could always be found in the Pan American timetables.

By December 1947 it was a fully-owned subsidiary of Pan American, although it had lost its mail contract on 1 September, 1940, the necessity for it being obviated by direct services from the USA through Barranquilla to Medellín and Cali. The airline was finally dissolved on 15 June, 1961, after the US Civil Aeronautics Board withdrew its certificate on 28 July, 1959.

SCADTA Supports the War Effort

During 1932 SCADTA became involved in a semi-military operation of great value to the Colombian Government. It was asked by the President to assist in supporting the Army and the Air Force in a logistics effort to supply the defence forces on the southern frontier. In an area which had no clearly-delineated

230

frontiers except those of natural features such as waterways, Peru was attempting to extend its frontiers northward. Later it was to succeed in replacing Ecuador as the sovereign power over a large expanse of Amazonian jungle which at the time seemed of negligible value, but was later to become the site of much prospecting for oil. In the course of pursuing its expansionist aims, Peruvian forces occupied the 'Leticia Trapezium', that territorial peculiarity which gave Colombia access to the banks of the Amazon.

If ever there was an isolated outpost, Leticia was it. It was separated from Bogotá by more than 1,000 kilometres of unmapped and featureless savannah—the llanos—which merged into impenetrable jungles. Except by taking a ship from Barranquilla to Belém, the Brazilian port at the mouth of the Amazon, and then an Amazon river steamer bound for Iquitos, Leticia was to all intents and purposes inaccessible from its own capital. On 2 September, 1932, therefore, the President called Herbert Boy to his office and asked him to organize a supply route to the Putumayo River, the southern boundary of Colombia bordering on Ecuador and Peru.

With the support of the SCADTA organization, Boy did all that was asked of him. He developed a supply route from the southern extremities of SCADTA's route system, Neiva, and set up successive air bases at Florencia, Tres Esquinas, and other places in the Provinces of Caquetá and Putumayo. His efforts were rewarded in many ways. He became a national hero, epitomising the precarious but dependable air lifeline between the isolated troop garrisons on the steaming banks of the Putumayo. Given the rank of major for the duration of the conflict, he was decorated by President Olaya Herrera, and a small community on the Caquetá River was named Puerto Boy. A mere landing stage for the Junkers floatplanes, it was no Lindbergh Field; but in the eyes of Colombians it was just as romantic a tribute, and far more valuable.

SCADTA's part in the affair consisted of supplying one F 13 and one W 34, which served Boy well, and did not drain the airline's commercial resources

The simple terminal building at Cali. It had a corrugated iron roof on which appeared the names SCADTA and CALI. (*AVIANCA*)

231

An early picture of Medellín Airport, situated at an altitude of about 1,500 metres, with SCADTA's Sikorsky S-38B amphibian C-47 *Olaya Herrera*. (*AVIANCA*)

unduly. In return it won a small bonus from the Colombian military budget, which, to meet the emergency and the influx of squadrons of aircraft purchased from the USA, had constructed an air base at Palenquero, conveniently en route between Bogotá and Medellín near the Magdalena River. The emergency ended in July 1933 and SCADTA's aircraft were thereafter able to use Palenquero and to dispense with the necessity of changing from floatplane to landplane at Girardot/Flandes for Barranquilla–Bogotá connections.

Fleet Modernization

Whatever may be said about the reasons for Pan American's entry into SCADTA's affairs, there can be little question about the results, which were entirely positive. By all accounts, the influence was efficient, well-mannered, and demonstrably beneficial. Its major contribution was to introduce new aircraft types which raised the standards, both technical and commercial, by several notches. At first, in the initial stages when the floatplane still reigned supreme because of the dearth of airfields, Sikorsky S-38s supplemented the Junkers types

Early view of the terminal area at Barranquilla's Veranillo Airport. The open-sided engineering shop with cantilevered roof was a feature of numerous Latin American airports. (*AVIANCA*)

of the earlier generation. This fitted in perfectly with the deployment of the type during the early 1930s on Pan American's own Caribbean routes along the northern seaboard of South America, and of its associate PANAGRA's down the Pacific coast. But the Junkers remained in command of the Magdalena River, where, however, they were fitted with Edo floats, which provided better hydrodynamics than the old Junkers design.

SCADTA's Fokker Super Universal C-44 *Medellín* starting its take-off run attended by military gentlemen on horseback. (*AVIANCA*)

On 27 June, 1932, at long last, Barranquilla attained the goal of a direct air service to Medellín, via Barrancabermeja and Puerto Berrío. This still involved a change of aircraft at the departure point from the Magdalena River, but the momentum for improvement was building up. The Medellín service went on to the growing city of Cali and thence to Buenaventura, where the new route connected with the Pacific coastal service. Then, on 15 July, 1933, the Línea Transandina was opened, finally connecting Colombia's two largest cities, Bogotá and Medellín. This was made possible by SCADTA's access to Palenquero, which provided the necessary staging point until aircraft with the necessary range for nonstop service became available. (See Map 23)

Pan American's scheduling organization exerted its influence at this point, to eliminate route segments of little productivity or those which had become redundant. Cali became the southern terminus of the Cauca River route. A rail service from Cali to Buenaventura was considered adequate; and the direct Barranquilla–Buenaventura service was suspended.

Even so, the rejuvenated SCADTA did not enjoy complete freedom of the Colombian skies; neither did it improve its safety record. There continued to be a number of accidents—in 1934 there was one to each of the major types in use, one Sikorsky S-38, one Junkers-F 13, and one Fokker Super Universal. The Sikorsky had the misfortune to crash in the jungles of the San Juan River region of Chocó Province, and gained notoriety when one of the passengers, Newton Marshall, managed to survive by a feat of self-preservation through applied jungle-craft which astonished everyone.

On 15 June, 1933, the **Servicio Aéreo Colombiano (SACO)** had been formed by Ernesto Samper Mendoza, and he quickly demonstrated that he was prepared to challenge SCADTA on its own terms, at least in equipment standards, even though its route network was small. Samper acquired Ford Tri-Motors to match those of SCADTA which were beginning to arrive through the auspices of Pan American. While SACO's routes numbered only two, at least they were good ones: direct service linking Colombia's three largest cities, Bogotá, Medellín, and Cali.

233

Samper himself was killed in the dramatic incident at Medellín on 24 June, 1934, when he was taking off in one of the Fords, apparently lost control, and crashed right into another waiting Ford of SCADTA (the *Manizales*). A total of seventeen people were killed in the disaster, which was a high figure for the time; but it was notable because one of the victims was Carlos Gardel, a famous and popular Argentine singer. The incident was one of the most talked about of all prewar air tragedies, comparing with the 1931 Knute Rockne crash in the USA (which led to the demise of the Fokker family of airliners in the United States) and which was perhaps eclipsed only by the *Hindenburg* holocaust in 1937.

Fritz Wilhelm Hammer (*left*) went to Colombia in 1920 as the technical representative of the Junkers company. An ex-naval pilot, he became the dynamic marketing director of the German Condor Syndikat, formed on 5 May, 1924, whose main task was to sell the products of the German aircraft industry to other countries. Hammer died in an aircraft crash in Ecuador on 5 March, 1938. Wilhelm Schnurbusch (*centre*) arrived in Colombia on the same ship as Hammer. An ex-naval aircraft engineer, he was SCADTA's technical director for twenty years. Ernesto Samper Mendoza (*right*) founded Servicio Aéreo Colombiano in 1933 but was killed a year later, as related in the text. (*Lufthansa and John W. Underwood*)

The arrival of the Ford Tri-Motors presented SCADTA with other problems, as the time had now come to face squarely the issue of replacing flying-boats and seaplanes with landplanes as the major aircraft type. But airfield building in Colombia, as with other South American countries, was slow. Because SCADTA had managed remarkably well with the Junkers floatplanes, there had not been the same incentive in Colombia for the airline, the Government, or the municipalities to build airfields. In fact, the military base at Palenquero was probably SCADTA's best field for several years. Thus, during the mid-1930s, the town of San Marcos, in Sucre Province about 200 kilometres south of Cartagena, became for a while an important station on the SCADTA network. The Junkers-W 34s still took off from Barranquilla—simply because there was no airfield—and alighted on the lake at San Marcos, whence the passengers were transferred to the Fords for onward connections to the cities of central and southern Colombia.

But this was a temporary expedient. In 1937 came the Boeing 247Ds, purchased from United Air Lines via Pan American. These fine aircraft had up to twelve seats—two less than the Fords—but were fast, had good range, and were versatile enough to use the grass strips being hurriedly prepared throughout Colombia. While this *Flota de los Conquistadores* was a second-hand fleet, the description should be seen in perspective. Only four years previously, the Boeing 247s had

A SCADTA Ford 5-AT, probably at Bogotá. A damaged and engineless Curtiss Condor can just be seen behind the Ford and on the right are two Junkers-Ju 52/3ms. (*AVIANCA*)

C-71 *Belalcazar* was one of several Boeing 247Ds introduced by SCADTA in 1936.

One of the less-well-known transport aeroplanes was the Clark GA-43. This SCADTA example may have been the only one to have operated as a seaplane. (*AVIANCA*)

C.110 was one of a pair of Lockheed 10-E Electras delivered to Servicio Aéreo Colombiano. These became part of the SCADTA fleet in 1939, passed to PAA's Alaska Division and at some time were in service with TACA. (*Lockheed*)

been the most modern aircraft ever put into service in the United States; and only the marginal superiority of the Douglas DC-2s, which entered service a year later, had displaced them in a hotly competitive market.

SCADTA had ten Boeing 247s and these gradually replaced most of the Ford, Junkers, Sikorsky, and assorted aircraft throughout the route system. The Junkers-W 34s continued to chug up and down the Magdalena, and the odd Ford was to be seen here and there. There was even a Clark GA-43J floatplane, one of the few GA-43s ever built, which plied between Barranquilla and Ciénaga. But the Boeing 247s were the flagships and the backbone of the fleet, not only routinely substituting for older aircraft, but opening up such nonstop routes as the Barranquilla–Bogotá Express; connecting Cúcuta and Barranquilla for the first time; and in January 1937 penetrating the llanos region of eastern Colombia, with two routes from Bogotá to Arauca, via Villavicencio and two or three tiny settlements.

Most of the Boeing 247Ds had nine passenger seats, plus one for the steward, an improved standard of comfort hitherto unknown in Colombia; but two of the aircraft were even more luxurious, with two of the seats being replaced by a toilet. Passengers still had to report to the SCADTA office for weighing some two or three days before the flight. By now, at last, Barranquilla had an airport, as befitted its status as the main air gateway to Colombia. Soledad Airport was opened in 1936, and from this time the service pattern was intensified.

Because of the difficult terrain, some cities still had to depend on surface connections with a neighbouring community favoured with a strip of land which lent itself more easily to the construction of an airfield. Thus, for a while, Cartago became an important point, serving the nearby larger cities of Armenia, Pereira, and Manizales by a train connection. Other rail links were used, but the most intriguing transfer must have been the one at Gamarra, a landing stage on the Magdalena about 300 kilometres south of Barranquilla. Here passengers wishing to travel to Ocaña, in Norte de Santander, were privileged to take the aerial cable car on a ride which lasted for seven hours.

SCADTA becomes AVIANCA

At about the time when the Boeing 247Ds were revolutionizing the SCADTA schedules, other revolutionary activities in the form of political upheavals were occurring in Europe. The Nazi war machine was on the move and Adolf Hitler was already making clear his aggressive intent by perpetrating the *anschluss* in Austria. Peter Paul von Bauer, who had retired to Austria after the 'gentleman's agreement' of 1931, became deeply disturbed by what was going on in Germany, so much so that he sold his castle at Klagenfurt, and returned to Colombia, via New York, where conversations took place with Juan Trippe.

The result was that von Bauer was reinstated as the President of SCADTA for a while, with the former chief of the Scientific Section Hermann Kuehl as the General Manager. Not that this carried the implied suggestion that the German influence in SCADTA was on the ascendant. Quite the contrary: on 26 May, 1938, Colombian Law No.89 obliged all air companies to organize its staff so that 25 per cent of the employees were Colombian citizens. From 1943 the percentage was raised to 50 per cent, and then from 1948 to 75 per cent.

The last years of the 1930s decade were characterized by route consolidation, and better integration of fleets, with the accent on the Boeing 247D. Accidents still took their toll, as a constant reminder that the Colombian terrain had not yet surrendered to the challenge of air transport. An important event in 1939 was when, on 27 October, agreement was reached to merge SCADTA and SACO. This was ratified at a stockholders' meeting on 23 February, 1940, and confirmed by Public Notary Advice on 3 October of that year.

But far more critical developments were afoot. The United States, with Pan American as its agency in matters where air transport might play a part in international statesmanship and strategy, decided that the time had come to exert political pressure in South America to stop what it considered to be the ominous spread of German influence through the medium of airline control. Juan Trippe procrastinated as long as he could. The German staff of SCADTA were good workers. More important, they were paid only about one third of the contemporary US wage scale. But further delay would have been regarded by the US State Department as almost treasonable. A delegation from Washington, representing the State Department, bluntly reminded the Colombian authorities that SCADTA was regarded as a risk and that, in the interests of continental security, it should be nationalized. The Colombian Government was apparently unaware of the 'gentleman's agreement'. Still holding four-fifths of the stock, Pan American held the whip hand legally, and the Government complied without demur. Von Bauer retired to Chile, where he lived for the remainder of his life.

On 8 June, 1940, in a shattering *coup de grâce*, all German employees were dismissed overnight. A total of about eighty skilled pilots, craftsmen, mechanics,

This picture of Peter Paul von Bauer and his family was presumably taken soon after his arrival in Colombia in 1921. He infused new life and energy into SCADTA, augmented its finances from his own resources, and showed great vision in surveying an air route to the USA in 1925. He sold his control of SCADTA to Pan American Airways in 1930, an act which was not publicly announced until 1940. Von Bauer died in Chile some years later.

(AVIANCA)

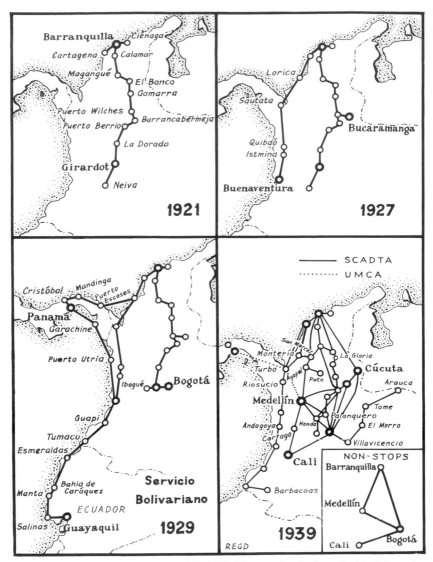

23. SCADTA Route Development, 1921–1939. After starting the first scheduled air service in South America that was sustained for more than a few years, SCADTA's expansion was restricted by the precipitous Andes, because of the altitude limitations of its aircraft. Thus new routes took the line of least resistance, along river valleys and the coasts. Attempts to add international services were terminated when Pan American took control in 1931, but Colombian domestic service was intensified.

The entrance to SCADTA's Barranquilla marine airport, with a SCADTA passenger bus on the left. The arch on the right of the photograph can be seen at top centre on the air view on page 221. (*AVIANCA*)

and administrators were informed that their services were no longer required. Some of them learned of their fate when they arrived home from work. They were immediately replaced by a group of Pan American employees who had been travelling incognito on SCADTA routes for several weeks before the blow fell. And so almost callously came to an end the contribution of the German pioneers who had been partners in the formation of the oldest airline in the Americas. Their work was finished, and political rather than industrial or commercial circumstances had brought about their abrupt demise. But this was no time for sentiment. There was some evidence that Nazi agents were trying to penetrate SCADTA. Although for the United States war was still more than a year away, the drums were rolling, and the change was inevitable.

The seal was put on the transaction when, on 14 June, 1940, all implications of German association were obliterated when the name SCADTA (with the first A proclaiming the German connection) was replaced by the now more appropriate Aerovías Nacionales de Colombia (AVIANCA).

An early AVIANCA Douglas DC-3. It is C-100 in the old system before HK became the Colombian national registration. (*AVIANCA*)

CHAPTER TWELVE

Colombian Consolidation

A New Start

Although the almost instantaneous replacement of German personnel by Pan American appointees and the official change of name of SCADTA did not occur until June 1940, the name AVIANCA began to come into general use at the beginning of the year. The legal transactions and negotiations took a little time, but on 14 June an official Notary Advice No.714 was published in Barranquilla to put things in order. Pan American, which had formerly held—unknown to almost everyone in Colombia, including the incumbent President—about four-fifths of the stock, retained 64 per cent. The Colombian Government had 15 per cent, while Colombian citizens and business interests held the remainder, including von Bauer's until he withdrew from the aviation scene.

In one respect, the influence of Pan American became immediately apparent, and wholly beneficial. The flying equipment was upgraded, and the Colombian public began to receive increased airline inter-city and local service, with improved standards of comfort and greater availability of seats. The most important contribution to the fleet was the addition of a number of 21-seat Douglas DC-3s with the ability to fly nonstop from Barranquilla to Bogotá, an achievement which could be regarded almost as a watershed of route development within Colombia.

The Pan American management tried to rationalize the route system to make the best use of the total inventory of aircraft. The single Clark GA-43 was used on the coastal route from Barranquilla to Ciénega, serving Santa Marta; Fords and Junkers were used on local routes; and the Boeing 247s continued to be the backbone of the regional fleet as the DC-3 was deployed on the busiest inter-city routes.

The need to use surface connections to reach some of the larger cities of Colombia was still a feature of the domestic air route system. Cities such as Manizales or Armenia benefitted from air and rail integration, and the unique aerial cable-car connection from Gamarra to Ocaña, mentioned in the previous chapter, continued to operate.

Early in 1942, a link with SCADTA's pioneering past was broken when the Junkers-W 34 floatplane service up the River Magdalena was curtailed at Barrancabermeja, and the Girardot station closed down. This terminal for both land and waterborne aircraft had served the company well for 21 years, and its closure must have been the occasion for many a sentimental gathering of some of the old-timers in the company, even though many of them were still *persona non grata* in AVIANCA.

There were some problems with the Boeing 247s during 1944, caused more by the still fairly primitive meteorological facilities than by the aircraft's shortcomings (although flying above 8,000 ft did not come easily to the 247). However, with the reinforcement of more aircraft from the United States, including three more DC-3s, normal services settled down again, to the exclusion of more of the old types. The Ford Tri-Motor still operated on the Interocean Line from Barranquilla to Buenaventura and Tumaco, and the Junkers-W 34 still made its familiar trips up the Magdalena. These latter aircraft were retained only because the airfields needed to replace the seaplane stations had not yet been built, a construction process which was eventually completed and the era of the floatplanes came to an end. The Ford Tri-Motors were withdrawn in 1946, to be replaced in some places by Sikorsky S-38 amphibians as an interim step, pending the final closure of all the seaplane bases. The schedules serving the Pacific coast were changed so that connections to the southwest were made at Medellín and Cali, thus eliminating the Interocean service that had been SCADTA's second trunk route.

The final break with a famous past came in 1947. Six new DC-3s, fitted with 28 seats to cope with the fast-growing demand, arrived in Colombia to permit the elimination of all the Boeing 247s, and—another sentimental occasion—the retirement of the Junkers-W 34s from the Magdalena route, to be replaced by the S-38s, whose amphibious capability enabled them to fly on to the important hub of Medellín without the inconvenience of a river-to-air transfer at Barrancabermeja.

AVIANCA's 'Hi-Per DC-3' HK-118 *Ciudad de Magangué* taking off from Bogotá in 1965. This aircraft was built as the C-47 41-38723, passed to AVIANCA as C-118, was converted to Hyper-DC-3 and lost in a collision with a light aircraft in October 1965.
(*Gordon S. Williams*)

ARCO

Even before the night of the long knives of 8 June, 1940, a few German employees of SCADTA had left the company to start their own airline in the llanos region. Capt Hans Hoffman and Capt Fritz Herzhauser founded **Aerovías Ramales Colombianas (ARCO)**—'ramal' means branch line—in Villavicencio on 30 October, 1939. With a small staff of half a dozen airline veterans and various helpers, they started a small operation with the single-engined Ford 8-AT *Santander*, purchased from the Iscuande gold-mine near Guapi on the Pacific coast; a Ford Tri-Motor, *Bolívar*, purchased from the Texas Oil Company; and a Beech 17 biplane. With this assortment of aircraft, Capt Hoffman proceeded to operate a small network serving the plains northwest of Villavicencio, stretching as far as the Venezuelan frontier at Arauca and Puerto Carreño.

Hoffman's Fords were fitted with an overhead hatch door so that large loads could be lowered by crane straight into the fuselage, which could carry two tons. In addition to the wide range of goods which flights to remote areas such as these inevitably carry, Hoffman also claims to have been the first to uplift the now firmly-established zebu cattle to the eastern ranches. These were the breed of hardy animals, imported from Asia, which were found to be the solution to the cattle-producing problems of the llanos, superseding other breeds which could not flourish in the special conditions of tropical terrain and climate.

ARCO's passengers included police and relief troops travelling to the outer perimeter of Colombia's frontier regions. Their presence might have been regarded as adequate grounds for security; nevertheless, possibly under pressure from United States sources, with military strategy demanding that no chances were to be taken which might imperil logistics supply routes from South America to the north, ARCO was purchased by AVIANCA on 25 April, 1941.

Developing the Llanos Network

The first route to Arauca, to inaugurate service to the llanos, had been started in January 1937 by SCADTA, and continued, primarily for the carriage of mail, during the brief interlude of parallel operations by ARCO. In the autumn of 1941, by which time Douglas DC-3s were deployed on services to the major cities of Colombia, steps were taken to improve and expand the service to the llanos and Ford Tri-Motors were transferred to Villavicencio for that purpose. There followed an interesting chapter in the history of the development of that region, one which vividly illustrates the point that the phrase 'from pack-mule to plane', used to describe Colombia's dramatic transition in transport, was no idle example of hyperbole.

One of the German pilots dismissed in 1940 had been Franz Series, who had gone to the llanos and taken up a career in construction. He built, for example, the first church in Yopal, now the capital of Casanare Province, but at that time only a dusty village on the open plains to the east of the populated part of Boyaca Province. Just about the same time as Capt Hoffman sold ARCO to AVIANCA, Series was approached by a gentleman from the US Rubber Development Corporation based at Villavicencio with a proposition to combine his building knowledge with his aviation background, and to undertake the survey and construction of additional airfields in the eastern Colombian plains.

Accordingly, he bought 17 mules, two horses, hired an invaluable assistant, Santiago Moreno, and himself adopted the alias of Francisco Gonzales—the idea of a German building airfields in the llanos might conceivably have raised some eyebrows in certain military circles at the time. The mules carried everything except the money, which was securely strapped in a belt around Moreno's waist. They moved from place to place, with supplies, materials, and tools, the largest of which were wheelbarrows, always carried on the top of the mules' loads. At each site selected by Series, local workmen were hired, usually between 15 and 25 in number, and the airstrips were quickly built. They required the clearing of all vegetation, and the approximate levelling of the red earth of the region, which was porous enough to permit excellent natural drainage. Series built a total of fifteen airstrips for AVIANCA, plus many more under private contract for the growing farming community which was beginning to populate the llanos farm country. He was eventually rehired by AVIANCA after the end of the war, and retired many years later in a pleasant hacienda not a stone's throw from Villavicencio airport, reflecting on the irony which caused him to perform the very task which had at one time been considered to be a good reason for dismissing him.

The First International Services of AVIANCA

Repeating to a certain extent the experience of about fifteen years previously, AVIANCA started its first international service to Ecuador on 21 March, 1946. On this occasion, however, the connection was by direct landplane—a DC-3—southwards from Cali to Quito, the capital, rather than by floatplanes around the coast. An extension was made to Guayaquil on 10 May. On 4 January, 1947, another route was started to Balboa (Panama Canal Zone) in parallel with the still-operating UMCA, which was, however, now something of an anachronism. The need to protect the corridor between a United States territory of great strategic value and a potential enemy stronghold no longer existed.

Shortly thereafter, on 22 January, 1947, an AVIANCA Douglas DC-4 opened the first long-distance Colombian overseas route, nonstop to Miami. It had been 22 years since Dr Peter Paul von Bauer had made his first attempt to establish a trans-Caribbean air route flying the Colombian flag. Except for Aerovias Brasil, which had been operating since the war years along the island chain of the eastern Caribbean, this was only the second service by a South American airline to reach the United States, and the first to provide a direct connection to the Andean countries of the west coast.

AVIANCA's Douglas C-54A HK-171 was originally the USAAF's 42-107442. After release from the Air Force it became American Airlines' NC90411 *Flagship Detroit*.
(*Gordon S. Williams*)

243

Nevertheless, AVIANCA's service was still very much a part of the Pan American system, and was promoted as such. Furthermore, although some local services were operated within Ecuador, to serve Cuenca (22 July, 1947), Manta (23 July, 1948), and Tulcan (10 January, 1950), these were suspended in 1951 along with all AVIANCA flights south of Colombia, in accordance with mutual scheduling agreements which gave PANAGRA a virtual monopoly in that country.

On 20 April, 1949, the Miami route was extended to New York, although no traffic could be carried between the two US points—the United States did not surrender cabotage rights as easily as it obtained them overseas. The biggest step forward in international route expansion followed soon afterwards. On 6 March, 1950, AVIANCA inaugurated trans-Atlantic service, to Lisbon, Rome, and Paris, also with DC-4s, and the same aircraft began flying to Jamaica on 17 September, 1950. During the next ten years, with the arrival of Lockheed Constellations AVIANCA added Madrid (3 July, 1951), Hamburg (17 April, 1953), and Frankfurt (24 April, 1954) to its European terminals, with Caracas (30 April, 1954) and San Juan (30 June, 1957) as intermediate stops. A completely new route was added to the south, to Lima, via Quito, on 1 June, 1957, by which time the Model 1049G Super Constellation had become the Colombian flagship.

AVIANCA's Lockheed Model 749 Constellation HK-163 was lost in the Azores in August 1954. Markings were dark blue with thin red outline slightly separated from the blue. The company name was in blue and the badge comprised a gold condor superimposed on a blue, red and yellow map. (*Lockheed*)

AVIANCA was making good use of its geographical position, at the crossways of important natural route arteries in the northwestern corner of the South American continent. Through service was offered from New York to Lima, and from Caracas to Panamá, with Barranquilla a key interchange point, to make full use of the so-called Sixth Freedom traffic rights which Colombia was fortuitously able to utilize, and which its promotional literature emphasized.

244

Energetic Postwar Competition in Colombia

Before the war came to its close, the resources of the United States in military supplies and material, including aircraft, had expanded at an almost explosive rate. Transport aircraft were pouring from the production lines of Douglas, Curtiss, and Lockheed factories, together with bombers and fighters, so that in some parts of the world, the latest arrivals at the operational bases superseded the older types, which were disposed of quickly as a matter of expediency. This process ran riot in South America, and a number of enterprising individuals picked up the surplus aircraft and went into business as commercial airlines, primarily to carry freight.

Colombia, with its uncompromising topography making surface transport still an inconvenient, if not a dangerous or difficult experience, was an ideal environment in which such small companies could find enough potential business to justify a precarious existence. Even though AVIANCA was vigorously expanding and strengthening its domestic route network, and carrying more freight than the surface carriers, there was always room for additional capacity.

For a few brief years, therefore, from 1944 until about 1947, a few names flitted across the historical chronology: **Aerovías Mundo, Sociedad Occidental de Transportes Aéreos (SOTA)**, **Taxi Aéreo Colombiano (TACO)**, and **Transandina**, followed by **Associación Interamericana de Aviación (AIDA)**, and **Aviación Refrigeración y Pesca (Afrypesca)**. These companies were predictably shortlived, their survival limited by their inability to maintain and fly successfully the fleets of Lockheed Lodestars, Noorduyn Norsemen, and miscellaneous types which they had been able to purloin from war-surplus supply sources.

Some of the newcomers lasted a little longer, especially if they were backed by an overseas parent company, such as was the case with **Líneas Aéreas TACA de Colombia**, one of the international chain of TACA's which was springing up in South America at the time. The Colombian TACA was formed on 17 November, 1944, and began service on 2 January, 1945, operating a nonstop DC-3 service from Bogotá to Caracas in co-operation with its sister company in Venezuela. On 17 July, 1946, TACA was granted a permit to operate to Miami even before AVIANCA received one, but never operated the route, as by early the following year it was losing money heavily and crashing DC-3s at an alarming rate. TACA withdrew its interest on 13 January, 1947, and the airline discontinued operations in May. By this time, AVIANCA was already poised to start its Miami service.

TACA's equipment—three DC-3s—was auctioned, and acquired by **Sociedad Colombiana de Transportes Aéreos (SCOLTA)**, which continued to operate from Bogotá and Medellín to Cartagena and Barranquilla for a year or two.

Another well-capitalized company—3 million pesos ($1·7 million)—started with a flourish. **Vías Aéreas Colombianas (VIARCO)** began operations in 1947 with seven converted Douglas C-47s and two Consolidated PBY-5A Catalinas, linking Bogotá, Cali, Medellín, and eight other points. In that year it reported carrying 57,000 passengers, but, like the others, it too succumbed to economic pressures and closed down.

An even more substantial operation was that founded by Ernesto Recaman, a pilot, together with associated Colombian interests, under the name of **Limitada Nacional de Servicio Aéreo (LANSA)** on 5 May, 1945. Initially, the capital was 135,000 pesos, but this was increased on 2 January, 1946, to 523,000. LANSA began to build up a domestic network and on 21 January, 1947, reached agreement with LAV, the Venezuelan national airline, for a joint service between Bogotá and Caracas. Service began soon afterwards, at first through an

245

interchange at Maracaibo, but on 27 May LANSA took over the entire operation. On 13 June, the company changed its status to that of a Colombian corporation, and changed its name to **Líneas Aéreas Nacionales, S.A.**

By 1947, LANSA was carrying half as many passengers as AVIANCA and continued to grow from strength to strength. By 1950 it had obtained permission to issue its own stamps, primarily for domestic routes, but also for an international route to Havana, Cuba. As with so many enterprising ventures in Colombia, however—even those showing great promise and conducted with energy and enthusiasm—LANSA ran into financial problems, and increasing deficits forced it into a merger with AVIANCA, signed on 10 September, 1951. For almost three years, the two companies operated services in parallel, until AVIANCA completely absorbed LANSA on 1 May, 1954.

At this time, AVIANCA found itself holding almost a monopoly position in Colombia. For a few months, at least, it was the only passenger airline, after it took over the operations of **Sociedad Aérea de Tolima (SAETA)**, which had been established in 1947 by a group of businessmen in Ibagué, capital of the Province of Tolima, with a capital of 570,000 pesos. AVIANCA subscribed 30 per cent, the rest mostly coming from the local populace. It had a fleet of three C-47s, and ordered two more, providing a service for the province giving direct connections to Bogotá, Medellín, and the Caribbean coast. It also maintained a station, among other feeder points, at Girardot, recalling distant memories of that former hub of the SCADTA network. AVIANCA took over SAETA in 1952.

Medellín Affirms its Presence

The city of Medellín has always been more than simply a provincial city of Colombia. Capital of the important Province of Antioquia, its stature within the country has always been considerable, amounting almost to a rivalry with the capital, Bogotá. Antioquia was a mining area, was rich agriculturally, and was more accessible than Bogotá to the remainder of the country, especially the Caribbean. After the war, Medellín began to develop as an important manufacturing centre, specializing in textile production, and became identified with the commercial world, while Bogotá remained the seat of government.

Medellín, in fact, had witnessed the historic meeting on 16 September, 1919, when Don Alejandro Echavarría assembled a group of friends to found the first airline in the New World. Subsequently, one of those original pioneers, Gonzalo Mejía, had had the inspiration of a trans-South American air route which, while never consummated, at least gave him the honour of providing the first regular link with Panamá, through the foundation of UMCA in 1931. The 'M' stood for Medellín, an indirect reminder of the importance of the Antioquian capital as a pivotal point in the centre of Colombia.

History was to repeat itself to a certain extent. In 1944, one of the entrepreneurs who lined up to buy second-hand aircraft from the United States armed forces was a Capt Dennis C. Powelson, formerly with the US Air Force, together with Arthur Taylor, who had a mining background. Powelson bought some Curtiss C-46s, and incorporated **Sociedad Aeronáutica de Medellín, S.A. (SAM)** in October 1945, as an all-freight airline. The authorized capital was a million pesos, equivalent at that time to about $600,000.

Air freight service between Medellín and Miami began on 1 September, 1946, and was extended to some domestic points. These included the city of Montería, capital of the Province of Sucre, and a rich cattle-raising district, where a slaughter-house which provided some steady business to the newly-formed SAM was owned by Pedro nel Ospina, son of one of the founders of C.C.N.A. in 1919, and none other than Gonzalo Mejia.

Although SAM's initial thriving business did not continue into the 1950s, as competition grew, and the large international trunk airlines were able to provide more freight capacity on their passenger aircraft, Powelson's company escaped the fate of his contemporaries who went bankrupt or merged with AVIANCA. Nevertheless, business declined, and an opportunity for diversifying SAM's operations into the passenger-carrying business was welcomed. It came in the form of an approach, in 1954, by the Dutch airline KLM.

It formed a case-book study of the efforts of a well-established international airline with worldwide ambitions trying to circumvent the limitation of the Five Freedoms of the Air. These basic principles laid down by the International Civil Aviation Organization (ICAO) were enthusiastically upheld by those countries which regarded the expansionist aims of older and larger rivals with apprehension, if not suspicion. KLM, for its part, had been a pioneer in its own right in the Caribbean and felt that it should be able to develop a network in northern and western South America as well as in the area radiating from the Dutch Antilles, centred in Curaçao. But it was frustrated by the inability to obtain Fifth Freedom rights through Colombia, that is, the right to pick up or set down passengers and freight to and from Colombian cities.

It sought a workable solution by an association with a Colombian airline, and accordingly formed, in January 1955, a new company, **Rutas Aéreas de Colombia Ltda (RAS)**, in conjunction with SAM. By this time, the Colombian airline had gained some respite by obtaining permission to start passenger services within Colombia, including the islands of San Andrés and Providencia, in 1956; and had been awarded a permanent foreign air carrier permit to operate air freight services to the United States, with terminals in Miami, New Orleans, and New York, via intermediate points, in 1957.

The device of a joint Dutch-Colombian international service was initially successful. RAS was designated as the official carrier between Bogotá and Rio de Janeiro, via Manaus, in July 1958, under a new bilateral agreement between Brazil and Colombia; and on 28 December, 1958, it inaugurated *El Trans-americano* service on the route, using Douglas DC-4s.

Early in 1960, RAS took over the domestic services of SAM; on 5 December the Brazilian route welcomed São Paulo as a co-terminal point with Rio; and in October 1961 opened the all-important link between Bogotá and Curaçao. The way seemed to have been open for consolidating the whole system, and to profit by the international co-ordination. But it was not to be. The domestic system was subjected to severe competition from AVIANCA, established by this time almost as a national institution, and itself consolidating successfully the fleets, routes, and organizations of LANSA and SAETA. Also, while the route from Bogotá to Rio and São Paulo looked most attractive on a route map, the traffic was not substantial. Indeed, the entire operations of RAS were losing money, and the joint airline went out of business in August 1962.

Finally, in September 1963, SAM itself went into liquidation, and AVIANCA bought the stock from Capt Powelson's widow. The transaction was made through AVIANCA's own subsidiary, Aerotaxi, and the assets included three DC-4s, and three C-46s, a welcome addition to the national airline's fleet. AVIANCA's new rival airline, Aerocondor, charged that this constituted unfair practice, at least in the manner in which AVIANCA conducted its affairs and

247

those of SAM. The latter was a non-IATA airline and could therefore charge what fares and rates it liked, whereas AVIANCA was an IATA carrier, and bound by the rules. It was argued that AVIANCA could use SAM to undercut rates and tariffs, and thus provide unfair competition with other non-IATA airlines. With a hidden subsidy from the parent company, these could be forced out of business and thus leave AVIANCA as the sole remaining airline, able to do as it pleased, without challenge. The arguments were inconclusive. Certainly, the Colombian Government took no sides, having awarded in 1962 the Miami route to the four airlines existing at the time, RAS, Lloyd, Aerocondor, and AVIANCA. Equally, the United States C.A.B., after careful consideration, saw nothing irrevocably wrong, and awarded SAM a three-year permit on 15 April, 1964, receiving the President's signature on 6 August of that year. From this time SAM has remained part of the Colombian aviation scene, as a partner to AVIANCA.

The Start of the Second Level

From time to time, in seeking permission to operate routes, certain Colombian airlines implied that the authorities were taking sides, favouring one company or group against another, but this does not appear to have been a chronic shortcoming. Indeed, a review of the history of entry and exit of Colombian airlines shows that participation has been widely spread. The Government's attitude, in general, has been one of *laissez faire*, taking a pragmatic view that, because of the problems of surface travel, apparently almost insuperable, air transport of any kind was to be encouraged. If a group of investors wished to purchase a few transport aeroplanes and try to run an airline, then they should be given a fair chance, subject to assurances of sound commerical practice and adequate technical standards to ensure service and safety.

There are arguments to the effect that the Colombian Government's attitude to these standards has been far too liberal, and over-lenient to transgressors. This may be so; but stricter regulations would, in a country like Colombia, be difficult, if not impossible, to enforce without an army of inspectors and a bureaucratic edifice which the country could not in any case afford. Also, under such a regime, the level of air service would certainly not have advanced to what it is today, as few airlines have had the resources to run their businesses other than on the proverbial shoestring.

Thus, although with the acquisition of SAETA, AVIANCA found itself in a monopolistic situation, this was with the cognizance of, but not the encouragement of the Colombian Government. And as soon as other interests were prepared to fill the breach left open by the demise of LANSA and SAETA, permission to go into operation was not hard to obtain.

The first new entrant, to what in retrospect seems to mark the beginning of a new class of airline—the Second Level—in the Colombian air transport scene, was **Lloyd Aéreo Colombiano (LAC** or **Lloyd)**, formed by a group of investors in 1954. At the time, this airline received tacit support from the Government of the day, and was able to obtain authority for overseas routes with comparative ease. Starting with a small fleet of Curtiss C-46s, equipped with JATO (Jet Assisted Take Off) auxiliary power, Lloyd supplemented its small network of domestic routes by opening, on 19 April, 1956, a route from Bogotá to Cochabamba, Bolivia, via Leticia (in the southeastern corner of Colombia) and Riberalta (in the northwestern corner of Bolivia). The prospects of such a route enjoying commerical success were remote, even though it followed closely along the transcontinental path once visualized by Gonzalo Mejia. Traffic between Colombia and Bolivia simply was not sufficient, and the bizarre experiment closed down on 3 November, 1956, after six months of operation.

Undaunted, in 1957 LAC ordered three Vickers Viscounts from Great Britain, and obtained a United States C.A.B. foreign air carrier permit to operate to Miami. But by November of the same year, the Viscount order had been transferred elsewhere. Also, the Colombian Government had changed, and LAC lost support from the new administration. Even though it struggled on with its domestic services, and even shared in the blanket award by the Colombian Government in 1962 which permitted four Colombian airlines to fly to Miami, this latter action was almost irrelevant, as the airline closed down in 1964.

Second of the new generation of airlines to make its mark during the latter 1950s was **Taxi Aéreo de Santander (TAXADER)**, originally founded in Bucaramanga in 1947, to operate Cessna aircraft in the northeastern provinces, where airfields were still usually too small for larger equipment. When LANSA ceased operations in 1954, the owner of TAXADER, Dr Herman Gómez Gómez, decided to widen his horizons. The capital was raised to 3 million pesos (about $250,000), five Douglas DC-3s were purchased, and a network of routes established from Bogotá to the Bucaramanga area and to the northeast of Colombia, including Barranquilla.

In 1960, TAXADER augmented its fleet with three Curtiss C-46s, converted to passenger use at a level of comfort sufficient to permit the description 'Super C-46'. The route network was extended to include Cartagena and San Andrés Island in the north, and Pereira and Cali in the south. This was further extended to Popoyán and Pasto, near the Ecuadorian frontier, in 1962, the year in which the company purchased two DC-4s, each fitted with 70 seats. Almost as its last effort to attain national stature, in 1963 TAXADER was restructured as **Líneas Aéreas**

Taxader's Douglas C-47 HK-793 at Santa Marta. Aircraft markings are very dark blue.
(*Gordon S. Williams*)

Taxader, and introduced Douglas DC-6B service from Bogotá and Barranquilla to Miami in October 1964, the necessary permit having been obtained the previous year (possibly superseding LAC's). Advertised with flair as *El Cafetero* (*The Coffee Tree*) it should have operated at a frequency of two a week; but it is believed to have made only one scheduled flight. Although it had been proudly billed as 'Colombia en los Aires' TAXADER shut down in 1965.

In Medellín, **Aerovías Pilotas Associados (AVISPA)** was founded in 1956 by Carlos Amortegui, Juan White, and Jaime Castro. AVISPA operated two DC-3s from Medellín to Puerto Berrío, Caucasia, and Chigorodó, but closed down in 1962. Castro continued to operate on his own, founding a company **Cessnyca**, which operated Beech C-45s, DC-3s and two DC-6Bs until 1974.

Aerocondor

On 3 February, 1955, a group of ex-AVIANCA pilots, headed by Juan Millon and Luís Donado, founded **Aerovías Condor de Colombia, Ltda (Aerocondor)** in Barranquilla. Following familiar practice, Condor acquired a fleet of Curtiss C-46s and went into business as an air freight operator, making its first scheduled flight from Barranquilla to Bogotá on 7 October, 1955. Several years passed before it began passenger service, on 12 January, 1960, but thenceforward its progress was swift.

One of Aerocondor's colourful Lockheed 188A Electras at Bogotá. The colours were yellow upper stripe and tail, orange centre line and red. (*R. E. G. Davies*)

By 1962, Condor was operating DC-4s on the trunk domestic route, and also to San Andrés. Having obtained the necessary authority from both the Colombian and United States Governments, it introduced DC-6B air freight service from Bogotá, Medellín, and Barranquilla to Miami, twice weekly, in 1963. In the following year, some flights to Miami were routed via San Andrés, a new service was opened to Aruba and Curaçao, and the C.A.B. permit was amended to allow Aerocondor to carry passengers to Miami.

With the demise of TAXADER, Aerocondor took over some local services in the northeast of Colombia in 1966, but these were soon left to an affiliated air taxi company as the parent company wisely concentrated on the more profitable task of serving only the major cities of Colombia, connecting these with Miami, the

A Boeing 720-023B of Aerocondor at Bogotá. (*R. E. G. Davies*)

gateway to North America, and providing service to the popular San Andrés, the Colombian equivalent of Las Vegas.

By 1969, Aerocondor was enjoying a measure of success not previously attained by any of the previous airline aspirants hoping to share some of AVIANCA's business. It opened an effective publicity drive, adopted a bright and attractive new paint scheme for its aircraft, and introduced Lockheed Electras (bought from American Airlines) on 1 May, 1969. These aircraft were sensibly deployed only on trunk domestic routes connecting Bogotá, Barranquilla, and Medellín, and to Miami, Aruba, and Curaçao. By the end of the year, Aerocondor had four Electras, enough to justify the retirement of the piston-engined DC-6s. Its competitive strength was now established and effective, to the extent that it forced AVIANCA's Second Level partner SAM to follow Aerocondor's lead. SAM quickly obtained its own Electras, exchanging five of the propeller-turbine aircraft (bought from Eastern Air Lines) for its old unpressurized DC-4s in October 1969. SAM boldly called its new fleet Astrojets, a semantic inexactitude, but indicative of the competitive battle raging in Colombia at the time. In 1972, an understanding was reached between the two rivals to arrange schedules in such a way that self-destructive competition was avoided; but this did not stop Aerocondor from pursuing its ambitions to improve its stature. At the end of 1972, the maverick airline introduced a turbofan-powered Boeing 720B, thus placing itself on a technical level closer to SAM's senior partner, AVIANCA.

This Airbus A300B4, F-WNDD, was operated for a short period by Aerocondor as HK-2057 *Ciudad de Barranquilla*. (*Airbus Industrie*)

251

The First Jet Services in Colombia

AVIANCA had started its first jet service on 16 October, 1960, with a flight to New York with a Boeing 707 leased from Pan American, pending delivery of its own jet aircraft. This latter, a Boeing 720B, entered service to Miami, via Kingston, on 1 December, 1961, and by 19 January, 1962, the Colombian national airline could claim that all its international schedules were by jet. The Constellations were transferred to domestic trunk services, by the familiar pattern of relegation.

With modern equipment, AVIANCA extended its Latin American network, adding a route to Mexico City, via Panamá, in October 1962, and extending the Lima route to Buenos Aires—an important stage in the quest for Sixth Freedom traffic, as AVIANCA could now offer through service from New York or Mexico to the Argentine capital, then the largest city in the southern hemisphere.

By the mid-1960s, all domestic trunk services were scheduled at frequencies of six or seven a day each way, a remarkable indication of the spectacular growth of travel in Colombia—when SCADTA became AVIANCA in 1940 a once-daily service was normal. All the trunk routes were served by four-engined equipment, a policy which in most countries would have been considered undesirable because of the additional operating costs incurred by the use of four-engined aricraft. But Colombia was different: the terrain alone demanded the attraction of multiple engines as a psychological as well as a technical aspect of security, and the high altitude of many of the airfields, especially the most important one of Bogotá, emphasized the preference.

When AVIANCA eventually selected a jet aircraft for its domestic routes, therefore, its choice was a compromise between the desire to have something better than a twin; at the same time recoiling from the prospect of operating four-engined jet aircraft on short domestic routes. The three-engined Boeing 727 was chosen and it entered service on 1 January, 1966.

AVIANCA's red and white Boeing 727-21 HK-1717 *Coronel Boy*, seen at Bogotá, was delivered in October 1974 and had previously been Pan American's N315PA.
(*R. E. G. Davies*)

HK-1409, AVIANCA's Hawker Siddeley HS.748 Series 2 is seen with red-topped fuselage and tail and black and white markings. (*T. R. Waddington collection*)

Staying firmly with Boeing, AVIANCA introduced the improved Model 707-320B, with 189 seats, on its international routes on 1 April, 1968, at the same time giving further thought to the problem of the domestic routes, where the 727, though operationally an emphatic success, was proving to be somewhat costly and difficult to show profits at the low average fare levels in Colombia. In December 1968, AVIANCA bought two of Boeing's twin-engined 737-100 short-haul airliners, with 99 seats; but these were not a success, the rigorous conditions of the Colombian topography proving them unsuitable. At the same time, to deal with a special airfield restriction at Bucaramanga, two twin-engined propeller-turbine Hawker Siddeley HS.748s were added to the fleet.

In 1966, AVIANCA moved cautiously into new territory, with a service to Manaus, Brazil, via Leticia; and the following year added Santiago, Chile, to the southern arm of its long-distance routes. But in fact, the map of the international route system had not substantially changed for many years, and the addition of Los Angeles on 2 July, 1969 was a welcome departure from traditional patterns, and opened up Colombia to the potentially lucrative markets of California and the North American west coast.

During this period, the old piston-engined aircraft were progressively retired, the Constellations in 1968 and the old Douglases in 1974. These latter, consisting of a number of veteran DC-3s and DC-4s, had been transferred hither and thither, with mixed success. Sometimes they had filled a need in low-productivity areas where the operation of jets was operationally impossible or economically futile; and the older aircraft, incurring low costs in fuel and crew expenses, their purchase price already lost in the mists of time, could provide minimum service. But the costs were high in other respects, for example in maintenance, because spare parts were increasingly difficult to obtain, and growing more expensive. Also the notorious Colombian Andes continued to be cruelly demanding of near-perfection in all aeronautical departments, and the time came when to maintain such standards became too costly to make economic sense. The pattern of relegation repeated itself once again, and the small airlines of Colombia lined up to carry on where AVIANCA left off.

During this period also, the administration of Colombia's flag carrier underwent a gradual change. The acquisition of LANSA and SAETA had been more than mere book transactions, some of the assets of these companies being in the form of capable executives who took their rightful places in the running of the airline. At the same time, Pan American's controlling interest was progressively reduced. In 1951, when LANSA was merged, the US company's interest dropped just below 40 per cent. By 1968 it was 25 per cent, and by 1975 was down to little more than 11 per cent. AVIANCA had gradually turned itself into an independent Colombian airline, and it demonstrated its self-assurance and confidence by adopting, in 1970, a completely new paint-scheme for its aircraft, superseding the old muted markings and Pan Am style lettering by a dramatic eye-catching red which did much to draw public attention to Colombia's presence in the international airline world.

During the 1970s, AVIANCA moved steadily with the march of civil airline progress. The European services were strengthened and expanded to serve new cities: Zürich on 28 April, 1971, London on 3 May, 1978, and re-opening service to Rome on 26 October of the same year. A new route was added on 17 January, 1972, by direct service to São Paulo and Rio de Janeiro, adding to the concentration of routes with Bogotá as the hub. Less publicised, but important nevertheless, was the addition of all-cargo international jet service in 1976, with a pallet-equipped Boeing 707 capable of carrying 40 tons (see Map 26, page 268).

AVIANCA's Boeing 747-124 *Eldorado* seen on a test flight while bearing the Colombian registration HK-2000 and US test registration N747AV. (*The Boeing Company*)

Colombia confirmed its stature in the airline world at the end of 1976, when, on 6 December, a Boeing 747 wide-bodied jet, dressed in AVIANCA's striking red colours, entered service on what had by now developed into the most important route on the system: Bogotá–Frankfurt, via San Juan, Madrid, and Paris. The day previously, the aircraft had made a ceremonial visit to the four major cities of Colombia: Bogotá, Medellín, Cali, and Barranquilla, exactly 57 years after the foundation of SCADTA.

SATENA Fills a Social Need

During the pioneer years of SCADTA, and the postwar developing years of AVIANCA, the vital role played by air transport in Colombia's economy had been emphatically demonstrated. In every category of carrying people or in transporting mail and goods, the commercial aircraft and the organizations behind them had become an essential national institution, linking the peoples of Colombia in the social as well as the geographical sense. The commercial airlines had served to make Colombia a truly united country.

But as time went on, it became apparent that, if the process was to continue to encourage the development and growth of new communities, for example in the llanos or the selva regions, then special steps would have to be taken. Throughout the history of Colombian air transport, no airline has ever received a direct subsidy—although in the early days, mail revenues constituted a priceless privilege to SCADTA and helped it through some difficult financial times. Consequently, in an untrammelled free enterprise system, the tendency was for private airlines always to seek the profitable routes and areas of operation. During periods of development, necessity permitted the setting of rates which could be attuned to costs, and this applied often to the remoter regions of Colombia as well as the industrial cities. But inevitable economic forces drew operators more and more to the inter-city routes. The wealth and the commerce and the consequent need to travel were all concentrated in the cities; and it became more profitable, for example, to await full loads of freight between Bogotá and Barranquilla, or to carry a load of weekend fun-seekers to San Andrés, than to perform praiseworthy—but financially crippling—good works in the llanos. It was no coincidence that the outstanding survivor of the airlines formed after the war was Aerocondor, which wisely concentrated on serving only the major cities, San Andrés, and Miami.

When therefore, in 1960, Executive Decree 1721 created both the Department of Civil Aeronautics and the National Council of Civil Aeronautics, one of the major problems it faced was how the airlines should serve Colombia as a complete nation—as opposed to fulfilling the narrower commerical need for the big cities—without erecting a complex and potentially corruptible system of subsidy which would be necessary to fill the deficit between costs and revenues on the feeder and Third Level routes. The problem was a fundamental one, and presented a paradox. Exactly as happened on a much larger scale in Brazil, the little airlines may have operated austerely, improvised maintenance, re-used rebuilt spare parts, and generally provided standards of service which would shock the technicians who wrote the manuals; but they did achieve a minimum standard which the communities whom they served were prepared to accept. The unpleasant alternative was no service at all; and at the beginning of the 1960s, especially with AVIANCA giving serious thought to retiring all the DC-3s and DC-4s, the air authorities found the prospect of Colombia becoming divided into two nations—the have-air service and the have-not-air service—staring them in the face.

Against this background, a solution was found by the creation of the **Servicio Aeronavegación a Territorios Nacionales (SATENA)**—literally an air service for the national territories, comprising those areas in eastern and southern Colombia which were still underdeveloped to the extent that they did not yet enjoy provincial status and were governed by, and largely dependent upon, the capital, Bogotá. SATENA's status was that of a semi-governmental agency, operated as a matter of expediency by the Colombian Air Force, the Fuerza Aérea, and using its equipment—DC-3s, C-47s, and sundry small aeroplanes. Regular services began on 1 June, 1962, and SATENA set about the unenviable task of providing air service to all those places in Colombia where nobody else wished to fly.

In the early years, the traffic carried by SATENA comprised essential supplies and personnel, determined by the needs of the communities themselves and by government agencies, including the Air Force, which combined SATENA's civil role with its own logistic and troop transporting requirements. But in due course, the value of the service was recognized to need more flexibility; and on 30

December, 1968, Law No.80 reorganized SATENA to become a public service, to be operated as an autonomous unit directly under the control of the Secretary of Defence. From this time onwards, the public could buy tickets and consign goods with SATENA in the same way as with a commercial airline.

Although the trusty DC-3s were the mainstay of the fleet, and later augmented by DC-4/C-54s, SATENA also purchased new aircraft in an effort to upgrade the quality of its service, at the same time retaining essential economies of operation and the ability to land on small unprepared airstrips. This was no easy task, as the rugged old DC-3 continued to defy all attempts to replace it in terms of sheer versatility. However, the addition of four Hawker Siddeley HS.748s in 1972 came close to reaching this almost unattainable objective.

Under its mandate, SATENA had to take on many and varied chores, all with the common denominator of serving outback communities, and contributing to their well-being and development. The HS.748s provided the main link between Bogotá and SATENA's DC-3 bases at Cali, Neiva, and Villavicencio. The DC-3s from Cali served the Pacific coastal area, and those from Villavicencio the llanos ranch stations which had finally been given up by AVIANCA in 1974. These latter had witnessed the coming and going of many and varied aircraft and airlines since the Boeing 247s and Ford Tri-Motors of SCADTA had first appeared in 1937. AVIANCA had, in 1948, handed over the responsibility of these services to its newly-founded subsidiary **Aerotaxi**, which had continued to serve the feeder and Third-Level routes with a fleet of twenty de Havilland Canada DHC-2 Beavers, sturdily built for rigorous Canadian conditions. Although they were equally adaptable to the demands of Colombia, and Aerotaxi adopted the slogan 'Don't ask us where we fly, tell us where you want to go!' some of the pilots took the slogan too literally and expected miracles of versatility out of the Beaver, and many landings were attempted in places which any self-respecting bird would have avoided. After a study of economics in the llanos, and after Aerotaxi had ceased operations in the mid-1970s, AVIANCA discovered that its break-even load factor of the DC-3 was 140 per cent, and that of the HS.748 120 per cent; and so handed over the service to SATENA as an economic necessity.

At Neiva, the DC-3s have been able to play their part in a repetition of history. In the territory of Caquetá, around the towns of Florencia and San Vicente, a new llanos region is developing, the conditions of the latter 1970s in that region a distant echo of those in the northeastern llanos in the latter 1930s. From Neiva, SATENA maintains a small DC-3 network to these places whose settlement is so

SATENA's Hawker Siddeley HS.748-260 bearing Colombian Air Force serial FAC 1101 and the Air Force fuselage marking. The livery comprises two shades of blue.
(*R. E. G. Davies*)

Aerotaxi's de Havilland Canada Beaver HK-1009 in rugged country.

recent that they are not yet marked on many Colombian maps, a vivid illustration of the constructive role being played by Colombia's semi-military airline.

One more example of SATENA's work epitomises both the transport problems and the progress which has been made. When, in 1954, well before SATENA's time, the first asphalt surface was laid at the airport of Leticia, near the banks of the Amazon in Colombia's southeastern tip, the material was manufactured as a by-product at the oil-producing region of Barrancabermeja, on the Magdalena River. It was transported by riverboat to Barranquilla, trans-shipped around the coast to the mouth of the Amazon, at Belém, and thence up the mighty river to Leticia. Twenty years later, the material for resurfacing was carried on sixty flights by SATENA C-54s, each with six or seven tons of asphalt.

SATENA's administrators are philosophical about their role in Colombia's air transport system. They are well aware that, because they fly continuously in inhospitable territory, danger is always present; yet providing a social service as they do, they cannot simply withdraw on the grounds of economics or operational difficulty. Thus, their exposure to risk is greater than with most airlines, and their accident record suffers from over-emphasis thereby. SATENA does not consciously try to expand its network for the pleasure of drawing an impressive map. It simply performs a social service to Colombia, and if a private airline wishes to take over any of its routes, every move in that direction is warmly welcomed, sometimes with relief, by the military officers in Bogotá whose unenviable task is to continue the tradition of replacing muletrains with aircraft (see Map 24, page 258).

Second Level Development

After a period of about ten years during the 1960s, when there was little activity by small airlines, AVIANCA, SAM, Aerocondor and SATENA began to receive competition at many levels of domestic and even international operations from a variety of carriers which comprised a new wave of commercial air activity. To place these newcomers in definite strata, using terms such as Second or Third

Level, or Trunk and Feeder, would to some extent be misleading. The small airlines took traffic where they perceived an opportunity, either by operating a route which appeared to be receiving inadequate service, or one which SATENA was happy to hand over; by finding a niche in the trunk system by offering a lower-fare service in parallel with the senior airlines; or by concentrating on

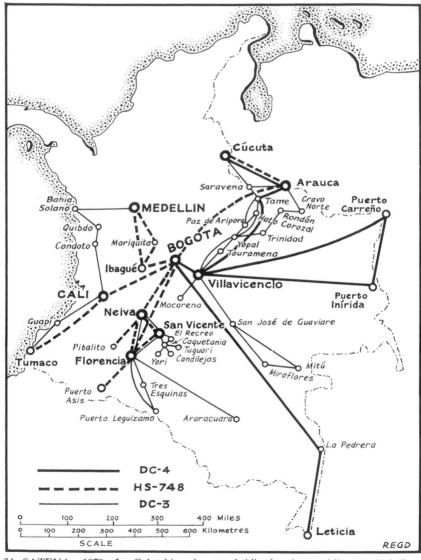

24. SATENA, 1979. In Colombia, the unsubsidized private airlines – including AVIANCA—could not be expected to operate unprofitable services to small communities. Consequently, the Government supported such service through a special arm of the Air Force, SATENA.

258

A Líneas Aéreas La Urraca Douglas DC-3 at Pistón in May 1972.
(*Henry Janscrite, courtesy Barrie James*)

specialized cargo services, notably in the air freighting of thousands of tons of cut flowers, mainly carnations, annually to Miami. They obtained cheap aircraft where they could, second- or third-hand, from abroad and from home territory, including AVIANCA.

It would be almost invidious to select particular airlines for special comment, but in the interests of historical reporting, attention should be drawn to a few, as they contribute in a small way to the constantly developing saga of Colombian air transport.

A familiar name for almost a quarter of a century was **Líneas Aéreas La Urraca**, a name pictured by the magpie emblem which pertly proclaimed the airline's intentions to steal traffic wherever it could find it, especially at the expense of the established airlines. La Urraca was founded in 1955 in Villavicencio by Capt Alvaro Henao Jaramillo and his brother Fernando, a pioneer pilot of the llanos. They competed vigorously for the specialized and limited traffic in the region, dealing with contingencies such as passengers who were inclined to bring live boa constrictors on board with only flimsy wrapping or, in one reported case, of a client who insisted that his cow should be treated as hand baggage.

The Henaos relied, as a thousand aspiring airline owners throughout the world have done, on the DC-3, supplemented by sundry other types; but they began to seek further outlets, including scheduled service, during the mid-1960s. They suffered during the process a number of setbacks which would have deterred all but the most determined or obstinate, and attempts to add three C-46s met with tragedy when Fernando was killed on a ferry flight from Miami. A DC-3 was hijacked to Cuba. And when, in 1970, La Urraca bought three Handley Page

Aerolíneas TAO's Vickers-Armstrongs V.745 Viscount HK-1057 served with Capital Airlines, Philippine Air Lines, Hawaiian and Alitalia before going to Colombia. In this picture it retains the fuselage stripes of Alitalia but with red outer bands and red rudder and in the original photograph its old Italian registration, I-LIRT, can still be read on the nosewheel door. (*T. R. Waddington collection*)

Heralds to supplement its four DC-3s, and to break into the trunk air route business, the elevation into the senior operational strata proved too much, and after two crashes Capt Alvaro withdrew to the llanos, where he felt more at home.

La Urraca kept going—even adding two Britten-Norman Islanders—until 1979, when the company was closed down by the Colombian Government for conduct which even the lenient regulations of the free-wheeling Colombian aviation authorities would not countenance; and a colourful character withdrew from aviation. But La Urraca is well remembered, not least by the tiny community of Mitú, way out on the Brazilian frontier in the territory of Vaupés, where a small obelisk displays a plaque as a tribute to Captain Fernando 'Benefactor del Vaupés'.

One other small airline had its own counter at Bogotá airport during the 1960s. **Taxi Aéreo Opita Ltda (TAO)** was formed by some citizens of Neiva, capital of

One of Aeropesca's Vickers-Armstrongs Viscounts seen at Neiva on 26 April, 1979, during a special flight to mark the Year of the Child. (*Hernando González*)

260

Aerotal's Boeing 707-331C seen here still bears part of its former TWA red livery and US registration N15710. (*T. R. Waddington collection*)

Huila Province, the company's name being derived from the familiar term used to refer to the inhabitants of the province. In 1963 it had expanded its taxi service to include a DC-3 route from Bogotá to Neiva, under the title of 'La Ruta Cordial del Sur'. Reaching further to the skies, TAO purchased two second-hand Viscounts in 1969 and began to serve other points in Colombia beyond the local confines of Huila. But TAO, as so many others before, had over-reached itself, and ceased operations in 1974.

In the passenger field, the next airlines to get under way in the early 1970s in Colombia were Aeropesca, Aerotal, and TAC. **Aeropesca** had actually gone into business on 14 October, 1960, specializing uniquely in the transport of fish from the River Amazon to the capital. The full name of Aeropesca was Aerovias de la Pesca y Colonización del Sureste Colombiano, and for the first ten years of its existence concentrated on the route from Leticia to Bogotá. Then in September 1971 Aeropesca branched out by opening a service, for passengers as well as freight, from Bogotá to Popayán and Pasco, in the south of Colombia, and to Medellín, Cúcuta, Barranquilla, and Cali. The equipment consisted of Viscounts—C-46s were no longer acceptable for passenger work—and Aeropesca has established itself firmly in the southern market.

Aerotal was founded originally in 1971 as **Taxi Aéreo Llanero (TAL)**—the taxi operation was often the proving ground for many a future airline. After a few

TAC's Sud-Aviation Caravelle VIR HK-1812 was acquired in October 1976. This aircraft had been delivered to Iberia and later served with Aviaco. Markings are very dark blue with red lower band. (*R. E. G. Davies*)

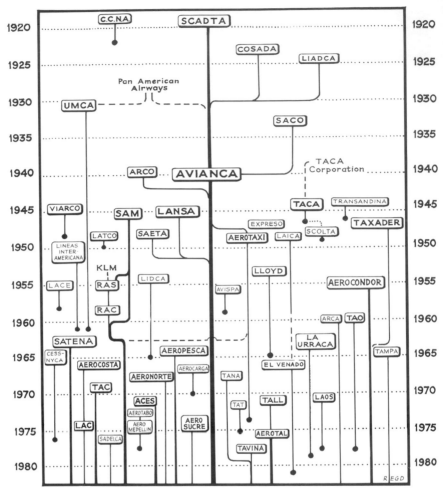

6. Genealogy of Colombian Airlines. Nowhere in Latin America has the spirit of private enterprise been preserved more than in Colombia, where liberal regulations permitting entry into the air transport business have helped to make Colombia one of the most air-minded nations in the world.

years, as TAL moved into the scheduled inter-city business, it became known as **Aerotal**, short for **Aerolíneas Territoriales de Colombia, Ltda**. It began freight operations internationally with a Boeing 707-320, an impressive departure for a small Colombian airline, and established domestic jet services between all the major cities with a fleet of four Caravelle VIR's purchased from LAN-Chile.

Pursuing a similar course, **Transportes Aéreos del Cesar, Ltda (TAC)** was founded in Valledupar, El Cesar Province, by Dr Alfonso Sanchez Lopez. Starting cautiously with light aircraft, TAC quickly moved into larger passenger types by putting into service a Fairchild F-27, later replacing this with Viscounts. Still concentrating on serving Valledupar from Bogotá, TAC has expanded also to Barranquilla, Medellín, and a few other points; has put into service four

Aerosucre's Curtiss C-46F HK-751 was previously Flying Tiger's N67995.
(*R. E. G. Davies*)

Loading or unloading the Líneas Aéreas de Caribe Douglas DC-6A HK-1702. This aircraft
was built as the C-118A 53-3299 and delivered to the USAF in December 1955.
(*R. E. G. Davies*)

ARCA's Douglas DC-8-43F HK-1854 was Alitalia's DC-8-43 I-DIWP. It went to ARCA
in October 1976 and was converted to cargo configuration.

Aerocosta's Curtiss C-46D HK-1282 photographed in June 1969. The upward-opening port-side cargo doors can just be seen above the fuselage. (*Gordon S. Williams*)

ACES' de Havilland Canada Twin Otter 300 HK-2215. (*R. E. G. Davies*)

TAVINA's Swearingen SA.226TC Metro II HK-2176. The aircraft is light grey overall with blue badges and company name, the forward fuselage band is blue and the rear band yellow. On the rear fuselage the yellow band is uppermost. (*R. E. G. Davies*)

Caravelle VIRs, matching Aerotal, and in the latter 1970s claimed to be the fourth largest airline in Colombia, after AVIANCA, Aerocondor, and SAM. In January 1980, it changed its trading name to Aerovías del Cesar, or more briefly **Aerocesar**.

And so the parade of Colombian Second Level airlines goes on, a reflection of the air transport potential in a country with a surface terrain like Colombia's. Current newcomers include **Aerolíneas Centrales de Colombia (ACES)**, founded by Alvaro Arango and the Coulson family in Manizales in 1971, and now operating a substantial fleet of aircraft, based in Medellín. Starting with three Saunders ST-27s and a de Havilland Heron, and tried an F.27, it had by 1981 built this up to sixteeen Twin Otters and two Boeing 727s.

Trans-Colombiana de Aviación (TAVINA) was founded by Gabriel Echavarría Obregón in Bogotá in 1975, subsequently taking over Taxi Aéreo Nacional Ltda (TANA). Like most airlines at this level, TAVINA's fleet has undergone frequent changes, the DC-3s and Swearingen Metros giving way to Twin Otters and Britten-Norman Islanders. These operate local services from both Bogotá and Barranquilla.

El Venado's yellow and red liveried Douglas Hyper-DC-3 HK-140 provides shelter from the rain at Mitú. The oil drums in the foreground had been flown in in HK-140 and unloaded by dropping them onto a rubber tyre. This aircraft was built as DC-3A N34961 for Pan American but was delivered to the US Navy as an R4D-1. It went to Colombia as a civil aircraft, crashed, was rebuilt, became AVIANCA's C-140 and later HK-140 and was converted to what AVIANCA called a Hi-Per DC-3. (*R. E. G. Davies*)

The Lower Echelons

The Colombian air transport industry today is indeed a many-splendoured thing. At Bogotá's El Dorado Airport, AVIANCA's latest Boeing 747 lines up cheek-by-jowl with a SATENA DC-4, the first bound for the capitals of Europe, the second for the capital of the llanos. The Twin Otters of ACES jostle for ramp position with the brightly-hued Viscounts of Aeropesca and the Caravelles of Aerotal and TAC.

Down in the sultry plains, the SATENA DC-4 makes the connection with the hardy breed of bush pilots who have served eastern Colombia for almost four decades. These have included **Transportes Aéreos Colombianos (TAERO)**, which

25. El Venado, 1979. Typical of the lower echelons of airline service in Colombia was El Venado. Based at Villavicencio, a Colombian frontier town and the gateway to the *llanos*, its DC-3s continued the same kind of service as in the 1940s. Other aircraft and other airline structures have been unable to match the versatility of the veteran Douglas airliner.

El Venado's Britten-Norman BN-2A Islander HK-849 was previously N132JL.
(*R. E. G. Davies*)

operated Noorduyn Norsemen between 1944 and 1947; and **Líneas Aéreas Interiores de Catalina (LAICA)** which continued the good work from 1948 with two Catalinas and a DC-3. At Villavicencio, the entrepôt of the llanos, the tradition has been maintained by Capt Alejandro Salamanca, whose Taxi Aéreo **El Venado** (Spanish for Deer—a pert bambi on the aeroplanes' tails symbolizes the eternal optimism of these unique airlines) provided the vital lifelines to places like Mitú, Miraflores, and San José de Guaviare, where the airstrip can still become flooded in five minutes by a tropical storm. Salamanca operated at one time or another three C-54s, eight DC-3s, two Beech Queen Airs, a

A little known transport aircraft is the Evangel 4500/300 nine-seat passenger and cargo STOL monoplane designed for bush operations. Built by Evangel Aircraft Corporation of Ohio and powered by two 300 hp Lycoming IO-540-K1B5 engines, the type first flew in June 1964 and it was certificated in July 1970. Seven had been built by 1974. The example illustrated in El Venado's yellow and red livery is HK-1355 and it is seen at Villavicencio.
(*R. E. G. Davies*)

Britten-Norman Islander, and—for those places where the strips were only as long as some runways are wide—an Evangel 4500/300 with STOL performance.

Neither should the all-freight airlines be forgotten. Just as Colombia always seems to suffer from a shortage of air passenger seats, so the cargo airlines have seemed to fall short of adequate capacity. Consequently there is always sporadic business to be picked up by enterprising owners of C-46, C-47, or other freight aircraft, often trying to keep pace with the insatiable appetite of the United States for cut carnations. These freight operators are listed in Table 14 and their place in Colombian airline history illustrated in the Chart on page 262.

The Diamond Jubilee

The sixty years of air transport in Colombia have seen many changes, not least the spectacular increase in the population, surpassing in growth rate that of most countries in the world. When SCADTA was founded in 1919, Colombia had about five million people; now it has five times that number. Most dramatic has been the growth of the cities. The capital, Bogotá, has grown in 60 years from about 350,000 inhabitants to more than four million. Provincial cities such as Medellín and Cali have grown from 80,000 and 45,000 to almost two million and 1½ million, respectively. The port of Barranquilla, formerly second city of Colombia because of the sea and river trade, has almost a million people. Colombia has, during half a century, transformed itself from a primarily agrarian, largely primitive society, with few roads but many mules, to a sophisticated industrial community which enjoys inter-city airbus services and uses them with as much ease as most countries use cars.

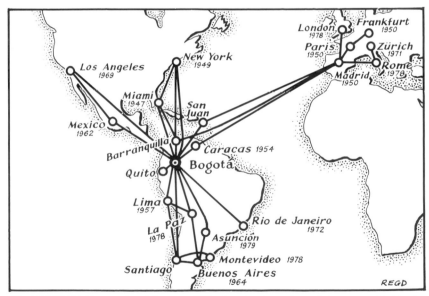

26. AVIANCA International Routes, 1979. Starting from the solid base provided by its predecessor SCADTA, the Colombian flag carrier has expanded steadily to provide international services to the Americas and to Europe. Geographically, Bogotá is well situated as a hub, although its 8,000 ft (2,500 m) elevation can provide problems.

TABLE 14
Colombian Cargo Airlines

Airline (and abbreviation)	Period of Service	Routes	Fleet	Remarks
Líneas Aéreas del Caribe (**LIDCA**)	1954–1964	Extensive services from Barranquilla and Bogotá	11 C-46 3 C-82	Founded by Alfonso R. Aria
Aerovías Colombianas, Ltda (**ARCA**)	1960–	At first locally from Villavicencio. Then Bogotá–Cúcuta (passenger). Finally, all-cargo, serving main Colombian cities and Miami	2 C-47 1 DC-6 3 DC-8	Founded by Capt Hernando Gutiérrez Sanchez
Aerovías del Norte, Ltda (**Aeronorte**)	1966–	Cargo services throughout Colombia	1 C-54 3 C-46	Founded by Capt Alvaro Cote Hernandez
Transportes Mercantiles Panamericanos (**TAMPA**)	1971–	Based in Medellín. Contracted with SAM to operate cargo flights to Miami	2 DC-6A 3 Boeing 707	Founded by Oscar Posada
Líneas Aéreas Orientales (**LAOS**)	1971–1978	Local network centred on Villavicencio, mainly to Mitú	3 DC-3 1 C-46	Founded by Manuel Borde and Alfredo Betancourt
Aerocosta	1972–1976	Services to Miami, Panamá, Aruba, Margarita Island (Venez) from Barranquilla; and to main Colombian cities	4 C-46 4 Electra 6 DC-6 1 DC-7	
Aerosucre, Ltda	1975–	Freight services from Barranquilla to Bogotá, to San Andrés, and to the Dutch Antilles	4 C-46 1 C-54 1 C-47	Founded by Jorge Juan Carlos Solano Recio
Aerolíneas Medellín, Ltda	1976–1979	Freight services from Medellín to main Colombian cities	3 C-54	Founded by Gilberto Villa Olarte, taking over Transportes Aéreos de Bolívar (**Aerotabo**)
Líneas Aéreas de Caribe (**LAC**)	1976–	Took over routes (but not assets) of Aerocosta (see above)	7 DC-6A 2 DC-8	Founded by Capt Luís Carlos Donado Velilla
Sociedad Aérea del Caquetá (**SADELCA**)	1977–	Services from Bogotá and Neiva	3 C-47 1 C-54 1 C-46	Founded by German Cuellar S.

The special nature of Colombia's geography has created a natural environment for the commercial airliner, overflying mountains and rivers which were almost insuperable barriers to easy access by surface means. The joint enterprise of Colombians and foreign associates ensured the firm foundation for growth. Government policies permitted the expression of free enterprise and encouraged innovation, at the same time insisting that the airlines should stand on their own feet. In Colombia there has never been a need for Deregulation, which has shaken the foundation of United States regulatory practices; simply because, perhaps by the successful application of the unwritten rules of Trial and Error, the delicate balance between freedom and control has always been preserved to everyone's satisfaction.

The year 1979 marked the sixtieth anniversary of the foundation of AVIANCA's ancestor airline SCADTA. With a continuous history of operation, Colombia's national airline epitomises the vigorous health of the airline industry. The Boeing 747s of today are a far cry from the diminutive Junkers-F 13s of 1920. While all the original SCADTA aircraft have long disappeared, at least one, a veteran Junkers-W 34, is enshrined by the Fuerza Aérea as a mute witness to the passing show of aircraft which has made Bogotá's El Dorado Airport the showcase of air transport progress in the New World. In some respects, Colombia should honour the old Junkers with the same reverence as the prize exhibits in the Gold Museum; or as Lindbergh's *Spirit of St Louis* is honoured at the Smithsonian in Washington.

Ecuatoriana's *Jet Cargo* Boeing 707, seen here at Simón Bolívar Airport, Guayaquil, is thought to be the Model 321C HC-BGP/FAE19273 named *Manapi* and formerly N451PA with Pan American and N451RN with Iran Air.

CHAPTER THIRTEEN

Ecuador

The First Airline Services

Air transport in Ecuador began as the result of expansionist aspirations by the Colombian airline SCADTA, controlled mainly by German nationals and Colombians of German descent. After survey flights along the Colombian Pacific coast in 1927, SCADTA began regular services to Guayaquil, calling at Ecuadorian coastal points, on 30 July, 1928. The pioneer of this route was Herbert Boy, a famous German pilot who became a hero of his adopted country, and whose favourite Junkers-F 13 seaplane was the *Boyaca*—the name derived from a province of Colombia, which may well have appealed to the pilot.

The route to Ecuador allowed SCADTA to co-opt the name **Servicio Bolivariano de Transportes Aéreos**, evoking comparisons with the former dream of the liberator Simón Bolívar to link the three nations of northwest South America into one unit. But the scheme was even more short-lived than Bolívar's. Even though sorties were made further south into Peru, Boy's work was overcome by developments which resulted in SCADTA and the Servicio Bolivariano coming to an abrupt end on 17 December, 1930.

The direct cause was the juggernaut-like advance of Pan American Airways, under the dynamic and at times ruthless leadership of Juan Trippe. The United States airline, backed by its Government as the chosen instrument for overseas airline route development, swept aside (or devoured) every barrier in its path, which included embryo airlines in Santo Domingo, Peru and Chile, a rival US-owned airline in Brazil, Compañía Mexicana, and SCADTA. Trippe could not, however, sweep aside the W. R. Grace Corporation, whose various trading activities, including a flourishing steamship line, was possibly the strongest single

271

power along the South American west coast—and that description even included some of the national governments whose stability was too often shaken by frequent revolutions.

A compromise was reached by the formation of Pan American Grace Airways (PANAGRA) on 25 January 1929, by which time Pan American had already established a foothold in Ecuador. On 16 September, 1928, Trippe bought a half-interest in Peruvian Airways, formed originally by Huff-Daland Dusters, an American crop-spraying company which had established itself in Lima. Three days earlier, a Peruvian Airways Fairchild FC-2 four-seat monoplane had made the first scheduled flight as far north as Talara. On 30 November of the same year, the route was extended to Guayaquil. The flight carried passengers and messages from the President of Peru and the US Ambassadors of Peru and Chile to President-elect Hoover on board the USS *Maryland*.

Thus, in Ecuador, with a certain amount of appropriate pomp and ceremony, PANAGRA signalled its era of supremacy of the airways of western South America, to last unchallenged for a decade, to become a keystone of the United States war effort, and to establish a tradition of reliability and service which is still remembered today. PANAGRA adopted the slogan 'The World's Friendliest Airline' and although some members of SCADTA would probably not have agreed as they watched their route network contract to within the frontiers of Colombia, the countries along PANAGRA's trunk route from Cristóbal, Panamá, to Santiago and Buenos Aires had no cause for complaint.

Ecuador had the honour of witnessing the first upgrading of equipment standards, when PANAGRA's first Ford Tri-Motor was assembled in Guayaquil on 11 August, 1929. These all-metal landplanes replaced the Sikorsky S-38 amphibians which had started the first through service from Miami to Peru on 14 May, arriving in Lima on 19 May. Passenger service was introduced on 16 January, 1930. Subsequently, PANAGRA was always among the first group of airlines to introduce modern equipment. By 1935 the trunk route was being flown by a combination of Consolidated Commodores (originally built for NYRBA and taken over by Pan American) and Douglas DC-2s, the first Commodore from Cristóbal arriving at Guayaquil on 16 July and the first DC-2, already operating primarily on the busy trans-Andean route between Santiago and Buenos Aires, reaching the Ecuadorian port city from the south on 24 August. Sikorsky S-43s replaced the Commodores on 21 June, 1936, and Douglas DC-3s were delivered in time to start the new consolidated schedules on 1 November, 1937.

SEDTA

At this time, PANAGRA's position of absolute dominance in the area was threatened once again by the initiative of German interests, in this case directly from Germany, and not from German emigrés. On 24 July, 1937, the **Sociedad Ecuatoriana de Transportes Aéreos** (SEDTA) was established in Guayaquil by none other than Fritz Hammer, one of the original founders of the Condor Syndikat, which had promoted airlines in Brazil and Peru, and had assisted many others throughout the continent. The airline, though German-owned—Deutsche Lufthansa had the majority shareholding—at least proclaimed itself as Ecuadorian. This was an acceptable gesture to the Government which allowed the threat to PANAGRA and took the risk of irritating both the US Government and Trippe. Nevertheless, Ecuadorian tolerance did not include the granting of mail payments or any other kind of subsidy.

272

SEDTA therefore had to operate by its own merits and from its own revenues; and these were not enough to cover the costs of operating the small fleet of Junkers-W 34s and Ju 52/3ms which went into service during the Spring of 1938. Sadly, the first months were marked by tragedy, when, on 5 March, 1938, Fritz Hammer was killed in a W 34 crash in the mountains, ending the career of one of the true pioneers of commercial aviation in Latin America, a man of immense drive and vision, and whose death was clouded by approaching political problems which tended to obscure his reputation and record of achievement.

One of SEDTA's Junkers-Ju 52/3ms at the opening of La Toma Airport at Loja in the mountains of Ecuador. (*Lufthansa*)

Had he lived, Hammer would have found himself in the centre of a political confrontation which had far-reaching repercussions. With Deutsche Lufthansa overtly in control, SEDTA made modest increases in its Ecuadorian domestic network (see Map 27) and sounded alarm bells in Washington when it proposed, in May 1940, to open a route to the Galápagos Islands. Possibly over-reacting to a hypothetical speculation, the United States Government took steps to curtail what it regarded as unnecessary and unjustified—and therefore suspicious—expansionist moves by a German airline which was uncomfortably close to the Panama Canal, hub of US defensive strategy in Central and northern South America. On 2 November, 1940, the United States C.A.B. authorized PANAGRA to operate in parallel with SEDTA's Ecuadorian domestic routes. Though technically an Ecuadorian airline, SEDTA was German-owned, so that the entry of PANAGRA resulted in not one cabotage airline—rare enough in itself—but two cabotage airlines in the same country, possibly a unique occurrence in Latin America.

PANAGRA began local service between Guayaquil and Quito, using a DC-2, on 8 November, 1940, and on other domestic routes on 16 March, 1941. The technical struggle was one-sided. The elderly Junkers aircraft of SEDTA were no

273

match for PANAGRA's DC-2s. Furthermore, PANAGRA was given an annual subsidy of $180,000, in exchange for which it undertook to improve airfields, erect passenger buildings, and provide radio facilities. The Ecuadorian Government cut off SEDTA's aviation fuel supplies.

The final blow to SEDTA came on 5 September, 1941, when the remaining fleet of two Junkers-Ju 52/3ms were requisitioned by the Ecuadorian Government. On 28 March, 1942, it signed a five-year contract with PANAGRA, guaranteeing a 32¢ per pound mail payment for such services, and the local operation was renamed **Aerovías del Ecuador (ADEP)**, thus re-establishing the national identity first bestowed by SEDTA.

The End of the Cabotage Services

When PANAGRA acquired its fleets of Douglas landplanes—DC-2s in 1934 and DC-3s in 1937—it began to replace its flying-boat bases along the coast by land airports. During a transition period, Sikorsky S-43 amphibians were re-routed on the Colombia–Ecuador section, with Cali substituted for Buenaventura on 18 July, 1937. Quito was added on 19 November, 1938, providing parallel service on one or two days a week with SEDTA and then augmented into a local network within Ecuador in 1940 and 1941. Five additional Ecuadorian points were served, and although Salinas and Loja were omitted during the late 1940s, Manta, Cuenca, and Esmeraldas were retained on PANAGRA's network until November 1959.

During the wartime period, Guayaquil had been privileged to be one of the points served on Latin America's first commercial all-cargo service, when the US Civil Aeronautics Board granted a special certificate to PANAGRA to operate two converted Douglas DC-2s between the Canal Zone and Lima in Peru. This notable first service started on 28 August, 1942.

During 1946 the curious situation of two cabotage airlines flying domestically within Ecuador was repeated. On 1 April, 1946, the Colombian national airline **AVIANCA** started to operate to Quito from nearby Cali, now a fast-growing industrial and commercial centre, and on 1 July the route was extended to Guayaquil. Early in 1948 AVIANCA added Manta and Cuenca to its Ecuadorian network and later included Esmeraldas and Loja also; but this incursion by the Colombian airline into foreign territory was short-lived, and the local services were terminated late in 1951.

The First Ecuadorian Airlines

Until the end of the war, Ecuador never had an airline which it could call its own. The operations both to, from, and within the country had been conducted by foreign airlines enjoying cabotage rights, that is the right of a company to operate entirely within the frontiers of another territory or state. PANAGRA, SEDTA, and AVIANCA all had this privilege, and PANAGRA's domestic tenure lasted for almost twenty years. But in 1946, about the same time that AVIANCA became active south of its border, an airline was founded in Ecuador which, although having some United States citizen participation, was not controlled by a foreign airline in the same way that Pan American, for example, was still in control of AVIANCA.

Aerovías Nacionales del Ecuador, S.A. (ANDESA) was founded on 6 May, 1946, and started regular passenger and freight services within Ecuador, using three Curtiss C-46s and two Grumman Duck aircraft. In September, ANDESA

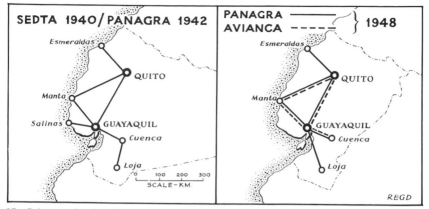

27. Cabotage Services in Ecuador, 1940–1948. As a relatively small and poor country, Ecuador was unable to support airlines of its own during the first stages of development. German, United States and Colombian airlines successively provided cabotage routes.

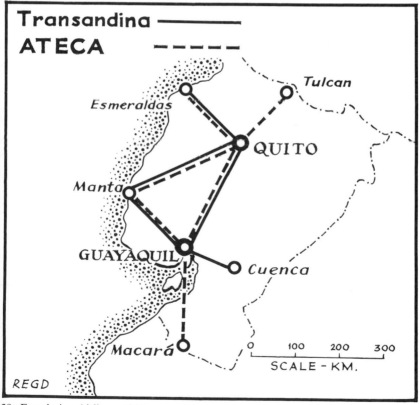

28. Ecuadorian Airlines, 1948. Two of the early Ecuadorian national airlines operated parallel routes during the late 1940s, and merged to form AREA shortly afterwards.

bought a fourth C-46 and two Noorduyn Norseman aircraft from ATCO, a US non-scheduled company, and the following month signed a contract with the Shell Oil Company to carry supplies to the Oriente region of Ecuador, where energetic oil prospecting was in progress—the first stages of a development which was to transform the economy of the country. Unfortunately for ANDESA, Shell terminated its contract on 24 April, 1947, and although an attempt was made to continue local public services, operations were suspended in October, and all assets sold on 11 February, 1948.

But a precedent had been set, and other companies entered the Ecuadorian domestic scene. Encouraged by the ready availability of second-hand and war-surplus US aircraft, two more small airlines got under way. In November 1947, **Aero Transporte Ecuatoriana, C.A.** (ATECA) was founded by seven Ecuadorian citizens, who assembled a fleet of two Douglas DC-3s, eight Stinson 108s, and two small Pipers. Shortly thereafter, on 15 March, 1948, **Transandina Ecuatoriana** began operations, duplicating ATECA's services with a DC-3 and a C-46 (see Map 28). The following year, the two companies very sensibly got together and merged their interests to form **Aerovías Ecuatorianas, C.A.** (**AREA**) and proceeded to seek wider horizons.

The first pressurized airliner to go into service was the Boeing 307 Stratoliner, produced for Pan American and TWA. The example illustrated was one of two operated by Aerovías Ecuatoriana. It bears the registration HC 004 and the name *Quito*. (*Gordon S. Williams*)

In the summer of 1951, AREA began a weekly service from Guayaquil to Miami, via Panamá, using two Boeing 307 Stratoliners, and later in that year consolidated its domestic service pattern when the Ecuadorian Government gave practical support by suspending AVIANCA's cabotage rights. It also granted the airline a $1,000,000 short-term loan. In spite of this assistance, however, the competition from PANAGRA on the trunk route between Quito and Guayaquil was such that AREA was forced to suspend all its operations late in 1954.

During an age when national sovereignty was being asserted everywhere in the world, with the international forum of the United Nations Assembly giving the smaller nations greater hope and aspirations, PANAGRA's retention of the trunk route of a foreign country (to the USA) was something of an anachronism. But such was the power of the W. R. Grace company in the region that the Government of Ecuador did not make a diplomatic issue of the matter, and awaited the expiration of signed bilateral agreements which gave to the US airline what would today be considered over-generous operating rights.

During the early 1950s, a few other attempts were made to start airlines in Ecuador. Companies called **CIASA, Aerodesa, Americana**, and the **Sociedad Anónima Nacional de Transportes Aéreos (SANTA)** made brief and unremembered appearances. In February 1957, however, another new airline was formed which was to survive them all. **Compañía Ecuatoriana de Aviación, S.A. (C.E.A.)** was formed by a group of Ecuadorians, holding 81 per cent of the shares, with a US citizen, Elly Heckscher, holding the remaining 19 per cent.

By the end of that year, C.E.A. had joined the group of airlines assembled by C. N. Shelton, a US resident of Honduras who was turning TAN into an airline with a reputation for offering the lowest fares from Miami to Central and western South America. The Ecuadorian company made representations to the US Civil Aeronautics Board in the same manner as other Latin American airlines had done: that PANAGRA's service, though excellent operationally, was commercially unrealistic, except for US businessmen, affluent US tourists, and an élite few Latin American businessmen and diplomats. The average Latin American, wishing to visit relatives in the USA, would willingly exchange pressurized comfort for lower fares, even if this meant multiple stops in twin-engined Curtiss C-46s—not noted for outstanding performance but able to carry good loads.

Accordingly, at the end of 1957, in association with TAN of Honduras, Aerolíneas Peruanas (APSA) of Peru, and sometimes Aerovías Panamá (APA) or Lloyd Aéreo Colombiano (LAC), C.E.A. opened C-46 service between Miami and Lima, via Panamá, Cali or Quito, and Guayaquil. The following year the southern terminus was extended to Antofagasta, Chile, but this was later curtailed in 1961 to Talara, Peru. By this time, C.E.A. had acquired a Douglas DC-6, and the consortium of airlines integrated their aircraft according to availability and scheduling convenience.

Certainly, the low-fare innovation was effective. With a round trip Guayaquil–Miami fare of $198 against PANAGRA's or Braniff's $351, C.E.A. increased its traffic from under 6,000 long-haul passengers in 1959 to over 20,000 in 1961.

Competitive Struggle for Survival

C.E.A. had been formed at a time when its predecessor, AREA, was in a state of suspended animation. But the latter was not completely defunct; indeed, it showed signs of renewed initiative when it introduced a new aircraft type into Ecuador on 9 July, 1959, when a Fairchild F-27 began service on the trunk route from Quito to Guayaquil, an event which is commemorated to this day by a plaque at Quito Airport. AREA also supplemented the F-27 flights with DC-3 services to smaller cities, but received a blow to its enthusiasm when its propeller-turbine flagship crashed in November 1960.

Undeterred, AREA plunged into the international fray, buying at first a Douglas DC-4 from Northwest Airlines in 1961 and then—to pose a real threat to C.E.A.—three Douglas DC-7Bs, formerly of Continental Airlines, in June 1964. Shortly thereafter, AREA resumed service on the Miami route and announced all kinds of ambitious plans to acquire jet aircraft and to start a service to Europe. C.E.A. countered by intensifying its domestic services between Quito and Guayaquil, meanwhile suspending service to Cali. At the same time, AREA offered to merge with its rival, but C.E.A. declined the offer.

In 1966, AREA made good its promise of jet service by introducing an ex-BOAC Comet 4—described in the publicity campaign as the 'Rolls-Royce Jet'—on a service to Miami via Bogotá. The DC-7Bs were transferred to the

277

Quito–Guayaquil line, while the trusty DC-3s continued the feeder services. C.E.A. countered this in the following year by introducing the Lockheed Electra, and extending its trunk service southwards as far as Santiago, Chile. It also reopened service to Cali in December 1967.

AREA continued to score points in the promotional, if not the operational battle. In October 1967 it announced authorization to operate routes to Madrid—route unspecified, although Belém, Dakar, and Casablanca had previously been mentioned as intermediate points—and to Montevideo, via La Paz and Asunción. At the same time, AREA made overtures towards the possible acquisition of a Lockheed Hercules, to support the heavy demands being made especially by the oil prospecting companies in the Oriente region.

In 1968, the competition came to a head. In March, C.E.A. expanded its Electra service to Mexico City, via Panamá. AREA's Comet was impounded at Miami, but, undaunted, the airline rebounded from this blow by opening its announced service to Montevideo (via La Paz and Asunción) with a Convair CV-990A, acquired in some fashion from Alaska Airlines, but this flight is believed to be the only one made by the Convair jet. AREA's finances were in bad shape, and its struggle to keep alive by desperate measures collapsed as it went into receivership towards the end of 1968.

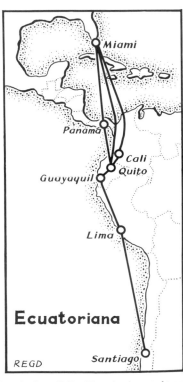

29. Ecuadorian International Airlines, 1967. During the late 1960s, Ecuador boasted two nationally sponsored routes to Miami. AREA managed to operate a de Havilland Comet for a short period, but C.E.A. (Ecuatoriana) survived longer, co-operating at first in a consortium with TAN of Honduras and other airlines.

Only one other airline had posed a competitive threat to C.E.A. as PANAGRA finally withdrew from domestic involvement in Ecuador, while the international service became a choice between the high fares and better amenities offered by the US airline against the no-frills service of C.E.A. and its Shelton-inspired partners. **Línea Internacional Aérea (LIA)** was formed in June 1958 and was designated soon afterwards as Ecuador's second international airline. It operated services between Guayaquil and Quito, and from Guayaquil to the Galápagos Islands, using two Curtiss C-46s, and official recognition was given in the form of a subsidy for the latter route.

On 29 April, 1960, it was designated as the Ecuadorian flag airline on a South American trunk route from Buenos Aires to Miami, plus a route to Los Angeles; and the US Civil Aeronautics Board recommended a permit later that year. But LIA ran into difficulties in raising the capital to purchase long-range aircraft, and although it was reported to have acquired a second-hand Boeing Stratocruiser, there is no record of the airline operating regularly on international trunk routes, or of surviving domestically beyond 1963.

Left now to continue without the constant threat of AREA splitting Ecuador's market share of the traffic passing to and through Guayaquil and Quito, C.E.A. continued a precarious existence. Emphasizing its national identity by adopting the name **Ecuatoriana**, it concentrated on the route to Miami, the main point of entry into the USA for all travellers to and from the west coast of South America. In January 1972 Bogotá was added to the network, but on 28 June of the same year, service to Santiago was suspended because of political difficulties in Chile. C.E.A. owed its survival at the expense of AREA largely to a better fleet procurement policy. Though not as dramatic a performer as AREA's Comet, which could handle the 10,236 feet (3,120 metre) altitude of Quito Airport with ease, C.E.A.'s Electra was adequate to do a more economical job; while the latter's Douglas DC-6s and DC-6Bs were more reliable than the DC-7s of AREA. Also, C.E.A. did not concern itself with unremunerative local routes, although the retention on its books of an old Douglas B-23 bomber was an historical peculiarity.

Nevertheless, these relative advantages over its former rival were only marginal, and C.E.A. found itself in difficulties, both with its accountants and with the Ecuadorian Government. To try to halt a deteriorating situation, the Government stepped in and on 15 August, 1972, acquired 52 per cent of the shareholding, and announced the formation of a mixed stock company in which the capital would be raised to 100 million sucres, of which the Government would hold 51 per cent, and the public would hold the remainder.

A National Airline for Ecuador

Government involvement in commercial aviation in Ecuador had begun in 1962. On 17 December of that year, following the initiative of Major José María Montesinos, and with the support of the President of Ecuador, a transport division of the Ecuadorian Air Force (Fuerza Aérea Ecuatoriana—F.A.E.) was established. This was called **Transportes Aéreos Militares Ecuatorianos (TAME)**. Its fleet consisted of two Douglas DC-3s, allocated by the Air Force, and operations were started immediately, both on the Guayaquil–Quito trunk route, and to provincial cities (see Map 30). As a matter of policy, the fares charged were lower than those set by the private airlines; but the amenity standards were lower, and in the early years all operations were from military fields.

279

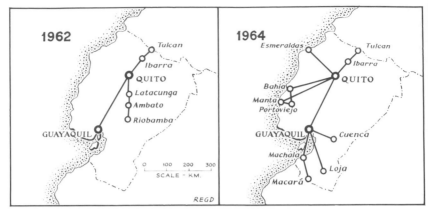

30. TAME, 1962–1964. The Government airline, operated as a commercial enterprise by the Ecuadorian Air Force, supplemented the efforts of the private companies. Later, TAME asserted greater influence on the course of air transport affairs.

In 1963, TAME made some intermittent flights to Baltra (Galápagos Islands), approximately once per month, using the DC-3s which required full tanks to make the flight with adequate reserves. Although some years were to pass before further developments occurred, TAME can take credit for pioneering one of the last remaining links to Pacific islands by commercial air transport.

The next year, on 9 January, a new management took over. Their first act was to change and expand the domestic service pattern (see Map 30) and to negotiate TAME's official status as an airline, recognized by Supreme Decree No.1020. Operations stabilized, and thoughts were then turned towards the expansion of service to the Galápagos. TAME acquired a long-range aircraft, a 62-seat Douglas DC-6B which duly began a once-monthly service to the Islands in April 1967.

The big problem in operating to this naturalists' and zoologists' paradise was that there was no hotel there and not even a water supply; the problem was eventually solved, in co-ordination with Metropolitan Touring de Quito, a tourist agency, whereby a once-weekly TAME DC-6B linked with a floating hotel which toured the islands by night, and remained anchored offshore during the day.

TAME's Boeing 727-2T3 HC-BHM/FAE078 *Cotopaxi* seen on test before delivery.
(*The Boeing Company*)

At the end of 1969, TAME transferred its operations from military airfields to civil airports at Quito and Guayaquil, and shortly afterwards stressed its changing role by becoming a mixed stock company on 19 January, 1970. Regrettably, this transformation was accompanied by an unusual occurrence: a double hi-jacking, when two DC-3s were diverted to Bogotá and Havana on 6 December, 1969, and the co-pilot of one of them was killed.

In 1970, TAME bought two Hawker Siddeley HS.748s, each equipped with 42 seats, and offering superior standards of service to the feeder route system, compared with the old DC-3s. Such was the growing demand for travel within Ecuador when these airliners were introduced in September 1972 that the 62-seat DC-6B was pressed into service when demand exceeded HS.748 capacity.

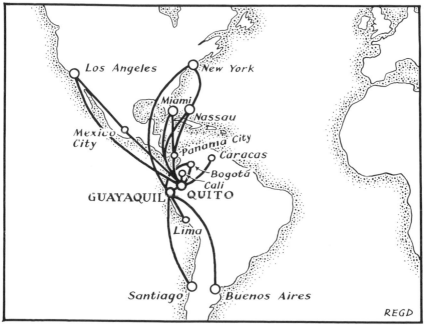

31. Ecuatoriana, 1979. By the late 1970s, the unstable airline situation in Ecuador had been resolved. Ecuatoriana emerged as a national flag carrier, operating to a commendable number of foreign destinations.

Around this period, the national flag carrier C.E.A. was running into serious trouble and came to a grinding halt on 16 April, 1974. All operations were suspended and the Government stepped in and nationalized the airline. By Decree No.742 of 31 July, 1974, almost the entire shareholding of C.E.A. was taken over by TAME, acting on behalf of the Government. TAME took over the Electra fleet and put one into service on 10 August, 1974, (to celebrate Ecuador's Liberation Day) and the second on the Galápagos route on 25 October, 1974, (to mark the 54th Anniversary of the foundation of the F.A.E.)

Meanwhile, C.E.A. took on a new lease of life. In August it acquired two Boeing 720Bs from Israel Aircraft Industries and reinstated service to Miami on 1 September, 1974. Others quickly followed to restore the network to its former stature. To remind the travelling public of its existence, and of its determination

TAME's Lockheed 188A Electra HC-AZL/FAE1050 *Guayas* at Guayaquil. The upper part of the fuselage and the fin are light blue, the fuselage stripe dark blue and lettering black.

to assert its position as an aggressive company—the trading name Ecuatoriana having already become familiar to the travel business—aircraft were painted in a remarkably vivid colour scheme which dazzled the eye and caused comment everywhere—which was precisely Ecuatoriana's objective.

Progress thereafter was swift. With the Government firmly in control of the airline, and with the appointment of General Carlos Banderas as President, Ecuatoriana went from strength to strength. Not only did it expand its international services to serve all the places which had been the subject of Ecuadorian airline aspirations during the past twenty years; it expanded its long-range fleet of Boeing 720Bs and Boeing 707s, at the same time improving its operating and administrative efficiency to the stage whereby good profits were made. One interesting development was to open a service in 1978 to Nassau, in the Bahamas, to connect with the low-fare trans-Atlantic services of Bahamasair,

In 1974–75 Ecuatoriana described itself as *La línea aérea en el corazón del mundo* but in place of the second letter o in corazón had a silhouette of a heart. It was presumably in line with these feelings that the airline adopted the livery illustrated here for its Boeing 720-023Bs. The basic fuselage and tail surfaces of HC-AZP, illustrated, were white or pale grey and the superimposed markings were red, yellow, black, pale blue, medium blue, dark blue and green. There was at least one other equally unusual scheme.

(*Harold G. Martin and T. R. Waddington*)

282

an associate of the pioneer airline in discount fares, Loftleidir.

Wisely, Ecuatoriana concentrated on the national priority of establishing overseas routes for Ecuador, leaving domestic services to the entrepreneur community. Several small companies were engaged in fixed-base operations, carrying freight, or offering charters on demand. A few managed to sustain scheduled operations towards the late 1960s and early 1970s. **Compañía**

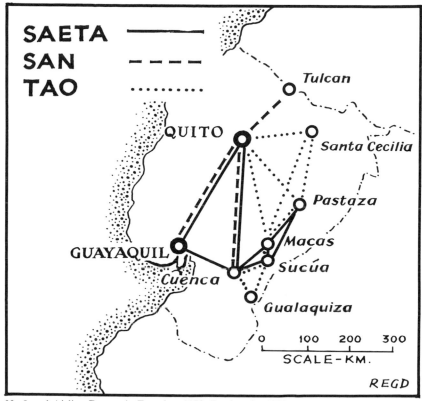

32. Local Airline Routes in Ecuador, 1972. During the 1970s, several small airlines were established. SAETA and SAN particularly provided efficient, competitive services between the main cities of Ecuador.

Ecuatoriana de Transportes Aéreos (CEDTA), Líneas Aéreas Nacionales, S.A. (LANSA), and **VIANSA** all provided local services to coastal towns north and south from Guayaquil. Aerotur operated in the mountain region between Quito and Cuenca, with links to Guayaquil, while **Transportes Aéreos Orientales (TAO)** flew from Quito and Cuenca to the jungle regions of eastern Ecuador, serving the oilfields. All these companies failed to survive but two other small airlines showed enough staying power to take their place permanently in the Ecuadorian commercial airline scene.

Servicios Aéreos Nacionales, S.A. (SAN) and **Sociedad Aérea Ecuatoriana de Transportes Aéreos (SAETA)** were the two private airlines which have supplemented Ecuatoriana and TAME to meet accelerated passenger demand as the commercial life of Ecuador expands with its growing national income derived

SAETA's blue and white Sud-Aviation Caravelle VIN HC-BDS was originally delivered to Alitalia as I-DABV. (*R. E. G. Davies*)

from the oil revenues. SAETA was founded late in 1966 by a group of ex-army officers, headed by Colonels Carlos Najera and Eduardo Sandoval. It started modestly with a Piper Aztec service from Quito to Cuenca in March 1967, and gradually expanded to include Tulcán and Guayaquil (see Map 32). In April 1970, SAETA acquired two Viscount 785s from Alitalia, and with these quickly expanded its traffic, reaching the 50,000 passenger mark by 1971. Going to the same source for equipment in September 1975, three Caravelles were added, so that SAETA was able to operate a jet shuttle service between Quito and Guayaquil.

Although founded earlier, in May 1964, SAN did not enter the scheduled service business until October 1967, a few months after SAETA. SAN used DC-3s, and also expanded to points in the Oriente, and then matched SAETA's modernization by buying Viscount 828s from All Nippon Airways, fitted with 68 seats, compared with its rival's 52. In the true spirit of direct competition, SAN

Servicios Aéreos Nacionales' Vickers-Armstrongs V.828 Viscount HC-ATV, seen at Guayaquil, was previously All Nippon Airways' JA8209 and last but one of all the Viscounts built. Markings were dark blue with yellow fuselage band and tail disc. (*R. E. G. Davies*)

ANDES' Canadair CL-44-6 HC-AYS was originally delivered to the Royal Canadian Air Force as 15903 and later served Canhellas as CF-CHC. (*Harold G. Martin*)

also bought Caravelles at the same time as SAETA; and the route between Guayaquil and the Ecuadorian capital was able to boast one of the most frequent and efficient inter-city air services in the whole of Latin America.

To round off a review of Ecuadorian airlines, mention should be made of **Aerolíneas Nacionales del Ecuador, S.A.**, with the appropriate acronym of **ANDES**, which was founded by Capt Alfredo V. Franco del Monaco in 1961. This was an all-freight airline which acquired an all-cargo certificate from the US Civil Aeronautics Board, and is one of the very few in the whole of Latin America to hold such a document. ANDES began its scheduled operation with Curtiss C-46s in 1964, between Miami and Lima, via Panamá, Quito, and Guayaquil, and steadily improved its fleet with DC 6As in 1968, Canadair CL 44 Yukons (*i.e.* non-swing tail) from the Canadian Armed Forces in September 1973, and moving to a DC-8-33F in the late 1970s.

Ecuador is a relatively small country compared with its neighbours. But it has

This view, taken at Simón Bolívar Airport, Guayaquil, shows Aerolíneas Condor's Fairchild F-27 HC-BGI and the Fuerza Aérea Ecuatoriana's Hawker Siddeley HS.748-285 which is camouflaged and bears civil registration HC-BEY and Air Force serial FAE739.

nearly eight million people and the advantage of being one of the world's oil-producing nations. Its commercial airlines balance well the requirements of State and private enterprise, with Ecuatoriana and TAME representing the former, and SAETA, SAN, and ANDES representing the latter. These were joined recently by **Aerolíneas Condor**, another company serving the cities of the high cordillera. Formed on 3 January, 1978, Condor began F-27 operations on 12 March, 1979. Today, Ecuador's small but vigorous air transport industry serves its people efficiently and without extravagance. In this respect and bearing in mind the severe operating conditions with extremes of climate and terrain, Ecuatoriana's perfect safety record is especially commendable.

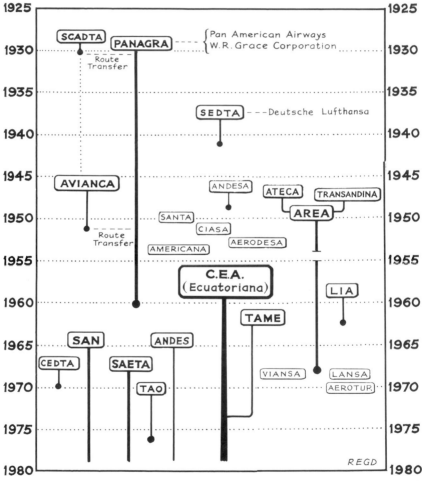

7. Genealogy of Airlines in Ecuador. After two uncertain decades of foreign-dominated airline activity, and after a few false starts, Ecuador possessed its own national airline, supported by a group of small domestic operators.

This extremely primitive form of transport in the Andes formed the competition for early Peruvian air transport. (*Faucett*)

CHAPTER FOURTEEN

Peruvian Airlines before the Second World War

A Formidable Challenge

To understand the problems which faced the early pioneers of commercial aviation in Peru, an appreciation of the basic geography is essential, together with a full recognition of the position of Peru—the third largest country in South America—in the world of economics and commerce during the interwar years. As in many other Latin American countries, much of the business was either owned by, or controlled by foreign interests—the mining industry in particular being largely United States-owned.

The centre of the Peruvian business world was Lima, which had remained the focal point of the South American west coast since its days as the proudest city of the Spanish empire in the New World. The contrast between the sophistication of Lima and the poverty of the rest of Peru was emphatic, as was the statistical fact that Lima's population was greater than that of all the other Peruvian cities put together. Indeed, when commercial aviation began, no other city in Peru could boast more than 50,000 people.

The facts of physical geography were as remarkable as those of the demographic. Successive ranges of the Andean Cordillera effectively cut off the major part of Peru from its capital. Even along the coast, the quickest means of

This undated photograph, probably taken in the early 1930s, shows Cuzco Airport which is situated at an elevation of 10,656 ft. (*Pan American World Airways*)

transport during the 1920s was by ship, as the roads were quite inadequate and there was no coastal railway. Yet paradoxically, Lima did have access to some cities immediately inland, thanks to an outstanding feat of railway engineering. A line from Lima to La Oroya, built early in the century, about 300 km long, contains 22 switchbacks, 65 tunnels, and 67 bridges, and crosses the Cordillera Occidental divide at a height of 15,665 ft (about 5,000 m). A similar railway in the south links the coastal town of Mollendo with Arequipa, and thence to the shores of Lake Titicaca and the historic city of Cuzco. By means of a ferryboat service across Lake Titicaca, it provided Bolivia, a landlocked country, with one of its outlets to the ocean.

Vast areas of Peru were therefore virtually inaccessible to the capital. Not only were there thousands of square miles of mountainous territory in which lateral valleys were separated by impenetrable ranges; the extensive *montaña* region in the east of Peru, which includes the lower eastern slopes of the Andes, plus the equatorial forest, or *selva* region, adjoining the Brazilian jungles of the Amazon Basin, were even more isolated. The stimulent to start the first air service in Peru was to provide reasonable access to these regions.

The Peruvian Naval Air Service

Although the Peruvian Government had published regulations governing civil aviation as early as 15 November, 1921, it was not until 20 September, 1926, that a commercial service was specifically authorized. Curiously, the route operated by the Peruvian Naval Air Service was entirely inland, albeit following the course of rivers, and using waterborne aircraft. The objective was to provide a mail and passenger service from the Peruvian capital to the most remote city, Iquitos, situated on the Amazon River about 1,500 miles (2,500 km) from the Atlantic, yet—confirming the title 'mighty' customarily attached to that great natural waterway—served by shipping lines with direct links to London and New York. Accordingly, a route was established on 3 January, 1928, which started at San

Ramón, on a tributary of the Ucayali River (itself a branch of the Amazon) and only about 100 km past La Oroya, linked directly with Lima by both road and rail. From San Ramón, the route crossed a small spur of the eastern Andean foothills to follow another tributary of the Ucayali River, and thence due north to the Amazon itself at Iquitos (see Map 33).

Six Keystone aircraft were supplied from the USA, two landplanes and four seaplanes, equipped with two passenger seats, and able to carry also 400 lb of mail or baggage over a range of 400 miles (650 km). During the year of 1928, 140 passengers and 14,000 lb of baggage were carried during 80,000 miles of flying; an achievement which led to further government support in the form of an allocation of almost $200,000 to support the Iquitos Air Line, as it was popularly called. The subsidy was well worth while. Before the inauguration of the Naval Air Service, the claim that the quickest way to travel from Lima to Iquitos was via the Panama Canal and up the Amazon was no exaggeration.

Foundation of Faucett

On 1 May, 1928, a group of Peruvian citizens applied to the Government for authority to operate a regular passenger and cargo air service. The group comprised Santiago Acuña, Armando Fabbri, Manuel Gallagher, P. Winder, and Ernesto Ayulo. They were inspired and led by a United States emigré, Elmer J. Faucett, who was destined to join the distinguished group of airline pioneers who are honoured by posterity in the names of the companies they founded. 'Slim' Faucett had arrived in Peru on 28 June, 1920, as a representative of the Curtiss Aviation Corporation. The young mechanic showed initiative beyond the limitations of maintenance routines, and on 15 October, 1922, he made a noteworthy flight from Chiclayo to the Amazon River in a Curtiss Oriole, for which exploit he was almost canonized when he arrived at Iquitos. When, in the later 1920s, enthusiasm for aviation escalated all over the world, stimulated by

Elmer Faucett's Curtiss Oriole at Arequipa on 18 September, 1926, after a 5½ hr flight from Lima. Faucett used the Oriole on a number of pioneering flights in Peru before beginning scheduled operations.

289

flights such as Lindbergh's and various Polar explorers', Faucett was among the first to see the practical possibilities in Peru.

On 4 June, 1928, the Faucett group received the necessary operating permission by Supreme Resolution No.736. On 15 September, regular flights of **Compañía de Aviación Faucett** began on a coastal route from Lima to Chiclayo, quickly extending to Talara in the north and Arequipa in the south. Aircraft used were two Stinson Detroiter six-seat monoplanes which, by the end of the year, had carried 242 passengers and had flown 30,000 miles.

In 1929 the northern and southern termini were extended to Tumbes and Tacna respectively, and in June of that year the initial capital of the company was increased from the modest 100,000 soles ($700 US in 1978 values) to 450,000 soles. The source of this financial injection was none other than Clement M. Keys, the promotor of multi-million dollar aviation corporations in the United States (including Curtiss, North American, and T.A.T.) during the late 1920s.

Peruvian Airways

Competing with Faucett along the coastal route was another airline whose momentum was originally generated by a United States organization. **Huff Daland Dusters, Inc** was a company which specialized in crop-dusting, particularly in the Peruvian cotton fields, drawing experience from its record of similar activity in the southern states of the USA. (The same company provided the basis for the original foundation of Delta Air Lines, now one of the world's largest). On 28 May, 1928, on the initiative of Harold R. Harris, Huff Daland's operations manager, and C. E. Woolman, the chief entomologist (and, incidentally, a good salesman) the company received permission to establish mail, passenger, and freight air services both within Peru and to the United States. Meanwhile, on 4 September, **Peruvian Airways Corporation**, was formed by the Haydon Stone group in New York.

Regular weekly service started on 13 September, 1928, under the terms of the Huff Daland concession—two days before Faucett—on a route from Lima to Talara, using a five-seat Fairchild FC-2. At first, this single aeroplane did not carry any markings that revealed its ownership or identity. The main purpose of the service was to save time on the mail route to the United States. The Peruvian authorities imposed a mail surcharge for the privilege. Peruvian Airways could leave Lima a day after the US-bound steamer and overtake it at Talara. On 16 September, 1928, the Aviation Corporation of the Americas (the Pan American parent organization) bought a half-interest in Peruvian Airways, which then became a mere pawn in the game of airline power politics being played by the dominant figures in the United States international airline expansion at that time. All the Huff Daland permits were transferred to the Peruvian Airways Corporation on 28 November, 1928.

This was the era of Juan Trippe, the driving force behind the foundation and expansion of Pan American Airways, and who was steamrollering his way throughout the entire South American continent, as inexorably as the metaphor implies and at a much faster pace. Simultaneously locked in battle with NYRBA on the east coast, Trippe had to settle for a half-share compromise on the west, as he was confronted by a giant corporation which was already firmly entrenched, holding a grip on commerce from Panamá to Santiago more powerful than governments themselves. The W. R. Grace Corporation controlled, amongst other activities, the shipping lines; and they were not prepared to allow a

This PANAGRA Fairchild FC-2W2 NC8039 has also been described as a seven-seat Fairchild 71. (*Pan American World Airways*)

newcomer, even Trippe, to poach on their transport territory. Accordingly, on 25 January, 1929, **Pan American-Grace Airways Inc (PANAGRA)** was formed, with Grace and the Aviation Corporation of the Americas each holding a half-share of the $1,000,000 stock. Peruvian Airways was absorbed on the same day and ceased to exist as a separate entity.

By this time, however, progress had been made within Peru. By the end of 1928, 135 passengers had been carried and 24,800 miles flown—comparable with Faucett's achievement—and the line had been extended northward, on 30 November, to Guayaquil, in Ecuador. On the day before the creation of PANAGRA, the line was extended along the whole length of the Peruvian coast, as far as Mollendo (see Map 33). Notably, the itinerary of Peruvian Airways concentrated on longer segments, while Faucett served every city of importance in the coastal zone of Peru.

The Faucett company, though inspired by a United States-born citizen, always identified itself as a Peruvian airline, and indeed Faucett himself became something of a local folk-hero, not only for his early exploits in exploratory flying, but for his apparent sincerity in trying to build up a transport organization which—in contrast to other airlines in the area—was concerned with serving Peruvians rather than visiting or transient foreigners. But the problems of physical geography weighed heavily against his endeavours.

The Ford 5-AT-D NC433H *San Felipe*, seen here at Trujillo in Peru, served PANAGRA from 1932 and crashed at Lima in December 1935. (*Pan American World Airways*)

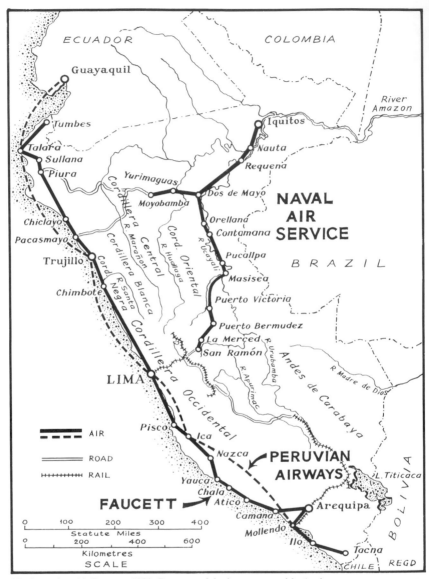

33. Peruvian Air Routes, 1929. Because of the insurmountable Andes, many years were to pass before Peru was to have its own trans-Andean air route. At first, the route from Lima to Iquitos involved three forms of transport: rail, road, and air. But two companies competed on the coastal route.

292

Nothing daunted, and reflecting no doubt that, if a Curtiss Oriole could reach the Amazon at Iquitos in the early 1920s (broadly equivalent to crossing the Himalayas in a Dragon Rapide) then the aircraft of the 1930s should be able to emulate that accomplishment. Tentatively, on 11 June, 1932, he made a flight from Chimbote to Yungay, penetrating the well-populated valley of the Río Santa. Passengers were carried on the Yungay service on 2 December of that year, but it was not sustained. Faucett also carried freight to such destinations as Puno in the south, a gateway to Bolivia; but his greatest opportunity came through political events in the area. Peru became involved in military conflict in the north with both Colombia and Ecuador—the boundaries were in dispute—and Faucett offered his services to the Peruvian military forces, providing connecting flights between the coast at Lima and the terminus of the Peruvian Naval Air Service at San Ramón.

By this time, the Naval Air Service had been combined with the Army Service to become the **Línea Aérea Nacional (LAN)**, provisionally on 22 February, 1929, and finally made permanent on 1 January, 1930. The Army section was based at Las Palmas, while the Navy section was at Ancón, under the command of Ben H. Wyatt, of the US Naval Mission. All air services in Peru were under the command of Capt Harold B. Grow, so that there was a strong North American element about the Peruvian commercial air programme. In 1931, a coastal route from Talara to Tacna was started, approximately parallel to those of Faucett and PANAGRA, but this lasted only a few months, because of inadequate equipment. More permanently, the Amazon service sprouted a branch line to link Iquitos with Moyobamba, via Yurimaguas, thus narrowing the gap between the Atlantic waterway and northern Peru.

From 23 April to 1 July, 1933, Faucett's operations were actually suspended during the period of emergency, while he provided valuable logistics service to the Peruvian Army, gaining, as an incidental bonus, however, some valuable experience in mountain flying, especially in the locating and preparation of airfields. To complement the improvement of ground facilities at the inland points, he now turned his attention to improving his aircraft. By judicious tinkering with his Stinson Number 5, he raised its speed from 105 to 130 mph. Thus encouraged, he then obtained the rights to build Stinson aircraft in Lima, assisted by a Stinson engineer, Gale Alexander, who used the basic Stinson design to build an aircraft especially suited to Peruvian operating conditions. This Faucett-Stinson F. 19 made its first flight on 20 September, 1934, and was so

Compañía de Aviación Faucett's Faucett F.19 eight-seat monoplane designed for high-altitude operation. These aircraft were developed from a Stinson design and frequently referred to as Faucett-Stinsons. This example is OB-PAH.

successful that thirty were built during the next twelve years, in the Faucett workshops at Lima, not only for the airline, but also for the Peruvian military support squadron.

Further United States Involvement

The year 1935 was to witness further participation by United States promoters in Peruvian commercial aviation, even though Faucett became wholly Peruvian-owned. **Cóndor Peruana de Aviación S.A.** was formed on 7 October by Hughie Wells, who had been nominated as chief engineer of NYRBA in its closing days before the Pan American takeover. Apparently he had later parted company with the US flag carrier to launch an airline of his own.

Cóndor Peruana's Curtiss BT.32 Condor OB-IIA loading tobacco at Tarapoto for the 5½ hr flight to Lima. The airline was renamed Línea de Aviación Cóndor.

The parent company of Cóndor was the newly-formed **Tampa-New Orleans-Tampico Air Lines Inc**, of New York City, which cherished the ambition of opening a route from New Orleans to Buenos Aires, via Bogotá, Quito, Lima, and La Paz. Rightly judging that a secure base in strategically situated Peru was essential, Wells obtained permission on 23 February, 1937, to import four twin-engined Curtiss Condor biplanes—the type which had inaugurated sleeper services on the US transcontinental air route. Unfortunately, both the US and the Peruvian Governments feared that these aircraft might be diverted for use in the Bolivian–Paraguayan war, then in full swing, and perhaps lead to some delicate diplomatic complications. Wells therefore had to bide his time by using them for photographic surveys, freight operations to remote and isolated mining communities, and for hauling tobacco from trans-Andean plantations to Callao, the port for Lima.

While Wells was bringing in the Condors, PANAGRA improved its services down the South American west coast. On 17 September, 1934, the first Douglas DC-2 had made a daylight flight from Cristóbal to Lima, replacing the ponderous Ford Tri-Motors. Five DC-2s were based in Lima so as to speed up and intensify the air service through to Buenos Aires. This meant, however, that the stops at the smaller cities of Peru had to be discontinued if full advantage was to be taken of the Douglas airliner's range and speed. All the Peruvian Airways permits were therefore transferred to PANAGRA on 23 October, 1934. Subsequently, on 8 August, 1934, PANAGRA established a subsidiary, **Cía Aerovías Peruanas**,

294

The PANAGRA hangar at Limatambo Airport, later used as Lima's general aviation airport. The nearest aircraft is PANAGRA's Douglas DC-3 NC18936. The centre aircraft is the airline's DC-2 NC14272 which was delivered to PANAGRA in September 1934 as P-30 *Santa Lucia* and crashed in Chile in July 1938. The furthest aircraft is an unidentified Ford 5-AT. (*Pan American World Airways*)

PANAGRA's Douglas DC-3 NC25652 at Lima. This aircraft was later acquired by the Peruvian Air Force. (*Pan American World Airways*)

295

which obtained an operating permit on 23 July, 1935, and maintained two services weekly from 1 November to all the coastal towns, linking up with the DC-2s at Talara, Piura, Chiclayo, Trujillo, Lima, and Arequipa only. On 1 May, 1936, a branch line was opened inland from Lima to Huancayo and, on 1 December of that year, the southern terminus was extended to Tacna. On a special contract, PANAGRA/Aerovías Peruanas transported 350 metric tonnes of mining equipment from Huamachuco to Piaz between 28 June and 26 August, 1936.

These activities apparently met with official Peruvian displeasure, as this was directly competitive with Faucett, Peru's own adopted airline; and although the concept of cabotage had not yet been the subject of international jurisdiction, or even discussed at international aviation forums, PANAGRA was clearly in a weak position to protest too heavily. A compromise solution to the problem was found. The operations of Aerovías Peruanas were transferred to Faucett on 26 April, 1938, in exchange for a 20 per cent interest, ending a period of stiff competition between Faucett and United States airline interests.

Meanwhile, Faucett had been making progress, in company with the Government's Línea Aérea Nacional, which by the mid-thirties was concentrating solely upon serving the *montaña* region beyond the Andes. In 1936 the two companies combined to establish a trans-Andean air service in the north of Peru. Faucett opened a branch line from Chiclayo to Yurimaguas, to connect with the LAN route from Iquitos to Moyobamba, thus closing the gap between the Amazon and northern Peru. Clement Keys sold his interest to the Sperry Corporation in 1934, and this eventually passed into Peruvian hands in 1936. Faucett thus became completely Peruvian.

Elmer Faucett (*left*), a US citizen, was one of the few airline pioneers who gave his name to the company he founded. Faucett became famous in Peru in 1922, when he made a pioneering flight from Lima to Iquitos. He redesigned the standard Stinson SM-6B monoplane to adapt it as the F.19 for hazardous trans-Andean flying conditions. Clement M. Keys (*right*) was a former *Wall Street Journal* editor who was one of the leading instigators of the United States aviation boom of the late 1920s. When the economic bubble burst in 1929, he invested in Cía de Aviación Faucett, then after the war in Peruvian International Airways. (*right-hand picture courtesy The Smithsonian Institution*)

In 1938 Wells's company, reorganized as **Línea de Aviación Cóndor Tampa**, eventually managed to begin scheduled services, the Curtiss Condors opening a route from Lima to Iquitos, via Huánuco, Tarapoto, and Yurimaguas, in 1938. The company claimed, with unabashed modesty, to have been operating for five years over the Sub-Stratosphere Route. A southern line from Lima to Cuzco followed, the first air link between the two cities, and a notable accomplishment for Cóndor Tampa, bearing in mind that the airport at Cuzco was at an altitude of 13,000 ft, one of the world's highest. PANAGRA had attempted a Lima–Cuzco service in 1934, but the route was flown only between 13 and 27 May of that year.

Praiseworthy though Wells's efforts were, he was unable to obtain material assistance from the Peruvian Government, which did not see its way clear to subsidize a foreign-owned operation, in spite of the obvious service being provided to the travelling public within Peru. He was unable to maintain schedules with regularity, and ceased operations altogether in April 1941. All assets were expropriated on 23 May, 1941, because of 'lack of spares holding which creates a danger to the public'.

German Intervention

In 1936, LAN opened a branch line from Masisea on the Ucayali River southeastwards to Puerto Moldonado, on the Río Madre de Dios, which provided a waterborne connection into northern Bolivia. This service was maintained, however, for only two years, and the Bolivian connection was then established by a direct route between La Paz and Lima, via Puno, by no less than a Peruvian branch of the German national airline Deutsche Lufthansa (DLH), which received permission from the Peruvian Government on 23 July, 1935, to begin service.

Although widely publicized, because of subsequent considerations of military strategy involving Germany's expansionist activities on the South American continent, this was not the first European incursion into Peru. Some time earlier, in October 1930, the French **Aéropostale** company had started a service from Arica, in northern Chile, to La Paz, Bolivia, calling at Tacna, the southernmost city of Peru. This service ceased after six months of operation as the empire of Marcel Bouilloux-Lafont collapsed under the pressures of political intrigue within France itself. But during the last few weeks of Aéropostale's unfortunate demise, that great pioneer airline is believed to have made the first few flights from Tacna to Lima, in preparation for a French west coast South American service.

On 24 May, 1938, **Deutsche Lufthansa Sucursal en Perú** began operations over this strategic segment of what had become a German transcontinental air service, starting at Rio de Janeiro by the Brazilian Condor airline as far as Corumbá, and thence by the Bolivian airline LAB to La Paz. The action attracted some interest in political circles, as DLH had also founded a similar branch airline in Ecuador during the previous year. With Nazi aggression on the rampage in Europe, the United States became apprehensive. Some observers noted the proximity of the Panama Canal, and a possible German supply route by means of Condor-LAB-Sucursal, should that nation ever cast covetous eyes towards the Isthmus.

Although the two Junkers-Ju 52/3ms of DLH Sucursal en Perú extended the network slightly in the south (to Arequipa), the connection with SEDTA of Ecuador was never made; and it came as no surprise when pressure from the United States caused the Peruvian Government to withdraw the operating permit in February 1941. Operations were suspended on 31 March, 1941, and the services replaced the next day by PANAGRA, which in fact was already operating a parallel service.

During the early 1940s, when most of the world was at war, Peruvian aviation marked time, except that some progress was made by the two surviving airlines, Faucett and Línea Aérea Nacional. Faucett acquired two PBY-5 Catalinas in 1943 to serve the US Rubber Development Corporation. During four years of service, these aircraft carried 6,800 passengers and 580,000 kg of rubber—a vital commodity for the United States war effort—plus 1,375 tonnes of cargo.

Lufthansa Sucursal en Perú's Junkers-Ju 52/3m OA-IIID taking off from Arequipa in southern Peru. (*Lufthansa*)

This service was concentrated of course on the *selvas* region where the rubber trees flourished, adjacent to those on the Brazilian side of the frontier. During this period also, in October 1944, Panair do Brasil extended its Amazon service from Tabatinga to Iquitos, thus completing, with the Peruvian connection, another transcontinental air route in South America.

Overshadowing even this achievement, however, in terms of Peruvian transport progress, was the opening in 1940 of the Pan-American Highway, which for the first time enabled heavy truck and bus traffic to complete the whole Peruvian coastal route. Some of the local air connections were thus rendered partially redundant, an uncommon reversal of the normal process.

CHAPTER FIFTEEN

Postwar Progress in Peru

A New Start

Postwar development in Peru proceeded at a much faster pace and over a much broader base. Various advantages derived from the country's status as a United States source-of-supply led to the emergence of different strata in the economy, including a consumer market. The war had brought about a revolution in aircraft standards, and although pressurized types did not operate domestically for several years, at least there was no longer any doubt about their ability to fly any Peruvian route nonstop from Lima, thus aiding the dispersal of commercial activity away from the intense concentration in the capital. One of the by-products of the wartime supply activities was the improvement of airfields, perhaps none more important than the new construction at Iquitos. This enabled flights to be made directly from the nation's capital, in place of the change of gauge which was previously necessary via the seaplane base at San Ramón.

Faucett extended its Yurimaguas route to Iquitos in 1946 and, with the delivery of war-surplus C-47/DC-3s, was able to add direct flights to the Amazon port from Lima. In 1947 the share capital was increased to 5 million soles, and further routes were opened on a spoke pattern to link every city of regional importance with Lima. By the time 'Slim' Faucett went into honourable retirement on 7 August, 1951, Faucett could rightfully claim to be Peru's national airline.

The Government airline was active also. On 8 May, 1946, Línea Aérea Nacional (LAN) was transferred to the 41st Transport Squadron of the Peruvian Air Force as the **Transportes Aéreos Militares (TAM)** and it also started a trans-Andean service to Iquitos, via Pucallpa. TAM, like its predecessor, was primarily a service for government personnel, emergency supply, and social flights; but this situation changed gradually so that only the local waterborne

Compañía de Aviación Faucett's Douglas C-47B OB-PAT bears the number 200 on its fin and was reregistered OB-R-200. Markings were red and black. (*Faucett*)

299

aircraft along the Amazon and its tributaries remained active in that role. TAM supplemented the commercial services of Faucett, specializing in low-fare, spartan standards of travel appropriate to a community whose per capita income was very low. During the late 1940s the name was changed to **Transportes Aéreos Nacional de la Selva (TANS)**. In 1951, the organization became known as the **Grupo de Transportes Número 41**.

As with so many developing economies, there was a marked increase in urbanization in Peru during the postwar period, an increase which, moreover, was to accelerate in later decades. However, it was immediately after the war that Peru ceased to be effectively a one-destination country for foreign travellers, as the improved accessibility of Cuzco brought the magnificent Inca ruins of Machu Picchu within reach of international tourists. And although the inevitable demographic magnetism of the capital caused an explosive population growth (Lima-Callao trebled its population between 1940 and 1960) there emerged also provincial cities of moderate size, not only along the coastal strip, where Chimbote, for example, grew from a village to a city of 60,000 during the same period; but also inland, where Pucallpa was fast becoming a commercial centre, thanks to its strategic position as the terminus of the trunk road across the Andes completed in 1943.

34. Postwar Establishment of a Peruvian Domestic Network, 1951. As in many Latin American countries, private airlines existed alongside government-supported operations. Faucett continued its fine work, while the Naval airline's descendant maintained the Amazon route after the war.

The First Peruvian International Airline—PIA

Until the late 1940s, then, for the international traveller, the commercial world of Peru was centred almost entirely on Lima, the transport hub of all roads, railways, and feeder air services to the rich mines of the *sierra*, with minor international ports of call such as Talara in the north, site of the International Petroleum Company's richest oil deposits in Peru. For international air services, PANAGRA reigned supreme, the joint manifestation of both the W. R. Grace

Peruvian International Airways' Douglas C-54A OB-SAF—actually owned by PIA's subsidiary Aeronaves S.A.—made the first scheduled arrival at New York International Airport, on 9 July 1948. It is seen here on that occasion.

Corporation and of Pan American Airways in commercial air dominance on the west coast of South America.

This remained an effective monopoly for almost three decades, only occasionally interrupted by aspiring interlopers on PANAGRA's hallowed ground. The company served the international business world of Peru well throughout the period, and although competition was almost non-existent, to criticize PANAGRA for displaying the evils of monopoly would be churlish. While in its latter years, it was to meet increasing challenges from other locally-based airlines down the Andean chain for the low-fare market which began to emerge during the 1960s, the fact that there was no low-fare market before that period is sometimes forgotten by critics of PANAGRA. When the low-fare services got under way, there were some limited numbers of people who could take advantage of them; but, in the developing years of PANAGRA, the average income levels throughout the western coast of South America were such that even low air fares, at any economic level, would have been too high. Neither had tourism reached the intensity of today's group-packaged volumes. In the 1940s and 1950s, tourists had to make individual arrangements with travel agents or with the airlines, and tours to Machu Picchu were normally within the grasp of only the more affluent—and the more adventurous—citizens of North America.

Only one airline caused any ripples on PANAGRA's pool during the early postwar years. On 14 January, 1946, **Peruvian International Airways (PIA)** was founded by a group of investors from three countries: Peru, Canada, and the United States. Its main promoter was none other than C. M. Keys, of North American/Curtiss/T.A.T. fame in the 1920s and early 1930s, and who had been the source of additional capital for Faucett in its formative years.

With a capital of $4,000,000, PIA began service on 14 May, 1947, using Douglas DC-4s, on a route to Havana, via Panamá. This was extended southward to Santiago, via Antofagasta, on 18 August, and north to Washington and New York on 26 September of the same year. With great enthusiasm, an increase of stock was approved in October to double the capital; but PIA seems already to have

301

been riding for a fall, and it was a classic case of an airline trying to run before it had learnt to walk—or whatever is the flying equivalent of that metaphor. For by 9 February, 1949, after less than two years of well-promoted operations ('La Avenida Aérea de Las Américas'—The Airway of the Americas—was its confident slogan) Peruvian International Airways ceased operations. Not least of its problems was undoubtedly the introduction by PANAGRA of pressurized Douglas DC-6 service from New York to Buenos Aires, via Panamá, Lima, and Santiago only, on 1 July, 1947; and the final blow was Braniff's entry into the Latin American market with a service to Lima on 4 June, 1948.

One of PIA's stranger claims to fame was to have been the world's first airline to operate radar-equipped airliners, on 4 April, 1946, during trials at Morrison Field, West Palm Beach, Florida.

APSA

Interest began to stir in Peru during the 1950s to establish its own international airline. With the Chileans to the south, and the Ecuadorians to the north, showing their countries' flags at the Miami Gateway to the United States, Peru was beginning to look like a poor relation in the eyes of its near-neighbours. There was considerable satisfaction in Lima, therefore, when on 16 September, 1956, the formation was announced of **Aerolíneas Peruanas S.A.** (**APSA**).

Dr Emilio Rodriguez Larrain and ex-Air Force General Carlos Washburn approached a United States citizen, C. N. Shelton, resident in Honduras. Shelton was to become the driving force behind the enterprise. An airline entrepreneur who owned TAN Airlines of Honduras, he was one of the band of cavalier airline promoters who claimed—with a certain amount of logic to support his conscience—that bilateral agreements set up between certain countries were mere devices to protect an international cartel of privileged airlines. Accordingly, he set about constructing his own private cartel, by forming associated airlines in other countries, through nominees, and evading the strict ICAO-approved definitions of Fifth Freedom rights. Even more important, by the device of segmenting multi-stop international routes between the various airlines under his control, but arranging through-plane service, he achieved the so-called Sixth Freedom, much in the same way that Icelandic Airlines turned the geographical location of its country to commercial advantage.

APSA performed the key role of responsibility for services south of Lima, connecting northward with another Shelton-initiated airline, Cía Ecuatoriana de Aviación (C.E.A.) at Talara and Guayaquil. C.E.A. overlapped to Lima, but provided the northern links both to Miami and to Tegucigalpa, TAN's headquarters, where it made connections throughout Central America. APSA began service on 17 June, 1957, to Santiago, Chile, via Antofagasta, using an old Curtiss C-46, then on 6 August to Tegucigalpa via Talara and Managua.

The APSA/C.E.A./TAN interchange ingeniously circumvented international regulations, and at first was quite successful, mainly with end-to-end traffic. Shelton's organization could offer through service from Miami to Santiago or Buenos Aires, substantially undercutting the IATA-based fare structures of the official flag carriers of the United States and other participants in the west coast South American market. Clearly, however, Shelton was on shaky ground, as although the Sixth Freedom traffic was not in itself illegal (except by the self-imposed rules of IATA) it was seen through the eyes of the United States C.A.B. as a contravention of the spirit of the law, if not a flagrant breach.

302

Some complex and fascinating litigation then ensued, when, to try to come more closely within the US policy guidelines, and at the time it extended its service to Buenos Aires, APSA applied to the C.A.B. in August 1958 for its own route to Miami. The question of Shelton's control of the Peruvian airline was vigorously raised by Pan American and PANAGRA, but—rather like the problems surrounding litigation in some of Howard Hughes's affairs—this could not be settled because of Shelton's refusal to leave Honduras to testify in Washington at the hearings.

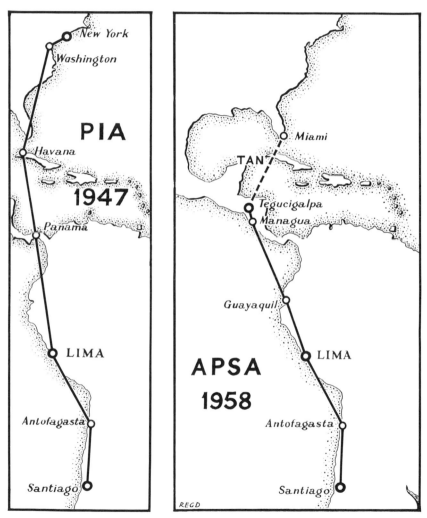

35. The First Peruvian International Air Routes, 1947–1958. Peru's first venture into the international air scene, PIA, was short-lived, although operating radar-equipped Douglas DC-4s. After a gap of several years, a new company, APSA, was able to provide substantially the same service, in co-operation with the Honduran airline, TAN.

APSA's Convair CV-990A OB-R-925 was originally American Airlines' N5612.
(*T. R. Waddington collection*)

The C.A.B. compromised and on 27 October the Examiner recommended a temporary one-year certificate to enable APSA to divest itself of foreign interests. The case was then reopened on 28 January, 1959, when Pan American introduced fresh evidence to support its case that Shelton controlled APSA; but in February 1960 the C.A.B. recommended a two-year permit, subject to adequate financial and statistical reporting, and other special requirements. These included the termination of single-plane services to Miami by APSA/C.E.A./TAN, and satisfactory evidence that APSA had cleared its debts to the Shelton-owned service organization based in Panama, the Compañía de Servicios Aerovías, S.A., Shelton immediately took steps to transfer his shares to new shareholders in Peru.

During this tendentious litigation, the C.A.B. was probably conscious of the aspirations of Peru to start its own airline, and that a bilateral agreement existed between the two countries. Also, some of the members of the Board may possibly have remembered that, in its time, Pan American had indulged in practices very similar to those that it was now condemning; and in fact much of Juan Trippe's airline empire had been built by methods similar to Shelton's. At all events, the C.A.B. gave APSA the green light on 23 June, 1960, and DC-6 service began to Miami, with only one stop, at Panamá, on 13 July.

APSA meanwhile had, in February 1960, ordered two Lockheed 188 Electras but had cancelled the order when that aircraft ran into its wing structure problems. The Panamanian airline APA withdrew from its short-lived association with the Shelton group, and steps were taken to put APSA's house in the kind of order that was necessary to satisfy the US authorities. To show that Peru was serious about its intentions, APSA applied for a renewal of the permit before the time limit had expired, adding a request for the addition of Bogotá (to which city service began in 1961), plus an extension beyond Miami to Washington and Montreal. This was approved by the C.A.B. in February 1964, but by this time APSA had already moved into a satisfactory position. In November 1963 it leased a Convair CV-990A from Fred B. Ayer, the well-known US aircraft dealer, and jet service began on 1 December, supplementing the Douglas DC-7Bs which had been acquired instead of the Electras. At the same time, a special arrangement was made with Northeast Airlines, a US trunk airline operating to Florida from northeastern USA, to provide the necessary connection to New York. APSA in fact never did operate north of Miami, but offered the first low-fare jet service to South America, at $273 one way, a saving of $31, from Miami to Buenos Aires.

304

On 7 November, 1964, APSA began to spread its wings, and to establish itself more firmly in the South American market, added a new route, to Rio de Janeiro, with the CV-990s providing a one-stop service from Miami to Rio, via Lima. This route was later consolidated with stops at Panamá and São Paulo, so that APSA was now serving most of the important cities of South America, with the geographical position of Lima working to its advantage. During 1964, La Paz, Asunción, and Montevideo were also added to the network.

C. N. Shelton, incidentally, died in March 1965. Had he lived a little longer, he would have witnessed a complete transformation of the airline he sponsored in 1956. The Shelton trustees retained 23 per cent of APSA's stock, while 33½ per cent each was held by the *Popular y Porvenir* insurance group, and the Cisneros industrial group, with 10 per cent in the hands of private citizens. APSA in fact became a model of respectability, joining IATA in 1965. It adopted as its mascot-symbol a pert little Indian maiden, a mythological personage, Antarqui, who possessed the ability to fly. She will long be remembered by the South American travelling public, most of whom have never heard of Shelton.

During the late 1960s APSA presented the outward appearance of a highly successful airline, zealously promoting its services throughout Latin America, and with a well-organized agency in the USA. Receiving a second Convair CV-990A in February 1965, it added some important new routes: to Mexico City and Los Angeles on 18 August, 1966; and to Europe, terminating in London, via Madrid and Paris, in 1969. It acquired more aircraft, not only CV-990s but also a Douglas DC-8-52, leased from Iberia, the Spanish national airline which was beginning to make arrangements with the Spanish-speaking nations in Latin America, so as to expand its influence there in competition with non-Spanish-speaking European airlines.

But the impressive expansion was deceptive. APSA was running deeply into debt, partly because it was paying uneconomic rates for the lease of its aircraft, few of which it owned. When APSA's services were abruptly suspended on 3 May, 1971, it was reported to owe $22,000,000, of which $19,000,000 was to General Dynamics, manufacturers of the CV-990s, some to Fred Ayer, and some to Iberia. It was a sad ending to Peru's first entry into the international field, and APSA's demise left shock waves throughout the aviation business on the west coast. Three years were to pass before Peru's flag was to be seen at a foreign airport again.

APSA's Douglas DC-8-52 OB-R-931 had been Iberia's EC-ARC. After service in Peru the aircraft went back to Spain. (*T. R. Waddington*)

305

Domestic Airline Developments

While APSA was having its hours of glory, events at home went their own quiet way, by devious and meandering paths. There were no clear-cut directives from the Government, and airline development continued on an opportunist basis typical of Latin American countries. Faucett remained as the national airline in practice, but the Government airline maintained its share of the action, especially after the military government took power in 1968. Additionally, many smaller companies appeared on the scene, mostly to survive only briefly.

Faucett drew large dividends from its long traditions, keeping faith with the aims originally set down by Faucett himself: operating its routes with steady reliability, acquiring aircraft in a sensible succession and with well-planned financing, and maintaining them commendably. Faucett had become so much a part of the Peruvian economic system that even a government seeking to transfer or to allocate some of the aviation spoils to its own agency could not bring itself to harm Faucett significantly, largely because of popular sentiment.

A Faucett Douglas DC-6B at Arequipa with the 19,200 ft El Misti in the background. (*Courtesy Esso Air World*)

Faucett's only questionable act—questionable in the sense of lack of judgement—was its sortie into the international arena. Almost the same day that Elmer Faucett died in April 1960, the Peruvian Government gave the Compañía de Aviación Faucett permission to operate international routes. With the first pressurized DC-6 being delivered in July of that year, designated for the Lima–Cuzco route, Faucett was technically able to operate a service to the USA—always a prerequisite for United States C.A.B. authority, which was duly granted in October 1961. Although this appeared to have been consummated with some alacrity, compared with the long-drawn-out negotiations with APSA, the C.A.B. still wished to have the matter over PANAGRA's 20 per cent shareholding in Faucett cleared up, and therefore limited Faucett's licence to a provisional five-year term.

Nothing happened. Faucett did not start an international service of any kind; and PANAGRA became the subject of internecine warfare between the joint owners, with the result that, with the C.A.B.'s blessing (and possibly behind-the-scenes persuasion) the entire airline was sold to Braniff International Airways. This immediately upgraded the Dallas-based airline to the stature of a

Faucett's Boeing 727-063 OB-R-902 was delivered in 1968. (*Courtesy Barrie James*)

major force in commercial aviation in South America, offering a competitive challenge to both the indigenous airlines and to Pan American itself. When Braniff acquired control of PANAGRA on 31 January, 1967, it obtained 1,160,000 shares of Faucett, equivalent to 17·77 per cent of the capital.

In February 1967, the C.A.B. granted a five-year extension to Faucett's international permit; but although the Peruvian airline received delivery of a Boeing 727 trijet, it placed this on domestic services, rather than on the international route. Finally, in June 1969, it filed notice of intention to serve Miami, but when Faucett aircraft finally arrived there in the Spring of 1970, they were Douglas DC-4s operating cargo services only.

Possibly Faucett had kept a wary eye on APSA's sorry plight, and decided that it was better to continue doing the things it knew how to do well than to risk doing badly the things it knew little about. At any rate, in August 1973, passenger rights to Miami were withdrawn, and there were no protests from the airline. Much was happening in Peruvian politics at this time, of direct application to Peruvian airline affairs, and no doubt Faucett felt that its future should not be complicated by unnecessary involvement.

Meanwhile, the domestic services developed steadily, with improvements in flying equipment, from DC-4 to DC-6B, then a Boeing 727, and two BAC One-Elevens purchased in 1971. But many routes still continued to be operated by the DC-3; and even more remarkably, a few Stinsons were still to be seen on local services between Arequipa and Tacna, and between Talara and Tumbes, until the early 1960s.

Faucett's BAC One-Eleven-476FM OB-R-953. (*T. R. Waddington collection*)

The SATCO Douglas DC-3 OB-XAD at Lima in 1965. (*Gordon S. Williams*)

SATCO

More or less parallel with Faucett, the Peruvian Government transport wing, also known locally as the **Grupo de Transportes Número 8**,* operated a few trunk routes to major cities during the 1950s, using the DC-3 and C-46 which had replaced de Havilland Dragon Rapides throughout Peru including the feeder services in the Amazon region. These latter, however, were handed over to another branch of the Air Force in 1960, and the Grupo concentrated on commercial operations. In 1963, the change was emphasized by changing the name to **Servicio Aéreo de Transportes Commerciales (SATCO)** and acquiring further DC-3 and C-46 aircraft. It began to see itself as a competitor to Faucett, rather than as a complementary agency of the Peruvian Government. Though its services were not so frequent as Faucett's, its influence and position in Peruvian domestic airline affairs were now on a different scale than in the days of the Línea Aérea Nacional, the Transportes Aéreos Militares, or the Grupo de Transportes. In fact, its route mileage was almost as great as Faucett's.

In 1966 SATCO introduced DC-4s, and in connection with earthquake relief work, added four DC-6s and three Lockheed Hercules to its fleet, a formidable addition to its cargo-carrying capability, and superior to that of any other airline in Peru—or, for that matter, in many neighbouring countries. It also conducted a competition for the replacement aircraft for its domestic trunkline routes, choosing the Fokker F.28 in March 1973 over both the Douglas DC-9 and the BAC One-Eleven, because of its demonstrated superiority in being able to use the restricted airfields at some cities.

For a time, ominous political clouds seemed to darken Faucett's future, as President Velasco had announced a five-year plan in 1968 which had as its objective the transfer to State ownership of most industrial, commercial, and agricultural sectors of the Peruvian economy. And when, in May 1973, the newly-formed State airline AeroPerú took over SATCO as its domestic division, the outlook became even more threatening. But a reprieve came when putting ambitious schemes into practice proved difficult and Faucett survived by default. Because of ill health, President Velasco gave way to President Morales Bermúdez in 1975; and the sweeping reforms were superseded by more moderate evolutionary steps.

*Grupo de Transportes Número 8, should not be confused with Grupo de Transportes Número 41, with which it was, however, affiliated with the Air Force organization.

This Lockheed L-100-20 was originally delivered to the Peruvian Air Force as FAP396. In this view it carries SATCO's livery, the civil registration OB-R-956 and its Air Force number. (*Harold G. Martin*)

AeroPeru's Fokker F.28 Fellowship Series 1000 OB-R-1018 had earlier been OB-R-398. The aircraft is seen with a mixture of AeroPeru and SATCO livery. (*Harold G. Martin*)

The Smaller Airlines of Peru

As with almost every Latin American country, large or small, affluent or impoverished, Peru was destined to have a multiplicity of small, precariously-supported airlines as soon as a transport need was established and cheap second-hand aircraft became available.

The small Peruvian airlines which have come into being since the war are summarized in Table 15.

Happily there are occasional examples which manage to emerge from the pack, through a combination of hard work, fortuitous continuity of contracts, and the ability to survive in disturbed political waters. But only two airlines in Peru could be said to qualify for special mention beyond the confines of a tabulated summary.

One of these had an eventful history. **Líneas Aéreas Nacionales S.A. (LANSA)** was founded in 1963 by a group of bus operators based in Lima. With some additional investment late in 1965 from a powerful source in the United States, Eastern Air Lines, which acquired a $33\frac{1}{3}$ per cent interest, LANSA started to expand service to the main cities of Peru which had begun in January 1964. Its

TABLE 15
Minor Airlines of Peru
(In Order of First Service date)

Airline (and abbreviation)	Date of Foundation (Date of First Service)	Routes	Fleet	Remarks
Transportes Aéreos Peruanos, S.A. (TAPSA)	June 1946	Lima–Trujillo–Tarapoto–Iquitos, plus feeder services in Andes and Selva	Various types, including 4 Anson 4 Norseman 2 Lockheed 4 C-46	Ceased operations, 1959
Compañía Aéreo Mercantil, S.A. (CAMSA)	February 1947	Feeder services from Tingo María	1 Douglas B-18 1 C-82 6 Cessna T-50	Intermittent operations, 1947–1951, 1952–1957
Aerovías Nacionales del Sur (ANDES)	6 April, 1948 (12 May, 1948)	Lima–Tacna, Iquitos, Pucallpa	4 C-46	Operations terminated, March 1951
Rutas Aéreas del Perú, S.A. (RAPSA)	January 1955		1 C-82 1 B-17	Ceased operations, late 1956
Expreso Aéreo Peruano, S.A.	May 1956	Cargo charter services, Lima to Central America	3 C-82	Ceased operations, March 1962

Empresa Andoriente, S.A.	November 1960	Ad hoc charter services in Andes	3 B-17	Ceased operations, April 1965. Bankrupt February 1966
Aerovías Amazonas, S.A.	(April 1961)	Cargo: Iquitos–Quito–Bogotá–Panamá–Miami	3 C-46	Ceased operations, 1965
Rutas Internacionales Peruanas, S.A. (RIPSA)	March 1961 (March 1962)	Cargo: Lima–Panamá–Miami	2 C-46 1 DC-4 1 L-749A	Ceased operations, 1967
Transperuana de Aviación (Transperuana)	1 October, 1961 (1964)	Iquitos–Trujillo–Chiclayo	5 C-46 1 C-82 2 DC-3	Air taxi service until 1964. Non-scheduled 1964–1967. Permits expired July 1969. Declared bankrupt 25 Sept, 1970
Compañía Peruana Internacional de Aviación. S.A. (COPISA)	July 1964	Lima–Cali–Panamá–Miami (and Iquitos–Maracaibo, 1967)	3 L-749	Suspended operations, July–Sept 1967; ceased 1973
Aerovías Trans América Perú, S.A. (ATAPSA)	February 1964 (September 1965)	Ad hoc services to Iquitos, Pucallpa, Tingo María, Tarapoto, Leticia (Colombia), Manaus (Brazil)	1 DC-3	Ceased operations, 1967

Note: In addition to the above companies, *Aero Taxis, S.A* operated taxi services with Cessna T-50s from 1954 to the mid-1960s; *Aglo, S.A. (AGLOSA)* used C-46s for business purposes only 1966–1967; *Aerovías Siesta del Perú, S.A.* was founded in 1968 to operate Douglas DC-7C aircraft Lima–Easter Island–Tahiti–Sydney. Government approval was obtained in June 1969, but the airline never operated.

LANSA's Lockheed 749 Constellation OB-WAA was originally Eastern Air Lines' N117A.
(*Harry Gann*)

speciality was to promote vacation flights and tours for visitors who wished to see Machu Picchu, Chan-Chan (the ruins near Trujillo), Iquitos, and Arequipa. Its fleet included Model 749A Constellations, acquired in February 1964, to which were added three ex-Braniff Electras and four Nihon YS-11s, delivered in the summer of 1967. The last two types especially offered good comfort and good operating economics and incidentally forced Faucett to upgrade its equipment. Nevertheless, LANSA was often in poor financial shape and actually had to suspend service during the summer of 1966. When therefore an Electra crashed in 1970, killing 99 people, this was bad news indeed.

Further disaster followed, when on 24 December, 1971,—the incident dramatized even further by the festive occasion—another Electra crashed in the Amazon jungle near Iquitos, LANSA's days were literally numbered. The Peruvian Government cancelled the airline's operating certificate on 4 January, 1972, stating that the company had exhausted its working capital. It had also presumably exhausted the patience of the licensing authorities in terms of its safety record; while the travelling public cannot have been too enamoured with an airline which lost most of its fleet, and almost 200 people, in little more than a year.

LANSA's YS-11A-120 was delivered new and in this view taken at Seattle it still bears its Japanese registration JA8676. It became OB-R-857. (*The Boeing Company*)

In the second accident, 91 people lost their lives. But a remarkable story surrounds the sole survivor. Miraculously, a 17-year-old girl, Juliane Koepcke, made her way through the treacherous jungles and constructed a raft in which she navigated the waterways. Her ordeal to the nearest habitation lasted ten days, and she was sustained by a Christmas cake which she had brought with her as a present for her father. Her survival ranks among the classic escapes such as Guillaumet's trek to safety in the early days of Aéroposta and the incredible incident in which, after an inflight explosion in 1972, Vesna Vulović, a Jugoslav airline stewardess fell 25,000 feet, and—thanks to a perfectly angled snow slope—lived to tell the tale.

The cargo Douglas DC-8-43 OB-R-1143 *San Martin de Porres* is shown while being jointly operated by AeroPeru and Aeronaves del Perú. Previously this had been Alitalia's DC-8-42 I-DIWA.

Soon after LANSA entered the scene, another new airline was organized by ex-Air Force personnel to operate domestic services. Originally called Compañía de Aviación Aeronaves de Perú, S.A. (AAPSA) on its foundation in 1965, it became known simply as **Aeronaves del Perú** when it was permitted to start services while awaiting operating licences. It was no more successful in breaking into an already over-populated airline market than any of its other contemporary aspirants, but it did not close down altogether, turning instead to international cargo operations. In 1969, it was designated by the Peruvian Government as an all-cargo flag carrier to the United States, with the restrictions that the licence would be reviewed after five years, and that the fleet should not exceed two aircraft. In June 1970, Aeronaves del Perú received the coveted foreign air carrier permit from the United States C.A.B. which enabled it to substitute its charter services to Miami by a twice-weekly scheduled operation.

AeroPerú

After a two-year hiatus following the abrupt demise of APSA in 1971, a new Government-owned airline was founded in May 1973 as the Peruvian national flag carrier. It immediately absorbed the existing organization of SATCO, the Government's domestic airline which traced its origins to the Peruvian Naval Air Service of 1928. In fact, the first **AeroPerú** official flight was on 28 July, 1973, on the anniversary of Peru's independence, and was merely the substitution of the new name for SATCO's services.

The full name of Peru's new airline was Empresa de Transportes Aéreos del Perú and the new administration thankfully resisted the temptation to add to the confusing list of acronyms by which so many Latin American airlines are identified. At least, with AeroPerú potential travellers knew to which country their aircraft belonged. AeroPerú's first service with its own aircraft, other than those taken over from SATCO, was in May 1974, with a Boeing 727-100 bought from United Air Lines. It operated nonstop routes from Lima to Cuzco, Arequipa, Chiclayo, and Iquitos.

The new airline moved quickly to recover Peru's international standing, filing an application with the United States C.A.B. early in April 1974 for a scheduled service to supplement the non-scheduled and charter services already approved for SATCO by President Nixon. The C.A.B. Law Judge approved this on 12 June, but restricted the permit to three years, matching a similar restriction placed on foreign airlines by the Peruvian Government. Three weeks later, when Braniff asked for landing rights in Lima on a new flight from Miami to Rio de Janeiro, and the Peruvian Government refused, this seemed to be a straw in the wind of possible political problems affecting the airlines. And although President Nixon approved AeroPerú's routes to Miami and Los Angeles on 26 July, 1974, this was only the lull before a political storm.

AeroPerú wasted no time in putting its authority into effect. On 29 July, with a small fleet of Douglas DC-8s, it began international service to Buenos Aires and Santiago, plus Guayaquil. On 16 September, these routes were extended northward to Miami, thus restoring Peru's route to the USA and beginning the hard road back to regain the market share which APSA's departure had lost. But the political clouds began to gather to put the new service in jeopardy.

The threat of a suspension of services because of a stalemate in traffic rights negotiations became a real possibility. Discussions in Lima were suspended on 16 January, 1975, and the C.A.B. moved to revoke AeroPerú's operating rights on 24 February. Peru retaliated by warning the United States that, in its turn, it would suspend Braniff's rights in Peru, and it was left to the two airlines, rather than the politicians, to try to pour oil on troubled waters. However, on 29 April Peru rejected Braniff's compromise offer, on 27 May the C.A.B., supported by the White House, threatened to cancel AeroPerú's US authority, and two days later the Peruvian Government announced that Braniff's authority into Lima would be limited to one token flight a week.

Fortunately, things went from bad to better. After six months of hard and often bitter argument, an agreement was reached on 28 June, 1975. Braniff was granted local traffic, *i.e.* Fifth Freedom rights southwards from Lima; and in return AeroPerú received authority to serve New York. The agreement meant that there would be 15 round trips weekly between the United States and Peru.

The New York authority was a major achievement for AeroPerú. Although Miami was the natural gateway for South Americans entering the United States, New York was their ultimate destination in most cases, and the New York area was the origin point of the greatest number of North Americans visiting Peru, both on business and pleasure. But service was not inaugurated immediately. First priority was given to completing the network originally planned, and on 4 October, 1975, through service by AeroPerú DC-8s started from Rio de Janeiro and São Paulo to Los Angeles, via Lima and Mexico City.

Progress was not spectacular, as AeroPerú had to work hard to recover the Peruvian national share of the market, in the face of competition not only from a well-organized and -directed Braniff, but also from many European and South American airlines operating down the west coast of South America. Nevertheless, by May 1978 Bogotá and Caracas, and also Quito, had been added to the route system.

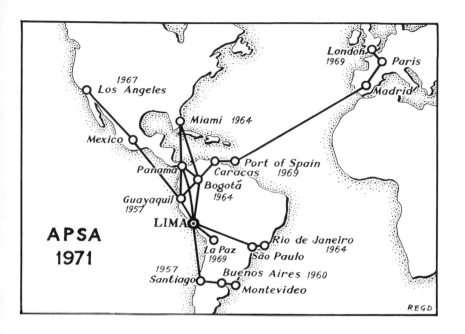

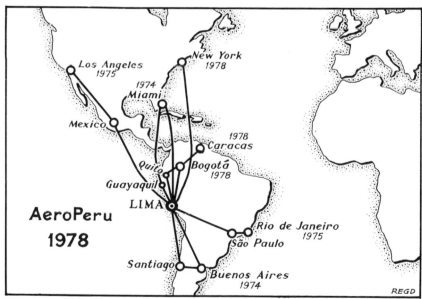

36. Peruvian International Route Development, 1971–1978. APSA advanced from being part of a loosely-knit international consortium to become Peru's flag airline, with an impressive route network. But it outgrew its strength, and in a repetition of history, ceased operations. When AeroPeru was formed as a national carrier, its international plans concentrated on the Americas.

While AeroPerú was securing its various footholds and consolidating a network closely resembling (except for the European route) that of the late APSA, preparations were in hand to elevate its standard of equipment so as to join the ranks of wide body operators to match the likes of Lufthansa, Air France, and other operators of Douglas DC-10s and Boeing 747s destined to become standard equipment throughout the trunk routes of Latin America.

When the time came, AeroPerú's decision was decisive. It took full advantage of Lockheed's precarious position as the least successful of the wide-body manufacturers and negotiated a good financial deal. Lockheed delivered two L-1011 TriStars formerly ordered for the Californian airline PSA and, although intended for US domestic operation, these were converted for over-water use, pending eventual delivery of longer-range aircraft. AeroPerú introduced the L-1011 to open the New York route on 15 December, 1978.

One of the Lockheed L-1011-100 TriStars that was leased by AeroPeru. The livery was white with two shades of red and the badge on the fuselage was gold. (*Courtesy Barry James*)

With three airlines competing for Peru's national traffic, there followed an uneasy period of a few years, with Aeronaves del Perú strengthening its relative status, to the extent that, in April 1982, it came to the forefront. The Zanetti family, already owning 58·8 per cent of the Aeronaves stock, purchased Faucett for $4 million. The latter airline was reported to have suffered from mismanagement to the extent that its debts totalled $18 million, almost half of which were owed to British Aerospace, suppliers of half the domestic fleet.

Zanetti promptly transferred one of Aeronaves del Perú's Douglas DC-8s to Faucett for its route to Miami, and continued to examine ways of avoiding unnecessary duplication of domestic services against AeroPerú. This airline, too, was not thriving. It has not been able to sustain the TriStar service, returning the wide-bodied aircraft to Lockheed, and maintaining the service to New York with Douglas DC-8s. Such is Faucett's reputation in Peru that, if (as seems logical) Aeronaves del Perú and Faucett were to merge, the name Faucett would survive to maintain a long tradition in air transport in Peru, and as a tribute to one of the great pioneers of Latin American air transport.

Perhaps the supreme irony was that, in 1982, the once powerful Braniff, which had acquired PANAGRA on 19 January, 1967, ceased operations altogether on 13 May, 1982. But Faucett lived on to meet the new competition from Eastern Air Lines, designated immediately by the United States C.A.B. to take over Braniff's Latin American routes.

CHAPTER SIXTEEN

Bolivian Airlines

A Topographical Challenge

Descriptions of South American countries tend to be punctuated by the use of superlatives. Each one seems to claim either the highest waterfall, or the longest river, or the most volcanoes, or the biggest swamps or jungles in the Americas, if not the world. The landlocked country of Bolivia has its fair share of most of these geographical features which make it unusual, not to say unique, in many ways. The main physical characteristic having far-reaching effects on the entire development of the country itself, and in its relations with neighbouring states, is the high plateau, formed between the two ranges of the mighty cordillera of the Andes, and occupying about one third of Bolivia.

The average altitude of the plateau ranges between about 7,000 ft and 12,000 ft (2,000–4,000 metres), and though possessing a somewhat dry climate and rather mixed vegetation, is rich in minerals, especially valuable ores such as silver and tin. Consequently, colonial settlers, ever since Spanish times, have preferred this

Line-up of Lloyd Aéreo Boliviano's Junkers-F 13 fleet at Cochabamba in April 1928. The aircraft are early production examples with unbalanced tail surfaces but have the broad-chord triangular fins. The fourth and fifth aircraft from the left are *Mamoré* and *Charcas*. For several years LAB's fleet bore names instead of registrations. (*LAB*)

317

area to the jungles and grassy plains which occupy most of the eastern and northern two-thirds of the country.

Bolivia has never been a prosperous country, and in spite of its mineral wealth, the majority of its citizens have ranked amongst the world's poorest by the normal criteria of comparison. Of the approximately five million population, about 85 per cent are of indigenous Indian stock, and this percentage applies also to the literacy level as a whole. The country is run therefore, both politically and commercially, by an élite few, drawn from traditional family hierarchies or military juntas. Bolivia's history has been one of constant instability and territorial misfortune. Whether by war or treaty, Bolivia always seems to have come off second best. It lost its sea coast in wars with Chile at the end of the nineteenth century; it lost the Acre Territory to Brazil at the beginning of the twentieth; and in a crippling war with Paraguay in the early 1930s, lost a stretch of territory—the Chaco—to Paraguay.

On the whole, therefore, Bolivia would seem to have been an unlikely candidate for the role of a pioneering airline country in Latin America. Yet, in defiance of much economic logic—though certainly not in terms of the genuine need for transport of any kind, road, rail, or air—the national airline of Bolivia can lay true claim to being the second oldest surviving airline in the Americas. For the historian, this airline provides a neat subject, in the sense that throughout its history of more than half a century it has retained the same name and identity; has never been party to a merger and consequent complications; and has progressed (albeit unsteadily from time to time) in almost case-study fashion from the proverbial one-plane, one-route trail-blazer to become a worthy representative of its government and nation in the modern international jet arena.

Foundation of Lloyd Aéreo Boliviano

In the month of July 1925, three visitors of German nationality arrived in Bolivia. The small team comprised Willy Neuenhoffen, a pilot of good reputation; Franz Schoenmetzler, a mechanic; and Ing Walter Jastram, the President of the South American Junkers Mission which had already made successful demonstrations in Argentina. Another arrival, by the long train journey from Buenos Aires, was a Junkers-F 13 monoplane, disassembled in three parts: the fuselage and the two wings. The team supervised the transport of the pieces from the railway station at Cochabamba to an improvised landing field at San José de La Banda, a farm on the outskirts of town, where it was prepared for its first proving flight, successfully accomplished on 27 July.

A few days afterwards, these three, together with Ing Raúl Peró as co-pilot, and Ing Alberto Cornejo as Bolivia's first fare-paying passenger, made an historic flight to Sucre—at that time taking its turn as the capital—as a dramatic contribution to the Centennial celebrations of Bolivia's independence. It is recorded that Ing Peró's role as co-pilot was in no way connected with actually taking control of the aircraft. His presence was necessary because he was the only one who knew the way!

Further proving flights were made to demonstrate the sturdy F 13 to various other cities in Bolivia, and shortly thereafter a group of German residents who formed the small expatriate colony in Bolivia met on 15 September, 1925, to form **Lloyd Aéreo Boliviano (LAB)**. Led by its first President, Guillermo Kyllman, the company purchased the Junkers, and persuaded the Bolivian Government to provide a small subsidy to begin operations. In a large country, starved of

Dr Aníbal Peña (*left*), a director of LAB; (*centre*) Hermann Schroth, technical director and later chief pilot of LAB; and the airline's second ranking pilot, believed to be named Helmers. They are seen in front of one of the company's Junkers-F 13s at Cochabamba.

communications, it was for Bolivia an epoch-making step forward, and a commendable fusion of free enterprise and official initiative.

A few months later, on 24 December, a regular service began between Cochabamba and Santa Cruz with the Junkers-F 13, named *El Oriente*. The distance of about 200 miles was covered in 2 hr 20 min, comparing very favourably with surface modes, which varied between four days and two weeks, depending on the weather and the condition of the vehicle. Although Cochabamba is by no means the highest city in Bolivia—by local standards, its elevation of over 8,000 ft is not remarkable—the flight to Santa Cruz, down on the plain, could be termed to be all downhill in one direction, and uphill in the other.

Mamoré, one of LAB's Junkers-F 13s seen as a floatplane while working in the north of Bolivia. This picture, taken at Riberalta, also shows the 300 hp Fiat-engined Glisador *The Oquendo* which was capable of 40 km/h.

319

Early Route Expansion

By this time, LAB had gained, on 7 November, 1925, official recognition by Supreme Resolution of the Bolivian Government, and by the end of the year had purchased three more F 13s. With the augmented fleet, new routes were extended to provincial cities, hitherto so distant in surface journey time that they might as well have been in another country. The opening of LAB service to Trinidad, in the potentially rich arable province of Beni, on 28 October, 1926; and eastwards from Santa Cruz to Puerto Suárez, on the Brazilian frontier, opposite Corumbá, in February 1928: these were important contributions to the development of Bolivia. This was an occasion when the aeroplane preceded the road or the railway, and even today the railway planned to traverse Bolivia from east to west has not been completed.

Encouraged by the success of its initial expansion, LAB added more F 13s in 1928 which, after some losses, brought the fleet total to six. These were *Oriente II, Charcas, Mamoré, Illimani, Chaco,* and *Beni III.* Two of these were equipped as floatplanes for use in the northern regions, laced with tributaries of the Amazon. It was with such a floatplane that a new route to the northern city of Riberalta was added on 3 June, 1928, while landplanes linked Santa Cruz with Yacuiba, on the Argentine frontier to the south, on 8 June; and Cochabamba with La Paz, via Oruro, later in the year.

This last route is notable in that, although Cochabamba, at more than 8,000 ft, would be high enough by most standards, Oruro is nearly 4,000 ft higher, and the destination, La Paz, the commercial capital of Bolivia, and its largest city by some margin, is famous for being one of the highest in the world, at about 12,000 ft. Yet the city is built in a valley, and the airport is on the plateau, some 1,500 ft higher still, on the desolate *altiplano* area of the Bolivian high plateau.

Apart from the interesting variety of cargo in the foreground, this photograph is of great historic value because the Lloyd Aéreo Boliviano Junkers-Ju 52/3mde *Juan del Valle,* together with *Huanuni,* were the first production or pre-production Ju 52/3ms and the first to go into service. The first Ju 52/3m was built from a single-engined Ju 52 airframe. The Bolivian Ju 52/3ms were delivered in 1932, had narrow-chord engine cowlings, a cockpit canopy resembling that of the G 31, long cabin windows with sliding panels and a horizontally divided double cargo door, the lower part forming a loading platform. Apart from normal airline operation these two aircraft served as military transports and for casualty evacuation in the Gran Chaco war.

LAB's Junkers-Ju 52/3m *Illampu* was later registered CB-22.
(*Pan American World Airways*)

Fleet Development and a Crisis

Lloyd Aéreo Boliviano made the next logical step in fleet development in March 1929, when it acquired a larger-capacity aircraft, a Junkers-W 34, and named it *Vanguardia*. With its sister-ship *Tunari*, added in 1930, this was an improved version of the F 13, with more powerful engines, cleaner lines, and could carry six passengers compared with the F 13's four. Then, two years later, LAB moved into multi-engined equipment. Possibly reacting also to the need to play its part in the national emergency as the first blows of the 1932–1935 Chaco War with Paraguay were heard, the airline bought the Ford Tri-Motor *Cruz del Sur* in September 1932, and its first Junkers-Ju 52/3m, *Chorolque,* a month later. These three-engined aircraft could carry up to about 16 passengers (or more on certain occasions) and were obviously superior to the single-engined types which had served so well to establish a national Bolivian airline. Unfortunately, the Ford crashed after only a few months of service.

By 1933, Bolivia was embroiled in a crippling war with Paraguay. The territory of El Chaco had long been disputed between the two countries, and the problem had surfaced in 1926, only to subside into an uneasy truce, with both sides agreeing to submit to arbitration. But war broke out in 1932, draining the resources of both Bolivia and Paraguay, both of whose economic ability to sustain a military conflict was pitifully small.

One contribution on the Bolivian side was a gift to the Bolivian Government of two Junkers-Ju 52/3ms by Señor Patino, the Bolivian tin millionaire. The Government then supplied the aircraft to LAB, in exchange for a capital shareholding, and with the understanding that the armed forces had first call on the LAB resources for logistic support as long as hostilities continued. Two more of the single-engined Junkers were also added, W 33s (differing only from the W 34s in the type of engine used) and then two more Ju 52/3ms, so that by 1936 the LAB fleet consisted of three F 13s, a Sikorsky S-38B, three Ju 52/3ms and four W 33/34s.

The Pacific-Atlantic Route

In the spring of 1937, the Bolivian airline took a notable step up the equipment ladder by acquiring the handsome Junkers-Ju 86, named *Illimani*, and which was among the most modern aircraft in service in the world at that time. It could certainly lay claim to being one of the fastest, cruising as it did at about 190 mph (310 km/h); but its operating economics could not have been too attractive, as it carried a maximum of only 10 passengers—the Ju 86 was primarily a military aircraft. LAB only ever owned one of this type, and that could not have been too efficient a fleet size either.*

Lloyd Aéreo Boliviano operated several Junkers-Ju 86s each powered by two Pratt & Whitney, or BMW-built, Hornet engines. One LAB Ju 86 was named *Illimani* but that is not the aircraft illustrated. In service with Lufthansa and South African Airways the Ju 86s had accommodation for ten passengers, but the LAB example here is clearly one of the bomber versions. Not only do the covers protect the engines and crew compartment windows, for the front cover is hiding the forward machine-gun installation. Between the flaps and the starboard wheel can be seen the under-fuselage 'dustbin' gun position. This photograph was taken at Cochabamba.

Nevertheless, the performance of this aircraft undoubtedly contributed to the success, short-lived though it was, of the trans-South American route operated as a partnership between three countries and three airlines whose common denominator was the ownership of Junkers airliners and—in the case of two of the partners—direct influence, amounting to partial control in one case and complete ownership in the other, by Deutsche Lufthansa, the national airline of Germany. At this period of history, DLH was fast becoming an economic agency of the Nazi commercial drive throughout the world, acting as a valuable propaganda medium, showing the flag much in the same way as 'sending a gunboat' used to do in more blatant colonial times.

Lloyd Aéreo Boliviano was legally independent of the German State airline, but, in many important respects, it might as well have been a subsidiary. It operated German aircraft almost exclusively; they were technically supported by ground staff trained by and assisted by German-trained technicians, either from

---

*LAB also operated three Ju 86K-7 military aircraft from mid-1938 until they were transferred to the Fuerza Aérea Boliviana in 1940.

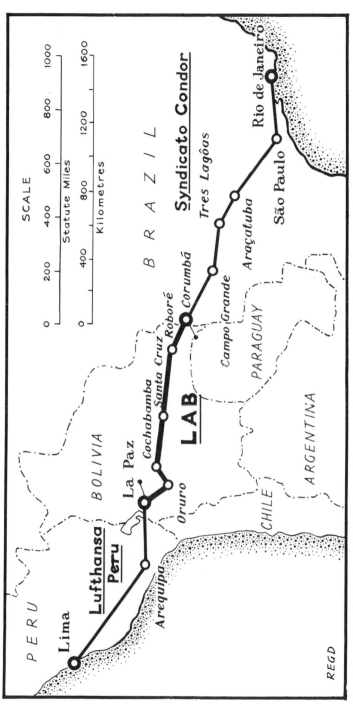

37. Coast-to-Coast by Junkers, 1938. An impressive transcontinental route across South America was fashioned before the Second World War, supported and equipped entirely from German sources. LAB of Bolivia was the middle section of a trio of airlines controlled by, or working in association with Lufthansa, and connecting with that airline's trans-Atlantic route from Europe at Rio de Janeiro.

Germany or from the German-owned Condor line of Brazil; and the main trunk route was integrated with those of the two German associates. Nevertheless, the subtleties of politics apart, the trans-South America coast-to-coast route was a considerable achievement in organization and operation, considering that the terrain in the Andean section was frightening, and that navigational aids, including the most elementary radio communications, were often entirely lacking over some critical sections of the route.

The journey from Rio de Janeiro—connecting with the mail service to Europe via Deutsche Lufthansa—to Lima took three days, divided neatly between the Brazilian Syndicato Condor (Rio–Corumbá), LAB (Corumbá–La Paz) and Lufthansa Peru (La Paz–Lima). LAB's contribution was the most arduous, flying above the awesome gorges and between the peaks of the Andes, with stops at Roboré, Santa Cruz, Cochabamba, and Oruro. The service was inaugurated on 24 May, 1938, and lasted for about three years, until PANAGRA took over the operation on 3 June, 1941, as a defensive measure by the United States, working in conjunction with South American governments, to put a stop to what it considered to be unjustified control by a foreign power of strategic air activity over the South American continent.

PANAGRA Takes Over

The United States became increasingly apprehensive about German incursions into South America during 1941, eyeing particularly the trans-South American all-Junkers, all DLH-influenced route. This gave Germany a second air transport connection to the South American west coast and the Pacific Ocean, and the strategic position of Lima, plus the ominous presence of another German airline in Ecuador (see page 323), made the USA nervous. The chosen instrument to 'snuff out any axis dream of acquiring commercial air supremacy in South America' (as a brochure described the objective) was mainly PANAGRA, with Panair do Brasil acting as an accessory. PANAGRA systematically replaced the German-controlled airlines in the Andean region, as a covert exercise in foreign intervention by the US State Department even though it was not yet committed as a belligerent in the war.

In May 1941, Lloyd Aéreo Boliviano was nationalized by the Bolivian Government, ostensibly on the grounds that the airline had not given consistently reliable service. During the liquidation proceedings, it was revealed that the Bolivian Government appeared to own 64 per cent of the stock, and the original shareholders only about 20 per cent, the remainder being represented by patriotic contributions made during the Chaco War. At all events, all the German employees were discharged, and PANAGRA took over on 3 June, 1941. Politics apart, the official report also stated that LAB's technical organization was good, making it possible to prolong the life of old aircraft. It also commented on the dearth of weather stations, which must have somewhat perturbed the PANAGRA staff.

The take-over having been ratified by Supreme Resolution of the Bolivian Government on 31 July, a loan was obtained from the United States on 2 August, and PANAGRA was given a five-year contract to provide management services. Part of the fees consisted of 23 per cent of the stock, and the US airline took over in its entirety the trunk service from Cochabamba to Puerto Suárez, with LAB continuing to provide the feeder services within Bolivia. Three 12-seat Lockheed Lodestars were acquired to replace the aging and spares-hungry Junkers, which

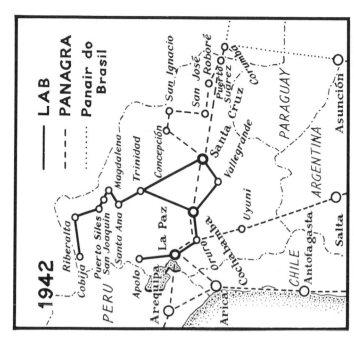

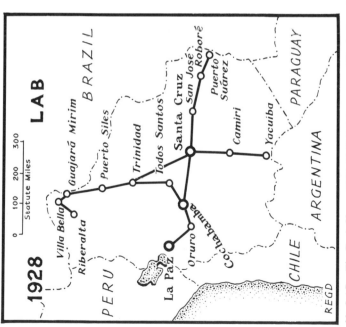

38. LAB—The Early Years, 1928–1942. LAB was one of Latin America's first permanent airlines, and remains today as one of the world's oldest still operating under its own name. During the war, and because of its German connections, LAB's network was restricted to feeder routes within Bolivia.

were either gradually retired or sold—one went to Aeroposta Argentina in 1943 and one to VASP in May 1944.

This arrangement worked well, and the Lodestars were supplemented by the Douglas DC-3, the first arriving in August 1945. Nineteen of the Douglas workhorses were acquired from various sources during the next twenty years, and these were to provide the backbone of the Bolivian airline fleet for several decades, while many other types passed across the Andean scene.

PANAGRA's contract expired on 2 August, 1946, but a second contract was negotiated on 26 November, with reduced participation. PANAGRA management was withdrawn, but technical support was retained. The distribution of stock at this time was PANAGRA 19·8 per cent, the Bolivian Government 55·4 per cent, with the rest held by private citizens.

Passengers boarding LAB's Lockheed Model 18 Lodestar CB-26 at Oruro between Sucre and La Paz. (*Pan American World Airways*)

A Slow Recovery

In 1948, the capital shareholding was increased to 50 million bolívars, and LAB painstakingly began to rebuild the airline. In 1950 it acquired the first of eleven Boeing B-17 Flying Fortress bombers, and converted them for commercial cargo operations. The four-engined Boeing bombers were considered to be suited to the arduous Bolivian conditions, but the record shows that five crashed or were written off within the next nine years; only three were left in the mid-1960s, and two remaining aircraft were sold in 1970, to end one of the historical oddities of airline fleet inventories. In 1949 the first of eight Curtiss C-46s, fitted with between 20 and 26 seats, arrived.

They were valued cargo-carrying aircraft, with double the capacity of the more reputable C-47/DC-3. Produced during the war and rushed into service without the normal meticulous testing and modification programmes which normally accompanied the introduction of US aircraft, the C-46 had put in a meritorious service record flying the 'Hump' between India and China to support the Chinese armies in the fighting against the Japanese; and the Bolivian Andes matched the formidable mountain crags of western China. But C-46 take-offs from Cochabamba and Oruro, not to mention the 4,000-metre altitude La Paz, were agonizingly long and with an imperceptible climb gradient, reminding witnesses of 'a fully-loaded freight train ascending a steep hill.' Only one C-46 was left by the mid-1960s, and curiously the B-17s outlived them all.

LAB operated several Boeing B-17 Flying Fortresses. CP-627, seen at Cochabamba, was the B-17G c/n 22166 (ex-44-6393) acquired with two others in 1956. (*Gordon S. Williams*)

With the limited aeroplanes at its disposal, and with corresponding weaknesses in its ability to service and maintain them (because of the dependence on PANAGRA during the war) LAB set about the task of rebuilding a national route network to serve the provincial area better, and to develop air connections with neighbouring countries.

On the east-west trunk route, an agreement was made with the Brazilian Government in 1951 to permit Cruzeiro do Sul (formerly the German Syndicato Condor, but now completely Brazilian) to extend its service westwards from Corumbá and to permit traffic rights (cabotage) within Bolivia. This complemented the PANAGRA service, and the three airlines co-operated for a few years before the US company withdrew its cabotage flights east of Santa Cruz on 19 November, 1959. Meanwhile, LAB introduced its own service, with DC-3s, from Cochabamba to Puerto Suárez in 1957, taking over Cruzeiro do Sul's cabotage service. The latter continued to serve Santa Cruz directly from Corumbá.

Having restored its domestic service to a respectable level, LAB began to build cautiously in the international field. On 20 March, 1954, the east-west route was extended to Arica, Chile, the Pacific port at which, under treaty since the Bolivia-Chile war of the late nineteenth century, Bolivia was exempt from customs obligations. Two Douglas DC-4s were added in April 1955, and, modest though these unpressurized aircraft were by comparison with the fleets of some

LAB's Douglas C-47A CP-591 at Cochabamba. The upper stripes (above the flight deck and on the fuselage sides) were blue and the lower stripes, company name and registration red. LAB was black and the bird crest (not seen here) on the fin and rudder was blue.
(*R. E. G. Davies*)

327

LAB's Fairchild F-27M CP-862 was delivered in August 1969.

neighbouring countries, LAB continued to expand. Two direct flights to Brazil were added, to Corumbá on 9 July, 1957, and to Pôrto Velho on 28 January, 1958; while Asunción, Paraguay, received DC-4 service between 1 April, 1958, and 1 July, 1959. The four-engined Douglas aircraft was used mainly for the busy route between La Paz and Cochabamba, and on to Santa Cruz, which was now beginning to expand as an important regional centre.

LAB spread its wings further by extending to Buenos Aires on 2 July, 1959, and, with the aid of four Douglas DC-6Bs acquired in 1960, to Lima in March 1961. Also, in May 1963 these new aircraft, the first pressurized type to fly the Bolivian flag, began to serve São Paulo, Brazil; but this was the limit of LAB's route expansion for many more years.

A Struggle for Survival

In spite of the apparent growth of the route network, LAB was sorely troubled during the 1960s. PANAGRA's contract terminated completely in 1963 and the Bolivian airline faced every kind of problem: a shortage of aircraft because of

LAB's Lockheed 188A Electra CP-853 at Cochabamba. Markings are blue and lettering red. This Electra had been American Airlines' N6134A *Flagship Memphis*, it was acquired by LAB in 1968 and in 1974 passed to Transporte Aéreo Militar. (*R. E. G. Davies*)

328

crashes and other accidents, the inability to service and properly maintain those aircraft which were still flying, and an acute shortage of funds to correct these shortcomings. In desperation, LAB had signed an agreement on 2 November, 1955, with Lloyd Aéreo Colombiano to provide service from Bogotá to Cochabamba, via Riberalta; but this lasted only from 19 April to 3 November, 1956, and had no significant effect on LAB's declining fortunes.

The British Handley Page Dart Herald was demonstrated to LAB in the summer of 1959; but the exercise was academic, for the airline had no funds, was living from day to day, receiving competition when it least needed it from other Bolivian non-scheduled airlines, and was still losing aircraft and suspending service at some points.

A silver lining in this almost overpowering cloud of misfortune appeared in October 1963, when the United States Local Service carrier, North Central Airlines, was awarded an $800,000 contract by the United States Agency for International Development (A.I.D.) to provide managerial and technical assistance for a period of two years. Then, in 1966, the Systems Analysis Research Corporation (SARC) a management and research consultancy firm of Washington, D. C., was called in to advise on the choice of new equipment.

Their recommendation was the 36-seat Fairchild F-27, the twin-engined Fokker propeller-turbine airliner being built under licence in the United States, and which won the selection by a narrow margin over the Herald and the Hawker Siddeley HS.748. LAB had kept going on its international services with a Lockheed 188 Electra placed in service on 19 September, 1968, and the addition of the F-27s on 9 October of the following year began to provide an air of respectability. As if living under some kind of curse, however, this period of transition to modern airliners was marred by the worst air accident in Bolivian history, when a DC-6B crashed on a flight between Santa Cruz and La Paz, killing all 74 of its occupants. The Andean ranges in Bolivia had taken a severe toll over the years of those who dared to challenge the hazards of terrain and climate, without proper navigational or ground aids. But mercifully, this sad story of tragedy and frustration was now to give way to a new era.

There has been only one scheduled airline in Bolivia. Indeed, the air passenger traffic potential from the limited Bolivian clientèle, that is to say the literate minority, numbering only a few hundred thousand people, has hardly justified more than one. Because of Bolivia's peculiar geography, however (matching Tibet's or Nepal's in its remoteness from the world's trade routes) there has always been a ready market for international air cargo; while the fearsome terrain within the country has always been a strong deterrent to surface travel.

Thus, numerous hardy non-scheduled companies have been established over the postwar years, mainly to carry cargo, mostly in C-46s, but offering limited passenger service when there was no reasonable alternative way to travel. During the latter 1960s, **Aerolíneas Abaroa (ALA)** and **Cía Boliviana de Aviación (BOA)** carried a few thousand such passengers, in addition to freight.

One company's aircraft were to been seen from time to time at Miami. **Transportes Aéreos Benianos, S.A. (TABSA)**, also known as **Bolivian Airways**, was founded by the owners of the Crillon Hotel of La Paz in July 1963. Its small fleet of C-46s flew directly from the ranching country around Trinidad to neighbouring countries, and to Miami, on authority from the US C.A.B. TABSA obtained Super Constellations for this long-haul route, started in April 1968, but disappeared from the record books in 1977. Some of its derelict C-46s joined the assembly of battered and toil-worn aircraft at the windswept La Paz airport, high

329

This Curtiss C-46A, CP-987, was registered to Transportes Aéreos Illimani Ltda but in this view, taken at Trinidad in Bolivia, the title reads Transaéreos Illimani. Markings were red. By 1978 this aircraft was operated by Transaéreos Frimo of La Paz.

Bolivian Transporte Aéreo Militar Douglas C-47 TAM-25 plays its part in the overall transport system. The location is not known but the photograph was taken in 1973. The Bolivian colours on the rudder (reading down) are red, yellow and green. (*DIA*)

on the *altiplano*, having paid their dues to the cause of air transport in a manner which would be scarcely credible outside Bolivia.

Jet Service

On 14 March, 1970, Lloyd Aéreo Boliviano put into service its first jet airliner, a Boeing 727-100, with 119 seats, on the Cochabamba–La Paz domestic trunk route. Subsequently, the Boeing took over all the international mainline services, from Arica to São Paulo and Buenos Aires, while the Electra maintained the Cochabamba connection, with the 727 flying directly from La Paz to Santa Cruz. The Electra gave way to the DC-6B in 1971.

Gradually, LAB began to settle down to a stable existence, with its more modern fleet enabling it to cope with day-to-day problems of scheduling and maintenance, as its staff acquired more skills and experience, and the single 727 managed to cope with all the demands made upon it. Encouraged by its achievement of stability, LAB announced the purchase of two more Boeing 727s on 18 September, 1975, and began service almost immediately, in October, on a route to the United States.

The problem of La Paz's 4,000-metre airfield altitude had always presented a severe challenge to any airline planner with thoughts of developing long-range services from Bolivia. Desirable though it was to fly directly from the country's largest city and commercial centre, the altitude was too restrictive on the payload-range characteristics of most aircraft. The necessary reduction of fuel load to permit safe take-off normally limited the practical range of flights from La Paz to the capitals of the nearest countries. LAB found the solution to its problems by centring its long-range operations on the city of Santa Cruz, comfortably situated at an altitude of some 1,400 ft, down on the plains, and incidentally close to the geographical centre of South America, if the desolate Mato Grosso region of Brazil is excluded from the reckoning.

The Boeing 727—not normally used for long-distance flights—stopped at Panamá en route to Miami, and was demonstrated to be perfectly adequate to perform the role. Showing commendable enterprise, LAB built upon this success. In April 1977 it ordered two Boeing 727-200s—the stretched version— fitted with the higher-thrust Pratt & Whitney JT8D-17R engines, permitting full operations at La Paz.

With the augmented fleet of five Boeing 727s, Lloyd Aéreo Boliviano expanded its links with the South American continent by opening a new service to Miami on 1 December, via Manaus, Brazil,—where it connected with Air France's intercontinental route from Paris—and Caracas. The following month, Cali, in

An early morning line-up of LAB Boeing 727-100s at Cochabamba. The first three aircraft (*left to right*), are CP-1070 previously with Braniff and Trans International, CP-1223 previously with Braniff and BWIA, and CP-861. (*Photo Iriarte, courtesy Barrie James*)

LAB's Boeing 707-323CF CP-1365 cargo aircraft was acquired in 1977. This aircraft was originally American Airlines' N7558A *Astrojet Detroit*. (*T. R. Waddington*)

331

Colombia, was added as an additional stopping point on the western routeing, via Panamá.

With a well-balanced fleet of efficient jets for its international services, complemented by the economical F-27s for its domestic services to smaller cities (even Trinidad, once little more than a cattle station in the early days of LAB, has enjoyed 727 service since 1975) LAB faces the future with great confidence. A far cry from the distant days of the little Junkers-F 13s during the 1920s, the airline has survived many crises with great determination, to become a worthy agency of the Bolivian national economic system, as that once impoverished country takes its place among the enlightened developing nations of today.

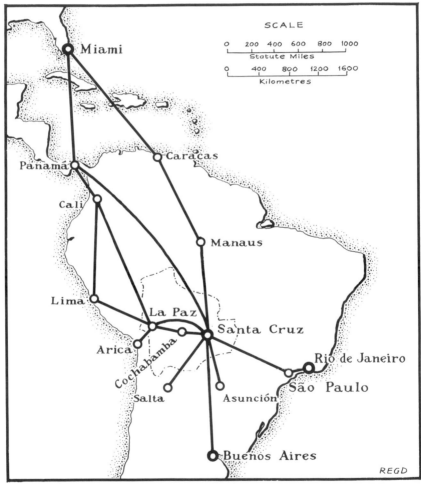

39. LAB International Routes, 1978. During recent years, LAB has made great strides. Taking advantage of the strategic position of Santa Cruz as a crossways of air routes, service was offered from the USA to both Brazil and Argentina. The 13,000 ft elevation of the airport at the capital, La Paz, made necessary the use of the provincial city, at a comfortable 1,000 ft elevation.

The Dornier Wal flying-boat P-BAAA *Atlântico* was an early example of the type. It was one of two purchased by the Condor Syndikat which made a Central America survey flight in 1925. It went back to Germany and became Luft Hansa's D-1012 and then went to Brazil where it received the first Brazilian registration. It was operated by Syndicato Condor, passed to VARIG as described in the text and was sometime reregistered PP-CAA. (*VARIG*)

CHAPTER SEVENTEEN

Foundation of Airlines in Brazil

Prelude

During the first half of the Twentieth Century, while Brazil was apparently dragging its economic and industrial footsteps, the cynics used to observe knowingly that 'Brazil is a country of the future—and always will be!' Even allowing for an element of the legendary Hearst newspaper instruction to the effect that the truth should always be sacrificed in the interests of a neat turn of phrase, progress in the largest country of South America was agonisingly slow.

Today the cynics would find it difficult to validate their statement. No longer does this vast country lack progressive exploration of undiscovered resources. The majority of its economically-productive population used to cling to a 50-mile-wide coastal strip. Its trade balance was dependent upon only one export—coffee. In dramatic contrast, the last quarter of the Twentieth Century sees Brazil as one of the world's leading commercial and industrial powers, still developing energetically. And if the historians analyse the economic stimulants which changed frustrating stagnation into dynamic growth, much of the credit will have to go to the airlines, which provided the vital nerve system to the body of the invigorated adolescent.

With its immense distances and inadequate means of communication between centres of population, Brazil was an obvious arena for the establishment of an airline network. The road system was of little relevance in linking major cities, while the railways were sadly fragmented and could serve only local purposes.

333

Although in 1926 there were almost 20,000 miles of railway line, half of this total was concentrated in the central states of Rio de Janeiro, São Paulo, and Minas Gerais. Furthermore, companies used different gauges. Other progressive states in the south were connected by a single line which, however, bypassed the state capitals; while the railways in the north, centred on such important cities as Recife, Salvador, Fortaleza, São Luis, and Belém, were not only isolated from the centre and the south, but also from each other. As for the vast Brazilian interior, where untold riches were suspected to be hidden, the iron road was only just beginning to extend its tentacles towards the states of Goiás, Mato Grosso, and Amazonas.

The scene was thus set for the foundation of a healthy airline industry, and it was a remarkable commentary on the lack of direction that existed in commercial life in Brazil at the beginning of the twentieth century that the start was delayed until 1927.

Exploratory Steps

There had been some early attempts to establish airlines. During 1919, several individuals or companies were granted permission to undertake, at their own expense, the formation and operation of air services between the principal cities of Brazil (see Table 16). Among these stillborn efforts, the name of Handley Page appears, indicating early British interest. This company planned to start services as early as July 1919, using two Norman Thompson N.T.2B flying-boats, an Avro 504K, and an S.E. 5 fighter aircraft. But nothing came of this venture, and all the machines were donated to the Brazilian armed service, the last in August 1920.

Not mentioned in the Table, because it did not receive a Government Certificate of Operation, the Società Italiana di Trasporti Aerei (or Sociedade Italo-Brasileira de Transportes Aéreos) was also active in 1919. The Italians arrived in Rio de Janeiro in November of that year, with a Macchi M.7, a Macchi M.9 (both flying-boats) and a Caproni bomber. The Macchi M.9 ended in tragedy when an English pilot from Handley Page, John Pinder, was drowned when making a forced alighting on a lagoon in South Catarina whilst attempting to fly from Rio to Buenos Aires. The Caproni and the M.7 were also donated to the military, on 21 February, 1920, and 2 November, 1920, respectively.

Apart from these brief ventures, the only air transport development in Brazil in the early 1920s was the extension of João Varzea's certificate until 1925. But none of the companies listed in Table 16 ever went into operation.

Previous legal authority granted by the Brazilian Government in the field of aeronautics had been confined to permission to fly balloons—to José Passos de Faria, in 1882; awarding credits to the national aviation hero, Alberto Santos Dumont; and to establishing airfields and aero clubs. Although not covered by any official recognition, there is also a record of a Commander Nelson Guillobel trying to create the Compagnie de Transports Aériens du Valé de l'Amazonas in 1912. Bearing in mind that flying aircraft of any kind in the Amazon basin was still hazardous some twenty or more years later, the Commander's efforts with the equipment of the day must have been ambitious, not to say courageous, in the extreme.

TABLE 16
Brazilian Government
Certificates of Airline Operation
1918–1919 (Prior to enactment of Civil Air Transport Regulations)

Date	Decree	Company or Individual(s)	Routes or Areas specified	Remarks
23 Oct, 1918	D.13,244	João Teixeira Soares and Antonio Rossi	Between principal cities of Brazil	Did not operate
12 March, 1919	D.13,504	João Baptista dos Santos and Augusto de Araújo Góes	Between principal cities of Brazil	Did not operate
26 April, 1919	D.13,566	Davidson, Pullen & Company	Between different points in Brazil and to foreign points	Re-confirmed by D.14,087, 29 July, 1920. Did not operate
26 April, 1919	D.13,567	João Varzea	Between principal cities of Brazil and to foreign points	Re-confirmed by D 14,087, 29 July, 1920. Renewed for two years by D.16,046, 22 May, 1923. Renewed for one year D.15,084, 1 Nov, 1924. Did not operate
26 April, 1919	D.13,568	Francisco do Rego Barros Barreto Filho	Between principal cities of Brazil	Amended by D.13,702, 21 July, 1919; and by 13,749, 3 Sept, 1919. Did not operate
26 April, 1919	D.13,569	Handley Page Ltda	Between principal cities of Brazil	Authority to foreign points added by D.13,630, 28 May, 1919. Reconfirmed by D.14,087, 29 July, 1920. Did not operate

Source: Coletânea de Legislação Aeronáutica, 1955

The Latécoère Mission

The British Handley Page company never followed up its early interest in Brazil. Nevertheless, the first positive steps which were eventually to lead to success were initiated in Europe. The French **Compagnie Générale d'Entreprises Aéronautiques (C.G.E.A.)**, the airline associate of the Latécoère aircraft manufacturing company of Toulouse, was planning to extend its West African services across the South Atlantic.

In November 1924, a Latécoère mission arrived in Rio de Janeiro for the express purpose of surveying and planning a French air service in South America. The mission comprised two Latécoère directors, a team of pilots and mechanics, and three Breguet 14 biplanes, representing by the standards of that time the deployment of considerable resources.

On 14 January, 1925, an experimental flight, carrying mail and newspapers, and led by Paul Vachet, the chief pilot, was successfully accomplished. Three Breguets set off southwards from Rio de Janeiro, and the two which completed the journey arrived at Buenos Aires after 36 hr elapsed time, including six stops. On 5 February, the two surviving Breguets made a similar flight northward from Rio de Janeiro to Recife, again under Vachet's command, with three stops. To round off the survey, on 6 March, 1925, Vachet, supported by the pilots Roig and Hamm, and accompanied by Prince Murat, a Latécoère director, set off on a successful round trip all the way from Buenos Aires to Recife, stopping where necessary on the beach by moonlight.

Two Latécoère Breguet 14s on the beach at Santos on 23 January, 1925, during the course of experimental flights by the Latécoère Mission. The aircraft on the right is the Breguet 14 Torpédo F-AECT which bore the Latécoère number 149. The text on its fin reads 'Lineas Aéreas Latécoère. Linha Pernambuco–Rio de Janeiro–Montevideo–Buenos Ayres.'

The Latécoère Mission had difficulty in obtaining operating permission from the Brazilian Government, and in persuading the authorities to grant a subsidy for performing the valuable service to the nation of carrying air mail between all the main cities; but the official procrastination may have been simply because there were as yet no properly defined operating rules for airlines, as Brazil did not yet have any.

In any event, this shortcoming was quickly corrected, under the provisions of Law No.4,911, enacted on 12 January, 1925. Presidential Decree No.16,983, promulgated on 22 July of that year, created Brazil's first Civil Air Navigation Regulations, to be administered by the Ministry of Transport and Public Works. Chapters of the Regulations covered air space, civil aircraft, crews, ground installations, air traffic, air transport, and other aspects. While inevitably to be amended and improved later, it was admirably comprehensive for its time.

The Latécoère Breguet 14 F-AGBX at Rio de Janeiro on 11 March, 1925, after making the first flight from Rio de Janeiro to Pernambuco and back. The crew comprised Joseph Roig (Director), Paul Vachet (pilot) and mechanic Estival. To the left of Vachet is the Portuguese Admiral, who, as Captain Gago Coutinho, made with Commander Sacadura Cabral, the first flight across the South Atlantic, in 1922.

Latécoère was the first beneficiary under the new regulations. It had set up a Brazilian associate, **Companhia Brasileira de Empreendimentos Aeronáuticos**, to take care of its Brazilian activities and to comply with Brazilian law. Accordingly, the legal way was now clear, and on 1 October, 1925, Decree No.17,055 granted a concession to the Latécoère associate, led by Prince Murat and M. Portait, to operate a route between Recife and Pelotas, with intermediate stops at Maceió, São Salvador, Caravelas, Vitória, Rio de Janeiro, Santos, Paranaguá, Florian-

Believed to have been taken during the Latécoère mission in 1925 this picture shows (*left to right*) the pilots Etienne Lafay, Paul Vachet and Victor Hamm by the tail of the Breguet 14 F-ALXE. This aircraft bore the Latécoère fleet number 118.

ópolis, and Porto Alegre, with the rights to extend later to Natal, Fernando de Noronha, and the Roche dos São Pedro e São Paulo (St Peter and St Paul Rocks) in the South Atlantic. Frequency was to be a minimum of one round trip a week, for the carriage of passengers, mail, and cargo.

Unfortunately for Latécoère, this generous authorization was not approved by the Law Courts (Tribunal de Contas) and negotiations had to be resumed with the Brazilian Government, causing a delay. Meanwhile in Germany, a new development in air transport was taking place. Although at first unrelated to Brazil, it was to have far-reaching consequences on the subsequent expansion of airlines in that country.

The Condor Syndikat

On 5 May, 1924, the **Condor Syndikat** was formed in Berlin for the exclusive purpose of promoting the sale of German commercial aircraft overseas. It was sponsored by Deutscher Aero Lloyd, A. G., one of the leading German airlines and an ancestor of Deutsche Luft Hansa (DLH), together with Schlubach Theimer, a Hamburg trading company, and Peter Paul von Bauer, an Austrian emigrant to Colombia who had been persuaded to join the Sociedad Colombo-Alemana de Transportes Aéreos (SCADTA) of Barranquilla, Colombia, to promote commercial aviation. Von Bauer held 10 per cent of Condor's capital (equivalent to $200,000) to protect SCADTA's interests. The driving force behind the company's marketing thrust was its Director-General, Fritz Hammer.

Condor's initial ambitions were twofold: to support and assist von Bauer in developing an air network throughout the Caribbean as far north as the USA and to support Aero Lloyd's ambitions to cross the South Atlantic. The Syndikat bought two Dornier Wal flying-boats, the *Atlántico* and the *Pacífico*, names which epitomized the vision and confidence which characterized German commercial airline enterprise at the time. This was despite the handicap of provisions of the Treaty of Versailles, which restricted the power of any German aircraft to a single

Furthering its aim of operating air services linking Germany with South America, Luft Hansa made numerous survey flights during the period 1928–31. In this picture fuel is being unloaded to be rowed out to the Dornier Wal D-1647 *Bremerhaven* in Gando Bay, Gran Canaria, Canary Islands. (*Lufthansa*)

338

engine, and that, moreover, limited in output. Although the sturdy little Junkers-F 13 scraped through under the regulations, the Dornier Wals, and other larger aircraft, had to be built in other countries to evade the provisions of the Treaty. *Atlántico* and *Pacífico* were built at Pisa in Italy.

In pursuance of von Bauer's plans to survey the route from Barranquilla to Miami, the two flying-boats were shipped to the River Magdalena base of SCADTA in Barranquilla and set off on their flight to Miami on 10 August, 1925, to arrive, by way of the countries of Central America, in Havana on 19 September. Political difficulties then obliged von Bauer to abandon his plans and *Atlántico* was shipped back to Germany.

Meanwhile, an important development was under way in Brazil, inspired by a Brazilian of German ancestry, Otto Ernst Meyer. Meyer worked for a Recife textile company with subsidiaries and associates in other parts of the country, and he was greatly inconvenienced by the extensive travel necessitated by the unco-ordinated and incomplete railway system. At that time, it was quicker (and safer and far more comfortable) to travel from Recife to Rio de Janeiro by ship than by land. Meyer clearly recognized the need for an airline system, and backed his resolve by moving to Porto Alegre, partly because, in the state of Rio Grande do Sul, there was a large German emigrant population from whom he hoped to obtain practical support.

Though he was not to know it at the time, Meyer's choice of name for his yet unborn airline was eventually to become well-known in airline circles throughout the world. Even before its official recognition, however, **S.A. Empresa de Viação Aérea Rio Grandense (VARIG)** was familiar to businessmen in Porto Alegre, as Meyer assiduously sought their support. He first went to the local Chamber of Commerce, whose President, Major Alberto Bins, then assisted him to obtain an audience with the State President, Dr Antonio Borges de Medeiros, who thereupon urged the State Assembly to support the fledgling airline by a tax levy.

To obtain flying equipment and experienced staff, especially flying crew, for his airline, Meyer naturally went to the German commercial aircraft industry which was then producing the world's most advanced load-carrying aeroplanes. Meyer's visit to the Condor Syndikat in Hamburg, in November 1926, was to culminate in an agreement to allocate 21 per cent of VARIG's shares to Condor in exchange for the *Atlántico,* now returned to Hamburg, plus the necessary technical support.

The precise relationship between Meyer and VARIG on the one hand and the Condor Syndikat on the other, was somewhat obscure. While Meyer undoubtedly played an important part in the introduction of Condor into Brazil, subsequent developments strongly suggest that the German company's ambitions went much further than, and were independent of, Meyer's. For one reason, Meyer's financial resources were limited, and he depended upon local support—fifteen years were to pass before VARIG's route network expanded beyond the confines of its parent State; Condor, on the other hand, recognized the entrée into Brazil as a golden opportunity and seized the chance with calculated efficiency, thereby providing new impetus to the commercial air transport industry in Brazil.

The Linha da Lagôa

On 19 November, 1926, the first commercial aircraft which was to fly a revenue-earning service in Brazil arrived at Rio Grande, having left Buenos Aires two days earlier. It had been shipped, at the newly-formed Deutsche Luft Hansa's expense, from Hamburg to Montevideo, and flown to Buenos Aires. The aircraft was the route-seasoned Dornier Wal *Atlántico*, and the crew consisted of Fritz Hammer, Max Sauer, and Herman Teegen. With a sense of occasion, the Dornier carried as a passenger the former Chancellor of Germany, Dr Hans Luther, who had resigned from office in May that year.

The Dornier flying-boat had already attracted much favourable publicity when it was chosen by Major Franco, of the Spanish Army, to make an historic flight across the South Atlantic earlier that year, between 22 January and 9 February. Now the 'Luther Flight' added a political rubber stamp to Fritz Hammer's ambitions, for to carry a leading personality such as Luther was to give credence to the claims for safety and reliability of transport aircraft.

The next day, further detailed regulations were issued by the Ministry of Transport and Public Works, covering professional examinations, under different classifications of crew members. Brazilian official recognition of civil aviation was getting into its stride.

On 27 November, 1926, the *Atlántico**, still under German registration as D-1012, arrived at the Ilha das Enxadas, in Guanabara Bay, to demonstrate its capability in Brazil's capital city, having already received a warm welcome from the German emigrants in Florianópolis, São Francisco, and Santos en route. The scene was set for an eventful year to come.

On New Year's Day 1927, the *Atlântico* made a demonstration flight from Rio de Janeiro to Florianópolis, via Santos. The pilot was Capt Rudolf Cramer von Clausbruch, newly arrived from Germany, who had flown in the Baltic region for Deutscher Aero Lloyd and for Deutsche Luft Hansa, the new German national airline founded as an amalgamation of the many smaller companies. Other crew members were Franz Nuelle and Herr Wirz, but more important to Condor on that occasion were the illustrious passengers: Dr Victor Konder, the Brazilian Minister of Transport; Raul Portugal and Machado Florence, journalists; Alberto Botelho, of Botelho Films; accompanied by Fritz Hammer, taking the opportunity of explaining the Dornier Wal's features, including its eight-seat capacity, and its twin engines. (All Latécoère aircraft were single-engined.)

Victor Konder must have been suitably impressed, for on 26 January the Condor Syndikat received authority from the Ministry, under Notice No.60/G, to operate air services for a period not to exceed one year. The Syndikat was represented in Brazil through the agency of the firm Herm Stoltz and Company, of Rio de Janeiro. The routes designated were from Rio de Janeiro to Rio Grande, via Santos, Paranaguá, São Francisco do Sul, and Florianópolis; Rio Grande to Porto Alegre, via Pelotas; and Rio Grande to Santa Vitória do Palmar.

Three days later, the *Atlântico* was transferred to Porto Alegre, in preparation for one of the major events in the history of South American air transport. One of the passengers on the positioning flight was Otto Ernst Meyer, founder of VARIG.

On 3 February, 1927, the 'Linha da Lagôa' was inaugurated in the Lagôa dos Patos, the lagoon which stretched halfway along the coast of the State of Rio Grande do Sul. The passengers were Guilherme Gastal, João Oliveira Goulart, and Srta Maria Echenique, who was the official courier of greetings from the Mayor of Porto Alegre to the Mayor of Rio Grande.

Although this flight is commemorated as the beginning of commercial aviation in Brazil, it was not the first regular service. The *Atlântico* had to stay in Rio Grande for refurbishing, and scheduled services actually started on 22 February.

* To be accurate *Atlántico* (Spanish) became *Atlântico* (Portuguese) when it went to Brazil.

Incidentally, on 9 March, 1927, the French **Cie Générale d'Entreprises Aéronautiques, Lignes Latécoère**, finally received its official permission to operate, under Notice No.197/G of the Ministry of Transport and Public Works. But its service inauguration, under another name, was still eight months away, and the Brazilian-German activities in the South were stealing all the headlines.

On 28 March, 1927, Condor flew the first postal service of the Linha da Lagôa, once again with von Clausbruch and Nuelle at the helm, and by 17 May the 50th flight had been entered in the log-book.

Shortly afterwards, another important step forward was made, when the Condor Syndikat augmented its fleet by the addition of a three-engined Junkers-G 24, the *Ypiranga*, which made a commercial flight (though not yet the start of regular service) from Porto Alegre to Rio de Janeiro on 3 June, 1927. The crew was Capt Heinz Puetz and Otto Schollkopf. *Ypiranga* made the return flight on 9 June, 1927.

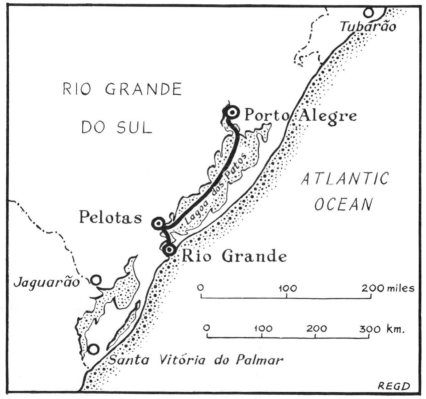

40. The Linha da Lagôa, 1927. On this route, the German Condor Syndikat began the first regular Brazilian air service, using the Dornier Wal *Atlântico*, which had also participated in the SCADTA survey flight from Colombia to Florida in 1925. The line was later taken over by VARIG, and a Brazilian company, Syndicato Condor, was formed as a subsidiary of the German enterprise.

Significantly, the line was already becoming known as the Syndicato Condor, and indeed the tenure of the company under the German name was approaching its end. On 15 June, the Linha da Lagôa and the *Atlântico* were officially transferred to VARIG, while Rudolf von Clausbruch and Franz Nuelle were temporarily seconded as technical advisers. Condor took a substantial shareholding, with Fritz Hammer and Max Sauer among VARIG's first directors. Between 22 February and 15 June, the Condor Syndikat had completed 63 flights and had carried 800 passengers on the Linha da Lagôa, so the demonstration could fairly be judged a success.

The Condor Syndikat officially ceased operations on 1 July, 1927, and later went into liquidation, but **Syndicato Condor**, the new Brazilian company which was to succeed it, was allowed to begin flying a fixed timetable on the Rio de Janeiro–Porto Alegre route on 9 November. The round trip was completed in four days, allowing for an extension from Porto Alegre to Rio Grande. By the end of the year, 22 flights had been completed, carrying 160 passengers, on this new route.

With the addition of two more Dornier Wals, *Santos Dumont* and *Bartholomeu de Gusmão,* the Condor Syndikat retained a slender foothold in Brazilian air transport by making efforts to expand northwards from Rio de Janeiro. Notice No.620/G, of 20 August, 1927, gave the necessary permission, and two round trips were completed experimentally to Recife before the end of the year, carrying 13 passengers in the process.

Incorporation of VARIG

Otto Ernst Meyer, having already made initial progress by giving his proposed airline a name, called the first general meeting of Empresa de Viação Aérea Rio-Grandense (VARIG) on 1 April, 1927, composed mostly of citizens of Porto Alegre or other cities of the State of Rio Grande do Sul. Shortly afterwards, on 7 May, VARIG was officially registered under the laws of the State as a private company, with a capital of 1,000,000 reis, in 200-reis shares. Share certificates and

Syndicato Condor's Junkers-G 24 PP-CAB *Ypiranga* at Floriano, Piauí, in 1937. This aircraft had previously been registered P-BABA and D-1287 and was one of the aircraft used on the Buenos Aires–Montevideo services by the Junkers Mission.
(*Courtesy Martin Bernsmüller*)

342

Otto Ernst Meyer (*right*) was the first President of a small airline Viação Aéreo Rio Grandense (VARIG), which he founded in the southernmost State of Brazil in 1927. His colleague, Rubem Berta (*left*) became the second President in 1941 and made it the largest airline in Latin America (measured by passenger-km flown) and one of the world's great airlines. Berta died in 1966, to be succeeded by Eric de Carvalho. (*VARIG*)

additional funds, mainly from the Condor Syndikat, brought the total to 2,297,000 reis, of which Condor's share was estimated to be 21 per cent.

On 10 June, Presidential Decree No.17,832 authorized VARIG's operations along the coast of Santa Catarina, throughout the whole of Rio Grande do Sul, and subject to permission from the Government of Uruguay, to Montevideo. This was the first authorization to a Brazilian airline, although earlier official sanction had been granted to companies or persons, which had come to nothing; and of course it had been preceded by the Condor Syndikat and an associate of Latécoère, both foreign and the latter not yet operational. Condor terminated regular service three weeks after VARIG's certificate was issued, so that for about six months the Porto Alegre airline was the only one in Brazil.

As already mentioned, the *Atlântico* was transferred from Condor, in exchange for 1,050 shares, or 435 milreis (about $50,000) on 15 June, 1927, and re-registered under the new Brazilian aircraft registration system, the very first, as P-BAAA. The Linha da Lagôa was transferred to VARIG. A month later the technical contract with Condor expired, although von Clausbruch and Nuelle were still retained as advisors. As a matter of interest, the staff of VARIG included by this time a young man named Rubem Berta.

VARIG's first flight, beginning its regular schedule to replace the Condor service, took place on 22 June, 1927, from Porto Alegre to Rio Grande, via Pelotas. The *Atlântico* took two hours for the first segment, and twenty minutes for the second, cruising over the Lagôa dos Patos at an altitude of between 20 and 50 metres. The fare from Porto Alegre to Rio Grande was 220 reis one way, or 360

Syndicato Condor's Dornier Merkur P-BAAB *Gaucho* was originally D-936 acquired by VARIG. It was later registered PP-CAC. (*VARIG, courtesy Mário B. de M. Vinagre*)

round trip. Except for an isolated flight to Tapes, on the shore of the lagoon a little south of Porto Alegre, this was the only route flown regularly by VARIG during the first year of its existence.

In these infant days of VARIG, Meyer had his problems, and a great deal of the responsibility must have rested on the pilots, for the aircraft were not very reliable. On 13 July, *Atlântico* was taken out of service for repairs to the wing skin and during this period the Junkers-G 24 *Ypiranga* (P-BABA) was leased from Condor until 24 September. In October, VARIG received its second aircraft, a Dornier Merkur, named *Gaucho*, and registered as P-BAAB. This 6-passenger seaplane was purchased directly from Dornier, and entered service on the Linha da Lagôa on 24 November, just six days after the *Atlântico* had again been taken out of service for a complete overhaul. Then *Gaucho* had to be retired, on 1 December, 1927, for structural reasons, at the insistence of the insurers. Brazil's first airline was certainly not short of problems during its baptismal year.

The Aéropostale Mail Service

The Compagnie Générale d'Entreprises Aéronautiques (C.G.E.A.)—Lignes Latécoère—finally got under way in Brazil on 14 November, 1927, to forge one more link in the chain of mail routes which the French company wished to construct from Europe to South America.

Frustrated by constant procrastination and even obstruction by various South American authorities, Latécoère had met, on 3 December, 1926, a French industrialist, resident in Brazil, who had built up a business empire which included port installations, railways, docks, mines, banks, property, and even small towns. His name was Marcel Bouilloux-Lafont, and he became attracted by the potential of an air transport system which could serve his business interests. More than that: he was an intense patriot, and realised that he could use his influence to counter the spread of German interests in Brazil.

On 9 March, 1927, the Brazilian Government, under the terms of Aviso No.197, finally granted special authority to C.G.E.A. to operate the same route as outlined in Decree 17,055 of 1 October, 1925, minus the extensions. On 11 April, Bouilloux-Lafont purchased C.G.E.A. for 30 million francs. He took complete control, and Latécoère effectively retired from active participation. With characteristic energy and drive, Bouilloux-Lafont set in motion an extensive development programme, with a budget of $1·5 million (US), extending to several countries in South America.

When, therefore, C.G.E.A. started regular services between Natal and Buenos Aires on 14 November, 1927, the line was under completely new management. On 30 April the name had been changed to **Compagnie Générale Aéropostale (C.G.A.)**. Decree No.18,009 of 6 December confirmed the action of Aviso 197, and the change of name was officially recognized by Decree No.18,113 of 14 February, 1928.

C.G.A., or Aéropostale as it quickly became known locally, made a promising start. Operating once a week, a regular link was established from Natal, on the northeastern tip of Brazil, all the way to Buenos Aires. Flights originated from the base at Rio de Janeiro, flying northward and southward. During the first six weeks of operation, the average flight time for the northbound journey, Buenos Aires–Natal, was 29 hr 22 min; and for the southbound 26 hr 20 min. This was a praiseworthy effort, and the pilots Vachet, Roig, Hamm, and their colleagues, achieved such timing by having a generous supply of aircraft.

The contrast between the German and French policies was interesting. Whereas Condor put its faith in multi-engined flying-boats, with a passenger capacity of seven or eight, the Aéropostale aircraft were all single-engined landplanes: two Breguet 14s, for mail only, two Latécoère 17s and nine Latécoère 25s, the Latécoères having four seats. What the French lacked in capacity they made up in numbers, and of course their goal was less stringent, in that they did not attempt to carry passengers on a regular basis or as priority load.

On 13 December, 1927—a month after Aéropostale had launched its service—the Brazilian *Diario Oficial* announced the establishment of the Companhia Aeronáutica Brasileira to provide ground installations and services, and to construct landing fields at points served by Aéropostale. At Rio de Janeiro, facilities were made available by the War Ministry for the use of the airfield at Campo dos Afonsos, and the Military Aviation School. At this juncture, therefore, the development of an infrastructure to serve the needs of commercial aviation in Brazil appears to have been undertaken more in co-operation with,

Compagnie Générale Aéropostale's Latécoère 25 R2 c/n 650 photographed at Cricklewood, North London, where it was fitted with Handley Page slots—seen here in the open position. The metal propeller was another modification. (*Flight International*)

345

41. Brazilian Air Routes, 31 December, 1927. By the end of 1927 air transport was getting under way in Brazil. The Latécoère mail line—soon to be renamed officially as Aéropostale—operated along most of the Brazilian coast; while German-sponsored lines carried both passengers and mail in the south.

and for the support of, Aéropostale, rather than Condor.

After six weeks of operation, that is, by the end of 1927, Aéropostale had completed 25 one-way flights between Buenos Aires and Natal, flying 69,415 kilometres, and carrying 156,421 kg of mail, plus four passengers. Such a demonstration of regularity and reliability was a prelude to even greater achievement. Bouilloux-Lafont was about to inaugurate the fast mail service between France and South America and on 7 March, 1928, the Ministry of Transport and Public Works reconfirmed the details of the Aéropostale concession, renewing it at annual intervals thereafter.

346

Formation of Syndicato Condor

The Condor Syndikat had officially ceased operations on 1 July, 1927; but its survey flights continued, with quasi-scheduled service between Rio de Janeiro and the south, and occasional sorties to Recife. Presumably, during this period, there was considerable negotiation between the German executives of Condor and the Brazilian authorities, who were anxious to bring Brazil and its aviation fraternity as quickly as possible to the forefront of commercial airline operation.

Thus, on 1 December, 1927, the Syndicato Condor was registered as a Brazilian airline, although the name had already been in use for about six months. The directors were almost the same as those of its German predecessor: Fritz Hammer, as Director-General; Max Sauer, Technical Director; and Hans Wilkens, Commercial Director. The capital was subscribed by Hammer (7 contos de reis); Herm Stoltz (5); Sauer (4) and Conde Pereira Carneiro, a Brazilian (4).

On 20 January, 1928, Decree No. 18,075 granted Syndicato Condor the rights to establish air routes throughout the country. At first, the Rio de Janeiro–Porto Alegre route was maintained twice weekly, using the three-engined Junkers-G 24, but an accident to the second Dornier Wal, *Santos Dumont*, at Guanabara Bay, on 3 December, delayed development in 1929.

However, on 15 July of that year, a new route was opened: Salvador–Ilhéus–Belmonte, at a weekly frequency, using the sturdy Junkers-F 13 seaplane *Pirajá* (P-BAKA), flown by Capt Fred Hoepken and Xaver Greiss. The same crew inaugurated service to Valença and Santarém, two small towns between Salvador and Ilhéus, on 2 September. Syndicato Condor was beginning what was to become a familiar pattern: establishing bases and route segments at the further extremity of a trunk route, and then filling the gap subsequently.

As in many parts of Latin America, so in Brazil did the pioneer all-metal Junkers-F 13 play a major role in establishing air transport. The example seen 'up-country' was built in 1920. After service in Germany as D-347 it went to Syndicato Condor in January 1929 as P-BAJA *Iguassú*, having been fitted with the 1926-type balanced tail surfaces. Later this F 13 was registered PP-CAJ. Its original BMW IV engine was replaced by a Junkers-L 5. (*Lufthansa*)

TABLE 17

Brazilian Government Certificates of Airline Operations 1925–1928

(After Civil Air Transport Regulations enacted)

Date	Decree (D) or Notice (N)	Company	Routes or Areas specified	Remarks
1 Oct, 1925	D.17,055	Cia Brasileira de Empreendimentos Aeronáuticos	Recife to Pelotas, via Maceió, Salvador, Caravelas, Vitória, Rio de Janeiro, Santos, Paranaguá, Florianópolis, and Porto Alegre, with subsequent possible extension to Natal, Fernando de Noronha, and the St Paul Rocks	Company was the Brazilian associate of Cie Générale d'Entreprises Aéronautiques, Lignes Latécoère, of Paris (see N.197/G below). Did not operate.
26 Jan, 1927	N.60/G	Condor Syndikat	1. Rio de Janeiro to Rio Grande, via Santos, Paranaguá, São Francisco, Florianópolis. 2. Rio Grande to Porto Alegre, via Pelotas. 3. Rio Grande–Santa Vitória do Palmar, with possible subsequent extension to Montevideo, Uruguay	Condor Syndikat, of Berlin, represented in Brazil by Herm, Stoltz & Company

Date	Decree	Company	Route	Remarks
9 March, 1927	N.197/G	Cie Générale d'Entreprises Aéronautiques, Lignes Latécoère	Fernando de Noronha to Sta Vitória do Palmar, via Maceió, Salvador, Caravelas, Vitória, Rio de Janeiro, Santos, Paranaguá, Florianópolis, Porto Alegre, and Pelotas	French company, of Paris. Confirmed by D.18,009, 6 Dec, 1927. Change of name to Cie Générale Aéropostale recognized by D.18,113, 14 Feb, 1928
10 June, 1927	D.17,832	S.A. Empresa de Viação Aérea Rio Grandense	Coast of Santa Catarina, State of Rio Grande do Sul, with possible extension to Montevideo, Uruguay	Brazilian company, of Porto Alegre
20 Jan, 1928	D.18,075	Syndicato Condor, Ltda	Throughout Brazil, with possible extension to Uruguay and Argentina	Brazilian company, of Rio de Janeiro. Certificate amended by D.19,331, 29 August, 1930, to cover foreign countries in general
13 March, 1928	D.18,156	The Aircraft Operating Company	(Not specified) Specialized in aerial photography	British company, of London. Did not operate

Source: Coletânea de Legislação Aeronáutica, 1955

TABLE 18
The Brazilian Commercial Aircraft Register
31 December, 1927

Registration	Manufacturer	Type	Seaplane or landplane	Serial number	Airline
P-BAAA	Dornier	Do J Wal	sea	34	VARIG
P-BAAB	Dornier	Merkur	,,	92	,,
P-BABA	Junkers	G 24	sea	944	Condor Syndikat
P-BACA	Dornier	Do J Wal	,,	83	,, ,,
F-ALXE	Breguet-Latécoère	14 Limousine	land	118	C.G.E.A.— Lignes Latécoère
F-AGBX	,, ,,	14A.2	,,	307	,, ,,
F-AIGJ	Latécoère	17.4.R	,,	618	,, ,,
F-AIGK	,,	,,	,,	620	,, ,,
F-AIEK	,,	25.2.R	,,	610	,, ,,
F-AIFU	,,	,,	,,	615	,, ,,
F-AIFV	,,	,,	,,	616	,, ,,
F-AIFX	,,	,,	,,	619	,, ,,
F-AIJZ	,,	,,	,,	631	,, ,,
F-AIKG	,,	,,	,,	633	,, ,,
F-AIKH	,,	,,	,,	634	,, ,,
F-AIKO	,,	25.3.R	,,	635	,, ,,
F-AIKP	,,	25.2.R	,,	636	,, ,,

Source: Relatório da Viação, 1927 and European Transport Aircraft (Stroud).

This occurred on 5 February, 1930, when the complete coastal route from Rio de Janeiro to Natal was inaugurated, once a week, via Vitória, Caravelas, Belmonte, Ilhéus, Salvador, Marció, Recife, and Cabedelo. On the first half of the inaugural flight, as far as Salvador, Capt von Clausbruch (now returned from VARIG) flew the Dornier Wal *Olinda* (P-BALA), while the segment north of Salvador was taken over by Capt Hoepken, flying the Junkers-F 13 *Pirajá*.

The Condor achievement in matching Aéropostale's route along the entire coast of Brazil from Natal to Rio Grande was a vital link in the composition of long-distance routes being orchestrated by Deutsche Luft Hansa. With the ready co-operation of other German transport organizations, both shipping and aviation, DLH aimed to help the German aviation industry achieve its logical reward for producing the most efficient transport aeroplanes of the day. The significance of Condor's role was dramatically demonstrated less than two months after regular scheduled services had opened to Natal, and is recorded in the next chapter.

In September 1930, Fritz Hammer, Condor's founder, departed. His place as Director-General was taken by Paul Moosmeyer, under whose stewardship, Syndicato Condor—known familiarly simply as Condor—was to lead Brazil to the forefront of commercial aviation in South America.

CHAPTER EIGHTEEN

Brazilian Partnerships Overseas

Legal Refinements

In today's world of airlines, international control and regulation by some supranational authority such as the International Civil Aviation Organization (ICAO), or by some kind of co-operative union such as the International Air Transport Association (IATA) are taken for granted. In the late 1920s they either did not exist or were confined to Europe. Such problems as the Five Freedoms of the Air had not yet been thought about, much less given careful consideration with an attempt at definition.

Three of the outstanding pioneers of French air services to South America. *Left to right*: Jean Mermoz, Jean Dabry and Léonard Gimié. They were respectively pilot, navigator and radio operator on the 12–13 May, 1930, ocean crossing by the *Comte de la Vaulx*. Mermoz was lost on 7 December, 1936, in the Latécoère 300 *Croix du Sud* while making his 24th South Atlantic crossing.

351

Thus, in its formative years, Brazilian commercial aviation was in a unique situation. The country was one of the world's largest, but did not have an international airline, or even a nationwide national airline. Yet not only did foreign airlines regard Brazil as a major destination in its own right; but it also lay directly athwart the main routes from both the United States and Europe to Argentina, then the most prosperous and commercially influential country in the whole of Latin America. The capital, Buenos Aires, the 'Paris of South America', was the magnet for shipping and air transport interests alike, and Brazil was en route or in the way, depending on individual relations with that country.

The unique nature of Brazil's position should be stressed. Other large countries, or empires, had their own developing airlines. The USA, USSR, and Australia, had self-contained embryo air networks. Although meandering halfway round the globe, the British, French, Dutch, and other colonial powers faced few problems of politics, navigation, or traffic rights from smaller or weaker powers. But Brazil was different. Some 3,500 miles (5,000 km) of coastline alone was a slice of territory too large to be glossed over in a few words or by a handshake. Thus, during the period of the late 1920s and the early 1930s, Brazilian legal authorities sought to work out a formula by which the development of air transport could be allowed to progress unhindered. During the transitional period, this had to be undertaken by foreign companies, as Brazil's technical resources were inadequate; but the national interests and independence had to be protected, especially the development of the vast interior whose enormous wealth potential was being dimly realised.

The solution was found by permitting a series of international partnerships, under which foreign companies were allowed free passage to and through Brazil. But operations within Brazil had to be under the control of Brazilian-based companies which, however, could be subsidiaries of the foreign parents. In the beginning there was undoubtedly some inadvertent—and often deliberate— evasion of the strict letter of the law, as there was much interchanging of both equipment and payloads, to say nothing of joint use of crews and ground staff. But in the last resort, the Brazilian authorities had the power to invoke the precise wording of the Presidential Decrees under which each company operated. And in some cases, eventually, they did.

Ironically, the French airline, C.G.E.A., Lignes Latécoère, later Aéropostale, which first tried to operate within Brazil in 1925, was the last to obtain full legal authority. The US company, NYRBA, was the first to obtain both foreign and domestic rights, but survived only a few months before Pan American eagerly engulfed it. Condor had been registered in Rio de Janeiro, with only nominal Brazilian representation, almost from the start, and so the Germans had a slight legal edge.

The complex succession of Brazilian government authorization to foreign airlines under these Decrees is summarised in Table 19 on page 376.

A Man and His Dream

Although Brazilian airliners began to fly to neighbouring countries during the decade which was to follow the first coastal service from Rio Grande to Natal, the establishment of completely independent Brazilian intercontinental service did not occur until after the war. However, the history of the two major prewar Brazilian airlines is so interwoven with foreign interests, especially in their earlier periods of route expansion, that it is impossible to place the early development in

Ralph O'Neill (*left*) created the New York, Rio, and Buenos Aires Line (NYRBA) in 1929. Backed by a formidable array of US industrial magnates, he was thwarted, however, by Juan Trippe (*right*) Pan American's chief executive, whose influence with the US Post Office enabled him to win the coveted East Coast mail contract. O'Neill died in California on 23 October, 1980, and Trippe, on 3 April, 1981.

proper perspective without reference to the exciting—sometimes adventurous exploits of the foreign airlines which helped to promote Brazilian air commerce during the formative years.

Indeed, the chronology of Panair do Brasil, a name which was synonymous with Brazilian overseas airline involvement for 35 years, has to begin with an account of the fulfilment of one man's dream. Ralph O'Neill, a United States citizen possessed of considerable foresight, recognized the possibilities of commercial aircraft in speeding up the mail and passenger service between the great cities of North and South America. From his inspiration, and after much corporate in-fighting, Panair do Brasil was eventually born.

O'Neill was a much-decorated veteran airman of the First World War, who had spent five years organizing the Mexican Air Force and, in 1927, had become the Latin American concessionaire for the products of the Boeing Airplane Company. At the end of March 1928, he arrived in Rio de Janeiro to explore the possibility of creating an airline to link South America with the United States, thereby promoting aircraft sales—presumably Boeing's. He was granted an audience with President Washington Luis, who arranged for him to see Victor Konder, the Minister of Transport, with whom he established a good rapport.

O'Neill had arrived in Rio by ship, but he quickly became airborne, demonstrating the Boeing F2B fighter to the military authorities in Rio. He then attempted to beat the record flight time between Rio de Janeiro and Buenos Aires by flying the F2B over the route entirely in the daylight hours. Unfortunately he crashed in Uruguay, almost losing his life, and completely losing his job with Boeing, who blamed him for negligence and the loss of the aeroplane. Undaunted, on recovery from his injuries, he pursued his original plans, and was granted an audience with President Hipolito Irigoyen of Argentina in June. He also did some research on mail loads northbound from Buenos Aires, and these were impressive enough to persuade him to ask the Argentine Government for a contract to fly air mail to the United States and intermediate points. He then returned to Rio de Janeiro to further his cause in Brazil.

Empresa de Transportes Aéreos (E.T.A.)

Here, in July 1928, he had his first stormy confrontation with the promoters of a Brazilian airline, whose existence was in O'Neill's view only a myth. While the attitude of the small local company may have appeared over-ambitious, even presumptuous, the cold facts are that it came into legal existence before O'Neill's company.

Empresa de Transportes Aéreos (E.T.A.) was founded by Ruy Vacani and the brothers Benjamin and Alexandre Braga on 10 August, 1928. Their plans were modest compared to O'Neill's. They aspired to fly only between Rio de Janeiro and São Paulo, to Campos, and to Belo Horizonte and Pirapora. For these routes they acquired three Klemm open-cockpit monoplanes, one an L 20 (P-BBAA) and two L 25s (P-BBAC and P-BBAD). These were properly registered with the Brazilian authorities in December 1928.

It was about this time that O'Neill arrived back in Rio. He had been extremely active during the summer in obtaining solid financial backing for his enterprise from the wealthy James Rand, of the Remington Rand Corporation. Rand promoted the airline as Trimotor Safety Airways, but O'Neill prevailed upon him to imitate railroad practice in favour of the more geographically descriptive **New York, Rio, and Buenos Aires Line**, or **NYRBA**. Reuben Fleet, of Consolidated Aircraft, undertook to supply a number of twin-engined Commodore flying-boats, while O'Neill's friend in the Navy, Admiral Moffett, had also given him the assurance of early delivery of Sikorsky S-38s to cover operations while the Commodores were being built. Although NYRBA was to operate Ford Tri-Motors, the majority of the fleet was twin-engined, so that Rand's choice of name would have looked distinctly odd.

On 24 December, 1928, O'Neill had his second stormy confrontation with E.T.A., who produced documents from New York, in the name of NYRBA, which in effect was a partnership contract. E.T.A. had, in fact, visited New York, and convinced some of the NYRBA directors that it had an exclusive contract to operate within Brazil and to overseas points. E.T.A. had been paid $10,000, with the further commitment by NYRBA to invest $250,000 in cash and/or equipment. E.T.A. was to have exclusive rights in Brazil, NYRBA for overseas routes. O'Neill called for his lawyers, who assured him that such a contract was worthless under Brazilian law. They were right. E.T.A.'s claims were exaggerated and premature. On 1 March, 1929, Presidential Decree No.18,625 authorized the Sociedad Mercantil Brasileira, Empresa de Transportes Aéreos, Eta & Companhia Limitada, to operate air services. The provisions specifically excluded monopoly or other privileges, as they did for all such certificates, and restricted operations to within Brazil.

Formation of the New York, Rio, and Buenos Aires Line (NYRBA)

O'Neill, on the other hand, had been given the assurance of President Coolidge that the South American mail route would be open to competitive bidding, and had received the good news at the end of February that the Argentine Government had granted him the precious mail contract. On 17 March, 1929, the New York, Rio, and Buenos Aires Line (NYRBA or NYRBALINE) was formally incorporated in Delaware. In addition to Rand and Fleet, further formidable support was forthcoming from Frank C. Munson, of the Munson shipping line; William B. Mayo, of the Ford Motor Company (whose election to a directorship in May was accompanied by an order for six Ford Tri-Motors); J. E.

354

Reynolds of International Founders; and Lewis Pierson, of Irving Trust. Later, two renegades from previous Pan American internal battles, Richard Bevier and J. K. Montgomery, representing American International Airways (a paper company) came on board. NYRBA represented an $8,500,000 investment.

Between 11 June and 13 July, 1929, O'Neill completed an historic proving flight from the Hudson River, New York City, to Buenos Aires, using the Sikorsky S-38 *Washington*. This was no record-beating headline-seeking adventure. At every point along the route, carefully selected for maximum efficiency in future regular operations, discussions were held with the appropriate influential authorities, including Presidents of various countries, to assure the establishment of first-class flying-boat bases, mainly in the form of floats in protected harbours, to serve the Commodores when they went into service. In Rio de Janeiro, Victor Konder advised O'Neill to set up a subsidiary company, NYRBA do Brasil, so as to comply with Brazilian law, in the letter as well as in the spirit.

NYRBA's Sikorsky S-38B amphibian NC113M *Porto Alegre*. This aircraft passed to Pan American Airways, was stolen and crashed near Rio de Janeiro on 25 September, 1932. (*United Technologies Corporation*)

Possibly unknown to O'Neill, Pan American Airways, his arch-rival in the United States, had already obtained a certificate of operation in Brazil, under Decree No.18,768, on 28 May, 1929, although, at the time, Pan Am's ability to operate the route was highly questionable.

Little E.T.A. had also been active in a modest way. On 12 June it had obtained authority from the Brazilian Post Office to carry mail from Rio de Janeiro to São Paulo and to Campos, and the first mail-carrying flight was made to São Paulo on 29 July. E.T.A.'s plans were to fly twice a week, without attempting a round trip in one day—unambitious by O'Neill's standards—and there is no evidence that even this limited schedule was sustained for long. In any event, one source reported the sale of E.T.A. to NYRBA on 13 August, and the Klemm aircraft were sold to VARIG on 16 November, so that the maverick Brazilian company appears to have quietly faded away. Well, not quite, as a later incident was to prove.

NYRBA Starts Service

After a demonstration flight across the Andes in the newly-delivered Ford Tri-Motor on 1 August, 1929, NYRBA got its first services under way. First, the Sikorsky S-38 *Washington* began the daily shuttle service across the River Plate between Buenos Aires and Montevideo on 21 August. This connection soon became popular, and when a second S-38, *Montevideo*, arrived on 28 September, it was immediately put into service to provide extra capacity. By the end of the year, frequency was twice daily. The regular once-weekly trans-Andean route

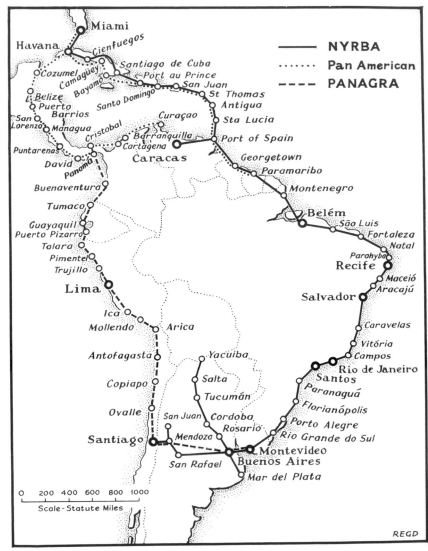

42. United States Airlines in South America, 1930. At the beginning of 1930, three US airlines aspired to reach Argentina, at that time the most prosperous country in the whole of Latin America. The front runner was NYRBA. Pan American Airways, at first confined to the Caribbean, quickly gained ascendancy by forming PANAGRA as a partnership with the Grace shipping line, by purchasing its east coast rival, and winning the vital US Post Office mail contract.

356

began on 1 September, the first transcontinental air service in South America, with a Buenos Aires–Santiago journey time of 7 hr 15 min. Frequency on this route too was increased, to twice weekly, by the end of the year.

Things were moving along nicely. On 1 October, Mrs Hoover, wife of the US President, named the first Commodore flying-boat *Buenos Aires* at Anacostia. On 15 October, NYRBA received its Brazilian operating certificate under Decree No.18,951. The Buenos Aires–Yacuiba (Bolivia) service started on 29 November, although traffic to and from the smaller cities in northern Argentina was predictably low. An important political figure, William P. McCracken, formerly Assistant Secretary of Commerce for Aeronautics, became Chairman of the NYRBA Board on 4 December. And to round off the year, the Buenos Aires–Rio de Janeiro route was inaugurated on 23 December, just in time for Christmas.

Although Pan American Airways and its affiliated, half-owned company, PANAGRA, announced the beginning of a Miami–Buenos Aires service, via the west coast of South America and across the Andes from Santiago, O'Neill did not take this to be a serious threat, as the trans-Andean flight was altogether too hazardous and challenging for aircraft such as the Fairchild FC-2 which PANAGRA was deploying on that section of the route.

The New Year began well. On 24 January, 1930, the Brazilian Government issued another certificate of operation, under Decree No.19,079, to NYRBA's subsidiary, **NYRBA do Brasil,** which authorized commercial operations within Brazil and to the neighbouring countries of Uruguay, Argentina, and the Guianas. A few weeks later, now under pressure to match its words with deeds, O'Neill made another historic inaugural flight.

Buenos Aires–Rio–New York

O'Neill's airline might have been more aptly named if the initials had been BARNY; for its launching depended upon mail contracts from the southern end of the trunk route. The early services radiated from Buenos Aires, and the first revenue-earning mail flight was northbound. This was as full of incident as any inaugural flight could absorb, and only the superb ground services and organization which had been meticulously built up by O'Neill's team enabled it to take place at all.

In spite of enough operational problems to have daunted most pioneers, O'Neill completed the inaugural NYRBA service from Buenos Aires to Miami during a hectic journey between 19 and 25 February, 1930. Although he left Buenos Aires in grand style in the Commodore *Rio de Janeiro* and arrived equally gloriously in a sister ship *Cuba,* this concealed the fact that the mail had been successively transferred in the intervening period between no less than eight different aircraft, plus a road trip from Santos to Rio de Janeiro, and then by launch to Niterói, to avoid some machiavellian activity by E.T.A., which managed to obtain attachment papers to the S-38 based at Rio. Three of the aircraft were damaged in some way, and only ingenious relay operations by back-up aircraft enabled the mail to fly through.

Nevertheless, the mail service and NYRBA's ability to do the job had been demonstrated, and, on 26 February, the second service began and was continued with admirable regularity. Progressively, the Commodores took on a greater portion of the total journey, and the entire operation began to work smoothly, in spite of the long distances and the problems of spares supply.

The elegant Consolidated Commodore (*top*), originally designed for the US Navy, was built in its commercial version in 1929 to the specification laid down by Ralph O'Neill, of NYRBA. Able to carry 27 passengers over short distances, the Commodore was ahead of its time, and some were still flying in the Bahamas after the war. The faster Consolidated Fleetster 17 (*bottom*) was used to carry the mails from Buenos Aires for the initial segments of the long East Coast route to the USA. Leaving a day after the Commodore, it would overtake the slower flying-boat, thus enabling NYRBA to fulfil its mail contract with Argentina which stipulated an eight-day transit time. (*Lower picture R. H. Fleet*)

Sadly, NYRBA lacked the key element to financial success in those days when no commercial aircraft could produce a profit without subsidy, direct or concealed, from some external source. NYRBA badly needed the United States mail contract; but this it could not obtain, for the simple reason that Walter F. Brown, the Postmaster General appointed by President Hoover, wanted to give it to Pan American. NYRBA might even then have survived had not the Wall Street crash of October 1929 severely affected the potential traffic—ironically during the time that O'Neill was solving most of his problems in the south. Mail contracts from South America alone could not compensate for the heavy investment and operational costs, and when, in April 1930, NYRBA's Board Chairman McCracken actually decided to talk about a merger with Pan American, O'Neill's days were numbered.

After much acrimonious debate and argument during the summer over respective net worths, Pan American Airways gained control of NYRBA, under terms grossly unfavourable to the latter, on 19 August, 1930. The next day, Pan American, as the 'chosen instrument' of the US Post Office, was granted the US Mail Contract (FAM-10) for the entire east coast of South America, at the maximum rate of $2 per mile. On 15 September, the formal absorption of NYRBA was completed, by a transfer of stock, and on 17 October, the name of the Brazilian associate, NYRBA do Brasil, was changed to **Panair do Brasil**, and recognized under its new name by Decree No.19,417 on 21 November, 1930.

Thus was born one of Brazil's great airlines. But as it did not itself fly overseas until after the war (such services being undertaken by its parent company, Pan American) the continuing history of Panair will be covered in the next chapter.

The First South Atlantic Air Mail Service

The pioneering **Aéropostale** service across the South Atlantic (more correctly the Central Atlantic, as the Equator crosses the route) should strictly be called an Accelerated Mail Service, rather than a purely Air Mail Service, as the trans-ocean section was carried out by a fleet of ships. By operating these between Dakar, Sénégal, on the western bulge of Africa, and Natal, Brazil, the time taken to carry mail between Paris and Buenos Aires was reduced from 16 to 8 days.

When Aéropostale began its pioneering rapid mail service between France and South America, the trans-ocean segment between Dakar and Natal was beyond the range of commercial aircraft. It was served, therefore, by a small fleet of *avisos* (*top*), fast destroyers formerly in the French Navy, and leased to the airline. Later, Marcel Bouilloux-Lafont, Aéropostale's owner, ordered four specially-designed ships (*bottom*), which went into service after Air France had absorbed Aéropostale in 1933. (*Air France*)

The Paris–Buenos Aires through service was inaugurated on 1 March, 1928, on a semi-regular schedule, as a natural sequel to starting the Natal–Buenos Aires segment on 14 November, 1927. The Paris–Dakar service had been in operation since 1 June, 1925, and the extension marked the first of many great achievements which can be credited to Marcel Bouilloux-Lafont. For the sea journey, Aéropostale leased from the French Navy a fleet of six submarine-chasing destroyers: *le Révigny, l'Épernay, le Reims, le Lunéville, le Péronne,* and *le Belfort*. Although not entirely without problems (one caught fire in Natal, and boiler tubes were inclined to blow up) these improvised mail-carriers worked the 3,200 km route steadily for about 2½ years, maintaining an average block time between Dakar and Natal of a little over 100 hr, or about 4½ days. Latécoère landplanes completed the journey southwards.

The destroyers were replaced towards the end of 1930 by a fleet of specially-designed ships, named *Aéropostale I, II,* etc, which were not only faster, but also more efficient in fuel consumption and manpower. Each had a crew of 36, and could complete the Dakar–Natal trip in 36 hr. Some idea of the considerable investment needed to maintain the service can be drawn from the fact that, in addition to the mail-carrying ships, four other supply vessels were commissioned: *le Bemtévi, le Becfigue, le Cicogne,* and *le Phocée.*

Bouilloux-Lafont was active all over South America at this time, signing mail contracts, surveying routes, and ceaselessly negotiating with governments in pursuit of his goal of constructing an air network without equal in the world at the time. Extension of the Aéropostale trunk route to Santiago on 15 July, 1929, to Comodoro Rivadavia on 2 October, and other routes in Peru, Bolivia, and Venezuela, are dealt with appropriately in other chapters in this book.

Meanwhile, on the Natal–Buenos Aires segment of the route, between 1928 and 1930, times were gradually improved from 79 to 43 hr southbound, and from 66 to 40 hr northbound, with a best time of 32 hr on one southbound trip. For the period this represented a considerable technical achievement, partly by the innovation, for example, on 16 April, 1928, of night flying as a regular routine. On that date, Jean Mermoz flew a Latécoère 26 from Campo dos Afonsos, in Rio de Janeiro, taking off at night, flying through the whole of the next day, and arriving at Buenos Aires late in the evening. By such enterprise, the 8- or 9-day Paris–Buenos Aires schedule was achieved with remarkable frequency and regularity. By 1930, for every flight which took longer, there was one which kept well within the exacting timetable.

But all this sustained effort was eclipsed in public esteem by the spectacular flight on 12/13 May, 1930. A Latécoère 28 seaplane, the *Comte de la Vaulx,* piloted by Jean Mermoz, with Jean Dabry as navigator, and Léopold Gimié as radio-operator, made the Atlantic crossing from Saint-Louis, Sénégal, to Natal in 21 hr 15 min. The difficulties of navigation, then a science still in its infancy, were taken in their stride. The mail consignment from France on this flight left Toulouse at 06.10 hr on Sunday, 11 May, 1930, reached Rio de Janeiro at 23.00 hr on Tuesday, 13 May, and was triumphantly delivered in Buenos Aires at 19.25 on Wednesday, 14 May. To this day, the flight, together with Mermoz's esteem as a pilot, ranks in France as Lindbergh's solo Atlantic flight ranks in the USA.

Just prior to Mermoz's flight, incidentally, Aéropostale had taken the necessary legal step to permit the carriage of mail and passengers within Brazil by forming a subsidiary, the Companhia Aeronáutica Brasileira, authorized on 14 February, 1930, by Brazilian Government Decree No.19,115, with subsequent change of name to Cia Aeropostal Brasileira on 11 July of that year.

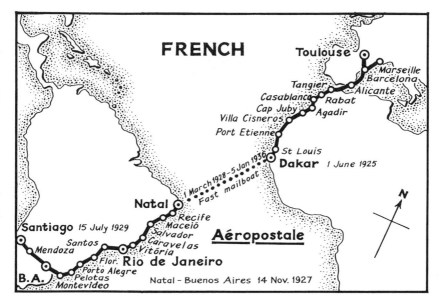

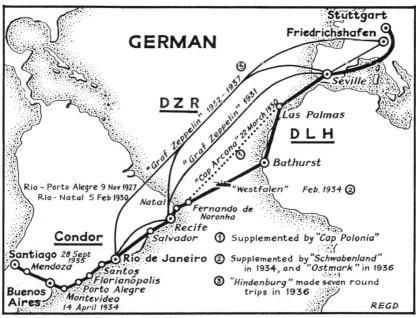

43. The South Atlantic Air Mail Service—Pioneers and Developers, 1927–1937. The rivalry between French and German airline enterprises is illustrated by these maps. The French Aéropostale mailboat made possible the first predominantly-air mail service between Europe and South America. Subsequently, however, the Germans displayed more versatility, with the airship service becoming the regular and reliable choice for passengers until 1937.

361

The Aéropostale Latécoère 28-3 F-AJPF was a sister craft of F-AJNQ *Comte de la Vaulx* in which Jean Mermoz flew the ocean sector of the first experimental all-air mail from Toulouse to Rio de Janeiro. The ocean crossing from St Louis, Sénégal, to Natal, Brazil, was made on 12–13 May, 1930, and took 21 hours.

German Ingenuity

The German reply to the French efforts took many forms. At the beginning, the idea of carrying the mail by surface ship was also pursued, in co-operation between **Syndicato Condor** and its parent organization, Deutsche Luft Hansa, of Berlin. On 22 March, 1930, the first link-up was completed off the island of Fernando de Noronha, when mail was transferred from the Condor Dornier Wal *Jangadeiro* (P-BAMA) to the fast German passenger liner *Cap Arcona,* flagship of the Hamburg Sudamerikanische Line. This first transfer was made under slightly hazardous conditions, on the high seas off the island; but subsequently, from July, the mail was transferred in the relative security of the protected bay on the island shore, with the *Cap Arcona* alternating with the *Cap Polonio* (see Map 43). By this means, Germany could claim a two-day advantage in carrying mail from Europe to Buenos Aires.

Although not yet operating on a regular basis, there was an even more dramatic demonstration of German air transport progress two months later. On 22 May,

On 22 March, 1930, mail from South America to Europe was exchanged at Fernando de Noronha from a Syndicato Condor Dornier Wal to the Hamburg-Sudamerikanische passenger liner *Cap Arcona*. This later picture shows an exchange at Fernando de Noronha between the Wal P-BALA *Olinda* (ex-D-1488) and a passenger liner. (*Lufthansa*)

362

1930, the famous airship *Graf Zeppelin* arrived at the Giquia landing field at Recife, having left Friedrichshafen on 18 May. On 25 May the *Graf Zeppelin* arrived at the Campo dos Afonsos field in Rio de Janeiro, where mail was distributed by Condor to other points in southern Brazil, especially to the German communities in the southern states.

At this time, the great airship was operated by Luftschiffbau Zeppelin GmbH (the builders) and the Hamburg Sudamerikanische Line, in co-operation with Luft Hansa and Condor.

While the ship-to-plane transfers were proceeding and plans were being made to turn the success of the *Graf Zeppelin* into a commercially viable operation, careful preparations were being made to train Luft Hansa pilots for a daring technical venture. During this era of aviation development, a preference for seaplanes or flying-boats over landplanes for over-water flights was almost universally accepted, and Germany was no exception. Aircraft were not yet big enough, and consequently unable to carry sufficient fuel to provide long range. Nevertheless, Luft Hansa systematically began to train a special group of pilots, who had previous experience in flying over the Baltic, for eventual South Atlantic deployment. Beginning on 23 March, 1929, these Luft Hansa pilots started to receive their 'Licence for High-Seas Long-Range Navigation.'

The *Graf Zeppelin*, LZ 127, began regular service between Friedrichshafen and Recife on 20 March, 1932, and was the first aircraft to operate transoceanic passenger services. The Zeppelin is seen here at Recife. (*Lufthansa*)

But some time passed before they were to need this qualification. The *Graf Zeppelin* service was performing well, and holding out good prospects for success. Strange though this may appear half a century later, in these formative years of long-range air transport, the lighter-than-air dirigible was seriously considered by many aviation specialists to be the answer to the problem of trans-oceanic flight. Certainly the *Graf Zeppelin* had no range limitations, which—landplane or seaplane—was the heavier-than-air machine's greatest shortcoming.

In August, September and October of 1931, the airship made three round trips between Friedrichshafen and Recife, where Condor took over both passengers and mail. On 20 March, 1932, the first of nine round trips during the year was begun, according to a widely advertised timetable which bore a striking similarity

LUFTSCHIFFBAU ZEPPELIN G. M. B. H., FRIEDRICHSHAFEN A. B.

Nicht übertragbar. Not transferable. Intransferible. Intransmissivel. Personnel.

ZEPPELIN-FAHRSCHEIN NR. 0054

TICKET NO. ◇ BILLETE NO. ◇ BILHETE NO. ◇ CONTRAT DE PASSAGE NO.

Bett Nr. / Berth No. / Cama No. / Cama No. / Couchette No.

Der Luftschiffbau Zeppelin G. m. b. H. übernimmt auf Grund seiner Beförderungs-
bedingungen (siehe Rückseite) die Beförderung von

In accordance with the conditions concerning the conveyance of passengers (see overleaf)
the Luftschiffbau Zeppelin G. m. b. H. is taking charge of the air-transport of

Según las condiciones de transporte (véase al dorso) la Luftschiffbau Zeppelin G. m. b. H.
toma a su cargo el transporte aéreo del

Segun do as condições de transporte (vide o verso) a Luftschiffbau Zeppelin G. m. b. H.
encarrega-se do transporte aereo de

Le Luftschiffbau Zeppelin G. m. b. H. s'engage à transporter, conformément aux termes
énoncés dans ses Conditions de Transport

Herrn/Frau Fräulein   **Herr Nicolas T. Heyman Perrée**
Mr./Mrs./Miss / Sr. Sra./Srta. / Snr./Snra. / Mr./Mme./Mlle.

mit dem Luftschiff   **" Graf Zeppelin "**   am   **20. August 1933**
by the airship / en el dirigible / no dirigivel / par le dirigeable   on / el dia / em / le

von   **Rio de Janeiro**   nach   **Friedrichshafen**
from / de / de / de   via / a / para / via

über   **Pernambuco**
to / via / via / à destination de

Das Fahrgeld von **Rs.6:590$000 ....** ist ordnungsgemäß bezahlt.
The amount of El importe de   has been duly paid. ha sido pagado de conformidad.
A importancia de Le montant du passage, soit   foi devidamente paga. a été payé.

Zur Einschiffung versammeln sich die Fahrgäste   For embarkation passengers will meet
Para el embarque, los pasajeros deben reunirse / Para o embarque os passageiros devem reunir-se
Pour l'embarquement les passagers se réunissent

am **10. August 33** um ⁴˒³⁰ A.M. Uhr im   **Avenida Rio Branco 79/81**
on / el / em / le   at a las às à   at en no à

Ort **Rio de Janeiro**   Datum **9. August 1933**
Place / Lugar / Logar / Lieu d'émission   Date / Fecha / Data / Date

                                        Luftschiffbau Zeppelin G. m. b. H.

Bitte Rückseite beachten!   in Generalvertretung:
Please note the back hereof! Véase al dorso!
Veja-se o verso! Voir au dos!   Hamburg-Amerika Linie.

Luftschiffbau Zeppelin ticket, 1933. This historic ticket, sold in Rio de Janeiro in 1933, was for a regular *Graf Zeppelin* flight to Germany. This ticket, for departure on 10 August, 1933, was made out for Herr Nicolas T. Heyman Perrée to travel to Friedrichshafen via Pernambuco and the price is shown as Rs. 6: 590 $000. Passengers had to report at the city terminal in Avenida Rio Branco at 4.30 am.

364

Zeppelin-Passagiere sind immer guter Laune

Los pasajeros del Zeppelin están siempre de buen humor

Os passageiros do Zeppelin estao sempre de excelente humor

Zeppelin passengers are always in cheerful mood

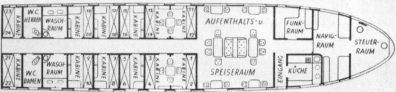

Der Kabinenplan des Luftschiffs
El plano de camarotes de la aeronave
A planta de camarotes do dirigivel
The cabin plan of the airship

Im Zeppelin fühlt man sich geborgen wie zu Hause. Die Fahrt ist immer ruhig und gleichmäßig, so daß bis jetzt noch niemand luft- oder seekrank geworden ist.

En el dirigible Zeppelin se siente uno tan seguro como en su propia casa. Su marcha es siempre tranquila y uniforme; hasta ahora nadie se ha mareado en él.

No dirigível Zeppelin sente-se o viajante tão seguro como em sua propria casa. A marcha da aeronave é sempre tranquilla e uniforme; até agora ninguem tem soffrido de enjôo nestas viajens.

When you are travelling by Zeppelin, you feel as safe as if you were at home. The airship proceeds ahead steadily and uniformly, and no case has ever been known of anyone becoming airsick or seasick.

Extract from Graf Zeppelin leaflet. This extract from a 1934 publicity leaflet illustrated the layout and the accommodation standards of the famous German airship on the South Atlantic route.

to steamship practice. Normal journey time was a regular $4\frac{1}{2}$ days to Rio de Janeiro by the airship-Condor connection, Recife being reached in three days. The Brazilian authorities thought enough of the airship service to prepare for greater things, and allocated a large sum of money to build a magnificent airship terminal at Santa Cruz, near Rio de Janeiro. In fact, the last three airship flights in 1932 went through to Rio, without the aid of Condor.

The year 1933 was an eventful one for the German group of airlines. Not only did the *Graf Zeppelin* continue to maintain its regular schedule of nine round trips per year, with a stop at Seville in Spain—and plans to stop in the future at Barcelona—but also the ingenious plans to put flying-boats into service came to fruition. The reason was quite simple; the airship, for all its attractions, was relatively slow, averaging little more than 60–70 mph. Not only did the German group wish to improve on this for its own technical self-esteem; but the French, under Bouilloux-Lafont, had been threatening to supersede their mail-boat connection with flying-boats which would cover the Dakar–Natal segment of the route nonstop.

Thus, after much technical experiment, one of the boldest and most enterprising ideas for furthering long-distance air mail services in the whole history of air transport was put to the test. By May 1933, the depôt ship *Westfalen*, an old cargo steamer which had been chartered in 1932, now completely re-equipped with some astonishing apparatus, was in position at Bathurst in West Africa, which was the German port of call on that continent, equivalent to France's Dakar.

The most noteworthy feature of the *Westfalen's* structural engineering was the enormous compressed-air catapult which occupied the entire front half of the ship. Although previous catapults had launched smaller aircraft off the liners *Bremen* and *Europa,* in an attempt to speed up North Atlantic mail services, this device was a giant by comparison. 42 metres long, it had to project a Dornier Wal, weighing 8–10 tonnes, into the air at a speed fast enough to permit the flying-boat to remain airborne without stalling. To position the aircraft, it had to be retrieved from the water by a crane, capable of lifting 15 tons. Finally, as a further refinement, a 'drag-sail' was towed behind the ship onto which the Wal could taxi, to be raised partly out of the Atlantic swell.

This elaborate engineering worked well. On 29 May, 1933, the Dornier Wal *Monsun* made an experimental catapult-assisted take-off from the *Westfalen* and alighted on the drag-sail in the open sea near Bathurst. On 2 June, Capt Jobst von Studnitz flew the *Monsun* to an anchorage at Bathurst. Then, on 6 June, the real dress rehearsal took place, this time with the *Westfalen* at its mid-Atlantic rendezvous about 1,500 km southwest of Bathurst. The *Monsun* was hauled on board, refuelled, and catapulted off again, to arrive at Natal next day. A little later, in October, another experiment had one Wal flying to the *Westfalen*, where a second Wal was ready on the catapult to complete the journey after a swift transfer of mail. In fact, the efficiency of the whole operation on board the depôt ship was such that this latter routine was unnecessary, as the entire operation could be completed within half an hour.

By any standards, the German trans-Atlantic Wal service was extraordinary. The normal cruising altitude was only between 5 and 10 metres—to take advantage of ground effect (if this term can be applied to the ocean), which Capt von Clausbruch claimed increased the speed by about 15 km/h, as at higher altitudes the wind component always seemed to be adverse. The catapult launching must have been a daunting affair. The powerful catapult, specially

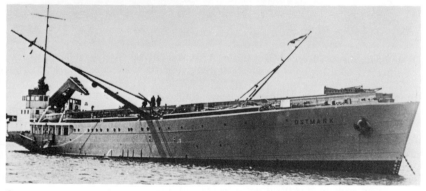

German perseverance in developing the depotship-based catapult technique is shown in this series of pictures. The *Westfalen* (*top*) was a converted merchant ship used in the first experiments at Bathurst in 1933. The *Schwabenland* (*centre*) added in 1934, permitted ships at both ends of the trans-Atlantic segment. Then the *Ostmark* (*bottom*), introduced in 1936, was specially built for its unique purpose. The crane could lift the Dornier Wal directly on to the catapult sled, while the twin masts could be lowered on each side to clear the way for take off. A fourth depotship, the *Friesenland*, was used only for the North Atlantic trial flights between the Azores and New York. (*Lufthansa*)

Deutsche Lufthansa's Dornier Do J IIaBos 8-ton Wal D-2069 *Monsun* on the catapult of the *Westfalen* (*top*) and just after launching from the same ship. (*Lufthansa*)

designed and built by Heinkel, pushed the Wal to 140 km/h in about two seconds—or so the pilots claimed—which may account for reports that on the *Westfalen* there was a 'double re-fuelling': strong spirit for the pilot as well as the Wal.

The Wal was as sturdy as any flying-boat built at that time, withstanding a great deal of stress from its unique mid-ocean alighting and take-off routine. The pilots had an affection for it, although the propellers were a little dangerous—'they could chop your fingers off if you reached up too far.'

It was well that the arduous years of trial and testing were now fulfilling their promise; for on 16 January, 1933, before *Westfalen* had left Germany, the French Aéropostale had made an experimental flight with a new landplane, the Couzinet 70 *Arc-en-Ciel,* which flew nonstop from Saint-Louis to Natal in 14 hr 27 min. But the aircraft was not entirely satisfactory, and this gave the Deutsche Luft Hansa-Condor partnership an opportunity to consolidate its position, maintaining its faith in the flying-boat.

Accordingly, on 3 February, 1934, the first all-air regularly-scheduled trans-Atlantic air mail service was inaugurated from Berlin. The Dorner Wal *Taifun* took over the southbound mails at Bathurst on 7 February (where they had arrived by Junkers-Ju 52/3m, which, in turn, had picked them up from a fast Heinkel He 70 at Seville) and made the now-perfected refuelling stop in mid-ocean and was catapulted from *Westfalen* to arrive at Natal in a shore-to-shore time of 14 hr 10 min. The Condor Junkers-W 34 *Tiéte* then carried the mail onwards, reaching Buenos Aires in 26 hr 51 min from Natal.

Improvements were made in the Spring of 1934. An additional depôt ship, the *Schwabenland,* was stationed off Bathurst, and the *Westfalen* transferred further southwest close to the island of Fernando de Noronha; in 1935, another vessel, the *Ostmark*, replaced the *Schwabenland* when it was transferred to the North Atlantic to take part in further experiments there. Fulfilling its share of the expansion programme, Condor extended its service from Porto Alegre to Montevideo and Buenos Aires on 14 April, 1934.

Concurrently with the Wal mail flights, the airship service continued to make progress. On 31 March, 1934, Luftschiffbau Zeppelin was granted its operating certificate in Brazil under Decree No.24,069. The *Graf Zeppelin* completed twelve round trips in 1934, one of which continued to Buenos Aires. The following year, the status of the airship company—and hence the partnership—changed slightly, when on 22 March, 1935, the Luftschiffbau Zeppelin and Deutsche Lufthansa* founded the **Deutsche Zeppelin-Reederei**, with the famous airship designer Hugo Eckener as its chairman. In that year, no less than sixteen round trips were completed to South America.

On 30 March, 1935, by the introduction of night services on the South Atlantic route, the regular Berlin–Rio de Janeiro DLH-Condor schedule was speeded up to three days, with an additional half a day to reach Buenos Aires. On 25 August, the 100th scheduled flying-boat crossing of the South Atlantic was celebrated, and on 28 September Condor extended its route to the Pacific, with a Buenos Aires–Santiago flight, with a stop at Mendoza. Mail could now be delivered from Berlin to Santiago in four days. The German-Brazilian partnership was now gathering momentum, with Deutsche Lufthansa also permitted to fly within Brazil, under the terms of Decree No.142 of 30 April, 1935.

Air France Swallows Aéropostale

Meanwhile the French efforts had been handicapped by a crisis in Aéropostale's affairs. Marcel Bouilloux-Lafont had negotiated with the French Air Ministry an understanding that the annual subsidy, amounting to a substantial portion of the revenue, should be guaranteed for a period of at least ten years. The former agreement negotiated with Pierre Latécoère had been renewable every year, and, as Bouilloux-Lafont pointed out, was totally unacceptable from the point of view of long-term financing. Having obtained the agreement, he then proceeded to invest his fortune into building Aéropostale into the world's biggest airline organization, not only with new aircraft but ground installations and equipment, airports, and radio facilities, not to mention a team of air and ground staff. To supplement his own investment, he also floated a bond issue with his bank in France, and raised further funds in Brazil.

*Deutsche Lufthansa was used in this form from 1 January, 1934.

When Pierre Latécoère first sought to start an airline from France to South America, he was unable to negotiate mail contracts and operating rights with Latin American governments. Disheartened, he sold his airline in 1927 to Marcel Bouilloux-Lafont (*left*) a French industrialist who, with great vision, quickly built the re-named Aéropostale into the greatest airline in the world at that time. One of his closest associates was the French pilot, Jean Mermoz (*right*), acclaimed in his own country as Lindbergh is in the USA. Bouilloux-Lafont died, forgotten by the airline world, in Rio de Janeiro in 1940.
(*Air France and Mme de Bure*)

Early in 1931, as the result of political intrigue in France, where governments were changing frequently, the French Chamber of Deputies refused to ratify the long-term subsidy agreement made by the former Air Minister. Bouilloux-Lafont suddenly faced a crisis, as his vast investment programme was based on the presumption of support from his government, and the expectation of the success which would inevitably follow a visionary plan. Suddenly, the Aéropostale empire was faced with collapse. Disillusioned and betrayed, Bouilloux-Lafont was forced ignominiously into *liquidation judiciaire* on 31 March, 1931.

At the time of the disaster, the Aéropostale route system extended to nine countries in Latin America, protected by firm contracts for routes, for the carriage of mail and passengers. New services had opened as far north as Trinidad and as far west as Tacna, Peru.

A new twin-engined flying-boat, the Latécoère 38, with range and load-carrying performance superior to that of the Dornier Wal, had been ordered specifically for the South Atlantic route. For reasons never satisfactorily explained, Aéropostale's Laté 38, although ready for delivery at Biscarrosse early in 1931, was allowed to rot away at the back of the hangar.

Plans were afoot to extend the latter route to Lima, and in an astounding political coup, Bouilloux-Lafont had acquired the exclusive rights to the Azores from the Portuguese Government, in preparation for an attack on the North Atlantic route, for which Jean Mermoz had already been briefed. Why the French Government should have chosen this time to destroy the man who had, almost single-handedly, given France a secure foothold for the development of air transport in half the world will possibly never be known. What is known is that Aéropostale's route network was curtailed to the single route to Buenos Aires, and the other routes, including the subsidiary organizations so elaborately fashioned to comply with local conditions and laws, were abandoned. The exclusive rights to the Azores, which had caused palpitations at Pan American Airways and Imperial Airways, and near-apoplexy in Luft Hansa, were allowed to lapse by default. A caretaker commission maintained Aéropostale for two years, but when the newly-created **Air France** took over the remnants on 30 August, 1933, it was only a shadow of what it might have been.

It was said at the time that, with the French Government working against Bouilloux-Lafont, and the German Government supporting Luft Hansa, Condor, and Zeppelin, with generosity and foresight, there could be little doubt as to which of the two great airline countries would emerge with the Latin American spoils. While the French were tearing down the house, rather than putting it in order, the Germans took timely advantage and started their regular air service, via the *Westfalen,* in February 1934. Nevertheless, the tradition of airmanship and innovative design enabled Air France to begin to pick up the pieces from the ruins of Aéropostale. Bouilloux-Lafont was left in exile in Rio de Janeiro, trying to salvage the vestiges of a once-great empire, and to redeem his debts in as honourable a fashion as his reduced circumstances would allow.

On 31 December, 1933, a new flying-boat, the Latécoère 300 *Croix du Sud,* specially designed for nonstop crossings of the South Atlantic with a mail payload of 1,000 kg, flew nonstop from Marseille to Saint-Louis, Sénégal, covering the 3,679 km in just under 24 hours. On 3 January, 1934, it made its first trans-oceanic flight from Saint-Louis to Natal. By this time, the Couzinet 70 landplane had been extensively modified as the Couzinet 71, and, with the famous Jean Mermoz in command, made its first Saint Louis–Natal crossing on 28 May.

Having secured the necessary Brazilian authority, under Decree No.24,030 of 22 March, Air France used both of these advanced aircraft (possibly trying to make its choice between landplane or flying-boat) when it began regular monthly crossings on 24 July, 1934, alternating between the two types. The destroyer service continued to operate three times a month. By the end of the following year, three production models of the flying-boat had been delivered as Latécoère 301s, so that from 5 January, 1936, Air France was able to announce that the surface link between Dakar and Natal (or Fernando de Noronha) was suspended, and that henceforth the weekly mail service would be entirely by air.

Regrettably, during 1936, two of the Latécoère flying-boats were lost, one Laté 301, the *Ville de Buenos Aires*, on 10 February, and the original Laté 300, the *Croix du Sud,* on 7 December. The pilot of the latter, Jean Mermoz, making his 24th Atlantic crossing, died with his crew. The Couzinet 71 had been withdrawn, but the landplane emerged as the mainstay of the Air France South Atlantic service, when the four-engined Farman F.2200, *Ville de Montevideo,* entered service on 5 October. A second Farman, *Ville de Mendoza,* was added towards the end of the year, and two more, *Ville de St Louis* and *Ville de Natal*, in 1937, although one was lost. By 4 July, 1938, Air France was able to announce its 300th crossing of the South Atlantic, the aircraft for the occasion being a later version of the Farman, the F.2220 *Ville de Dakar.*

German Setback

The year 1936 was undoubtedly the zenith of German/Brazilian achievement in maintaining the passenger and mail service between Europe and South America. During the year, sixteen airship round trips were completed, carrying 1,006 passengers—almost twice as many as in 1935. This larger number was partly the result of substituting the 50-passenger *Hindenburg* for the 24-passenger *Graf Zeppelin* on seven of the sixteen trips after the former had completed its impressive North Atlantic programme. In May, Frankfurt-on-Main replaced Stuttgart as the German terminal for both mail and passenger services—a prophetic choice, as that city was to become the air traffic centre of the postwar German Federal Republic. Possibly the most important development was the transfer of the new Dornier Do 18 long-range flying-boats from North Atlantic experimental operations in November 1936, to start nonstop flights between Bathurst and Natal.

Pride comes before a fall. Justly exhilarated by the success of the two airships, and the great promise of the Dornier Do 18, the Germans entered the year 1937 with great confidence. But their hopes and expectations were shattered by the disaster of the *Hindenburg* which was destroyed in the historic conflagration at Lakehurst, New Jersey, USA, on 6 May. The impact on the general public and airline authorities alike was so emphatic that all commercial airship flights were cancelled shortly thereafter. The *Graf Zeppelin* was actually en route from South America, but Capt Hans von Schiller elected not to inform the passengers of the tragedy until arrival at Friedrichshafen. The Luftschiffbau Zeppelin line was suspended by petition of the company on 17 June, 1937, while the Serviço Aéreo Transoceanico Condor-Lufthansa was also obliged to change its routeing from Seville to Lisbon because of the Spanish Civil War.

For the remainder of the period before the Second World War the South Atlantic route was continued. The Germans operated the fine Dornier Do 18s, the French mainly the Farman F.2200s: flying-boat against landplane. In 1938, the larger Dornier Do 26 was introduced by Deutsche Lufthansa, and made 18 round trips before the war started. The French kept faith with the landplane, supplementing the trans-oceanic Farmans with Dewoitine D.338s on the Natal–Buenos Aires section of the route on 16 March, 1939.

One notable feature of the period was the continuation of the pooling arrangement between the German and French interests which dated back to the improved Berlin–Buenos Aires timing of 31 April, 1935. This was put into more formal dressing in July 1937, and of course, with the cancellation of passenger flights by airship, was confined to mail services. Political considerations aside, the German and French rivalry, though fierce in responding to the challenges of technology, navigation, and operations, was not marred by the bitterness of fanatical competition. Even before the pooling arrangements, there was much mutual respect amongst the participants, not least among the crews, who were a rather special brand of flyers, possessing great stamina and good judgement. Unfortunately the same could not be said about the early USA–Brazil efforts which ended in acrimony.

Italian Postcript

It is sometimes forgotten today that, in air transport's adolescent period, the mere appearance of an aeroplane, especially one which carried more than just the pilot, was enough to bring the citizenry to the streets. The impact of some of the Condor

Syndikat's early aircraft such as the *Atlántico,* and of the enormous *Graf Zeppelin* on its survey flights has already been mentioned. Although operationally unsuccessful, the sheer size of the Dornier Do X twelve-engined flying-boat (which had already carried 169 people on a one-hour demonstration flight in Germany) was enough to draw headlines in all the newspapers when it visited Rio de Janeiro in 1931, even though the Do X was always having technical problems and was not a success.

In that same year, the Italians also put on a great aviation show. Under the command of Marshal Italo Balbo, an Italian Air Force squadron of no less than eleven Savoia Marchetti S.55 flying-boats completed the flight from Rome to Rio. Subsequently, three Savoia Marchetti S.79 bombers, known as the *Sorci Verdi* (*Green Mice*) crossed the South Atlantic in the record time of 8 hr 20 min. The pilots were Col Attilio Biseo, Capt Nino Moscatelli, and Commander Bruno Mussolini, the son of Italy's dictator.

In March 1938, Ala Littoria, Italy's national airline, made a survey flight with a Cant Z.506 seaplane, making a round trip from Rome to Buenos Aires. The aircraft was piloted by Signor Umberto Klinger, head of Ala Littoria, who took the opportunity to negotiate the necessary rights for his company to operate to South America. This was successful, to the extent that a provisional operating certificate was granted by Brazil on 23 December of that year, under Decree No.3,481, and Argentine permission followed on 6 March, 1939. Full Brazilian authority was confirmed, by Decree No.1,401, authorizing a coastal route from Natal to the extreme south of Brazil, on 3 July, 1939.

Meanwhile, the Italian Air Ministry placed its best pilots with Atlantic experience at the disposal of Ala Littoria, including Colonel Biseo and Commander Bruno Mussolini. Arrangements were also made to transfer the terminus from Buenos Aires to Santiago.

At this point, there seems to have been some internal reorganization within Ala Littoria. For the special trans-oceanic division which had been set up by Signor Klinger, Ala Littoria Linee Atlantiche, which had taken delivery of its first three-engined Savoia Marchetti S.M.83A six/ten-passenger landplane, underwent a corporate metamorphosis, emerging as the **Linee Aeree Transcontinentali Italiane (LATI)**.

Under this company's colours, Italy opened its first passenger aeroplane service across the South Atlantic on 21 December, 1939. To achieve this, the S.M.83 had to avoid British and French territory, as the war had started, and Italy was not exactly on friendly terms with the Allies. The route was thus via Seville, Villa Cisneros, Sal Island, Natal, and Recife. A special version of the aircraft, the S.M.83T, with increased fuel tankage at the expense of payload, flew the trans-Atlantic segment. It was restricted to 500 lb of mail, and some VIP passengers were occasionally carried. LATI used the S.M.83A from Natal onwards.

For the inaugural LATI service, one aircraft left Rome and another took off from Rio, but unfortunately the northbound flight ended in tragedy, as the aeroplane crashed near Mogador, French Morocco, killing the crew and three guest passengers, all reporters. But LATI continued its weekly service, avoiding the Allied blockade, and gained official recognition in Brazil by receiving its own certificate (the previous ones had been in Ala Littoria's name) on 15 August, 1940, under the terms of Decree No.6,108. Although there was a second fatal accident in January 1941, LATI received its Argentine permission in February, and extended its route to Buenos Aires in September of that year.

The Savoia Marchetti S.M.83 I-AMER was one of the three used by Ala Littoria S.A. Linee Atlantiche on the Recife–Rio de Janeiro sector of the Italian South Atlantic service.

But the sands were running out. In the April, Brazil had already imposed a fine of $1,000 on LATI because of an extended over-ocean flight, suspected to be related to the departure schedule of Italian ships attempting to run the Allied blockade. The LATI aircraft were alleged to be informing on the position of British naval vessels, an act which was against the terms of its operating certificate.

Things went from bad to worse. On 11 December, 1941, the United States cut off fuel supplies, and on 22 December, LATI ceased operations, Trans-Atlantic service was substituted by Pan American, but not of course with through flights to Rome. All LATI's assets in Brazil were requisitioned on 13 February, 1942.

The End of Condor

Simultaneously with LATI's demise, Syndicato Condor was running into trouble with the Brazilian authorities, now clearly favouring the Allied cause, although not yet a co-belligerent. On 19 August, 1941, the name was changed to **Serviços Aéreos Condor, Ltda.**, by Decree No.3,523. Between December 1941 and April 1942, there was a progressive transfer of power from the partial German control; but the need to train new Brazilian staff, together with the total breakdown of fuel supplies, obliged Condor to cease operations altogether for a short period.

Condor owed Deutsche Lufthansa $2,700,000 (or 55 milion cruzeiros—a great deal of money in those days) and a group of Brazilian businessmen bought control of the company from the Germans, with political support directly from the President, Getulio Vargas. Dr José Bento Ribeiro Dantas was appointed Director General on 6 January, 1942.

Although many Germans were summarily dismissed, some essential technicians were retained, leading to a certain amount of speculation, especially by United States observers of the Brazilian air transport scene, that somehow Condor was being used by Germany for political and military purposes. The strategy was said to be that the airline could provide a logistics and technical base for possible German military expansion. It was even alleged that the ultimate aim was to provide, through the agency of Condor, a trans-South American chain of airfields which could be used by Nazi bombers as refuelling and technical stops en route to the Panama Canal.

Support for this theory, though not documented, had an element of plausibility. Condor had always appeared to be interested in developing route networks in remote areas such as northeast Brazil and in the Acre Territory, rather than in the denser traffic areas of the more prosperous and populated states of central and Southern Brazil. On closer inspection, however, this theory does not stand up to analysis. Other airlines were active in these areas, so that Condor was simply looking for business opportunities where competition would be less severe, at the same time pioneering air transport in new areas. In any case, Condor's expansion into the underdeveloped parts of Brazil was not only welcomed by the local State authorities, but given official recognition and support by Brazilian Government subsidies.

Certainly, Condor performed maintenance and overhaul services for all German-controlled or -supported airlines in South America, except LAB of Bolivia. These included not only VARIG and VASP in Brazil, which used German equipment, but also airlines in Peru, Ecuador, and Argentina. A glance at the map could suggest an ambitious bid to control, and to provide bases to support a choice of strategic bomber routes from Europe, via the Brazilian northeast, across to the west coast, and thence to Colombia, where German influence in AVIANCA, formerly SCADTA, was still strong.

Supporting this theory was the fact that the Focke-Wulf Fw 200 Condor was a bomber design, and was exported to Brazil by the Germans at a time when there was every reason to build up air fleets in Germany. Condor's two Fw 200s were alleged to have made long detours on the Buenos Aires–Rio de Janeiro route, flying out to sea on what were believed to be reconnaissance missions to warn blockade runners. This too could be defended by Condor, because Brazil was still officially neutral in 1941, and the aircraft were, in any case, probably carrying precious spare parts for Condor.

Dr Leopoldo Amorim, who became President of Cruzeiro do Sul (Condor's Brazilian successor) in 1969, maintains that this elaborate case made against Condor was absurd. During the critical period of 1940–41 the German technicians were being reduced in number, to be replaced by Brazilians; furthermore, not more than five per cent of these Germans were in the slightest degree interested in politics or military ideas. They were simply aviation people, charged with the pioneering spirit which possesses all those involved with the excitement of airline expansion.

An impartial verdict must lean towards Dr Amorim's viewpoint, as all the evidence against Condor was circumstantial and hypothetical. While the potential for a spectacular military adventure can be discerned from the map of German airline associates in South America, nothing ever happened to suggest that such an ambitious plot was even contemplated. In any case, Brazil declared war on Germany in August 1942, all the German employees of Condor were dismissed, and the assets (along with those of Deutsche Lufthansa A.G.) became Brazilian property, under Decree No.4,614 of 25 August, 1942.

By another Decree, No.5,197 of 16 January, 1943, the illustrious name of Condor, which during a critical period of development in Brazil had epitomized the contribution which an airline could make to the national economy, was erased for all time. The airline became **Serviços Aéreos Cruzeiro do Sul, Ltda**, a name symbolizing the southern hemisphere, but also—fortuitously—the small city of Cruzeiro do Sul, in the Acre Territory, the westernmost point on the airline's network.

By this Decree, Brazilian airline partnerships with European companies came to an end. Not only did Condor lose its name and change its identity, but the writing was also on the wall for the Brazilian partnership with North America. Panair do Brasil, Pan American's associate, announced the first sale of stock to Brazilian investors in 1942, thus terminating the Pan Am monopoly ownership. Majority control by Brazil was to be delayed, however, until after the war.

TABLE 19
Transocean Airline Partnerships
Brazilian Legal Chronology (1)
(Original Government Decrees, excluding normal extensions)

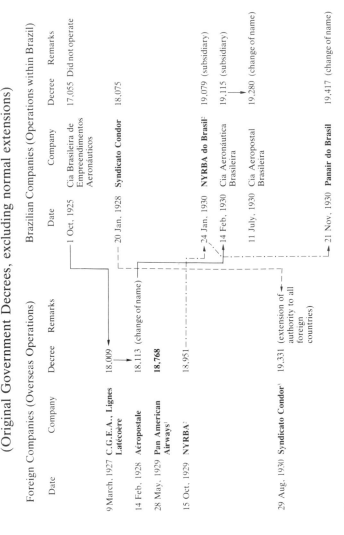

Foreign Companies (Overseas Operations)				Brazilian Companies (Operations within Brazil)			
Date	Company	Decree	Remarks	Date	Company	Decree	Remarks
				1 Oct. 1925	Cia Brasileira de Empreendimentos Aeronáuticos	17,055	Did not operate
9 March 1927	C.G.E.A., Lignes Latécoère	18,009					
14 Feb. 1928	Aéropostale	18,113	(change of name)	20 Jan. 1928	Syndicato Condor	18,075	
28 May 1929	Pan American Airways[1]	18,768					
15 Oct. 1929	NYRBA[2]	18,951		24 Jan. 1930	NYRBA do Brasil[2]	19,079	(subsidiary)
				14 Feb. 1930	Cia Aeronáutica Brasileira	19,115	(subsidiary)
				11 July 1930	Cia Aeropostal Brasileira	19,280	(change of name)
29 Aug. 1930	Syndicato Condor[3]	19,331	(extension of authority to all foreign countries)	21 Nov. 1930	Panair do Brasil	19,417	(change of name)

Notes:
1. Pan American granted cabotage rights (operations wholly within Brazil by a foreign-based airline) on 2 May 1934 (Portaria 364).
2. NYRBA and NYRBA do Brasil purchased by Pan American 15 September 1930.
3. Syndicato Condor registered in Rio de Janeiro, but majority of capital was German.

TABLE 20

Transocean Airline Partnerships
Brazilian Legal Chronology (2)
(Consolidation of Operating and Route Authority)

Date	Airline	Decree (D) or Order (Portaria) (P)	Remarks
21 Feb. 1934	**Pan American Airways**	179 (P)	Allowed to operate on coastal route within Brazil, but no traffic rights within the national territory.
5 May, 1934		364 (P)	Special permission to operate between points in Brazil (cabotage). Effective 28 September, 1934.
(18 Feb. 1938)		282 (D)	(Authorization to extend service to Asunción)
22 March, 1934	**Air France**	24,030 (D)	Succeeded **Aéropostale**
2 July, 1934		526 (P)	
6 March, 1939		1,136 (D)	
31 March, 1934	**Luftschiffbau Zeppelin, GmbH**	24,069 (D)	Specified 20 round trips per year. Special credit of 11,206,800 milreis to support airship operations, including construction of hangar at Santa Cruz. Elaborate regulations specifically for airships. Contract signed on 9 May, 1934
30 April, 1935	**Deutsche Lufthansa**	142 (D)	(Revoked by Decree No.4308, 18 May, 1942)
9 March, 1936		170 (P)	Natal designated as terminus, but allowed flights to continue southward to facilitate rapid transport of mail. But not cabotage rights, *i.e.* between points in Brazil.
6 March, 1939		1 135 (D)	
23 Dec. 1938	**Ala Littoria S.A.**	3 481 (D)	Rights from Natal to Porto Alegre but no cabotage.
3 July, 1939		1 401 (D)	
15 Aug. 1940	**S.A. Linee Trans-continentali Italiane (LATI)**	5,108 (D)	

TABLE 21
Pioneer Europe–South America Air Services

Date	Companies and Aircraft (plus ancillary service)						Remarks	Journey Time Europe–Buenos Aires
	France		Germany		Italy			
	Company	Aircraft	Company	Aircraft	Company	Aircraft		
1 March, 1928	**Aéropostale**	Latécoère 25 (plus fast destroyer)					Irregular mail	8 days
11 May, 1930	**Aéropostale**	Latécoère 28 (seaplane)					Experimental only (Mermoz)	4 days
22 March, 1930			**DLH** Hamburg Amerika	Heinkel 70 Junkers 52/3m (ocean liner) Dornier Wal			First experiment	
			Condor					
July 1930			(as 22 March, 1930)				Regular, every two weeks	6 days
18–25 May, 1930			**Luftschiffbau Zeppelin**	*Graf Zeppelin*			Survey flight	7 days (to Rio)
20 March, 1932			" "	" "			Regular passengers and mail	4½ days (to Rio)

Date	Airline	Aircraft	Airline	Service	Duration
16 Jan, 1933	Aéropostale — Couzinet 70			Survey flight	3 days
6 June, 1933		Heinkel He 70, Ju 52/3m, Dornier Wal W 34	DLH	First experiment with mid-Atlantic depot ship *Westfalen*	4 days
		⎰ (as 6 June, 1933)	Condor		
3 Feb, 1934				Regular, every two weeks	4 days
30 March, 1935				Trans-ocean night flights	3½ days
3 Jan, 1934	Air France — Latécoère 300			Survey flight	
24 July, 1934	,, — Laté 301, Couzinet 71, Blériot 5190			Regular, monthly, alternating with destroyer service	3½ days
5 Jan, 1936	,, — Laté 301, Couzinet 71, Blériot 5190			Destroyer service eliminated	3½ days
5 October, 1936	,, — Farman F. 2200			Landplane service	3½ days
Nov 1936		Dornier Do 18 (flying-boat), Dornier Do 26 (flying-boat)	DLH	Depot ship eliminated	3 days
1938					,, ,,
March 1938			Ala Littoria — Cant Z.506	Survey flight	
21 Dec, 1939			LATI — S.M.83A and 83T	Weekly landplane service	2½ days

Syndicato Condor's Junkers-G 24 P-BAHA *Potyguar*, seen operating in Brazil under primitive conditions, was built in 1925, served Luft Hansa as D-950 *Persephone* and went to South America in 1928. (*Lufthansa*)

CHAPTER NINETEEN

Bandeirantes of the Air

The Bandeirante Tradition

One of the essential stopping points on a guided tour of the city of São Paulo is the memorial to the Bandeirantes, an impressive structure of sculpture, representing a group of pioneers and evocative of a great struggle. This commemorates the *bandeirantes*, or members of the *bandeiras*, who were groups of true pioneers, and deserve to be so honoured. With São Paulo as their base, during the latter part of the 16th Century these armed columns set out to seek wealth in the form of minerals, including precious metals, and to bring back Indian slaves. In the early decades, they were comparatively unsuccessful, except in the latter category—though this is not the place to make moral judgements on their objectives.

During these treks, which often lasted several years, so that they amounted to temporary migrations, entire families took part. Ultimately, they found more than Indian slaves. Towards the end of the 17th Century—1693 to be exact—gold was discovered in what is now the State of Minas Gerais, and a gold rush began which compared with that of the mid-1800s in California and Australia, or of Alaska half a century later.

Until this time, Brazil's mineral wealth was totally undiscovered and its extent beyond anyone's wildest imagination. To the Portuguese, the colony of Brazil was simply a source of agricultural products, mainly timber and dye-wood. To state, therefore, that the bandeirantes revolutionized the economy of Brazil is not too much of an exaggeration.

Hitherto the entire population, except for indigenous Indian tribes, lived along the littoral, and São Paulo was the only city of any size which was not on the coast

380

or along a coastal waterway. The bandeirantes changed all this. A mass trek to the new mining country ensued which almost denuded some parts of the coast of its people. New towns sprang up almost overnight, much as they did in the gold rush days of the western United States and Victoria, Australia, 150 years later. Also, the name of the new State, Minas Gerais—General Mines—was apt, as there was more than gold in those mountains. Precious stones were discovered, in an abundance which has yet to be measured; for unlike many a gold rush, the deposits of diamonds, amethysts, and other gems have not yet been exhausted.

In spite of the widening of Brazil's economic base which the discovery of the minerals brought about, the country did not profit by its new-found wealth, as the vast interior was not fully exploited immediately. Economic progress was to be intermittent and sporadic, punctuated by political uncertainty and financial instability for about 250 years.

Not until after the First World War did the full commercial potential of Brazil come to be realized, or even dimly understood, either by Brazilian or world economists. The interior was still regarded as a place for adventure, or isolated exploitation such as in the rubber boom of the late 19th Century. But gradually, the expansion of railways began to have an effect, even though these were constructed as if Brazil was a collection of several separate countries. Also, the influx of enterprising new waves of colonists from Europe, especially Germans in the southern states, and Italians in São Paulo, added new initiative. Agricultural plantations, including coffee, sugarcane, and cotton, were laid out in areas which were formerly beyond the limits of convenient communication or transport. And the administrators began to realise that beyond the immediate hinterland of ports and coastal cities there were enormous land resources.

In this environment, the airlines of Brazil began to expand during the 1930s in a manner consistent with Brazil's new goals. Efficient and fast transport was essential for expansion, especially bearing in mind the long distances involved; and the successful participation of Condor, Panair do Brasil, and VASP during this period was a major factor in achieving this objective.

Into the Mato Grosso with Condor

Although the spread of air transport throughout the interior of Brazil was accomplished by airlines backed by German and United States interests, the first exploratory steps were taken by the French. In August 1928, Jean Mermoz, in a Latécoère 26, made a direct reconnaissance flight for Aéropostale from Rio de Janeiro to Corumbá and back. But it was an isolated sortie. The first permanent route was established by **Syndicato Condor** on 18 September, 1930, with a Junkers-F 13 seaplane, the *Pirajá,* piloted by Capt von Clausbruch, of Linha da Lagôa fame. The route was northward from Corumbá, rail terminus of the E. F. Noroeste do Brasil, to Cuiabá, State capital of Mato Grosso. A call was made at the river station of Porto Jofre, and the line operated once a week.

The choice of route was partly fortuitous. The aircraft had already been transferred to Corumbá, via Buenos Aires and Asunción, during the emergency of the Paraguay-Bolivia war, and Condor enterprisingly found a good use for the aircraft without bringing it back to Rio de Janeiro.

On 1 June, 1932, the route was extended eastwards to Campo Grande, a community on the railway, halfway across southern Mato Grosso, and a growing ranching centre. Here, the flights connected with the night trains to São Paulo. On 8 September, 1933, the final air link was completed, and Condor service began

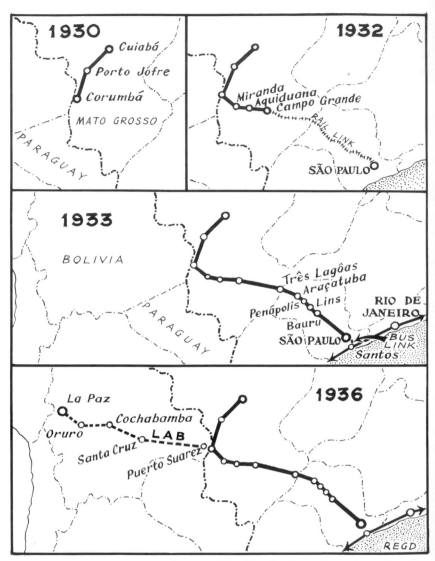

44. Into the Mato Grosso with Condor, 1930–1936. Syndicato Condor's first Brazilian inland route was isolated from the coastal service. A few years later, an extension from the coast replaced the rail link, but a bus was still necessary to connect São Paulo with Santos, as the latter had no land airport. This route to the Mato Grosso was eventually to become a vital section of a German-sponsored transcontinental air route, in association with Bolivian and Peruvian airlines.

between São Paulo and Cuiabá. Strangely, at this time, there was no direct air connection between the new route and the rest of Condor's network, as São Paulo, being inland and elevated on a plateau, offered only airfield facilities, and Junkers-F 13 landplanes had to be used. A special bus service connected São Paulo with Santos, where Condor's flying-boats and seaplanes provided the coastal service to the south and north.

In April 1936, this Mato Grosso service of Condor was co-ordinated with the main route of Lloyd Aéreo Boliviano (LAB), connecting at Corumbá with the eastern terminus of the Bolivian airline at Puerto Suárez, across the Paraguay River. LAB had been founded twelve years previously, and had used mainly German equipment, so that the association with Condor had technical advantages as well as operational ones.

The Military and Naval Post Services

A substantial part of the credit for developing inland airline services must go to the Brazilian armed forces, which performed considerable pioneer work in the true *bandeirante* tradition throughout the 1930s. The idea of a military mail service was first conceived by a group of War Ministry officials, notably Eduardo Gomes, Lemos Cunha, and Casimiro Montenegro, with tacit support from the Minister of War, General José Fernandes Leite de Castro. The idea was also supported with much enthusiasm by the military pilots who were confined to training within a 10 km radius of the Campo dos Afonsos, the military airfield in Rio de Janeiro.

At first the new service was called the Serviço Postal Aéreo Militar (SPAM), but this was soon superseded by the name **Correio Aéreo Militar (CAM)**, or Military Air Post.

In May 1931, Major Gomes formed the Grupo Mistos de Aviação, using a small fleet of Curtiss Fledglings. Some of these had been acquired by the Brazilian Government for use during the emergency of the revolution of 1930, while others were from the Força Publica de São Paulo, based at the Campo de Marte in that city.

The Fledglings were well-named. Having already seen service in the United States, they were slow, frail-looking, open-cockpit biplanes, seemingly far too fragile to undertake the formidable tasks which Gomes had conceived for them in the Brazilian outback.

In preparation for the main tasks, the first CAM flight was made on 12 June, 1931, by Lieuts Casimiro Montenegro and Nelson F. Lavenère-Wanderley, carrying mail from Rio de Janeiro to São Paulo. Returning on 15 June, the service was maintained at a frequency of three a week. Then Montenegro left Rio by land to arrange for the preparation of landing fields along the route of the railway line to Goiás (later renamed Goiânia), the capital of the state of that name, and at the perimeter of the populated area of south central Brazil.

The inaugural flight was to have been made on 12 October, when Montenegro and Wanderley left the Campo dos Afonsos in the Fledgling K.263. Unhappily, they had to make a forced landing before even reaching São Paulo, and the aircraft was damaged. However, over a week later, on 21 October, 1931, the CAM was successfully launched, when Wanderley and Lieut Araripe reached Goiás safely, having flown for two days, with night stops at São Paulo and Ipameri, and five other intermediate landings. Regular service began on this, CAM's first postal route, on 1 November (see Map 45).

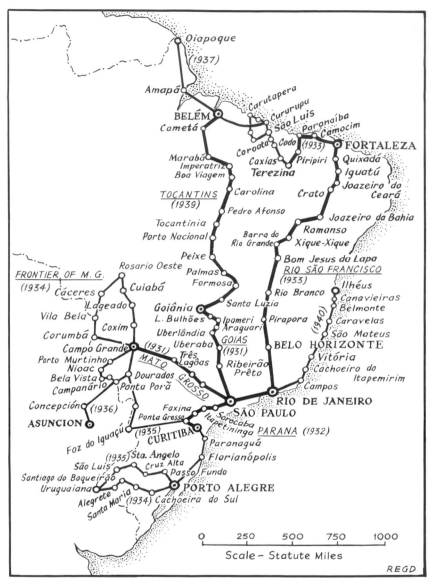

45. CAM, 1931–1940. The Correio Aéreo Militar played an important role in developing many difficult air routes into the inhospitable interior of Brazil. Operated primarily as a mail service, it did, however, also carry essential government personnel needed for administrative and other social services. In this map, the names of the major route subdivisions are underlined.

This pioneer effort proved to be an exacting training ground for a large number of pilots to gain priceless experience in mastering the techniques of taking off and landing at poor airfields, flying and navigating in erratic weather, and making the proper corrections to inaccurate maps and unreliable instruments. A notable navigational aid was introduced early in 1932 when all the stations along the railway line were identified with large white letters painted on the roofs; while beyond the terminus of the line (which had not yet reached Goiás) large letters were laid out on the ground at key points.

During the summer of 1932, the service was interrupted by another revolution in São Paulo, but when this emergency was over, the CAM was reinforced by the addition of a new fleet of Waco CSO biplanes, allocated by the War Ministry.

From this time, the CAM steadily expanded its postal route network. By the end of 1932, a route had been opened to the State of Paraná, terminating at the capital, Curitiba, and to Campo Grande, in the State of Mato Grosso. Then, on 15 February, 1933, the CAM spread its wings widely by opening a long route. It followed the course of the São Francisco River, northwards out of the State of Minas Gerais, for the first time reaching the Central Atlantic coast of Brazil by the direct air route, rather than circuitously around the coast, as flown by Panair do Brasil and Condor. After preparatory work on the surface terrain by Montenegro and Lieut Sampaio Macedo, Wanderley and Macedo made the first flight to Fortaleza, with two overnight stops at Bom Jesus da Lapa and Crato, plus eleven other stops, in two days. In December the line was extended to Teresina.

Further strengthening in many ways occurred in 1934. Twenty-five Waco Model C cabin biplanes arrived to augment CAM's growing fleet. With a range of 800 km, cruising at 200 km/h, and able to carry 200 kg of mail and passengers, they were a great improvement over the older equipment. This was demonstrated when, on 16 August of that year, a Model C flew from Fortaleza to Rio de Janeiro in only one day, between 03.30 and 19.00, yet stopping at every mail pickup point on the way.

By this time, the CAM was accepted as an integral part of Brazil's airline system. Although primarily a postal service, with the carriage of mail as its official role, it was also used to transport essential supplies to remote communities, and occasionally to carry special passengers such as doctors, government officials, or prospectors. The original postal regulations covered by Law 4,911 of 12 January, 1925, were imprecise; but on 28 April, 1933, President Vargas signed Decree No.22,673 which tightened the legal framework, at the same time simplifying an uncertain combination of ad hoc instructions. A uniform standard of air post rate-setting was established, with three levels: intra-state, inter-state, and international. Payment was charged by weight and air post services were administered by the Director General of Posts and Telegraphs, in association with the Ministry of Transport and Public Works.

Significantly, and giving fresh authority to CAM, on 6 July, 1934, Decree No.24,603 authorized it to carry mail, under the same conditions as any commercial airline. With its widening network of pioneering routes, the CAM was seen to be a priceless asset to Brazilian aviation, not only in providing rigorous training for aircrew in a country which was to depend so much on air transport for its future economic development; but at the same time providing a practical service to the community by carrying the mails.

Expansion continued. Lines were opened in the State of Rio Grande do Sul, on 23 July, 1934, and to the frontier of the Mato Grosso, adjacent to Paraguay, in August. Both of these took the form of circular services which aimed to bring air postal service to the maximum number of communities in those regions. On 23 March, 1935, a new line linked Curitiba and the Iguassu Falls (Foz do lguaçú), at that time separated from the developed area by extensive forested terrain.

And so the development continued. Thirty Waco F-5 aircraft were delivered during 1935. The Fortaleza–Teresina segment of the northern route was extended to the mouth of the Amazon at Belém on 14 July, 1935, and on 14 November a survey flight was made along the Tocantins River, in the northern part of the State of Goiás, hitherto considered to be virtually inaccessible, and possibly dangerous because of Indian tribes.

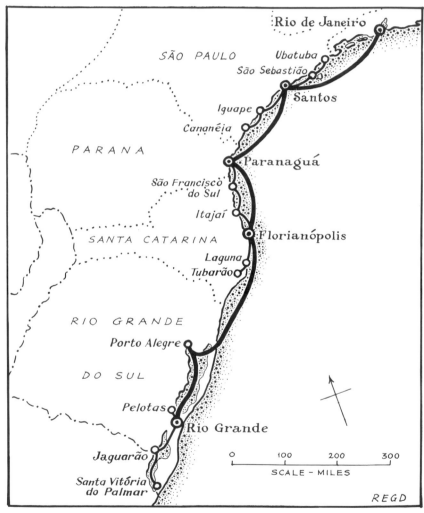

46. CAN, 1934–1940. Although not operating as extensively as the CAM, the Brazilian Navy also contributed to the provision of air mail services along the coast. In 1941, it combined with the military operation to form Correio Aéreo Nacional.

In 1936, in addition to two more survey flights on the Tocantins route, CAM made its first international sortie, when a Waco Model C flew from Rio to Asunción in Paraguay. In a commendable example of co-operation, when the Waco was damaged at Asunción, the Paraguayan Air Force lent a Breda aircraft to the Brazilian crew in which to carry the return mails as far as Campo Grande, where a connection was made with another CAM Waco. During the year CAM carried 23,907 kg of mail, and made 6,450 flights, maintaining a weekly schedule over most of the routes operated.

On 22 July, 1937, CAM reached even further north, with a Belém–Amapá link, and this was extended to Oiapoque, on the frontier with French Guiana, on 4 August. Finally, to complete a formidable programme of route development, the Tocantins River route was finally started on 31 January, 1939, when Major Hortencio Pereira de Brito and Capt Roberto de Assis Jatahy flew a Bellanca from Goiás to Belém, with twelve intermediate stops.

During this period of ceaseless expansion by the Military Postal Service, the Brazilian Navy also made its contribution, albeit in a more modest dimension than the impressive map of routes which adorned the walls of the CAM administrators' offices. The **Correio Aéreo Naval (CAN)** initiated service along the coast of Brazil in 1934, the first flight being made by a Waco CSO, fitted with floats, from the Galeão naval base in Rio de Janeiro harbour, as far as Florianópolis. The pilots were Capt Tenentes Ismar Brasil and Alvaro Araujo.

In 1936, this line was extended as far south as Rio Grande, and the trunk route was complemented by a number of short routes radiating from the main staging points, at Santos, Florianópolis, Paranaguá, and Rio Grande (see Map 46). CAN's fleet consisted of Waco CSOs, supplemented by Waco Cs and F-5s, landplanes as well as floatplanes.

In March 1936, the Aircraft Division of the Naval Post Service was created, with headquarters at the Naval Aviation Base at Rio de Janeiro, and responsible directly to the Director General of Aeronautics. This later became known as the Postal Aircraft Group of the Southern Route.

Both the CAM and the CAN were eventually absorbed into the new organization, at the creation of the Força Aérea Brasileira (FAB) under the terms of Decree-Law 2,961 on 20 January, 1941. The mail service provided by the amalgamation of the two former services became known as the **Correio Aéreo Nacional (CAN)** and its work was to continue until the commercial airlines had developed to a stage whereby it became redundant.

Panair do Brasil Penetrates the Amazon

The bitter infighting which characterized the foundation of **Panair do Brasil** had finally ended with Juan Trippe's *fait accompli,* with the Brazilian airline a wholly-owned subsidiary of Pan American Airways. The fleet assigned to the Brazilian register consisted of four Consolidated Commodores and four Sikorsky S-38s, all flying-boats. Their duties were to provide the essential coastal link from Belém (the terminus of Pan Am's own service through the eastern Caribbean and the Guianas) southwards along the entire coast of Brazil.

The first aircraft under the Panair flag carried the mails from Belém to Santos on 28 November, 1930. The company headquarters were established in Rio de Janeiro, the maintenance base at Belém, and the aircraft at first had all-US crews.

On 2 March, 1931, passenger service was introduced on this section of the route, the journey time from Belém to Rio de Janeiro being five days, a fairly

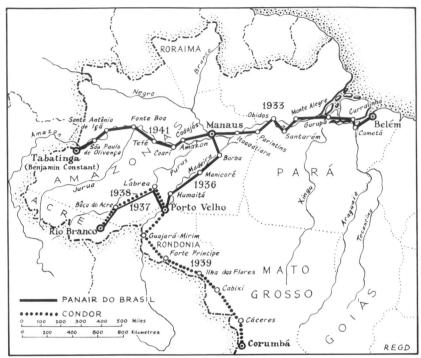

47. Panair do Brasil and Condor in the Amazon Basin, 1933–1941. Panair do Brasil, then a subsidiary of Pan American Airways, pioneered the air routes along the Amazon and Madeira Rivers during the mid-1930s. Then Syndicato Condor extended its Mato Grosso route to the Acre Territory, and Panair reached the Peruvian/Colombian frontier so that air transport served to open up the most remote corners of this vast country.

leisurely affair, with night stops. But this was soon augmented by an extension, on 23 November, as far south as Buenos Aires. The longer route still took only five days to fly, with night stops at Fortaleza, Salvador, Rio de Janeiro, and Porto Alegre. By this time, the Panair fleet had grown to five Commodores and five S-38s. The graceful Commodores were the flagships of the line, offering the kind of comfort and, for the period, the kind of reliability which Ralph O'Neill had originally visualized.

The following year was comparatively uneventful, except for a bizarre incident which resulted in the loss of one of the S-38s. One of these amphibians, P-BDAD, was stolen on 25 September, 1932, by a group of São Paulo revolutionaries who, however, forgot to take the precaution of taking a qualified pilot with them. The aircraft flew for about 25 km, and then crashed.

In 1933, Panair do Brasil entered the ranks of the aerial bandeirantes when it started a service in the north which echoed the pioneering spirit of Condor's westward sortie into the Mato Grosso. In October 1933, the first Sikorsky S-38 scheduled service was completed from Belém to the city of Manaus.

This, the State capital of Amazonas, was situated 900 miles (1,500 km) from the estuary of the Amazon River. Such was the magnitude of this great waterway that ocean-going ships called at Manaus, and even at Iquitos, Peru. Although some of

Panair do Brasil's Sikorsky S-38B amphibian P-BDAD *Pernambuco* was originally a NYRBA aircraft and it is likely that the name was only used by NYRBA.

the products, notably rubber, of the enormous jungle territory were no longer significant to Brazil's economy, and Manaus, with its once-busy waterfront, and city amenities which boasted an opera house, was only a shadow of its former self, there was still much commerce along the Amazon. Thus, Panair supplied a real need, and the Belém–Manaus service was to become almost a main route, with other feeder lines radiating from the Amazonian metropolis.

Meanwhile, the coastal service was expanding steadily, with the US airline partnership consolidating its position, in competition with the French and German enterprises. In March 1934, a second weekly coastal service was added, and effective from 28 September of that year, Pan American was granted the cabotage rights to join with its subsidiary, Panair, in carrying passengers and freight between any points along the Brazilian coast. In 1935, the first Brazilian pilots took over from the US crews, and the following year a maintenance hangar was completed, with office buildings, at the new Santos Dumont Airport built on the reclaimed land in Guanabara Bay in Rio de Janeiro, only a shortish walk from the commercial centre of the city.

In February 1936 two new amphibian flying-boats were delivered to Panair do Brasil. These were the Fairchild 91, or XA-942A, with about the same

This little known amphibian was one of a small batch of eight-passenger aircraft ordered by Pan American Airways for high-speed services in South America and China. They were built by Kreider-Reisner Aircraft Company, a Fairchild subsidiary, and known as Fairchild 91s or XA-942s. The first was completed in early 1935. The XA-942A model, seen here at Belém in 1937, was one of at least two operated by Panair do Brasil. The engine was a Pratt & Whitney Hornet or Wright Cyclone.

389

payload-carrying ability as the S-38s, but faster, even though single-engined. Although they were called 'flying pipes' by some uncomplimentary aircrew, they served Panair well under difficult operating conditions. One of them, PP-PAP, led an eventful life. On 8 May, 1939, it sank in the Amazon at Santarém, but was salvaged. Then in 1942, after an accident at Belém, it was shipped by sea to Rio for repair, but was too corroded and was written off. The other one plodded on (if such a term can be applied to an amphibian—perhaps 'paddled' is more appropriate) until retired in 1945.

The addition of the two Fairchilds augmented the fleet strength of Panair's Amazon squadron so that the Belém–Manaus line could be extended to Porto Velho, the city which had been created under unusual circumstances. Under a treaty agreement with Bolivia after a boundary dispute at the turn of the 20th Century, a railway had been built from this, the furthest navigable point on the Madeira River, to Guajará-Mirim. The unnavigable cataracts of the Madeira and Guajará Falls were thus by-passed, and the fertile Beni cattle country of Bolivia gained more convenient access to the sea. Just as Condor had reached Bolivia from the south, Panair do Brasil now served the same inland country from the north.

Early in 1937, an even longer tentacle of the meandering amphibious route took the Panair house-flag as far as Rio Branco, the capital of the Acre Territory; but this segment was transferred to Syndicato Condor the following year.

VASP links the Big Cities

While a map illustrating the expansion of air routes in Brazil during the 1930s rightly emphasizes the contribution made towards opening up the interior, the airlines were also active in the heavily-populated and more developed south central area, where the major cities were progressive and wealthy, and showing signs of realising the opportunity to expand commercial activity.

This area comprises the States of Rio de Janeiro, São Paulo, Paraná, and the southern half of Minas Gerais. Although, by a considerable margin, São Paulo and Rio de Janeiro, capitals of the States of the same name, were the largest cities, the first inter-city link was between São Paulo and Curitiba, the capital of Paraná.

Early in 1933, **Aerolloyd Iguassú** was founded in Curitiba by the firm of Mate Leão, which acquired two small Klemm Kl 31A three-seat monoplanes, registered in June as PP-IAA and PP-IAB. On 30 June, Government Decree No.22,878 authorized operations, and the Curitiba–São Paulo route was inaugurated at a frequency of four a week on 20 July. Although one of the Klemms crashed in December, Iguassú extended southwards in 1934 to Joinville, and in 1935 to Florianópolis, both in the State of Santa Catarina, having added three five-seat Stinson Reliants to its sole remaining aircraft.

Unfortunately, the airline was not profitable, and the owners of Mate Leão lost their enthusiasm, finally selling the company to VASP on 28 October, 1939 (Decree No.4,812).

Little Aerolloyd Iguassú was overshadowed by its near-neighbour in São Paulo, where a combination of powerful interests was able to put together the necessary financial backing to found a wholly Brazilian firm of some substance. **Viação Aérea São Paulo, S.A. (VASP)** was organized on 4 November, 1933, by the City, State, and Municipal Bank of São Paulo. Seventy-five per cent of the capital was from the City and State, so that this was more than simply a private venture, seeking to make money. It could be termed as an experiment in communications by public administrative agencies, whose interest was in development of the State, and who recognized the importance of fast transport.

VASP's first two aircraft were acquired on 12 November—only a week after the company was founded. They were imported from Britain, two small Monospar ST.4 three-seat monoplanes, named *Bartholomeu de Gusmão* (PP-SPA) and *Edu Chaves* (PP-SPB). Operating authority duly received on 31 March, 1934, by Decree No.20,070, VASP began scheduled passenger and mail service on 16

48. VASP and Iguassú, 1933–1940. Aerolloyd Iguassú was the fourth airline to start commercial air services in Brazil, but it was absorbed by the more powerful VASP, which was backed by the richest city, the richest State, and the richest bank in Brazil, all centred on São Paulo.

April on two routes: São Paulo–Ribeirão Prêto–Uberaba, and São Paulo–São Carlos–Rio Prêto. Service had to be curtailed after a few months, however, as the airfield at Ribeirão Prêto was condemned.

VASP was not deterred by such minor inconveniences. In November 1934 a six-seat de Havilland 84 Dragon biplane (PP-SPC) arrived, at the time the largest landplane in Brazil. More difficulty was then experienced, as the Campo de Marte airfield in São Paulo was flooded, interrupting operations; but it's an ill wind . . . a decision was made to build a new airport at Congonhas, on a low plateau close to the edge of what was then the outer limits of the city. Congonhas was to become to São Paulo what Santos Dumont was to Rio de Janeiro, both airports being within very convenient distance from the city centres. They quickly became the focus of commercial activity much in the same manner as when railway stations were established in the world's big cities at the time.

At the end of 1933, VASP ordered two Junkers-Ju 52/3m landplanes from Theodore Wille and Cia, a German importing firm closely connected with the Condor organization. These two 17-passenger, three-crew aircraft arrived in July 1936 and were named *Cidade de São Paulo* (PP-SPD) and *Cidade de Rio de Janeiro* (PP-SPE) They went into service on 5 August, 1936, inaugurating a new passenger route between São Paulo and Rio de Janeiro, and thereby starting a new era in the chronology of Brazilian air transport.

The service frequency was six a week, and the journey time for the 373 km was 100 minutes, later reduced to 75. This compared very favourably with the fastest rail time of 15 hr by the Central do Brasil, effectively offering the choice between a two-hour trip or the waste of a whole day. The State Government of São Paulo granted a generous annual subsidy to sustain the service.

VASP's luck with its operations was no better than that of the other early struggling airlines of Brazil, all of whom had their problems. VASP did it in style—both Junkers aircraft sustained minor damage on the first day, and did not resume service until 30 November. However, the service was immediately popular and business was soon brisk; in July 1937 a second daily frequency was added, and a third Junkers-Ju 52/3m ordered, the *Cidade de Santos* (PP-SPF), which was put into service in September.

VASP's de Havilland 84 Dragon II PP-SPC is seen at Rio de Janeiro on 1 November, 1934, after its first flight from São Paulo.

VASP's Junkers-Ju 52/3m PP-SPE *Cidade do Rio de Janeiro* at São Paulo. (*VASP*)

While VASP was establishing what was, within a few years, to become one of the world's busiest air routes, Panair do Brasil also turned its attention to inter-city business traffic. In October, a complete modernization of the fleet was undertaken, with Sikorsky S-43 eighteen-seat flying-boats—the 'Baby Clippers'—gradually replacing the Commodores, and Lockheed 10E Electra ten-seat landplanes opening up new possibilities for route expansion into the interior, other than following river routes such as in the Amazon basin.

On 23 March, 1937, the Lockheed 10E PP-PAS opened the first service from Rio de Janeiro to the State capital of Minas Gerais, Belo Horizonte, one of Brazil's emerging modern cities, which then became the focal point of other routes. In 1939 new routes radiated to Uberaba, to Governador Valadares, and, most importantly, direct to São Paulo, via Poços de Caldas, a summer health resort. São Paulo had already replaced Santos on the Rio–Porto Alegre route, so that Panair was in the privileged position of being able to offer scheduled air service on all sides of the triangle formed by the three largest and most prosperous cities in central Brazil. By 1940 the Rio–Belo Horizonte frequency was daily, and the Rio–São Paulo route was flown five days a week.

By this time a milestone had been reached by Panair do Brasil, when in September 1938 all the remaining US pilots were replaced by Brazilians. But perhaps an even more far-reaching event was the arrival in June 1940 of Panair's first 14-passenger Douglas DC-2 (PP-PAY).

Feeder Services in the Northeast

After completing its route from São Paulo to the Bolivian frontier in 1934, Condor spent the next three years consolidating and expanding its trunk coastal route, now integrated with the German South Atlantic Mail Service. The Rio de Janeiro—Porto Alegre route was extended to Montevideo and Buenos Aires on 14 April, 1934, and onward to Santiago, Chile, on 28 September, 1935. In the north, the coastal route was extended from Natal to Fortaleza in December of that year, and on 11 April, 1936, the three-engined Junkers-Ju 52/3m, on floats, began a two-day service between Rio de Janeiro and Belém, with an overnight stop at Recife.

Having reached out as far as the under-developed northeast, where surface transport could boast only a few lines of railway and very few roads, Condor now turned its attention to that region by developing feeder services to the main route, thus providing a vital social service to the community. Once again, the trusty Junkers-F 13 was used. On 18 October, 1936, a route from Parnaíba, on the Atlantic coast, was opened along the River Parnaíba as far south as Floriano, stopping at small landing stations along the route, including one at the State capital of Piauí, Teresina.

A year later, the route was systematically extended westwards to the Tocantins River, at Carolina, which was reached on 14 December, 1937. Finally, early in 1939, the Tocantins, like the Parnaíba, became the highway for the F 13—succeeded by the Ju 52/3m—and the route extended northward, to complete three sides of an irregular quadrilateral, to terminate at Belém.

The Junkers-F 13 *Pirajá* of Syndicato Condor opened the first airline service in the interior of Brazil, on 18 September, 1930, following its transfer to Corumbá, via Buenos Aires and Asunción, during the Chaco war between Paraguay and Bolivia. (*Lufthansa*)

But the usefulness of the F 13 in the Brazilian Northeast was not ended. On 23 October, 1939, more feeder services were started with F 13 landplanes to provide air travel to almost every town in the State of Maranhão, mainly into areas where railways did not exist, roads were unsurfaced, and even the rivers—often the main source of transport—were quite inadequate. Exactly one year later, the same innovation was made in the State of Ceará, linking up with the Parnaíba River route, and on 3 May, 1941, an additional circular route was added in Maranhão.

Needless to state, these Condor services were received with great enthusiasm by the local administration, and by the people of the States of Maranhão, Piauí, and Ceará. An impartial examination of the conditions under which the air routes were established, and of the ground installations, suggests that any possible plan to provide landing grounds for German bombers—a theory advanced by some US military strategists—would have required a far more substantial establishment and organization than the modest grass fields for F 13s which characterized the operation. And in any case, the first services into the northeast had been by the CAM, for whom the landing strips were first prepared. On the other hand, all this frantic activity by Condor in an area directly athwart an important United States strategic supply route raised justifiable suspicions among US military observers who could see no reason for an airline to open uneconomic routes when it was already financially unsound.

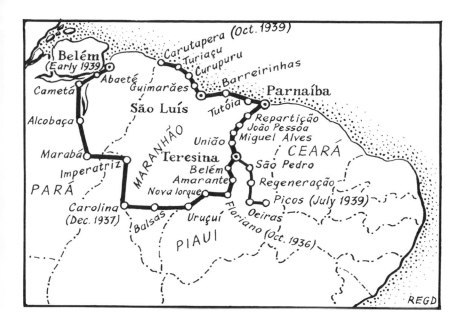

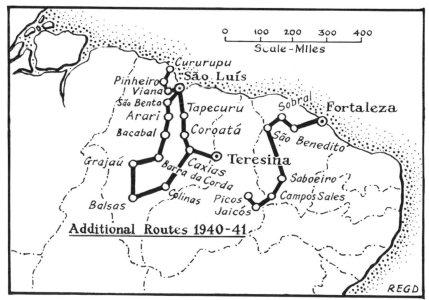

49. Condor Development in the Northeast, 1936–1941. Syndicato Condor continued its tradition of developing feeder routes as well as trunk lines, especially in the northeast of Brazil, where communications were poor. Associated as it was with the German national airline, then controlled by the Nazi Government, the Junkers aircraft which performed such useful service nevertheless caused some apprehension among United States observers.

Beyond the Brazilian Pale

Towards the end of the 15th Century, during the early years of the English occupation of Ireland, the great earldoms of the Irish were separated from the area around Dublin. Within this area, which became known as the Pale, about the size of a large county, mediaeval English law and order prevailed, but the area Beyond the Pale was regarded as something less than civilized, if not barbaric.

The same analogy could be applied to the Acre Territory, a strip of land bordering Bolivia and Peru, far off in Brazil's wild west, and where the Brazilians had been in conflict with the original settlers, Bolivian rubber-planters. After a dispute, the Acreanos actually set up a small independent republic in 1899, but the area fell under Brazilian rule in 1903 by purchase from Bolivia.

Into this far-off land eventually came Syndicato Condor, on a survey flight by the Junkers-W 34 seaplane *Taquary* which arrived at Rio Branco, the newly-established capital of the Territory, on 5 May, 1936. Military strategists later suggested that this sortie, too, was part of a plan to establish bases for German aggrandisement; but in fact Panair do Brasil was the first airline to serve the Acre Territory, although it did not sustain the service.

Condor took over only after Panair withdrew, making its first flight between Rio Branco and Porto Velho, the important port on the Madeira River, on 15 November, 1938. Once again, the *Taquary* was on hand, making the journey simultaneously with its sister aircraft, the *Tibagy*, in opposite directions. Condor connected with Panair's Amazon service at Porto Velho.

Shortly afterwards, on 6 February, 1939, another Condor Junkers-W 34, *Tiéte*, completed the link southward from Porto Velho to Corumbá, following the courses of the Mamoré and Guaporé Rivers. Although it is highly doubtful if anyone made the attempt, or even contemplated such an expedition, a circular air tour of Brazil, covering about 10,000 km, was now a practical possibility.

The Last Frontier

By a curious historical paradox, the last State of Brazil to receive regular airline service, apart from that originally provided in 1931 by the Correio Aéreo Militar, was Goiás. Only twenty years later it was to accommodate the new Federal Capital, Brasília, the site for which had already been selected before the days of air transport. The first railway did not penetrate this land of savannah and scrub until the late 1920s, and communication from the capital, Goiás (later Goiânia) to the central coastal states was partly by mule-train.

The Ministry of Transport and Public Works was authorized by Decree-Law No. 144 of 29 December, 1937, to establish a route from Uberaba (Minas Gerais) to Goiânia. A contract was then signed with Viação Aérea São Paulo (VASP) on 4 April, 1938, which included a provision for a subsidy of 3 milreis per kilometre. VASP started service on 1 August, 1938.

All was not well, however. The Government expressed concern over the standards of service, questioning whether the de Havilland Dragon used was adequate, and emphasizing the need for good radio-communication. It thereupon suspended VASP's certificate, under the terms of Decree-Law 760, until 31 December, 1938. This date was postponed by Decree-Law 1,137 of 6 March, 1939, presumably while VASP was coping with the heavy traffic on the São Paulo–Rio route, and planning its expansion to the south, through the take-over of Aerolloyd Iguassú.

The problems were finally settled on 14 October, 1939, under the terms of Decree-Law 1,682, whose specific clauses indicated the concern displayed by the Brazilian aviation authorities—although the citizens of São Paulo, always vigorously independent, would probably claim that this was a case of a Federal Government thwarting the energies and enterprise of an individual State—a situation familiar to all large countries.

This important decree recognized that, for the practical operation of an Uberaba-Goiânia route, the service should start from a metropolis such as São Paulo—it will be recalled that VASP had been obliged to suspend its service as far as Uberaba because of airfield problems en route. A subsidy was granted at the rate of 6 milreis per kilometre, and the aircraft used was specified to have three engines and 17 seats, which was tantamount to nominating the Junkers-Ju 52/3m for the job. Interestingly, the Decree stressed the strategic importance of Goiânia as a gateway to the far west and the far north, a visionary clause, bearing in mind that twenty years later, a mass migration to the State of Goiás was to herald the building of Brasília, and the city of Goiânia itself was to multiply several times.

And so VASP finally received its contract, on 21 December, 1939, and started service, with the Ju 52/3m, on 2 January, 1940. Further expansion occurred when the São Paulo–Curitiba–Florianópolis route taken over from Iguassú, and begun under VASP's colours on 30 November, 1939, was extended further to Porto Alegre on 28 November of the following year. With service frequency on the São Paulo–Rio route up to three a day each way, a handsome fleet of four Junkers-Ju 52/3ms, with two more on order, and service between the capital cities of the six richest southern states of Brazil, in addition to reaching northward to Goiânia, VASP seemed to be heading for great things. Some idea of the obvious potential for airline enterprise in Brazil at this time can be deduced from the competitive schedules between São Paulo and Curitiba, capitals of the two richest coffee states: train 27 hr, car 10 hr, VASP 1½ hr.

But this success was dampened by several events: a tragic crash, the worst in Brazilian air history at that time, occurred when on 8 November, 1940, one of VASP's Junkers-Ju 52/3ms (PP-SPF) collided in flight with an Argentine de Havilland 90 Dragonfly over Botafogo Bay, immediately after taking off from Rio's Santos Dumont Airport. Although two new aircraft were delivered in the summer of 1941 (one of them running the Allied blockade in the process) there were great difficulties with spares, and VASP had to improvise by making its own. Nevertheless, service on the whole route south of São Paulo had to be suspended later in the year, such was the strain on VASP's resources.

Back at the Ranch

With such extraordinary efforts being made throughout Brazil by a number of airlines plus the Military and Naval Post Service, the relative introversion of VARIG, the one remaining airline still not mentioned in this chapter, seems inexplicable, bearing in mind that it was to become one of the world's greatest airlines by the 1960s. Nevertheless, the facts are that, from its birth in 1927 until 1942, **Viação Aérea Rio-Grandense (VARIG)** never ventured out of its parent State of Rio Grande do Sul; and not until 1946 did it provide service to another Brazilian State.

VARIG was founded by loyal citizens of Rio Grande do Sul, largely of German origin, who nevertheless were known by other Brazilians as *gauchos*, a term strictly applicable to those of mixed Spanish and Indian stock, but one which

397

implied grudging respect for a people of great endurance and dignity. Certainly VARIG was to draw upon reserves of the former quality, even though there were times when it seemed a little hard-pressed for the latter.

For more than a decade after its dramatic involvement with the foundation of the first air route in Brazil, VARIG's ambitions did not spread further than to operate an airline which would faithfully serve the State of Rio Grande. Its finances were not extensive, and in those days there was not a commercial aircraft built which stood a chance of making a profit without some kind of subsidy. Thus, VARIG was partly dependent on outside help, mainly from the State or the cities of Rio Grande do Sul; and if the State was in financial difficulty, then so was VARIG. However, the little airline cut its coat accordingly, and modestly restricted its operations to serving the main cities of the State and their citizens.

The early years were not helped by the Brazilian political revolution in October 1930 which brought Getulio Vargas to power. This event was not the best traffic stimulant, and during this period, VARIG kept itself alive by keeping its fleet to the barest minimum. Although two Klemm L 25s (P-BBAC and P-BBAD) were acquired from Empresa de Transportes Aéreos (E.T.A.) on 16 November, 1929, these small craft were hardly a good substitute for the Dornier Merkur *Gaúcho* and the Dornier Wal *Atlântico,* both of which were sold back to Condor in the summer of 1930. To complicate matters, one of the Klemms crashed on 17

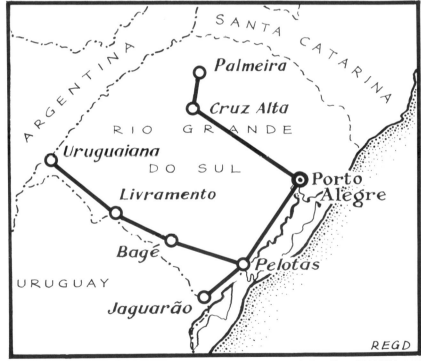

50. VARIG, 1938. Before the war, Syndicato Condor, Panair do Brasil, and VASP began to develop into airlines of considerable stature, comparable with those in Europe or the USA. VARIG meanwhile remained within its home state of Rio Grande do Sul as a diminutive feeder airline.

The Junkers-F 13 *Santa Cruz* served VARIG from 1932 until 1948. First introduced in Germany in July 1919, this was the last F 13 in regular airline service. (*VARIG*)

September, 1930, so at the end of that year VARIG subsisted on one small aeroplane and in fact for a short while stopped operations altogether.

At the beginning of 1931, the company staggered to its feet again. On 3 January, *Gaucho* (presumably leased from Condor) resumed service on the single route Porto Alegre–Pelotas–Rio Grande; two small aircraft, a Morane-Saulnier MS.130 trainer and a Nieuport-Delage 641 six-seater were acquired, and then, on 18 January, the Junkers-A 50 Junior (P-BAAE) entered service, and actually opened a new route, Porto Alegre–Santa Cruz–Santa Maria, on 23 February.

But this heady expansion was short-lived. The Junkers crashed in April, after only three months service, and sadly the pilot Franz Nuelle, one of the original Condor Syndikat demonstration crew of the Linha da Lagôa, was injured so badly as to never fly again. By the end of the year, VARIG was in dire straits again, and at the beginning of 1932, underwent a complete reorganization, with the help of the State Government, which lent the money to purchase two Junkers-F 13s from Germany. The F 13 *Livramento* (PP-VAF) entered service on 18 April, 1932, to be joined shortly afterwards by its sister aircraft, the *Santa Cruz* (PP-VAG).

The fleet thus augmented, new routes were added, from Porto Alegre to Cruz Alta, and to Santana do Livramento, via Bagé, both by *Livramento* on 18 and 19 April respectively. The Cruz Alta route was extended to Palmeira in 1933, by which time two more Junkers-A 50s had been delivered during 1932, but of which one had been quickly written off.

However, the news from VARIG was not all bad. In 1936, during which year Santa Cruz was added to this strictly local service network, the Rio Grande airline became the first airline in Brazil to operate a daily service, when its frequency between Porto Alegre and Pelotas was increased to eight a week. Apparently bent on testing the products of every German manufacturer of commercial aircraft, a four-seat Messerschmitt Me 108B Taifun was added in the autumn of 1936, but was cancelled from the register shortly afterwards, after a crash landing. Then a larger ten-passenger Messerschmitt M 20b entered service on 30 April, 1937, and the Livramento route was extended to Uruguaiana.

At last VARIG was beginning to see some relief from its struggles during the early and mid-1930s. In May 1938, a splendid 17-seat Junkers-Ju 52/3m, the *Mauá* (PP-VAL), was purchased from South African Airways, and went into service on 6 July. Later that year, VARIG participated in an interesting transport exercise.

When, late in 1938, it extended the Pelotas route to Jaguarão, on the frontier of Uruguay, this segment became part of a unique air-land-sea route between Porto Alegre and Buenos Aires, making use of no less than four different transport

399

VARIG's Messerschmitt M 20b2 PP-VAK *Aceguá*, seen at Pelotas, was formerly Lufthansa's D-UKIP (earlier D-2341) *Harz*. It entered service with VARIG on 30 April, 1937. (*VARIG*)

modes, involving a combination of land vehicles—motor coaches and trains (Ferrocarriles del Estado e Central del Uruguai) in Uruguay, and a ship connection from Montevideo across the River Plate.

Another innovation was a holiday route, with the Ju 52/3m, northwards from Porto Alegre to Tôrres, a seaside beach resort at the northeast corner of the State of Rio Grande, to meet a special seasonal demand; but the construction of a new road eased the surface travel problem, so the route only operated for one season.

For a small airline, VARIG kept itself in the local news one way or another. In 1941—the same year that Rubem Martin Berta was elected President of the company—two Focke-Wulf Fw 58s were leased from Condor. In 1942, the *Mauá* crashed, to be replaced by the six-seat Fiat G.2 trimotor, the only one of its kind built, and acquired from the Italian Air Ministry. But the Fiat (PP-VAM) had its hour of glory: no doubt deputising for the *Mauá*, it had the honour of opening VARIG's first route outside the State boundary—an international route moreover—by inaugurating the service to Montevideo on 5 August, 1942. Shortly afterwards, VARIG departed from its normal source of aircraft (possibly trying to protect itself from single-source spares and support problems) by adding a de Havilland 89A Dragon Rapide eight-seat biplane to its fleet. This aircraft entered service on 18 August, 1942, almost simultaneously with Brazil entering the war.

The sole example of the Fiat G.2 first flew in July 1932 and saw service with Avio Linee Italiane. It was purchased by VARIG in May 1942 to replace the Junkers-Ju 52/3m *Mauá*. It was the Fiat which opened VARIG's Montevideo service on 5 August, 1942. (*VARIG*)

400

The Need for Subsidy

However admirable the exploits of the bandeirantes of the air, these sturdy individuals were certainly not self-financed philanthropists or rich adventurers. Someone had to foot the bill. In the early days, much of the direct financial support came from foreign countries, particularly Germany, which sought outlets for the products of its aircraft industry, and without an overseas empire to provide a captive market. The French had already established a secure foothold in Brazil for their route to Buenos Aires, where they had an associated company; while the United States, anxious to maintain the spirit of the Monroe Doctrine, supported its chosen instrument, Pan American Airways, together with its subsidiary Panair do Brasil, with generous mail subsidy, to match European enterprise.

Also, as already observed, the Brazilian Government supported air routes by an indirect subsidy through mail payments, with an important Decree in 1933 providing a logical and workable framework for such payments.

These were not enough, however, to finance the routes to the interior. On the coastal route, the existence of large cities, all engaged in thriving commerce, generated substantial mail traffic, and hence mail payments, to contribute towards the support of the airlines. In contrast, the routes into the heartland of Brazil, almost devoid of people, except Indian tribes, could not generate much mail traffic. Thus, a system of direct subsidy payments gradually came into effect.

These are summarized in Table 22, which shows that, beginning with the Condor feeder routes in the northeast, all the interior routes of the Brazilian commercial air network were progressively taken care of. Decree No.1,106 was particularly important, as it specifically stated the purpose: to extend and augment the air routes, or to increase the capacity on such connections as Parnaíba to Belém, via Floriano; Belém to Porto Velho, via Manaus; São Paulo to Corumbá and Porto Velho.

The route covered under Decree No.1,106, if superimposed on a map of Europe, would link Helsinki, London, Barcelona, Venice, and Istanbul. But to demonstrate that distance alone was not the sole objective of the Brazilian authorities dedicated to support air transport, the little airline in the south, VARIG, was also granted a special payment in 1940.

In addition to the direct subsidy, the indirect contribution of mail payments was also augmented on 27 June, 1939. On that day, two important Decrees, Nos.1,446 and 1,447, were promulgated. The first authorized the grant of 3 million milreis to the Ministry of Transport and Public Works, in association with the Department of Posts and Telegraphs, for the issue of air mail stamps; the second supplemented this with a direct credit of 4,087,000 milreis to cover the costs of carrying air mail. A further 2,127,000 were later credited by Decree No.2,107 on 4 April, 1940.

Certainly, during the formative years of the establishment of a Brazilian national air network, covering every State and territory, the airlines could not complain of lack of official encouragement. From the Government's point of view, the positive support was a visionary approach to the gigantic problem, and was repaid a thousandfold. For in a country of great distances, where roads and railways were, at best, fragmented and unco-ordinated, the existence of an air network was vital to any programme of economic development in the interior. Without the bandeirante-inspired airlines during the critical years of the 1930s, the emergence of Brazil as an industrial country of world stature might have been delayed several decades later than the 1960s, when this stage of development was universally recognized.

TABLE 22
Subsidy Legislation in Brazil 1937–1940

Date	Govt Decree	Northeast (Condor)	Central (VASP)	Route Acre (Condor)	Amazon (Panair do Brasil)	West Central (Condor)	South (VARIG)
21 May, 1937		Parnaíba–Floriano (until 7 June, 1940)					
6 Sept, 1937		São Paulo–Floriano (Military Post Line)					
29 Dec, 1937	144		Uberaba–Goiânia (3 milreis/km)				
25 Aug, 1938	646			Porto Velho–Acre (6 milreis/km)			
22 Dec, 1938	978			Porto Velho–Xapuri	Manaus–Porto Velho		
19 Jan, 1939	8 G/M	Floriano–Belém				Corumbá–Porto Velho	
12 Feb, 1939	1,106	Parnaíba–Floriano			Belém–Manaus	São Paulo–Corumbá	
4 May, 1939	1,242			Rio Branco–Xapuri (58,500 milreis special credit)			
19 May, 1940							(500,000 milreis special credit)
31 May, 1940	1,585			Rio Branco–Xapuri			
7 June, 1940	2,863	Floriano–Belém					

Panair do Brasil used a small fleet of Sikorsky S-43 and S-43B Baby Clipper amphibians on the Amazon River services. Here PP-PBN has been converted to pure flying-boat with consequent gain in performance and payload.
(*Pan American World Airways, courtesy Martin Bernsmüller*)

CHAPTER TWENTY

Brazilian Airlines in Transition

The Achievement of the 1930s

War began on 1 September, 1939, when Germany invaded Poland, and it attained world-wide dimension when Japan attacked the USA at Pearl Harbor on 7 December, 1941. Germany's Lufthansa discontinued trans-Atlantic service at the outbreak of war, and its local Brazilian services were taken over by Condor, which also inherited the six locally-based Junkers-Ju 52/3ms. Even though Brazil did not formally declare war on the Axis Powers until August 1942, this event was foreshadowed from 1939 as world trading patterns took an ominous turn, mainly because of the Allied or Axis blockades; and Brazil suddenly found itself isolated from many of its natural trading partners in Europe. Of all Brazil's emerging commercial enterprises, aviation was particularly vulnerable, and the war came just as the airlines were reaching a level of maturity ahead of their national time, ranking with that of other countries far more industrially advanced.

At the beginning of 1942, Syndicato Condor, for example, possessed a handsome fleet with which it hoped to lead Brazil's airlines into the century's fifth decade with considerable élan. It was operating sixteen 17-passenger Ju 52/3ms, two new four-engined Focke-Wulf Fw 200s, two Focke-Wulf Fw 58s, six

Syndicato Condor's Junkers-Ju 52/3m floatplane PP-CBB *Tupan* in the airline's floating dock at Buenos Aires. (*Lufthansa*)

Junkers-W 34s, and two Junkers-F 13s, these last proving themselves to be the trusty 'old faithfuls' of the fleet. Panair do Brasil had twelve Lockheed Lodestars, the most modern US aircraft in South America, plus two Lockheed Electras and six Sikorsky S-43 'Baby Clipper' flying-boats. São Paulo's VASP had a tidy fleet of five Ju 52/3ms, contrasting with VARIG's situation whose operations were too limited to permit a large fleet, but kept going with a mixed bag of one Ju 52/3m, two Junkers-F 13s, one Messerschmitt M 20b, plus two Focke-Wulf Fw 58s leased from Condor. When VARIG's flagship Ju 52 crashed in February 1942, it acquired the Fiat G.2 from Italy and one de Havilland 89A Dragon Rapide from a local source, so that by mid-1942 it had seven aircraft, from five manufacturers, from three countries. While its predicament was unusual, it was symptomatic of the biggest problem which beset the whole Brazilian industry, that of supply.

Nevertheless there was much achievement to be recorded. Brazil possessed a network of air routes which outstripped in pace and imagination much of the economic development for which the airlines were the communications nerve system. Every State of Brazil, indeed every city of measurable size (outside the immediate vicinity of the more densely-populated parts of the south and south central areas) was served by one or more airlines, giving swift connections for mail, freight, and passengers to the important cities of commerce and government, and thence with the world.

To operate these routes, Brazil could boast a well-trained and experienced pool of pilots, technicians, and commercial airline men. These were all Brazilian, and

Syndicato Condor's Junkers-Ju 52/3mge PP-CBR *Uirapurú*, seen at Rio de Janeiro, was Lufthansa's D-AQUQ *Adolf v. Tutschek* on lease. This aircraft also served with SEDTA in Ecuador as HC-SAC. (*Eric Hess*)

this was itself an achievement, considering that only ten years previously, on 1 May, 1933, Capt Severiana Primo da Fonseca Lins had become the first Brazilian to pilot a Syndicato Condor aircraft. Now, VARIG had to request special permission to employ foreign crews when they needed pilots qualified to fly the Ju 52/3m.

These airline men had to cope with complex flying problems. Like Brazil, other countries or semi-continents were also vast; but Brazil's was a special kind of vastness: unpopulated for the most part, with areas of featureless terrain, thousands of square kilometres in extent. Thus, flying by normal visual flight rules was at best difficult, at worst dangerously deceptive. Huge expanses of savannah or dense forest offered no recognition points. In the Amazon basin, every meandering tributary looked almost identical with the next, and there were no visible human settlements, roads, railways, or cultivated land, which could be used as landmarks or direction indicators. Except on the coastline there were no radio or navigational aids. So the Brazilian airline crews who flew the aircraft of Condor, Panair do Brasil, VASP, the CAM, and the VARIG *gauchos* in the south, were a very special breed.

VARIG's de Havilland 89A Dragon Rapide PP-VAN *Chui* was purchased from Cía Fabril de Juta. (*VARIG*)

Impact of War

Even before Brazil became a co-belligerent with the Allied Powers in August 1942, it had become clear that the circumstances of the war, already being savagely waged in the Atlantic, would have a profound effect on the Brazilian airlines. Only Panair do Brasil, as a subsidiary of Pan American, and dependent exclusively on the parent company for the supply of aircraft, could face the new situation with equanimity. All the others, Condor, VASP, and VARIG, were almost completely dependent upon German equipment, and the Allied sea blockade effectively cut off their essential supplies, not only of new aircraft, but, possibly more critical, vital spares to keep the ones they had in airworthy condition.

Condor was particularly vulnerable. Although not quite on the same basis as the original Condor Syndikat, which had been the marketing vanguard of German civil aircraft sales and support in South America, Syndicato Condor had inherited the role of Brazilian partner to both the German industry, in the export of aircraft and spares, and to the German national airline, Deutsche Lufthansa. Thus, Condor acted as a supply depot for German aircraft spare parts for the entire continent, and even performed maintenance services both for Brazilian users of German aircraft and for similarly-equipped airlines in Bolivia, Peru, Ecuador, and Argentina.

Some indication of the severity of the problem was indicated in 1941, when the pride of the fleet, the two Focke-Wulf Condors, had to be grounded because of shortage of spares. Ironically, when on 16 January, 1943, the name Condor was finally abandoned and the airline became Serviços Aéreos Cruzeiro do Sul, with the Brazilian Government taking over debts and full financial responsibility, all the aircraft were German although not a German technician remained.

The other airlines managed the best they could. VARIG desperately went shopping for other aircraft, and found itself with a mixed fleet of British, German, and Italian types, none of which could be described as modern. VASP still had its Ju 52/3ms, but was reliant upon Syndicato Condor for spare parts—and Condor no doubt had its own priority system in that respect. Thus VASP found itself improvising to make its own spare parts. In these difficult times, an unflyable, condemned aircraft of German origin was almost as valuable as a flyable one, just for the spare parts obtained by cannibalization.

VASP's predicament was illustrated by the enforced modifications made on its last Ju 52/3m, acquired from LAB, Bolivia. This aircraft (PP-SPJ) had DC-3 wheels, hydraulic brakes, and constant-speed propellers, none of which was standard equipment, and each of the three engines was differently rated.

Tribute to German Influence

An objective assessment of Condor has to be that it was almost completely a straightforward venture. The airfields it built were usually no more than wooden landing stages on rivers which only the versatile F 13s or W 34s could negotiate; while the landing fields were originally prepared, for the most part, by local authorities for the pioneering efforts of the CAM.

Thus, while there may have been individuals in the airline with Nazi sympathies, the emotional case against Condor must give way to according it credit for the positive contribution it made to Brazilian air transport.

The Focke-Wulf Fw 200A-08 Condor PP-CBI *Abaitará*, seen here at Santos Dumont Airport, Rio de Janeiro, was one of two BMW-powered Condors supplied to Syndicato Condor. Later these aircraft were fitted with Pratt & Whitney engines, and remained in service until April 1947. (*Lufthansa*)

406

For more than a whole decade, throughout the Brazilian airlines' infancy and adolescence, German supply and support was almost synonymous with survival and development. The F 13s, the W 34s, and especially the Ju 52/3ms, became for Brazil as the DC-3 for the United States, the epitome of air transport practicability, and the bandeirante spirit. For the isolated prospectors and settlers in distant territories 2,000 km from a metalled road, the corrugated metal fuselages were a welcome sight indeed, bringing mail and news from the outside world. To all intents, the Junkers floatplanes *were* the outside world.

This is not to detract from the contribution also made by Panair do Brasil, and its US-built aircraft, which conquered the mighty Amazon and made this great artery its own special province. But the German influence was dominant.

Syndicato Condor's acquisition of the long-range Focke-Wulf 200 Condors was designed to enhance German prestige abroad. These were the world's first modern four-engined long-range landplanes capable of trans-ocean flight. They would have been used to start the first scheduled trans-Atlantic passenger services by heavier-than-air aircraft, had war not intervened. And the Brazilian airline Condor would have been one of the participants in that achievement.

Cruzeiro do Sul Looks to the North

When Dr José Bento Ribeiro Dantas, formerly Condor's lawyer, took over as Director General of Syndicato Condor on 6 January, 1942, one of his first tasks was to arrange for alternative sources of supply of aircraft and equipment. Even though Brazil did not declare war until August 1942, Europe as a supplier was clearly out of the question as long as the Atlantic remained a battle zone. Thus Condor was forced to look to the United States, which in any case was taking a technical lead over airliner manufacturers in Europe.

During 1942, after Brazil had assumed control of the airline, and had altered the name to Serviços Aéreos Condor, representatives of United States airlines, including TWA and Colonial, approached the Brazilian shareholders and tried to persuade them to sell their shares. These airlines presumably had aspirations to expand overseas, no doubt casting envious eyes on the mail subsidies received by Pan American and its monopoly control over Panair do Brasil.

The first meetings were held in a tense atmosphere, as the Brazilian airlines (except for Pan American's subsidiary, Panair) could not obtain fuel. Standard Oil would not supply any, and Condor obtained only meagre supplies from the Brazilian Air Force. The Brazilian negotiators rejected emphatically the assertion that they were merely holding shares as nominees for German interests, and the discussions then centred around the question of what could be arranged to everyone's mutual benefit. This included a consideration of the strategic aspects involved in maintaining Condor's established value as a transport organization whose resources would be harnessed to support the United States war effort, including the supply of war materials, such as, for example, Brazilian rubber. Thus, the issue became one of aircraft supply, and the US negotiators came up with an offer of four Lockheed 18 Lodestars—matching those of Panair do Brasil's growing fleet of that type.

Condor rejected this offer, and the US team demanded an explanation, claiming that the Brazilians did not possess the necessary experience of US aircraft to make comparisons of different types. Dr Bento's reply was quite simple: if the Lodestar was so good, then why did all the leading US airlines operate the Douglas DC-3?

Condor must have argued its case persuasively, for the offer was changed to four DC-3s. The US delegation conceded that they had misjudged Condor's desire to create a Brazilian airline, underestimating the stress on independence; but they requested a change of name as a gesture of intent and integrity. They also pointed out, with complete justification, that the DC-3, or its military version the C-47, was now in tremendous demand as a logistics transport aircraft in the USA. The US airlines themselves were deprived of their civil fleets to support long lines of supply routes, and to allocate this precious war machine to an airline whose name was synonymous with German aspirations would be embarrassing.

Condor agreed, but laid down two conditions: (a) It should be taken off the US 'black list', (b) there should be prior delivery of the four DC-3s, plus technical support. Apparently, tacit agreement was finally reached, at least on the principles of these conditions, although the actual timetable was delayed.

Cruzeiro do Sul's 29-passenger Douglas DC-3A PP-CBT *América do Norte*, seen at Santos Dumont Airport, Rio de Janeiro, was delivered on 2 November, 1943. (*Cruzeiro do Sul*)

On 16 January, 1943, by Presidential Decree No.5,197, Condor's name was changed to **Serviços Aéreos Cruzeiro do Sul, Ltda**, and the following month, the first DC-3 was flown to Brazil for demonstration. The pilot was Capt Dan Beard, Chief Engineer of American Airlines, and Francis L. Duncan, who had been one of the original negotiators acting on behalf of Colonial, remained in that capacity on behalf of the USA.

In March 1943, the DC-3 returned to the USA, carrying as passengers Dr Bento, who had vigorously defended Condor's case throughout the arduous negotiations, and Engineer L. Amorim, who was to be trained in US maintenance and overhaul procedures.

They were received in Washington by Stockley Morgan, head of the US Defense Supplies Corporation, a Government organization. At the end of March, after a week of detailed discussions, Dr Bento signed a contract for four Douglas DC-3s, with a clause in the contract which specified the training of 25 Brazilian aircraft technicians. Duncan was named head of the technical group, which included Dick Fagan, chief pilot of American Airlines, based in New York.

During the following months, Amorim led a group of Cruzeiro do Sul technical staff and crew to visit Pratt & Whitney, to study the engines; American Airlines, to study line maintenance; and United Air Lines, at Cheyenne, to cover overhaul procedures.

On 24 September, 1943, the first Cruzeiro do Sul DC-3 arrived in Rio de Janeiro, loaded with spare parts, including two spare engines. The aircraft went into service in November.

One interesting aspect of Cruzeiro's problems of maintenance was that its base was at Cajú, established to maintain floatplanes, although the DC-3s operated from the new airport at Santos Dumont. The difficulty was solved by floating the DC-3s by barge along the waterfront in Guanabara Bay until an adequate maintenance base could be built at the airport.

By the end of the year, all four DC-3s had arrived, and the fuel supply problem was easier. The new aircraft were put into service on the main routes along the coast, linking the big cities, and thus released some of the Ju 52/3ms to open new routes.

At the end of 1943, the first flight was made with the Ju 52 from Porto Velho, near the Bolivian frontier, and in the heart of the rubber producing country, to Boa Vista, in the Territory of Roraima in the far north of Brazil, bordering on Venezuela. At the end of 1944, a second survey flight was made, starting at Manaus, and flying through to Caracas, the Venezuelan capital, via Boa Vista, Santa Elena, and Ciudad Bolívar (the latter two settlements in Venezuela). This survey work, maintaining the best bandeirante tradition, culminated in the opening, in 1945, of a joint service between Rio de Janeiro and Caracas, by the direct inland route, in conjunction with LAV, the Venezuelan airline.

Panair do Brasil Swings the Pendulum

Cruzeiro do Sul had to struggle for its very existence, trying to obtain a supply of new aircraft to replace the old. For all their ruggedness, the Junkers types succumbed to the inevitable wear and tear of difficult operating conditions, improvised spares, and the loss of experienced staff. The US-owned **Panair do Brasil** thus found itself in the happy position of being able to gain the ascendancy under the benevolent custodianship of an affluent parent, Pan American Airways.

A typical scene during the 1930s was the flying-boat base at Belém. It was originally built in 1929 by Ralph O'Neill's NYRBA, whose subsidiary company became Panair do Brasil. A key staging point during a critical development period, passengers from Pan American's Clipper flying-boats were normally ferried to the shore by launch.

During this period, with greater obligations incurred by the airlines because of the demands of war, a new element was added to the factors which prevented the advance of airline activity. This was the need to build better airfields. In the past, limited aid had been provided by the Brazilian Government or the States to help the airlines on the ground, by constructing small landing fields or river and shore bases. But the expenditure had been relatively modest, except for the grandiose—but almost stillborn—Bartholomeu da Gusmão airship base at Santa Cruz, south of Rio de Janeiro; and the modern city airports at Rio and São Paulo, which were supported largely by the municipalities. Indeed, throughout the country, a great debt was still owed to the two pioneer airlines, NYRBA and Aéropostale, which had built the early infrastructure but which never survived to reap the benefits.

This Panair do Brasil Lockheed Model 18-10 Lodestar, PP-PBK, was one of a batch of ten acquired by the airline. The markings on Panair do Brasil aircraft were green. (*Lockheed*)

The newer and larger aircraft demanded better runways. The old Ju 52/3ms could take off from any reasonable grass field—the veteran pilots managed with 600 metres at most, even fully loaded, and less when lightly loaded. But the new US aircraft being delivered in the early 1940s were more demanding of the airports. While a hard grass or earthen strip was acceptable to a Lockheed Lodestar in good, dry weather (provided it was well cared for), a concrete or tarmacadam surface with a good foundation was not only preferable, but absolutely essential in poor weather when the ground was soft or waterlogged through rain.

Thus Panair do Brasil, or rather its Pan American parent, found itself in the position of having to build its own airfields if it wished to operate big aircraft. This task was accomplished mutually with the Brazilian Government, which recognized the expertise of Pan American in construction techniques and was prepared to work out a scheme by which Pan American and Panair do Brasil could be compensated for the work and cost of airport construction through the imposition of taxes upon other users.

Already, Pan American had demonstrated what could be done by completing a new airport at Barreiras, in the far west of the State of Bahia, in September 1940. Wishing to introduce its new four-engined landplanes, the Boeing 307 Stratoliners, on South American routes, Pan Am realised that to attempt to fly from Belém, where the airport was adequate, to Rio de Janeiro nonstop, was just too risky without a midway airport, either for landing regularly, or for emergency. Accordingly, the airline undertook the formidable task of building a modern

410

Until 1940, Barreiras was an unknown community in the westernmost part of the Brazilian State of Bahia. Then Pan American Airways built an airport there because it was almost exactly halfway on a direct line between Belém and Rio de Janeiro, permitting landplanes such as the DC-2 and the Boeing 307 to cut hundreds of kilometres off the circuitous coastal route.

airfield at a point about 700 km inland, where surface transport was by riverborne craft up the São Francisco River and its tributaries.

All material was first brought to Joazeiro, a railhead about 300 km from the mouth of the São Francisco; then brought by barge up the river and its tributary, the Grande; then trucked to the site. Several near-disasters included an incident when a raft carrying a vital tractor capsized on a sandbar; the tractor was successfully raised, disassembled, dried out, rebuilt, reloaded, and finally helped finish the first temporary runway. This was then discovered to be unsatisfactory because of terrain problems, and the new Barreiras airport was completed on a plateau nearby.

Pan American's hard-earned success, which enabled Douglas DC-3s to provide one-stop service between Rio de Janeiro and Belém, probably encouraged the Brazilian Government to work closely with the US airline in the matter of airfield

Panair do Brasil's Lockheed Model 10-C Electra PP-PAS, seen at Poças de Caldas, Minas Gerais, on the Rio de Janeiro–Belo Horizonte route, had a varied career with Panair do Brasil, Pan American Airways, Mexican carriers and finally VARIG. It crashed at Porto Alegre in 1944. (*Courtesy Martin Bernsmüller*)

411

construction. Perhaps as a direct consequence, Decree No.3,462, of 25 July, 1941, authorized Panair do Brasil to construct, improve, and equip airports at Amapá, Belém, São Luis, Fortaleza, Natal, Recife, Maceió, and Salvador, and provisions were made for lighting and other equipment. Natal was to become a joint sea and land base. The cost of the project was to be covered by a grant from the Government to the value of 27 million milreis, over a period of five years, the money to be recovered by airport taxes.

On the same day, by Decree No.3,463, Panair do Brasil was granted permission to operate new routes: Rio–São Paulo–Curitiba-Foz do Iguaçú–Asunción–Corumbá–Campo Grande–São Paulo–Rio, and Rio–Belo Horizonte–Patos–Goiânia. There were other extensions to the network in the north. The Amazon route was extended to Tabatinga/Benjamin Constant, at the junction of Brazil's

51. Twilight Era of the Flying-boat—the 'Barreiras Cut-off', 1940. Pan American Airways engineers built a new airport in western Bahia at a point almost exactly halfway between Belém and Rio de Janeiro. This enabled landplanes—DC-3s primarily—to save considerable time over the Sikorsky flying-boats plying the longer coastal route.

PP-PCY was one of a small number of Consolidated PBY-5A amphibians operated by Panair do Brasil on Amazon services linking Belém, Manaus and Iquitos—a route stretching some 2,000 miles.

frontiers with Peru and Colombia; while the ex-Condor routes in the States of Ceará and Maranhão were transferred to Panair. The unfortunate Condor no doubt suffered from having been controlled by an agency now at war with Brazil, even though this association had been abruptly and emphatically severed; but Panair's substitution in some of Condor's former spheres of influence was also because, with an assured supply of aircraft, it was—to use a term familiar in US aviation circles—fit, willing, and able to take over.

The basic fleet of Panair do Brasil in the war years was the Lockheed 18 Lodestar. Although in June 1940 it acquired from Pan Am its first Douglas DC-2, and a second one the following year, these were quickly transferred to Uruguay, in favour of the Lodestar, an airliner of about the same all-up weight and capacity as the DC-2, but smaller and faster, being of later design. Altogether, between April 1941 and January 1945, Panair do Brasil obtained a total of fourteen Lodestars, although the casualty rate was fairly high—six were lost, mainly through crashes, and the maximum number in the fleet at any time was ten. There were also two smaller Lockheed 12s in 1945 but these were soon sold; while the Fairchild XA-942As and Sikorsky S-43 flying-boats remained in service to deal with Panair's commitments in the Amazon River basin. Here, the airline was indispensable to the wartime Rubber Development Corporation, when Brazil's resources in this commodity were suddenly in demand as the rubber of Malaya and elsewhere in Southeast Asia fell under the domination of the Japanese.

Navegacão Aérea Brasileira

Towards the end of 1939, a wholly-Brazilian airline, **Navegacão Aérea Brasileira (NAB)** was formed and incorporated as a public company on 28 February, 1940. Its first two aircraft arrived by ship in Rio de Janeiro on 2 January, 1941. These were two Beech 18s (PP-NAA and PP-NAB) and were put into service on a route from Rio to Recife, via Belo Horizonte, Bom Jesus de Lapa, and Petrolina on 28 March. NAB built its own airfields at Lapa and Petrolina, and provided its own radio stations and beacons. By this means, it apparently established its own proprietary rights to the route, although official operating authority was not granted until 5 May, under Decree No.7,126.

The fact that a Brazilian airline could be formed, equipped, and in service in little more than a year was itself an achievement, and perhaps symptomatic of the growing momentum of Brazilian air transport. Not since VASP, founded in 1933, had there been an addition to the ranks of Brazilian airlines, although Aerobrasil, Ltda, and Transporte Aero-Brasileiro, Ltda, had received operating authority on 16 October, 1936 (Decree No.1,152) and 27 August, 1937 (Decree No. 1,921) respectively. Neither of these, however, operated (although the latter did acquire aircraft) and when NAB was founded, about seventy per cent of the airline traffic of Brazil was generated by Condor and Pan Am/Panair do Brasil, both of them foreign-owned or controlled.

On 6 September, 1941, NAB opened service on the coastal route to Recife, although this was not sustained as its two Beech 18s (plus two other small aircraft, a Beech 17 and a Fairchild 24) were inadequate. However, on 4 November, by Decree No.3,792, the Government stepped in with a subsidy of 5·5 milreis per kilometre. This was followed on 21 May, 1942 (Decree No.4,315) with a further special credit of 1,796,000 milreis, and yet another on 11 August (No.4,566) of 6 million milreis.

Thus fortified, NAB was able to augment its small fleet, and early in 1942, it acquired two Lockheed Lodestars and a Stinson Reliant. Frequency of service was increased and the northern route extended to Belém, by a branch from Lapa, via Teresina. On 29 July, 1944, the airline received yet another handsome subsidy, of 8 million cruzeiros, with the conditions that it should fly at least two million kilometres per year, and should acquire three more Lodestars.

NAB's record with its Lodestar fleet was brittle. Although it bought a total of five, it never operated more than four, and ironically saw this reduced to two within a few months of the 1944 subsidy award. Yet on 24 March, 1945, by Decree No.7,414, it was awarded another credit of 25 million cruzeiros, to be paid in ten annual payments, starting in that year. Certainly, NAB could not complain of lack of practical encouragement from its Government.

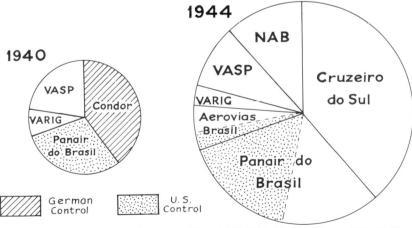

8. Brazilian Airline Ownership in Transition, 1940–1944. Until the Second World War, control or ownership of Brazilian airlines was almost evenly split between German, United States, and Brazilian interests. By the end of the war, however, about 80 per cent of the industry was in Brazilian hands. (Charts based on passenger-miles).

414

52. NAB and Aerovias Brasil, 1944. Two new airlines made significant contributions to airline development in Brazil during the early 1940s. They were the first airlines to be initiated from individual sources of finance, in contrast with State, Government, or foreign sponsorship of the earlier airline generation.

Aerovias Brasil

On 26 August, 1942, another company of substance joined the growing ranks of Brazilian airlines. As part of an ambitious plan to establish an integrated international empire of national airlines throughout Latin America, the TACA organization of Central America established Empresa de Transportes Aerovias Brasil, S.A., in Rio de Janeiro. Lowell Yerex, the owner of TACA, owned 42 per cent of the shares; one of his vice-presidents, Charles E. Matthews a further 18 per cent; while the remaining 40 per cent was held by two Brazilians, the brothers Oscar and Roberto Taves.

Aerovias Brasil (or Brazilian International Airlines, as it was sometimes called) began operations in October 1942 with two Lockheed 14s (PP-AVA and PP-AVB) and received authority to do so by Presidential Decree No.11,160 of 29 December of that year. Although it lost one of these aircraft in February 1943, it managed to provide freight services, on a charter basis, from Rio de Janeiro to Miami, via Uberaba, Goiânia, the Tocantins route to Belém, and thence via Paramaribo, Port of Spain, and Ciudad Trujillo. Maintenance was provided by the TACA organization, which also owned British West Indian Airways, based at

415

Port of Spain; while it also co-operated closely with NAB, and interchanged equipment and services. Again, as with the other airlines providing the direct overland links northward from the southern and central states of Brazil, Aerovias Brasil carried valuable supplies, notably quartz crystal, as its contribution to providing the United States with precious and scarce raw materials.

In 1944, Aerovias Brasil's headquarters was transferred to São Paulo, and it continued to operate its freight service to Miami sporadically with its one remaining Lockheed 14. It also began a Brazilian domestic service from Rio de Janeiro to Carolina, another of the new airports which had been constructed at strategic points on the direct overland route between Rio and Belém. The main service was provided by two Lockheed 12As, while two Fairchild 71s filled in with a stopping service through the State of Goiás, between Goiânia and Carolina, via points on the Tocantins River.

Prelude to Peacetime Expansion

To use the mildest of proverbs which could be applied to that holocaust, the Second World War was an ill wind which blew good only to a privileged few. In civil aviation terms, Brazil could be identified as one of the countries which emerged at the end with a widened and positive viewpoint upon the world. Much of this change of attitude took the form of a growing awareness of its place in world commerce, partly because the war forced the airlines both to re-orientate and to modernize themselves, and thus to bring Brazil much closer to other continents.

This took various forms during the eventful years between 1940 and 1945. Airline ownership, for example, underwent a complete reversal from pre-dominantly foreign to the precise opposite (see Chart 8 on page 414). The control of the former Syndicato Condor changed almost overnight from German to Brazilian. On 7 December, 1943, Pan American's complete ownership of Panair do Brasil was reduced to a 58 per cent shareholding. VASP and VARIG were already Brazilian, and of the two new companies of stature added to the airline lists, one was 40 per cent Brazilian, and the other completely so.

The change of ownership had an immediate effect on the composition of the airline fleets. When Brazil entered the war in 1942, Panair do Brasil had only just begun to bring in more US-built landplanes to supplement the two Lockheed 10E Electras acquired in 1936. All the other aircraft were either Sikorsky S-43 or Fairchild XA-942A flying-boats. As these were used entirely in the Amazon region, an impartial observer at the busy terminal aprons at Santos Dumont in Rio de Janeiro or at Congonhas in São Paulo would have been forgiven for assuming that all the commercial landplanes in Brazil were German.

As Table 24 shows, the next two years brought about a dramatic change. By the summer of 1944, when the invasion of Normandy by the Allied forces signalled the approaching end of the war, the end was also in sight for German aircraft in South America. Although arithmetically the German-built fleets exactly equalled those of the United States, it was the end of the line for Junkers and Focke-Wulf, and the beginning of an era in Brazil for Lockheed and Douglas. Of Cruzeiro do Sul's twenty-six aircraft, the old Junkers-W 34s were either retired or grounded, and the two Fw 58s had been requisitioned by the Government on 29 September, 1942. The aircraft from the United States, on the other hand, were the harbingers of a great flock of Lockheeds and Douglases which were to migrate southward, to form the foundation of many a mushrooming airline industry in the immediate

Among the various aircraft which passed into VARIG's hands during the war was the four-seat Italian Cant Z.1012, previously owned by the Italian Embassy in Brazil. Delivered to VARIG's Porto Alegre base by train, because the wings were allegedly warped, on its trial flight the crew forgot to lower the undercarriage, and the Cant was heavily damaged.
(*VARIG*)

postwar years.

In the extreme south of Brazil, the sad story of one aircraft epitomized the struggle of smaller airlines to keep going during a time of desperate shortages of almost everything connected with airline equipment. In January 1943, VARIG managed to lay claim to a small Italian three-engined monoplane, a four-seat Cant Z.1012, previously used by the Italian Embassy in Rio de Janeiro. It had been in Brazil since 1939, and was despatched to VARIG's base in Porto Alegre by train, as the pilots complained that the wings were warped and it was unflyable. Unfortunately, on the first test flight at Porto Alegre, the crew forgot to lower the undercarriage, and the Cant was heavily damaged, and never went into service. VARIG quickly acquired some Lockheed Electras, and from then on underwent a change of fortune, as Rubem Berta, elected President in 1941, began to exert a firm control, and its small share of the subsidies granted from the Government enabled it to remain financially sound.

The availability of commercial aircraft from the USA became easier as the war went on. Literally hundreds of aircraft swept down the Central Atlantic coast to Natal, which became one of the busiest airports in the world, located as it was in the extreme northeast tip of Brazil. Thus situated, it was the take-off point for all trans-Atlantic aircraft on the vital supply lines from the United States (the aircraft arsenal for Allied transport aircraft) to Africa, Europe, and the Middle East combat zones. Towards the end of the war, C-47s and C-46s began to accumulate at Natal, as demand in the Eastern Hemisphere declined but production continued and the transport pipeline continued to function. The physical presence in Natal of scores of war-surplus aircraft was one of the contributory factors towards the creation of dozens of small airlines in Brazil as soon as hostilities ceased.

If aircraft availability pointed the way towards a new postwar domestic airline trend, a small event in 1943 carried far-reaching implications. Decree No.13,172 of 17 August, 1943, granted to Panair do Brasil the right to extend its route network to all American countries, and specifically designated Iquitos, Peru, as the terminus of an extension to the Amazon trunk line which had been extended to the Peruvian frontier in 1941. While this was not likely to catch the attention of the airline world at large, it provided a mandate for expansion and a hint from the Government that it would encourage the Brazilian airline industry to seek new horizons.

417

TABLE 23
Brazilian Aircraft 1927–1943
(Acquired up to Brazil's entry into the Second World War)
Summary

Germany			United States			Other European		
Type	Airline	No.	Type	Airline	No.	Type	Airline	No.
Dornier Wal	Condor/VARIG	1	Consolidated Commodore	Panair do Brasil	7	**British**		
	Condor	5						
" Merkur	VARIG	1	Sikorsky S-38	"	7	Monospar ST.4	VASP	2
Junkers-G 24	Condor	3	" S-43	"	7	DH.84	VASP	1
" F 13	Condor	4	Lockheed Air Express	"	1	DH.89A	VARIG	1
	VARIG	2				British sub-total		4
" W 33	Condor	1	" Electra Model 14	Aerovías Brasil	2	**French**		
					2	Latécoère 25	Aéropostale	2
" W 34	Condor	6	" Lodestar	Panair do Brasil	12*	Morane-Saulnier MS.130	VARIG	1
				NAB	4			
" A 50	VARIG	3	Fairchild XA-942A	Panair do Brasil	2	Nieuport Delage 641	VARIG	1
" Ju 46	Condor	2	Douglas DC-2	"	2	French sub-total		4

Type	Operator	Number
" Ju 52/3m	Condor	16
	VASP	6
	VARIG	1
Klemm L 20	ETA	1
" L 25	ETA/VARIG	2
" Kl 31A	Iguassú	2
Messerschmitt		
" Me 108B	VARIG	1
" M 20b	VARIG	1
Focke-Wulf		
" Fw 200	Condor	2
" Fw 58	"	2
Sub-totals	Condor	42
	VARIG	9
	VASP	6
	ETA	3
	Iguassú	2
Totals		62

Type	Operator	Number
Beech 18	NAB	2
Beech 17	"	1
Fairchild 24	"	1
Stinson Reliant	Iguassú	1 3

Note: First six Commodores, first four Sikorsky S-38s and Lockheed Air Express registered under Panair's former name. NYRBA do Brasil

	Operator	Number
Sub-totals	Panair do Brasil	40
	Aerovias Brasil	2
	NAB	9
	Iguassú	3
Totals		54

Italian

Type	Operator	Number
Fiat G.2	VARIG	1
Cant Z.1012	"	1
Italian sub-total		2
Sub-totals	VARIG	5
	VASP	3
	Aéropostale	2
		10

*Includes aircraft orders, delivered up to February 1943. Others acquired later.

TABLE 24
Brazilian Airline Fleets
Mid-1944

Aircraft Type	Cruzeiro do Sul	VASP	VARIG	Panair do Brasil	NAB	Aerovias Brasil	Total
German							
Focke-Wulf Fw 200	2	—	—	—	—	—	2
Junkers-Ju 52/3m	10	5	—	—	—	—	15
,,　　 F 13	2	—	2	—	—	—	4
,,　　 W 34	5	—	—	—	—	—	5
,,　　 Ju 46	1	—	—	—	—	—	1
Total German	20	5	2	—	—	—	27
Italian							
Fiat G.2	—	—	1	—	—	—	1
Total Italian	—	—	1	—	—	—	1
British							
De Havilland 89A Dragon Rapide	—	—	1	—	—	—	1
Total British	—	—	1	—	—	—	1
USA							
Lockheed 10	—	—	2	—	—	—	2
,,　　 12	—	—	—	—	—	1	1
,,　　 14	—	—	—	—	—	1	1
,,　　 18	—	—	—	8	5	—	13
Beech 18	—	—	—	—	1	—	1
Douglas DC-3	4	—	—	—	—	—	4
Fairchild XA-942A	—	—	—	2	—	—	2
,,　　 71	—	—	—	—	—	2	2
Sikorsky S-43	—	—	—	4	—	—	4
Total USA	4	—	2	14	6	4	30
Brazilian Total	24	5	6	14	6	4	59

Panair do Brasil's Douglas DC-3A PP-PCJ seen at Santos Dumont Airport, Rio de Janeiro, is not as close to the 407 m high Pão de Açúcar (Sugar Loaf) as it appears. This famous landmark is 3½ km from the 02 runway thresholds. (*Eric Hess*)

CHAPTER TWENTY-ONE

Postwar Airline Fever in Brazil

A Proliferation of Airlines

At the end of the last chapter attention was drawn to the supply of war-surplus aircraft left at Natal and disposed of under favourable terms when war came to an end in 1945. Although not the only source of supply to enterprising Brazilian entrepreneurs—some British Avro Ansons, de Havilland 89A Dragon Rapides and Percival Princes were interspersed among the DC-3/C-47 and Lodestar acquisitions—the aircraft lined up at Natal were undoubtedly a factor in the emergence of many small airlines in Brazil during the five years immediately following the cessation of hostilities.

After the establishment between 1927 and 1933 of the four veteran airlines, VARIG, Syndicato Condor, Panair do Brasil, and VASP, only two more names were added to the list during the next ten years, NAB in 1939 and Aerovias Brasil in 1942. Aero Geral had been authorized to operate by the Air Ministry on 10 February, 1942, but was unable to get under way because no aircraft were available. In contrast, starting with VASD which was founded two years later, no less than 23 new companies began scheduled service during the five years from early 1945, while one more was formed as a non-operating company, and another started fixed-base operations preparatory to starting scheduled flights later in the 1950s.

Although this mushroom-like period of airline growth has been variously reported as featuring 30 or 40 airlines, there were actually never more than 18 operating in any one year, including the well-established older airlines.

Nevertheless, at this time, new names appeared with bewildering frequency on the fuselages of, mainly, the assortment of C-47s to be seen at the new airfields appearing all over Brazil. The 25 new airlines are summarized in Table 25, which is notable for the fact that not a single company listed therein survived beyond 1961, except as a semi-autonomous unit of a larger consortium.

Santos Dumont and Transcontinental

The first of the new generation was **Viação Aérea Santos Dumont (VASD)**, first organized with a capital of 30 million cruzeiros* on 18 January, 1944. By all accounts, this was an ambitious project, as a large auditorium in Rio de Janeiro was hired for the first meeting of the 7,000 shareholders. Two PBY-5 Catalina flying-boats and one Budd Conestoga landplane freighter were purchased from the Rubber Development Corporation at Belém for the initial fleet, and during 1944 a series of experimental flights was made. Early the next year, the Catalinas were flying regularly northwards from Rio along the coastal route as far as Fortaleza, and the Budd flying southwards to Porto Alegre.

VASD's fortunes waned, however. Although Brazilian Government Decree No.20,213 of 17 December, 1945, granted operating authority on the same basis as that to other established airlines, the directors resigned twelve days later, and on 4 January, 1946, the Budd was damaged, never to fly again, and the Catalinas were grounded. The company, in fact, was only able to keep going by operating in conjunction with another airline from March 1947.

Linha Aérea Transcontinental Brasileira (variously known as **Transcontinental**, or **TCB**, or **LATB**) was formed on 22 July, 1944, with a fleet of five Avro Ansons, and like VASD, made some experimental flights during 1945. In January 1946, three Douglas C-47s were purchased and sporadic operations started primarily with these aircraft, on 1 February.

On 27 August, 1948, the Government authorized scheduled service over two routes: Rio–São Paulo and the coastal route to Recife; and on 1 October of that year, Transcontinental (LATB) part-amalgamated with VASD in the first example of joint co-operation in Brazil, and possibly setting the example for many more to follow. Transcontinental and Santos Dumont shared commercial and technical resources, but retained their separate indentities—much in the same way as VARIG and Cruzeiro do Sul were to do on a vastly greater scale almost thirty years later.

In the same month, on 23 October, Col Dulcidio Espirito Santo Cardoso, Director-President now of both LATB and VASD, was also elected to the same office of **Viação Interestadual de Transportes Aéreos (VITA)**. This was an amorphous organization founded on 26 November, 1946, with a capital of 10 million cruzeiros, the biggest shareholder being Jevenil Rocha Vaz. Although authorized to operate on 3 December of that year, and officially registered as an airline, VITA did not own any aircraft, and never operated a service.

On 1 February, 1948, VITA purchased Linhas Aéreas 'Natal' but disposed of this holding on 6 September, 1949, its operating authority having been cancelled by the Brazilian Government on 6 June.

LATB meanwhile continued with modest success. In 1949 a fairly respectable network was beginning to develop. An alternative route to the northeast was added, via Conquista, Salvador, and Paulo Afonso to Fortaleza, and two local

*In 1942, the name of the Brazilian currency unit was changed from the milreis (= 1,000 reis) to the cruzeiro.

routes were started to points in the State of Minas Gerais. A Curtiss C-46 was acquired to develop the freight potential between Brazil's two major cities, Rio de Janeiro and São Paulo.

But this was the limit of LATB's ambitions. It sustained two crashes within six months, the C-46 in August 1950 (later rebuilt and sold to Lóide) and a DC-3, one of two leased from NAB, in January 1951. A few months later, in August, LATB was sold to REAL which acquired a fleet of three C-47s and a Beech D-18 in the process. VASD appears to have retained its autonomy, temporarily at least, and was absorbed by Nacional in April 1952.

A Little Independence

If the activities of the impressively-named Transcontinental and the honourably named Santos Dumont seemed small by comparison with the national networks of Cruzeiro do Sul or Panair do Brasil, they were at least more successful than some of the almost diminutive newcomers.

Companhia Meridional de Transportes (Meridional) was founded late in 1944 and made some trial flights in August 1945 with a fleet of three Avro Ansons purchased from Canada. On 4 October, 1945, scheduled services began on short routes from Rio de Janeiro to Campos and Vitória, but within two months, one of the Ansons crashed into a mountain near Rio, and Meridional ceased operations by going into bankruptcy in March 1946.

With a life span approximately equal to Meridional's, **Aerovias S.A.** (not to be confused with Aerovias Brasil) was founded in the State of Minas Gerais in 1944, and opened service in November 1945 with two Stinsons (an SM-8 Junior and an SR-8 Reliant) and the ex-VARIG Fiat G. 2. Later the fleet was improved with the addition of two Douglas DC-2s and two Douglas C-39s but the company was bankrupt by 1949.

Another airline with a small operational radius was **Viação Aérea Bahiana**, authorized to operate on 12 December, 1945. Bahiana purchased two Lockheed Lodestars from Panair do Brasil, which also provided technical and administrative assistance. In February 1946, operations began on routes from Salvador to Aracajú and to Ilhéus. The fleet was augmented in December 1947 by three DC-3s and a Boeing 247D purchased from AVIANCA, the Colombian airline. But on 22 June, 1948, one DC-3 was lost at Ilhéus and on 4 November Bahiana ceased operations. The aircraft were repossessed three years later by AVIANCA and passed either to other Brazilian airlines or were sold to the United States.

Viação Aérea Arco-Iris, S.A. was authorized to operate in March 1945, and purchased six de Havilland 89A Dragon Rapides, to begin operations on 12 July, 1946, from São Paulo to cities in the western part of the State, where at this time surface transport was virtually non-existent. Arco-Iris was the first airline to serve Londrina, the city in the State of Paraná which was emerging as the centre of a prosperous new coffee-growing region, and later to become the focal point of many local air services.

By the end of 1948, the familiar pattern of heavy financial losses brought Arco-Iris to an end. But the airline bowed out in dramatic style. The original owners sold the company to a new group in Rio Grande do Sul, and transferred the company's base to Caxias do Sul (Rio Grande do Sul) where the mayor was persuaded to build a hangar. But Arco-Iris never revived, as the D.A.C. would not authorize operations with the Dragon Rapides. In spite of an Air Ministry edict that airlines could no longer increase share capital by public subscription, an

423

PP-AIB was one of seven de Havilland 89A Dragon Rapides purchased by Viação Aérea Arco-Iris.

attempt was made by some of the directors to sell new stock. They were reported to have been saved from lynching through the intervention of the local constabulary of Caxias, as it was their misfortune to pick on some of the original stockholders (unaware of the sale) as potential new subscribers. Not surprisingly, Arco-Iris joined the ranks of cancelled authorizations in June 1950.

If ever pride came before a fall, this should have applied to **Linhas Aéreas Brasileiras, S.A. (LAB)**. Authorized by the Air Ministry in November 1943 to start selling shares, first discussions in 1944 led to extensive promotion. The first shareholders' meeting, held at the headquarters in Belém on 9 February, 1945, drew support from all over Brazil. The management ordered six second-hand Douglas C-47s from a broker in New York in May 1945, and LAB was officially constituted in Belém on 14 July, 1945.

Scheduled services began on a coastal route from Rio de Janeiro to Salvador on 8 December of that year, and from Rio to São Paulo, with an extension to cities in northwest Minas Gerais shortly afterwards. But for all its imposing title, LAB did not expand any further, and began to acquire a reputation for unreliability. Application to increase frequency was made in March 1948 but refused on the grounds that the existing advertised ones were not being flown. Employees complained about their terms of employment—such as the absence of wages—and a crisis was reached, a new board of directors being elected on 27 April, 1948.

But the end was in sight. The aircraft were impounded by LAB's insurance company in August 1948 and eventually sold to other airlines in Brazil in September 1949.

As if to keep the flag of complete independence alive, with no concessions to mergers or sellouts, two small airlines came into a mayfly existence when Bahiana and LAB disappeared into oblivion. **Universal Transportes Aéreos (Universal)** was founded at the end of 1947 by Col Presser Bello, and started operations early the following year with two ex-Panair do Brasil Lodestars on a route from Rio de Janeiro to Belo Horizonte, via São Lourenço and Lavras. Although extending to São Paulo in July, one of its aircraft crashed on 8 September and Universal went into bankruptcy on 1 December. It had operated for six months.

Another small company, **Transportes Aéreos Sul-Americanos (TASA)** acquired a DC-3 and two Douglas B-18s in February 1948. The B-18s were a deep-fuselage bomber development of the DC-2. Service began in July 1948 on a three-stop route from São Paulo to Goiânia, but the operation ceased at the turn of the year, after a life-span even shorter than Universal's.

A Family Affair

Many of the new Brazilian airlines of this period had names varying from the spectacular to the grandiose, from the colourful to the neatly appropriate. None, however, was so curious as the airline founded in the city of Juiz de Fora, in the State of Minas Gerais, on 3 July, 1946.

Linhas Aéreas 'Natal' S.A. was organized by Julio Alvares de Assis, with a capital of 5 million cruzeiros. The idea was conceived by Cmte Cyro Novais Armando, a former VASP pilot, and a friend of Julio's. The capital was put up by Julio's uncle, the head of a textile company in Juiz de Fora, and the name 'Natal' relates to this circumstance, not to the city in northeast Brazil. 'Natal' was simply (or not so simply) an acronym for Navegação Aérea Theodorico Alvares de Assis Ltda, in a praiseworthy attempt to give credit to Uncle Theodore.

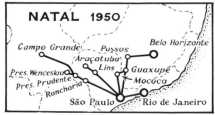

53. REAL Ancestors, 1948–1950. Three small airlines founded during the 1940s were absorbed by the highly successful and ambitious REAL.

The Air Ministry granted permission to begin operations on 30 July; four C-47s were imported from Canada, and the first service, from Rio de Janeiro to São Paulo was flown on 7 December, 1946. Some time after this, at the suggestion of Capt Abel Pereira Leite, the acronymic source of the airline's name was changed to Navegação Aérea Trans-Americana Ltda, a little ambitious perhaps, but quite suitable under the circumstances, as four more routes had been opened to the west of São Paulo, including one as far as Campo Grande.

'Natal' began to change hands, first on 1 February, 1948, when control passed to VITA, then on 6 September of the same year to Capt Aguiar. By May 1950 the airline was operating within the REAL consortium, and at the end of the year, 'Natal', its network of routes, and its C-47s were wholly incorporated into that fast-growing company.

Redes Estaduais Aéreas Ltda (REAL)

Of all the postwar airlines to be formed in Brazil between 1945 and 1950 none was more successful, or had more influence than REAL. Although formed as **Redes Estaduais Aéreas, Ltda.**, its acronym became so well known that the name was soon changed officially to **REAL S.A.**—Transportes Aéreos on 13 December, 1946. By this time it was so firmly established that, almost alone of the postwar airline generation, the name was as familiar to the Brazilian travelling public in the busy Rio de Janeiro–São Paulo–Curitiba triangle as those of the prewar companies such as Cruzeiro do Sul, Panair do Brasil, or VASP.

Linneu Gomes (*left*) founded REAL in December 1945 with a fleet of three C-47s. By shrewd mergers and acquisitions, he built his airline into the largest in Brazil, and by 1960, his consortium ranked tenth in the airline world, measured by passengers boarded. But Gomes out-reached himself and REAL was purchased by VARIG on 16 August, 1961. Claudio Hoelck (*right*) was originally the traffic manager of Transportes Aéreos Nacional Ltda, and was instrumental in building up this Brazilian domestic airline to serve 74 cities in Brazil as well as Asunción in Paraguay. Hoelck and Nacional joined Linneu Gomes's REAL Consortium on 2 August, 1956.

The inspiration for REAL went back several years, when in 1943 Vicente Mammana Neto tried to start an airline, Cia Santista de Aviação, using the Stinson aircraft formerly owned by Aerolloyd Iguassú, and which were redundant after VASP bought that company in 1939. This venture, however, never became operational. Two years later, Linneu Gomes, a former co-pilot of TACA (the Central American company with tentacles all over Latin America) decided to join the airline ranks. He bought three Douglas C-47s in November 1945 and obtained authority from the Air Ministry to operate as an airline on the last day of that month. Gomes and Mammana then joined hands, and formed Redes Estaduais Aéreas Ltda, in São Paulo in December 1945, with a capital of 3 million cruzeiros.

426

This view of São Paulo's Congonhas Airport shows its proximity to the city's suburbs. The airport is at an elevation of 2,631 ft (802 m), has parallel 16/34 runways and is officially 3·8 nautical miles south of the city. By 1977 the airport was handling more than 115,000 aircraft movements and 4½ million passengers a year. Just visible to the right of the terminal buildings are three aircraft including two VARIG Lockheed 188 Electras. (*R. E. G. Davies*)

Based at the bustling Congonhas Airport, Gomes piloted the first flight to Rio de Janeiro on 7 February, 1946, and followed this with an extension soon afterwards to Curitiba, the fast-growing State capital of Paraná. The densely-travelled São Paulo–Rio de Janeiro route at this time was served by many companies, all trying to emulate the incumbent pioneer, VASP, and REAL was prominent among these, obtaining permission to increase frequency to three a day on 26 June, 1946.

For a short period, REAL augmented its seating capacity by adding to its fleet two aircraft with substantially more seats than the 24/28-passenger C-47/DC-3s. On 17 October, 1946, the first Bristol 170 Wayfarer was delivered, and promptly went into service four days later on the São Paulo –Rio de Janeiro route, offering 36 seats, the highest of any aircraft operating domestically in Brazil at the time. The Wayfarer, or the Freighter, as it was called when equipped for air cargo, was an Ugly Duckling, with its bulbous nose lacking aesthetic appeal. But, for a limited period of operation, it did its job well. The two aircraft were able to give REAL almost as much capacity on the inter-city shuttle as four DC-3s.

REAL's Douglas DC-3/C-53 PP-AVJ, seen at Congonhas Airport, São Paulo, in 1954, served the USAF as 42-15538, TACA as YS-21 and TI-75, passed to Aerovías Brasil as PP-AVJ and with the Aerovías Brasil/REAL merger changed registry yet again. Among the later operators was VARIG who used it as PP-VDM. (*Mário B. de M. Vinagre*)

427

This action released the DC-3s for other work. A new service opened to Londrina on 15 May, 1947, and the Curitiba route was extended to Porto Alegre on 10 November. Early in 1948, a local service started to Rio Prêto, via intermediate points, the first of a rapidly expanding network in the States of São Paulo and Paraná, whose economic progress and prosperity demanded an efficient and comprehensive transport system.

The Bristol Wayfarers' life with REAL was short. Possibly because Gomes's concentrated operational pattern, with its frequent landings and invariably heavy loads, demanded more structure strength than was built into the design, one Wayfarer sustained a spar failure at the end of 1947, and both aircraft stopped flying. But at this time, REAL had a dozen DC-3s, and experience had given it the organizational flexibility to cope with such eventualities.

Except for the main inter-city routes, the Brazilian Government, through the process of route certification by the Air Ministry, did not encourage, indeed did not allow, direct competition on any one feeder route, rightly believing this to constitute uneconomic duplication of resources. Permission was quickly forthcoming for a proposed new route to a community hitherto without airline service. But, generally speaking, these opportunities were fraught with difficulties, because the airfields were usually poor (or even non-existent, with the airline having to build a strip) and the traffic low, simply because all the larger places able to generate good loads were already well served by firmly established companies. The development of a concentrated domestic route network during the hectic five-year period following the war was therefore characterized by many multi-sector routes, as the airlines sought to fill their aircraft by stopping several times on the same flight. Fortunately for the airlines, at least for a few years, the alternative surface transport, both in quantity and quality, was abysmally poor. Even the progressive State of São Paulo possessed few metalled roads, and this shortcoming was acute throughout Brazil. Railways too served primarily the main cities, and this only by a disjointed system because of different gauges.

For the airlines it was a case of survival of the fittest, in an exacting interpretation of the phrase. As has already been observed, none of the companies actually lasted more than a few years, partly because the ambitious hopes stirred by the dreams of success were seldom fulfilled. At the primitive airstrips and the sometimes half-deserted station buildings the small and mostly poor communities were not yet ready or able to support air transport in the fullest sense. And the days of generous operating subsidies were over, the Government confining support mainly to sponsoring airfield construction at big cities.

The concept of survival penetrated at all levels, besides those of management. The story of just one DC-3—actually an ex-American Airlines DST—epitomised the unstable operating environment. PP-YPS had 36,000 hr behind it when REAL bought it from American for $16,000 in June 1949. By the time it was transferred to TAS, a REAL associate, in September 1958, it had added another 12,000 hr. This would not rank highly in the utilization tables, but the fact that it sustained two accidents during the period deserves consideration. Underlining the point that survival was the watchword for pilots as well as aircraft, the pilot in both cases was a certain Capt Yasuda, leading to the unofficial assertion that the aircraft's registration stood for 'Yasuda pede sucovo'—'Yasuda needs help.'

The bottom of the potential route barrel was scraped to the point where every possibility of a new air route was exhausted. Thanks to the slow progress in road building, the situation was reached where adjacent small towns, only a few miles apart, received air service before a road was built, and there was many an instance where the pilot could see his destination airstrip immediately after taking off from the last stop.

As in every walk of commercial life, the bigger fish swallowed the smaller, not only as a means of expansion for its own sake, but as a device to acquire new routes. REAL's first acquisition was quite modest. **Linhas Aéreas Wright** had started flying from Rio de Janeiro to Santos on 1 April, 1947, using two Lockheed Lodestars. But on 17 March, 1948, REAL took over Wright, and the aircraft were later sold to H. Aguinaga, a Nacional shareholder.

It could be that Wright was doomed from the start. It had been founded by Francisco 'Chico' Ribeiro Wright and his brother; and to expect that the Wright Brothers could ever succeed in the land of Alberto Santos Dumont was perhaps challenging national sensitivity just a little too far.

In 1950 came the first of REAL's airline acquisitions which augmented not only its fleet but also its network. During the latter part of 1949 and in 1950, Gomes was able to absorb the routes of 'Natal', the Juiz de Fora company which connected São Paulo with Belo Horizonte, the important capital of Minas Gerais, and operated as far west as Corumbá, Mato Grosso, on the Bolivian frontier. Four extra C-47s were added to REAL's fleet, bringing the total to 20.

The next important development was to buy Linha Aérea Transcontinental Brasileira (LATB) for 34 million cruzeiros in August 1951. REAL's total capital was raised at the same time to 70 million. This gave Gomes access to all the major cities of the northeast of Brazil, including six State capitals. During the same year, on 10 December, permission was received from the Paraguayan Government to operate to Asunción, providing REAL with its first international route, which was opened shortly afterwards, from São Paulo to Asunción, via Curitiba and the Iguassú Falls.

This spectacular waterfall—'South America's Niagara'—had first been served by REAL in 1950, and it now assumed greater importance, positioned as it was close to the frontiers of three countries, including Argentina. Also, the REAL service provided access to a potential tourist destination, the full benefit of which was eventually to pass to the heirs of the REAL empire. Paraguay, a relatively poor country with limited resources at this time, granted REAL what was tantamount to national recognition as a quasi-Paraguayan airline, awarding on 4 February, 1954, operating rights from Asunción to Uruguaiana, via Encarnación; and on 15 November of that year to Corumbá, via Concepción. This was one of the rare cases in airline history of cabotage rights, that is, the right to operate a domestic route wholly within the territory of a foreign country.

REAL-Aerovias Brasil

All these acquisitions, Wright, 'Natal,' and LATB, however, were of relatively minor significance compared with the triumph achieved in 1954, when Linneu Gomes negotiated the amalgamation of REAL with **Aerovias Brasil,** one of the airlines affiliated with the corporation for which he had formerly worked, TACA. Aerovias was not one of the pioneer airlines of Brazil; but it was older than most, and had built up considerable prestige, authority, experience, and influence.

When the war ended, Aerovias Brasil was already an established airline of considerable stature, integrated with the widespread TACA group, and with a record of having operated non-scheduled wartime flights to the United States. It thus held, albeit tenuously, 'grandfather rights' for international operation to North America. While these were being translated into legal terms, however,

Aerovias consolidated its Brazilian trunk network, and in April 1946 was granted rights covering all the major coastal cities from Porto Alegre to Belém, resulting in access to thirteen State capitals, service to which was inaugurated during 1947.

The development of the United States route will be dealt with in the next chapter and the narrative confined here to domestic expansion and the REAL association. For while the international aspirations overshadowed domestic activity, this latter was none-the-less important.

By August 1948, having disposed of two DC-2s acquired in 1945, Aerovias's fleet of fifteen C-47s/DC-3s was bigger than REAL's. Its national network included, in addition to the coastal route, several intermediate points on its trunk route from Rio de Janeiro to Belém via Goiânia and Anápolis. In 1947 it had started a cargo service to Manaus, paralleling Panair do Brasil, but this was suspended in November 1948. The following month, however, this loss was compensated for by the transfer of another important north–south inland route linking the big cities of the south with the northeast, when the luckless NAB was forced to suspend its operations via Lapa and Petrolina.

In January 1949 Aerovias Brasil increased its DC-3 fleet to nineteen, when it acquired the assets of Empresa de Transportes Aéreo Brasileiro, Ltda, a non-operating company. Shortly thereafter, Aerovias itself was purchased by the Government of the State of São Paulo on 17 February, and then went through a complete reorganization on 29 September, when the majority stockholder of VASP (the Municipal Bank of São Paulo) took over effective operational control. The name Brazilian International Airlines was officially registered as an alternative title, and the new board took office on 3 November, 1950. The authorized capital was raised to 60 million cruzeiros. During this transitional period of ownership, the first two or three Saab Scandia aircraft were delivered to Brazil in Aerovias Brasil markings, the first arriving in Rio de Janeiro on 11 August, 1950; but all the Scandias were transferred to VASP on 21 December.

In 1951, Aerovias Brasil's fleet consisted of twenty-four DC-3s, four Curtiss C-46s, and three Douglas DC-4s, specially purchased to operate a new international route to Montevideo and Buenos Aires. Two years later, Aerovias

REAL-Aerovias Brasil's Douglas C-54 PP-AXR at Congonhas Airport, São Paulo. Originally the USAF's 44-9024, this C-54 passed to Chicago & Southern Airlines as NC54361 *City of San Juan* and, after service with Aerovias Brasil and REAL, went to Lóide Aéreo Nacional and VASP. (*A. Fortner*)

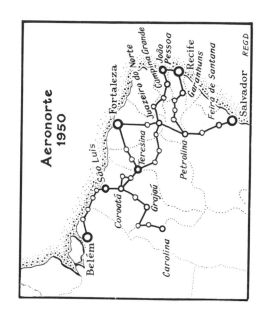

Aeronorte 1950

Belém
São Luís
Coroatá
Grajaú
Carolina
Teresina
Fortaleza
Juazeiro do Norte
Campina Grande
João Pessoa
Recife
Garanhuns
Feira de Santana
Petrolina
Salvador

REGD

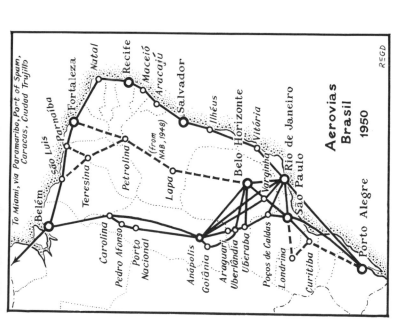

To Miami, via Paramaribo, Port of Spain,
Caracas, Ciudad Trujillo

Belém
São Luís
Parnaíba
Fortaleza
Natal
Recife
Maceió
Aracajú
Salvador
Ilhéus
Belo Horizonte
Vitória
Rio de Janeiro
São Paulo
Porto Alegre

Teresina
Petrolina
(from NAB, 1948)
Lapa
Carolina
Pedro Afonso
Porto Nacional
Anápolis
Goiânia
Araguari
Uberlândia
Uberaba
Poços de Caldas
Varginha
Londrina
Curitiba

Aerovias Brasil 1950

REGD

54. Aerovias Brasil and Aeronorte, 1950. Brazil's international airline, Aerovias Brasil, and its later associated company, Aeronorte, were both incorporated into the REAL air transport empire in 1954.

431

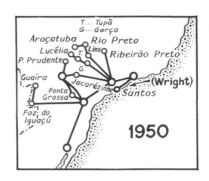

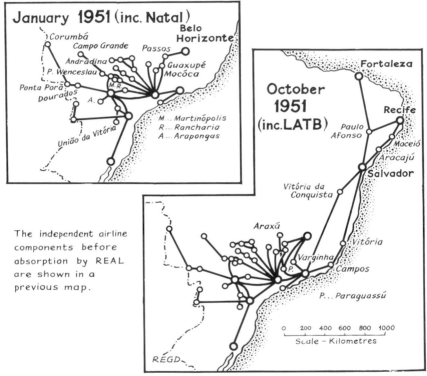

55. Early Growth of REAL, 1947–1951. The early growth of REAL, including its acquisition of small airlines, is illustrated in these maps.

acquired control of **Empresa de Transportes Aéreos Norte do Brasil, Ltda (Aeronorte)**, which operated feeder services in the northeast shoulder region of Brazil.

Aeronorte was founded in São Luis, Maranhão, late in 1949, and was authorized to start operations on 30 December of that year. The company took delivery of three Percival Prince aircraft, imported from Britain, and also bought

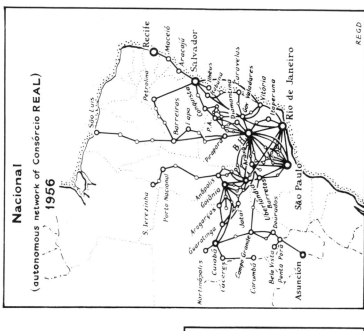

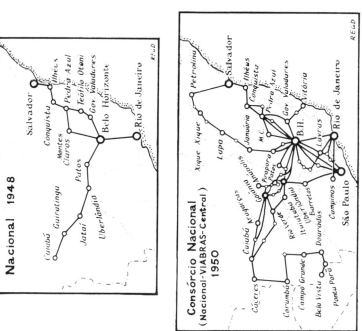

56. Growth of Nacional, 1948–1956. Nacional expanded from its base at Belo Horizonte into neighbouring states, and was operating a large network of feeder routes with REAL in 1956. (B.H. = Belo Horizonte, M.C. = Montes Claros, P.A. = Pedra Azul).

three Lockheed Model 10 Electras from VARIG. When operations eventually began in December 1950 on multi-stop routes from São Luis to Belém, Carolina, Fortaleza, Recife, and Salvador, Aeronorte leased one of VASP's old Ju 52/3ms.

When Aerovias took over in 1953, the Percival and Lockheed fleet had been depleted by crashes, and these were replaced by some all-purpose DC-3s transferred from Aerovias, and by six leased French-built Norécrin single-engined monoplanes. When REAL absorbed Aerovias Brasil in 1954, Aeronorte continued to operate as an autonomous unit, and was shown as such in the timetables, which referred to the 'REAL-Aerovias-Aeronorte Group' in recognition of the special nature of local airline work in the northeast.

Linneu Gomes negotiated the purchase of 87 per cent of the Aerovias stock on 10 September, 1954, having obtained full approval from the directors on 24 May. Then on 8 July the first of six Convair CV-340 pressurized twin-engined 40-passenger aircraft was handed over at the San Diego factory in California. The combined Aerovias-REAL fleet was now fifty-eight C-47/DC-3s, three DC-4s, and six Convair CV-340s.

Nacional

To proceed with the complex tale of mergers, acquisitions, and associations, it is first of all necessary to narrate the story of another consortium which had been fashioned during the early 1950s, under the control of **Transportes Aéreos Nacional Ltda.** By the time REAL took over Nacional in 1956, that company had assembled the routes and aircraft of seven other small airlines, and thus considerably strengthened REAL's stature at one stroke.

Transportes Aéreos Nacional, Ltda, was founded towards the end of 1946 by Hilton Machado and Manuel J. Antunes, two pilots. Most of the airline organization was placed in the care of Claudio Hoelck, the traffic manager, who was to play an influential role in Brazilian domestic aviation circles during more than thirty years of continuous involvement. Nacional obtained operating authority on 26 February, 1947, acquired its first fleet of two Douglas C-47s soon afterwards, and began regular services in January 1948, on a network centred on Belo Horizonte, providing connections with Rio, Salvador, and Cuiabá.

After two years of unobtrusive activity, during which time São Paulo was added to the route system and the C-47 fleet increased to six, Nacional made its first real expansionist move, by forming a consortium agreement with VIABRÁS. **Viação Aérea Brasil, S.A. (VIABRÁS)** had been founded on 11 April, 1946, by Arnoldo Raposo Murtinho, obtaining Air Ministry operating authority on 16 August, and beginning scheduled services with a fleet of three C-47s on 12 March, 1947—well ahead of Nacional's own progress. The original route was from Rio de Janeiro and Belo Horizonte to Rio Verde, via Uberlândia in western Minas Gerais, and Goiânia, the capital of Goiás. By the end of 1949, VIABRÁS had extended even further west, as far as Cuiabá and to Nortenópolis, in Mato Grosso, so that it virtually duplicated Nacional's services in that direction. The consortium, therefore, was eminently sensible, cutting out wasteful duplication where traffic volume could not justify competition.

Nacional had by this time opened a new route to Salvador, via Januária in northern Minas Gerais, and inland points in the State of Bahia as far north as Petrolina, following the course of the São Francisco River. It also consolidated its identity in Belo Horizonte by bringing a local airline, OMTA, into the consortium.

Organização Mineira de Transportes Aéreos (OMTA) was authorized to operate as an air taxi service, based in Belo Horizonte, in January 1946. Its first fleet was four de Havilland D.H.89As but these were supplemented by no less than nineteen Beech Bonanzas between 1947 and 1952. OMTA became a unit of the Nacional consortium, operating as an autonomous unit, in August 1950.

Two months later, Nacional brought into the consortium another airline which specialized in services to Mato Grosso. **Central Aérea, Ltda,** had been formed in March 1948, immediately after being granted an operating certificate on 29 March, 1948. It bought three Douglas C-47s in May, and started scheduled services on 11 June on a circuitous route from Rio de Janeiro to Belo Horizonte, via several cities in northern São Paulo State. By the end of the year, the network was extended to the States of Goiás and Mato Grosso, as far as Corumbá. In April 1950, more Mato Grosso points were added, so that the whole of the southern half of that extensive and remote State was connected with the industrial area of Brazil.

In April 1952, Nacional absorbed VASD (Santos Dumont) which had retained its corporate independence while operating in association with Transcontinental. Transcontinental went to REAL, but Nacional, by the new addition to the family, obtained access to Recife. During this period, the organization became known as the Consórcio Nacional de Transportes Aéreos; during 1953 and 1954 the C-47 fleet was increased to 20; and the consortium was incorporated as a limited company on 20 November, 1953.

By the end of 1954, another tentacle to Nacional's now extensive route network had been added, to São Luis, via some remote points in the States of Piauí and Maranhão. More C-47s were purchased, to bring the total to twenty-eight. Twelve thousand unduplicated route miles served 74 cities in Brazil, plus Asunción, Paraguay. Two more airlines came under its control, the first **Cia Itaú de Transportes Aéreos (Itaú)**, an all-cargo operator formed on 30 September, 1947, with a capital of 7½ million cruzeiros. Itaú had started operations in 1948 with a fleet of nine Curtiss C-46s, and by 1950, served important cities such as Belo Horizonte, Salvador, Recife, Fortaleza and Campo Grande, from both Rio de Janeiro and São Paulo. Nacional purchased Itaú in October 1955, by which time, however, the C-46 fleet had been depleted, through crashes, to five.

A few months later, Nacional also took over **Transportes Aéreos Salvador (TAS)** which had been founded by Capt Parreiras Horta in 1949 in Salvador as a charter and fixed-base operator. In 1953, TAS had obtained a certificate from the Air Ministry to operate scheduled services in the State of Bahia, by which time its fleet consisted of two de Havilland Herons and four Beech Bonanzas. During 1955, Panair do Brasil attempted to buy TAS, so as to secure a larger traffic base in Bahia; but these negotiations apparently were unsuccessful, and TAS went to Nacional early in 1956. This was a temporary arrangement, as later on TAS was to fall into Omar Fontana's grasp.

All these mergers had turned Nacional into an airline of substance, although its aircraft fleet, consisting entirely of twin-engined, unpressurized aircraft, did not permit it to participate in long-distance inter-city routes. It was, nevertheless, a valuable acquisition to Linneu Gomes's REAL consortium, when he acquired 85 per cent of Nacional's shares on 2 August, 1956. As was customary in Brazil, because of regulatory practice, Nacional continued to operate for a while as an autonomous unit, and even obtained further routes and aircraft under its own name. Six new Convair CV-440s, delivered between March and September 1957, were also registered under Nacional's numerical series.

435

PP-SLF was the third production de Havilland 114 Heron 1 and was the first of two acquired by Transportes Aéreos Salvador in 1952–53. It was sold in July 1955. (*British Aerospace*)

The End of REAL

By augmenting the airlines under his control into the Consórcio REAL-Aerovias-Nacional, Linneu Gomes had built himself an air transport empire. His route network stretched to every state in Brazil, mostly with both trunk inter-city and feeder routes. The combined domestic fleet totalled eighty-six C-47/DC-3s, six Convair CV-340s, plus six more Convair CV-440s due for delivery under a Nacional contract; while three DC-4s were allocated to international operations, which, however, had reached the stage of development when replacements were clearly essential. In fact, during the five years following the acquisition of Nacional, REAL turned its attention to developing its routes to North America and to the Pacific, an important and challenging process which is dealt with in the next chapter.

REAL-Aerovias Brasil's Convair CV-340-62 PP-YRD with passengers boarding via the forward airstairs. REAL's livery was green and black. In 1961 this aircraft was sold to Linjeflyg in Sweden. (*REAL*)

436

To Miami
Caracas
Port of Spain

CONSORCIO
REAL-AEROVIAS BRASIL
February 1955

Belém
São Luis
Parnaíba
Camocim
Fortaleza
Teresina
Natal
Recife
Carolina
Pedro
Afonso
Petrolina
Maceió
Paulo Afonso
Aracajú
Pôrto
Nacional
Lapa
Salvador
Cuiabá
Ceres
Anápolis
Conquista
Ilhéus
Goiânia
Uberlândia
Corumbá
Catalão
Araguari
Uberaba
Passos
Governador
Valadôres
Ytuporanga
Lucetba
Aracatuba
Dracena
Vitória
Campo Grande
Maracajú
Pôrto
Murtinho
Douraao
Rio Preta
Alfenaringa
Vargainha
Campos
Ponta
Porã
Paranavai
Maringa
Campo Mourão
Apucarana
Rio de Janeiro
Concepción
Cascavel
Ponta
Grossa
São Paulo
Santos
Asunción
Foz del
Iguaçu
Palmas
Campos
Encarnación
União da Vitória
Curitiba
Uruguaiania
Florianópolis
C. ... Catanduva
R.P. .. Ribeirão Preto
P. ... Penápolis
S. ... Sertanópolis
C.C. .. Cornélio Procopio
J. ... Jacarézinho
A ... Arapongas
M ... Mandaguari
T ... Tupã
R ... Rancharia
P.P. .. Presidente Prudente
P.W. .. Presidente Wenceslau
G. ... Guaxupé
Ca. .. Cambará

Pôrto
Alegre
Buenos
Aires
Montevideo

0   250   500   1000
Miles
0   200   400   600   800   1000
Kilometres

REGD

57. Consórcio REAL-Aerovias Brasil, 1955. After taking control of Nacional and Aerovias Brasil in the mid-1950s, the REAL Consortium began to assume the stature of a major airline. For a short time it ranked tenth in the world, measured by the number of passengers carried.

437

At home, REAL concentrated on consolidating the complex assembly of routes and services, having, with Nacional, to digest a corporate meal compared with which previous takeovers had been mere snacks. Nevertheless, the process of stabilizing and simplifying routes, and eliminating duplication, made good progress. On the main inter-city services, REAL gave the travelling public excellent service: in 1956 there were sixteen daily flights between Rio de Janeiro and São Paulo, twelve between Rio and Belo Horizonte, seven between São Paulo and Curitiba, and three from São Paulo to both Londrina and Belo Horizonte. But perhaps the most important route of all to be opened in the late 1950s was when on 3 May, 1957, REAL introduced the first air service to Brasília. This new national capital, the dream of President Kubitschek, was under construction in the State of Goiás to the northeast of Anápolis, and lacked communication with the rest of Brazil.

But REAL had outgrown its strength—or the ability of the mercurial Gomes to control it. Running into severe financial problems, he was compelled to sell half of his interest in Aerovias Brasil to VARIG on 2 May, 1961; and only a few months later, on 16 August, 1961, REAL was taken over in its entirety by VARIG, by a transfer of 90 per cent of the shares.

In many ways it was the end of an era. During its meteoric career, REAL became, in terms of passengers carried annually, one of the ten leading airlines in the world, carrying upwards of two million at the time of the Nacional merger. But the honeymoon for airline proliferation in Brazil was over. Paradoxically, the dearth of surface transport had given the airlines their first opportunity; now the fortunes were reversed.

In 1957 the car manufacturing industry was established in São Paulo, and the Brazilians' eager demand for road travel created an enormous stimulant for road building, funded both by the Federal Government and by the States. People who had been accustomed to making journeys to the nearest city by air suddenly found it was not only cheaper, but just as convenient, to go by road. In a curious way, REAL, whose early expansion had drawn strength from Brazil's inadequate surface transport, later became the victim of the latter's equally dramatic improvement.

The Lóide Consortium

While fourteen airlines went through the complicated manoeuvring which culminated in the eventual formation of the REAL consortium, another group, smaller in magnitude but lacking nothing in the tortuous intricacies of corporate manipulation, evolved on the other side of the Brazilian airline fence. This group was centred on Lóide, an airline which was founded in Anápolis, Goiás, as **Transportes Carga Aérea, S.A., (T.C.A.)** on 22 December, 1947, with a capital of 30 million cruzeiros. The President was Rui Vacani, one of the original owners of E.T.A. (the company which gave NYRBA so much trouble in 1929) and prominent shareholders were Roberto Taves and Marcilio Gibson Jacques. This company had a brief existence under this name, operating non-scheduled charter flights with a fleet of three C-47s, of which two crashed.

T.C.A. was then reorganized on 24 August, 1949, with a capital of 30 million cruzeiros, changing its name to **Lóide Aéreo Nacional.** It was authorized to import nine Curtiss C-46s and these began to fly regular services on two routes northwards from Rio and Belo Horizonte to São Luis, via Carolina, and to Fortaleza, via Lapa. The São Luis route also included a stop at Formosa.

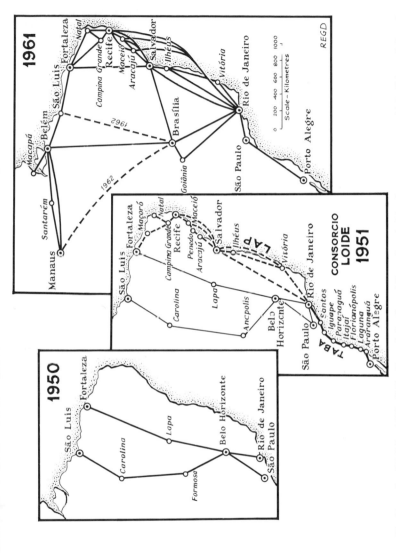

58. Growth of Lóide, 1950–1961. One of the few airlines founded in the postwar era which did not fall under REAL's control was Lóide Aéreo Nacional, which itself formed a small consortium. Later it was sold to VASP.

439

Within a few months of the reorganization, Lóide initiated discussions to form a technical consortium, consisting of pooled maintenance and operating facilities, with two other small airlines, **Linhas Aéreas Paulistas (LAP)** and **Transportes Aéreos Bandeirantes (TABA)**. Recognizing the presence of excessive competition within Brazil, this arrangement was consolidated into a complete consortium, under Lóide's name, on 24 August, 1951.

LAP was older than Lóide, having been founded late in 1943, with a capital of 50 million cruzeiros, but did not hold its first general meeting of shareholders until 9 February, 1945. Some evidence of the enthusiasm for airline investment in those days is provided by the *Diario Oficial*, which needed sixty pages to list the shareholders.

In June of that year the Air Ministry awarded LAP its operating permit, at which time the fleet consisted of a single Lockheed Hudson; but a year later, four Douglas DC-3s were acquired, and services started from São Paulo to Recife and Campina Grande, Pernambuco, via the coastal route. In February 1947 LAP became yet another airline to operate between São Paulo and Rio de Janeiro on a turnaround basis as well as a part of its trunk route. Experiencing some difficulty with its northern terminal—curtailing the route to Maceió in October 1948 and extending to Natal and Fortaleza in April 1950, LAP was operating a single route as far as Natal when it joined Lóide in 1951.

TABA was really little more than an airline name, as it operated intermittently for only a few months. Nevertheless, its history was somewhat unusual. Originally it had been founded as **Transportes Aéreos Bacia Amazonica**, just after the war, by Capt Alberto Martins Torres. He was a former well-known Air Force pilot who had been with Transcontinental and VASD, and who visualized the development of the Amazon region around Manaus. He ran into all kinds of problems, however, both economic—the price of rubber fell drastically, effectively delaying Manaus's progress as a regional centre; and regulatory—the Brazilian Government disapproved of company names which had strongly regional connotations. TABA infringed on the latter on two counts: the 'Amazonica' and the fact that TABA meant 'Indian village'.

Martins was obliged to re-structure his airline, changing the name to Transportes Aéreos Bandeirantes, thus retaining the same initials, with the emotive inclusion of 'Bandeirantes' no doubt dampening official objections. He also moved the focus of operations southward, and in April 1948 began to fly two PBY-5A Catalinas, originally purchased for the Amazon, from Rio de Janeiro to Laguna, Santa Catarina. This route was later extended to Porto Alegre, and although TABA was not even operating when it joined Lóide in 1950, the route to Porto Alegre was a valuable asset.

During the early 1950s Lóide established itself as an operator of substance, and by 1956 had a fleet of nineteen C-46s, of which three were all-freighters. Its routes extended to all the main State capitals, except that of Mato Grosso, but, unlike most of the other companies, had no ambitions to serve any of the feeder routes to small communities. By Brazilian domestic standards, Lóide was strictly long-haul. To some of the leading airline executives of the major companies, the Lóide route network seemed to pose the threat of uneconomic duplication over too wide an area, and this led to an interesting experiment.

On 22 November, 1956, Lóide signed an operational agreement with Panair do Brasil, for a limited period of two years, with possible renewal if the idea met with success. The basis of the agreement was a plan to subdivide Brazil into spheres of influence, or geographical zones, in which one major airline would be dominant,

440

Lóide Aéreo Nacional's Curtiss C-46A PP-LDX at Campo de Marte, São Paulo, during the commemoration of Semana da Asa. (*A. Fortner*)

so as to eliminate wasteful competition. Panair do Brasil and Lóide would join forces for long-haul routes to the north and northeast; REAL and Cruzeiro do Sul would assume responsibility for the central region and short-haul routes to the north; while VARIG and VASP would share the spoils in the south. Although the scheme did not succeed, there was a certain logic to it, as at the time Panair and Lóide had equipment well suited to the longer routes. Indeed, Lóide demonstrated its faith in the agreement by investing in no less than ten four-engined Douglas aircraft during 1957.

In February, four DC-6A (passenger-cargo convertible) aircraft were ordered, with the understanding that these would be leased to Panair do Brasil for international flights. At the same time, Panair undertook not to compete with Lóide on the long-haul domestic routes with comparable equipment, thus leaving Lóide a clear field in which to deploy its six DC-4s, bought during the year from Western Airlines and United Air Lines.

The agreement did not fulfil its early promise, partly through differences between the two participants, partly because it was too far-reaching an idea for the period; although events a decade or so later were to suggest that in principle they were on the right track organizationally. Clearly, there were too many

Lóide Aéreo's Douglas DC-6A PP-LFA was delivered in December 1958, leased to Panair do Brasil 1959–61 as *Garcia de Arica* and returned to Lóide as *Amazonas*.

airlines chasing too limited a traffic volume, even though in Brazil at the time this was considerable. However, the idea did not receive official support and the agreement was formally ended in July 1958.

Lóide then continued its way independently—and quite eventfully. The DC-6As duly arrived in February 1959 and were in fact leased to Panair for a while but went into service on Lóide's own routes in March 1961. A cargo service to Miami started in June 1959, and more DC-4s were purchased to replace two which had crashed. At the end of 1960 Lóide was showing considerable enterprise in a battle for low-fare traffic by offering a day tour from Rio de Janeiro to Brasília, including lunch, for 5,500 cruzeiros ($290 at the official rate of exchange).

Thus, although Lóide's days as an independent airline were numbered, the airline did not go under without a struggle. Indeed, on 24 October, 1961, it bought NAB, the oldest of the 'new' airlines, but now sadly ailing. NAB continued to operate as an independent unit, but the matter was academic, as in January 1962, the entire Lóide group was taken over by VASP.

The Perils of Pauline (NAB)

For most of the airlines formed during the hectic postwar period, the development usually followed a standard pattern: precarious establishment, followed by either mushroom-like growth or rapid demise. With **Navegação Aérea Brasileira (NAB)**, the airline which had been formed much earlier than most, the story was repeated not once, but several times.

Emerging from the war with a small fleet of Lockheed Lodestars, NAB bought two Douglas DC-3s in May 1946 directly from the manufacturer, one of them, PP-NAM, being the penultimate DC-3 off that distinguished and record-breaking production line. A third DC-3 was added early in 1947, during which year about 2½ million kilometres were flown over a network linking Rio de Janeiro and São Paulo with the cities of the northeast. By March 1948, however, services had been suspended because of financial difficulties, and the company was declared bankrupt on 17 August, 1948. The Brazilian Government took over the airline to give the creditors a chance to recover their money, and steps were taken to restrict NAB's activities to a scale which it could handle. Accordingly, two DC-3s were leased to LATB and with the remaining one a small local route network was established in the area north of Rio de Janeiro, as far as Montes Claros and Governador Valadares in Minas Gerais, and to Vitória in Espírito Santo.

By 1954, even this diminutive network had been reduced to two short routes, but somehow NAB survived. During the summer of 1957, it purchased two Curtiss C-46s, in November of that year the company was completely reorganized, and in July 1958, the shares were sold to Dilvo Perez, for 60 million cruzeiros. Ten DC-3s were purchased from Panair do Brasil, which also passed over some internal routes in the Recife area, and an operational agreement was concluded between the two companies. The local services in the Rio area were abandoned and NAB once more began to spread its wings over a trunk network echoing the days of its former brief prosperity in 1946.

Augmenting its C-46 fleet to eleven aircraft, NAB proceeded in 1960 to promote low-fare, austerity-standard services, in an effort to gamble on success or disaster, at high stakes. A so-called 'coach service' was launched at 45 per cent of economy fares prevailing in Brazil at the time, with a further 20 per cent off for round-trip tickets. In August, NAB was advertising coach service from Rio to Belém at 6,842 cruzeiros one way ($360 at the official rate of exchange), and

12,350 round trip. In 1961, in an effort to attract revenues at any price, a 'Coach cargo' service was advertised, in association with Exmar Transportes Rapidos Ltda, but this was the last desperate effort to defy all the laws of airline operating economics.

Lóide purchased NAB on 24 October, 1961, and the bewildering cycle of changing fortunes came to an end. NAB is remembered in Brazilian aviation circles with a curious affection. In spite of its uneviable reputation—its acronym was alleged to stand for 'Nao Anda Bem' (It doesn't go well)—it at least flew safely, which is more than could be said for almost every one of the other airlines whose chronology was punctuated by an annual accident or two.

Southern Incursions

Two companies in the Southern region of Brazil tried to establish State airlines, but both were doomed to failure from the start, for basically the same reasons as all the others which had chosen the industrially active Central region around Rio de Janeiro, São Paulo, and Belo Horizonte. The history of the two airlines ran parallel, and both shared the same fate.

SAVAG's Douglas C-47A PP-SAE also served with Cruzeiro do Sul.

S.A. Viação Aérea Gaucha (SAVAG) was started by private interests on 25 November, 1946, to operate scheduled services in the State of Rio Grande do Sul. Formed with a capital of 3 million cruzeiros by Dr Augusto L. Otero and Capt Gustavo Cramer, with support from Industrias Leal Santos, a canning company, SAVAG purchased three Lockheed Lodestars from Panair do Brasil in January 1947 and by the end of the year had inaugurated services between Porto Alegre and Bagé, Pelotas, and Rio Grande. In 1948, the network was augmented by a service to the north of the State, and the following year a DC-3 was added to the fleet. This aircraft was purchased by Cruzeiro do Sul, and transferred to SAVAG, offering fairly strong evidence that the latter operation was a device to enable Cruzeiro do Sul to penetrate southwards in the territory hitherto recognized to be the exclusive domain of VARIG. Unlike Cruzeiro, Panair, or VASP, VARIG had been content to restrict itself to a modest postwar route network within its home State and to immediately adjoining areas.

Presumably there was some controversy about this, and, late in 1952, the Department of Aeronautics gave SAVAG notice to terminate most of its routes, because of excessive competition with the incumbent airline. From this time, SAVAG was virtually a paper operation, as Cruzeiro do Sul had acquired a controlling interest in the company, handled all reservations, supplied the aircraft

443

and maintained services, and advertised flights—which were now confined to a route from Porto Alegre to Curitiba—jointly with its own.

More or less the same process was repeated in the State of Santa Catarina, immediately to the north of SAVAG's sphere of influence—if such a modest challenge to VARIG's hegemony could be so described. **Transportes Aéreos Ltda (TAL)** was founded in Rio de Janeiro in December 1947, and began operating two C-47s on a route from Curitiba to Rio de Janeiro in May 1948. In August 1950, the name of the company was changed to **Empresa de Transportes Aéreos Catarinense, S.A. (TAC)** and the headquarters transferred to Florianópolis. Cruzeiro do Sul began to provide technical assistance and flight personnel, much in the same manner as with SAVAG.

Effectively, the combination of SAVAG and TAC gave Cruzeiro do Sul more exposure to the public in areas which it felt it lacked competitive strength, but the pretence gradually became little more than an academic recognition in the airline timetables. On 1 January, 1966, both SAVAG and TAC ceased to exist, and their operations were completely absorbed by Cruzeiro do Sul, their mentor for two decades.

Aero Geral

During the frantic period of airline proliferation throughout the first half-decade of the postwar era, the established airlines, with histories going back to the 1920s and 1930s, generally remained aloof from corporate entanglements. They watched from afar, making only occasional forays, usually to pick up the pieces and restore order after some minor combatants had exhausted each other. Of the Establishment, Panair do Brasil never acquired, or took a financial interest in another company. VASP's action was confined to absorbing Lóide after that consortium ran out of stamina. Cruzeiro do Sul contented itself with setting up quasi-subsidiaries in the south to create an irritant for VARIG. This latter company which (unbelievably, in the light of its later record) did not fly northwards beyond the Rio Grande do Sul State boundary until 1946, remained very much a local-service operator during a period when other ambitiously-named companies were proclaiming objectives which, if fulfilled, would have culminated in widespread national, if not international, networks.

VARIG waited in the wings, conscious of its potential strength, watching lesser mortals strain to deploy their limited talents to a public and an industry which demanded higher performance and quality. With good husbandry, VARIG survived while others wilted. This story is told in the next chapter, but one significant episode is appropriate here, as it relates to an airline whose absorption by VARIG—the only acquisition by that company during the 1950s—was to have far-reaching consequences.

Aero Geral was originally founded in the Amazon region with a single small aircraft, a Monocoupe 90A. On 10 February, 1942, it was authorized to begin scheduled operations, but was unable to do so, because the Monocoupe was inadequate. Business activity ceased in 1944.

Then, in January 1947, the airline was re-established, when A. F. McLaren, assisted by another ex-Panair do Brasil pilot, planned to start an airline in the Amazon region. They had heard that Panair was planning to close its Amazon routes and sub-contract them. But Panair changed its plans, continued to operate, and the two pilots thereupon purchased Aero Geral's operating certificate, and simultaneously applied for permission to operate elsewhere.

444

VARIG's Douglas C-47A PP-VBP in smart blue, white and black livery. (*VARIG*)

They were successful in obtaining the rights to operate a coastal route from Santos to Natal, serving every main city en route. They bought four Consolidated PBY-5 Catalina amphibians from the War Surplus Commission at Natal, and began services to that city, at first from Rio de Janeiro, in March 1947, and extending to Santos in May. Aero Geral operated steadily and without major incident for four years, during which time it acquired a Curtiss C-46 and two DC-3s. Then, on 2 June, 1951, one of the Catalinas crashed, and this may have led to the decision to sell the remaining amphibians, and to wind up the company.

In May 1952, VARIG bought Aero Geral, which continued to operate under its own identity for about a year until the acquisition was finally approved by the Department of Civil Aeronautics in July 1953. This transaction was only one of dozens which occurred in the stormy postwar decade, but it was possibly the most far-reaching in its ultimate effect. For although VARIG acquired only one DC-3 and one C-46 in the takeover, it gained an extension to its route network which effectively doubled its influence in Brazil and its stature as an airline. By its shrewd decision, VARIG ceased to be a regional airline and became a national one, to measure against the hitherto dominant Panair do Brasil and Cruzeiro do Sul. And this was only the beginning.

VARIG's Curtiss C-46A PP-VCG is seen here with underwing Turboméca Palas turbojets which provided increased take-off power. This aircraft had several owners and at one time was REAL's PP-YQI. It was sold in 1969. (*VARIG*)

TABLE 25
New Brazilian Airlines 1945–1950
(In order of first service date)

Airline	Date Founded	Date of First Service	Fleet	Route Network	Date of Termination	Reason for Termination
Viação Aérea **Santos Dumont** (VASD)	18 Jan. 1944	Feb 1945	2 Catalina 1 Budd Conestoga 3 DC-3	Rio–northern coastal route to Recife	April 1952	Absorbed by Nacional
Cia **Meridional** de Transportes	Late 1944	4 Oct, 1945	3 Avro Anson	Rio–Campos and Vitória	March 1946	Bankruptcy
Linhas Aéreas Brasileiras, S.A. (**LAB**)	9 Feb, 1945	8 Dec, 1945	7 C-47	Rio–northern coastal route to Natal; Rio–São Paulo	Sept 1949	Bankruptcy
Linha Aérea Trans-Continental Brasileira (**Transcontinental**, or TCB, or **LATB**)	22 July, 1944	1 Feb, 1946	5 Avro Anson 5 C-47 1 Beech D-18 1 C-46	Rio–northern coastal route to Recife and Fortaleza; also to points in Minas Gerais	Aug 1951	Purchased by REAL
Viação Aérea **Bahiana**	12 Dec, 1945	Feb 1946	3 DC-3 1 Boeing 247D 2 Lodestar	Local routes in Bahia	4 Nov, 1948	Bankruptcy
Redes Estaduais Aéreas Ltda (**REAL**)	Dec 1945	7 Feb, 1946	(Many—see text and Fleet Appendix)	Rio–São Paulo; then rapid expansion to become national and international network	18 Aug, 1961	Absorbed by VARIG

446

Company			Aircraft	Services		Disposition
Organização Mineira de Transportes Aéreos (OMTA)	Jan 1946	March 1946	4 D.H.89A Bonanzas	Local services in Minas Gerais, mainly on air taxi basis	Aug, 1950	Absorbed by Nacional
Viação Aérea Arco-Iris, S.A.	March 1945	12 July 1946	7 D.H.89A	São Paulo–Paraná	28 Dec, 1948	Bankruptcy
Linhas Aéreas Paulistas (LAP)	Late 1943	July 1946	5 DC-3	São Paulo–Rio–northern coastal route to Fortaleza	24 Aug, 1951	Joined Lóide consortium
Linhas Aéreas 'Natal' S.A.	3 July, 1946	7 Dec, 1946	4 C-47	São Paulo and neighbouring states	May 1950	Purchased by REAL
Transportes Aéreos Nacional Ltda	26 Feb, 1947	Jan 1948	31 C-47	Extensive network based in Belo Horizonte, expanding to São Luis, Recife, and Mato Grosso	2 Aug, 1956	Purchased by REAL
Viação Aérea Brasil S.A. (VIABRÁS)	11 April, 1946	12 Mar, 1947	6 C-47	Rio–Belo Horizonte–Goiânia–Cuiabá	Aug 1950	Absorbed by Nacional
Aero Geral Ltda	10 Feb, 1942	Mar 1947	5 Cataiina 2 DC-3, 1 C-46	Coastal route, Santos–Natal	May 1952	Purchased by VARIG
Linhas Aéreas Wright, Ltda.	Early 1947	1 April, 1947	2 Lodestar	Rio–Santos	17 Mar 1948	Purchased by REAL
Viação Interestadual de Transportes Aéreos (VITA)	26 Nov, 1946	—	(Did not own aircraft)	—	23 Oct, 1948	Purchased by LATB

Airline	Date Founded	Date of First Service	Fleet	Route Network	Date of Termination	Reason for Termination
S.A. Viação Aérea Gaucha (SAVAG)	25 Nov, 1946	Oct 1947	3 Lodestar 2 DC-3	Local service in Rio Grande do Sul, later to Curitiba and São Paulo	1 Jan, 1966	Absorbed by Cruzeiro do Sul
Transportes Aéreos Ltda (TAL). Name changed to Empresa de Transportes Aéreos Catarinense, S.A. (TAC) in Aug 1950	Dec 1947	May 1948	5 C-47	Curitiba–Rio; later to Porto Alegre	1 Jan, 1966	Absorbed by Cruzeiro do Sul
Universal Transportes Aéreos	End 1947	Early 1948	2 Lodestar 1 C-46	Rio–Belo Horizonte, São Paulo	1 Dec, 1948	Bankruptcy
Transportes Aéreos Bandeirantes (TABA)	Early 1948	April 1948	2 Catalina 1 DC-3	Rio–Porto Alegre	Feb 1950	Joined Lóide consortium
Transportes Aéreos Sul-Americanos (TASA)	Feb 1948	May 1948	2 Douglas B-18 1 DC-3	São Paulo–Goiânia	Jan 1949	Bankruptcy
Central Aérea Ltda	29 Mar, 1948	11 Jure, 1948	4 C-47	Rio–Goiânia–Cuiabá–Corumbá, and points in São Paulo State	Late 1950	Absorbed by Nacional

Transportes Carga Aérea, S.A. Name changed to **Lóide** Aéreo Nacional, S.A., 24 August, 1949	22 Dec, 1947	July 1948	(Many—see text)	Rio de Janeiro and São Paulo to São Luis and Fortaleza, via Belo Horizonte	Jan 1962	Purchased by VASP
Cia Itaú de Transportes Aéreos (**Itaú**)	30 Sept, 1947	1948	10 C-46	Freight services, Rio–São Paulo–Salvador–Recife, Fortaleza, Campo Grande	Oct 1957	Purchased by Nacional
Empresa de Transportes Aéreos Norte do Brasil Ltda (**Aeronorte**)	30 Dec, 1949	Late 1950	3 Percival Prince 3 Lockheed 10 Electra 5 Norécrin Some DC-3s from Aerovias Brasil	Local services in north-east states, from Belém to Salvador	1965	Aerovias Brasil acquired control in 1953
Transportes Aéreos Salvador (**TAS**)	1949	1950	2 D.H. Heron 4 Bonanza 1 Beech AT-11 3 DC-3 6 C-46	Local services in Bahia	1962	Absorbed by Sadia

Dr Paulo Sampaio (*left*), Panair do Brasil's President from 1943 until 1955, transformed the airline from its status as a Pan American subsidiary into an intercontinental flag carrier which did much credit to its country. Sampaio ordered the early Comet jet airliner, whose tragic crashes in 1954 led to his failure to be re-elected as President in 1955. Doctor José Bento Ribeiro Dantas (*centre*) was appointed head of Syndicato Condor in 1942 when the Brazilian Government took over the German-owned airline and changed its name to Serviços Aéreos Cruzeiro do Sul Ltda. It was still the leading Brazilian domestic airline when he died suddenly on 20 April, 1969. Eric de Carvalho (*right*) accepted the formidable task of succeeding Rubem Berta as President of VARIG in 1966, by which time the Brazilian airline had taken its place as a world leader. (*Eric Hess; Carlos; VARIG*)

CHAPTER TWENTY-TWO

Brazilian Airlines Overseas

Divestment of Foreign Control

In an earlier chapter, dealing with the progress of Brazilian airlines during the influential years of the Second World War, the transition from predominantly-foreign to predominantly-Brazilian ownership was observed (see especially Chart 8 on page 414). This was accomplished, on 6 January, 1942, by the complete take-over of Condor and its overnight change of status to become a Brazilian airline; the termination, on 7 December, 1943, of Pan American Airways' complete ownership of Panair do Brasil to allow 42 per cent of the shares to pass to Brazilians; and by a 40 per cent initial shareholding of Aerovias Brasil on its formation on 26 August, 1942.

Parallel with these direct actions to reduce foreign control, progress was also made to secure a stronger Brazilian base for future international negotiations when the war was over. Legal steps were taken, first of all, to eject any protracted involvement by the Axis powers. On 12 February, 1942, under Decree No.4,109, the operating permit of Luftschiffbau Zeppelin GmbH to operate airships

450

between Brazil and Germany, was revoked, and at the same time title of the airship base and facilities at Santa Cruz (Bartolomeu de Gusmão) passed to the Air Ministry. Shortly afterwards, on 18 May, by Decree-Law 4,308, the same fate befell Deutsche Lufthansa, and, on 14 June, 1945, under Decree-Law 7,642, Ala Littoria, S. A. Meanwhile, on 11 May, 1945, under the provisions of Portaria 145 of the Air Ministry, the material assets of Air France and Brasil Aérea Limitada, its Brazilian associate, were requisitioned by the Brazilian Government.

By this time, the important Bermuda Agreement between the United States and Great Britain had been signed on 11 February, 1945, and this had provided a model for future such agreements. Before the war, intercontinental or trans-oceanic travel was operated under conditions which were not critically demanding of international law. Most of the long-distance routes were operated by European airlines which served to link overseas colonies, dependencies, and dominions with the motherland (or fatherland, depending on national psychology). Matters of over-flying or landing rights were not needed too often, especially by the British, whose territory was almost continuous throughout most continents. In other cases, there was a mutual exchange of rights, sometimes covered only by a simple memorandum of understanding, or even an unwritten 'gentleman's agreement', such as between the British and the Dutch in southeast Asia, where both countries needed each other's territory for flights to Australia. The postwar world, however, was different. Not only was the course of nationalism gaining momentum so that countries were either seceding from the European empires, or were demanding greater autonomy and control; but aircraft were capable of much longer range, and it was becoming practically possible for almost any nation with a strong commercial airline to contemplate direct service against a background of vastly increased airmindedness on the part of the travelling public. Above all, most nations feared the potential dominance of the United States, whose airline industry had prospered while others had languished under the rigours of wartime austerity and restriction.

Following this trend, a bilateral agreement was signed between Brazil and the United States, on 2 October, 1946, under Decree No.21,888. This followed closely the provisions of Bermuda, exchanging basic flying rights according to the 'Five Freedoms', agreeing on fare structures under the aegis of IATA, and designating routes with agreed capacity limitations to prevent excessive competition. One clause permitted airlines on both sides to employ the device of 'change of gauge' for multi-stop routes in the respective foreign territories to avoid providing excessive capacity on some segments, at the same time ensuring that cabotage rights were not abused.

By Aviso 96 of the Air Ministry, on 21 October, conditions were laid down for the Brazilian airlines which aspired to operate overseas on the routes covered by the bilateral agreement. This covered standards of capitalization and competence, including proof of Brazilian control, e.g. at least 51 per cent shareholding, and proof of experience, specifically a past record of at least 2,000 mn annual kilometres of flight, and two years of continuous scheduled service.

Fortunately, Panair do Brasil had already qualified for the ownership clause. On 19 September, 1946, when the capital was increased from 80 million to 100 million cruzeiros, Pan American sold 400,000 shares to Brazilians, thus giving Brazil a majority 52 per cent shareholding of its major airline.

The way was now open for Brazil to show the flag overseas on the tails of its own commercial airliners.

The First Route to the USA

The terms of the bilateral agreement with the United States allowed the designated US airline to operate to Brazil by two routes: Belém–Barreiras–Rio de Janeiro–Porto Alegre, and beyond, and Manaus–Goiânia–Guaíra and beyond, as well as allowing onward rights to Africa, via Belém and Natal. The Brazilian carrier(s) were granted, in return, routes to the United States mainland, via Puerto Rico, to New York or Washington; Miami and Chicago; and Miami and New Orleans. Also, provision was made to serve third countries via these points, by any reasonably direct route.

Aerovias Brasil was now able to consolidate its existing non-scheduled service into a scheduled route under the terms of the bilateral agreement. The airline was chosen as one of two international operators by the Brazilian Government, and continued to operate to Miami from Belém, via Paramaribo, Port of Spain, and Ciudad Trujillo (Santo Domingo). The multi-stop nature of this route was imposed by the equipment. Although Aerovias Brasil purchased two DC-2s in 1945, and thirteen DC-3s in 1946, the twin-engined aircraft did not have the range to permit more direct service.

The terms laid down by the Brazilian Air Ministry were met by the purchase, on 11 January, 1947, of the TACA shares in Aerovias Brasil by a group of São Paulo industrialists, so that the airline became 91 per cent Brazilian. Shortly afterwards, the overland route to Belém, via Goiânia, Porto Nacional and Carolina, was supplemented by a coastal route via all the major cities; and a US C.A.B. permit, issued on 27 August, 1947, set the seal on Aerovias's grandfather rights to the route.

Five weeks later, on 2 October, **Cruzeiro do Sul** was named by the Government as the second of the two new airlines designated to serve the United States. Permission was granted to open a route to New York and Washington, via San Juan. In 1946, Cruzeiro had increased its capital from a nominal amount to 20 million cruzeiros and, on 2 May of that year, taken delivery of three DC-4s, converted from C-54 wartime transports. It was thus in a good position to inaugurate service.

During 1948 and 1949, Cruzeiro do Sul operated about 30 survey flights to New York and/or Washington; but Dr Dantas, the Director General, refused to start public service without subsidy, and the issue became one of principle between Cruzeiro do Sul and the Government, with neither side giving way. In 1949 the three DC-4s were sold, for $600,000 each, and the money allocated towards the

Cruzeiro do Sul's Douglas C-54B PP-CCI *Sirius* was delivered in 1946, and is seen in natural metal finish, with the Brazilian green and yellow colours running diagonally across the fin and rudder. (*Cruzeiro do Sul*)

Panair do Brasil's Lockheed Model 049 Constellation PP-PCF *Manoel de Borba Gato* was originally Pan American's NC88849. (*Lockheed*)

purchase of a fleet of four pressurized Convair CV-340s. Later, in May 1952, the Ministry of Aeronautics cancelled Cruzeiro's US authorization, because of lack of adequate equipment, and the route was ceded to VARIG, which was prepared to operate without subsidy.

By this time, Aerovias Brasil had, in 1950, officially registered an alternative name for overseas applications: Brazilian International Airlines; and had bought three DC-4s for use on its overseas routes, and to Buenos Aires. Cruzeiro do Sul contented itself with more modest foreign ambitions, in 1953, with a route to Georgetown, British Guiana, via Cayenne, French Guiana; and to Santa Cruz, Bolivia, in co-operation with Lloyd Aéreo Boliviano.

To consider the long-term effect of Dr Dantas's firm—some would term it obstinate—stand is an interesting speculation, in the light of subsequent events. The principle upon which he took it was vindicated when the Brazilian Government later granted subsidies on a kilometres flown basis. But this was not until 1950 and did not help Dantas in 1947. Ironically, the airline which inherited the prestige route to New York was VARIG, which ultimately bought Cruzeiro do Sul. Had Fate taken a slightly different course in the immediate postwar years, the positions might well have been reversed.

Panair do Brasil to Europe

By the time **Panair do Brasil** was in full compliance with the Brazilian-majority stipulation by the Air Ministry it was already established as a trans-ocean airline, representing its country on the prestige routes to Europe, formerly operated only by European companies. Having taken delivery of its first Lockheed 049 Constellation in March 1946, service was inaugurated to London on 27 April; and as further aircraft were delivered, additional services were started to Paris and Rome on 1 July and 3 October respectively. The next year, on 5 June and 16 November, Cairo and Istanbul were included on the map, while on 9 March, 1948, the Paris service was extended to Frankfurt, at which time Panair do Brasil also turned its eyes southwards, with service to Montevideo and Buenos Aires.

Panair do Brasil had been preceded on the South (or more correctly mid-)Atlantic regular postwar crossing only by the newly-formed British South American Airways (BSAA) which, however, operated converted bomber designs and, at best, interim commercial aircraft which were clearly inferior to the modern US four-engined pressurized types such as the Constellation. Although other European airlines and Aerolineas Argentinas joined in the competition, Panair do Brasil was the pace-setter, and its achievement of completing 1,000 South Atlantic crossings on 29 April, 1949, was more than an academic notation in the record books. It was solid evidence that the Brazilian airline industry was a new force to be reckoned with, and that trans-oceanic scheduled service was no longer the exclusive privilege of North American and European airlines.

Although the momentum of this rapid entrance into the intercontinental airline scene could not be sustained, steady progress was made. After a brief suspension, the Istanbul service was resumed on 3 August, 1950, and extended to Beirut on 5 October, 1950, and the following year, Santiago, Chile, and Lima, Peru, were added to the South American network. This last station, incidentally, was not Panair's first incursion into Peru. In 1945, the Amazon local service had been extended westward along the upper reaches of the River to reach Iquitos.

During this period of consolidation on the European route, the Lockheed Constellation was Panair do Brasil's flagship, the fleet building up ultimately to twelve aircraft by 1957. Panair's experience with this fine piston-engined aircraft included, on the debit side, three serious crashes, but nevertheless, on 30 December 1953, the Brazilian airline was able to claim the world's longest regularly scheduled nonstop air route, on the 4,837-mile (7,784 km) southbound segment from Lisbon to Rio de Janeiro, in a flying time of 21 hr 40 min. Hamburg and Düsseldorf were added to the European network on 31 August, 1953, and 22 March, 1954, respectively.

This was an era of air records and, in the commercial airline field, many were being set by the world's first commercial jet airliner, the British de Havilland Comet, which had astonished the airline world by going into service on the London–Johannesburg route on 2 May, 1952, and moreover demonstrating— albeit for less than two years—a very high standard of reliability.

Panair do Brasil, under the energetic leadership of Dr Paulo Sampaio, staked its claim to be among the world leaders by placing an order, on 20 March, 1953, for four Comet 2s, which had longer range than the first Comet, together with an option for two Comet 3s, the even longer-range version which had also been ordered by Pan American Airways. Now firmly established as Brazil's leading overseas flag-carrier, Panair do Brasil terminated at about this time many domestic services in the south, and the Barreiras–Carolina route to Belém, retaining only the Amazon services in which it was a specialist.

But pride came before a fall, as it did with the British BOAC which had sponsored the Comet. Two fatal accidents early in 1954 resulted in the discovery of design faults which led to the withdrawal of all Comets then in service with four airlines, and the cancellation of orders for five more. In an important statement made on 1 October, 1954, while the British Court of Inquiry was holding a meticulous post-mortem on the exact causes of the Comet crashes (primarily metal fatigue) Dr Sampaio stated that he still had faith in the Comet, in spite of the crashes; and that although Panair do Brasil was to have opened service with the new jet aircraft in September 1954, this auspicious day would not be cancelled, but simply postponed.

This faith received harsh treatment not only from Brazilian public opinion but also from the Panair do Brasil shareholders. On 25 May, 1955, after twelve years as President of Brazil's biggest airline, Sampaio was summarily replaced by Dr Argemiro Hungria da Silva Machado—an event, incidentally, which ironically was followed by two Constellation crashes within three weeks. But the die was cast, and Panair do Brasil sought immediate alternative sources of long-range

Panair do Brasil's Douglas DC-7C PP-PDL *Bandeirante Fernão Dias Pais* was delivered in April 1957 and scrapped after veering off the runway at Belém on 14 October, 1961.

aircraft, turning to the Douglas Aircraft Company with an order for four piston-engined DC-7Cs. The substantial monetary deposit on the Comets was transferred to Douglas as a down payment on the four 'Seven Seas', reputedly with the longest range of any commercial aircraft of the day.

The first of these was delivered on 16 April, 1957, and went into service shortly afterwards. The next year, Panair leased some more Douglas aircraft from Lóide, four DC-6Cs, and with the eight aircraft was able to maintain a daily service, starting in March 1959, between Brazil and Europe, plus the routes to Argentina, Chile, and Peru.

The USA Route—Second Phase

As Cruzeiro do Sul's aspirations to serve the United States petered out in 1953, its northern foreign route stopping short at Georgetown, British Guiana, the Brazilian Government nominated **VARIG**, the airline from Porto Alegre, as the second national representative of Brazilian air transport in North America. In

VARIG's Lockheed Model 1049G Super Constellation PP-VDE. (*Lockheed*)

455

February 1953 it awarded the New York route to VARIG, which immediately ordered three Model 1049G Super Constellations from Lockheed.

For VARIG, this was a remarkable development. Only a year previously, its fleet had consisted of twin-engined, unpressurized, second-hand Douglas DC-3s and Curtiss C-46s, and only five years previously, in 1948, had honourably retired its last Junkers-F 13, diminutive survivor of the 1920s. Until 1942, the route network had been confined to its home state of Rio Grande do Sul. Before 1952, when the acquisition of Aero Geral gave it a coastal route to northern Brazil, VARIG's route system had not extended further north than Rio de Janeiro, or further south than Montevideo. Now, suddenly, in 1953, it came into an unexpected inheritance.

VARIG started its New York service in grand style, on 2 August, 1955. The first Super Constellation flew from Rio via Belém, Port of Spain, and Ciudad Trujillo, and immediately set higher standards of service on a route which the US airline Pan American had come almost to regard as its own, because of previous Brazilian default. The 'world's most experienced airline' suddenly faced powerful competition from South America, where hitherto it had invariably controlled the course of events because of technical dominance or through political influence. VARIG's new service was as epoch-making, therefore, as Panair do Brasil's first European service had been in 1946, and served further to consolidate Brazil's position in the higher echelons of international air transport.

When, however, in November 1955, VARIG was granted a subsidy for the route, which was now doubled and extended southwards to Buenos Aires, this action would seem to have confirmed Dr Dantas's view that any Brazilian airline charged with operating such a prestige—and therefore costly— route would need official financial help. And the executives of Cruzeiro do Sul must have cast some rueful and envious glances in the direction of Porto Alegre.

As if to demonstrate also that misfortune did not fall only upon Panair do Brasil, VARIG lost one of its Super Constellations in a crash—on a test flight—and in 1957 services had to be curtailed to the 1955 level of twice weekly, even though, in the previous year, it had increased frequency to thrice weekly, with the extra refinement of a joint scheduling arrangement with the German airline, Lufthansa, for a triangular route linking Europe, Brazil, and the USA.

While VARIG was going through its metamorphosis from regional to intercontinental status, another airline expanded Brazilian access to the United States. On 10 September, 1954, **REAL** had purchased the original Brazilian overseas airline of wartime days, Aerovias Brasil, and had inherited the route to Miami as one of the valuable assets. On 15 September, 1956, REAL reinforced its position by adding a route to Chicago (originating at its home base, São Paulo) thus implementing another of the designated routes to the United States under the terms of the bilateral agreement of 1946.

Although REAL ceased to exist only five years after this event, its imminent demise would have been difficult to detect, if its energy in developing its route network and improving its fleet were any indication. In February 1958, three Lockheed 1049H Super Constellations were delivered, and soon, on 19 November, 1959, a new service began to the United States west coast, terminating in Los Angeles, on a route via Manaus, Bogotá, and Mexico City. This was consolidated on 2 May, 1960, by the inclusion of Brasília, giving North Americans a direct route to the new capital; and REAL achieved a notable Brazilian 'first' on 9 July, 1960, by opening a trans-Pacific route to Tokyo as an extension beyond Los Angeles, with a stop at Honolulu.

REAL's Lockheed Model 1049H Super Constellation PP-YSA.

But this was the last flame from the dying embers of an airline which outgrew its own strength. It was obliged to terminate its service to Chicago, and then on 2 May, 1961, to sell Aerovias Brasil, its international division, to VARIG, Presidential approval being granted on 28 June, 1961, giving to the latter airline the entire North American continent as its sphere of overseas influence, together with the important trans-Pacific extension. Having taken one seven-league stride by flying to New York in 1955, VARIG now took another, adding three more US routes, although the Pacific crossing was deferred until 26 June, 1968.

Jet Service Overseas

On its routes to the United States, VARIG introduced jet aircraft in an unusual manner. Although it had originally ordered three Boeing 707s in September 1957, and two Caravelles for mainline domestic routes one month later, the circumstances of the manufacturers' delivery positions resulted in the Caravelles arriving first. VARIG took a calculated gamble by putting these into service to New York, on 12 December, 1959, even though the aircraft were not designed for such long hauls. The Caravelles, however, demonstrated commendable versatility by linking Porto Alegre with New York with stops only at São Paulo, Rio de Janeiro, Port of Spain, and Nassau; and on 20 January, 1960, a new schedule included Brasília as an en-route stop, by which time the total frequency on the route had grown to five, three by Super Constellation, two by Caravelle.

This interim step served its purpose of giving VARIG the nominal right to advertise jet services to the USA, and to gain valuable experience in jet operations. In any case, the real thing was not long delayed. The first two Boeing 707-441 Rolls-Royce Conway-powered jets arrived in Rio on 23 June, 1960, and nonstop service between Rio and New York began only five days later, with the Brasília stop included on one frequency on 2 July.

On 18 November, 1961, a new Boeing 707 service began: Rio de Janeiro–Lima–Bogotá–Mexico City–Los Angeles, but REAL's old route extension across the Pacific was suspended until 1968. By this time, another momentous airline event had been put into the record books. On 12 February, 1965, VARIG took over the routes and material assets of Panair do Brasil, the

457

VARIG's Boeing 707–341C PP-VJT was delivered in March 1967. (*The Boeing Company*)

latter including some jet equipment. This complex story is recounted in the next chapter.

Panair's fleet had been augmented in the early 1960s by the addition of two jet types: short-haul Sud-Aviation Caravelles and long-haul Douglas DC-8s. The first of the latter entered service on the European routes on 20 April, 1961, and to Buenos Aires and Santiago, Chile, on 4 November of that year. Two of these DC-8s remained with VARIG after the Brazilian authorities had ruled on the disposal of Panair's assets.

A third long-range jet had been ordered by Brazil. The ill-fated REAL had selected the Convair CV-880, which at the time (1960) was claimed to be the fastest commercial jet in the world. These hopes were not fulfilled, however, and the order was changed to a later purchase of the modified Convair CV-990A. When VARIG acquired REAL's subsidiary Aerovias Brasil in May 1961 it tried to cancel the order, on the grounds that the aircraft did not meet its performance guarantees. When the Convair CV-990s became due for delivery, however, VARIG agreed, on 1 March, 1963, to accept three of them.

VARIG's Convair CV-990A-30 PP-VJE was delivered in March 1963 and went to Alaska International Airlines in 1967 as N987AS. (*VARIG*)

Thus, in the early 1960s, when the second wave of jet aircraft was sweeping into world service to start a new era in air transport, Brazil's three overseas airlines each chose a different manufacturer and type: VARIG the Boeing 707, Panair do Brasil the DC-8, and REAL/Aerovias the Convair CV-990. All were in service by the mid-1960s, and all with VARIG, which inherited practically everything after the dust had settled on the turbulent airline battles of that period. To have three different four-engined, long-range jets, moreover with three different engine types, was not the most efficient way to enter the jet age; but unfortunately for VARIG, in that sense if in no other, the Brazilian chronology of aircraft procurement was not co-ordinated with corporate manoeuvres towards the formation of a national airline.

A Brazilian World Airline

Some airlines were born great; some became great; and some had greatness thrust upon them—to paraphrase a well-known observation on degrees of attainment. VARIG's beginnings were humble enough to disqualify it for the first possibility; but thanks to astute direction and management, backed by driving leadership, it rapidly combined the latter two alternatives during the eventful years after 1952. Only then did it reach northwards beyond Rio de Janeiro, yet by 1965, after the takeover of Panair do Brasil, its network spread three-quarters of the way around the world.

By an extraordinary chain of circumstances, of this impressive route map only one route—to New York—was actually started by VARIG itself. The pioneering airlines were Aerovias Brasil/REAL and Panair do Brasil but, like long-distance runners who set too fast a pace in the early laps, they ran out of stamina; and there was VARIG, nursing its reserves of strength, to come through to take the honours in a spectacular finish at the post.

The old aphorism could thus, in VARIG's case, carry a supplement: some were able to acquire greatness by default. VARIG may have lacked initiative in the earlier days, but there can be little criticism of the way in which Brazil's national flag carrier conducted its affairs after it found itself with the world at its feet. Progress was steady and methodical, the airline resisting temptations to expand its route network merely for the sake of drawing more lines on a map. It did, on the other hand, concentrate on good housekeeping, particularly to match its varied fleet to the route requirements, both domestic and international, even though it possessed innumerable types because of the nature of its expansion through corporate acquisition.

Intercontinentally, the Boeing 707 fleet grew to a total of sixteen by 1975, most of these the improved 707-320C with Pratt & Whitney turbofans. With a lone DC-8, these sustained all the demands made of VARIG's network until, after a two-year evaluation, the Douglas DC-10-30 wide-body jet was selected in November 1972 as its next generation of airliners. The DC-10 entered service on the European routes on 24 June, 1974, and started to serve New York on 1 July.

Route expansion during this period was relatively modest. For five years after the Panair do Brasil acquisition, only minor changes were made, such as a new destination in Europe, when VARIG opened service to Zürich on 1 November, 1966. Otherwise, in that continent, development was aimed to consolidate existing services and to operate them profitably, in the face of stiff foreign competition from many airlines. The only other new point to be served in Europe was Copenhagen, on 15 April, 1968.

One new continent was added to the four already served. Boeing 707s began to fly to Johannesburg on 21 June, 1970, with a technical stop at Luanda in the westbound direction (because of payload restrictions from the high-altitude Johannesburg airport). Seven years later, having flown a semi-scheduled freight service, specializing in the shipment of meat, since 23 February, 1976—Boeing 707s started a full passenger and freight once-weekly service to Lagos on 26 June, 1977.

VARIG's McDonnell Douglas DC-10-30 PP-VMA was delivered in May 1974. (*McDonnell Douglas Corporation*)

Around this time, VARIG suffered a setback which was none of its own doing. Having been the beneficiary of Brazilian Government policy, it now became the victim—a case of taking the rough with the smooth. On 4 June, 1976, as a measure to reduce the country's serious balance of payments deficit, the Government introduced a special exit tax on overseas flights. Under the terms of Decree No.1,470–76, all travellers except government employees and students had to deposit 12,000 cruzeiros with the Bank of Brazil. This was bad enough, but to pour salt on the wound, the deposit had to be left in the bank for one year, without interest. In a country with continuous double-digit inflation, would-be travellers had to weigh the advantages of the trip against a possible loss of up to a quarter of their deposit in real money value.

Curiously, because of favourable exchange rates of the cruzeiro against certain other currencies, the exit tax was not imposed for travel on routes to Argentina, Chile, Uruguay, and Paraguay. For northbound international flights, businessmen could obtain permission by going through the bureaucratic channels, but the process took as many as forty days. Needless to state, VARIG's international traffic figures showed a sharp decline from mid-1976.

But for every action, there is a reaction. In spite of the unorthodox fiscal policies followed by the Brazilian Government and national banks, under which inflation was bluntly recognized and made part of the economic prosperity drive,

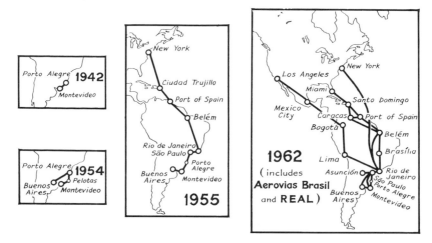

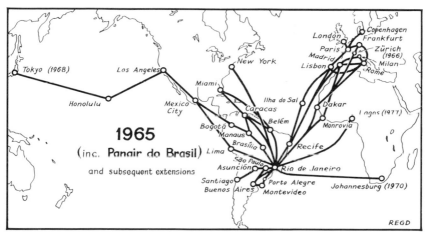

59. Growth of VARIG International Network, 1942–1965. Until 1955, VARIG's participation in international markets was modest, reaching only to the River Plate, close to its home State of Rio Grande do Sul. Subsequently, however, progress was swift, both by its own initiatiave (to New York) but primarily by acquiring the route franchises of other airlines which fell under its ownership or control. Later extensions also shown.

there was plenty of discretionary income to be absorbed by the airlines, as middle-class city dwellers sought to travel for pleasure. Thus, neatly counterbalancing near-disaster on international routes, VARIG, in company with other airlines, experienced a boom on its domestic services.

These had grown considerably since the feverish years of the unstable postwar period to the extent that Brazil possessed, by the mid-1970s, a many-tiered airline society, mature and efficient. This befitted President Kubitschek's vision of Brazil as a sleeping giant rising to take its place among the world's great industrial and economic powers. Jucelino would have been well pleased with VARIG's part as a stimulant to that awakening.

TABLE 26
Development of Brazilian Intercontinental Network
(Inauguration dates on major routes)

Date	Area	Destination	Aircraft	Airline	Remarks
July 1946 (already operated on semi-scheduled basis)	USA	Miami	Douglas DC-3	Aerovias Brasil	Taken over by REAL 10 Sept. 1954, but operated as Aerovias Brasil from 9 Nov. 1959, then acquired by VARIG 2 May, 1961
27 April, 1946	Europe	London	Lockheed 049 Constellation	Panair do Brasil	All routes taken over by VARIG 12 Feb, 1965
1 July, 1946		Paris	"	"	
3 Oct, 1946		Rome	"	"	
16 Nov, 1947		Istanbul	"	"	
9 March, 1948		Frankfurt	"	"	
31 Aug, 1953		Hamburg	"	"	
22 March, 1954		Düsseldorf	"	"	
5 June, 1947	Middle East	Cairo	"	"	
5 Oct, 1950		Beirut	"	"	
2 Aug, 1955	USA	New York	Lockheed 1049G Super Constellation	VARIG	
15 Sept, 1956	USA	Chicago	Douglas DC-4	REAL	Taken over by VARIG, 16 Aug, 1961
19 Nov, 1959	USA	Los Angeles	Lockheed 1049H Super Constellation	"	
5 July, 1960	East Asia	Tokyo	"	"	Suspended 1961–66
1 Nov, 1966	Europe	Zürich	Boeing 707	VARIG	
15 April, 1968		Copenhagen	"	"	
21 June, 1970	Africa	Johannesburg	"	"	
26 June, 1977		Lagos	"	"	

View looking approximately north across Rio de Janeiro's Santos Dumont Airport. The 02/20 parallel runways are extremely closely spaced and the entire area between the runways and the terminal area is used for aircraft parking. The Navy Yard is on the left beyond the airport and the bridge is the Ponte Rio Niterói. A Lockheed Electra can be seen making a climbing turn just after take off. (*Fokker B.V.*)

CHAPTER TWENTY-THREE

Brazilian Air Transport Reaches Maturity

After the Feast

The Brazilian compulsion to form airlines right, left and centre, finally subsided, partly because the potential speculators learned from the experience of the earlier entrepreneurs, and shied away from the air transport industry as a pathway to instant riches. Almost all the many new independent companies disappeared by the mid-1950s, either by bankruptcy or were taken over by REAL or Lóide. It was a painful process although, from the national point of view, the balance sheet was not entirely depressing. Between 1945 and 1950, the number of commercial aircraft registered by the Air Ministry doubled, from 1,036—itself a colossal increase on the prewar count—to 2,227, thus providing a foundation for further growth.

Nevertheless, the glut of airlines became a matter of history, and this was no bad thing. The surviving airlines tried to co-ordinate the enormous Brazilian domestic route network into some semblance of cohesion, but it was an uphill task. Although the aircraft were great in numbers they were generally poor in quality. The vast majority had been acquired second-hand, with a record of tough military service, and even subsequent bush service, to test the integrity of the airframes to the utmost. Also, as observed in Chapter 21, Brazilian surface transport was beginning to develop from almost primitive standards to the nucleus of an integrated rail and road system. This, possibly more than any other reason, was responsible for the termination of large numbers of air routes in the central and southern regions of Brazil. However, because of the latent demand for transport of any kind, to cater for a nation breaking out of industrial and commercial lethargy, the airlines were secure in the knowledge that the sheer size of the country would always sustain them, provided they kept their house, and their books, in order.

Thus, there arrived a period of sober reflection, conservative decision-making, and cautious progress. Most of this was in the hands and minds of the few survivors from the melée of the late 1940s, a privileged few who competed for the now almost stagnant Brazilian airline traffic of the late 1950s.

The First Pressurized Equipment

The leading aircraft used for domestic routes at this time was the Convair-Liner, the twin-engined, pressurized 40-seater which supplemented the DC-3. The Convair-Liners did not replace the DC-3s, for on the majority of routes on the feeder networks, the airfields were just not good enough for the heavier wheelloadings of the Convairs, which were therefore confined to serving the main cities. Cruzeiro do Sul bought the first Convair CV-340 on 18 March, 1954, turning an international misfortune into a domestic advantage, after having withdrawn its interest in flying to the United States.

Cruzeiro do Sul's Convair CV-340 PP-CDW *Sirius* was delivered in March 1954 and crashed at São Paulo on 3 May, 1963. (*Cruzeiro do Sul*)

REAL was the first airline to follow Cruzeiro's lead, when it took delivery of its first two CV-340s at the Convair plant in San Diego, California, on 8 July, 1954, putting them into service shortly thereafter. VARIG was next, when it bought five CV-240s from Pan American in September, but REAL, competing vigorously for domestic technical supremacy, supplemented its Convair fleet by adding the improved CV-440s in June 1956. By this time, Cruzeiro do Sul had also added four CV-440s to match its CV-340 fleet, and had then acquired ten CV-240s from American Airlines in 1955, making a total of eighteen of all three Convair-Liner series. VARIG purchased more CV-240s in the latter 1950s, so that, after purchasing REAL in 1961, it had a total of twenty-nine, including seventeen from REAL. There were thus almost fifty of the Convair twins to provide the standard Brazilian inter-city equipment until the first jets came along. With the Convairs, Brazil moved out of the DC-3 era.

VARIG's Convair CV-240-2 PP-VCY, acquired in October 1957, had been Pan American's N90668. (*VARIG*)

During this period, Panair do Brasil was withdrawing from the domestic scene, and concentrating on international services to Europe, at the same time having big problems with long-haul equipment. It did not, therefore, influence the course of affairs within Brazil. But the other powerful survivor, the São Paulo-based VASP, certainly did. It had remained aloof from the DC-3/Convair-Liner progression, having gained some advantage before the Convair era by introducing the Swedish-built Saab Scandia in 1950, and then ignoring the first jet generation by buying the British Viscounts in 1958. But before continuing the story of the rise of VASP, it is perhaps expedient at this point to deal with the only new airlines to be formed after the amalgamations of the late 1940s and the early 1950s.

Aerovias Brasil's Saab 90A-2 Scandia as PP-XEI before delivery. It was reregistered PP-AXM and passed to VASP as PP-SQF. This was a Saab-built example and the markings were red and dark blue. (*Saab*)

465

Paraense

During the 1950s, for various reasons, the meteoric growth of Brazilian air traffic slowed down to rates consistent with the rest of the world. Yet, defying all logic, an airline started to operate at a time when the majority of airlines had disappeared, and those that remained were contemplating close associations, if not outright mergers, so as to conserve resources and maintain financial viability. Somehow or other, by drawing upon resources of determination which kept them going long after most promoters would have thrown in the sponge, Paraense survived for thirteen years.

Paraense Comercial Ltda was originally founded by Antonio Alves Ramos Jr, on 22 February, 1952, and made its first flight with an ex-Aero Geral Catalina PBY-5A from Belém to Pedro Afonso, in northern Goiás, on 30 March of that year. Ramos's objective was to transport food, principally meat, from the cattle country in that area to ready markets in the cities. Although the first flight was to Belém (Paraense's base) the chief target was the industrial heart of Brazil, especially the huge urban concentrations around São Paulo and Rio de Janeiro.

The longer-haul southern extension, however, was not started until later, in 1955, when the company had been renamed **Paraense Transportes Aéreos, S.A.** Then on 4 September, 1957, two Curtiss C-46s were acquired to start regular scheduled flights—previous service having been non-scheduled—on a route from Belém to Rio de Janeiro, via Pedro Afonso, Cristalândia, and Brasília. Paraense was one of the first airlines to serve the nation's new capital, which began to supplement Goiânia as the major air staging point in central Brazil.

In August 1958, Paraense was awarded an important new route from São Paulo to Rio Branco (Acre Territory), via Cuiabá and Porto Velho, but did not go into

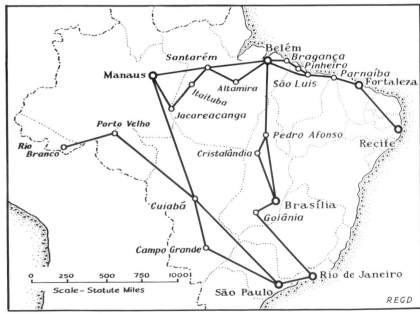

60. Paraense, 1966. Paraense, a Belém-based airline, survived precariously for a few years in the 1960s, even opening long domestic routes.

466

Paraense's Fairchild Hiller FH-227B PP-BUH *Rio Tapajós* was delivered in February 1968, taken over by the Ministry of Aeronautics in July 1970 and leased to VARIG until 1975. *(Gordon S. Williams)*

operation until 1960. By this time, the meat transport was no longer the main source of income, and Paraense's revenue base was split between passengers and general freight. But there was, perhaps, another reason why the start was delayed: a chronic shortage of airworthy aircraft.

It is a matter of record that Paraense proceeded to lose aircraft with alarming rapidity and regularity. For example, between 1957 and 1959 a total of eight C-46s were acquired; yet not a single one remained by the end of 1965. Six had crashed, at various points on the network, one had exploded in flight, and one was destroyed on the ground.

The trail of misfortune was not confined to the C-46s. Of three Douglas C-54/DC-4s acquired in 1962 and 1963, two had gone by April 1964. More spectacularly, the single C-47/DC-3 bought on 7 February, 1963, came to an inglorious end when it made a forced landing in the jungle near Porto Velho. There were no injuries among the thirty passengers and the four crew, but they were stranded, and had to wait for help for many days. After some sensational headlines in the Brazilian press, they were all eventually rescued, one by one, by a small Cessna private aircraft. Against this background of uncertainty, Paraense bought and sold aircraft and somehow managed to remain in the airline timetables, advertising, for example, nonstop four-engined service from Belém to Rio de Janeiro and between the major cities on its network during the 1960s.

Then, after evaluating various twin-Dart-engined aircraft, Ramos selected the Fairchild Hiller FH-227B, which in Brazil was called the Hirondelle. At this time, the aircraft must have been on the shelf, and possibly a good bargain, as the order was placed in November 1967 and all five arrived in Belém in January 1968, with a sixth on lease, pending delivery, for training and route proving. In some ways, it was an extraordinary choice, almost as if to proclaim Paraense's character as a non-establishment free spirit. Already, all three of the other twin-Dart powered aircraft were established in service: the Hawker Siddeley HS.748 with VARIG, the Handley Page Herald with Sadia, and the Nihon YS-11 with Cruzeiro do Sul. Whatever may have been the reason for choosing the Hirondelle, it was certainly not the desire for standardization or co-operative airframe maintenance.

Unbelievably, Paraense's experience with the Hirondelle was no better than its previous record. Within a year of introducing the type, some were grounded through lack of spares. Then, on 14 March, 1970, one crashed in the mouth of the Amazon near Belém, and 36 people were killed. On the very same day, another Hirondelle was hit by a vehicle at Belém Airport, and put out of action; while a third aircraft was already grounded. Thus, out of a fleet of five new aircraft, and after only two years of service, Paraense was left with but two—and one of these had been returned to the USA for overhaul.

The Brazilian Government must have decided that this was enough. It reviewed Paraense's finances, which were, not surprisingly, in a precarious state, and withdrew the airline's operating authority on 29 May, 1970. The end came on 15 July of that year, when the Government took over the four remaining aircraft. These were flown to São Paulo, where they were repainted by VARIG and used on the Ponte Aérea.

Omar Fontana and Sadia

There are many examples in the history of air transport of a gifted individual being possessed of a rare combination of talents: vision, nerve, resolution, and a vigorous sense of independence. This last quality has frequently come into prominence when the individual has battled against tradition and vested interests, frequently identified with State-owned, or at least State-recognized institutions.

Thus, in the United Kingdom during the 1930s, Edward Hillman challenged the established order of Imperial Airways; in postwar Australia, Reg (later Sir Reginald) Ansett fought first for survival, then achieved equality with the State airline; Grant McConachie struggled for recognition of the private sector in Canada; and in the United States Slim Carmichael challenged the might of the Big Four giants, coming close to becoming one of the Big Four himself. In recent times, the Englishman Freddie (now Sir Freddie) Laker, with his courageous promotion of a new form of no-reservation air service, has made his name a household word, not only in his own country, but throughout the world of air travel.

Omar Fontana (*left*) started his own airline, Sadia, in Santa Catarina in 1955. Sadia merged with TAS and later became Transbrasil. Vigorously independent, Fontana's is the only postwar Brazilian trunk airline to survive. He also holds a controlling interest in the regional airline Nordeste. Colonel Marcilio Gibson Jacques (*centre*) was formerly one of the leading promoters of Lóide. In 1976, he founded TABA Transportes Aéreos Regionais da Bacia Amazônica, S.A., establishing an airline which is now identified with good air service throughout the Amazon Basin. João Lorenz (*right*), like Fontana and Gibson, is also President of a regional airline, but with a far different background. One of the earliest staff members of VARIG before the war, he rose to become its Economic Director, and played a prominent part in guiding its fortunes. Today he directs the affairs of Rio Sul as well as continuing his work with VARIG.

468

Sadia's Douglas DC-3A PP-ASJ was originally delivered to Pan American as NC33612. It served with Panair do Brasil and was acquired by Sadia in April 1955. PP-ASJ is seen here at Congonhas Airport, São Paulo, in the mid-1950s in early Sadia livery.
(*via Mário B. de M. Vinagre and Alberto Fortner*)

In Brazil, Omar Fontana is one such free spirit. Since the general exodus of the early 1950s, he alone has founded a new airline and retained complete independence. His problems have not simply been a case of free enterprise against State control, although this is partly true. Brazil's airlines have no direct federal ownership, although VASP is owned by the State, City, and Bank of São Paulo. His achievement was to start from scratch in an apparently fully saturated industrial environment, and by innovative ideas, strategic commercial dealing, and courageous aircraft investment, thereby infiltrate into the big leagues of the Brazilian airline industry.

Fontana worked in his father's meat-packing factory in the small city of Concórdia, Santa Catarina. Seeking to improve product distribution for his firm, S.A. Industria e Comercio Concórdia, he formed a private airline on 5 January, 1955, obtained a second-hand DC-3, and built himself a landing strip at Concórdia. He called his airline **Sadia**, a condensation of the first two and last three letters of his father's company. On 3 August he received his certificate of operation from the Ministry of Aeronautics, followed by a further mandatory certificate of technical competence on 20 January, 1956—Brazil does not allow the business of commercial air transport to be entered into without due process.

Thus armed with the necessary documentation, Fontana began his first scheduled service on 16 April, 1956, as a supplement to hauling meat from Concórdia to the big cities. The route was modest enough, and hardly one guaranteed to generate heavy traffic: São Paulo–Joaçaba–Videira–Florianópolis. But it was a start, and another route was soon added, from Joaçaba to Londrina, the big coffee centre of Paraná State, and to Bauru and Ribeirão Prêto in northern São Paulo State. The following year, Sadia joined the ranks of the many airlines operating to Brasília.

In November 1957 he took an important step by forming a close association with the mighty REAL, at that time completely dominating the air routes of central Brazil, but not, in fact, serving the State of Santa Catarina, except at Florianópolis. Gomes received 50 per cent of Sadia's stock, and Fontana joined REAL's management, where he obtained priceless experience of airline operations on a national scale. Sadia moved to São Paulo and integrated its services with REAL's, but continued under its own name. As part of the agreement it expanded to Rio de Janeiro and Porto Alegre. The fleet grew modestly, to consist of five DC-3s and two Curtiss C-46s.

469

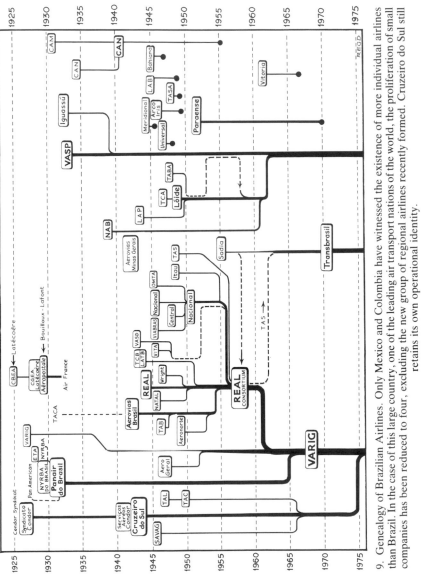

9. Genealogy of Brazilian Airlines. Only Mexico and Colombia have witnessed the existence of more individual airlines than Brazil. In the case of this large country, one of the leading air transport nations of the world, the proliferation of small companies has been reduced to four, excluding the new group of regional airlines recently formed. Cruzeiro do Sul still retains its own operational identity.

This association was short-lived, as after four years, in August 1961, the REAL empire collapsed, and by mutual agreement, Omar Fontana bought back the stock formerly held by Gomes, and sought fresh capital. At that time, it was stated that VARIG did not want, or did not need Sadia, but this may have been a way of saying that it did not want the maverick Fontana, who, with whatever good intentions, may not have fitted in with the policies of the larger company.

At the end of 1962, after having acquired more aircraft, Fontana made what can be seen in retrospect as the most important and far-reaching single decision in his career. He merged with **Transportes Aéreos Salvador (TAS)** of the State of Bahia, based in Salvador. TAS had been acquired by the company Charqueada Santa Maria do Araguaia, owners of territory along the Tocantins River, and operators of C-46 cargo aircraft between its base and Belém. The merged group became at first two operating units, Sadia and TASSA, with a combined fleet of twelve DC-3s and three C-46s. Fontana could list 54 cities in his new domain.

Handley Page Herald 210 PP-SDG was leased to Sadia and is seen at Santos Dumont Airport, Rio de Janeiro. (*Denir Lima de Camargo*)

Whether by good fortune or shrewd judgement, or a combination of both, the Sadia-TAS merger could not have occurred at a better time. For within two months, in January 1963, the Brazilian Government introduced a new system of subsidies, in which the uneconomic feeder routes were designated the Rede de Integração Nacional (RIN). This gave the Fontana airline group, which might otherwise have shared the same fate as the small airlines of the previous generation, a new lease of life. Sadia's route system was composed almost entirely of routes which qualified for subsidy, and he also acquired a few more, including a coastal route from Rio de Janeiro to Salvador, by default because the other airlines found it operationally convenient to remove them from their national systems.

Omar Fontana then turned his attention to the study of a replacement aircraft for the ageing DC-3s, which had seen long and faithful service, and were becoming somewhat of an anacronism when seen alongside the modern types used for the trunk and secondary routes. He therefore resolved to find a propeller-turbine airliner which would be able to serve his RIN network, with adequate airfield performance, better comfort, including pressurized cabins, yet at the same time matching the low operating costs of the fully-depreciated DC-3s. After much analysis, he finally chose the British Handley Page Herald, and set about the formidable task of obtaining all the necessary certificates and licences to operate.

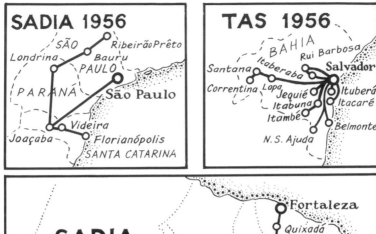

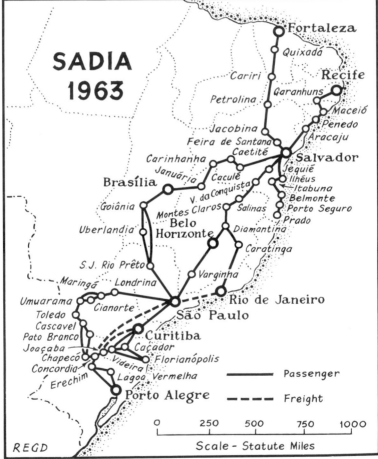

61. Early Development of Sadia, 1956–1963. Sadia was a maverick airline which dared to challenge the Brazilian airline establishment. By an ingenious manipulation of route authority, it managed to fashion the small spoke networks of two regional airlines into a nation-wide system.

472

At first, the Government would not permit the purchase, and so, in February 1964, he borrowed two Heralds, one from the manufacturer, one from the near-bankrupt Cruz Airways in the Philippines, and operated them on combined route proving and demonstration flights. Fontana was able to prove his point. Not only was the Herald able to perform well, it was also economical. Accordingly, he was permitted by the Department of Aeronautics to classify the Herald within the piston-engined fare structure—otherwise the higher propeller-turbine tariffs would have been counter-productive when applied to the RIN network, depressing traffic, and thus placing heavier demands on the subsidy arrangements.

The frustrating process of Herald acquisition gradually unfolded. On 6 January, 1965, Sadia placed an order for five Series 200 aircraft, equipped with 46 seats, at a cost of £1,500,000 ($4,200,000), including spares. By this time, the airline had undergone a reorganization, by introducing a form of worker-ownership, by which the employees could purchase stock in the company. The route network was rationalized to exclude some of the minor cities and reduce the number of points served from 54 to 28. Towards the end of 1965, Sadia joined in the Rio de Janeiro–São Paulo Ponte Aérea, albeit with a minimum service pattern, having been admitted to that admirable consortium, possibly because Fontana was making noises about introducing a low-fare service on the route with the Heralds.

Final official approval for the Heralds was not forthcoming until February 1966, by which time they were firmly established in service. The capital of Sadia was increased from 750 to 1,000 million cruzeiros, with the Fontana family, however, maintaining control. Although still the smallest, by some margin, of the Brazilian airlines, Sadia lacked nothing in impact, mainly through the personality of its owner who, by his innovative methods, aided somewhat by his unorthodox approach to negotiation and promotion, was able to consolidate his airline as a permanent feature of the Brazilian domestic airline network. Characteristically, Fontana's next step was not long delayed, and his part in introducing further new aircraft types is discussed later.

VASP and the Viscount

Chapter 21 described the succession of airlines which appeared on the scene during the postwar period as feverish, but observed at the same time that the older established airlines usually bided their time, carried on steadily, and weathered the various storms which burst upon the over-ambitious aspirants. Perhaps the steadiest of all, if not the most ambitious in terms of route expansion, was the São Paulo State airline, **Viação Aérea São Paulo (VASP)**.

Having relied upon the German Junkers-Ju 52/3m for its fleet in the late 1930s, the airline barely survived the war with enough airworthy aircraft, and kept flying only by taking desperate measures. Immediately upon the cessation of hostilities, however, it quickly put its house in order by introducing the Douglas DC-3 (converted C-47) in January 1946, building up a fleet of sixteen within two years. New routes were added into the northwest of São Paulo State, to Presidente Prudente and Tupã; and to Londrina and Maringá, in the new coffee-growing area of northern Paraná.

On 17 February, 1949, the Governor of São Paulo, Ademar de Barros, acquired the stock of Aerovias Brasil and the control was vested in VASP, the State flag carrier. Aerovias had ordered a quantity of Saab Scandia twin-engined

473

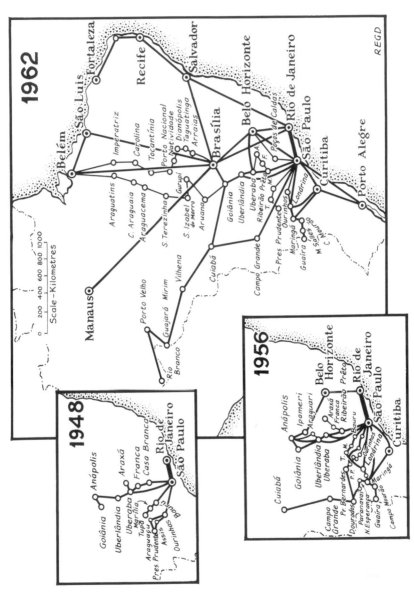

62. Postwar Growth of VASP, 1948–1962. For many years the São Paulo airline served only its own state and neighbouring cities, but in the 1960s, by the acquisition of Lóide and NAB, it became a Brazilian national domestic airline, alongside Cruzeiro do Sul and VARIG. (A. = Araxá, F. = Franca, M. = Marília, P.P. = Presidente Prudente, T. = Tupã.)

aircraft from Sweden, and although the first two were flown out to Brazil in the colours of that airline, they were delivered to VASP, and complete ownership of the fleet of five passed to the latter on 21 December, 1950. In 1951, nine more DC-3s were acquired, to make a total fleet of twenty-five, and another Scandia. The capital of VASP at this time was 100 million cruzeiros, divided between the State of São Paulo (34·2 per cent), the Municipality (33·3 per cent), the State Bank (8·4 per cent), and private citizens (24·1 per cent).

During the mid-1950s, VASP consolidated its position as a reliable airline, with a commendable record of reliability and punctuality. In 1953, it offered fifteen round trips a day on the São Paulo–Rio de Janeiro route. Its route expansion was aimed sensibly at the larger cities, rather than the myriad of small localities which were the target of most of the newcomer airlines. Curitiba, the rapidly-growing prosperous capital of Paraná State, came into the network in 1955, and routes to Campo Grande and Cuiabá, the largest cities in Mato Grosso, plus Belo Horizonte, Minas Gerais, which had become the third largest city in Brazil, were added in 1956. On 28 July, 1955, four more Scandias helped VASP to keep pace with the expansion.

VASP's Douglas DC-3 PP-SQP was built as a DST (Douglas Sleeper Transport) with starboard passenger door. It was United Air Lines' NC18104 *Mainliner Fresno* and impressed as a C-48B. It went to VASP in July 1951 and was destroyed in a hangar fire at Congonhas on 26 November, 1964. Markings were medium blue. (*Gordon S. Williams*)

The period was one in which many factors combined to make life difficult for the Brazilian airline industry, and although VASP was not burdened with a surfeit of uneconomic routes or stations, it nevertheless had to take prudent measures to maintain financial health. It disposed of Aerovias Brasil to REAL, and its rather precarious situation was publicised in February 1956 with a rumour that the company was up for sale; but this was never pursued, and a rational solution to some of the problems of excessive costs was found by concluding, on 20 October, 1956, an agreement with VARIG, to co-ordinate traffic and sales offices, and maintenance and training facilities.

This protection against possible extravagance during a period of comparative traffic stagnation may have contributed to VASP's decision, on 10 May, 1957, to order five British propeller-turbine aircraft, from Vickers-Armstrongs. The Viscount 827 had four Rolls-Royce Dart engines, carried 56 passengers, and had already demonstrated that it was versatile enough to serve both short- and medium-haul routes. By this bold purchase, VASP stood to achieve equipment superiority over its piston-engined competitors, whose Convair-Liners had an edge over VASP's Scandias.

VASP's Vickers-Armstrongs V.701 Viscount PP-SRN, seen at Congonhas Airport, was originally BEA's G-ANHB. It was withdrawn from service in 1969. (*Fernando Tibiriçá*)

During the same year as the Viscount order, two important new routes were opened: to the new capital of Brasília, where REAL, Nacional, and Cruzeiro do Sul had narrowly beaten VASP for the privilege of opening the first service, and the key coastal route from Rio de Janeiro to Natal, via the intermediate State capital cities. To reinforce the fleet and to cope with the new demands, eight more Scandias were purchased from SAS to make a total of nineteen.

Thus, when the first Viscount went into service on 3 November, 1958, it was reinforcing a company which was expanding its influence in the Brazilian airline world. Only two years previously, VASP was regarded as the Paulista airline which had pioneered the São Paulo–Rio de Janeiro route but not much else beyond a few local intra-state routes, with the occasional branch into an adjoining state. Now, VASP served ten State capitals, plus Brasília, so that the introduction of the first turbine-powered aircraft on to domestic routes in Brazil was something of a landmark. Even though eclipsed a few years later by the pure-jet Caravelle, this did not prevent VASP from echoing publicity and promotion elsewhere in the world and unashamedly advertising the Viscounts as jets.

The Ponte Aérea

As air transport grew during the first forty years of its existence, the route patterns which emerged were many and varied, long- medium- and short-haul; inter-city, secondary, and third level; trunk and feeder. They also varied in traffic density, from those which generated only a handful of passengers per week, to the other extreme which demanded frequent flights, up to the accepted ideal of 'on-the-hour, every hour', or more.

The busiest air routes in the world were invariably short-haul, a consequence of the gravity theory which applies to all transport movements, in that the potential volume varies directly with the terminal populations and inversely with the distance. While a precise formula cannot be set—for other factors are involved—the statistical record shows that, almost without exception, the most densely travelled air routes are those which link two large cities or metropolises when these are between 200 and 500 miles apart. In Europe, London–Paris is the best example, with traffic topping the million mark in spite of crippling fare levels; in Australia, Sydney–Melbourne; in Japan, Tokyo–Osaka and Tokyo–Sapporo; in the USA, New York–Boston, New York–Washington and Los Angeles–San Francisco, all fall into this category while Riyadh–Jeddah and Riyadh–Dhahran have recently reached these levels of passenger demand. Brazil, too, had its São Paulo–Rio de Janeiro route, where the traffic became so dense as to demand special measures to cope with it.

The conditions for stimulating air travel were ideal. The distance—about 230 miles, or 370 km—was far enough to justify the air journey as in the 1950s neither road nor railway permitted a round trip within a day. Even today this would be regarded as something of an accomplishment. The cities qualified naturally to create high demand. Each had a population exceeding five million even then, with São Paulo challenging Buenos Aires for the claim to be the largest and richest metropolis in the Southern Hemisphere. São Paulo, with its cordillera of skyscrapers, energetic business activity, and pulsating commercial life, had to have adequate transport to link it with Rio de Janeiro, resort city *par excellence*, Brazil's biggest seaport and major international air hub, and at the time the centre of government.

To add even greater stimulation to travel, both cities had contrived to provide airports which were almost on the businessmen's doorsteps. São Paulo had its Congonhas, built on a small plateau-shaped hill not twenty minutes' drive from the heart of the business quarter; Rio had its Santos Dumont, built on reclaimed land in a corner of Guanabara Bay, and literally within walking distance of the world-famous Rio Branco, the business centre of Rio. Congonhas had been used by VASP as early as 1936, with the modern passenger station opened on 26 January, 1955. Santos Dumont was opened on 1 November, 1938, in grand style, representing a notable landmark in air transport progress in Latin America. These airports were busy from dawn until midnight, with airliners queuing up to handle the endless stream of passengers. Reservations procedures were maintained miraculously, in a manner understood and achievable only by Latin Americans, but the sheer volume of traffic led to discussions by the airlines as to whether this was all necessary. And thus was created the first non-reservations

Santos Dumont Airport, Rio de Janeiro, in its early period. The airport is almost surrounded by Guanabara Bay. At the northwest corner (on the right) is the flying-boat slipway and hangar.

VASP's Saab 90A-2 Scandia PP-SQU, seen at Congonhas Airport, São Paulo, was a Fokker-built aircraft and the last of the eighteen examples produced. It was delivered to SAS as SE-BSL *Folke Viking*, withdrawn from service at the end of the summer in 1957 and sold to VASP. On the right is Scandia PP-SQC which was originally ordered by Aerovias Brasil. (*Pedro Zoboli*)

service in the world, the Ponte Aérea (Air Bridge), pre-dating the better-known Eastern Air Lines Air-Shuttle by two years.

On 6 July, 1959, VARIG, VASP, and Cruzeiro do Sul signed a pool agreement for the joint operation of the São Paulo–Rio route. VARIG and Cruzeiro used Convair-Liners and VASP used Scandias, fifteen of each, both types twin-engined, designed specifically for short routes and able to use the two downtown airports which, though ideally convenient for travellers, were operationally limited in that their runways were not long enough for many larger types. The biggest and most attractive aspect of the agreement was that reservations could be

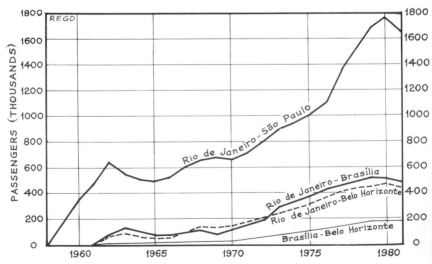

10. The Brazilian Air Bridges. Brazil's *Ponte Aérea* no-reservation air shuttle service between Rio de Janeiro and São Paulo was the first true airbus service in the world. Opened in 1959, this route was later augmented by others on Brazil's densest short-haul routes.

made only up to 24 hours before departure. After that, passengers could go straight to the airport, buy a ticket, and walk on to an aircraft of one or other of the partner airlines. It was almost certain that not only would an aircraft be waiting but that there would be a seat on it; if not, there would be another one in half an hour, or even sooner in the rush hours.

Some idea of the volume of traffic on the route can be judged by the fact that, for many years in the 1950s and since, the *Guia Aeronáutico*, that admirable air guide which serves as the Brazilian passenger's primary timetable reference, has devoted a whole page to list the services. At their height, these numbered as many as seventy flights in each direction. The biggest single operator at the time of the formation of the Ponte Aérea was REAL, providing about 15 daily services each way, against the combined VARIG/VASP/Cruzeiro's 25 or so; but this competition evaporated when REAL merged with VARIG in 1961, while the other airlines on the route, Panair, Lóide, and NAB, all disappeared within the next few years, to be replaced only by a nominal contribution from Sadia.

The Ponte Aérea was a landmark in the furtherance of air transport as a means of travel in which the customers' needs were given priority. Later, other countries were to adopt similar ideas, particularly Eastern Air Lines, already mentioned, which added the benefit of actually guaranteeing a seat, even if this involved calling up a standby aircraft. On such short routes, the matter of competition and basic economics had to be treated in a distinct way. The competition of speed was not significant, as, over 200 miles, the difference between the time taken by a 600 mph jet and a 250 mph piston-engined type is surprisingly close, because of the longer climb and approach patterns demanded by the jets, together with the higher cruising altitudes. Thus, older, even obsolescent, aircraft could be used, and indeed were; but the passengers who were getting a good bargain did not complain. And above all, the effective removal of reservations resulted in substantial economies in overhead costs.

Nevertheless, the question of equipment was not to be dismissed lightly, and there was pressure to improve upon the old piston-engined types. For several years, aircraft manufacturers, notably the British Aircraft Corporation, tried to persuade the Brazilian air authorities that jet aircraft could use Congonhas and Santos Dumont Airports with complete safety; and although this was conceded in the case of the São Paulo terminus, it was denied at Rio de Janeiro. Consequently, when jet aircraft began to appear on Brazilian domestic routes, the Ponte Aérea, for technical rather than commercial reasons, relied upon the well-proved propeller, in the propeller-turbine powered Lockheed 188 Electra. The record of the Ponte Aérea is illustrated in Chart 10, page 478, and in the next chapter.

The First Domestic Jets

Although VARIG used its first Caravelles in December 1959 to accelerate its jet début on the prestige international route to New York, some of these were transferred to major domestic routes as soon as the Boeing 707s were delivered in June 1960. The French jet continued to operate the stopping service to Miami, via Brasília, Belém, Port of Spain, Caracas, and Santo Domingo, until the Convair CV-990s, inherited after some dispute from REAL, arrived in the spring of 1963. VARIG, however, was never enthusiastic about the Caravelle, and sold its small fleet in 1964.

The main protagonist of the Caravelle was Panair do Brasil. Having ordered four Caravelle VIRs in October 1961 (at a time when VARIG was busily

An unidentified VARIG Sud-Aviation Caravelle I leaving the factory at Toulouse.
(*VARIG*)

reorganizing REAL) it was able to put the first one into service less than a year later, on 15 September, 1962. Panair then proceeded to promote the Caravelle vigorously, emphasizing the reduction of journey time on the long-distance domestic routes, particularly to Salvador, Recife, Fortaleza, Belém, and Manaus. As the balance of the flights was served with four-engined Constellations, Panair's competitive impact on the national aviation scene during the early 1960s was considerable.

The third Brazilian Caravelle operator was Cruzeiro do Sul, which had been the first to introduce pressurized equipment on domestic services. By 1955 it had augmented its fleet of Convair-Liners to eighteen, and after a period of marking time, flirted with the idea of keeping that type with a propeller-turbine modification, which would have replaced the trusty Pratt & Whitney piston engines with the new British Napier Eland. By this device, Cruzeiro do Sul could have continued to rely upon a solid airframe, at the same time keeping pace with advancing engine technology. But the Napier engine was not a success, and although a few modified Convairs flew in limited service in North America in 1960, the whole project was a failure.

Cruzeiro do Sul's search for a new type occurred during the late 1950s, when in spite of the welcome stimulant of the creation of Brasília, domestic traffic growth was not spectacular, and aircraft procurement was not a burning issue. Cruzeiro

Cruzeiro do Sul's Sud-Aviation Caravelle VIR PP-CJD was delivered in July 1963. It is seen here, in the airline's turquoise-blue and white livery, at Rio de Janeiro International Airport in February 1971. (*via John Wegg*)

480

gave some consideration to the Frye F-1 Safari, a United States project which aimed to produce a true 'DC-3 Replacement'; but like so many other attempts, this came to nothing. In 1958 Cruzeiro did, however, take delivery of eight Fairchild C-82 *Vagôes Voladores* (Flying Boxcars) which were used partly to carry spare engines. One of these finished its days ignominiously as a night club in Rio.

Cruzeiro do Sul eventually ordered four Caravelles in 1961—matching Panair do Brasil in its timing—and began service in January 1963, emphasizing the speed, comfort, and smooth ride of the new jets. Not long afterwards, the fleet was increased to seven, when, by government order, Panair do Brasil's routes and aircraft were distributed to VARIG and Cruzeiro do Sul.

An interesting postscript to the Brazilian Caravelle story is that, unlike the Convair-Liner, which at least expanded its numerical base, the French aircraft never consolidated its early success and public acceptance. This was mainly because VARIG apparently regarded the Caravelle only as an interim type, or at least was not satisfied with its economics, and instead chose the propeller-turbine Lockheed Electra for many of its mainline services, complementing the DC-6Bs and CV-990s inherited from REAL, as well as sundry C-46s and DC-3s, which were still to be seen in the most unlikely places.

VARIG's Lockheed Model 188A Electra PP-VJM, acquired in 1962, had been American Airlines' N6104A *Flagship Washington*. (*VARIG*)

VARIG's choice was a bold one, and is an indication of the shrewdness and care with which it made its purchasing decisions. At the time, the emotional impact of the word 'jet' and the fact that the Caravelle was very popular with the public, could have persuaded the airline to stay with the ones it already had, and expand the fleet. Although REAL had opened negotiations with Lockheed for the propeller-turbine Model 188 Electra, there was no contractual commitment by VARIG when it purchased REAL. Furthermore the Electra had only just emerged from the harrowing experience of having its wings completely rebuilt, to avoid being grounded by the United States FAA following at least two fatal crashes attributed to structural failure.

Nevertheless, VARIG ordered five Electra IIs almost simultaneously with the take-over of REAL, and these entered service on the inter-city coastal routes on 2 September, 1962, the same year in which all twelve of REAL's Convair CV-440s were sold. VARIG has never regretted its Electra decision. Although the

481

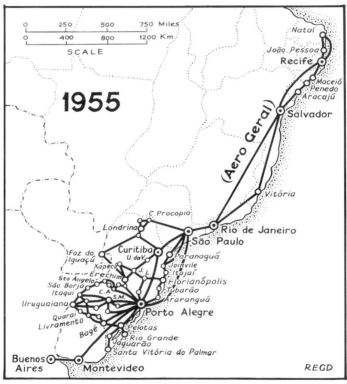

63. Growth of VARIG Domestic Network (1), 1927–1955. For almost thirty years, VARIG's progress in route expansion was confined to the southern States of Brazil. Only in 1952 did it reach northward, when it acquired Aero Geral. (C.A. = Cruz Alta, J. = Joaçaba, L. = Lajes, S.M. = Santa Maria, U. do V. = União do Vitória.)

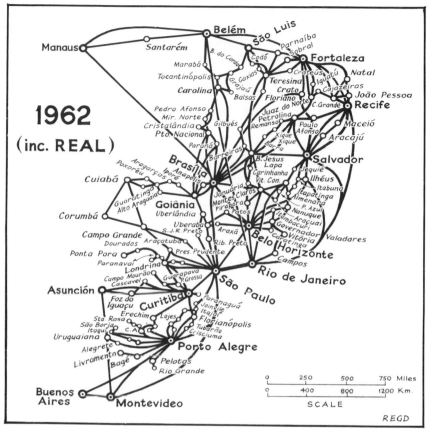

64. Growth of VARIG Domestic Network (2), 1962. VARIG's route mileage in Brazil suddenly grew to several times its former size when it engulfed REAL in 1961. Even after some sensible route rationalization, the residual network was a closely-knit web covering almost every part of Brazil except the far west. (C.A. = Cruz Alta.)

broad-bladed propellers were a constant and emphatic reminder that the Electra did not belong to the glamorous family of jet airliners, this was immaterial at Santos Dumont Airport, where the Electra was permitted to land and take off but the jets were not. For quite a while, VARIG could point to the fact that its Electras could bring passengers to Salvador, for example, just as quickly as the Caravelles, simply because Santos Dumont was the proverbial five-minute walk from downtown Rio, whereas Galeão, the jet airport, was an hour or more's dusty, congested, and irritating drive away from the city centre. Curiously, although the Electras gradually had to give way to the jets in public esteem, as new second-generation jets replaced the Caravelle, the improvement of the roads out to Galeão was also a factor.

So intuitive was VARIG's choice of the Electra, however, that its longevity in service was to threaten the record of previous famous types such as the Junkers-F 13 and the DC-3.

483

VASP Becomes a National Airline.

When VASP put its new Viscounts into service in 1958, it was just beginning to expand its network, and had proudly opened a coastal route as far north at Natal. Then in June 1960 a DC-3 route, following the paths of the CAM in earlier years, provided a stopping service through central Goiás, to put Belém on the VASP map. Simultaneously this was augmented by a direct service to Belém with the Viscounts, from both São Paulo and Rio de Janeiro, stopping only at Brasília, where connections were made to Fortaleza and other cities of the northeast. Possibly VASP was able to acquire such important connections to the north, in spite of the existence of incumbent operators who provided adequate service, because it was also prepared to take its share of the uneconomic feeder services. The Brazilian Government urgently wished these to be continued, and if possible expanded, yet was reluctant to subsidize without being absolutely sure it was getting its money's worth, and that there was no duplication. Thus, on 7 August, 1961, VASP took over from Cruzeiro do Sul two new central routes to the north, the Linha do Tocantins and the Linha do Araguaia, multiple-stop social services flown by the ever-faithful DC-3, from Goiânia to Belém.

To establish its national position even more solidly, and encouraged by the Government, which was pursuing its goal of reducing the number of airlines to create a more rational system, the São Paulo Governor Carvalho Pinto announced on 7 January, 1962, that VASP had bought Lóide. This airline had itself formed a consortium with two other airlines, NAB and TABA, and owned Lemke S. A. Industria e Comercio, an engine overhaul plant. Lóide's route network covered substantially the same area as VASP's, so that the Government's objective of reducing the number of airlines without reducing service to the public was realised (VARIG had acquired REAL the previous year).

The networks were completely integrated and the merger officially recognized on 4 April, 1962. A new route was opened to the Acre Territory, as an extension of the Cuiabá route, with also a direct link with Brasília. VASP now served 72 cities in 21 States and two Territories.

Changing the Route Structure at Petrópolis

On 27 November, 1961, the Department of Civil Aviation, together with other affected Government agencies, convened a Conference at the Castelo Country Club in Petrópolis for twelve days to discuss with the airlines and three major banks the problem of maintaining a viable Brazilian air network which would serve the country at a time when it was poised for dramatic commercial and industrial expansion. There was a dire need to try to reconcile the needs of the public with the aggression of the independent airlines in a way which, while preserving all the virtues of competition and free enterprise, would at the same time maintain some sort of order in a complex situation which could easily get out of hand.

The biggest problem was one of subsidies. Traditionally, Brazil had followed a careful course, granting aid to airlines which were seen to be providing a genuine social service to communities which otherwise would be deprived of any kind of transport. Indeed, in the furtherance of some of its aims to open up new frontiers in remote inland areas, the airlines had been encouraged, even requested, to provide such service; and usually a bargain was struck which was acceptable to all parties.

But the postwar developments in Brazilian domestic aviation, spectacular though the growth may have been, was accompanied by a host of problems. A large number of feeder and bush routes had been operated only because the airlines could obtain cheap second-hand aircraft—mainly the DC-3; and often the airlines would fly these at shoe-string cost levels, to enable them to make money even without subsidy. Of course, if the subsidy was also available, so much the better. But as the aircraft grew older, and highways were built, and surface transport in the more densely populated states was no longer a time-consuming adventure, the natural reservoir of potential air traffic stagnated, and in many areas, declined. Compounding this difficulty, the costs started to soar as Brazilian fiscal policy produced one of the highest sustained rates of monetary inflation of any country in normal peacetime conditions.

Subsidy, therefore, was a burning issue, and a new formula had to be found. Accordingly, drawing advice from all sides, the Brazilian Government came up in due course with Decree No.52,693, dated 15 October, 1963, which created a distinct category of air routes, the Rede de Integração Nacional (RIN), broadly comparable with the Local Service Airline policy in the United States. These were closely controlled by the D.A.C. and, as with the US practice, would qualify for subsidy. They could be operated by all Brazilian airlines for a ten-year term, and had to be operated only by DC-3s and (in the case of the Amazon River routes) PBY-5 Catalinas. There were also special subsidies for international routes, and routes in the Amazon basin.

The RIN complemented the Rede Aérea Nacional (RAN) which comprised the main trunk routes, and the Rede Aérea Internacional (RAI). These were considered to be potentially profitable without the benefit of subsidy, provided that the tariffs were carefully controlled. In the tricky period of galloping inflation, the Government was not going to allow indiscriminate tariff wars. It therefore insisted that every effort must be made to relate fares to costs, and kept a careful watch over airline affairs to ensure that the policy was being carried out both in the letter and the spirit of the law.

Under the provisions of Portaria 221, the D.A.C. laid down precise tables of fares for all RAN routes, and specified the exact seating and level of tariff for every type of aircraft. Simplified, these were as follows: T1 Plus, for Caravelles, Electras, and any international jets used on connecting domestic routes; T1, for Viscounts, DC-6s, and Constellations; T2 for Convair-Liners and Scandias; T3 for DC-4s and C-46s; and RIN for DC-3s and Catalinas. There were subtle variations from this basic framework, such as being allowed to charge only RIN fares for the new Dart Heralds of Sadia; but the Government was correctly vigilant in demanding the strictest standards of cost control to ensure that the policy of 'true' tariffs was observed.

Other stimulants agreed at the Conferência do Castelo (or Conferência de Petrópolis) were airport tax concessions and special rates of exchange for importing aircraft and spares. And it was a sign of maturing air policy that the unique case of the Ponte Aérea received special attention, not only for the famous São Paulo–Rio de Janeiro connection, in vigorous operation since 6 July, 1959, but also by creating three new Pontes, started on 12 March, 1962: Rio–Belo Horizonte, Rio–Brasília, and Belo Horizonte–Brasília. Above all, the principle of reducing the number of airlines to a minimum was encouraged, but not so as to allow a monopoly, and areas of influence and control were agreed.

The new national capital was conceived in the mid-1950s as the political brainchild of President Kubitschek (albeit putting into practice an idea many decades old). That it should receive frequent and regular Air Bridge service so quickly was a great tribute to the energy and initiative of the airlines. For the record, the first to serve the area destined to be the Federal Territory was Cruzeiro do Sul, when it made a bi-monthly stop at Planaltina, on its central Goiás route, in 1954. Planaltina was a little to the north of the Territory, and frequency increased to once weekly in February 1957. Then REAL began the first scheduled service to Brasília itself on 3 May of that year, followed quickly by every airline except Panair and VARIG before the year was out. These latter two introduced Caravelles in 1960; and two years later Brasília had its own airbus service. The creation of the new Federal capital completely changed the Brazilian airline map.

The first of the new terminal buildings at Rio de Janeiro International Airport was dedicated by President Ernesto Geisel on 20 January, 1977, and VASP operated the first service from the terminal on 1 February. The control tower can be seen in the centre and the curved earthwork beyond indicates the location of the second terminal. Runway 09/27, commissioned on 20 January, 1979, can be seen under construction in the background. Aircraft of VASP, VARIG and Transbrasil are in the foreground. (*VARIG*)

The resultant effects of the cost v. tariff regulations were neatly in line with the economic theory of aircraft operations related to the so-called demand elasticity. On the shorter routes from the great urban concentrations of São Paulo and Rio de Janeiro to such nearby provincial cities as Belo Horizonte, Curitiba, even Salvador and Porto Alegre, the fares were a slight deterrent to traffic growth, as on such shorter stages the cost per mile was relatively high, and this was tied to the fare. But on longer routes, such as to Recife, Belém, or Manaus, the costs were lower down the curve, and fares were relatively cheaper as a consequence. So the RAN fare structure indirectly stimulated the longer-haul routes in Brazil.

CHAPTER TWENTY-FOUR

A World Airline and the Regionals

The End of Panair do Brasil

During the early 1960s, after making its mark on the domestic scene with successful deployment of the Caravelle fleet, it was business almost as usual for Panair do Brasil on the international front. There were one or two setbacks through accidents, both at night, one to a DC-8 taking off from Galeão, Rio de Janeiro, on 20 August, 1962, the other when a Constellation crashed in the jungle near Manaus on 14 December of the same year, killing 50 people. But Panair's record was no worse than many other airlines in South America, and drew no special criticism in world aviation circles.

During the same period, in October 1962, Panair bought two DC-3s from NAB for operations in the Amazon region, and in August 1963 two DC-7Cs were transferred from Pan American for the pooled Brazil–Lisbon service with TAP, the Portuguese national airline. This had been started on 30 October, 1960, and fares were discounted for passengers of Brazilian or Portuguese—*i.e.* Portuguese-speaking—nationality.

Pan American sold its last remaining shares in 1961, so that for the European services, Panair do Brasil was solidly established as a Brazilian airline, untainted by foreign shareholding. Its routes were fiercely competitive, against strong national airlines, so that it was wholly logical and prudent to sign a pool agreement, in November 1963, with some of the main rivals. The airlines involved were Alitalia, Aerolíneas Argentinas, and Lufthansa, so, bearing in mind that the Lisbon connection was already well taken care of, Panair should have been comfortably placed.

During 1964, in fact, the only news item of note was that the Brazilian Government granted authority to operate flights from Lisbon to Luanda, Angola, under charter to TAP, to provide extra capacity to the Portuguese carrier on its African colonial routes.

It came as an abrupt surprise, therefore, when on 10 February, 1965, Panair do Brasil's 21.00 hr European flight was cancelled only three hours before departure. VARIG, however, was ready with an aircraft, and immediately took over all Panair's services, without cancelling a single one. The next day, the Government cancelled Panair's operating authority, because of what was described as an 'irretrievable' financial position. It directed that all international services should be taken over by VARIG, and all domestic services by Cruzeiro do Sul. Panair was alleged to have got into financial difficulties with the Bank of Brazil and with the National Bank of Economic Development.

On 16 February, 1965, Panair do Brasil was declared bankrupt, with an overseas debt of $62,000,000. One DC-8 and one DC-7C, both on lease, were returned to Pan American, while two other DC-8s were re-leased from Pan Am at $75,000 per month for VARIG to maintain services, the implication being that a better deal was struck. Panair do Brasil employees' salaries were paid by the Air

Ministry for a week, but that was all.

The speed with which this massive transfer of airline power was executed was in striking contrast with the normal course of events involving Brazilian government agencies, not least those connected with aviation matters. The suspicion remains, therefore, that Panair had been under investigation for some time, and that to avoid far-reaching repercussions affecting Brazilian prestige in Europe, the matter was kept secret until a smooth transition of service responsibility could be assured. For although VARIG ranks today, and did in 1965, as one of the finest and most efficient airlines in the world, to add a new service at three hours' notice for another airline, and to continue the pattern without interruption, could only be achieved with some prior inkling that emergency action might be required of it.

For its part, Panair do Brasil was able to make a sturdy defence of its financial position, because the debt, though substantial, could be weighed against some positive factors, with substantial assets and the prospect of continued operating viability as security. The Bank of the State of Guanabara gave Panair do Brasil its support, and the Governor of the State, Carlos de Laserda, further suggested that the Bank should take over the ownership of Panair. The debt would thus be guaranteed, with the material assets, including the DC-8s and Caravelles, as security, much in the same way that the Bank of São Paulo gave a solid financial foundation to VASP. The Air Minister, Eduardo Gomes, denied this idea, and Panair showed its books to VASP, whereupon the Bank of São Paulo proposed to take over the ownership, presumably with a VASP-Panair merger in mind. This would have achieved the objective of reducing the number of Brazilian airlines, but there was a suspicion that domestic regional rivalries were also a factor.

In this vast country, as for example in the USA or the Soviet Union (even in smaller countries like Great Britain, France, and Germany) there are great differences in human character and behaviour between the regions, and the rivalry has always been especially strong between the Paulistas of São Paulo and the Cariocas of Rio de Janeiro. The latter could also usually draw on support from the other regions which were deeply suspicious—and possibly a little jealous—of São Paulo's dynamic growth, success, prosperity, and affluence. There existed a nation-wide apprehension that the Paulistas would take over everything, given half a chance. VASP always laboured under this undefinable, ever-present disadvantage when it came to matters as important as the elimination of one of South America's major airlines, with Brazil's national prestige at stake. At any rate, the São Paulo interests had no more success than those of Guanabara.

Panair in fact was buried without trace, was not even given a decent funeral, and the customary eulogies were absent. This was one of the sadder aspects of the whole affair, for the airline had been one of Brazil's unofficial ambassadors for thirty-five years, twenty of which had seen it as Brazil's flag carrier in Europe. The distribution of the effects, however, was dealt with in quick order.

At the time of the demise, most of the radio communications services in Brazil were provided by, or had been originally installed by Panair do Brasil, and these were taken over by the Government. In July 1965, Cruzeiro do Sul inherited the three Caravelles, plus the five Catalinas, to maintain the special Amazon services. The two remaining DC-8s went to VARIG, via the Government receiver. In August, the tribunal in charge of Panair's bankruptcy ordered that the DC-8 which had been purchased from Pan American, but on which no payments had been made, should be returned to that airline. Of the four DC-7Cs, acquired in 1963, two were returned to Pan American, and two were subsequently sold for scrap. Of the ten remaining Constellations, all except one were scrapped.

Panair do Brasil's Douglas DC-8-33 PP-PDT *Bras Cubas* was to have been Pan American's N820PA *Clipper Morning Star*. It failed to take off at Rio de Janeiro and ran into the sea on 20 August, 1962. (*Douglas Aircraft Company*)

In May 1966, the final curtain was drawn when the appeal of Panair do Brasil's directors to the Brazilian Supreme Court, calling for cancellation of the Decree of Bankruptcy, was denied. It had been an unhappy experience for all the Panair people. Perhaps special sympathy should be extended to the engineers and maintenance men at Galeão. Panair's base at Galeão, established many years before the war (when, in fact, Panair was a subsidiary of Pan American) was the only one in Brazil which was licensed by the United States C.A.A. for both airframe and engine overhaul, including US aircraft of US registry, both civil and US Air Force. That Panair should be accused by its most malevolent detractors as not having adequate maintenance was the unkindest cut of all.

New Aircraft Types

The Brazilian Government, either by direction, persuasion, or guidance, may have hoped to transform the airline industry from a proliferation of small companies into a privileged assembly of large corporations, and thus achieve a substantial measure of standardization and consequential economies and efficiency. If this was so, by whatever degree of emphasis, the policy was not extended to the exertion of influence over aircraft procurement policies. For while the number of Brazilian airlines steadily decreased from the 1950s to the 1970s, the number of aircraft types seemed to vary in inverse ratio. Indeed, during one decade, from 1964 to 1974, no fewer than nine different aircraft types were introduced in Brazil, eight of them for domestic use.

One of the most baffling examples of the apparently obsessive desire by the airlines to try one of everything was to introduce into service, within the period of only four years, all four twin propeller-turbine aircraft powered by the Rolls-Royce Dart engine. First in the field was the British Handley Page Herald, put into service by Sadia in February 1964. Omar Fontana's frustrating dispute with the authorities over this purchase was finally settled early in 1966, yet in the same year, in November, Cruzeiro do Sul signed a contract with the Japanese to purchase eight of the Nihon YS-11-200A. The YS-11 was larger than the Herald, with 60 seats against the Herald's 40, being equipped with the more powerful Series 10 Dart engines, and could thus be demonstrated to be marginally more economic to operate, provided the loads were forthcoming. Also, the Japanese, anxious to break into a new market, undoubtedly offered excellent terms, including the trade-in of all of Cruzeiro's ageing fleet of Convair-Liners. For Cruzeiro do Sul, it was a good deal; but hardly in line with the principles of aircraft

489

VASP's YS-11A-212 PP-SMM, seen at Santos Dumont Airport, Rio de Janeiro, was
delivered on 30 November, 1968.

standardization. VASP also ordered six YS-11As in February 1968.

Hard on the heels of this transaction, moreover, came the decision by VARIG
to buy the Hawker Siddeley HS.748, a rugged example of the twin-Dart family
which was also purchased by the Força Aérea Brasileira for transport purposes.
While VARIG's choice seemed to fly in the face of logic, in view of the previous
purchases by Sadia and Cruzeiro, it was in many respects the most sensible,
judged by subsequent events. The HS.748—known familiarly as the Avro,
because of its original design ancestry—was the best performer of all the
twin-Dart aircraft, displaying much versatility in coping with poor airfields with
bad surfaces. In this sense, therefore, it came closest of all to achieving the elusive
and long sought 'DC-3 Replacement' specification and capability. The same
aircraft are still being put to this stringent test, as VARIG's remaining fleet of six
HS.748s were sold to Bouraq Indonesia Airlines in 1976.

A Hawker Siddeley HS.748 in VARIG livery, with Copacabana below and Ipanema on the
left. Careful study of the original photograph has failed to reveal any identity of this aircraft
and it is not certain that this picture is genuine. (*British Aerospace*)

VASP's BAC One-Eleven 423ET PP-SRT was delivered in December 1967 and sold in the USA in 1974.

The fourth twin-Dart aircraft was the Fairchild Hiller FH-227B, a 48-seat version of the universally-accepted Fokker F.27 Friendship, and built under licence in the United States. The aircraft shared the ill fate of its owners, Paraense, the demise of which has already been narrated.

Perhaps the strangest aspect of the twin-Dart quadriplication of types was not simply that they were bought by four different airlines, but that they were all bought for essentially the same purpose: to operate feeder services into outlying parts of Brazil where operating economics were at a premium. The Herald and the FH-227B were both high-winged, which was an advantage to passengers who wished to view the never-ending panorama of jungle or savannah spread beneath on flights to the remoter parts of Amazonas or the Mato Grosso. They were thus more attractive than the HS.748 which, however, had superior airfield performance, a critical factor in some regions. The YS-11 was a little larger, and could thus serve a slightly wider band of routes, including those of higher traffic density than the average feeder network. Taking everything into account, this was one procurement situation in which the Government might have given firmer direction, even to the point of holding a national competition.

Almost simultaneously with the last of the twin-Dart aircraft came the first of the second wave of twin-jets—the Caravelle having represented the first in 1959. Initially, the British met with success, with the BAC One-Eleven. By vigorous promotion, they were in the happy position of seeing both São Paulo airlines, VASP and Sadia, vieing for the privilege of being the first to invest. With typical directness, Omar Fontana made the first public overtures by asking the Government for permission to purchase in May 1967. By the time he had made his final selection of the 94-seat 500 series One-Eleven, however, in February 1969, VASP had moved smartly by actually ordering two of the One-Eleven 400 series on 22 June, 1967. The contract was worth £3 million, and was the fifth BAC

Although this BAC One-Eleven 521FH is seen here at Congonhas Airport, São Paulo, in October 1970 with Sadia's name and the Brazilian registration PP-SDP, it was Austral's LV-JNR on lease and wearing Austral's livery. (*Denir Lima de Camargo*)

491

One-Eleven order in Latin America. BAC's success was, in some measure, at Handley Page's expense; as VASP had previously announced an order for ten Heralds on 21 April, 1965, but did not take delivery, and approximately the same investment was made in the One-Elevens. VASP put the aircraft into service on 8 January, 1968, well in advance of Sadia's 17 September, 1970, using a leased aircraft, pending delivery of its own BAC One-Eleven 500 on 17 October.

When the One-Elevens arrived in Brazil, the two big United States twin-jet manufacturers, Boeing and Douglas, had joined in the competition for this rich market. The Brazilian domestic network was seen at the time to be one of the largest in the world, with good growth potential, so the stakes were high, and a hard-fought contest developed. First off the mark was again VASP, ordering five Boeing 727-200s, late in March 1968. The State Governor of São Paulo, Abreu Sodre, signed the contract. As an indication of the growing prosperity of Brazil's airline industry, this order brought VASP's total investment in new aircraft to $50 million within the four years from 1966 to 1969. In fact, when final financing arrangements were revealed, the 727-200 order was changed to five twin-engined 737-200s, the first of which was delivered in July 1969.

VASP's cargo Boeing 737-2H4C PP-SMW at Congonhas Airport in September 1981 This aircraft was previously operated by Aloha Airlines and Southwest Airlines.
(*Nelson de Barros Pereira Jr*)

But the biggest battle was for the orders from Brazil's two largest airlines, VARIG and Cruzeiro do Sul. VARIG, now firmly established as the flag-carrier, was the sales target with most prestige. Boeing won the battle, and, it would seem from subsequent re-orders for its equipment, at the same time won the war. Cruzeiro do Sul ordered four Boeing 727-100s in December 1968, and VARIG ordered ten shortly thereafter. The basis of selection was performance at São Paulo's Congonhas Airport. The British Hawker Siddeley Trident was alleged to lack sufficient power, while the DC-9's twin engines were considered inadequate. Also, the Boeing 727 was enjoying considerable success all over the world, having won significant and crucial orders in Japan and Australia, to jeopardize the Trident's chances for world acceptance.

Cruzeiro do Sul put the Boeing 727-100 into service on 3 February, 1970, on routes from Rio to Brasília, and on the international service to Buenos Aires, a course of action which seemed strangely irrelevant to the reasons given for the choice. VARIG followed Cruzeiro into service with the Boeing 727 on 13 October, 1970.

The EMB-110 Bandeirante

Any one of the four twin-Dart propeller-turbine airliners intended to serve the outer regions and the smaller airfields of Brazil might have found a very large market, with the HS.748 as the best prospect, had it not been for the concurrent development of a small airliner built by the emerging Brazilian aircraft industry. Aircraft had been built sporadically by a number of individuals and companies in Brazil since 1910; but these had been mainly short-lived projects, or, particularly after the war, concerned with production of small communications or training aircraft under licence from foreign companies. In the 1950s and 1960s, the experience accumulated by a small nucleus of Brazilian aeronautical engineers enabled them to build from original designs, and to find a market with the Força Aérea Brasileira, in a mutually beneficial partnership.

In due course, the Centro Técnico de Aeronáutica (CTA) unveiled the prototype of a small propeller-turbine airliner, the IPD-6504, on 26 October, 1968, four days after the eight-seater made its first flight. Recognizing that this aircraft, more than all previous Brazilian designs, contained the basic market potential to justify a successful production line, and in default of adequate private capital sufficient for such production, the Brazilian Government intervened. After representations by Brigadier Paulo Victor da Silva, the Director of CTA at the time, a series of inter-departmental meetings were held, under the sponsorship of the Ministry of Aeronautics, and on 19 August, 1969, under the terms of Decree-Law 770 of 29 July, was born the Empresa Brasileira de Aeronáutica S.A. (EMBRAER), a joint-stock company, with the Brazilian Government holding 51 per cent, charged with the responsibility of producing the Bandeirante.

The Bandeirante, or EMB 110 as the production version was called by the newly-founded company, may not have been the ideal aircraft for the lowest level of Brazilian air service, previously served for so long on an ad hoc basis by the venerable DC-3. But no other project had come close. The basic problem facing all manufacturers still pursuing the elusive goal of building a DC-3 replacement

Two Embraer 110C Bandeirantes, seen at São José dos Campos in March 1973 before delivery to Transbrasil. The aircraft are PT-TBA and PT-TBB and they are finished in the airline's orange, black and mustard livery. (*via Mário B. de M. Vinagre*)

was that the contemporary labour and material costs, together with far more stringent certification standards, ensured that to build it would be so costly that no airline could purchase and operate a new aircraft and turn in a profit. The nearest to the solution were the twin-Dart types, but their 40-seat capacity was excessive for large segments of the Brazilian airline system. There were countless communities which could not generate such a load in less than a week, so that frequency could not be related to demand in a reasonable manner.

Thus, although small by comparison, the Bandeirante was able to fulfil a need. It could at least claim to offer a seating capacity which matched the sparse demand of the Brazilian outback; and its Pratt & Whitney PT6 Canadian-built engines offered well-proven reliability. Above all, it was made in Brazil, and its production would serve two purposes: it would be an unequalled training school for aspiring Brazilian aeronautical engineers, at the same time making Brazil self-sufficient in one segment (albeit a modest one) of the air transport industry, and save valuable foreign exchange.

EMBRAER found that much work had to be done on its promising inheritance. After prototype flying, the aircraft underwent a complete redesign, and production aircraft were larger, with a capacity of 12–16 seats. The first of these flew on 9 August, 1972, and the commercial airline version, the EMB-110C, was ordered by Transbrasil (formerly Sadia) and VASP in March and April 1973, respectively. Transbrasil's first Bandeirante (PP-TBA) went into service on 16 April and VASP's first (PP-SBA) on 4 November of that year on short-distance feeder services in the southern States. Henceforward, the Bandeirante was to become a familiar sight all over Brazil, and was to play a key role in another major development stage of the Brazilian airline structure. The EMB-110P version, with 18 seats, was introduced in 1976, and first went into service with TABA, one of the new regional airlines.

The Brazilian faith in its product was well justified. The EMB-110, in its different versions, has been accepted as a competitive commuter or Regional airliner all over the world, earning the ultimate compliment of the affectionate nickname, the 'Bandit'.

A Giant Recovers its Strength

During the late 1950s, in typically apt phraseology, President Kubitschek had used as a slogan the brave claim 'I Will Awaken the Sleeping Giant' but it was ironic that, after the first heady flush of traffic stimulated by the construction of Brasília, Brazilian air traffic statistics revealed a severe decline. In 1965, following a five-year period which witnessed the complete disappearance of three major airlines, REAL, Panair do Brasil, and Lóide, the number of passengers carried by Brazilian airlines was only about two-thirds of the number carried in 1960.

Recuperation began during the second half of the 1960s, the same period when the twin-Dart airliners and the first of the second-generation twin-jets arrived to transform the airline fleets from primarily piston-engine-powered to almost completely turbine-powered. The airlines began to reap the benefit of the properly structured tariff system and better commercial discipline was applied, with the support of the Federal Government. For example, the arrangement by which Government officials, from senator level down through apparently limitless strata of qualifying staff, could obtain free airline tickets, was abolished. The creation of a small aircraft industry able to produce its own airliner, the Bandeirante, was an important psychological factor. Concurrently, the Brazilian

Government re-structured the airport construction and maintenance organization on 12 December, 1972, (Law No.5,862) by creating Empresa de Infra-Estrutura Aeroportuária (INFRAERO) which embraced the activities of several previously unco-ordinated agencies. By 1974, Brazil had recovered its air transport strength to the extent that it ranked twelfth in the ICAO world listing of passenger-km flown, and to keep pace, the airlines embarked upon another round of jet airliner purchases.

A New Wave of Aircraft

Having taken a few years to absorb Panair do Brasil and become used to the idea of being a world airline, ranking with the long-established leaders in Europe and the United States, VARIG began to think about new equipment. Reliable though its fleet of Boeing 707s were, accelerating Brazilian international traffic growth demanded the introduction of one of the larger, wide-bodied types for its intercontinental routes. The big battle was once again between the traditional manufacturing rivals, Boeing and Douglas, and in this instance Douglas was the winner. After a two-year evaluation, VARIG selected the DC-10-30 over the Boeing 747 in November 1972, ordering three in May 1973. The DC-10 entered service on 24 June, 1974, on the European services, and on 1 July to New York. Ever since the start of its Constellation service to New York in 1955, VARIG had built up an enviable reputation for superb on-board service, and the DC-10 supplemented this competitive factor to consolidate Brazilian success on the South Atlantic service, where nine airlines vied for supremacy.

But VARIG did not abandon its traditional supplier, Boeing. Douglas's satisfaction at having put the DC-10 into service in Latin America, before the Boeing 747 had even chalked up an order, was dampened by VARIG ordering ten Boeing Advanced 737-200s, with uprated Pratt & Whitney JT8D-17 engines, in May 1974, part of a $135 million Boeing Brazil deal which also involved Cruzeiro.

VARIG put the 727-200 into service on 27 November, 1974, and Cruzeiro followed in January 1975. The tri-jet 727 and the twin-jet 737 now came to dominate the Brazilian domestic scene. Including orders for the Federal

VARIG's Boeing 737-241 PP-VMN, seen at Congonhas Airport, São Paulo, in February 1980. This version is known as the Super Advanced model. (*Mário B. de M. Vinagre*)

Cruzeiro do Sul's Boeing 737-2C3 PP-CJN in the airline's smart blue and white livery. The upper fuselage band is dark blue and the lower band and tail markings are turquoise blue.
(*The Boeing Company*)

Government, upwards of seventy of the two types were delivered to Brazil, to the total exclusion of the Douglas DC-9 and the near-extinction of the BAC One-Eleven. Although pressure or direction from the Brazilian Government probably had little to do with the decision, here had been an example of standardization of equipment which was in satisfactory contrast with earlier experience.

Boeing's success continued. In March 1977, VASP announced an order for two Boeing 727-200s, each equipped with 152 seats, the first of the so-called stretched 727s to be ordered by Brazil. But although more of the stretched Boeing tri-jet were added, some with Transbrasil, traffic demand on the booming Brazilian inter-city routes led to the introduction of an even larger type.

Cruzeiro do Sul's Airbus A300B4-203 PP-CLA at Congonhas Airport, São Paulo, on 19 July, 1980. The aircraft in the left foreground is TAM's Cessna 402B PT-IUX.
(*Mário B. de M. Vinagre*)

The European Airbus, the 230-seat A300 (B4 version), which had made its first acquaintance with Latin America when the energetic Omar Fontana made initial overtures in 1978, went into service on 1 July, 1980, with Cruzeiro do Sul, on the Rio de Janeiro–São Paulo–Buenos Aires route. Subsequently, under a pooling arrangement with VARIG, which now owned Cruzeiro but continued to operate separately, the Airbus was deployed throughout the primary domestic routes of Brazil, and to Caracas, Miami, and Asunción.

VARIG's Airbus A300B4-203 PP-VND landing at Congonhas Airport, São Paulo, on 26 September, 1981. (*Mário B. de M. Vinagre*)

Maintaining the growth on long-distance intercontinental routes also, VARIG introduced the 360-seat Boeing 747, mainly on Rio de Janeiro–New York, on 12 February, 1981, to supplement the fleet of DC-10s.

Meanwhile, an effective though unspectacular aircraft deployment programme was taking place which was of inestimable benefit to the airlines and the Brazilian travelling public alike. Airfield performance of new types at the key airports of São Paulo's Congonhas and Rio de Janeiro's Santos Dumont had long been a bone of contention. The São Paulo problem was less serious than that at Rio, where the runway ended abruptly in Guanabara Bay at the edge of the original landfill which had created the airport. Eventually, on 1 March, 1975, the Government decreed that all twin-engined aircraft should be withdrawn from the Ponte Aérea, thus excluding the twin-Dart types, the Boeing 737, and the BAC One-Eleven. The Boeing 727 needed more runway length, and so the Lockheed Electra, with propeller-turbines, came into its own. This type became standard equipment, with VARIG providing service for all participating airlines at an agreed fee, with the VARIG insignia removed appropriately from such aircraft.

The success of the Ponte Aérea continued, and in December 1976, VARIG bought two more Electras from Aerocondor, of Colombia, to bring its fleet total to twelve. This permitted a half-hour frequency between Santos Dumont and Congonhas, even every 15 min during the rush hours, plus extra sections, with the choice of seat reservation or non-reservation, and a standardized seating layout. Total daily frequency each way was 28, the allocation of revenues being split 52 per cent VARIG, 22 per cent VASP, 19 per cent Cruzeiro do Sul, and 7 per cent Transbrasil.

The Ponte Aérea came of age on 6 July, 1980, after completing 21 years of uninterrupted no-reservation airbus service between Brazil's two great cities. More than 18 mn passenger seats had been sold during the period, and 400,000 aircraft hours flown at a steady average of about 37 round trips per working day, and 22 daily at the weekends.

Two Airlines merge into Two

To them that hath shall be given. Already the beneficiary of two major amalgamations, by acquiring REAL and Panair do Brasil, VARIG now proceeded to absorb yet another. One of the few Brazilian airline survivors in the 1970s was Cruzeiro do Sul, claiming to be the direct descendant of the original Condor Syndikat of 1927 and thus the oldest airline in Brazil; and, in spite of VARIG's phenomenal growth, still the second largest. But by the middle of 1974, a combination of economic factors—the oil price increase of the winter of 1973–74, Brazilian economic instability generally, and excess capacity—almost brought this proud airline to its knees. It approached the Brazilian Government for temporary finance to see it through a crisis, and the suggestion was made that Cruzeiro should merge with **Transbrasil.** This latter company, having caught the headlines with its BAC One-Eleven promotion in the early 1970s, had also experienced financial difficulties, although with typical ebullience and commercial flair, Omar Fontana, the owner, camouflaged his problems. He had changed his company's name from the former Sadia to the more impressive Transbrasil, in line with an extended and expanded route network and the newly-acquired jets. He had moved his headquarters to Brasília, and adopted a completely new colour scheme, in which the entire fleet was painted in brilliant primary colours in a two-tone scheme for each individual aircraft.

Omar Fontana, as colourful in character as his aircraft, at first favoured the idea of the merger, and made an offer, but was unable to persuade the National Development Bank to guarantee the 42 per cent of the total sum required. Also, a possible third partner, an air taxi company, withdrew from the negotiations. The Government then altered its course and, aiming for a two-company domestic airline system, proposed that both Cruzeiro do Sul and Transbrasil should be sold. Cruzeiro started negotiations with VASP, which, however, made a poor initial offer, while Fontana was invited to join forces with VARIG. But Fontana felt by this time that his financial problems were not insuperable, and refused to sell to VARIG.

Another proposal being discussed was that there should be a three-way merger between VASP, Cruzeiro do Sul, and Transbrasil. This would certainly have met

Two of Transbrasil's Boeing 727s in the maintenance area at Congonhas Airport, São Paulo. The nearest aircraft is the 727-078 PT-TYR acquired in August 1976 after service with BWIA as 9Y-TCO and Braniff as N305BN. These 727s have canary yellow fuselages and the tails and fuselage flashes are magenta. The sunrays on the tail are canary yellow.

498

the Government's objective of preserving a two-airline balance of power, as VARIG would have retained 90 per cent of Brazilian international routes, while the merged triumvirate would have retained 68 per cent of the domestic routes. But this idea was not pursued very far.

Finally, after rumour, counter-rumour, speculation, and much burning of midnight oil, VARIG acquired control of Cruzeiro do Sul on 22 May, 1975. The VARIG owners, the Fundaçao Rubem Berta, bought, at first, 65 per cent of the shares, later increasing this to 98 per cent. In one very important aspect, however, this acquisition was different from other previous amalgamations. Cruzeiro do Sul continued to operate as a separate airline, with its aircraft retaining their own handsome paint-scheme. Many activities such as reservations and accounting continued as separate functions, but schedules and fleets were integrated to eliminate unnecessary duplication, while spares stocks and maintenance procedures were sensibly rationalized. There emerged from the amalgamation two airlines only subtly different from their predecessors, under one ownership, both operating with commendably improved efficiency, in friendly rivalry rather than in bitter competition.

As a postscript to the VARIG-Cruzeiro do Sul merger, the effect on the Brazilian domestic balance of power did not go unnoticed. VASP and Transbrasil feared the competitive dominance of a super-airline. The Brazilian Government was anxious to preserve a reasonable balance and to avoid possible allegations that it had conspired to create a monopoly. Accordingly, on 26 August, 1975, Portaria 088/GM–5 of the Civil Aviation Department allocated a maximum domestic traffic share, measured in seat-km, of 40 per cent to VARIG/Cruzeiro. This was in their competitors' favour, as VARIG and Cruzeiro combined had considerably more than 40 per cent, and the São Paulo airlines moved to increase their capacity accordingly.

The directive was modified on 10 March, 1976, by Portaria No.27, altering the VARIG/Cruzeiro share to 45 per cent—still less than the 52 per cent currently being achieved. By a carefully constructed formula, this share would be reduced only from future market growth, and not by actually reducing current service patterns or capacity. VARIG/Cruzeiro was to reduce its combined share by 3 per cent for every 15 per cent of market growth, and as the formula was based on seat-km, this still allowed for free competition by load factor. Later still, on 7 October, 1980, Portaria 1188/GM–5 set maximum shares of 40 per cent for VASP and 25 per cent for Transbrasil.

Throughout the world of commercial air transport, the question of the importance of retaining the spirit of free enterprise versus the need to guard against excesses by sensible regulation has always been a difficult problem. In its handling of the balance of power between four airlines, each able to make its own special contribution to Brazilian airline progress, the Brazilian Government appears to have made a shrewd decision, maintaining fair shares for everyone while at the same time stimulating growth.

The Regionals

Simultaneously with its balancing act involving trunk and secondary networks, the Government moved with commendable perception and authority at the other end of the airline operations spectrum. The need for action was urgent. While progress in the upper levels of air routes was substantial, with the most modern types of aircraft such as the Boeing 727 and 737 which were ideal for the job, the

TAM's Fokker F.27-600 PT-LAF had earlier served All Nippon Airways and Pertamina. (*Nelson de Barros Pereira Jr*)

TAM's Embraer 110C Bandeirante PP-SBH, seen at Congonhas in October 1981, was formerly operated by VASP. (*Nelson de Barros Pereira Jr*)

Rio-Sul's Embraer 110P Bandeirante PT-GKC at Londrina Airport, Paraná, in February 1981. Aircraft livery is blue and white with yellow lower fuselage band and black registration. (*Nelson de Barros Pereira Jr*)

TABA's Beech H-18 PT-KXG at Júlio César Airport, Belém, in July 1981.
(*Nelson de Barros Pereira Jr*)

TABA's Curtiss Super 46C, PP-BUB, seen at Júlio César Airport, Belém, in July 1981, had enlarged cargo doors and was acquired by TABA in 1976. (*Nelson de Barros Pereira Jr*)

TABA's Fairchild Hiller FH-227B PP-BUJ was ordered by Paraense and named *Rio Amazonas*. It was taken over by the Ministry of Aeronautics and leased to TABA in June 1976. The aircraft is seen in TABA's standard livery with white forward fuselage, fawnish-brown centre fuselage and blue rear fuselage, fin and rudder. In fawnish-brown on the tail are stylized representations of the Indian house known as taba.
(*Nelson de Barros Pereira Jr*)

501

VOTEC's Douglas DC-3 PT-KZF was originally American Airlines' NC15590 *Flagship Memphis*. It is seen here at Júlio César Airport, Belém, in May 1981.
(*Nelson de Barros Pereira Jr*)

lower levels were woefully short of the right equipment and a cost-to-revenue ratio which could turn in profits. The twin propeller-turbine aircraft, while able to perform well on most secondary routes, were often too large for the traffic on the sparser segments, or could not use some of the worst airfields. The 16/18 seat EMBRAER 110 Bandeirante had come along at the right moment but even this aircraft could not produce seat-km costs which could guarantee financial viability. Mainly because of this chronic aircraft incompatability, the Brazilian domestic airline network had gradually declined from serving between 350 and 400 destinations during the 1950s to less than 80 in the autumn of 1975, with the further prospect of even this modest number being halved by the end of the year. In fact, only the State capitals, plus a few other privileged cities, appeared to stand a chance of enjoying continued air service after 1976.

The irony of this situation was that the 1950s had been years of entrepreneurs exercising a cavalier approach to airline operation and management. Their success was later judged to be fortuitous, or at best secondary to more ulterior motives, such as making some quick easy money at the expense of good flying standards, concern for the passenger, or the hope of sustained service. Yet in spite of all these shortcomings, much had been accomplished with an assortment of aircraft, almost entirely second-hand, and mostly vintage DC-3s. They had been obliged to use airfields which were of poorer standard than in the 1970s. Whatever

Nordeste Linhas Aéreas's Embraer 110C Bandeirante PP-GKA at Congonhas Airport in February 1980. (*Mário B. de M. Vinagre*)

their faults, however, and with all the handicaps, the Nacionals, the VIABRÁSes and their contemporaries gave the Brazilian public an air service which extended to the furthest corners of the land. Now, a quarter of a century later, with all the advances of modern technology, computers, and managerial expertise, there were clear indications that this previous success could not be emulated.

With good timing, on 12 November, 1975, Decree No.76,590 established a system of Regional airlines, under conditions which would encourage continued or renewed service, and even further development of routes, to small cities and communities. The Sistema Integrado de Transportes Aéreos Regional, to give

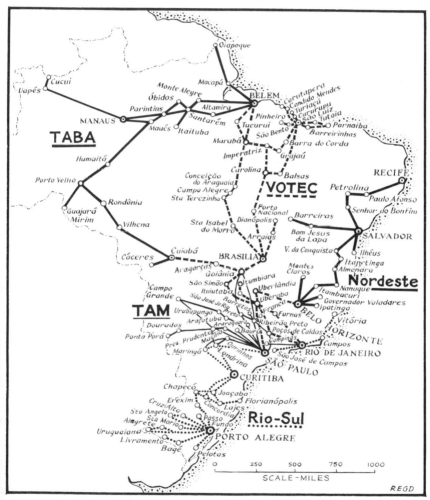

65. Brazilian Regional Airlines, 1976. During the 1960s, Brazilian airlines faced a crisis. Because of prohibitive costs, they were unable to sustain service over routes of low traffic density, mainly to small communities which were otherwise isolated. The airlines and the government worked out a scheme by which a federal subsidy was paid to new regional companies, working in association with the trunk carriers.

503

the plan its correct title, aimed to complement the trunk and secondary routes, and in particular to connect all outlying areas of Brazil with the heartland of the southeastern cities and industrial regions. A subsidy was to be paid from a special fund, financed by a 3 per cent surcharge on all tickets sold on mainline and secondary routes served by the larger—and, almost by definition, more economic—aircraft. The subsidy would be allocated on a load-factor based formula. Up to 33 per cent of the shareholding of each new airline set up under the regulations could be owned by one of the existing trunk lines.

The country was divided into five regions for the purpose of allocating routes: Amazon Basin, Tocantins-Araguaia Basin, São Francisco Basin, West Central Region, and the South or South-Central Region. Six weeks later the first new airline was in operation (as it was already in business) and within less than a year, all five were energetically regaining lost ground by opening up new routes. The five airlines are summarized in Table 27. Cynics might point to the fact that the Brazilian Government had provided a generous subsidy and an artificial incentive; but the alternative was inescapable: without the new airlines, and without some system of payment over and above the revenue which could be earned, even from inflated fares, much of Brazil would have been back to the mule-train and river canoe for its transport.

The record speaks for itself: within eighteen months of Decree No.76,590, the five airlines were serving 121 cities with 73 new routes spread throughout 26 States and Territories (see Map 65). They were operating some 60 aircraft (including 35 Brazilian-built EMB-110 Bandeirantes) on a total of almost 400 frequencies over more than 40,000 kilometres of a great new network, covering an area bigger than Western Europe, and as big as the contiguous United States. By any standards of airline development anywhere in the world, it was an impressive achievement. These airlines now operate 40/60-seat aircraft, including, F.27s, FH-227Bs, and C-46s. VOTEC deserves special mention for having rejuvenated the DC-3.

A Rational Airline System

To describe the establishment of an integrated Third Level airline system as the ultimate solution to Brazil's airline route problems may be somewhat premature, but there are grounds to assert that it symbolized the completion of a continuous programme of development which had taken half a century to achieve. Brazilian airlines now offered comprehensive service throughout all the complex strata of air routes: intercontinental, regional international, domestic trunk, secondary, and regional, with special categories such as the Ponte Aérea and air taxi. That the organizational problems needed to integrate all these diverse activities should have been rounded off during just the few years between 1973 and 1976 was a fitting coincidence. The establishment of the Third Level category on 12 November, 1975—some 50 years after the first Civil Air Navigation Regulations were enacted on 12 January, 1925—was the final step in a long, laborious, and often painful administrative process. The entry into service of the 270-seat Douglas DC-10 on VARIG's route to Europe on 24 June, 1974, was just about 50 years after the nine-seat *Atlântico*, VARIG's first aircraft, was being built at Pisa, in Italy, destined to fly southwards to inaugurate Brazil's first air service. The VARIG-Cruzeiro do Sul merger on 22 May, 1975, took place in time to consummate perhaps the last amalgamation between the airlines which had pioneered Brazilian air transport, before the industry moved into its second half-century.

All influences affecting Brazilian airlines during the mid-1970s, however, were not wholly positive. It was a sign of the increasing importance of air transport to the Brazilian economy that VARIG was tempting many Brazilians to fly to the United States. The adverse effect on foreign exchange resulting from such travel created a minor problem in Brazil's balance of trade, sufficient in fact to cause the Government to take action.

The provisions of Decree No.1,470–76, imposing an international travel tax, have been reviewed in a previous chapter. The effect of the imposition—12,000 cruzeiros deposit from 4 June, 1976, rising to 16,000 on 17 February, 1977—took several directions. Traffic on VARIG's northbound flights was directly affected; but the southbound destinations such as Buenos Aires and Montevideo were exempt, and consequently experienced a traffic boom. But even the northern routes were not depleted catastrophically, because a large proportion of VARIG's traffic was of foreign origin, and therfore unaffected by a Brazilian tax.

The reciprocal effect on domestic traffic has already been noted. VARIG and its new partner Cruzeiro do Sul saw a welcome increase in domestic travel over their routes in compensation for the loss internationally. But the bonus for VASP and Transbrasil was even greater, and a surge in their domestic statistics during the period could be traced indirectly to the effects of the exit tax. Fortuitously, it assisted the progress towards the revised domestic shares desired by the Brazilian Government.

Such economic causes and effects are inevitable in the complex balance between the need to regulate a healthy, competitive industry within the framework of an organized system of control, which has to relate to the nation's economy as a whole. The newly-established Regional airlines may be the next group to experience problems of some as yet unpredictable kind. The full effect of the introduction, late in 1975, of the laws governing Vão de Turismo Domestico (V.T.D.) services, imposing upon the airlines the obligation to offer a 40 per cent discount for travel groups of 25 or more has yet to be measured. The development of domestic tourism, encouraged by the continued imposition of the exit tax, would be considerably strengthened by the parallel development of hotels in all the main cities, and at resort areas such as the Iguassú Falls and Manaus. VARIG has already formed its own hotel company and may be on the threshold of a self-stimulating boom in package travel within Brazil, and slip into gear with a new industry, the inclusive air tour, already firmly established in Europe, the United States, and Japan.

Whichever direction is taken by Brazilian airline expansion, however, the foundation for further growth is secure. Regardless of temporary deterrents such as the exit tax, the prominent position which Brazil now holds in the world of commerce is a guarantee of continuous business traffic; while the expanding proportion of Brazil's 123 million people who will be able to fly for pleasure will supplement the business traffic to an increasing degree. In air transport, Brazil's position as a leader is no longer a matter for future speculation, any more than is its place as a strong industrial power.

TABLE 27
Brazilian Regional Airlines
(In order of first scheduled service)

Airline	Trunk Airline Associate (Region served)	Date of First Service	First Routes	Main Aircraft Types	Remarks
TABA (Transportes Aéreos da Bacia Amazônica)	(None) (Amazon Basin)	1 Jan, 1976	Belém–Itaituba Belém–Manaus	Bandeirante Fairchild FH-227B	Consolidated operations of TABA and NOTA (Norte Taxi Aérea Ltda.). Started operations in July 1975 with Beech 18. Chief shareholder: Col Gibson Jacques
Nordeste (Nordeste Linhas Aéreas Regionais, S.A.)	Transbrasil (33⅓%) (São Francisco Basin)	8 June, 1976	Salvador–Lapa– Barreiras; Salvador– Petrolina–Paulo Afonso–Recife	Bandeirante Fokker F.27	Took over routes already operated by Transbrasil. State of Bahia holds 33⅓% of shares
TAM Transportes Aéreos Regionais, S.A.	VASP (38⅔%) (West Central)	12 July, 1976	São Paulo—various points in São Paulo State	Bandeirante Cessna 402 Piper Navajo Fokker F.27	Táxi Aéreo Marília (TAM), which started in May 1961 as Transportes Aéreos Marília, and Copersucar are major shareholders
Rio-Sul (Empresa Rio-Sul Serviços Aéreos Regionais, S.A.)	VARIG (52%)* (South) *Possibly increased to full ownership	9 Aug, 1976	Rio de Janeiro–São José dos Campos. Porto Alegre—various points in State of Rio Grande do Sul	Bandeirante Piper Navajo Rockwell Sabreliner Fokker F.27	Nucleus of airline was TOP Táxi Aéreo. Two insurance companies, Atlântica Boa Vista; and Sul América Terrestres, Marítimos e Acidentes, hold substantial interests
VOTEC (Votec Serviços Aéreos Regionais, S.A.)	— (Tocantins– Araguaia Basins)	11 Oct, 1976	Goiânia–São Simão– Uberlândia	Bandeirante Britten-Norman Islander Douglas DC-3 Fokker F.27	Cláudio Hoelck, of Motortec (formerly of Nacional) is major shareholder. VOTEC originally formed on 23 September, 1966, as Voos Técnicos e Executivos S.A. (VOTEC). Autonomous division: VOTEC Amazônia Taxi Aéreo, S.A.

CHAPTER TWENTY-FIVE

Paraguay and Uruguay

The First Air Services to Asunción

For most of the 170 years since its liberation from the Spanish Empire in 1811, the history of the landlocked country of Paraguay has been sad. After a period of mild despotism, a war with its neighbouring countries from 1864 to 1870, involving incredible hardship, ended with its population reduced from 1,340,000 to a mere 220,000, of whom only 29,000 were adult males. Periodic outbreaks of revolution, war debts to Brazil, and another war with Bolivia during the 1920s, all combined to hinder Paraguay's commercial and social progress. Development of communications and transport has therefore been slow, and by modern standards, inadequate.

Paraguay's general level of national income did not permit the comparative luxury of entering the airline business during that industry's formative period in South America during the latter 1920s. It was left to foreign airlines to introduce a new, faster way of reaching Asunción from the major entrepôt of trading, Buenos Aires, in competition with the train service and the ocean-going ships which were able to reach the Paraguayan capital along the Paraná and Paraguay Rivers. The train journey was hitherto the fastest, theoretically 56 hr, including a ferry across the Paraná at Encarnación. A one-day visit either way involved an arduous week's travel.

After the Paraguayan Government had granted a mail contract on 14 September, 1928, the pioneer French company, **Aéropostale**, started mail service, twice weekly, with Latécoère 25s, on 1 January, 1929, operating under the control of Aéropostale's subsidiary, Aeroposta Argentina. Unfortunately, this was the time of deteriorating world economy, with the Wall Street Crash coming later in the year. The service to Asunción was terminated on 17 April, 1931, Aéropostale having been put into *liquidation judiciaire*. The Argentine authorities rightly concentrated on salvaging the domestic portion of the line and continued to provide service to Patagonia. Asunción was to be without air service for six years.

Pan American Airways was authorized to serve Asunción by the Decree of 21 June, 1937, and started a service to Paraguay in December 1937, flying Lockheed Electras from São Paulo, via Curitiba and Iguassú Falls, and on to Buenos Aires via Monte Caseros. Douglas DC-3s replaced the Electras the following year. The Argentine-Italian line Corporación began operations on 26 March, 1941 (Decree of 22 March). Under different ownerships and airline titles—ALFA (Decree of 9 October, 1946) and later Aerolíneas Argentinas (described in the Argentine chapter of this book), there has been continuous service by an Argentine airline to Asunción ever since. Panair do Brasil began Lodestar service to Asunción in 1941, and PLUNA was authorized by Decree of 9 October, 1942.

The First Paraguayan Air Routes and Airlines

Eventually, the Paraguayan Government felt that there should be a national air service designed to provide much-needed communication with the remoter parts of the country. Commercial activity, and most of Paraguay's population were concentrated in the southern quarter south of Asunción, much of it along the only railway line, to Encarnación on the Paraná River, via Villarrica, Paraguay's second city. To the north, only the Paraguay River provided any reasonable form of public transport. To fill the breach, and after some preliminary experimental services beginning in 1941, **Línea Aérea de Transporte Nacional (LATN)** was created by Government Decree on 12 July, 1944. In addition to providing service to outlying army posts, inherited from the Chaco War with Bolivia, and which retained the prefixes *fuerte* and *fortin* (Spanish for fort and blockhouse), LATN established public services on two other routes (see Map 66) on 9 October of the same year, following the first board meeting on 2 October, 1944.

On 6 February, 1945, LATN's authority was strengthened, and its military identification diluted, again by Government decree, which also laid down operating regulations for its modest collection of aircraft, three small Fleets and two Caproni AP.1s. Later, a Breda 44 and two Travel Airs were acquired, and LATN flew 1,689 hr in 1946, carrying 700 passengers.

Shortly afterwards, the TACA organization tried to expand its South American air empire by establishing Aerovías Paraguayas; but this was never more than an idea, and the company never became a reality.

The next attempt to expand air service in Paraguay came once again from an outside source. Paraguay still did not have the resources to invest in new equipment but its Government recognized the need to upgrade the air service standards between Asunción and the most important provincial points. Accordingly, under the Decree of 26 June, 1951, it granted to the ambitious Brazilian airline, **REAL**—always seeking ways to expand—the traffic rights to operate within Paraguay as an extension of a route from São Paulo to Iguassú Falls, with a stop at Encarnación authorized on 4 February, 1954.

REAL's cabotage authority was dated 15 November, 1954, and was from Corumbá, in Brazil's Mato Grosso Province, to Asunción, via Concepción, with additional stops at Iguassú Falls and Encarnación. Although the Paraguayan Government withdrew Asunción–Encarnación rights on 1 September, 1955, REAL was well established as Paraguay's main air outlet to the north and east by 1956. It maintained DC-3 service from Corumbá and from Iguassú Falls, as well as a nonstop Convair CV-340 flight direct from Curitiba. Additionally, in December 1951, REAL's subsidiary, Nacional, had also reached Asunción from Rio de Janeiro and São Paulo by a DC-3 stopping service, crossing the Paraguayan frontier at Ponta Porã.

REAL's ambitions to take the air services of Paraguay under its wings were cut short, however, by its own downfall. When VARIG bought REAL on 16 August, 1961, it was content to retain only the direct service from São Paulo to Asunción, via Iguassú Falls, which was in Brazilian territory and beginning to develop as a tourist destination.

The later 1950s represented a period of much uncertainty about the future of Paraguayan airline service. In May 1954, the **Transportes Aéreo Militar (TAM)** was set up as part of the logistics effort of the Paraguayan Air Force and funds were granted for the purchase of a fleet of transport aircraft under a Decree dated 27 September, 1954. TAM began operating Douglas C-47s in May 1955 in parallel

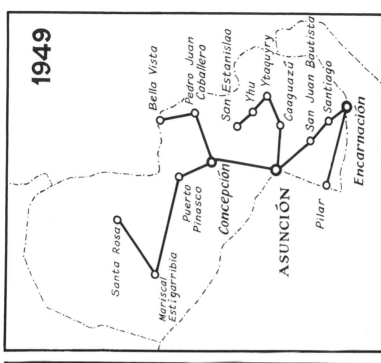

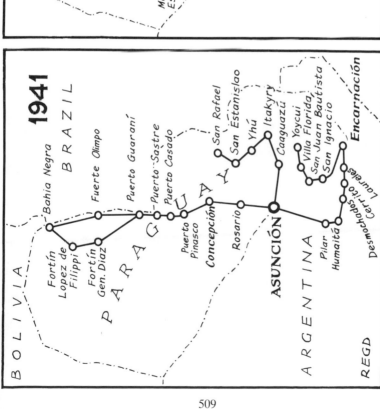

66. LATN (Paraguay), 1941–1949. For several decades, Paraguay did not have the resources to support its own airline. Air services were provided by a special squadron of the Paraguayan Air Force.

Paraguayan Transporte Aéreo Militar Douglas C-47 T-41 at Concepción on a regular 'civil' flight to Puerto Casado in the Paraguayan Chaco. (*John A. Kirchner*)

with LATN and in due course took over the regular service to twelve cities, and during 1956, carried 25,500 passengers and 330 tons of cargo. LATN's role was confined to serving the outlying military posts, together with air taxi and ambulance work using PBY-5As and Beech Bonanzas.

Then in October 1957 a private company **Servicios Aéreos del Paraguay**, with 52 per cent of the capital owned by Paraguayans, and equipped with a Douglas DC-4 and a Curtiss C-46, began services from Asunción to Rio de Janeiro, Montevideo, and Buenos Aires; but this enterprise disintegrated on 13 December the same year, losing its permit in 1958 because of financial problems and what was described as 'infringement of international regulations'—a phrase which could cover a world of sins and probably did.

Inspiration and backing for Servicios Aéreos was believed to have come from abroad, but its successor, **Lloyd Aéreo Paraguayo (LAPSA)**, formed on 14 September, 1960, was 88 per cent Paraguayan. In May 1961, LAPSA opened a service from Asunción to Rio de Janeiro, via Curitiba and São Paulo, a route that was fast rivalling the southern outlet to Buenos Aires as Paraguay's main trading corridor. LAPSA used 50-seat Curtiss Super C-46s on a twice-weekly frequency,

The standard military interior of TAM-Paraguay's Douglas C-47 T-41, seen on a flight from Concepción to Puerto Casado in November 1972. TAM advertisements in the Asunción press said 'Fly our comfortable Douglas DC-3s'. (*John A. Kirchner*)

510

and survived a little longer than most previous aspirants for the role of Paraguayan flag carrier. In January 1964, it purchased a Lockheed 049 Constellation for service to Buenos Aires and attempted to negotiate an agreement by which it would be guaranteed 35 per cent of the revenue. Although the Argentine authorities permitted a six-weekly frequency, they did not agree to either the 35 per cent or the Constellation, which was ferried from the USA to Rio, lost an engine at Campinas, and never flew again. LAPSA in fact did not survive much longer, being superseded by another Paraguayan airline which was at last to bring some stability to the national aviation scene.

Líneas Aéreas Paraguayas

Líneas Aéreas Paraguayas, S.A. (LAP) was formed in 1962 with a capital of 200 million guaranís (about £570,000). It was effectively an extension of theTransportes Aéreo Militar into the international arena. Two directors represent the Commander in Chief of the Armed Forces, two represent the Air Force, all under the direction of the Commander of Military Aeronautics. The airline was thus formed by military men, a common occurrence in many South American countries where the armed forces have a considerable influence on the course of national policies.

Líneas Aéreas Paraguayas' Lockheed Model 188A Electra ZP-CBZ was delivered in February 1969 having previously served Eastern Air Lines as N5539. The fuselage stripe was red, lettering black and the Paraguayan red, white and blue appeared on the rudder. (*Mário B. de M. Vinagre*)

LAP began operating full service to Buenos Aires, São Paulo, and Rio de Janeiro in August 1963, using two Convair CV-240s purchased from Aerolíneas Argentinas. Its network directly paralleled that of LAPSA, the frequency was twice a week, and more important, it quickly came to an agreement with Cruzeiro do Sul for representation, ticket agency, and other services at Brazilian points. Montevideo and Santa Cruz, Bolivia, were added to the network soon afterwards, so that Paraguay now enjoyed airline service under its own flag to every one of its neighbouring countries.

Steady progress was made. In February 1969, LAP acquired three Lockheed 188 Electras from Eastern Air Lines, and carefully prepared itself for further expansion. Largely directed by Operations Director Coronel Raul Calvet, LAP opened Electra service to Lima and Santiago in 1975 and began to explore more ambitious possibilities.

Calvet recognized that, like Bolivia, Paraguay's geographical position could be used by an enterprising airline to national advantage. If services to North America and Europe could be opened to Asunción, the Paraguayan capital could form the hub of a spoke network serving the whole of South America south of the Equator. No doubt the thought of differential fares was high on the list of factors considered, with cheap second-hand aircraft permitting a different economic equation from that resulting from the purchase of expensive wide-bodied types.

This project became a reality when, in October 1978, LAP purchased two Boeing 707-320s and promptly put them into service. The Lima route was extended to Miami on 17 November, 1978, and discussions were held with the United States to authorize the trading name of **Air Paraguay** for better national identification, especially bearing in mind that airlines in other countries had the same corporate acronym.

Líneas Aéreas Paraguayas' Boeing 707-321B ZP-CCF was originally Pan American's N415PA *Clipper Monsoon*.

Paraguay's airline industry could be said to have come of age on 2 November, 1979, when LAP opened a service to Madrid and Frankfurt, via Rio de Janeiro. This was 21 years after the low ebb of 1958 when Servicios Aéreos del Paraguay wound up its affairs after which for two years Paraguay had no airline of its own. LAP's achievement should also be seen in perspective: although Bolivia's LAB is one of the oldest airlines in the Americas, and has a flourishing service to Miami, it does not yet operate to Europe. Uruguay, for many decades a prosperous country when Paraguay was impoverished, still does not have a national route beyond neighbouring countries, although, to be fair, Montevideo is far more vulnerable to excessive competition from all the powerful trunk airlines operating the South Atlantic trunk air route.

Much of LAP's new prosperity and success stems from its country's growing affluence resulting from the construction of the world's largest hydro-electric project, in which the waters of the great Paraná River are being harnessed for the joint benefit of the three riparian countries, Brazil, Argentina, and Paraguay. President Alfredo Stroessner, the ex-army general who seized absolute political power in a 1954 coup, could regard the dam construction projects at Itaipu as his greatest achievement. Paraguay will receive half the power produced, although the other countries met the construction bill. Yet this power is surplus to its needs and can be sold back to the other countries. This energy boom is reflected in enormous foreign exchange earnings, out of all proportion to Paraguay's previously meagre income. As this boom continues, with 'white coal' replacing the more familiar oil as the source of prolonged prosperity, Paraguay may become

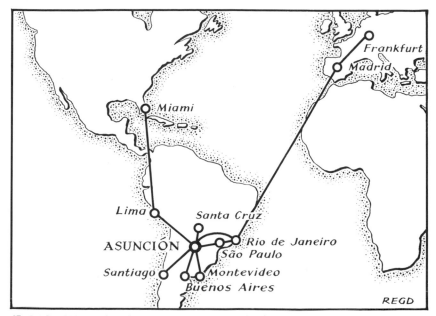

67. LAP, 1979. Against the expectations of many foreign observers, Paraguay became an international air nation in the 1960s, operating in competition with more powerful rivals in neighbouring countries. By the late 1970s, it had expanded its regional network to include routes to the USA and to Europe.

better known in the commercial and travel world. With LAP it now has an airline to provide the necessary air links in keeping with its new status.

First Air Services in Uruguay

Uruguay was a more prosperous country than Paraguay during the inter-war period of the 1920s and 1930s. Diminutive by South American standards, it is about the size of the State of Missouri or a little smaller than England and Scotland together. Its terrain lacks any conspicuous natural features, and its mainly agricultural people are engaged in livestock farming. About one quarter of the population is concentrated in the capital and port of Montevideo, from which all the road and rail systems radiate. Traditionally, most of the commerce used to be owned by or controlled by foreign interests, both North American and European, but Uruguay enjoyed a comparatively high standard of living and its literacy rate was—and is—the highest in South America.

Overshadowed across the Río de la Plata,* however, by the great city of Buenos Aires which was the magnet for the greatest volume of trade, communications, and travel in the whole continent, and situated, moreover, directly en route from the north to that metropolis, Montevideo has usually been known as the last port of call on the way to the Argentine capital, rather than as a destination it its own right.

Nevertheless Uruguay had the distinction of being the terminus of one of the

* Known in English as the River Plate.

first air routes in the Americas, when the **Compañía Río Platense de Aviación**, a joint enterprise of British and French aviation promoters in Buenos Aires, started a trans-Río de la Plata service to Villa Colón (now Colonia) on 17 December, 1921. This operation seems to have ended in 1924, but air services were resumed again when, after negotiating a postal contract with the Uruguayan Government on 16 June, 1927, the great French pioneering line **Aéropostale** began a mail service all the way from Natal, on the northeast tip of Brazil, to Buenos Aires, via Montevideo, using Latécoère 25 landplanes.

The French were joined by vigorous challengers from the United States soon afterwards. Capt Ralph O'Neill, displaying enormous drive and vision, persuaded financial interests in the USA to form the New York, Rio and Buenos Aires Line (NYRBA) which started a mail service from Buenos Aires to Montevideo on 21 August, 1929, as a preliminary to its great project of an air route joining the great cities of North and South America. Pan American-Grace Airways (PANAGRA) joined the fray on 30 May of the same year, albeit haltingly because of problems with equipment. The United States competition

While developing his plans for a service by NYRBA between New York and Buenos Aires, Ralph O'Neill was obliged to use the Sikorsky S-38B (*top*) while awaiting delivery of the larger Commodores. He used it on an historic survey flight over the whole route in the summer of 1929, and began scheduled service with it across the River Plate on 21 August. O'Neill's rival airline, PANAGRA, later used Loening Air Yacht amphibians (*bottom*).

was resolved by Pan American's acquisition of NYRBA on 15 September, 1930. PANAGRA opened passenger service on 5 October, 1931, by which time the Pan American empire encircled Latin America, and was to become synonymous with air transport throughout the continent for a quarter of a century.

Ironically, the true pioneers, the visionaries who first attempted to use a new transport mode, the commercial aeroplane, were all doomed to watch their initiative pass into other hands. Capt O'Neill suffered the acute disappointment of seeing his airline's name disappear along with others after the Wall Street Crash and with the connivance of the United States Post Office; while Marcel Bouilloux-Lafont, who had saved the Latécoère line by pouring his industrial fortune into the renamed Aéropostale, was the victim of political forces in France. These combined to withdraw the French subsidy (during a time when all long-distance air routes, without exception, depended on outside financial support, directly or indirectly) without warning or explanation, leaving Aéropostale to be put into *liquidation judiciaire*, later to be picked up for a song by Air France.

On 14 April, 1934, the Brazilian Syndicato Condor, in association with the German airline Deutsche Lufthansa, extended its Brazilian route network southward to Montevideo and Buenos Aires, using Junkers-W 34s. During the 1930s, Uruguay was thus generously served by no less than three major world airline systems, backed by French, German, and United States private and State finance, and was firmly on the world air map. Unfortunately, these foreign interests had no reason to develop air routes within Uruguay, and it was left to Uruguayans, with some overseas help, to provide that initiative.

PLUNA

Primeras Líneas Uruguayas de Navegación Aérea (PLUNA) was formed by a group of Uruguayan financiers led by the importers Alberto and Jorge Márquez Vacza, with some help from British associates, in September 1935. With a tiny fleet of two de Havilland D.H.90 Dragonflies—a scaled-down version of the Dragon Rapide, with only three passenger seats—PLUNA began service on 20 November, 1936. The two aircraft, *San Alberto* and *Churrinche*, operated on a route to the far north of Uruguay—a full 600 km—terminating at Artigas and Rivera on the Brazilian frontier. Competition was from the train service, which charged 27 pesos (the peso was roughly valued at one US dollar at that time) for a $22\frac{1}{2}$-hr journey, twice weekly. PLUNA charged 35 pesos for a four-hour journey, thrice weekly. There was no road service.

In November 1937, after one year of successful operation, the Uruguayan Government granted a subsidy of £6,000 to PLUNA, which promptly used this windfall to purchase a larger aircraft, a de Havilland D.H. 86B, fitted with twelve seats. Subsequently, after a few further uneventful years, a Government commission was engaged to study the country's total transport needs, and in January 1943, a law was passed to grant the Uruguayan Government a 49 per cent shareholding in a new mixed-stock corporation. The following month, unfortunately, a change of government upset all these plans. The law was rescinded, PLUNA's subsidy was withdrawn, and as a direct result, Uruguayan domestic air service was suspended on 15 March of the same year.

Airline service was not resumed until after the war, when the company was re-established on 15 September, 1945. The Government held 83·3 per cent of the stock, 1,000,000 Uruguayan pesos, or about $500,000, most of which went into

PLUNA's red and cream de Havilland 90 Dragonfly CX-AAS *San Alberto*. Standing in front of the aircraft is Alberto Márquez Vaeza, one of the founders of PLUNA and the General Manager.

the purchase of a small fleet of Douglas DC-2s and a C-47 to supplement the de Havilland machines. On 9 December, 1947, capital was increased to 3,000,000 pesos, with the Government share now 94·4 per cent, and a Douglas DC-3 opened an international route to Porto Alegre, Brazil, on 4 May, 1948. In 1951, the Government acquired the remaining shares of PLUNA, arranged for the purchase of four de Havilland D.H.114 seventeen-seat Herons, and opened a new route to Asunción, Paraguay, via Salto. More important, in 1956, PLUNA entered the competitive Buenos Aires air ferry market, with three daily services, also providing weekend connections to the growing resort city of Punta del Este, a mere half an hour's flight from Montevideo.

River Plate Competition

Until this time, either through commercial caution or by Government directive, PLUNA had not attempted to compete with the incumbent airlines on the air route across the Río de la Plata, this great inlet of the South Atlantic which forms

The prototype Potez 62-1 appeared in 1935 and ten were built for Air France. The prototype, F-ANQN, and F-ANQQ began working the Buenos Aires–Santiago route on 7 May, 1936, and in 1942 F-ANQN was acquired by PLUNA as CX-ADH. It retained its blue and silver Air France livery. (*Courtesy Barrie James*)

the estuary for the Paraná and Uruguay Rivers. Because of the problems of the marshy terrain along the lower courses of the rivers, bridge-building was economically impossible as well as technically challenging; so that the estuary positively beckoned aviation entrepreneurs seeking to demonstrate the efficiency of the aeroplane as a viable means of transport, given favourable circumstances. On each side of the river the business and commercial sections of both the cities of Buenos Aires and Montevideo are closely adjacent to the waterfront, so that the operation of flying-boats or floatplanes was a natural solution.

Thus, echoing the processes of a previous era (see the earlier reference to Río Platense) the **Compañía Aeronáutica Uruguaya, S.A. (CAUSA)** was founded on 29 December, 1936, by Luis J. Supervielle, head of the Uruguayan industrial enterprise of that name. Capital was 1,000,000 Uruguayan pesos (about US $530,000 at that time). Service started between the two port areas on either side of the 154-mile stretch of water between the two capitals on 12 March, 1938, with a fleet of two Junkers-Ju 52/3m seventeen-passenger floatplanes. In January 1940 an extension was made to Punta del Este.

CAUSA's Short Sunderland V CX-AKR *Capitan Bosio Lanza* on the slipway at Belfast after being converted from the military DP195. (*Short Brothers & Harland Ltd*)

In 1943, CAUSA opened a new route from Colonia, a point across the river immediately opposite Buenos Aires, only 45 miles away, and whence a connection could be made by bus to Montevideo. This was a novel development, made possible by better surface travel, both in the standard of the roads in Uruguay, and by the improvement in the comfort of the buses. The combination of the Buenos Aires–Colonia air route and the Colonia–Montevideo bus line permitted cheaper fares, compared with the direct air link.

After the war, conditions changed, with more competitive direct service between the two cities, and CAUSA improved its standards by introducing two converted Short Sunderland flying-boats, with seating for 40 people, and for several years shared the traffic with the Argentine operator ALFA, subsequently Aerolíneas Argentinas. This service took the form of a shuttle operation, and although not formally promoted as such, the twice-daily service could be patronized on a no-reservation basis, subject to the seats being available. It was so successful that CAUSA purchased more flying-boats of the same family, the so-called Bermuda type of BOAC, or Sandringhams,

This was in the mid 1950s, by which time the competition was beginning to strengthen in line with the booming commercial activity, together with increased

517

PLUNA's Vickers-Armstrongs V.769 Viscount CX-AQN was delivered in May 1958 and still in service in 1982. Fuselage band and company name were traffic blue.

tourist traffic as short weekend vacations in Uruguay became a habit among the more prosperous of the population of Buenos Aires, then about 8,000,000. CAUSA's first rival came from the home country, when PLUNA entered the market with three DC-3 round trips a day in 1956; and by 1961 had stepped up the pressure by introducing Vickers-Armstrongs Viscounts four times a day to the Aeroparque airport, almost as close to the centre of Buenos Aires as the port facilities served by the flying-boats.

One Uruguayan competitior should have been enough; but another airline joined in the fray. **Aerolíneas Colonia, S.A. (ARCO)** was founded on 9 January, 1957, the principal shareholder being ONDA, a Uruguayan bus company. Some years were to pass before air service began, but in July 1964 the organization got under way. It was not exactly a luxury affair, as the flying equipment consisted of two ex-CAUSA Curtiss C-46s—notorious for austere passenger amenities. These to some extent were compensated for by the surface element of the journey, which was provided by ONDA Super G.M. Jet Coaches.

In July 1966, ARCO ran into difficulties, when a heavy storm severely damaged its C-46 fleet at Colonia, and all operations had to be suspended for several months before resuming service four times a day, with a fleet augmented by twin-engined Convair-Liners, a marked improvement on the C-46s. By this time, CAUSA had fallen out of the competition, going into receivership in 1967.

Aerolíneas Colonia 'ARCO' Convair CV-600 Rolls-Royce Dart propeller-turbine conversion of a CV-240. Markings were goldish-brown. (*ARCO, via Barrie James*)

518

One interesting feature of the interplay between the various modes of transport was the introduction in 1964 of a fast hydrofoil service between Buenos Aires dock Darsena D and Puerto Colonia by an Argentine company ALIMAR S.A. This also was operated in association with ONDA, the Uruguayan bus operator, and offered competitive fares which matched up well with the opposition. Thus, although the hydrofoil took an hour for the Buenos Aires–Colonia trip, against the 15 minutes of CAUSA's flying-boats, the fare was only 1,000 m$s Argentine round trip. CAUSA and PLUNA charged 2,400 m$s round trip directly to Montevideo, but for that money ALIMAR-ONDA would offer three days in the Hotel California in Montevideo, including the cost of the journey via Colonia.

An Airline Industry in Transition

In retrospect, the lack of unity or co-operation among the Uruguayan airline interests, both private and government, led to a deterioration of the country's competitive stature, with inevitable consequences of financial losses. There was just not enough total traffic demand into and out of Uruguay to permit the luxury of three, even two airlines, and efforts to compete with the larger Argentine companies proved counter-productive. To try to obtain a good market share of the biggest route, measured in passenger numbers, was a natural aim, bearing in mind also that inbound traffic was often remunerative in other fields, such as

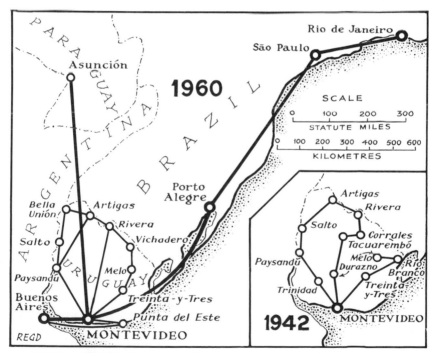

68. PLUNA, 1942–1960. Uruguay's airline activities have been quite modest. The country is small, overshadowed by two powerful neighbours, and almost every intercontinental flag carrier from Europe calls at Montevideo. However, PLUNA has managed to represent its flag over a regional network, with a commendable safety record.

accommodation and consumer spending. But a route as short as Montevideo–Buenos Aires was doomed to economic difficulty, if not disaster, for no other reason than that the basic cost structure works against profitability, with revenues always striving to offset the terminal expenditures, with marginal economical cruising distance in between.

By the mid-1960s, too, Uruguay was running into severe problems of currency convertibility. Government restrictions on hard currency exchange forced PLUNA to cannibalize its fleet to obtain spare parts, a process which, once started, quickly leads to an airline devouring itself. Quaintly, the sale of duty-free goods on board the trans-River Plate routes brought in disproportionate, though nevertheless welcome indirect revenue. Argentina's galloping inflation worked to Uruguay's advantage in this instance. But it was obscuring the essence of the money problem.

Transporte Aéreo Militar Uruguayo Fairchild Hiller FH-227D T-572/CX-BIM at Aeroparque, Buenos Aires, in July 1976. This aircraft was delivered to the Uruguayan Air Force in 1973, operated by PLUNA from August 1973 and returned to the Air Force.
(*Nelson de Barros Pereira Jr*)

The route to Rio de Janeiro and São Paulo had to be suspended, and PLUNA's international operations curtailed to Porto Alegre. However, a policy decision was made to compete vigorously on the routes to Buenos Aires, and a reorganization took place in 1974. PLUNA remained responsible only for Uruguayan international services, while the internal routes were handed over to the transport squadron of the Uruguayan Air Force, **Transporte Aéreo Militar Uruguayano (TAMU)** which operated in a manner similar to air force units in Paraguay, Peru, Colombia, and other South American countries. PLUNA first obtained three Viscount 827s from VASP, then proceeded to acquire one Boeing 737 in 1970 to introduce jet service. Two Boeing 727s were then purchased from Lufthansa in November 1978 to replace propeller-turbine aircraft with jets. Meanwhile TAMU provided economical internal services with 40-seat F.27s and FH-227s, 28-seat DC-3s, and 12-seat Embraer Bandeirantes, according to demand.

And so the pendulum has swung. During the early years of the development of air transport in South America, Uruguay was geographically in the mainstream of air commerce, even if it did not have its own airline. By the latter 1930s, Montevideo had two home-based airlines, while poor Paraguay—'poor' was indeed the operative word at the time—was struggling to recover from a war with

PLUNA's Boeing 727-30QC CX-BKA, seen at Congonhas Airport, São Paulo, was originally Lufthansa's D-ABBI *Mainz*, and the livery is basically that of Lufthansa. (*Nelson de Barros Pereira Jr*)

Bolivia, had no national airline or even thoughts of one, and was grateful to foreign companies for providing a branch line to Asunción. Today, the fortunes have reversed. Paraguay, with its new wealth from the Paraná hydro-electric project, can boast routes to both the United States and Europe, while Uruguay can provide only connecting flights, one of them, interestingly enough, to Asunción.

The Uruguayan flag was carred to other continents for a few years by a cargo airline operating in conjunction with Cargolux, the Luxembourg operator. **Aero Uruguay** was formed by that company and Uruguayan businessmen in 1977 and made its first flight from Montevideo to Puerto Rico on 12 November, using a leased Canadair CL-44. Its own cargo aircraft, a Boeing 707-331C, provided

PLUNA's Boeing Advanced 737 CX-BOO, photographed at Congonhas in 1982 with yet another new livery, mostly dark blue with red lower band. (*Nelson de Barros Pereira Jr*)

521

Aero Uruguay's Boeing 707-331C non-convertible freighter CX-BJV was originally TWA's N5771T. (*T. R. Waddington collection*)

service on charter flights to North America and Europe from 9 October, 1978, until June 1982. This was replaced by a leased DC-8-63CF until the airline was closed down in June 1982.

Atlántida Línea Aérea Sudamericana (ALAS) started operations in November 1978 to provide similar all-cargo and charter service, using an ex-Argentine CL-44. But this service lasted only until October 1979.

CHAPTER TWENTY-SIX

Airlines of Chile

Early Development

One glance at the map of Chile, stretched along more than half of the west coast of South America for more than 2,600 miles (4,400 km), evokes immediate visions of air service potential, simply because of the vast distance involved in travelling over the end-to-end, or even part of the north–south itinerary. East–west transport considerations are a matter of irrelevance, as the country is only 200 miles across at its widest point. Mostly it is about 100 miles, and as half of this is taken up by the Cordillera of the Andes, Chile is more or less confined to a narrow coastal strip varying between 50 and 80 miles in width.

About 70 per cent of Chile's population live in the central third of the elongated national territory. The northern third, however, contains the area of the Atacama Desert which,though uninvitingly arid, contains Chile's vast mineral wealth of nitrates and copper. The ports of Antofagasta, Iquique, Tocopilla, and others, flourish from the export of these products; but the links with the central part of

On 5 March, 1929, Commandante Arturo Merino Benitez formed Línea Aeropostal Santiago-Arica to fly passengers and mail between those two cities. At first operated as a division of the Air Force, and in co-operation with the French Aéropostale, this airline was to become the LAN-Chile of today. The Commandante also founded the Chilean Air Force, and Santiago's airport is now named after him. (*Esso Air World*)

Chile have been tenuous—the rail journey of 800 miles or so a formidable undertaking, to the extent that many travellers went by coastal ship. The southern third of Chile—its share of Patagonia—was remote and wild territory, without surface communications, and hardly a habitation of any kind except at the extreme south, where Punta Arenas maintained its claim as the southernmost city in the world.

Possibly because of its local importance—the nearest city of comparable size was 1,000 miles to the north—one of the earliest commercial aviation ventures in Latin America was projected here. In 1921, Aeronavegación Chilena-Argentina, S.A., was created in Punta Arenas to start an air service to Río Gallegos, then the southernmost town in Argentina. Some experimental flights were made, but the promoters lacked sufficient equipment to proceed.

Civil aviation came to Chile in 1929, when the new airfield of Santiago witnessed a succession of important dates in the annals of South American airline route expansion. On 5 March, the **Línea Aeropostal Santiago-Arica** was formed by Comandante Arturo Merino Bonitez to fly passengers and mail from the capital to the Peruvian frontier. Comandante Merino had founded the Fuerza Aérea Nacional (National Air Force) and was to become the first General del Aire. The line was at first operated as a division of the Air Force, and equipped with twelve de Havilland Moths, part of a total of 64 ordered by Chile. This little light aircraft had been setting some impressive height records during 1927 and 1928, and, with a wary eye on the craggy peaks of the Andes overlooking Santiago, the authorities no doubt set a premium on high flying.

The two-seat Moths soon inaugurated Chile's first air service, on the Santiago–Arica route, via Ovalle, La Serena, Vallenar, Copiapó, Antofagasta, Tocopilla, and Iquique. 762 passengers were carried during the first year of operations, and seven four-seat Fairchild FC-2s were then added to supplement the Moths.

A preserved de Havilland 60 Gipsy Moth, with non-standard exhaust pipe and bearing the title Línea Aérea Nacional on the fuselage, stands beside a LAN-Chile Boeing 707. A Cirrus-engined Moth was LAN's first aeroplane. (*Esso Air World*)

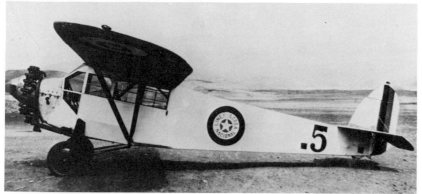

An unidentified Fairchild FC-2W2 with the early markings of Línea Aérea Nacional. It bears an early form of Chilean Air Force red, white and blue markings. (*Esso Air World*)

The Chilean Línea Aeropostal appears to have been organized to provide a vital link with the South American route of the French Aéropostale. On 15 July, 1929, the first regular flight by a Latécoère 25 of Aeroposta, the Argentine subsidiary, arrived in the Chilean capital from the eastward direction. This was to herald many famous exploits and adventures in the inhospitable Andean mountains, bringing fame to the intrepid pilots. But unfortunately the parent company suffered from an abrupt termination of support from the French Government and Aeroposta's service ended in 1931, to the great satisfaction of the German rivals.

However, a brave attempt had been made by the French enterprise to extend air service in western South America. A reconnaissance flight was made from Santiago to La Paz early in 1930 and on 2 October connection was established from the Chilean mail line's northern terminus, Arica, to the commercial capital of Bolivia, La Paz, via Tacna, Peru. This achievement was notable in that, over a distance of about 200 miles, the open-cockpit Potez 25s flew from sea level to an altitude of 13,000 feet (4,000 metres). The Aéropostale Arica–La Paz service ended in May 1931.

At this time, Santiago had suddenly become connected with the world's trunk air routes. PANAGRA, the company which had just been founded jointly by Pan American Airways and the W.R.Grace shipping company, began mail service, with a Fairchild FC-2, from Panamá down the west coast during 1929, reaching Santiago on 21 July. The persuasive Pan American president, Juan Trippe, had previously organized Chilean Airways on 21 December, 1928; but this was only a paper company, set up for tactical reasons to put the pressure on Grace, and it never owned or operated aircraft. PANAGRA soon substituted Ford Tri-Motors on the route, and operated the first through service to Buenos Aires on 8 October, 1929.

During 1930, following the precedent of PANAGRA, three Ford Tri-Motors were acquired by the Chilean Air Force for the use of the Línea Aeropostal, and the following year, trans-Andean flights were made to the Argentine cities of Mendoza and San Juan. The value of air transport to the economy and social services of Chile was now recognized to such an extent that, in 1932, the postal line became an independent Government agency, independent of the Air Force. Under the terms of Decree No.247, Línea Aeropostal Santiago-Arica became

One of the four Ford 5-ATs which were used by the Chilean Air Force. These Fords were numbered F-1 to F-4 but the identity of the example illustrated has not been established. There is evidence that at some time all four aircraft had ring-cowlings on their outboard engines. (*Esso Air World*)

Línea Aérea Nacional (LAN) and was granted a monopoly of all air routes in Chile, except that PANAGRA continued to enjoy virtually unlimited rights which were the heritage of the W.R.Grace company, one of the first examples of a commercial enterprise which held as much power as governments themselves.

After some political difficulties during the early 1930s, LAN opened a new route southwards to Puerto Montt in 1935. Such was the geography of Chile that this new endeavour almost doubled the unduplicated mileage. At about this time, the fleet of two Fords and two surviving Gipsy Moths was supplemented by some important additions, six Potez 56s and three Curtiss Condors, the latter large biplanes boasting comfortable passenger cabins. LAN further augmented these with three single-engined, four-seat Fairchilds, built in LAN's own workshops.

Thus equipped, sorties were made to the south, progress in which direction, however, was hampered by the absence of airfields, or even reasonable strips of land on which to build any. Thus, when an experimental service was opened to Puerto Aisén, some 300 miles south of Puerto Montt, it was operated by Vickers Vedette amphibians. For a short while, in September 1937, the final link was made all the way to Punta Arenas, but soon had to be abandoned through lack of facilities able to sustain either land or water operations. To establish air service in these latitudes was indeed an arduous task. The barren and rock-strewn terrain, indented with island-studded fjords, was difficult in the extreme to develop; but the climate also was inclement, marked by frequent storms and consistently-heavy rainfall. Thus, with no reason to establish settlements in an infertile and almost unpopulated region, the Chilean airline awaited a substantial improvement in commercial aircraft technology before pursuing its goal of providing a regular air link with Punta Arenas, which continued to be a remote outpost.

The first notable advance was the acquisition, in 1938, of three Junkers-Ju 86 twin-engined monoplanes. Fitted with Junkers Jumo diesel oil engines, this was a fast aircraft, cruising at 177 mph, but lacking the range to fly to the extreme south. The year 1938 probably marked the zenith of German aircraft industry marketing success in South America, and the outbreak of war, with the attendant problems of shipping blockades, abruptly terminated not only sales of Junkers and other German aircraft overseas but also cut off the supply of spare parts and engines.

Thus, on 11 March, 1941, the first of six Lockheed Model 10 Electras arrived from the USA, and on 1 September, 1943, the first of four 14-seat Lodestars augmented the Lockheed fleet.

During this period of aircraft modernization, domestic fares were lowered, producing a consequent increase in traffic. Although the route network had been reduced to the original Santiago–Arica line, and extensions to the south remained in abeyance, passenger journeys increased from 2,600 in 1940 to 27,000 in 1945. Thus encouraged, LAN began to prepare the way for considerable route expansion. At first a modest addition to its route mileage was made on 30 June, 1945, by opening an Electra service across the Straits of Magellan, from Punta Arenas to Porvenir, thus providing an air link to the Chilean half of the island of Tierra del Fuego. Then, in 1946, longer strides were made. The first route to a foreign capital was opened in March, when a LAN Lodestar began service to Buenos Aires, sharing frequencies on an agreed basis with the Argentine FAMA. Meanwhile, in common with scores of other airlines in the immediate postwar period, LAN took delivery of the first DC-3, war surplus but little used, and was at last able to open up the cherished route from Santiago to Punta Arenas.

Progress during the next ten years was steady, with LAN consolidating its newly expanded network. More aircraft were purchased to supplement the DC-3 fleet, now grown to ten. In 1947 four 40-seat twin-engined pressurized Martin 2-0-2s replaced the Lodestars on the trans-Andean route, which was extended to Montevideo, while, during the following two years, twelve eight-seat de Havilland Dove feeder airliners augmented the domestic fleet. A change in management in 1952 saw more routes to the south, and further development was planned. In 1953, LAN was granted permission to purchase three Douglas DC-6B four-engined pressurised airliners, so as to compete on equal terms with the Argentine and Brazilian companies, Aerolíneas Argentinas and Cruzeiro do Sul. The DC-6Bs began entering service early in 1955, and LAN—now becoming known as LAN-Chile, because of possible confusion with other South American companies with similar initials—embarked on a further programme of route expansion.

The de Havilland 104 Dove CC-CLW was one of six delivered in 1949. It was reregistered CC-CAA and sold in 1954. The fuselage band and nacelle markings were red with a thin dark blue outline. Lettering was also dark blue. The upper segment of the national marking on the tail was blue and the lower segment red. (*British Aerospace*)

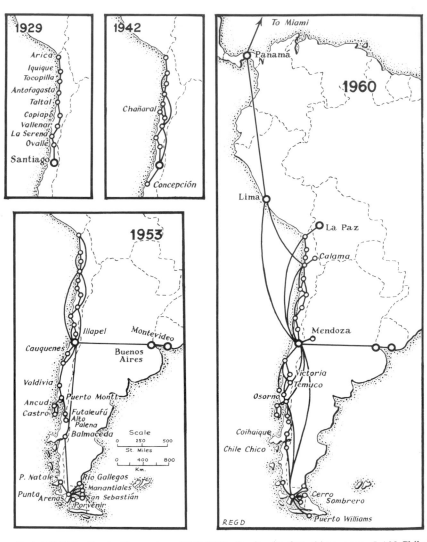

69. LAN-Chile Route Expansion, 1929–1960. During its first thirty years, LAN-Chile expanded its route system steadily, taking care not to extend its ambitions beyond the limitations of its resources.

LAN-Chile's Martin 2-0-2 CC-CLT over the Andes on the Santiago–Buenos Aires route. This aircraft was reregistered CC-CLMC.

The Strong Breath of Competition

In 1953, the Chilean Government permitted the entry of private airlines into Chilean air transport. Thus, into LAN's hitherto privileged pool, two awkwardly-shaped objects were dropped in the form of two Chilean airlines, formed with the backing of private interests, and whose declared objective was to break a restrictive price cartel imposed by the members of IATA, of which—in addition to LAN—the powerful PANAGRA, linked with even more formidable parents, Pan American and the W.R.Grace Corporation, was the prime practitioner. These newcomer airlines sensed that, while business traffic provided a steady and lucrative income for the incumbent airlines, there was a big reservoir of untapped traffic which could be generated by offering attractive fares to many South Americans who wished to go to the United States.

Best known among these maverick airlines was **Compañía Nacional de Turismo Aéreo (CINTA)**, founded in November 1953 as a subsidiary of a Chilean steamship company, Compañía Sud Americana de Vapores. Jorge Carnicero, an airline entrepreneur connected with many enterprises in South America, held some interest, and was responsible for much of the aggressive and effective promotion. At first operating domestically with Lockheed 10-A Electras, Lodestars and DC-3s, CINTA extended service to Miami, via Antofagasta, Arica, Talara, and Panama City late in 1957, using a fleet of two Douglas DC-4s.

These 55-seat unpressurized aircraft were painted in colours very similar to the traditional green paint scheme of PANAGRA's pressurized Douglas DC-6Bs. To

529

add insult to injury, the round windows of the DC-4s were actually camouflaged to look like the rectangular ones of the DC-6Bs. While such a practice raised questions of ethics, there was nothing illegal about it.

More controversial was the issue of fare levels—though again the question of legality was relative, and dependent upon different governments' interpretation of international obligations as they affected public transport. On its *Latin Americano* service—suspiciously similar in name, as well as camouflaged appearance, to PANAGRA's *Inter-Americano*—CINTA charged $394 round trip, compared with PANAGRA's $678 tourist, or $871 first class. This two-for-the-price-of-one offer was unprecedented in the 1950s (although ironically became accepted as common practice by the 1970s) and the effect on traffic was predictably positive. During the summer of 1957, CINTA was averaging about 500 northbound passengers a month, compared with PANAGRA's 250. Significantly—although in the heated debates at the time, the point was often missed—PANAGRA's passenger loads had been no higher during the previous year, before CINTA started its big drive, so that the new low fares demonstrably created a new market without invading the incumbent airline's preserves.

CINTA Chilean Airlines Douglas C-54B CC-CBO had been the USAF's 43-17179 and it passed to United Air Lines as NC30040 *Mainliner Yosemite* before going to Chile.
(*Harold G. Martin*)

CINTA was joined in 1954 by a second Chilean privately-owned airline, **ALA, Sociedad de Transportes Aéreos, Ltda**. This was a division of a prominent industrial firm of nitrate producers, Compañía Salitrera de Tarapaca y Antofagasta, and was formed by the merger of two non-scheduled airlines, Lyon Air and Air Chile, operating during the early 1950s with Curtiss C-46s and a Consolidated B-24 respectively. In May 1957, ALA started service to New York, using 54-seat Lockheed 049 Constellations leased from Cubana, with the occasional 1049G Super Constellation when the 049 was being overhauled. This pressurized equipment was the best used by the cut-price carriers—or even LAN—on the South American west coast, but the fares were comparable with CINTA's: New York–Santiago for $269 one-way, compared with IATA (tourist) $412, or (first-class) $542. Once again, two for the price of one.

But after the heady summer of 1957, with the accountants no doubt beginning to add up the costs of this flamboyant gamble, traffic was not sustained. Possibly in the first flush of success, CINTA and ALA had mopped up all the potential surplus market. At any rate, in December 1957 they took the step so common among airlines in trouble: they merged, handing over the domestic routes to a new company in the process of being formed, LADECO.

530

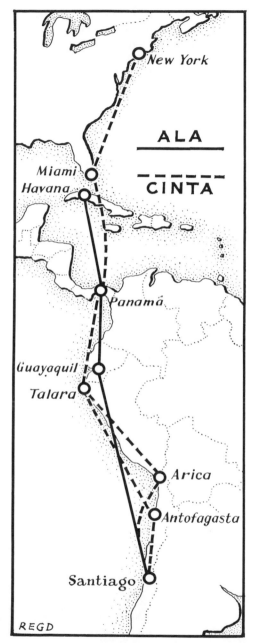

70. ALA/CINTA, 1957. The first challenge to PANAGRA, the established US flag airline backed by powerful organizations which controlled both air and surface travel down the west coast, came from Chile. Two independent airlines, with an aggressive policy of fare discounts, broke into the market.

The combined ALA/CINTA service continued for a while, using the Constellations as far as Havana, with connecting service to the United States. The DC-4s maintained a route from Santiago to Arica. But the revolution in Cuba, which brought Fidel Castro to power on 1 January, 1959, heralded the expulsion of foreign interests and the nationalization of private enterprises in Cuba. This spelt the death-knell for the Chilean renegades, dependent as they were on Cubana's aircraft. Service was suspended in the summer of 1959, and in February 1961, ALA/CINTA was declared bankrupt.

The Chilean enterprise, on the international scene, lasted only two years; but its impact was tremendous. Unlike some often unscrupulous airlines which managed to cut fares by operating obsolete equipment picked up for the proverbial song in the second-hand stores behind Miami Airport, ALA/CINTA provided good service. The Constellations were comparable with the best available at the time, while the on-board amenities were at least as good as the IATA standards, with free meals and drinks, and a generous baggage allowance. Even without the Cuban revolution, the airline may not have lasted long; but it brought a refreshing wave of commonsense thinking into the Latin American arena, and forced the Establishment out of its complacency, to recognize that there were other categories of air passengers besides well-heeled businessmen.

Although this was certainly the populist view, the IATA airlines defended their position by observing that they had pioneered the air routes, constructed the airfields, installed the navigation facilities (although, to tell the truth, these were few and far between on the South American west coast), created the marketing environment, and generally fashioned a certain level of airmindedness among the Latin American travelling public. Therefore, they argued, they were entitled to reap the harvest. As events turned out, the threat from the upstart airlines was more imagined than real. But the first erosion of time-honoured traditions had been made, and the most permanent of these, at least in Chile, was the recognition by the Government that private airlines could and should co-exist with the national airline, LAN-Chile.

Thus, when ALA/CINTA departed from the international scene, a new company arose to take over the remnants of the domestic network. **Línea Aérea del Cobre, Ltda (LADECO)** was formed in November 1958, in close association with the copper-mining interests of northern Chile. The northern terminus was Calama, a small city on the railway line from Antofagasta to Bolivia, but notable from an airline's point of view for possessing the nearest airfield to the richest open-cast coppermine in the world, Anaconda's enormous investment at nearby

The Douglas C-47 CC-CBK, seen in LADECO's blue and white livery and with modified door incorporating airstairs, was originally the USAF's 42-68737 and it served with United Air Lines before going to Chile.

TRANSA's Curtiss C-46A CC-CNC was acquired in November 1956 and crashed near Arica on 11 April, 1957.

Chuquicamata. Also, the stop at Potrerillos, south of Antofagasta, was the site of the Anaconda smelting plant serving another big mine at El Salvador; so altogether, by providing an essential travel service for the copper-mining personnel, LADECO had a ready passenger market and a virtual guarantee of traffic on its flights.

Nevertheless, it did not confine its activities to the copper-mining interests alone, and opened a new route to the south, to Puerto Montt, centre for some of Chile's beautiful lakes and vacation area. LADECO started with Douglas DC-3s, but began to expand steadily during the 1960s. It became an associate member of IATA on 1 October, 1964, and an active one on 1 December, 1967.

One other small airline in Chile during this period deserves mention. Early in 1960, **Sociedad de Transportes Aéreos de Chile S.A. (TRANSA)** started a regular air freight service from Santiago to Caracas, via Lima, Guayaquil, and Panamá, using Curtiss C-46s. It also flew domestic passenger and freight services along the whole length of Chile, from Arica to Punta Arenas. On the southern sector, flights were made to and via San Carlos de Bariloche, in the Argentine lake district—a rare exercise in international scheduling, in which a foreign point was used as an en route stop on a domestic service. Another interesting TRANSA venture was a PBY-5A Catalina service from Santiago to Juan Fernández Island, on which Alexander Selkirk survived alone for more than four years, to inspire the tale of Robinson Crusoe. Nevertheless, TRANSA's career was short, and the company went bankrupt after about a year's operations.

Another company participated in the Juan Fernández traffic. **Línea Aérea Taxpa, Ltda (TAXPA)**, founded in January 1967, expanded its air taxi services in the post-Allende period to operate a regular DC-6B schedule to the island, where it owned a small hotel. Scheduled routes were also added from Santiago to several nearby cities.

LAN-Chile Goes Intercontinental

While the entrepreneurs enjoyed their hours of glory in being the first Chilean airlines to operate to the United States, LAN was also granted Government approval in April 1958 as a second carrier. Equipped with new Douglas DC-6B long-range, pressurized aircraft, service had been opened to Lima during the summer of 1956, and this was now extended to Miami in August 1958. When the CINTA/ALA combination was forced into retirement because of events in Cuba

LAN's Douglas DC-6B CC-CLDE was delivered in August 1958, bore Fleet No.405 and was reregistered CC-CCH. (*McDonnell Douglas Corporation*)

at the end of that year, LAN was able to reap the benefit of the newly-created market to add to its own, and began to fulfil its role as the national flag carrier on the international scene.

LAN was able to provide a special contribution to Chilean national prestige and aspirations when, on 22 December, 1956, it made a special flight to Antarctica, in support of Chile's claims to territory on that continent. This was the forerunner of other flights many years later which had a more commercial objective, in the practical sense; but LAN's early exploratory flight was indicative of a bold approach to aviation problems and the willingness to try the unorthodox.

However, at this stage, LAN's tasks were somewhat less spectacular, as there had been much criticism of its failure to extend service to more points within Chile. LAN could argue that the feeder services always lost money, and only the trunk services to places like Antofagasta or Arica actually paid for themselves; so that to operate more of such services would incur further demands for subsidy, for which it was being criticised. While LAN lost one battle—private airlines were allowed to enter the domestic markets—it was able to publicise its case for obtaining better aircraft for its services both internationally and within Chile. As a consequence, the first Sud-Aviation Caravelle was delivered on 30 March, 1964, and went into service a few weeks later on the trunk route to Miami. At home, Hawker Siddeley HS.748 propeller-turbine aircraft replaced DC-6Bs, the first service being from Santiago to Puerto Montt, and on to San Carlos de Bariloche, on 6 January, 1967.

LAN's Sud-Aviation Caravelle VIR CC-CCP, Fleet No.502, was delivered in May 1964 and in 1975 was disposed of to Aerotal Colombia as HK-1779.

Considerable expansion took place during the late 1960s, changing the entire Chilean airline map, and giving LAN-Chile a new lease of life through the introduction of long-range jet equipment, as well as replacing the Caravelles. But the DC-6Bs still continued to give a good account of themselves. On 8 April, 1967, one of the four-engined Douglases began a service to Easter Island (Isla de Pascua) the 64 square mile speck in the eastern Pacific Ocean, belonging to Chile, and famous for its mysterious stone statues of a long-forgotten race of mankind. Considered at first to be a special case of providing a social service to a remote and isolated community, the operation, once proved to be a technical success, revealed greater possibilities. Not only was interest aroused in Easter Island itself, now that LAN-Chile had made it accessible; but the prospect of it being an important stepping stone for a route from southern South America across the Pacific became apparent.

LAN-Chile's Hawker Siddeley HS.748-234 CC-CEF, Fleet No.744, seen at Santiago, was one of nine delivered in 1967–69. (*Gordon S. Williams*)

LAN Chile showed its interest in the latter direction by extending the route to Tahiti on 2 January, 1968. Traffic grew enough to demand extra frequencies, and on 28 February, 1970, 144-seat Boeing 707s were introduced, after LAN had taken delivery of the second aircraft of this type.

The first Boeing 707 had given LAN-Chile new strength and stature by starting a service to New York on 15 April, 1967, (just a week after the inaugural Easter Island flight) and speeding up the end-to-end journey by including a Lima–New York nonstop segment from 25 March, 1968. On 2 November of that year, another schedule showed Buenos Aires–Santiago–Guayaquil–New York as an itinerary, a neat application of Sixth Freedom rights, which no doubt gave much satisfaction to the Chilean airline which had been on the worst end of such exchanges with Argentina for many years.

On the domestic front, the first Boeing 727 was delivered on 13 March, 1968, and went into service almost immediately. On 1 April it flew from Santiago to Punta Arenas nonstop and followed this with similar flights to Arica, so that the two Chilean cities at the extreme ends of the country were at last only a morning's or afternoon's flight from the capital. In the same year, on 8 July, a new service was opened to Balmaceda, on Lake Buenos Aires in southern Chile, close to the Argentine lake district, and where a new airport had been built by the Chilean Government in an effort to open up the scenic beauty of the southern Andes. Such was the attraction of this new destination that the HS.748s which opened the route gave way to DC-6Bs and then, on 27 September, 1969, to Caravelles.

In 1969, LAN-Chile turned its attentions to the achievement of another ambition: a route to Europe. The first exploratory sorties took the form of starting service to Asunción, via Antofagasta, on 2 May and to Rio de Janeiro ten days later as an extension from the Paraguayan capital. With the delivery of a second Boeing 707 at the end of the year, the jet route to New York had been supplemented by weekly jet flights to Easter Island, as already noted, quickly acquiring operational experience and expertise thereby, LAN-Chile opened a Boeing 707 service to Europe on 1 August, 1970. With the terminus at Frankfurt, Madrid and Paris were en-route European stops, and Buenos Aires and Rio de Janeiro service points in South America, Asunción becoming the terminus of a separate route. Chile thus joined the ranks of major South Atlantic trunk route airlines, moreover reminding the European travel world of the existence of a faraway country whose best-known direct transport route with Europe had been shipping cargoes of nitrate and copper ore from the northern Chilean ports, and made famous by some notable achievements by the great sailing ships.

LAN's Boeing 707-385C CC-CEB *Lago Ranco*, Fleet No.702, was delivered in December 1969. (*The Boeing Company*)

Political Interlude

Shortly after LAN-Chile had provided Europe with a direct route to the islands of the South Pacific via South America, thus consolidating an unusual intercontinental network, its fortunes were directly affected by revolutionary events—in the completely literal sense of the term—in Chile. On 4 November, 1970, after closely-fought elections in what was regarded as South America's most democratically governed country, Dr Salvador Allende, a declared Marxist politician, came to power. He immediately set about accelerating a number of reforms which the previous Fray administration had neglected, or, in the opinion of the left-wing factions, had suffered from unnecessary procrastination. Also, he embarked on a vigorous campaign to nationalize key industries; and although the United States-owned copper giants were the main target for Allende's revolutionary zeal, the airline industry also came under his scrutiny. The political effects on LAN-Chile were both direct and indirect. Directly, it was obliged to begin a service to Madrid, via Havana—Cuba now being a friendly nation; but this was shortlived after the inaugural flight on 17 July, 1971. Indirectly, as a result of the belligerent confrontation between the Chilean Government and the US copper interests, LAN actually had to stop service to New York on 18 February, 1972. Braden Copper, a subsidiary of Kennecott Copper, had won a court action to freeze Chilean assets in the United States, in default of a loan, and LAN's New York organization was included in the black list. But the crisis was overcome, and Braden allowed the airline to resume operations after a few days' suspension.

By Government decree, domestic fares were lowered during the Spring of 1972, as a measure to put air travel within a wider range of income levels. Even though inflation was already eroding almost everyone's real-value incomes in Chile, there was nevertheless a boom in traffic, so that high load factors were experienced throughout LAN's domestic system. Unfortunately, the fares were so low that it became impossible to cover costs, even at full loads; yet, paradoxically, LAN was under pressure to obtain larger aircraft to cope with the traffic.

The biggest problem facing LAN-Chile during this difficult period, however, was the edict, amounting almost to a Government decree, to obtain the Russian Ilyushin Il-62 long-range jet, either to replace or, at the very least, supplement the Boeing 707 fleet. This was clearly a politically-inspired order, but LAN-Chile resisted with a well-constructed and legitimate technical case against the aircraft. The Government wished to have a good direct link with Havana, which was the only nation in the Americas now holding out the hand of friendship to Chile. Why not, ran the argument, operate a direct Il-62 service from Santiago to Havana? LAN pointed out that the aircraft could not fly the route nonstop, and that a stop en route, though technically and operationally feasible, demanded special facilities—the Ilyushin needed a special grade of fuel, for example—and there might be practical, as well as political jeopardy by risking a stop (memory of the Braden Copper incident no doubt was still fresh).

A compromise in the debate was found by sending a delegation from the airline to Moscow in the summer of 1972 to make a thorough investigation into the true capabilities of the Il-62. Led by Jorge Hofer, LAN's Chief Engineer and almost indispensible member of the executive management, the delegation returned with a report which not only supported the airline's original contention that the payload restrictions on the Havana route would be crippling, but other matters came to light, such as the extremely low engine overhaul life, which, in the case of Chile, was especially threatening, because of the long distance from the source of supply. In the event, LAN-Chile did not order the Il-62. Whether or not further pressure may have been exerted when the aircraft was improved may never be known, as Dr Allende was assassinated on 11 September, 1973, ending a traumatic era in the country's history,—although the recriminations of the replacement Pinochet Government were another kind of nightmare.

Throughout the difficult period, LAN-Chile behaved with commendable wisdom, patience, and level-headedness. Weathering the storms of the political arena, it even managed to make some progress. During 1972, the frequency to Europe was doubled, and preliminary efforts were initiated to explore the possibility of an innovative trans-ocean service across the South Pacific. Talks were held with the Governments of New Zealand and Australia in 1971, but these were inconclusive, especially as the normal and most obvious route involved operating rights with France (Tahiti being still a French territory) and with Fiji, a sovereign state. Consequently, eyes turned to an unprecedented and original solution: a more southerly itinerary, calling at Punta Arenas, and then taking the southern Great Circle route via Antarctica, there being an operational airfield at McMurdo Sound, on the Antarctic continent, built by the United States Air Force, and open to any friendly power for Second Freedom, or transit rights. Early in 1973, LAN-Chile approached the pioneers of the Arctic Polar Route, Scandinavian Airlines System (SAS) for advice on this spectacular enterprise.

The first charter flight was made from Santiago to Sydney, via the Pacific islands, on 29 September, 1973, and operated at monthly intervals thereafter. On 9 February, 1974, an experimental flight was made from Sydney to Punta Arenas, over the Antarctic continent; but unfortunately the meteorological records showed that, as an alternate airfield for use in emergencies—mandatory procedure under internationally-enforced aviation law—McMurdo Sound was

71. LAN-Chile—Antarctic Route Possibilities from 1967. Displaying considerable initiative, the Chilean national airline ventured cautiously into the Pacific, first to Easter Island, then by subsequent extensions to Fiji. Its goal of a route to Australia has not yet been realised, but it has looked very carefully at the possibility of a southern trans-polar route.

not completely reliable. In particular, because of the prevailing extremely low temperatures, it was subject to intermittent low-lying ground fog which completely obliterated the runway, even creating the optical illusion of a false horizon, so that landing became hazardous. Because of these very real operational problems, LAN has never opened an Antarctic route but it did start a service to Fiji, as an extension of the Tahiti route, on 5 September, 1974.

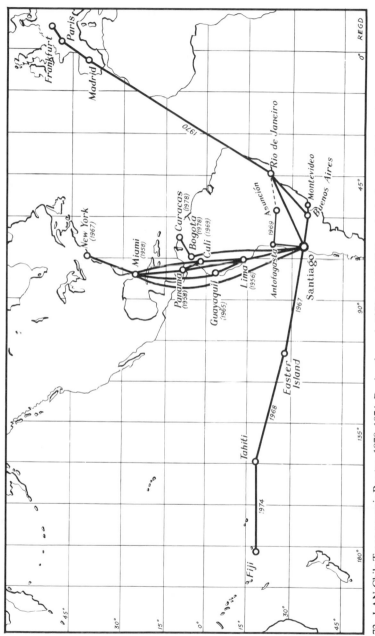

72. LAN-Chile Trans-oceanic Routes, 1970–1974. During the early 1970s, LAN-Chile embarked on a well-planned route expansion programme which transformed the airline into an intercontinental contender. To date it has been unable to complete the line to Australia, but even so it has carried many Australians to Europe by a fascinat ng itinerary, as an alternative to the traditional route via India.

LAN-Chile's McDonnell Douglas DC-10-30 CC-CJN *Santiago* had been National Airlines' N81NA *Renee*. The upper fuselage band is dark blue, the lower band and company title on the fuselage and registration are red. (*T. R. Waddington*)

Post-Revolution Adjustment

The latter 1970s were a time of consolidation for the Chilean airline. It had gone through a decade of massive expansion while surviving a period of dramatic political upheaval, and much operational and administrative dust had to settle. Further route expansion, therefore, was modest, compared with the great strides made previously. On 1 November, 1977, a nonstop service from Santiago to Miami brought the popular United States gateway even closer to the Chilean capital, and in June 1978, the South American network up the west coast was expanded to include Bogotá and Caracas (Cali had already been added as a

LAN's Boeing 737-2A1 CC-CHJ *Arica* bears fleet number 731. The upper paint band is blue, the lower band red and the company name on the fuselage is also in red.
(*The Boeing Company*)

540

Colombian point on 27 April, 1969). Because of the precarious finances of Chile, desperately recovering from almost record inflation and loss of foreign credit-worthiness during the Allende period, LAN's financial resources were slender, so that aircraft procurement was at first limited to two second-hand Boeing 707s. Subsequently, however, LAN-Chile gradually found the ways and means to modernize its fleet for domestic routes, acquiring Boeing 727s and 737s. By the lease of Douglas DC-10s in 1982, it also joined the ranks of wide-bodied operators in South America, and maintains its reputation for a service which does credit to its country.

While LAN-Chile was surviving as the national airline, the Chilean independent companies found a new lease of life after 1973. The Allende government, during its three-year existence, had nationalized or closed down almost every private enterprise of any substance, and these had included all the small air freight companies. The aircraft thus grounded, mostly C-46s, were lined up at Los Cerrillos, Santiago, like so many tombstones.

Of the former operators, few need to be recorded as having any pretensions to the term 'airline'. **Línea Aérea Taxpa (TAXPA)** (1957), **Línea Aérea Condor** (1959), **Línea Aérea Sud Americana (LASA)** (1964), **Transportes Aéreos Squella** (1964), and **Aerolíneas Flecha Austral (ALFA)** (1965) had all operated charters intermittently throughout Chile and to neighbouring points in Argentina. These had been mainly meat charters, all with the faithful workhorse of South America, the C-46, later supplemented by the DC-6. Squella, incidentally, named after its founder Oscar Squella, had taken over TRANSA's network. These were joined later by **Solastral**, whose two cargo DC-6s flew the trunk route from Santiago to Punta Arenas during the early 1970s.

After things had settled down a little when the Pinochet government took over on 1 January, 1973, Squella revived briefly until April 1976, as **Transportes Aéreos Suravia**. LASA and the others disappeared from the scene in 1978, but TAXPA appears to have a new lease of life.

On 14 August, 1978, another airline **Fast Air Carrier Ltda (Fast Air)** was formed to operate international freight services with an ex-TWA Boeing 707. On 27 November of that year this aircraft began a tramping trade up the South

LADECO's Boeing 737-2K6 CC-CIM with orange, red and black livery.
(*The Boeing Company*)

LADECO's Boeing 727-116 CC-CAG, seen at Congonhas Airport, São Paulo, in August 1981, had originally been delivered to LAN-Chile in February 1968.
(*Mário B. de M. Vinagre*)

American west coast and on to Miami, carrying Chilean agricultural produce, including wine, northward, and manufactured goods and Colombian coffee southward.

Domestically, several new companies were formed, taking advantage of the easing of restrictions. Predictably, most of these were based in Santiago. The largest, **AeroNorte-Sur (Aeronor Chile)**, founded in 1977, operates a small fleet of Fairchild F-27s to points northward as far as Arica, but mainly to Copiapó, via La Serena and Vallenar. **Línea Aérea Andina (Aeroandina)** operated a single Convair CV-600 to Concepción and La Serena from January 1980 to March 1981, and a DC-9-14 leased from the Spanish carrier Spantax later in the year; **Aeroguayacan, Ltda** and **Línea Aérea Icaro Servicios, Ltda (Icaro)** now operate locally with Beech King Airs and Pipers, respectively.

In the far north, **Línea Aérea Iquiquena** operates similar small aircraft types from Arica to points as far south as Antofagasta and Calama; while **Aerolíneas Cordillera Ltda (Aerocor)**, based at Coihaique, operates a DC-3 and a GAF Nomad to small towns in the Aisen province along the Argentine frontier.

Pride of place should go, however, to **Transporte Aéreo de Magallanes (TAMA)** which operates Beech Queen Air Excaliburs from Punta Arenas to Porvenir and Puerto Williams. This diminutive airline has the honour of being the most southerly-based scheduled operator in the world.

The small Chilean airlines still come and go. But the only one which has offered real competition to LAN-Chile during the post-Allende years has been LADECO which survived political uncertainties to enlarge its jet fleet from a single Boeing 727-100 to three 727s and three 737-200s, the latter all new, by July 1982. Its last DC-6B was withdrawn in 1979, the year in which it started international routes to Mendoza, and to Rio de Janeiro, via Asunción and São Paulo.

CHAPTER TWENTY-SEVEN

First Steps in Argentina

Cía Río Platense de Aviación

When air transport first got under way in the early 1920s, Argentina was, by some margin, the most prosperous country in South America, enjoying a standard of living, particularly in the cities, comparable with Europe and the United States. This was derived from a thriving economy, based on high production of staple food products such as wheat and cattle, for both of which Argentina and its bustling capital and chief port, Buenos Aires, were world-renowned. In the region immediately surrounding Buenos Aires, and across the pampas, the surface communications were excellent. Several efficient railways flourished—most were British-owned—and in the province of Buenos Aires and adjoining regions no community was more than 25 miles from a railway.

As the majority of Argentina's population lived in these areas, and outlying cities such as Mendoza or Tucumán were also connected by rail to the hub systems, the natural demand for an air service was not evident. Those communities which were remote from railheads, and at the same time were inland, and therefore lacking even a sea link with Buenos Aires, were too few, and too poor to justify the risk and investment needed to set up an airline service.

Nevertheless, some attempts were made to begin an air service, and the most successful was by an Englishman, Major Shirley H. Kingsley, formerly of the Royal Flying Corps (later to become the Royal Air Force). That the service should neither serve the more densely populated area, nor venture into the wilds

PANAGRA's Douglas DC-2 NC14268 *Santa Ana* over the Andes. This aircraft was delivered to Pan American Airways on 27 August, 1934, and six days later went to PANAGRA. After passing to Delta Air Lines it was acquired for the Royal Air Force by the British Purchasing Commission and was finally destroyed at Akyab in Burma on 13 April, 1942. (*Pan American World Airways*)

of Patagonia or the Gran Chaco was entirely consistent with the geographical and economic realities of Argentina in the 1920s.

Major Kingsley was an experienced airman, having received his brevet on 18 June, 1915, and completed 1,762 flying hours when he arrived in Argentina, representing George Holt Thomas's Aircraft Manufacturing Company Ltd of England, or Airco as it was called. Enthusiastically encouraged by a fellow compatriot, Brig-Gen Guy de Livingston, who believed in the future of civil aviation in its own right, as well as a means of generating work for otherwise idle military aircraft production lines, Kingsley began a series of demonstration flights with a de Havilland D.H.16 on 10 June, 1919. Always accompanied by two passengers, eleven trips were completed in five weeks between Buenos Aires and Montevideo, together with other sorties to Bahía Blanca, Rosario, Bell Ville, Gualeguay, Colonia, Córdoba, and one complete circuit of Uruguay.

Kingsley had made a neat appraisal of a natural air route. Buenos Aires was cut off from the nearest neighbouring country, Uruguay, by the 56-mile wide Río de la Plata, or River Plate. Uruguay was also at that time a prosperous nation but a journey to its capital, Montevideo, from Buenos Aires necessitated a 120-mile sea trip which took either all day or all night. A de Havilland D.H.16 could cover this distance in little more than an hour. While the aeroplane might not be able to compete with Argentina's excellent railways, it could challenge the shipping lane across the Río de la Plata.

Kingsley formed **The River Plate Aviation Company** on 1 August, 1919, and anxiously awaited delivery of his aircraft. These started to arrive at the end of the year: twelve wartime D.H.6 trainers, and two four-seat D.H.16s. Operations were started on a charter basis early in the new year. Failing to obtain much encouragement or material assistance from local authorities, River Plate set up its own installations—stores, workshop, hangars, and aero club—at San Isidro on 23 May, 1920, and it was from this airfield that, in due course, it began Argentina's first regularly scheduled air service. From 17 December, 1921, de Havilland aircraft maintained a regular daily service to Villa Colón, in Uruguay, serving Montevideo, until 30 April, 1922; but this was not until some reorganization had taken place.

As with every attempt to start air services in the early 1920s, the ambitious operators quickly found to their dismay that the aeroplane could not be flown cheaply enough to make a profit, even if full loads were always carried—which was seldom the case. The aircraft were usually too small, and basically too fragile, and therefore short-lived, to be economically viable. Like many of his contemporaries, Kingsley tried for a while to keep going but had to fall back on a familiar device: that of merging with another company of similar bent. In this case, it was a French concern, the **Compañía Franco-Argentina de Transportes Aéreos,** the operating division of a French marketing venture closely parallel with Kingsley's. River Plate and the French joined hands on 21 September, 1921, to form the **Compañía Río Platense de Aviación**, with a mixed fleet of de Havilland, Potez, Bristol, and Dornier aircraft.

According to the French *Indicateur Aérien* of June 1922, the Buenos Aires–Montevideo service was maintained twice a week in each direction, using "eight-passenger Rolls-Royce-engined de Havillands". It is of interest—bearing in mind the current schedule—to note that the published time from the Plaza de Mayo, in Buenos Aires, to the Plaza Constitución, in Montevideo, was $2\frac{3}{4}$ hr.

On 20 November of that year, the equipment was changed to Vickers Viking amphibians, which plied between Dársena Norte, the port of Buenos Aires, and

Lignes en Argentine

COMPANIA RIO PLATENSE DE AVIACION

Aérodrome San Isidro UT 145. — Administration Lavalle, 341, Buenos-Ayres.

SAMEDI	LUNDI		SAMEDI	LUNDI
13.00	7.30	Buenos-Ayres (Plaza Mayo)...........	14.45	9.15
15.45	10.15	Montevideo (Plaza Constitucion)	17.30	12.00

Appareils. — De Haviland — 8 passagers — moteur Rolls Royce.

TRANSPORT DES PASSAGERS

Tarifs.
Aller ....$ 80 m/n arg. ou $ 35 0/urug.
Aller et retour..................$ 140 m/n arg. ou $ 60 0/urug.
Nota. — 15 kgs de bagages gratuits, excédent $ 2 m/n arg. le kg.
— Le tarif comprend le transport en automobile de Buenos-Ayres (Plaza Mayo) à l'aérodrome de San Isidro et de Montevideo (Plaza-Constitucion) à l'aérodrome de Villa Colon.

Buenos Aires–Montevideo Service, 1922. This extract from *L'Indicateur Aérien* of 1922 shows that an adequate air service was provided across the River Plate in the earliest days of aviation in South America.

the Muelle (pier) Maciel, in Montevideo, a service which continued until 31 March, 1923. The reputation and record of the airline was now sufficiently good, apparently, for the Post Office to grant a subsidy of 4,500 pesos a month for the carriage of air mail, while the Ministry of War contributed an equal sum as a direct subsidy. On 28 December, 1923, the Post Office established an official air mail, issuing special stamps, with surcharge, effective from 1 January, 1924. The air fare at this time was 50 pesos single, 90 return.

One of the two Vickers Type 73 Viking IV amphibians delivered to the River Plate Aviation Company in February 1923 and used on the Buenos Aires–Montevideo service. Both aircraft were powered by 360 hp Rolls-Royce Eagle IX engines, were underpowered and difficult to get off calm water. The other Viking had an open cockpit. On the mooring raft (*left to right*) are Maj Shirley Kingsley MC (director), Maj Brian Ferrand DSO (chief pilot) and P. F. Hasselt.

545

Nevertheless, in spite of what appeared to be the running of the tide in their direction, Río Platense de Aviación did not survive another season, and there is no record of continued operations beyond 1924.

First Efforts in Patagonia

Contemporarily with Major Kingsley's activities, there had been some attempts to promote air services in the part of Argentina where they seemed to be most needed from the standpoint of serving the country's social needs. In Patagonia, the relatively undeveloped—and partly barren and unattractive—region to the south, only a few railways linked tiny towns and settlements with a few small ports; and these had meagre shipping connections with the industrial and prosperous areas of Buenos Aires and the pampas. Yet there was scattered wealth, including oilfields at Comodoro Rivadavia, and the aeroplane appeared to be the logical vehicle to serve the isolated communities.

Accordingly, several proposals were put to the Argentine Government for support in starting a Patagonian air service. First, in September 1920, Eduardo Bradley prepared plans for a service from Bahía Blanca, the southernmost large city of Buenos Aires Province, to Río Gallegos, near the southern tip of the peninsula, and sought official support in the way of subsidy. In this venture, Bradley was backed by the Sociedad Anonima Importadora y Exportadora de la Patagonia, and the Banco de Chile y la Argentina. The former was owned by the Menendez Behety family, which was also reputed to own most of Patagonia, and appears to have enjoyed the same relationship with the Argentine Government as the East India Company had with the British Parliament in the days of Clive. But in spite of this considerable leverage, Bradley's scheme was unsuccessful.

The British Vickers company presented a similar project in 1921, but was equally unsuccessful. Presumably, the intention was to use the Viking amphibians, which, however, were put to good use by the Anglo-French partnership on the River Plate service.

In 1922, Enrique (later General) Mosconi, who played a leading role in the development of oil prospecting and exploration in Patagonia, founded the Servicio Aeronáutico del Ejercito, to develop an air service from Carmen de Patagones, about 100 miles south of Bahía Blanca, to Ushuaia, on the island of Tierra del Fuego, and Argentina's southernmost habitation. But Mosconi suffered the same fate as his predecessors.

The Junkers Mission

While the trans-River Plate service and the proposed routes in Patagonia were natural objectives for commercial aircraft operation, the German sales mission in Argentina showed remarkable enterprise in locating another opportunity for an air route. Whereas the British and French identified a water barrier hindering fast surface transport, the Junkers Mission found a land barrier, in the shape of a range of mountains, the Sierra de Córdoba, which was a hindrance to convenient travel. While not reaching the formidable heights of the Andean Cordillera, the Sierra was nevertheless mountainous enough to prevent direct road or rail service to the westernmost part of the Province of Córdoba. The road journey to Villa Dolores, for example, took 7 hours. Accordingly, following a proposal by Admiral Don Alfredo Malbrán, an air service was started by the Government of the Province of Córdoba in co-operation with the Junkers Mission, under the name of **Lloyd Aéreo Córdoba**, with a capital of 75,000 pesos. The company was formed on 1 January, 1925, and services began later in the year, using two sturdy Junkers-F 13 cabin monoplanes, with five seats, from Córdoba across the mountains to Villa Dolores, and on to Río Cuarto, further south. A second service was added from Córdoba to the Laguna Mar Chiquita, about 120 km to the west. The service operated under the patronage of the local aero club (Córdoba was to become the centre of Argentina's aeronautical industry) and received a monthly subsidy of 7,000 pesos, from May 1925.

The two F 13s operated at a regularity of 98·2 per cent and with perfect safety. In 1926 Lloyd Aéreo was encouraged to add a third aircraft, a three-engined Junkers-G 24. Unfortunately, the company ran into some frustrating legal problems over the subsidy and patronage arrangement, and went into liquidation in 1927.

As its swan song in Argentina, the Junkers Mission took over the ailing route between Buenos Aires and Montevideo, now abandoned by Río Platense de Aviación. Between 1 March, 1926, and 7 October, 1927, using floatplanes, the Mission completed 436 flights (using Dárseña Norte as a base) at a regularity of 97·3 per cent. Frequency was three a week, and a subsidy of 3,000 pesos a month was received during the period of operation.

The Junkers Mission took its valuable assets elsewhere, the two F 13s to Bolivia, where they joined LAB's fleet, and the G 24 to Brazil, where it became VARIG's *Ypiranga*.

An unidentified Junkers-G 24 floatplane over Buenos Aires. This aircraft operated Junkers Aero-Lloyd's Buenos Aires–Montevideo service and is reported to have gone to Brazil as Syndicato Condor's P-BABA *Ypiranga* which identifics it as c/n 944, but it is just possible that there was more than one G 24 in Argentina.

Other Early Experiments

While very short-lived, four other small ventures into the risky world of regular airline service in Argentina during the latter 1920s are worthy of mention. From 18 March, 1925, the **Aero Club de Tucumán**, using a 160 hp Curtiss Oriole, operated for about a month between that northern city and Tafi del Valle—another example of the aeroplane substituting for surface transport, in difficult terrain. In 1928 the Tucumán Aero Club extended service to Valles del Oeste and Valles Calchaquies, using a Fairchild 71.

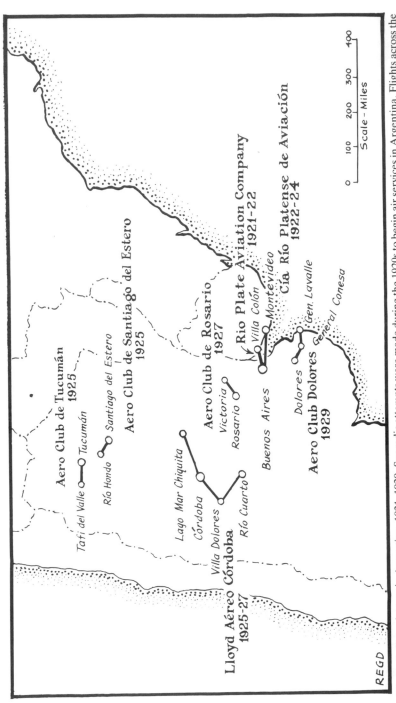

73. Early Experiments in Argentina, 1921–1929. Sporadic attempts were made during the 1920s to begin air services in Argentina. Flights across the River Plate were initially successful but not sustained. Elsewhere there was no co-ordinated plan, and competition from the well-organized railways postponed early development.

Then, in the same northern region, in the adjoining province, the **Aero Club de Santiago del Estero** operated to Río Hondo, a small community to the west, from 1 July to 30 August, 1925.

Two years later, on 22 January, 1927, the **Aero Club de Rosario** began a service from the city of Rosario—second only to Buenos Aires in size—to Victoria, across the marshlands of the Paraná River, thus linking the provinces of Santa Fé and Entre Ríos. In the absence of any road or railway in a section of the Paraná which constituted a formidable natural barrier, this was a shrewd choice of route but it did not last long.

The fourth aero club to try its hand at a regular service was that of **Dolores**, a city in eastern Buenos Aires Province. It provided service, from 16 November, 1929, when the roads were impassable through flooding, from Dolores to the neighbouring towns of General Conesa and General Lavalle, using Fleet, D.H. Moth and Curtiss Robin landplanes.

But admirable though the efforts of the clubs were in their small way, their sights were set only towards local horizons, and the history of Argentine commercial aviation from this time was mainly in the hands of a larger enterprise with far greater ambitions, and whose initial development was to provide the firm basis for future expansion not only within Argentina, but in linking the country by air with the remainder of South America and with Europe.

The First Aeroposta

The final steps which resulted in the establishment of much-needed regular air services in Patagonia had their origins in France, and date back to 1918, when Pierre Latécoère founded his famous pioneer airline in Toulouse, with ambitions to create a network linking France with South America. During his attempts to establish the necessary support, he had met, in Rio de Janeiro on 3 December, 1925, Marcel Bouilloux-Lafont, another French industrialist who had built up a commercial empire of railways, port installations, mines, banks, and real estate in South America. Just over a year after their first meeting, Latécoère sought Bouilloux-Lafont's assistance to overcome some bureaucratic resistance in Brazil, and the latter was so intrigued by the possibilities of adding to his empire a transport system with such prospects as Latécoère's that a deal was made.

They went to Buenos Aires and, together with the active participation of a popular Argentine aviator, Vicente Almondos Almonacid—known in his country as *el Condor de la Rioja*—were given an audience with President Alvear in January 1927. He granted the concession to carry 25 per cent of the mail between Argentina and Europe, and such was Bouilloux-Lafont's personal involvement by this time that he bought control of the Ligne Latécoère.

In April 1927, he changed the name to Aéropostale, invested the equivalent of about $1,500,000 in the venture, and proceeded to revitalize the company. He put in hand programmes of supply depots and airfield construction, initiated diplomatic negotiation for mail contracts, and set up subsidiary airlines in several South American countries: Brazil, Venezuela and Argentina. The last of these, **Aeroposta Argentina**, was founded on 5 September, 1927. The directors included French and Argentine businessmen and industrial leaders. On 14/15 November, Buenos Aires was linked by Aéropostale with Natal.

During 1928 preparations were made in Argentina for service: route planning, airfield construction and organizing facilities, training, and administration. During that year, beginning 1 March, the parent company, Aéropostale, started

Lignes Aériennes Latécoère's red and silver Latécoère 17 F-AIEI. This aircraft was later modified to Latécoère 25.3.R standard and survived to be taken over by Air France. A large number of Laté 17s and 25s was built and some were operated by Aeropostal Brasileira and Aeroposta Argentina. (*Air France*)

its historic Europe–South America air mail service, in which letters reached Buenos Aires only eight days after leaving Toulouse, having been carried partly by air, and on fast destroyers from Dakar to Natal. The famous French pilot, Jean Mermoz, inaugurated night take-offs and landings at Rio de Janeiro and Buenos Aires from 16 April to speed up the mails to gain maximum advantage.

On 13 January, 1929, Aeroposta Argentina opened a branch line northwards from Buenos Aires to Asunción, Paraguay, the necessary mail contract having been obtained from the Paraguayan Government on the previous 14 September. Service was twice weekly, the Latécoère 25s flying via Monte Caseros and Posadas. Paul Vachet, one of Aéropostale's veteran pilots, who had been put in charge of the Argentine organization, flew on the inaugural flight with his wife and with co-pilots Pedro Ficarelli and Leonardo Selvetti, both Argentine.

The Latécoère 25 F-AIEH of Aéropostale being run-up at Bahía Blanca before departure for Río Gallegos. This aircraft, c/n 603, was the prototype Laté 25.1.R, was later converted to 25.3.R, passed to Aeroposta Argentina as R 211, was reregistered LV-EAB, and has been preserved at Buenos Aires.

On 28 February of the same year, Mermoz and Collenot, with the Comte de la Vaulx as a passenger, made an historic proving flight across the Andes to Chile in a Latécoère 25, and on 15 July, Mermoz and Henri Guillaumet established the air link from Buenos Aires to Santiago, which was subsequently flown once a week via Mendoza. For this route the Laté 25 was replaced by the Potez 25, which had arrived in March, and could fly at an altitude of 6,000 metres, and was thus better able to overfly the soaring, unforgiving peaks of the Andes.

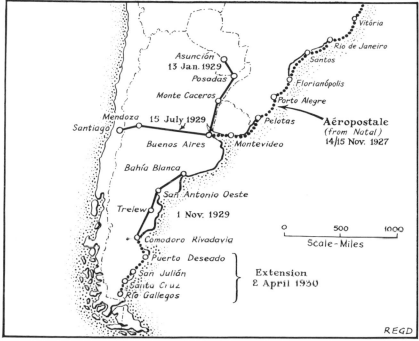

74. Aeroposta, 1929. The first trunk air routes in Argentina were started by a subsidiary of the pioneering French airline Aéropostale, with lines to Paraguay, Chile, and to Patagonia.

One of the main objectives during the early days of commercial aviation in Argentina was to open a regular service between Buenos Aires and Santiago de Chile. Although Aéropostale could claim to have first inaugurated the service on 15 July, 1929, this was for mail only. The race to start trans-Andean passenger service at the time was exclusively American, and featured a bitter rivalry between several factions from the USA.

Claiming the honour of making the first commercial flight was the pilot Harold MacMahon, flying for **American International Airways**. This company was formed by John K. Montgomery and Richard B. Bevier, the same partnership which had incorporated the original Pan American Airways in search of the US Air Mail contract from Key West to Havana. Thwarted by Juan Trippe's astute manoeuvring on behalf of the Aviation Corporation of the Americas, Montgomery and Bevier tried to set up an organization to challenge Trippe.

They acquired a Sikorsky S-37, a large landplane which, under the name *Ville de Paris* was to have been flown by the famous French pilot René Fonck in an

551

Sikorsky S-37. This rare Sikorsky landplane was originally built in 1927 as the *Ville de Paris* for Capt René Fonck's attempt to fly across the North Atlantic. It passed to American International Airways and was renamed *Southern Star*, with capacity for 20 passengers and weighing 14,500 lb fully laden. It made the first passenger flight over the Andes on 28 July, 1929.

attempt to win the Orteig trans-Atlantic prize after the Sikorsky S-35 had crashed. After Lindbergh's famous flight had rendered this venture superfluous, the aircraft passed to American International as the *Southern Star*. After an eventful flight from the Long Island factory, including replacement of the Gnome-Rhône-built Bristol Jupiter engines by Pratt & Whitney Hornets, the S-37 arrived in Santiago and flew across the Andes to Buenos Aires on 10 July, 1929, carrying eight passengers.

The company made a few flights between the two capitals before accepting an offer to join with Ralph O'Neill's **NYRBA**, which began regular trans-Andean mail and passenger service, using Ford Tri-Motors (with the S-37 as a back-up) on 1 September, 1929. Much to NYRBA's satisfaction, their Fords (which operated for a time under the name of **Trimotor Safety Airways**, were superior to those of **PANAGRA**, which was able to open service for mail only on 12 October, 1929, and could not carry passengers regularly until the following April.

PANAGRA's Buenos Aires base soon after the opening of the route from Santiago. In front of the hangar is the Ford 5-AT-C NC8416 which was operated by PANAGRA from mid 1929 until 1938. This Ford had numerous owners and survived into the 1940s. The Loening amphibian on the right is thought to be a C-2-C. (*Pan American World Airways*)

Aeroposta's greatest achievement came towards the end of the year, after Antoine de Saint-Exupéry had joined the Argentine contingent of Aéropostale, charged with establishing a route southwards from Bahía Blanca into Patagonia. This was duly achieved, the first regular flights starting on 1 November, 1929, using the Latécoère 25. The route was through barren country to Comodoro Rivadavia, via San Antonio Oeste and Trelew. While St-Exupéry did not have mountains to contend with—indeed, the terrain was boringly flat—he had his share of climatic problems, claiming that the winds were so strong that a headwind could result in flying at zero ground speed, and that—to paraphrase his literary account—the very stones in the ground took to the air in a storm.

One of the dramatic incidents in the pioneering days of air transport involved Henri Guillaumet and the Potez 25 F-AJDZ. On 13 June, 1930, Guillaumet left Santiago, Chile, for Mendoza with mail for Europe. Fierce snowstorms and heavy turbulence finally forced him down near Laguna Diamante at an elevation of 11,482 ft and the Potez overturned. Guillaumet walked for two days before he encountered help and several months later the Potez was recovered and put back into service. (*Air France*)

The annals of Aéropostale are filled with anecdotes of adventure. The early development of the route down the coast of West Africa as far as Dakar was punctuated by frequent incidents in which aircraft made forced landings in the desert, and their crews were captured by hostile tribesmen with such regularity that the paying of ransoms became a regular operational routine. Argentina, too, had its share of aviation stories, mostly concerning hair-raising escapes from death in the mountains. Few accounts of survival, however, can equal that of Henri Guillaumet's epic escape in the Andes, when, on 13 June, 1930, having made a forced landing, he trudged through the snows without stopping for 48 hr, until, at the end of his endurance, with frostbitten feet, he was rescued by an Indian peasant. His aeroplane, incidentally, a Potez 25, was recovered the following Spring, repaired, and put back into service.

553

On 2 April 1930, the Patagonia route was extended southwards from Comodoro Rivadavia to Río Gallegos, via Puerto Descado, San Julián, and Santa Cruz. This was as far south as it was possible to fly within Argentine mainland territory, without the final stage to the island of Tierra del Fuego, the extension to which was to take another five years. The inaugural flight to Río Gallegos was flown by a newly-delivered Latécoère 28, piloted by St-Exupéry, with the Aéropostale President, Marcel Bouilloux-Lafont, as passenger, and was greeted with great enthusiasm by the local populace who, quite understandably, had come to regard Buenos Aires as some remote northern city far away. It was the world's southernmost air service at that time.

Sadly, this achievement represented the zenith of Aeroposta's development during the early 1930s. Although during the summers of 1929 and 1930, supplementary flights were made from Buenos Aires to Mar del Plata, these were the years of a world economic depression, and from then on the airline's fortunes went into a steep decline. Bouilloux-Lafont had to fly back to France but was too late to save Aéropostale from going into liquidation on 31 March, 1931—ironically a few months after some of Mermoz's greatest exploits in long-distance flying across the South Atlantic. The service to Asunción was suspended on 17 April, 1931, and the one to Santiago in June. The French Government, for reasons which have never been satisfactorily explained, withdrew the vital subsidy from Aéropostale.

Recognizing, however, that the service to Patagonia deserved special consideration beyond the normal criteria of commercial book-keeping, the Argentine Director of Aeronautics, Señor Mundin Schaffter, tried to find a solution to the problem. By the Decree of 29 September, 1931, the assets of Aeroposta were loaned to the State, under the control of the Directorate of Civil Aeronautics. Under the name **Aeroposta Nacional**, the Bahía Blanca–Río Gallegos service was maintained under the control of the Argentine Post Office from 2 October, 1931, to 31 March, 1932. Special arrangements were made for the payment of rent to Aeroposta for the lease of material, personnel, and infrastructure. During the period, this second-generation Aeroposta carried 208 passengers and 2,725 kg of mail.

The company was rejuvenated soon afterwards, by the Decree of 31 May, 1932, and resumed activities as **Aeroposta Argentina, S.A.** under arrangements made with Aéropostale—still being operated under French control—but with substantial assistance by the Argentine Government, which granted a monthly subsidy from 1 June until 31 December, 1932, and made special provisions for the supply of fuel from the oilfields at Comodoro Rivadavia, which became the southern terminus of the line. Then on 24 March, 1933, a further Decree increased the subsidy to 180,000 pesos a month, and confirmed the concession for ten years, thus giving the stamp of authority and permanence to a service which had demonstrated its value as a national asset.

CHAPTER TWENTY-EIGHT

Development of an Argentine Airline System

Reorganization of Aeroposta

Argentina's only airline, Aeroposta Argentina, S.A., still partly foreign-owned through the residual French interests from the former Bouilloux-Lafont enterprise, managed to survive as an operating entity during the early 1930s, but its footholds in Patagonia were precarious. Even though a token extension was made south of Río Gallegos to Río Grande, on the island of Tierra del Fuego, in November 1935, there was an urgent need to put this valuable transport service on a firmer footing.

Much credit for the furtherance of the air transport cause in southern Patagonia should go to the local authorities in the Territory of Santa Cruz, whose Governor Gregores, assisted by Gustavo Costabel, created a network of airfields, supported by radio installations, throughout the Territory (Santa Cruz had not yet reached provincial status). Regular services were initiated on 31 May, 1934, by **Servicio Aéreo Territorial de Santa Cruz**, using a Lockheed Vega 1, which, however, crashed at Cóndor on 11 July, 1935. The Argentine Navy then supplied a Huff Daland Pelican, with which a fortnightly service was maintained from Río Gallegos to all the inland settlements in the lake district at the foothills of the southern Andes within the Territory.

This little air service continued to provide the lifeline for the otherwise isolated communities of Santa Cruz, until Aeroposta (which had passed down a Latécoère 25 for the use of the Territory in 1938) took over the responsibility in 1945.

Help came to Aeroposta in 1937 from a powerful financial source, the Pueyrredon commercial group, which controlled banks, insurance companies, and various other business affairs, and which presumably viewed the acquisition of Aeroposta in much the same way that Bouilloux-Lafont had done ten years

LV-AAH *Pampa* was one of a small fleet of Junkers-Ju 52/3ms operated by Aeroposta Argentina.

earlier. On 1 February, 1937, the line passed under Pueyrredon control, with Dr Ernesto Pueyrredon taking a personal interest and acting as the first President of the now all-Argentine airline. The Government continued both to take responsibility and exert some control by the payment of a subsidy of 1.50 pesos for each kilometre flown—a slight change in the subsidy arrangements which gave some incentive for route and service development.

On 14 October, 1937, Pueyrredon arranged for the supply of three Junkers-Ju 52/3m aircraft through the co-operation of Deutsche Lufthansa, the German national airline which was competing strongly in friendly though rigorous rivalry with the French for pride of place on the South Atlantic air mail route. For both nations, Buenos Aires was the prime destination, and both airlines operated extensions across the Andes to Santiago. Although the French had long since abandoned ambitions to reach the southernmost tip of South America, and indeed, the Germans could have had little commercially strategic reason for doing so, the complete transfer of influence was most satisfactory from the point of view of German commercial efforts to become the chief source of supply of aircraft throughout the South American continent.

With the modernized, three-engined Junkers equipment, augmented to a fleet of five, Aeroposta maintained the Patagonian trunk route, extending southwards again to Río Gallegos and on to Río Grande, and with the important modification that the northern terminus was transferred from Bahía Blanca to the airport of Quilmes, a suburb of Buenos Aires, and thus provided direct connection with the intercontinental routes to Europe and the United States. And for almost the remainder of the decade, this was the only Argentine commercial air service of substance, apart from those operated by foreign companies.

Further Airline Ventures in the Thirties

During the early 1930s, a few private individuals, clubs, and associations had helped to popularize commercial aviation in the northern provinces of Argentina. These, together with the pioneer aero clubs of the 1920s, already referred to in the previous chapter, are summarized in Table 28.

Special mention should be made of the continuity of interest at Tucumán. When that city's aero club could no longer sustain its local operation, the Department of Civil Aviation took over on 1 December, 1931, and maintained the service until 31 May, 1932, using a Bellanca monoplane. Then in 1934, the **Sociedad de Transportes Aéreos (STA)** was created by Dr Miguel Figueroa Roman. He reinstated the service from Tucumán to Tafi del Valle and Santa Maria from 5 September, 1934, for three more years, at first with aircraft from the Aero Club and later with a Ryan Brougham, belonging to the Department of Civil Aviation, and loaned to STA.

However, the development of small airlines in Argentina was sporadic and mainly transient, each small venture seldom lasting more than a few months, and almost invariably localized in nature. This was mainly because of the excellence of the railway system, which linked almost all the large cities (which in any case were grouped together within a relatively small area). Also the periphery of the country was sparsely populated by agriculturally-inclined settlers, with little motivation or indeed the wealth to travel. It was not until the early 1940s that, with the exception of major international connections, and the essential service down the coast to Patagonia maintained by Aeroposta, that Argentine civil aviation began to make headway.

Corporación

The Argentine population is descended from European immigrant stock, and the largest single source of immigrants has been Italy, even though Argentina is a Spanish-speaking nation. Indeed, between the middle of the Nineteenth Century and the inter-world war period, Italian settlers numbered almost as many as all the other nationalities combined. Italian influence was therefore considerable, and for an airline to be founded jointly by representatives of the two countries was almost inevitable.

Corporación Sudamericana de Servicios Aéreos was organized in 1938 by Ing Mauro Herlitska and Dr Mario Pastega, with participation from the Italian Government, which contributed to the assets by supplying Italian aircraft, crew, and technical support. This was entirely in the tradition of the way in which the French Aéropostale had originally started to build an airline empire, and in which the Germans had energetically expanded the Condor system to include satellites across the South American continent. Italy was spreading its intercontinental wings, with ambitions to match the French and German enterprise, and on 6 March, 1939, was finally granted permission by the Argentine Government to open a service to Europe. This was exactly a month after Corporación (as the company was generally known) had established a service from Buenos Aires (Dock A) to Montevideo, using Macchi C.94 flying-boats and Italian crews. A line was attempted to Rosario, starting on 15 May, 1939, but this lasted only three months.

On 26 March, 1941, the route to Asunción, Paraguay, via Santa Fé, Barranqueras (serving Resistencia and Corrientes) and Formosa was opened, but shortly thereafter, with the US entry into the war intensifying the pressures to restrict supplies to Axis nations and their national interests overseas, Corporación ceased activities. At the same time, the newly-formed Italian South Atlantic airline, LATI, whose aircraft had run into many difficulties, not the least the refusal of the US Government to supply fuel, ceased operations on 22 December, 1941, so that all Italian airline influence in Argentina evaporated.

One of the Corporación Sudamericana de Servicios Aéreos Macchi C.94 flying-boats over the Río de la Plata.

557

SANA

A small airline, **Sociedad Argentina de Servicios Aéreos (SASA)** operated for a short while in 1939 between Buenos Aires (San Fernando) and Concepción del Uruguay, via Gualeguay, but did not survive for very long. Slightly more permanent was another wholly-Argentine company, **Sociedad Argentina de Navegación Aérea (SANA)**. Founded in 1940 by Dr Pastega, one of the co-founders of Corporación, and with a capital approaching that of the well-established Aeroposta, SANA purchased three flying-boats from Pan American, one Sikorsky amphibian, and two Consolidated Commodores, honourable survivors of the pioneering NYRBA fleet of 1930. With this equipment, SANA opened a route on 5 June, 1940, from Buenos Aires to Colonia, across the Río de la Plata in Uruguay. This short hop connected with a bus service to Montevideo, and competed with the direct service between the two capitals provided by Corporación and CAUSA, the Uruguayan airline. However, the city-centre journey time of three hours was twice that of its rivals, and so SANA charged half the fare for the complete journey. In US equivalent currency at the time, this was less than four dollars one way, which seems to have been quite a bargain. SANA had ambitions to fly to Asunción, via Posadas, and to Jujuy, via Córdoba, Santiago del Estero, Tucumán, and Salto. The first of these routes is believed to have been operated for a short while; but the loss of the Sikorsky undoubtedly put an end to long-distance domestic aspirations; and indeed SANA terminated its single route on 16 August, 1943.

The Military Airlines

In common with other South American countries which sought the solution to promoting its air services by invoking direct government involvement, Argentina witnessed the entry of the Army Air Force into commercial operations in 1940. On 1 January, Observers Group No.1, part of the Agrupación Transporte of the Aviation Command of the Argentine Army, initated a series of experimental flights between Buenos Aires and Esquel, in southwest Argentina. After nine months the trial flights were consolidated into a regular service pattern, and on 1 September, the **Línea Aérea Suroeste (LASO)** was organized by the Argentine Air Force (Fuerza Aérea Argentina) and took over the route, under the provisions of Decree 67,777, dated 19 June. Actually beginning the schedule on 4 September, a single Junkers-Ju 52/3m flew once a week to Esquel, via Santa Rosa, Neuquén, and Bariloche.

Under the direction of General Zuloaga, LASO carried passengers, mail, and express, and, like its counterpart in Brazil and other countries, provided valuable training for the Air Force. Interestingly, although such airlines are formed mainly to provide so-called social services, to benefit communities which are relatively isolated from the capital or major cities by the inadequacy of surface transport, LASO served an area which was to become one of the world's major mountain-resort destinations, so its traffic was generated as much from the capital as from the outlying settlements—and for reasons unconnected with the normal justification for the indirect subsidy provided through the agency of the Air Force.

75. Argentine Airlines, 1943. During the early 1940s, the airlines of Argentina comprised a ▶ heterogeneous group. Each route of a spoke pattern radiating from Buenos Aires was flown by a different company. Some were private, some were semi-military, and one was a foreign company enjoying cabotage rights.

The Esquel service was increased to twice weekly, and a second service projected—once again to a resort destination. On 6 September, 1943, a reconnaissance flight was made from El Palomar airfield in Buenos Aires to the Iguassú Falls, and, under the terms of Decree No.9,235, service was started on 20 September. The route was dignified with a new name as a division of the commercial arm of the Air Force: **Línea Aérea Nor-Este (LANE)** on 6 January, 1944.

On 15 December, 1944, a subdivision of LANE was created: **Servicio Aeropostales del Estado (SADE)**. Although under the technical direction of the Air Force—single-engined aircraft were used—administration came under the direct control of the Director General of Civil Aviation, and was thus a predominantly civil, rather than a quasi-military service. On 4 May, 1945, LANE was authorized to extend its main route to Clorinda, the Argentine city across the Paraguay River from Asunción, and two weeks later another branch linked Posadas with Presidencia Roque Saenz Peña, via Resistencia, on the Clorinda route.

Yet another subdivision of the commercial arm of the Air Force had been added on 15 December, 1944, when the **Servicio a Mar del Plata** was inaugurated, between Buenos Aires and Mar del Plata, at a frequency of up to three times a day during carnival time and Holy Week. Until the service was taken over by Aeroposta this was another example of the Government providing air service to serve the public in its leisure activities, as well as providing essential transport to supplement the surface modes in the remoter regions of Argentina.

In 1945, the two main divisions, LASO and LANE, were consolidated under the title **Líneas Aéreas del Estado (LADE)**, which exists to this day. SADE and the Mar del Plata line remained as sub-divisions. LADE continued the now substantial network until 21 January, 1947, when, under Decree No.1,395 of that year, this was taken over by the newly-formed joint stock companies (see below). During this first stage of existence, from 1940 to 1947, LASO had carried 13,311 passengers, about 14,000 kg of mail, and 10,700 kg of freight. LANE carried 7,594 passengers, 3,500 kg of mail, and 2,350 kg of freight. Between 1944 and 1947, 10,166 passengers were carried on the Mar del Plata line, while SADE carried 10,850 kg of mail and freight.

Creation of Joint Stock Companies

Although not directly involved in the war, Argentina's commercial development had nevertheless been severely handicapped by its effects, both by the impossibility of acquiring suitable aircraft and by the presence and considerable influence of foreign airlines, both from Europe and the United States. These enjoyed wide operating privileges, not only having the right to carry all international traffic into and out of Argentina, but also exercising 'cabotage' rights, that is, carrying domestic traffic wholly within Argentina. This situation was clearly unsatisfactory, and in 1945, the Government took effective action. Law No.12,911, on 27 April, stated the nation's policy regarding air navigation. Article 5 of that Law established that 'internal transport air services . . . would be performed either by State or mixed stock companies' constituted according to Law 12,161, and Article 8 of Law 12,709 relating to air enterprises. The mixed stock companies were to be authorized by the Secretaría de Aeronáutica, and the shares identified as Argentine-owned, by citizens domiciled in Argentina. Cabotage routes, mainly those operated by the US airline PANAGRA, were to be taken over by the new companies.

560

76. Regional Allocation of Argentine Routes, 1947. After the war, and following a change of Government, a new plan was evolved to co-ordinate airline activity in Argentina. The country was divided into spheres of influence, to be allocated to new joint-stock companies.

Long overdue, Argentina quickly set up the new organization plan. Three new joint stock companies were formed in 1946; Aeroposta was converted from private to mixed capital in 1947; also in that year the routes of LADE were transferred to the new companies, and the cabotage routes transferred to Argentine control. The country was divided into six zones. In addition to its own territory (Zone I) Aeroposta acquired the old LASO route (Zone II); ALFA took over the old Corporación route (Zone VI) and the LANE territory (Zone IV); while ZONDA became responsible for developing services in the northwest, hitherto almost exclusive to PANAGRA (Zone V) and the trunk route directly westward from Buenos Aires to Chile (Zone III). (see Maps 75 and 76).

Each of the three airlines had access to two points in neighbouring countries: Aeroposta to Punta Arenas and Pilmaiquen, in Chile; ZONDA to Santiago and Antofagasta, also in Chile; while ALFA was allowed to fly to Asunción, Paraguay, and Montevideo, Uruguay. Complemented by a designated international airline, FAMA, it was a systematic system, and the four new companies set about the task of postwar reconstruction and development with vigour.

FAMA

Authorized by executive decree on 31 December, 1945, the first of the joint stock companies to be established was **Flota Aérea Mercante Argentina (FAMA)**, on 8 February, 1946, with a capital of m$n 150 million, of which the State was to provide one-third. In fact, few of the private shares were taken up, as there was considerable uncertainty in the financial and political world of Buenos Aires at the time, as Argentina was then ruled by a military government, before the rise to power of Juan and Eva Perón by the end of 1947. Prominent among the private interests was the Dodero shipping company, and Dr José Dodero himself had taken a lively interest in commercial aviation, setting up a subsidiary company, **Compañia Argentina de Aeronavegación Dodero** (see ALFA section, below).

Dodero had obtained four British Short Sandringham flying-boats, and as early as 15 February—only a week after FAMA's formation—the Sandringham *Brasil* left Buenos Aires for a three-day proving flight to Baltimore, via Montevideo, Rio de Janeiro, Natal, Trinidad, and Bermuda. Dodero acquired the Sandringhams to support his own personal objective of starting the first air service to Europe by a South American airline.

During the early months of 1946, preparations were made for FAMA to take its place among the world's intercontinental flag carriers. The Government had recognized it as such, and reciprocal agreements were made with LAN, the Chilean airline, and British South American Airways in March and May, respectively. A Douglas DC-4 began service to Santiago on 4 June, 1946, but for legal reasons a separate company was established in Britain, and one flight made by a Sandringham to the United Kingdom also on 4 June. A small fleet of Avro Lancastrians (Lancaster bomber conversions) and three Avro Yorks had also been obtained, together with five or six Vickers Vikings and three Bristol 170 Freighters for regional use to neighbouring countries.

Anxious to get into service as quickly as possible, Dodero had shopped around for aircraft with the earliest delivery and British wartime conversions came off the line quickly. But they were inadequate for the mission demanded. The Lancastrian offered cramped conditions in the long, slender bomber fuselage, while the York's performance was inadequate for long stages while carrying full loads. At this time also, the campaign was still being conducted, albeit fighting for a lost cause, to promote the virtues of the flying-boat over the landplane. Dodero, it could be argued, showed some business acumen in acquiring both types of aircraft. At least he did not pursue a rumoured order for the ill-fated Avro Tudor.

Despite Dodero's initiative, however, his conflict with the State interests were irreconcilable, and he parted company with FAMA in August 1946. Only a month later, on 17 September, the first service took off for Paris and London, not with the British aircraft, but with a Douglas DC-4, the same type which had inaugurated service to Santiago. This was the US civil version of the highly successful C-54 Skymaster military transport which owed its origins to a

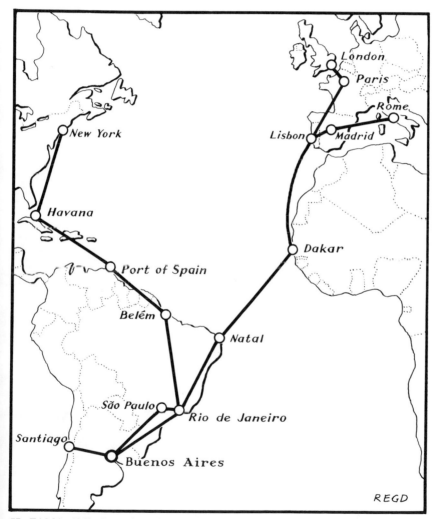

77. FAMA, 1949. Argentina's first airline to operate overseas routes was FAMA, which laid the foundations of what was to become the international division of Aerolíneas Argentinas.

563

FAMA's Avro 685 York C.Mk.1 LV-XGO was reregistered LV-AFY and sold back to the United Kingdom. (*British Aerospace*)

One of twenty Vickers-Armstrongs Vikings supplied to the Argentine Government, LV-AEW is seen in service with FAMA.

Seen in FAMA's livery with blue fuselage, tail and cowling markings, Convair CV-240-6 LV-ADP was actually delivered to Aerolíneas Argentinas on 27 February, 1949, and was named *Chacabuco*. It was acquired by the Paraguayan Air Force in 1962.
(*General Dynamics*)

specification set up in the early 1940s by the leading US airlines. Following the signing of a reciprocal agreement with Spain in September, service to Madrid began on 11 October, and Rome was added on 9 July, 1947.

Although the DC-4s were the flagships of the FAMA fleet, the Lancastrians and Yorks supplemented them on some services, while the Vikings operated to Porto Alegre, São Paulo, and Rio de Janeiro, and to Santiago. During 1947, considerable progress was made in training Argentine national crews, the year having begun with only one wholly Argentine crew.

Service to New York opened on 21 October, 1946, with a DC-4, via Rio de Janeiro, Natal, Belém, Trinidad, and Havana. Some unpressurized Douglases were replaced by the pressurized development of the famous series, the DC-6, in 1948. FAMA's six DC-6s were well fitted out, in a sleeper version with only 26 convertible seats, instead of the normal 46. The Lancastrians having been sold to the Air Force, FAMA's long-distance fleet was all-Douglas by 1949, with the DC-6s providing trunk service, and the DC-4s working the connection from Lisbon to Rome, via Madrid (Lisbon had replaced Madrid as the main European gateway), and the regional services to Chile and Brazil. (see Map 77)

FAMA established an honourable name for itself during the brief years of its existence and can take full credit for putting Argentina on the intercontinental air route map. Although officially taken over by the near-monopoly State airline Aerolíneas Argentinas in 1949, FAMA's young roots were deep enough for it to be still issuing timetables under its own name as late as the summer of 1950.

ALFA

Dr José Dodero's Compañía Argentina de Aeronavegación Dodero purchased the former Italian-sponsored airline Corporación early in May 1946. When, by Decree No.13,632/46, **Aviación del Litoral Fluvial Argentina (ALFA)** was formed on 8 May, 1946, it absorbed Corporación, which constituted the principle sharcholding, and thus Dodero held control. As has already been narrated, however, the shipping magnate withdrew from active participation in the airline business in August 1946, although he continued to be a shareholder.

ALFA began operations under its own name on 1 January, 1947, and on 9 January took over the routes of the military airline LADE which fell within the designated ALFA zones of influence. It also began trans-River Plate services to both Montevideo and Colonia on 15 April, 1947. Thus the LANE route to Posadas and Iguassú Falls gave access to the whole territory between the Uruguay and Paraná Rivers, running parallel as it did with the former Corporación route via Santa Fé and Resistencia to Asunción. Also, ALFA took over the postal services of SADE, so that, curiously, the component parts of the new joint stock company had been drawn from one private airline (Corporación), one military (LANE), and one under the control of the civil aviation authorities (SADE), truly a mixed ancestry.

Equally mixed was the ALFA fleet, resulting from the amalgamation of disparate assets. In 1947, ALFA had six Sandringham flying-boats (of which two were destroyed by a hangar fire on 24 December, 1948), two Douglas DC-3s, including one cargo C-47, seven Noorduyn Norseman, two Beechcraft C-18S, and the two old Macchi C.94s. The DC-3s and the Sandringhams shared the main routes, while the Norseman and Beechcraft shared the postal services.

In addition to the hangar fire which destroyed much equipment and installations, a serious accident to one of its flying-boats in Buenos Aires harbour,

The Short Sandringham 2 G-AGPZ *Argentina*, seen on Belfast Lough in November 1945, was built at Rochester in 1942 as the Sunderland DV964. After conversion at Belfast it was ceremoniously launched on 17 November, 1945, by Señora Dodero and then ferried to Buenos Aires. It operated with ALFA and passed to Aerolíneas Argentinas.

where maximum adverse publicity was the inevitable consequence, seriously damaged ALFA. It pruned its services, cancelling the flights to Rosario, as this was well served by train and the distance was not great. Attempts at recovery then became somewhat irrelevant, as in 1949, along with the other postwar companies, ALFA was taken over by Aerolíneas Argentinas.

ZONDA

The joint-stock company designated to serve the northwest was originally organized on 23 February, 1946, under the name **Líneas Aéreas Argentinas Noroeste (LAAN)** but in June this was changed because of confusion with the Chilean national airline, LAN. With a substantial fleet of seventeen DC-3s and ten de Havilland D.H.89As, plus three Beech Bonanzas and two Avro Ansons, LAAN spent most of its first year in training, making survey flights, and preparing its administration. First operations, still on an ad hoc basis, under the new name **Zonas Oeste y Norte de Aerolíneas Argentinas (ZONDA)** started in August, and the first revenue-earning service, from Buenos Aires (Morón) to Salto was completed in November.

Regular scheduled service began on 2 January, 1947, over a network which was basically the former cabotage network of PANAGRA. These included two nonstop prestige flights *Expreso El Cordobes* and *Expreso El Tucumáno*, thus contributing some much-needed flair in the approach to Argentine domestic schedules which had hitherto not been patronized with great enthusiasm by the traditionally railway-minded Argentines.

ZONDA had ambitions to fly local international services, as permitted under its charter, and a survey flight was made to La Paz, Bolivia, in February 1947. Authority to serve that city was forthcoming in September, as an extension of its northernmost terminus. Through traffic was permitted until such time as FAMA, the designated Argentine long-haul airline, could open direct service from Buenos Aires. However, ZONDA never did start service to La Paz, although in 1948 it did extend its route as far as Yacuiba, just across the Bolivian frontier.

Permission was also given to extend its Mendoza service to Santiago, Chile, in June 1947, and this was duly inaugurated in October 1947, so that there were thus two Argentine airlines serving the Chilean capital, FAMA having also started direct flights from Buenos Aires, using 44-seat Douglas DC-4s. At this time, ZONDA also opened a night service between Buenos Aires and Córdoba.

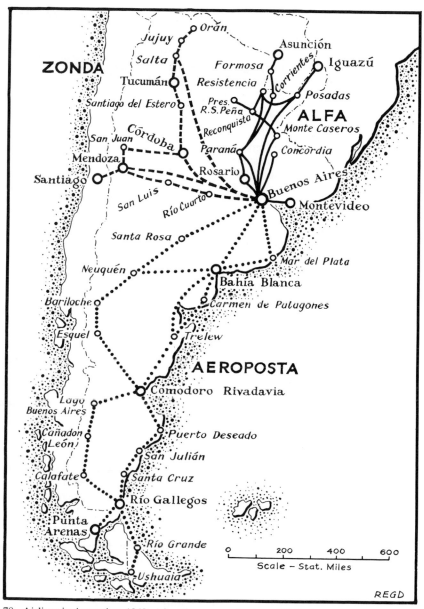

78. Airlines in Argentina, 1949. After the reorganization of 1947, three airlines shared the responsibility of providing domestic air services within Argentina.

Before the formation of Aerolíneas Argentinas, which engulfed ZONDA, negotiations had started to buy a small fleet of Convair CV-240 twin-engined, pressurized airliners to replace the DC-3s, especially for the route to Santiago and the named services to Córdoba and Tucumán. But although ZONDA placed the order, the contract was actually signed by FAMA, and delivery did not take place until after Aerolíneas Argentinas came into existence.

The Last Years of Aeroposta

Under the ownership of the Pueyrredon industrial group, and equipped with three-engined Junkers-Ju 52/3ms, Aeroposta concentrated on assuring reliable service along the important coastal route to the south of Patagonia, and this was its only route until February 1945, when a branch was opened inland from Comodoro Rivadavia. This route, formerly operated by the Territory of Santa Cruz, served the beautiful lake district in the frontier region of Argentina and Chile, along the southern Andes, before returning to the coast at Río Gallegos.

The Government decision of 12 April, 1946, to form mixed-stock companies meant that Aeroposta underwent yet another reorganization and change of ownership, the fifth in its chequered history. Originally named Aeroposta Argentina as a subsidiary of a foreign airline, the French Aéropostale, with operations dating from 1928, its routes had been taken over by the Argentine Post Office in 1931 as Aeroposta Nacional. Then, in 1932, the Argentine Government took a financial interest, enabling the line to continue as Aeroposta Argentina, S.A., until Pueyrredon purchased the company in 1936. Now came the joint stock company, formed on 13 February, 1947, with the Argentine Government acquiring 20 per cent of the shares.

Already, from 1 February, six Douglas DC-3s had augmented the five Junkers, and on 15 May two new routes were added by transfer from LASO, the southern arm of the military airline LADE. The main route was from Buenos Aires to Bariloche and Esquel, via inland points, and the Mar del Plata route also came within Aeroposta's responsibility under the allocated zone system. To the south, the terminus at Río Gallegos was extended to Ushuaia, on the southern side of the island of Tierra del Fuego, and about as far to the south of the continent as it was possible for an aircraft to land. By the time the Government formed **Aerolíneas Argentinas** on 3 May, 1949, additional aircraft had enabled Aeroposta to fill in the gaps in its route network, to co-ordinate its new acquisitions. The new national airline took over a route system which provided adequate service to every community south of Buenos Aires, and the basic network has changed only in minor details to this day. (See Map 78)

Survival of LADE

Under the same Decree No.1,395/47, which transferred all its commercial routes to the new joint stock companies, the military line LADE was reconstituted, with new terms of reference. Instead of opening routes like any other airline, LADE was henceforth charged with developing truly social services, providing flights to communities which could not economically support normal airline service. If, however, these developed into viable routes, LADE was obliged to hand them over to the joint stock companies—effectively Aerolíneas Argentinas, as the former group had ceased to exist by the time LADE route development had progressed to meet this requirement.

568

TABLE 28

Early Argentine Airline Experiments
(Service for less than one year)

Airline (and base)	Date of First Service	Routes	Fleet	Remarks
Aeroclub de Tucumán	(1) 18 March, 1925	Tucumán–Tafi de Valle, Tucumán–Valles del Oeste and Vallés Calchaquies	Curtiss Oriole	Service terminated April 1925
	(2) 1928		Fairchild FC-2	Service terminated after a few months. Resumed by DCA and STA 1931–1937 (see text)
Aero Club de Santiago del Estero	1 July, 1925	Santiago del Estero–Río Hondo		Service ended 30 August, 1925
Aero Club de Rosario	22 January, 1927	Rosario–Victoria	Morane-Saulnier	Service of short duration
Sociedad Franco Argentina de Transportes Aéreos	17 March, 1929	„ „	Potez 32	„ „ „
Aero Club Dolores (Dolores)	16 Nov, 1929	Dolores–Gen Lavalle–Gen Conesa	Curtiss Robin D.H. Moth	
José Elverdin & José Gatti (Rosario)	29 July, 1931	Rosario–Santa Fé–Paraná–Corrientes–Resistencia	Curtiss JN-4	One flight per week, passengers and mail. Service ended 12 October, 1931

Continued on page 570

569

Airline (and base)	Date of First Service	Routes	Fleet	Remarks
Eduardo & Carlos Regunaga (Salta)	27 August, 1931	Salta–Cafayate–Santa Maria–Amaicha del Valle	D.H.80 Puss Moth	One flight every two weeks. Service ended 21 October, 1931 when aircraft crashed (killing Eduardo Regunaga)
Servicio Experimental de Transporte Aéreo (SETA) (Córdoba)	8 February, 1934	Córdoba–Buenos Aires	Three Ae.T.1s	Operated by Aerotecnica (Military Aircraft Factory) by Exec Order 18 Jan, 1934. Service ended 1 October, 1934. 197 passengers carried
José Gatti, Celestino Corbelli, & Juan Arfinetti (Buenos Aires)	29 Sept, 1936	Buenos Aires (San Fernando)–Resistencia	Laté 26	Aircraft ex-Aeroposta. Service ended 31 December, 1936. Passengers, mail, freight
Transportes Aéreos Ranqueles, S.A. (TARSA) (Río Cuarto)	3 January, 1940	Córdoba–Río Cuarto–Vicuña Mackenna–Huinca Renancó	Beech 17	Founded 22 April, 1939, by Roberto Ripamonti. Frequency three a week. Service ended 30 December, 1940

Aerolíneas Argentinas Douglas DC-3 LV-ACD *Ibaté*.

CHAPTER TWENTY-NINE

Argentina Strikes a New Course

Formation of Aerolíneas Argentinas

By the time the newly-formed joint stock companies, created under Decree-Law No.12,911 of 27 April, 1945, had actually started operating, a new political wind was already sweeping through Argentina. Its cutting edge was soon felt, as the new Government, under Juan Perón, took a strictly nationalistic view on the use of all Argentine economic assets; and transport in all its forms was regarded as vital. Thus the lives of the new companies, ALFA, ZONDA, FAMA, and the reconstituted Aeroposta, were short-lived.

On 3 May, 1949, a new State Corporation, **Aerolíneas Argentinas**, was formed as an arm of the Ministry of Transport to take over the operations of the four airlines. The Government already held a 20 per cent share of the three domestic operators, and a 33 per cent share in FAMA. In future, it agreed to underwrite losses and to guarantee a surplus, in partial recognition of the fact that to merge four airlines, which had themselves only recently been formed and suffered the problems of early development, was to invite administrative complication and duplication of effort, if not chaos, on a widespread scale.

At least the new airline inherited a route network which did not suffer from needless overcapacity through duplication, thanks to the system of zoning which had been the keystone of the postwar plan. Thus, Aerolíneas Argentinas took over domestic and international systems which needed little realignment. In particular, the long-distance intercontinental routes, carrying the Argentine flag to Europe and the United States, experienced only the change of name from FAMA.

During its early months of existence, the management of the amalgamated company tried with some success to integrate the many different types of aircraft which it had inherited. Long-distance routes were operated by the FAMA DC-6s, backed up by DC-4s, with the former pressurized type entering service on the

New York route on 21 March, 1950, a date which is claimed to be the inaugural occasion, implying that FAMA's services had not been flown with complete regularity—a shortcoming, however, which was all too common among the first postwar airlines the world over. The old British converted bomber types had already been retired, but the Sandringhams were retained for routes along the Paraná and Uruguay Rivers to the north, as far as Asunción, and to Montevideo. In September 1950 the Convair CV-240s originally ordered by ZONDA went into service to the northwest and to the important cities of Córdoba, Mendoza, and Santiago, Chile. Elsewhere the trusty old DC-3s, ex-Aeroposta and other companies, continued to provide the lifeline to Patagonia and to cities where the landing weight of the new aircraft was still too much for the airfields.

By 7 December, 1950, the route system was completely integrated. In April 1952, the administration acquired greater autonomy by being transferred to the National Transport Corporation, which, under the Government of the day, was given supreme power over all forms of transport (the railways too, mostly British-owned, had also been nationalized, as was shipping). The following month, Aerolíneas joined IATA, but this did not herald any significant expansion overseas. Indeed, the only major route extension during the first decade of the airline's existence was to open a DC-4 service, early in 1953, to Santa Cruz, Bolivia, in conjunction with LAB. At this time, Santa Cruz did not enjoy a rail or road connection with the rest of Bolivia, although the rail link was completed a few months later.

An attempt was made in 1954 to extend the Santa Cruz route to Lima, Peru, but the northernmost point remained at La Paz, reached in 1955, where the paved runway could accept DC-6s, in spite of its 13,000 feet elevation. Santa Cruz, unfortunately, boasted only a dirt strip.

Politically, the 1950s were not exactly the best years for Aerolíneas Argentinas. Juan Perón was sent abruptly into exile when a military coup terminated the dictatorship on 16 September, 1955, and set up, in November of that year, a provisional government under General Aramburu, whose affirmed policy was to restore civil liberties, and to allow more freedom for private enterprise.

The Aerolíneas Argentinas Douglas DC-6 LV-ADS, seen over Buenos Aires, was delivered to FAMA in September 1948 and taken over by Aerolíneas Argentinas the following May and named *17 de Octubre*. It was renamed *Mariano Moreno* but names were removed from some aircraft after the overthrow of the Perón government. LV-ADS broke up in a storm while flying from Asunción to Buenos Aires on 7 September, 1960, and crashed near Salto in Uruguay. (*Aerolíneas Argentinas*)

The monopoly position held by Aerolíneas Argentinas came to an end on 12 July, 1956, when Decree-Law No.12,507/56 set down principles for granting temporary operating certificates to private airlines. Reinforced by Decree-Law No.1,256/57 and extended by 14,467/57, which gave definition to the manner of governmental control, including a system of subsidy, the measure was intended to be an interim step while a new Master Plan for Argentine air routes was being prepared. This, however, never materialized, as the operating environment was in something of a turmoil. During 1957, Aerolíneas Argentinas suffered badly in popular esteem when three of its aircraft crashed, with some loss of lives. Then, on 22 February, 1958, Dr Arturo Frondisi was elected President in the first free elections for twelve years, leading immediately to administrative changes in many quarters. In May 1958, the entire management of Aerolíneas Argentinas resigned, and the Government appointed a new airline President, Colonel Guiraldes, formerly with the Government airline LADE.

As a parting gesture, one of the last acts of the old management was to place an order, in April, for six de Havilland Comet 4 jet airliners, a visionary decision which was to come as a much-needed morale-booster for a sadly demoralized airline, affected as it was not only from its poor safety record, but also from the inroads made on its markets, both domestic and international, by a new breed of private airlines.

Transcontinental

One of the first, and certainly the one which provided Aerolíneas Argentinas with the biggest intercontinental challenge, was **Transcontinental, S.A., (TSA)** formed on 5 September, 1956, by a group of private Argentine investors, inspired by Jorge Carnicero, who was connected with a United States non-scheduled airline, California Eastern, which leased aircraft in exchange for a 25 per cent shareholding. All flight personnel were of US nationality, but these were to be replaced by Argentines by 1962.

Transcontinental began operations in 1957 with a fleet of four Curtiss C-46s and three Lockheed 1049H Super Constellations. The C-46s entered service on a domestic and local network which was notable for including the most desirable destinations: Córdoba, Tucumán, Salta, and Mendoza—some of the largest cities in Argentina—together with Mar del Plata, the seaside resort, and Montevideo, the Uruguayan capital. The Super Constellations opened a service to New York in September 1958 and to the mountain and lake resort of Bariloche, fast-growing in popularity, in February 1959.

Already, however, TSA had greater ambitions. In August 1958, it ordered two Britannia 305 propeller-turbine airliners from the Bristol Aeroplane Company (formerly ordered by Northeast Airlines), and these went into service on the New York route in March 1960. In October, Santiago, Chile, and Miami were added to the impressive network, while Asunción was included in 1961. Thus, the airline appeared to be going to 'all the best places'; moreover, its on-board service was good, and its schedules convenient. It demonstrated its confidence by ordering Convair CV-440s for domestic routes, and Convair CV-880s for international.

But pride came before a fall. Although a rescue operation was attempted in the Spring of 1961 by SABENA, the Belgian airline, TSA suspended operations on 8 November, 1961. Its finances were such that one of its Britannias was temporarily impounded in New York, but was later released on payment of $83,000 in cash owed for fees and fuel.

Negotiations began immediately for Transcontinental to be taken over by Austral, a new domestic airline whose fortunes were on a more even keel. In May 1962, Decree No.3,727/62 ratified this arrangement. Austral added the domestic routes to its network (though it lost Salta and Tucumán soon afterwards) while Aerolíneas Argentinas inherited the intercontinental—though this was an academic exercise, as no new points were actually served. Transcontinental was officially declared bankrupt in September 1962.

Aerolíneas Ini

About a year after the founding of Transcontinental, a second privately-owned Argentine airline got under way. Backed by Señor José Ini, a prominent and wealthy Argentine businessman, who owned 73 per cent of the stock, **Aerolíneas Ini y Cía** was formed late in 1957 and applied for permission to operate to the United States. In January 1960, a DC-4 service started to Miami, with fares substantially lower than those of the IATA members, and in September 1960 DC-6s were introduced to offer pressurized comfort.

Ini's route was via the South American west coast. At first, with the DC-4s, stops were made at Santiago, Antofagasta, Lima, Guayaquil, and Panamá; but with the longer range of the DC-6s, Santiago and Guayaquil were omitted. However, a stop was made at Córdoba, for traffic-generating reasons.

At this time, the struggle for airline markets was raging throughout Latin America. On the one hand was the Establishment, represented by the IATA carriers such as Aerolíneas Argentinas and Panair do Brasil—who, officially at least, complied with the fares and rates laid down by international agreement. On the other hand was a group of airlines who dared to challenge the established order, and, in an attempt to attract traffic, offered low fares to the public as an inducement. Down the west coast of South America, such competition was taking on new dimensions, with a group of airlines from different countries challenging PANAGRA's supremacy and dominance. While Ini's fare level was not at such a low rate, it was nevertheless low enough to make the whole operation financially precarious.

On 1 July, 1960, Ini appears to have changed its policy, and joined IATA; but its problems lay deeper than the mere setting of fares. By the end of 1963, the company reported a loss of $300,000 during the year, and was prepared to go into liquidation. The end was near. By the time IATA announced Ini's official resignation on 23 November, 1964, Aerolíneas Argentinas had already been given permission to operate Ini's route, which it proceeded to do in its own time a year later, with a Comet 4 service to Miami, with only one stop, at Lima.

Transatlántica

Third among the new international Argentine airlines was **Transatlántica Argentina, S.A. de Aeronavegación**, formed by a group of ex-Air Force officers in March 1958. After some delays in obtaining equipment and the necessary operating authority, both at home and overseas, service was eventually started on 21 September, 1960, using a fleet of three Lockheed 1649A Starliners on a route to Zürich, via Rio de Janeiro, Recife, and Lisbon. This route was later changed to serve Dakar instead of Recife, and, for a short while terminated at Tel Aviv, with Geneva substituted for Zürich.

Transatlántica joined IATA on 1 July, 1961, a somewhat academic exercise, as

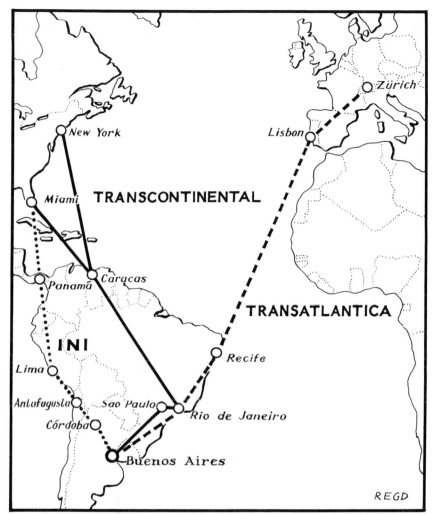

79. Argentine Independent International Airlines, 1960. For a short period during the 1960s, three private airlines were able to operate international routes from Buenos Aires.

by November its services were described as 'totally paralysed', its staff were not being paid, and there were accusations of fraudulent bankruptcy. All routes were suspended late in February 1962, and the operating rights transferred to Aerolíneas Argentinas. On 21 August, 1962, the airline resigned from IATA—less than a year after having joined—and ceased to exist.

The three new independent airlines, born as the direct result of the release from Perón's tightly-controlled state monopoly system when President Frondisi came to power, combined to enact a story of disappointment, at the same time carrying a simple lesson to other aspiring airline promoters. Theirs was a classic example of inexperience breeding over-confidence in entering a complex technological and commercial world, facing competition from tough, well-capitalized State or

575

The Aerolíneas Argentinas de Havilland Comet 4 LV-AHN *Las Tres Marias* seen flying on test with the temporary registration LV-PLM. (*British Aerospace*)

State-supported airlines, with no quarter asked nor given. Also, they entered the arena just when a new age of fast jet aircraft were appearing, so that DC-6Bs, Starliners, and even Britannias were no match for the glamorous new machines. Indeed, the Argentine national airline stressed this aspect only too emphatically.

The First Jets in South America

Aerolíneas Argentinas took delivery of its first Comet 4, named *Las Tres Marias*, on 2 March, 1959, and after proving flights on the main trunk routes, introduced the first commercial jet air service in South America on 16 April with regular service from Buenos Aires to Santiago. These were stirring times for an airline which had had to survive a painful period in its history, weathering the storm of criticism because of crashes and the uncertainty of a change of management. It was a source of pride, therefore, when, in quick succession, aircraft in the Argentine's light blue colours opened the world's first jet service both across the South Atlantic and between North and South America. On 19 May, the Comets started flying to Europe, alternating to Rome and Frankfurt, or Paris and London, after stopping at Rio de Janeiro, Recife, Dakar, and Madrid; and, on 7 June, began service to New York, via Rio de Janeiro and Port of Spain. In fact, among the world's trunk air routes, Aerolíneas jet service had been preceded only by BOAC's Comet 4s and Pan American's Boeing 707s on the North Atlantic,

One of the fleet of Hawker Siddeley HS.748s delivered to Aerolíneas Argentinas, LV-PIZ seen here carried the title Avro 748 on its fin. This example was delivered in January 1962, reregistered LV-HGW, named *Ciudad de Bahía Blanca*, and was written off at Corrientes in February 1970. (*British Aerospace*)

and by BOAC, Air France, and UAT Comet 1 operations; and by Aeroflot Tupolev Tu-104s.

Tragically, Aerolíneas lost two of its Comets within a year, happily without passenger fatalities. On 26 August, 1959, one crashed near Asunción, where it had been diverted because of runway work at Rio de Janeiro; and in February 1960, one was lost on a training flight at Buenos Aires. At this time, the Comets were averaging 10 hr a day in revenue service, a high level by any standards, and so the loss to the airline schedules was substantial. However, affairs kept on an even keel in 1961, which began by the welcome renewal of the United States operating permit in January. On 14 March the airline ordered nine Avro 748 twin propeller-turbine airliners for feeder services, followed by three Sud-Aviation Caravelle twin-jets in August for domestic trunk and regional routes. A point of interest in this latter purchase is that it was the first sale of the French short-haul jet to be completed through the agency of the Douglas Aircraft Company, with which Sud-Aviation had concluded a marketing agreement.

The Aerolíneas Argentinas Sud-Aviation Caravelle VIN LV-HGZ *Rigel* was delivered in October 1962 as LV-PVU, went to the Argentine Air Force in July 1963 as T-92 and in 1976 was sold in the United States.

Then fate frowned on Aerolíneas Argentinas once again, when a third Comet, the *Arco Iris*, was lost at São Paulo, leaving a fleet of only three. The political repercussions within Argentina were such that Brig Miguel Moraguez, President of Aerolíneas, who had ordered the Comets, was forced to resign. All things considered, the airline demonstrated considerable equanimity by pressing on with its modernization programme. The first Avro 748 flew from Buenos Aires to Punta del Este on 15 February, 1962, and went into service to Bahía Blanca on 2 April. The previous day, on 1 April, Caravelle service began to the resort city of San Carlos de Bariloche, and with the old Convair-Liners and Sandringhams being retired, Aerolíncas Argentinas took on a brave new look.

The Convair-Liners were sold to the Paraguayan Air Force at the end of the year, and the Sandringhams were simply phased out after seventeen years of honourable service across the Río Plata and up the big rivers. The Argentine travelling public was, in fact, loath to say good-bye to the old flying-boats, because, flying as they did from the Hidropuerto of Buenos Aires, close to the business area of the city, city-centre journey times still compared well with their faster replacements. At least for the short busy air trip to Montevideo, sentimental journeys could still be taken in the last of an aircraft dynasty by taking the Uruguayan CAUSA flight. The Argentine Sandringhams eventually went to the Cooperativa Asociación Argentina de Aeronavegantes.

577

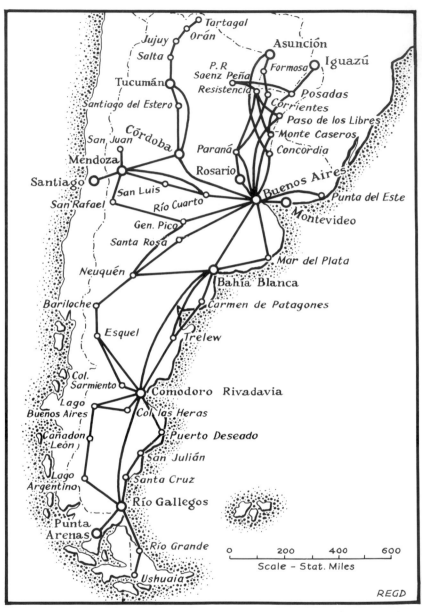

80. Aerolíneas Argentinas, 1962. After a period of unsettled political conditions, Aerolíneas Argentinas established a permanent domestic route structure.

Aerolíneas Argentinas was not quite out of the wood yet. On 28 August, 1962, there was a highly publicised incident when a door fell off an Avro 748 while in flight, with an apparently similar incident two days later when an engineer tried to reproduce the symptoms. The controversy raged for a few days until a group of 32 pilots took the unprecedented step of taking an advertisement in a Buenos Aires newspaper to express their full confidence in the aircraft. Their faith was fully justified. The Avros quickly clocked up an impressive record of reliability, flying at an annual rate of 3,000 hr, with some individual aircraft reaching 16 hr a day. Such utilization would be praiseworthy in normal operating conditions. The performance of the Avros was especially commendable, as the climate in Patagonia was no better than in the days when the winds blew St-Exupéry and his comrades of Aeroposta out to sea; and the airfields in the Andean foothills were often no more than cleared strips among open scrub country. At one of these, a visiting journalist remarked that he 'had heard of unprepared strips, but this one seemed positively taken by surprise.'

An Argentine Second Force Airline

While Aerolíneas's fortunes alternated between dizzy success and abject despair during the volatile years from 1957 to 1962, a new threat appeared in the form of one or two small airlines which, like their more ambitious contemporaries, Transcontinental, Ini, and Transatlántica, had been founded as a result of President Juan Perón's fall from power in 1955 and the conditions of Decree-Law No.12,507 and subsequent amendments. The first of these new aspirants to the commercial air business was **Aerotransportes Litoral Argentina (A.L.A.)**, formed the same year in Rosario by members of the Argentine Air Force Transport Command, who were also associated with Transatlántica. Starting with a small fleet of Aero Commanders, A.L.A. concentrated on providing a frequent service between Buenos Aires and Rosario, Argentina's second city, together with a few other short routes from Rosario. This operation was unsuccessful, and in 1958 the company was reorganized, and six DC-3s were acquired to replace the Aero Commanders. A.L.A. also entered into a co-operative agreement with another small airline, Primera Línea Aérea Santafecina (PLAS), founded in 1958 in Santa Fé, and which operated Lockheed Model 10 Electras to Buenos Aires.

Meanwhile, in February 1957, **Austral**, Compañía Argentina de Transportes Aéreos, S.A., was formed with the backing of two industrial companies, Luís de Ridder and Menendez Behety.

The latter was apparently reviving an interest in airline operations, long dormant since an unsuccessful venture in 1920. The company was originally named Aerovías Monder, founded on 14 December 1955, and registered as Austral on 23 June, 1957, and began to operate non-scheduled services to Miami, using Curtiss C-46s. In January 1958, Austral began scheduled services along the Patagonian coast to Río Gallegos. In November 1960, it was permitted to make the short international air link from Río Gallegos to Punta Arenas, Chile's important free port on the Straits of Magellan.

In November 1961, Austral doubled the area served by taking over the services of Transcontinental, when that airline suspended all services. Austral was permitted to integrate the routes and to acquire the assets, including the personnel, of the defunct airline, and Decree No.3,727/62 confirmed what was effectively a merger. The airline was, however, not in a position to benefit from its new authority to serve such cities as Córdoba, Tucumán, Mendoza, and Bariloche

579

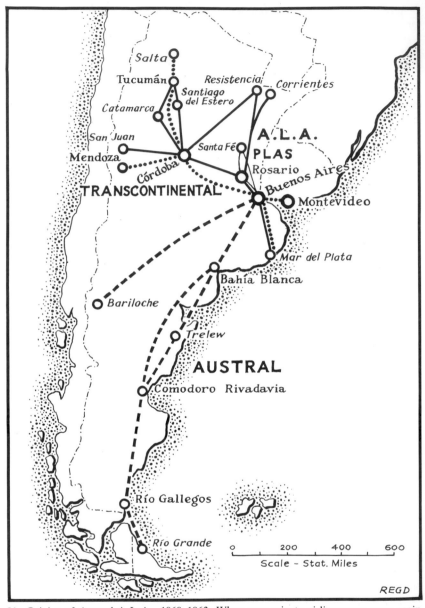

81. Origins of Austral-A.L.A., 1960–1963. When new private airlines were once again permitted to operate in Argentina in the 1960s, a second national airline was fashioned by combining the route structures of several small companies, including the residual domestic network of Transcontinental.

because it was still operating C-46s. Its State-owned rival, Aerolíneas Argentinas, on the other hand, had introduced the Avro 748s on domestic services, and had a clearcut advantage in technical excellence and passenger appeal. As a consequence, Austral's traffic declined severely. In 1963, only 71,000 passengers were carried, compared with 128,000 in 1961, and the nadir of the airline's fortunes occurred during the Spring of 1962 when it was unable to pay the salaries of its employees.

In 1963, the Argentine Government finally published its Master Plan for Argentine domestic air routes, through Decree No.8,528/63. Austral was compelled to withdraw from the northern route to Tucumán and Salta (one of the lines inherited from Transcontinental); but A.L.A. was permitted to fly to Montevideo, Uruguay, and to Asunción, Paraguay.

Airlines which operated within Argentina during the late 1950s had faced severe financial problems, as fares were very low, about £4 for the 400-mile flight from Buenos Aires to Córdoba, for instance. Fares were increased on 1 June, 1958, but this was still insufficient to cover costs adequately.

The Government authorized a subsidy of 53 million pesos to Austral and 37 million to A.L.A. to cover losses in 1962, and 51 million and 41 million respectively for 1963, giving a welcome relief from financial stringency. At this time also, Pan American Airways took an interest in Austral, amounting to 22 per cent of the shareholding, and Douglas DC-6B service replaced the aging C-46s on major routes. In 1966, Austral and A.L.A. began to work in co-operation, the latter airline having moved its headquarters to Buenos Aires. The arrangement gained favour with the Government, partly because it was a more efficient way of operating, and because the merged airline was one which stood a chance of maintaining financial viability, simply because of the greater economies derived from being a larger operating unit. One way in which the Government confirmed its approval was to award Austral-A.L.A. some mail contracts previously held by the railways.

The year 1967 was one of great significance to the Argentine domestic airline industry, as it was virtually the turning point at which the sharing of the route network between State and private companies was recognized on a permanent basis. Decree-Law No.17,285/67—known as the Código Aeronáutico—superseded Decree No.12,507/56 and confirmed the co-existence of State and private concerns, a move which was popularly interpreted as the Government's way of forcing Aerolíneas Argentinas to improve its efficiency. Effectively, Austral-A.L.A. became the second-force airline, and it moved immediately to consolidate its new-found strength.

Austral's BAC One-Eleven 420EL LV-JGY was delivered in December 1968 and written off at San Carlos de Bariloche in November 1977. (*Courtesy, Barrie James*)

Austral's NAMC YS-11A-309 LV-JII in 1974-style livery. (*Courtesy, Barrie James*)

In fairly quick order, Austral revolutionized its fleet. In June 1967, it signed a contract for four 74-seat BAC One-Eleven 400 twin-jet airliners from the British Aircraft Corporation, and put the first one into service in January 1968. In 1969, it acquired three 58-seat Nihon YS-11s for routes where the airfields could not accept the jets, and at the end of the year added four more BAC One-Elevens, the larger 500 series.

During 1967 also, Austral had acquired a majority interest in Lagos del Sur, S.A. which owned resort hotels and other amenities in the mountain lake region near Bariloche. On 1 January, 1971, the airline established Sol Jet S.R.L. for the purpose of operating inclusive air tours (viajes todo comprendido—V.T.C.) in close co-operation with Lagos del Sur. V.T.C. flights began on a systematic basis on 29 January, 1971.

Everything fell into place in 1971. Decree-Laws Nos.6,875/71 and 19,030/71 modified the system of subsidies, to the airlines' benefit. On 26 March, 1971, Austral and A.L.A. amalgamated to form **Austral Líneas Aéreas, S.A.**, gaining Government recognition on 10 May through the provisions of Decree No.1,119/71. This important measure preserved a fine balance of positive and negative articles in the published document. Austral was allowed to augment its capital to a total of 15 million pesos, to be subscribed in six annual stages, and the debts owed to State agencies, including the Y.P.F., the oil monopoly, were wiped out. On the other hand, in a 'once-and-for-all' clause, the Decree firmly restricted the merger to its joint assets at the time. The new Austral was not allowed to buy, sell, transfer, or lease any operating equipment, nor was it allowed to invest in any other companies. In a fascinating reversal of roles, Austral was now seen as a threat to the State airline, and the Government had found that, by encouraging Austral to provide that threat, the perky little penguin which was Austral's symbol was now showing shark-like tendencies.

McDonnell Douglas DC-9-82 N10027 was one of two DC-9-82s delivered to Austral on 8 January, 1981. The aircraft have overall white fuselages with red upper stripe, blue lower stripe and red and blue AU on the forward fuselage. (*McDonnell Douglas Corporation*)

582

In 1973, Austral started to make profits, and for two years rode the crest of a wave, until the depression of 1975/76, caused by political revolution and massive inflation, brought on a new crisis. The Argentine Government stepped in with more regulations, and caused havoc in the private sector by promulgating Decree No.986/74, which aimed to reduce Austral's influence by terminating certain concessions and redistributing some routes—in favour of Aerolíneas Argentinas. However, the tariff system was modified to relate revenues more logically with costs, and losses were permitted to be carried over into subsequent years. Both sides, private and State, criticised the Government, but the latter seems to have weathered the political storms of an extremely difficult period. Though both Austral and Aerolíneas Argentinas continually claimed that the other side had received unfair advantage, the fact that Argentine commercial aviation retained its equilibrium throughout very difficult times is an indication that the authorities distributed the spoils justly.

The Third Force

In addition to the three short-lived intercontinental aspirants and what was to become the Austral-A.L.A. partnership, no less than a dozen other small companies rushed to join the airline ranks in Argentina when Decree No.12,507/56 was seen by many investors to open the flood-gates to some easy business successes. As has happened so often, when a State-owned or dominant carrier has been imagined to be negligent and missing opportunities, most of the new private airlines which were founded during the five years following the change of government policy did not last the course, so that the national carrier and the resilient Austral benefitted by default.

The activities of the small companies are listed and summarized in Table 29. With a few exceptions, their impact on Argentine commercial aviation was slight, but a few are worthy of mention. **Aero Chaco,** for instance, has managed to survive to this day, providing as it does a valuable social feeder service to the communities in the north central plains of Argentina, mainly in Chaco Province. Founded at Resistencia by private capital, together with the provincial administration and the local aero club, Aero Chaco- Líneas Aéreas Chaqueñas started life in 1958 with two ten-seat de Havilland Canada DHC-2 Beavers. Its performance was such that it qualified for subsidy from the Argentine Government, as it was rightly considered to be providing essential transport in an area which lacked alternative surface communications.

Transportes Aéreos Buenos Aires (TABA) was another 1958 airline fortunate enough to receive subsidy from the Government in the early 1960s, although the justification does not appear to have been so clearcut as in the case of Aero Chaco. TABA operated mainly eight-seat Beech C-45s in the Province of Buenos Aires and, in spite of having to co-exist with reasonable road and rail networks, outlasted many other small feeder airlines.

Another small airline which looked likely to make the grade was **Líneas Aéreas de Cuyo**, which was granted a 15-year concession in 1958 to operate from the important western city of Mendoza, so as to provide hub services from the west to the north, south, and to the coast, without passengers having to travel circuitously via Buenos Aires. By 1959, Cuyo was operating a daily service from Mendoza to Buenos Aires, using Aero Commanders and a Lodestar. However, this promising enterprise ceased to exist in July 1960.

Apart from PLAS which operated in association with A.L.A. one other

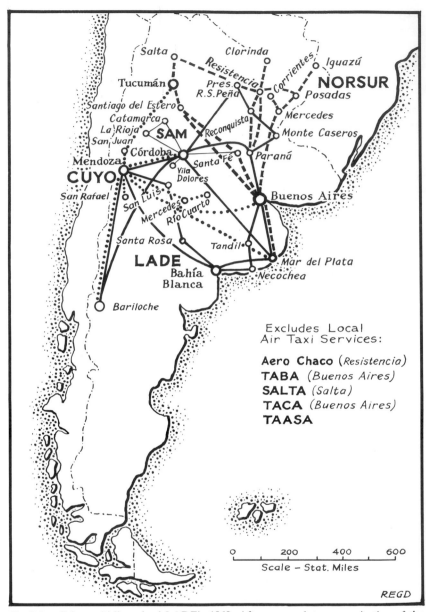

82. Other Private Airlines (and LADE), 1960. After a complete reorganization of the airline structure in Argentina, several small airlines operated limited route networks, supplementing those of the trunk airlines.

This ex-Canadian Armed Forces Canadair CC-106 Yukon was operated by Aerotransportes Entre Rios as LV-JSY from 1970 until it was written off in a crash at Miami on 27 September, 1975. (*Harold G. Martin*)

company established what was more than merely a local Third Level commuter network. **Norsur**, Compañía Argentina de Aeronavegación, also started in 1958 (the timetables must have been most confusing in that year to the Argentine air travellers familiar only with Aerolíneas Argentinas). Its fleet of three 14-seat Lockheed Lodestars duplicated to a large extent both those of A.L.A. and Aerolíneas, but the airline withdrew from the scene in the mid-1960s.

Aerolíneas Argentinas Consolidates

The early 1960s were years of stress and strain for Aerolíneas Argentinas. Although beset with the problems caused by the loss of half its Comet fleet, the dramatic saving of time on the South Atlantic route to Europe was such that its competitive advantage was maintained in spite of the handicap, to such an extent that its competitors exerted considerable pressure from both sides of the tariff-setting spectrum. On the one hand, non-scheduled and non-IATA airlines cut fares; yet IATA would not allow Aerolíneas to apply a special surcharge for jet travel (as, some years later, was allowed to British Airways and Air France for Concorde flights—the time-saving differential being of the same order). The dispute culminated in Aerolíneas Argentinas resigning from IATA on 7 June, 1963, a move which, in aviation circles, was the equivalent of a cleric renouncing the Holy Trinity.

Nevertheless, co-operation continued at the individual airline level, and during 1963–4 pool agreements were signed with Iberia, Alitalia, and Panair do Brasil. By this time, happily, the incipient challenge from the trio of intercontinental Argentine private airlines had evaporated, and although Aerolíneas did not need the routes to Europe, it gladly accepted the certificate previously held by Aerolíneas Ini. Government permission was granted in May 1964, and a Comet service to Miami, with a stop only in Lima, started the following year, by which time, one Comet 4C had been received to replace one of the crashed aircraft.

One reason why the Comet fleet was not augmented further was because a new management had taken over in June 1964. Reacting to powerful criticism of all kinds of irregularities, ranging from administrative bungling to smuggling, a complete new board of directors took over, under the command of Brig-Gen (R) Guillermo Zinny. The General set about his work with vigour, and one of his main goals was to invest in a new fleet of aircraft which could match the growing competition from larger jet aircraft. All the leading manufacturers of the day vied

The Aerolíneas Argentinas Boeing 707-387B LV-ISC *Betelgeuse* in the two-tone blue livery introduced in 1970.

for Aerolíneas Argentinas's favours, and Boeing won. An order for four Boeing 707-320Bs was placed on 5 February, 1965, and ratified by President Illía on 15 September. The occasion seems to have been celebrated by the airline making its peace with IATA, which it rejoined on 6 October, 1965, that august body having forgiven alleged fare violations.

Another political upheaval, in June 1966, brought in a new administration, with Brigadier (R) Arnaldo Tesselhoff at its head. Although the Decree-Law No.17,285/67—the Codígo Aeronáutico—kept Aerolíneas Argentinas's steel collar in place at home, 1967 was a year in which its horizons were much broader. On 15 December, 1966, the first Boeing 707 service had opened, to New York, and on 3 April, 1967, the 142-seat jets replaced the Comets on the routes to Europe. At the time, the Comets were averaging 72 per cent load factors, so the Boeings were able to consolidate on a firm traffic base. The Dakar stop was eliminated; and on one service, the Rio de Janeiro–Rome segment was the world's longest nonstop air route at the time—5,700 miles. Zürich was re-introduced as a European destination, and all the Comets were transferred from long-distance routes to regional services.

Negotiations began during 1968 to begin service to the west coast of the United States, and the necessary sanction was forthcoming in February 1969 when President Nixon approved a US foreign carrier permit to fly to Los Angeles, via Lima, Bogotá, and Mexico City. Such was Aerolíneas's mood at the time that an

The Boeing 737-287 LV-LIW was delivered to Aerolíneas Argentinas in December 1974.

586

extension to Tokyo was freely discussed. Boeing 707s opened service on 15 June, 1969, and shortly afterwards the fares were reduced to match those of non-IATA competitors.

On the home front, Aerolíneas Argentinas had to respond to the challenge of Austral's BAC One-Eleven jets, against which the sturdy Avro 748s, though splendidly able to cope with unprepared strips, were no match on domestic inter-city work. Two Nihon YS-11s met a capacity shortage during the peak holiday season in December 1967, on routes to Mar del Plata and Punta del Este, Uruguay, but this was only an interim step before placing an order worth $25 million for six 115-seat Boeing 737-200 twin-jets. These were destined to replace both the Comets and the Caravelles on mainline domestic services.

The 1970s witnessed more alarums and excursions in the efforts of Aerolíneas Argentinas to keep its affairs on an even keel. In March 1971, Lt-Gen Alejandro A. Lanusse took over the Argentine Presidency and ordered a return to civilian government; Decree No.19,030/71 superseded 12,507/56 to consolidate the rights of the private airlines to co-exist with the State corporation. After considerable manoeuvring, a general agreement was reached on 1 December, 1972, between Aerolíneas Argentinas and Austral. The internal routes of Argentina were classified into two categories, low- and high-load factor, effectively feeder and trunk. The former were divided between the two companies, while the latter were to be operated under a pooling system, avoiding the more ruthless aspects of competition, and to be presided over by a benevolent civil air administration. Austral surrendered operating rights to neighbouring countries, except Uruguay.

The Argentine Air Force's Fokker F.27-400M Troopship TC-72 was delivered in June 1969 and written off in March 1975. In 1981 a new TC-72 was delivered to LADE. When operating LADE services the F.27s were, at least on some occasions, simply marked Fuerza Aérea Argentina. (*Fokker B.V.*)

The Argentine Government airline, Líneas Aéreas del Estado (LADE) continued in its familiar role of providing much-needed social services in areas where other airlines were unable to operate under commercial conditions. By the late 1970s, LADE was operating mainly in Patagonia, with most of its activity centred on Comodoro Rivadavia. Its fleet consisted of propeller-turbine Fokker F.27 and de Havilland Canada DHC-6 Twin Otter, and Fokker F.28 twin-jets.

One of its routes, started in 1972, was to the Falkland Islands, a remnant of the former British Empire, situated about 400 miles east of southern Patagonia. This served as a valuable supply line to the islanders who were otherwise isolated from most of the creature comforts of the modern world. Argentina has, for many years, laid claim to the islands (called the Islas Malvinas in Buenos Aires) which no doubt prevented LADE from claiming to be an international airline. This useful service came to an abrupt and tragic end when hostilities erupted on 2 April, 1982, between Argentina and Great Britain, and the likelihood of its early resumption is remote.

While an uneasy harmony may have been achieved within Argentina, the battle standards were raised abroad. Having started a one-stop Buenos Aires–Los Angeles service, via Lima only, on 19 May, 1972, Aerolíneas then became embroiled in a squabble with the US authorities over the rights of Pan American and Braniff International Airways, both serving Argentina. On 14 August, the Argentine Government denied Pan American's request for expanded authority, and followed this on 7 September by informing Braniff that its Fifth Freedom rights from Buenos Aires to both La Paz and Santiago would be refused until the end of the year. Regarding this as a provocation, the United States imposed restrictions on Aerolíneas as a retaliatory measure which, if effective, would have cut services by 42 per cent. Cooler heads seem to have prevailed, and a modus operandi was agreed at the end of the year, partially resolving the areas of disagreement and 'reaching an accommodation for the time being'.

This settled, route development continued, with the addition, on 2 April, 1973, of the important trans-South Atlantic route to Cape Town, at a frequency of two a month, alternating with South African Airways. On 6 May, 1973, nonstop service to Miami began. Then the political storms blew up again. Hector J. Campora had been elected President of Argentina in March 1973, to be succeeded almost immediately—and dramatically— on 12 October by ex-President Juan Perón, returning from exile. Following Argentine custom, a new management took over the airline in December, under President Cesar Aurelio Guasco, a retired major-general with Air Force and civil aviation experience, supported by a director-general, Juan Carlos Pellegrini, formerly with Austral. Under this leadership, the commercial department was restructured, new airport facilities were commissioned, the transition to an all-jet fleet was accelerated, and a bright new look given to the company, including a modern paint scheme on the aircraft. Domestic fares at this time were increased by 50 per cent, to cope with galloping inflation, and a policy adopted under which the airline was not expected to operate internal routes as a subsidized social service, but on a strictly commercial basis.

Then began a long-drawn period of evaluation to acquire a fleet of wide-bodied jet aircraft. A statement was made in January 1975 that two Boeing 747s would be ordered, subject to Government approval. Two years later, the first Boeing 747 service, to Madrid, Rome, and Frankfurt, left Buenos Aires on 5 January, 1977, using a 364-seat version leased from Boeing, but it was not until June 1978 that the firm order was finally placed, for three 747-200Bs, worth $160 million. The order was not officially announced, in fact, until January 1979, such were the complications involved in a procurement decision of such magnitude.

Charter flights with Boeing 707s and 747s began across the Antarctic continent to Auckland, New Zealand, in April 1981. On 6 September, 1981, regular monthly flights began from Buenos Aires to Auckland nonstop, using the 747-200B, and occasionally the SP version. Thus, although the Chilean airline had pioneered the Antarctic route, Aerolíneas Argentinas had the honour of being the first airline to operate a scheduled air service across the world's 'last continent'.

Fleet modernization proceeded also in the lower echelons of the fleet list. Early

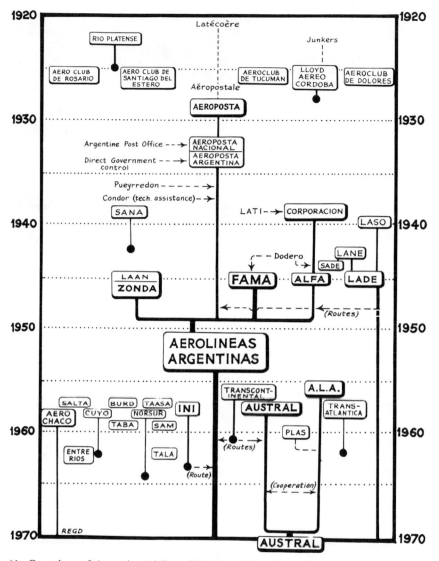

11. Genealogy of Argentine Airlines. This chart shows the complex development of the Argentine airline system during its first 50 years. Early experiments were short-lived. The first airline, Aeroposta, merged with others to form a monopoly. Then a change of policy allowed free entry to many aspirants to the airline business; but these too gave way to essentially a two-airline system.

This Aerolíneas Argentinas Boeing 747 does not appear to carry any identification markings. (*The Boeing Company*)

in 1975, three 65-seat Fokker F.28-1000 twin-jet airliners replaced the last of the Avro 748s still operating in the region between the big rivers, where airfields were still marginal for larger and heavier jets. In December 1978, the first Boeing 727-200s, fitted with 155 seats, arrived for service on major regional and domestic trunk routes.

Juan Perón died on 1 July, 1974, and his wife, Isobel, became President of Argentina until 23 March, 1976, when a military junta took over the reins of government. The airline structure remained unchanged.

Aerolíneas's world today is one of big business, travel to sophisticated tourist resorts, delicate international negotiations and rivalry, and precarious domestic politics. Unlike many other national airlines, whose progress has normally been favoured by stable and continuous government support, and whose management has changed only infrequently, Aerolíneas has had to suffer the frustrations and irritations of ever-changing management and control, see-sawing government policies, bitter domestic rivalries, and innumerable scandals, some real, some imagined. That it has come through these trials to continue to provide good public service, and to maintain Argentina's prestige on the world's air routes, often with distinction, betrays an innate devotion to a cause which has somehow survived every hazard. The perils of Aéropostale's Patagonian route in 1928 may have been more adventurous in the physical sense; but the inheritors of St-Exupéry's tradition may be judged to have weathered just as many perils, and to have emerged as a credit to the nation.

TABLE 29
Small Argentine Airlines
(Following Decree 12.507/56)

Airline	Date of Foundation	Routes	Fleet	Remarks
Taxis Aéreos Argentinas S.A. (TAASA)	1946	Buenos Aires to seven cities in province of Entre Rios	6 D.H.89A Fairchild 24 Stinson 108	Created by Decree 179/47. Began Service Jan 1949. Service ended 1959
Servicios Aéreos Burd	1957	Rosario–Victoria	2 Pipers	
Transporte Aéreo Costa Atlantica (TACA)	1957	Local network in province of Buenos Aires	1 Norseman 1 Cessna 170	Service ended 1962
Sociedad Argentina de Líneas de Transportes Aéreo (SALTA)	1957	Salta–San Pedro–Orán–Embarcación	1 Anson 3 Cessna T-50	Service ended 1959
Norsur	1958		8 Lodestar	Started operations March 1958
Primera Línea Aérea Santafecina (PLAS)	1958	Santa Fé–Rosario–Buenos Aires	2 Lodestar 2 Electra	Aircraft leased from Norsur. Operated in co-operation with A.L.A. Service ended about 1965
Líneas Aéreas de Cuyo (LAC)	1958	Mendoza–Buenos Aires, Tucumán, Córdoba, Mar del Plata, Bariloche	Lodestar	Service ended 1960

Continued on page 592

591

Airline	Date of Foundation	Routes	Fleet	Remarks
Transportes Aéreos Buenos Aires (TABA)	1958		1 Cessna 170 5 Beech C-45 1 Cessna T-50	Received subsidy during early 1960s. Service ended approx. 1969
Líneas Aéreas Chaqueñas (Aero Chaco)	1958	Local services in Chaco Province	2 Beaver 3 DHC-6	Received subsidy during early 1960s. Introduced two FH-227 (bought in Brazil) in 1978
Servicios Aéreos Mediterraneos (SAM)	1958	Local services based on Córdoba	Beech 18	Service lasted only a few months
Transportes Aéreos Fe, S.A. (TRAFE)	1970		Convair CV-240	Charter services. Also operated DC-8
Líneas Aéreas Privadas Argentinas (LAPA)	1977	Local services in province of Buenos Aires	3 Swearingen Metro II 1 PA-31T	
Astro	1979	Buenos Aires–Colonia; Buenos Aires–Carmelo	BN-2 Islander	

Bibliography

Basic background reading on Latin American airlines is contained in well-known reference books such as *Jane's All the World's Aircraft*, published annually since 1911. The less widely distributed *Aircraft Year Books*, published annually from 1919 to 1962, contained in the earlier years useful data about the embryonic progress of Latin American airlines. Also, such publications as Van Zandt's *World Aviation Annual* and Roadcap's *World Airline Record*, together with magazines such as *Flight International, Aviation Week,* and *Air Transport World*, are essential to keep pace with contemporary developments.

Additionally, much of the history of the airlines has been faithfully recorded by airline timetables, not only those issued by airlines, but also by specialist publishers. The *Guia Aeronáutico* published in Brazil and other airline *Guias* from Argentina, Colombia, Ecuador, Chile and Peru, have comprised a documented chronology of progress of airline commercial activity.

Other general books and reference material on air transport have already been noted in the bibliography to *Airlines of the United States since 1914*, the predecessor and companion volume to this book. This listing of books (invariably written in the language of the country of origin) is intended for the specialist student of Latin American airline history.

Argentina
La Aeronáutica Nacional al Servicio del País (Published by the Secretaría de Aeronáutica de la Nación, 1948).

Brazil
Coletânea de Legislação Aeronáutica (Published by the Divisão Legal da Directoria de Aeronáutica Civil, 1955).

Asas de Ontem, de Hoje, e de Amanha, by Abel Pereira Leite (Livraria Civilização Brasileira, 1957).

História de Fôrça Aérea Brasileira, by Tenente-Brigadeiro Nelson Freire Lavanère-Wanderley (Ministério da Aeronáutica, 1966).

A Construção Aeronáutica do Brasil, 1910/1976, by Roberto Pereira de Andrade (Editora Brasiliense, 1976).

Aviação Comercial Brasileira, by Dole A. Anderson (Editora Universitária, 1979).

A História da Panair do Brasil, edited by J. D. Madeiros (ETA-Editora Técnica de Aviação, 1980).

Os Avioes que Fizeram a Aviação Comercial Brasileira, by Carlos E. Dufriche (Sindicato Naçional dos Aeronautas, 1982).

South American Aviation News, formerly *Manche* (Published quarterly), edited by Mario B. de M. Vinagre.

Colombia
Una Historia con Alas, by Herbert Boy (Editorial Iqueima, 1963).
The Air Post of Colombia, by Eugenio Gebauer (Eugenio Gebauer, 1963).
Historia de la Aviación en Colombia, by Coronel José Ignacio Forero F. (Aedita, Editores, Ltda, 1964).
Los Primeros 50 Años de Correo Aéreo en Colombia, by Eugenio Gebauer and Jairo Londoño Tamayo (Eugenio Gebauer, 1975).

Costa Rica
Historia de la Aviación en Costa Rica, by Carlos Jiménez G. (1959).

Mexico
Breve Historia de la Aviación en México, by Ing José Villela Gómez (José Villela Gómez, 1971).
La Historia de la Aviación en México, by Salvador Novo (Compañía Mexicana de Aviación, 1974).
Resumen Historico de la Aviación en Yucatán, by Raul Rosado Espinola.

Peru
La Aviación en el Perú, by Capitán E. P. Alberto Fernández Prade E. (Lima, 1966).
Libro de Oro (Faucett 1928–1978) (Faucett Public Relations Office, 1978).

France
La Ligne, by Jean-Gérard Fleury (Gallimard, 1944).
Les Amériques et l'Empire des Airs, by Henry Mourer (Editions Internationales, 1949).
L'Atlantique Sud de l'Aéropostale à Concorde, by J. G. Fleury (Editions Denoël, 1974).

USA
The Struggle for Airways in Latin America, by William A. Burden (Council on Foreign Relations, 1943).
Under My Wings, by Basil L. Rowe (Bobbs-Merrill, 1956).
A Dream of Eagles, by Ralph A. O'Neill (Houghton-Mifflin, 1973).
The Perilous Sky, by Wesley Phillips Newton (University of Miami Press, 1978).
An American Saga, by Robert Daley (Random House, 1980).
Shelton's Barefoot Airlines, by Philip Schleit (Fishergate Publishing Company, 1982).

APPENDIX 1

Sixty Years of Air Traffic in

Latin America

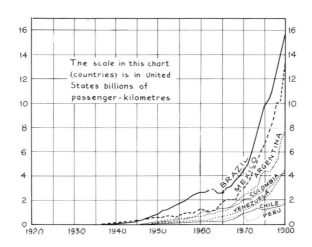

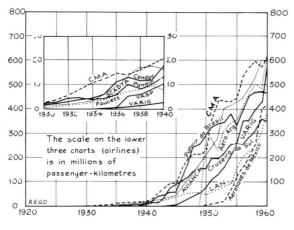

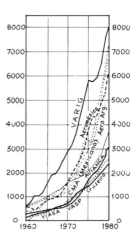

The Leading Airlines in Latin America

1930–1980

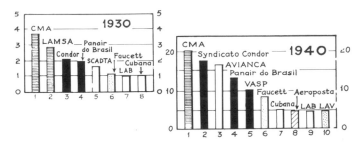

On the set of charts
on this page, the figures
on the vertical axes are
in millions of passenger-
kilometres

The charts are drawn
to different scales

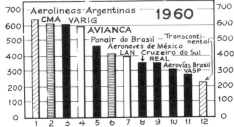

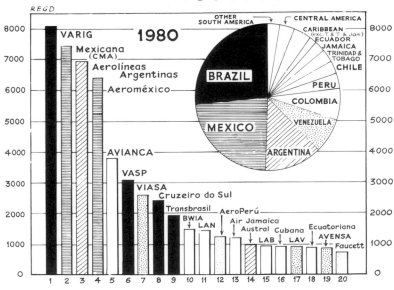

APPENDIX 3

Selected Airline Fleet Lists

The comprehensive fleet lists in this Appendix have been compiled only through the gracious and enthusiastic help of John M. Davis, of Wichita, Kansas, who specializes in aircraft research in the Spanish-speaking countries, and Carlos Dufriche, of Rio de Janeiro, who specializes in Brazil. Their exhaustive records were edited into this final form by the author and subjected to meticulous scrutiny by Putnam's indefatigable aviation editor, John Stroud. Significant contributions were also made by Franz Preuschoff, of Germany, Lennart Andersson, of Sweden, José Villela, of Mexico and Abel Leite, of São Paulo.

To some readers, these lists may appear to represent unnecessary attention to detail; to others they will probably not be detailed enough. The author and editor have therefore attempted a compromise solution which will serve to supplement the text with authoritative facts about the commercial aircraft which have played a vitally important role in creating the airline industry of Latin America.

The Junkers, Dorniers, Fairchilds, and Sikorskys, followed by the Douglases, Curtisses, Boeings and Lockheeds, pioneered air routes over frightening terrain and through treacherous weather, without navigational aids, and using landing strips which would barely be accepted as car parks today. But they were the vanguard of future flotillas of modern aircraft. They laid the foundations of a great industry which changed the face of a whole continent, and if for no other reason, they deserve to be remembered, and their existence recorded.

Where the facts are established, those aircraft which crashed or were written off for any reason during their period of operation with the named airline are indicated with an asterisk immediately following the registration. While the numbers are somewhat alarming in some cases, the miracle is that the casualties were not higher, bearing in mind the hazards of weather, terrain, and technical infancy.

The lists in this Appendix cover those periods of development within each country which can aptly be described as the formative years from the start of scheduled service. Although there are no exact criteria, the terminating date for inclusion is typically the last piston-engined fleet, or the last of the first generation jets such as the Comet and Caravelle, as the airline industry in each country reached maturity. But there is no hard and fast rule, and information believed to be of particular interest, regardless of period, is included. The lists thus comprise the prelude for the comprehensive tabulations and aircraft chronologies which are available in publications which specialize on the subject, and which normally concentrate on the airline fleets of the jet age.

The dates in parentheses following the aircraft type are those for the introduction of that type.

The fleets are listed alphabetically by countries and chronologically as:

Argentina

Aeroposta 1930–1949

Latécoère 25 (1930)

F-AIKP	c/n	636			From parent company. Not reregistered		
R 177		645			,,	,, ,,	Ex-F-AIQL
R 178		644			,,	,, ,,	,, F-AIQK
R 179		631			,,	,, ,,	,, F-AIJZ
R 180		643	Later	LV-DAB	,,	,, ,,	,, F-AIQF
R 181		635			,,	,, ,,	,, F-AIKO
R 182		642	Later	R 256	,,	,, ,,	,, F-AIQE
R 211		603	,,	LV-EAB*	,,	,, ,,	,, F-AIEH
R 212		649			,,	,, ,,	,, F-AISA
R 257		615	Later	LV-FAB	From Aeropostal Brasileira Ex-PP-AAA, P-BEAA, F-AIFU		
R 262		638			From Aeropostal Brasileira Ex-PP-AAB, P-BEAB, F-AIOO		

*This aircraft has been preserved

Potez 25A.2 (1930)

F-AJDZ   1522   Transferred from parent company

Latécoère 28 (1935)

F-AIJQ	906			From parent company. Not reregistered			
F-. . . .	918			,,	,,	,,	,, ,,
R 293	929			,,	,,	,,	Ex- F-AJUV
R 297	916	Later	LV-GAB	,,	,,	,,	
R 305	915	,,	LV-HAB	,,	,,	,,	
R 322	910	,,	LV-IAB	,,	,,	,,	,, F-AJOU
R 338	903	,,	LV-JAB	,,	,,	,,	,, F-AJIO

Potez 29-2 (1936)

R 299   1497   From parent company Ex-F-AIVX

Junkers-Ju 52/3m (1937)

R 344	5824	Later	LV-AAB	*Patagonia*	Reregistered	LV-AAG
R 345	5833	,,	LV-BAB	*Tierra del Fuego*	,,	LV-AAH†
R 346	5829	,,	LV-CAB		,,	LV-AAI
LV-AAN	4061			*Quichua*	Ex-LAB (Bolivia)	
LV-AXB	6800	Later	LV-AAJ	*Ibaté*	Ex-Condor (Brazil)	

†Sometime named *Pampa*

Cessna UC-78 (1946)

LV-ACR   3846   Ex-USAAF

598

Douglas DC-3 (1947)

LV-ACW	12057	LV-ACY	12291	LV-ADF	20158
LV-ACX	12387	LV-ACZ	–	LV-ADG	33430

Corporación Sudamericana 1939–1946

Macchi C.94 (1939)

LV-LAB	94008	Later	LV-AAD	*Río de la Plata*
LV-MAB*	94012	,,	LV-AAE	*Río Paraná*
LV-NAB	94010	,,	LV-AAF	

Short S.25 Sunderland 3 (1946)

LV-AAS	SH.6C	Bought by Dodero for CAUSA

SANA 1940–1943

Consolidated 16 Commodore (1940)

LV-DXA	2	LV-QAB	5	Later LV-AAL

Sikorsky S-38B (1940)

LV-OAB	414-13	Later LV-AAM	LV-PAB*

LADE* 1940–1975

Junkers-Ju 52/3m (1940)	Douglas DC-6 (1967)
Vickers-Armstrongs Viking (1947)	DHC-6 Twin Otter (1968)
Douglas DC-3 (1950)	Fokker F.27 (1968)
Douglas DC-4 (1958)	Fokker F.28 (1975)

*Civil transport arm of Fuerza Aérea Argentina. Fleet drawn from military pool. Full details not published.

FAMA 1946–1949

Douglas DC-4 (1946)

LV-ABI*	7445	LV-ABP*	7466	LV-AEU	10345	*Niña*
LV-ABL*	3080	LV-ABQ	7468	LV-AFD	10300	
LV-ABM	7462	LV-ABR	10315	LV-AFG*	7479	
LV-ABN	3101	LV-ABS	10371	LV-AGG	10333	
LV-ABO	10285	LV-ADH	7460	LV-AGH	10329	

Avro York (1946)

LV-AFV	1354	LV-AFZ	1356	LV-XIH*	1366
LV-AFY	1355	LV-XIG*	1365		

599

Douglas DC-3 (1946)

LV-ABT	18992	LV-ACG	33538	LV-AFW	19790
LV-ABU	19278	LV-AFE	6176		

Avro Lancastrian 4 (1947)

LV-ACS*	1382	LV-ACU	1402	LV-ACV	1403

Vickers-Armstrongs 615 Viking (1947)

LV-AEV	185	LV-AFF	191	LV-AFL*	192
LV-AEW	184	LV-AFI	193	LV-AFU	200

Bristol 170 Freighter Mk 1A (1947)

LV-AEX	12754	LV-AEY	12751	LV-AEZ	12753

Douglas DC-6 (1948)

LV-ADR	43030	LV-ADT	43032	LV-ADV	43034
LV-ADS	43031	LV-ADU	43033	LV-ADW	43136

Note: FAMA is believed to have used other Vikings delivered to the Argentine Government. A total of 20 were sold to Argentina.

ZONDA 1946–1949

Douglas DC-3 (1946)

LV-ABX	13435	LV-ACH	13027	LV-ACO	25277
LV-ABY	12850	LV-ACI	13156	LV-ACP	11920
LV-ABZ	13473	LV-ACJ	13336	LV-ACQ	13159
LV-ACD	13328	LV-ACL	12020	LV-ADD*	19545
LV-ACE	13373	LV-ACM	9490	LV-ADJ	13150
LV-ACF	25455	LV-ACN	12246		

De Havilland D.H.89A Dragon Rapide (1948)

LV-AEN	6864	LV-AER	6609	LV-AGV	6399	LV-AGY	6550
LV-AEO*	6789	LV-AES	6822	LV-AGW	6843		
LV-AEP	6892	LV-AGR	6581	LV-AGX	6942		

Beech Bonanza (1948)

LV-AGL	D-1138	LV-AGO	D-1435	LV-AGP	D-1450

Avro Anson V (1948)

LV-AGI	MDF-314	LV-AGJ	MD-17

Convair CV-240 (1948)

LV-ADM	35	LV-ADO	62	LV-ADQ	77
LV-ADN	50	LV-ADP	72		

ALFA 1947–1949

Macchi C.94 (1947)

LV-AAD	94008	LV-AAF	94010

Short S.25 Sandringham (1947)

LV-AAO	SH.1C	Mk. 2	*Argentina*	Ex-Dodero	
LV-AAP*	SH.2C	Mk. 2	*Uruguay*	,,	Crashed 29 July, 1948.
LV-AAQ	SH.4C	Mk. 3	*Inglaterra*	,,	
LV-AAR	SH.3C	Mk. 3	*Brasil*	,,	
LV-ACT	SH.43C	Mk. 2	*Paraguay*	,,	

Short S.25 Sunderland 3 (1947)

LV-AAS SH.6C *Río de la Plata* Ex-Corporación   Flown by CAUSA as CX-AKF

Noorduyn Norseman VI (1947)

LV-AAT	165	LV-AAV	563	LV-AAX	640	LV AFR*	768
LV-AAU	219	LV-AAW*	798	LV-AAY*	341		

Beech C.18S (1947)

LV-AAZ	4958*	LV-ABD	4542

Douglas DC-3 (1947)

LV-ABE	6015	LV-ABH	13621

Aerolíneas Argentinas 1950–1965

Avro York (1950)

LV-AFV	1354	Ex-FAMA	Retired upon acquisition.
LV-AFY	1355	,,	
LV-AFZ	1356	,,	

Beech D.18S (1950)

LV-ABD 4542   Ex-ALFA

Cessna UC-78 (1950)

LV-ACR 3846   Ex-Aeroposta

Convair CV-240 (1950)

LV-ADM*	35	*Yapeyu*	LV-ADO	62	*San Lorenzo*	LV-ADQ*	77
LV-ADN	50	*Uspallata*	LV-ADP	72	*Chacabuco*		

All ex-ZONDA

Douglas DC4 (1950)

LV-ABM	7462	Ex-FAMA	Retired on acquisition
LV-ABN	3101	,,	,, ,,
LV-ABO	10285	,,	,, ,,
LV-ABQ*	7468	,,	Crashed 17 June, 1953
LV-ABR	10315	,,	
LV-ABS	10371	*Teniente Origone* Ex-FAMA	
LV-ADH	7460	Ex-FAMA Retired on acquisition	
LV-AEU	10345	*Teniente Zanni*	Ex-FAMA
LV-AFD	10300	*Teniente Candelarias*	,,
LV-AGG	10333	*Teniente Benjamin Matienzo*	,,
LV-AGH	10329	*Jorge Newbery*	,,
LV-AHY	18341	*Vicente Almandos Almonacid* Ex-United Air Lines	
LV-AHZ*	27227	Ex-United Air Lines. Crashed 8 December, 1957	

Douglas DC-6 (1950)

LV-ADR	43030	Ex-FAMA	*Presidente Perón/Bernardino Rivadavia*
LV-ADS*	43031	,,	*17 de Octubre/Mariano Moreno*
LV-ADT	43032	,,	*Argentina/General Güemes*
LV-ADU	43033	,,	*Eva Perón/Manuel Belgrano*
LV-ADV*	43034	,,	*Pampero/General Paz*
LV-ADW*	43136	,,	*Presidente Perón/General San Martin*

Note: LV-ADU was for a time named *General Belgrano*.

Douglas DC-3 (1950)

LV-ABE	6015	Ex-ALFA	Retired on acquisition
LV-ABH	13621	,, ,,	,, ,,
LV-ABT	18992	Ex-FAMA	,; ,,
LV-ABU	19278	,, ,,	,, ,,
LV-ABX*	13435	Ex-ZONDA	*El Liberatador* Written off 1953
LV-ABY	12850	,, ,,	*Quichua*
LV-ABZ	13473	,, ,,	*Cuyano*
LV-ACD*	13328	,, ,,	*Ibaté* Crashed 16 July, 1956
LV-ACE	13373	,, ,,	*Patagonia*
LV-ACF	25455	,, ,,	*Norteño*
LV-ACG	33538	Ex-FAMA	
LV-ACH*	13027	Ex-ZONDA	*Puntaño* Crashed 30 December, 1950
LV-ACI	13156	,, ,,	Retired on acquisition
LV-ACJ	13336	,, ,,	*Guarani*
LV-ACL	12020	,, ,,	Retired on acquisition
LV-ACM*	9490	,, ,,	*Tierra del Fuego* Crashed 14 July, 1959
LV-ACN	12246	,, ,,	*Pampa*
LV-ACO	25277	,, ,,	*Chaco*
LV-ACP	11920	,, ,,	*Iguazú*
LV-ACQ*	13159	,, ,,	*Coya* Crashed 20 May, 1955

LV-ACW	12057	Ex-Aeroposta	*Tehuelche*	
LV-ACX*	12387	,, ,,	*Quilmes*	Crashed 23 April, 1954
LV-ACY*	12291	,, ,,	*Yagan*	,, 26 March, 1951
LV-ACZ	—	,, ,,		
LV-ADF	20158	,, ,,	*Chonó*	
LV-ADG	33430	,, ,,	*Querandi*	
LV-ADJ	13150	Ex-ZONDA	*Los Andes*	
LV-AET	19961	,, ,,	*Napuche*	
LV-AFE	6176	Ex-FAMA	*Araucano*	
LV-AFS	12025	Retired on acquisition		
LV-AFW*	19790	Ex-FAMA	Crashed 15 May, 1959	
LV-AGD	9162	*Ona*		
LV-AGE*	20083	Crashed 3 June, 1951		
LV-AGF	20405			

Short S.25 Sandringham (1950)

LV-AAO	SH.1C	Mk. 2	*Argentina*	Ex-ALFA
LV-AAQ	SH.4C	Mk. 3	*Inglaterra*	,,
LV-AAR*	SH.3C	Mk. 3	*Brasil*	,,
LV-ACT	SH.43C	Mk. 2	*Paraguay*	,,
LV-AHM	SH.71C	Mk. 6	*Almirante Zar*	Ex-SAS

Short S.25 Sunderland 5 (1951)

LV-AHG*	SH.70C	*Uruguay*	LV-AHH	SH.69C	*Río de la Plata*

De Havilland Comet 4 (1959)

LV-AHN	06408	*Las Tres Marias*	
LV-AHO*	06410	*Cruz del Sur*	Crashed 20 Feb, 1960
LV-AHP*	06411	*Lucero del Alba*	Crashed 26 Aug, 1959
LV-AHR*	06430	*Arco Iris*	Crashed 23 Nov, 1961
LV-AHS	06432	*Alborada*	
LV-AHU	06434	*Centaurus*	

Sud-Aviation Caravelle VIN (1962)

LV-HGX	19	*Aldebaran*	LV-HGZ	149	*Rigel*
LV-HGY*	127	*Sirius*	LV-I I I	180	*Antares*

Hawker Siddeley HS.748 (1962)

LV-HGW	1539	*Ciudad de Bahía Blanca*
LV-HHB*	1540	*Ciudad de Corrientes*
LV-HHC	1541	*Ciudad de Concordia*
LV-HHD	1542	*Ciudad de Salta*
LV-HHE	1543	*Ciudad de Resistencia*
LV-HHF	1544	*Ciudad de San Juan*
LV-HHG	1545	*Ciudad de Mar del Plata*
LV-HHH*	1546	*Ciudad de Neuquén*
LV-HHI*	1547	*Ciudad de Río Gallegos*
LV-IDV	1556	*Ciudad de Montevideo*
LV-IEE	1557	*Ciudad de Santa Fé*
LV-IEV*	1558	*Ciudad de Gualeguaychu*

De Havilland Comet 4C (1962)

LV-AIB 06460 *Presidente Kennedy*

Bolivia

Lloyd Aéreo Boliviano 1925–1969

Junkers-F 13 (1925)

El Oriente	769?	*Chaco*		*Mamoré*	634
Beni (I)	711	*Charcas*		*Oriente*	
Beni (II)		*Illimani*		*Beni* (III)	788

There is evidence to suggest that LAB had at least nine F 13s. *El Oriente* and *Oriente* appear in some records as *Oriente* and *Oriente II* but the names as listed here were painted in capital letters on the fuselage sides. There is also evidence to suggest that three F 13s were named *Beni*. The first *Beni* crashed in January 1926 and *Oriente* crashed on 26 August, 1929. Two F13s, c/ns 634 and 788, were from Lloyd Aéreo Córdoba in the Argentine. Two survived until 1942.

Junkers-W 34ci (1929)

*Vanguardia**	2607	New	Crashed 12 April, 1939
Tunari	2608	,,	Still in fleet January 1942

Ford 5-AT Tri-Motor (1932)

*Cruz del Sur**	100	Crashed shortly after delivery

Junkers-Ju 52/3m (1932)

CB-17*	4008	*Juan del Valle*	First production Ju 52/3m. Crashed 3 Nov, 1940
CB-18	4009	*Huanuni*	Second ,, ,, ,, ,, 15 Dec, 1937
CB-21	4061	*Bolívar*	Sold to Aeroposta (Argentina)
CB-22	5623	*Illampu*	Sold to VASP
—	4018	*Chorolque*	Crashed 17 Jan, 1936

Junkers-W 33 (1933)

CB-19*	2756	*Mururata*	New	Crashed 3 April, 1939
CB-20*	—	*Sajama*	,,	,, 13 March, 1937

Junkers-A 50 Junior (1933)

Acre	*Piray*	*Warnes*

Sikorsky S-38B (1933)

Nicolas Suárez	414-15	*Marihui*

Junkers-Ju 86 (1937)

CB-23 860013 *Illimani* New. Civil passenger version

Three Ju 86K-7s were delivered to Bolivia. Used for a time by LAB, they were *Mariscal Sta Cruz* (860234), *General Perez* (860237), *Mariscal Sucre* (860240).

Special Note: Bolivia was at war with Paraguay from 1932 to 1935 in a dispute over the Chaco region. LAB became effectively the logistics air support for the army. The missing registration numbers CB-1 to CB-16 have not been precisely identified as they were allocated retrospectively in 1939 or 1940. Initially names were used instead of registrations.

Grumman G-21A Goose (1938)

CB-24 1015 *Moxos*

Lockheed 18-10 Lodestar (1941)

CB-25	2088		CB-26	2098		CB-27	2169		CB-28	2217

Douglas DC-3 (1945)

CB-29	4980	Later CP-529		CB 73	4682	Later CP-573
CB-30	34351	,, CP-530		CB-83	9668	,, CP-583
CB-31*	13837			CB-84*	19226	,, CP-584
CB-32*	19445			CB-91	20200	,, CP-591
CB-33*	—			CB-100*	2181	,, CP-600
CB-34	12570	Later CP-607		CB-101	2182	,, CP 601
CB-35*	4867	,, CP-535		CP-605*	32542	
CB-36*	20619	,, CP-536		CP-734*	34312	
CB-68*	19024	,, CP-568		CP-735	33553	
CB-72	1549	,, CP-572				

Curtiss C-46 (1947)

CB-37*	433	C-46A		CB-51*	26369	C-46A
CB-38*	—	,,		CB-67	33283	C-46D
CB-39*	26488	,,		CP-540	33594	,,
CB-41*	33579	C-46D		CP-730*	33457	,,
CB-50	26397	C-46A				

CP-540 did not go into service.

Boeing B-17 (1950)

CB-70*	8296	B-17F	Later CP-570
CB-79	3119	,,	,, CP-579
CB-80*	9300	B-17G	,, CP-580
CB-97*		,,	,, CP-597
CP-620	8749	,,	
CP-621	8683	,,	
CP-623*	32391	,,	
CP-625*	10285	,,	
CP-627*	22616	,,	
CP-686*	6369	B-17F	
CP-891	22616	B-17G	CP-627 rebuilt

605

Consolidated C-87 (1951)

CB-89

Douglas DC-4 (1955)

CP-609*	10510	CP-610	10538	CP-682	27249

Douglas DC-6B (1960)

CP-698*	43273	CP-707*	43547	CP-715	43543	CP-740	43272

Lockheed 188A Electra (1968)

CP-853   1125

Fairchild F-27 (1969)

CP-862	127	F-27M		CP-1117*	118	F-27J
CP-863	128	,,		CP-1175	121	,,
CP-1116	111	F-27J		CP-1176	119	,,

Brazil

VARIG 1927–1970

Dornier Wal (1927)

P-BAAA	34	*Atlântico*	Ex-D-1012 of Condor Syndikat. To Syndicato Condor 1930

Dornier Merkur (1927)

P-BAAB	92	*Gaúcho*	New. To Syndicato Condor 1930

Klemm L 25 (1930)

P-BBAC	105	*Ruyzinho*	Ex-E.T.A. (Brazil) Later PP-VAA
P-BBAD	106	*Irma*	,, ,, ,, ,, PP-VAB

Morane-Saulnier MS.130 (1931)

P-BAAC	3310	Later PP-VAC

Nieuport-Delage 641 (1931)

P-BAAD	3	Later PP-VAD

Junkers-A 50 Junior (1931)

P-BAAE*	3354		New. Re-allocated PP-VAE (not used)
P-BAAH	3509	*Bagé*	,, ,, PP-VAH ,,
P-BAAI	3518	*Minuano*	,, Registration allocated but re-registered as PP-VAI and renamed *Bagé*

Junkers-F 13 (1932)

P-BAAF	2064	*Livramento*	New Later PP-VAF
P-BAAG*	2067	*Santa Cruz*	,, ,, PP-VAG

Messerschmitt Me 108B Taifun (1936)

PP-VAJ*	987

Messerschmitt M 20b (1937)

PP-VAK	546	*Aceguá*	Ex-DLH

Junkers-Ju 52/3m (1938)

PP-VAL*	4058	*Mauá*	Ex-South African Airways. Crashed 28 Feb., 1942

Fiat G.2 (1942)

PP-VAM	1	*Jacuí*	Ex-ALI and Italian Air Ministry

De Havilland D.H.89A Dragon Rapide (1942)

PP-VAN	6449	*Chui*	Ex-Cía Fabril de Juta

Cant Z.1012 (1942)

PP-VAO	Never entered regular service

Lockheed 10 Electra (1943)

PP-VAP	1042	Model E		PP-VAT	1029	Model A
PP-VAQ*	1008	,, C		PP-VAU*	1036	,, B
PP-VAR	1015	,, A		PP-VAV	1074	Y1C-36
PP-VAS*	1028	,, A		PP-VBD	1073	,,

Douglas C-47/DC-3 (1946)

PP-VAW	32690		PP-VBK	26823	PP-VCH	19972
PP-VAX	32754		PP-VBL	6014	PP-VCS*	19757
PP-VAY*	34276		PP-VBN	25360	PP-VDL*	4115
PP-VAZ	34287		PP-VBO	27138	PP-VDM	7333
PP-VBA	26183		PP-VBP	9666	PP-AVJ	7333
PP-VBB	35652		PP-VBR	4947	PP-AVN	27222
PP-VBC	32732		PP-VBT	25588	PP-AVT	13782
PP-VBF	10156		PP-VBV*	26889	PP-AXL	20463
PP-VBG	9209		PP-VBW	25989	PP-CDS*	4823
PP-VBH	34301		PP-VCD	9031		

Noorduyn Norseman VI (1947)

PP-VBE*   623   Purchased from Ted Coleman

Curtiss C-46 (1948)

PP-VBI*	33100	C-46D		PP-VCB*	26641	C-46A
PP-VBJ*	33481	,,		PP-VCC	27055	,,
PP-VBM*	134	C-46A		PP-VCE	30656	,,
PP-VBQ	33254	C-46D		PP-VCF*	30283	,,
PP-VBS	445	C-46A		PP-VCG	30454	,,
PP-VBU	33554	C-46D		PP-VCI	26919	,,
PP-VBX	30268	C-46A		PP-VCJ	27046	,,
PP-VBY	30243	,,		PP-VCL	30300	,,
PP-VBZ*	30400	,,		PP-VCM	26496	,,
PP-VCA	253	,,		PP-VCT*	260	,,

Convair CV-240 (1957)

PP-VCK*	39	PP-VCQ*	103	PP-VCW	19	PP-VCZ	91
PP-VCN	98	PP-VCR	44	PP-VCX	99	PP-VDG	67
PP-VCO	34	PP-VCV	14	PP-VCY	83	PP-VDH	65
PP-VCP	24						

Lockheed 1049G Super Constellation (1955)

PP-VDA*	4610	PP-VDC	4612	PP-VDE	4684
PP-VDB	4611	PP-VDD	4681	PP-VDF	4685

Sud-Aviation Caravelle I/III (1959)

PP-VJC	10	*Brasilia*	New	Series I, converted to III			
PP-VJD*	15		,,	,,	,,	,,	,,
PP-VJI	20		,,	,,	,,	,,	,,

Lockheed 188 Electra (1962)

PP-VJL	1024	PP-VJP*	1049	PP-VJW	1124	PP-VLC	1093
PP-VJM	1025	PP-VJU	1119	PP-VLA	1139	PP-VLX	1063
PP-VJN	1037	PP-VJV	1126	PP-VLB	1137	PP-VLY	1073
PP-VJO	1041						

Hawker Siddeley HS.748 (1967)

PP-VDN*	1625	PP-VDQ*	1628	PP-VDT	1631	PP-VDX	1634
PP-VDO	1626	PP-VDR	1629	PP-VDU*	1632	PP-VJQ	1535
PP-VDP	1627	PP-VDS	1630	PP-VDV	1633		

In 1961, VARIG acquired the entire fleet of the REAL Consortium. These aircraft retained the same registrations and are therefore not duplicated here—see separate REAL, Aerovias Brasil, and Nacional listings. Also, VARIG leased two ex-Panair do Brasil DC-8s from the Brazilian Govt.

608

Syndicato Condor (1927–1940)—Cruzeiro do Sul 1943–1970
Dornier Wal (1927)

P-BAAA	34	*Atlântico*	Ex-D-1012 Condor Syndikat, with VARIG June–July 1927. Later PP-CAA
P-BACA*	83	*Santos Dumont*	Crashed 3 December, 1928
P-BADA*	82	*Bartholomeu de Gusmão*	Destroyed by fire 11 February, 1928
P-BAIA	106	*Guanabara*	Later PP-CAI
P-BALA*	107	*Olinda*	
P-BAMA	108	*Jangadeiro*	

All except P-BAAA ex-DLH

Junkers-G 24 (1928)

P-BABA*	944	*Ypiranga*	Ex-DLH. Leased to VARIG July-Sept., 1927. Later PP-CAB
P-BAHA*	921	*Potyguar*	Ex-DLH
P-BAQA*	961	*Riachuelo*	,, Later PP-CAS

Junkers-F 13 (1928)

P-BAFA	750	*Bandeirante*	Ex-DLH	Later	PP-CAF
P-BAGA*	644	*Blumenau*	,,	,,	PP-CAG
P-BAJA*	584	*Iguassú*	,,	,,	PP-CAJ
P-BAKA*	725	*Pirajá*	,,	,,	PP-CAK

Junkers-W 33 (1928)

P-BAEA*	2511	Not in regular service. Crashed 1928

Dornier Merkur (1930)

P-BAAB	92	*Gaúcho*	Ex-VARIG. Later PP-CAC

Junkers-W 34 (1931)

P-BANA*	2593	*Tiéte*	New	Later	PP-CAN
P-BAOA	2594	*Tibagy*	,,	,,	PP-CAO
P-BAPA*	2595	*Taquary*	,,	,,	PP-CAP
PP-CAR*	2711	*Tapajoz*	,,	,,	*Turyassú*
PP-CAW	2791	*Tacutu*	,,		
PP-CBO	2608	*Tarauacá*	Ex-SEDTA		

Junkers-Ju 52/3m (1933)

PP-CAT*	4024	*Anhangá*		PP-CBD	5478	*Jacy*
PP-CAV	4038	*Caiçara*		PP-CBE	5120	*Yarassú*
PP-CAX	4043	*Curupira*		PP-CBF	4079	*Aracy*
PP-CAY*	4042	*Marimbá*		PP-CBG	4075	*Pagé*
PP-CAZ	5261	*Maipo*		PP-CBH	5109	*Moré*
PP-CBA	5283	*Aconcagua*		PP-CBL	5656	*Los Andes*
PP-CBB	4078	*Tupan*		PP-CBP	6800	*Ibaté*
PP-CBC*	5453	*Guaracy*		PP-CBR	5053	*Uirapurú*

Junkers-Ju 46 (1934)

PP-CAU*	2720	*Tocantins*	Ex-DLH
PP-CBK*	2744	*Tingúa*	,,

Focke-Wulf Fw 200 Condor (1939)

PP-CBI*	2996	*Abaitará*	Ex-DLH
PP-CBJ	2995	*Arumani*	,,

Focke-Wulf Fw 58 Weihe (1940)

PP-CBM	3102	*Aquiri*	Ex-DLH
PP-CBN	3103	*Cacuri*	,,

Douglas DC-3/C-47 (1943)

PP-AJA*	—			PP-CCZ	7404	*Caritiana*
PP-AJC	20402	*Itajaí*		PP-CDB	19008	*Ibagé*
PP-CBS	4963	*Três Americas*		PP-CDC	13764	*Erexim*
PP-CBT	4968	*América do Norte*		PP-CDD	26818	*Tupanciretã*
PP-CBU	4981	*América Central*		PP-CDG	19245	*Joá*
PP-CBV*	4977	*América do Sul*		PP-CDH	11730	*Yaraporanga*
PP-CBX*	11658	*Tupi*		PP-CDI*	4684	*Banzo*
PP-CBY*	11692	*Tamoio*		PP-CDJ*	19278	*Abalily*
PP-CBZ*	11767	*Tapuio*		PP-CDK	18992	*Guanandi*
PP-CCA*	27177	*Tabajara*		PP-CDL	6015	*Goitacas*
PP-CCB	32682	*Timbira*		PP-CDM	6193	*Arapuan*
PP-CCC*	32593	*Tupiniquim*		PP-CDN	13156	*Tuchaua*
PP-CCD*	32559	*Tupinambá*		PP-CDO	11790	*Anhembi*
PP-CCE	19829	*Tapira*		PP-CDP	3288	*Andradina*
PP-CCK*	4750	*Bugre*		PP-CDR	4891	*Curussá*
PP-CCL*	13802	*Bororó*		PP-CDS	4823	*Caajara*
PP-CCM	19613	*Botocudo*		PP-CDT	4442	*Coriamba*
PP-CCN	10042	*Bigua*		PP-CDU	13452	*Pyatá*
PP-CCO	12616	*Bacurau*		PP-CDV	26601	*Petrolina*
PP-CCP*	4226	*Juruena*		PP-CEB	20586	*Corsario*
PP-CCR	32609	*Baré*		PP-CEC	2079	*Morubixaba*
PP-CCT	4703	*Bugio*		PP-CED	7386	*Mero*
PP-CCV	20402	*Jarú*		PP-CES	11689	*Aniquim*
PP-CCW	34366	*Jamaú/Piquiri*		PP-PED	2134	
PP-CCX*	7341	*Caeté*		PP-SAD	13764	*Erechim*
PP-CCY	20126	*Carajá*				

PP-CEC was a C-39

Lockheed 12-A (1945)

PP-CBW	1209	*Saci*

Beech AT-11 (1946)

PP-CCF*	3090	*Batuira*		PP-CDA	1247	*Atobá*
PP-CCG*	3304	*Ibere*		PP-CDE	3546	*Jaó*
PP-CCH	3059	*Marreca*		PP-CDF	3698	*Tuyuyu*

Douglas DC-4 (C-54B) (1946)

PP-CCI	10441	*Sirius*	PP-CCS	27234	*Vega*
PP-CCJ	10483	*Canopus*			

Convair CV-340 (1954)

PP-CDW*	159	*Sirius*	PP-CDZ	167	*Vega*
PP-CDY*	166	*Canopus*	PP-CEA	175	*Antares*

Convair CV-440 (1958)

PP-CEN	466	*Castor*	PP-CER	494	*Procyon*
PP-CEO	467	*Pollux*	PP-CFE	471	*Altair*
PP-CEP*	493	*Alcion*			

Convair CV-240 (1958)

PP-CET	2	*Regulus*	PP-CEZ*	25	*Dube*
PP-CEU	4	*Aldebaran*	PP-CFA	33	*Rigel*
PP-CEV*	6	*Betelgeuse*	PP-CFB	36	*Belatrix*
PP-CEW	18	*Polar*	PP-CFC	87	*Alderamin*
PP-CEY	20	*Salph*	PP-CFD*	142	*Arcturus*

Fairchild C-82A Packet (1958)

PP-CEE	10144	*Hercules*	PP-CEI	10185	PP-CEL	10153
PP-CEF*	10200	*Centauro*	PP-CEJ	10156	PP-CEM*	10180
PP-CEG	10141		PP-CEK	10147	PP-CFF	10182
PP-CEH*	10115					

Sud-Aviation Caravelle VIR (1963)

PP-CJA	129	PP-CJD	168	PP-PDX*	126
PP-CJB	133	PP-PDV*	120	PP-PDZ	131
PP-CJC	62				

Consolidated PBY-5A Catalina (1965)

PP-PCW*	CV-429	PP-PEB	2007	PP-PEC*	91

NAMC YS-11 (1967)

PP-CTA	2041	PP-CTD	2044	PP-CTG*	2063	PP-CTJ	2081
PP-CTB	2042	PP-CTE	2054	PP-CTH	2064	PP-CTK	2082
PP-CTC	2043	PP-CTF	2055	PP-CTI*	2080	PP-CTL	2083

Panair do Brasil 1930–1965

Consolidated Commodore (1930)

P-BDAA	2	*Rio de Janeiro*	Later PP-PAA	New (NYRBA do Brasil)		
P-BDAE	5	*Santos*	,, PP-PAE	,,	,,	,,
P-BDAG	6	*São Paulo*	,, PP-PAG	,,	,,	,,
P-BDAH	9	*Argentina*	,, PP-PAH	,,	,,	,,
P-BDAI	10	*Miami*	,, PP-PAI	,,	,,	,,
P-BDAJ	1	*Buenos Ayres*	,, PP-PAJ	,,	,,	,,
PP-PAO	3			Ex-PAA		

Sikorsky S-38 (1930)

P-BDAB	414-6	*Porto Alegre*	Later PP-PAB	New (NYRBA do Brasil)	
P-BDAC	214-19	*Bahia*		,, ,, ,,
P-BDAD*	214-10	*Pernambuco*		,, ,, ,,
P-BDAF	214-20	*São Luiz*		,, ,, ,,
P-BDAK	414-2		,, PP-PAK	Ex PAA
P-BDAL*	214-16		,, PP-PAL	,,
PP-PAM*	214-4		,,

Lockheed Air Express (1930)

P-BDAH	65	*Maracá*	New (NYRBA do Brasil). Floatplane

Fairchild XA-942A (1936)

PP-PAP*	9402	New	PP-PAT	9403	New

Sikorsky S-43 (1936)

PP-PAR*	4307	New (via PAA)
PP-PAU*	4308	,, ,, ,,
PP-PAW	4304	Ex-PAA
PP-PBA*	4303	,,
PP-PBL	4322	,, (S-43B)
PP-PBM*	4316	,, ,,
PP-PBN*	4315	,, ,,
PP-PCQ	4316	S-43B. Rebuilt by PAB from three aircraft

Lockheed 10 Electra (1936)

PP-PAS	1008	Model 10-C	Ex-PAA
PP-PAX	1042	,, 10-E	,,

Douglas DC-2 (1940)

PP-PAY	1351	Ex-PAA	PP-PAZ	1324	Ex-PAA

Lockheed 18 Lodestar (1941)

PP-PBB	2080	PP-PBG	2081	PP-PBO	2216
PP-PBC	2082	PP-PBH*	2113	PP-PBP	2215
PP-PBD*	2083	PP-PBI*	2114	PP-PBQ*	2115
PP-PBE	2099	PP-PBJ	2116	PP-PBR	2133
PP-PBF	2112	PP-PBK	2117		

Douglas DC-3/C-47 (1945)

PP-PBS*	11747	PP-PCC	4703	PP-PCL	26052
PP-PBT	11743	PP-PCD	4544	PP-PCM	19524
PP-PBU	11683	PP-PCE	9137	PP-PCN*	3284
PP-PBW	4884	PP-PCH*	4087	PP-PCO	11775
PP-PBY	26183	PP-PCI	2197	PP-PCP	2134
PP-PBZ	32609	PP-PCJ	4103	PP-PCS	7387
PP-PCA	34283	PP-PCK	26158	PP-PCT	7396

Douglas DC-3/C-47 contd

PP-PCU	26272	PP-PED	2134	PP-PEE*	7396
PP-PCV	25871				

Lockheed 12 (1945)

PP-PBV	1259		PP-PBX	1227

Lockheed 049/149 Constellation (1946)

PP-PCB	2048	*Domingos Alfonso Sertão*	Ex-PAA	
PP-PCF*	2049	*Manoel de Borba Gato/*		
		Antonio Rodrigues Velho	,,	
PP-PCG*	2062			
PP-PCR*	2060	*Domingos Barbosa Calheiros*	,,	
PP-PDA*	2066		,,	
PP-PDC*	2056	*Domingos Dios Prado*	,,	
PP-PDD	2033	*Domingos Jorge Velho*	,,	
PP-PDE*	2047	*Estavão Ribeiro Bairo Parente*	,,	
PP-PDF	2038	*Garcia Rodrigues Paes Leme*	,,	
PP-PDG	2037	*João Amaro Maciel Parente*	,,	Model 149
PP-PDH	2050	*Manuel Prêto*	,,	,,
PP-PDI	2057	*Amador Bueno de Veiga*	,,	,,
PP-PDJ*	2032		,,	,,
PP-PDK†	2059	*Bras Cubas*	,,	,,
PP-PDP	2052	*Francisco Nimes de Siqueira*	Ex-Aeronaves de México	,,
PP-PDQ†	2059	*Jeronimo Fragoso de Albuquerque*	,,	,, ,, ,,

†PP-PDK leased to Aeronaves de México and later became PP-PDO

Consolidated PBY-5A Catalina (1948)

PP-PCW*	CV-429	*Pedro Teixeira*
PP-PCX	CV-240	*Antonio Pedroso de Alvarenga*
PP-PCY	CV-242	*Antonio Dias Adorno*
PP-PCZ	CV-282	*Jaycomo Raymundo de Noronha*
PP-PDB*	22021	
PP-PDR	1781	*Pedro Vaz de Barros*
PP-PEB	2007	
PP-PEC	91	

Douglas DC-7C (1957)

PP-PDL*	45122	*Fernão Dias Pais*
PP-PDM*	45124	*Antonio Raposo Tavares*
PP-PDN	45125	*Nicolau Barreto*
PP-PDO*	44872	*Bartolomeu Buena da Silva*
PP-PEG	45094	*Bras Esteves Leme*
PP-PEH	45091	

Douglas DC-6A (1959)

PP-LFA	45527	*Garcia de Avila*
PP-LFB	45528	*Bartolomeu Bueno da Siqueiro*
PP-LFC	45529	*Fernando de Camargo*
PP-LFD	45530	*Francisco Dias de Avila*

Douglas DC-8-33 (1961)

PP-PDS	45272	*Manoel de Borba Gato*
PP-PDT*	45273	*Bras Cubas*
PP-PEA	45253	*Garcia d'Avila*
PP-PEF	45271	*Bras Cubas*

Sud-Aviation Caravelle VIR (1962)

PP-PDU*	118	*Antão Leme da Silva*
PP-PDV	120	*Domingos Rodrigues de Carvalho*
PP-PDX	126	*Fernando de Camargo*
PP-PDZ	131	*Francisco Dias de Avila*

VASP 1933–1972

General Aircraft Monospar ST-4 Mk II (1933)

PP-SPA	24	*Bartholomeu de Gusmão*	*VASP 1* until 1937
PP-SPB	25	*Edu Chaves*	*VASP 2* until 1937

De Havilland D.H. 84 Dragon (1934)

PP-SPC	6085	*VASP 3*

Junkers-Ju 52/3m (1936)

PP-SPD*	5459	*Cidade de São Paulo*	New
PP-SPE	5465	*Cidade de Rio de Janeiro*	,,
PP-SPF*	5869	*Cidade de Santos*	,,
PP-SPG	6465	*Cidade de Goiânia*	,,
PP-SPH	6510	*Cidade de Curitiba*	,,
PP-SPI	6684	*Cidade de Cuiabá*	Ex- Colombian Petroleum
PP-SPJ	5623	*Cidade de Campinas*	Ex-LAB

Douglas DC3/C-47 (1946)

PP-NAM	42980	PP-SPS	26343	PP-SQG	1919
PP-NAT	11683	PP-SPT*	20543	PP-SQH	1545
PP-SPK*	32706	PP-SPU*	20729	PP-SQI*	13048
PP-SPL*	34274	PP-SPV*	25985	PP-SQJ	11863
PP-SPM*	34151	PP-SPW*	34364	PP-SOK	4347
PP-SPN	34296	PP-SPX*	12257	PP-SQL	2248
PP-SPO	34285	PP-SPY*	10102	PP-SQM	4621
PP-SPP*	27063	PP-SPZ*	4649	PP-SQO	19778
PP-SPQ*	27036	PP-SQA*	4742	PP-SQP*	1952
PP-SPR*	20544				

Saab Scandia (1950)

PP-SQB	90001	PP-SQV*	90106	PP-SQQ	90112
PP-SQF	90101	PP-SRA*	90107	PP-SQS*	90113
PP-SQC	90102	PP-SRB	90108	PP-SQT	90114
PP-SQE*	90103	PP-SQX	90109	PP-SQR	90115
PP-SQD	90104	PP-SQY*	90110	PP-SQZ	90116
PP-SQW	90105	PP-SQN	90111	PP-SQU	90117

Vickers-Armstrongs Viscount V.827 (1958)

PP-SRC	397	PP-SRE*	399	PP-SRG*	401
PP-SRD*	398	PP-SRF	400	PP-SRH	316

All bought new. PP-SRD was named *Armando de Salles Oliveira*

Curtiss C-46 (1962)

PP-BLE	246	C-46A		PP-NAP	83	C-46A
PP-LDG	26869	,,		PP-NMC	30543	,,
PP-LDL	33467	C-46D		PP-NME	30418	,,
PP-LDP	27046	C-46A		PP-NMF	26971	,,
PP-LDQ	30343	,,		PP-NMG	30450	,,
PP-LEP	26798	,,		PP-NMH	26508	,,
PP-NAO	32831	C-46D		PP-NML	26621	,,

Douglas DC-4 (1962)

PP-BLG	3062	*Sergipe*
PP-LEL	18383	*Pará*
PP-LER	27251	*Ceará*
PP-LES	10487	*Bahia*
PP-LET	18393	*Guanabara*
PP-LEW	10348	*Maranhão*
PP-LEY	18338	*Goiás*
PP-LEZ	27250	*Rio Grande do Norte*

Douglas DC-6A (1962)

PP-LFA	45527	*Amazonas*
PP-LFB	45528	*São Paulo*
PP-LFC	45529	*Rio Grande do Sul*
PP-LFD	45530	*Pernambuco*

Vickers-Armstrongs Viscount V.701 (1963)

PP-SRI	11	PP-SRM*	19	PP-SRP	61	PP-SRR*	66
PP-SRJ	15	PP-SRN	62	PP-SRQ*	65	PP-SRS	182
PP-SRL	22	PP-SRO	64				

All ex-BEA

BAC One-Eleven 422 (1967)

PP-SRT	119	PP-SRU	126

NAMC YS-11A (1968)

PP-SMI*	2059	PP-SMM	2079	PP-SMX	2043
PP-SMJ*	2068	PP-SMN	2084	PP-SMZ	2044
PP-SML*	2076	PP-SMO	2091		

Note: PP-SMJ named *Cidade de Cuiabá*

VASP also leased one DHC-6 Twin Otter in 1967, one Beech 99 in 1968 and one Swearingen Metro in 1972

Navegação Aérea Brasileira (NAB) 1941–1961

Beech 18S (1941)

| PP-NAA | 430 | New | | PP-NAB | 431 | New |

Beech D.17S (1941)

| PP-NAC | 314 | | From George F. Ryan (USA) |

Fairchild 24 (1942)

| PP-NAD | 114 |

Lockheed 18 Lodestar (1942)

| PP-NAE* | 2149 | PP-NAH | 2171 | PP-NAJ | 2212 |
| PP-NAF* | 2150 | PP-NAI | 2168 | | |

Stinson SR-9E Reliant (1942)

| PP-NAG | 5268 | | From Brazilian private owner |

Douglas DC-3/C-47 (1946)

PP-NAK	26601	PP-NAS	11743	PP-NAX	11775
PP-NAL*	42979	PP-NAT	11683	PP-NAY	2134
PP-NAM	42980	PP-NAU	4884	PP-NAZ*	7387
PP-NAN	4521	PP-NAV	4544	PP-NMA	7396
PP-NAR	26019	PP-NAW	9137	PP-NMB	26272

Curtiss C-46 (1957)

PP-NAO	32831	C-46D	PP-NMG	30450	C-46A
PP-NAP	83	C-46A	PP-NMH	26508	,,
PP-NAQ	27021	,,	PP-NMI	30344	,,
PP-NMC	30543	,,	PP-NMJ	30391	,,
PP-NMD*	242	,,	PP-NMK	30564	,,
PP-NME	30418	,,	PP-NML	26621	,,
PP-NMF*	26971	,,	PP-NMM	26486	,,

NAB became part of the Lóide Consortium in 1961.

Aerovias Brasil 1942–1961

Lockheed 14 (1942)

| PP-AVA* | 1405 | Ex-TACA | PP-AVB | 1401 | Ex-TACA |

Fairchild 71 (1944)

| PP-AVC | 671 | Ex-Roosevelt Flying Service |
| PP-AVD | 3501 | Ex-Bell Laboratories |

616

Lockheed 12-A (1944)

PP-AVE	1202	Ex-TACA		PP-AVF	1207	Ex-RCAF

Douglas DC-2 (1945)

PP-AVG	1245	Ex-TACA		PP-AVH	1252	Ex-TACA

Douglas DC-3 (1945)

PP-AVI	4825	*Mato Grosso*	Ex-TACA
PP-AVJ (V)	7333	*Bahia*	,, ,,
PP-AVK	4910	*Espirito Santo*	,, ,,
PP-AVL*	9886	*Paraná*	Ex-USAAF
PP-AVM*	32746		Ex-US civil
PP-AVN (V)	27222	*Pernambuco*	Ex-USAAF
PP-AVO*	19113	*Goiás*	,, ,,
PP-AVP	19214	*Rio Grande do Norte*	Ex-TACA
PP-AVQ	11653	*Piaui*	,, ,,
PP-AVR	19779	*Santa Catarina*	,, ,,
PP-AVS	19792	*Maranhão*	,, ,,
PP-AVT (V)	13782	*Rio de Janeiro*	,, ,,
PP-AVU	19389	*São Paulo*	,, ,,
PP-AVV	32785	*Minas Gerais*	Ex-Caribbean Line Inc
PP-AVW	4754	*Sergipe*	Ex-E. F. Drew & Cía
PP-AVY*	13632	*Rio Grande do Sul*	Ex-USAAF
PP-AVZ*	9156	*Ceará*	,, ,,
PP-AXD*	13326	*Paraiba*	Ex-TABA
PP-AXE	12356	*Alagoas*	,, ,,
PP-AXF	12147	*Pará*	,, ,,
PP-AXG*	25295	*Amazonas*	,, ,,
PP AXI	25235		From Adamastor R. Vergueiro
PP-AXJ*	6177		From M. B. Lima & Cía
PP-AXK	13636		From Maquinas Aerocom
PP-AXL (V)	20463		Ex-Don Cardiff
PP-AXT	13048		From José Oliviera Barros Jr
PP-AXV	4419		Via Florida Trading Company
PP-AXW	4957		,, ,, ,,
PP-AXY			Ex-International Airports Inc
PP-AXZ	20244		Ex-US Civil
YS-22*	11724		Leased from TACA

Saab Scandia (1950)

PP-AXM	90101	New

Curtiss C-46A (1951)

PP-AXN	30463	
PP-AXO	30549	*Territorio do Amapá*
PP-AXP	26515	
PP-AXU	26796	

Douglas DC-4 (1951)

PP-AXQ	18338	*General San Martin*
PP-AXR	27250	*George Washington*
PP-AXS*	7467	*Duque de Caxias*
PP-YRO	10348	

Aerovias Brasil came under the control of REAL in 1954, and continued its separate existence until purchased by VARIG in 1961, just before VARIG's purchase of REAL itself. Aircraft marked (V) were absorbed into VARIG's fleet.

REAL 1945–1961

Douglas C-47 (1945)

PP-YPA	19446		PP-YPQ	12985		PP-YQG	34272
PP-YPB	13658		PP-YPR	9659		PP-YQH	26683
PP-YPC (V)	20719		PP-YPS	1500		PP-YQJ	25228
PP-YPG	13776		PP-YPT (V)	13488		PP-YQK*	4732
PP-YPH	4692		PP-YPU (V)	12303		PP-YQL	2012
PP-YPI (V)	4361		PP-YPV	12190		PP-YQM	25871
PP-YPJ (V)	20179		PP-YPW	13371		PP-YQN (V)	1919
PP-YPK (V)	20181		PP-YPX*	9154		PP-YQO	2248
PP-YPL	4569		PP-YPY (V)	11670		PP-YQP	34373
PP-YPM*	4241		PP-YPZ*	11699		PP-YQQ (V)	4615
PP-YPN	4755		PP-YQA	13621		PP-YQR	9719
PP-YPO (V)	20529		PP-YQB	12025		PP-YQS	4914
PP-YPP	19176		PP-YQF	34292			

Note: By 1957, REAL had formed an operating consortium with Aerovias Brasil, Nacional, and other airlines which had been absorbed already by those companies. Their aircraft usually retained their first registrations. Including these and allowing for write-offs, REAL's total fleet of DC-3s reached 86 by 1957.

Bristol 170 Wayfarer Mk IIA (1946)

PP-YPD	12740	New	PP-YPF	—	Ordered, but never delivered
PP-YPE	12743	,,			

Curtiss C-46A (1951)

PP-YQC	26798	PP-YQD	30283	PP-YQE	30393	PP-YQI	30454

Convair CV-340 (1954)

PP-YRA (V)	189	PP-YRC (V)	195	PP-YRE	199
PP-YRB*	191	PP-YRD (V)	196	PP-YRF	200

Convair CV-440 (1956)

PP-YRG	333	PP-YRJ	469	PP-YRL	499
PP-YRH	349	PP-YRK	498	PP-YRP	388
PP-YRI	468				

Passed to VARIG with same registrations.

Lockheed 1049H Super Constellation (1958)

PP-YSA	4833	PP-YSB	4834	PP-YSC	4837	PP-YSD	4838

Passed to VARIG with same registrations.

Aero Commander (1959)

PP-YQT	560E-602-36		PP-YQU	680E-858-77

Convair CV-990*

PP-YSE	PP-YSF	PP-YSG	PP-YSH

*These four aircraft were ordered, but never delivered to REAL. VARIG purchased three aircraft, in fulfilment of the contract, after it took over REAL in 1961.

Lockheed 188A Electra (1961)*

PP-YJF	1037	PP-YJG	1024	PP-YJH	1025

*These three aircraft were purchased from American Airlines, and were delivered direct to VARIG after the takeover.

Douglas DC-6B (1961)

PP-YSI	44166	PP-YSL	43746	PP-YSN	43824
PP-YSJ	43745	PP-YSM	43822		

Passed to VARIG with same registrations.

Aircraft indicated (V) were acquired by VARIG when it purchased REAL in 1961.

Nacional 1947–1957

Douglas DC-3/C-47 (1947)

PP-AKA (V)	20193	PP-ANG (V)	4307	PP-ANQ	20519
PP-AKB	33573	PP-ANH*	20187	PP-ANR	4704
PP-AKC	27069	PP-ANI*	34293	PP-ANS	4280
PP-AKD	20136	PP-ANJ	20182	PP-ANT (V)	9714
PP-AKI (V)	11743	PP-ANK*	13773	PP-ANU (V)	1545
PP-ANA	9203	PP-ANL (V)	19871	PP-ANV (V)	
PP-ANB	19238	PP-ANM	4365	PP-ANW	
PP-ANC	4306	PP-ANN (V)	1992	PP-ANX*	13048
PP-AND	9004	PP-ANO*	19830	PP-ANY	4756
PP-ANE	34299	PP-ANP (V)	4341	PP-ANZ (V)	13822
PP-ANF	19438				

Curtiss C-46A (1956)

PP-AKE (V)	26758	PP-AKF*	295	PP-AKG (V)	26729

Convair CV-440 (1957)

PP-AQA (V)	371	PP-AQC (V)	443	PP-AQE*	456
PP-AQB (V)	389	PP-AQD (V)	444	PP-AQF (V)	457

Nacional was acquired by REAL in 1956. In turn REAL was acquired by VARIG in 1961. Those aircraft which became part of VARIG's fleet, same registration, indicated (V)

Lóide Aéreo 1948–1962

Douglas C-47 (1948)

PP-ASA*	19843	Ex-USAAF
PP-ASB*	20467	Ex-USAAF
PP-ASC	20200	Ex-USAAF Later PP-LDA

Curtiss C-46 (1949)

PP-LDB*	30204	C-46A		PP-LDR	27021	C-46A
PP-LDC*	30443	,,		PP-LDS	27051	,,
PP-LDD*	30346	,,		PP-LDT	30393	,,
PP-LDE*	446	,,		PP-LDU	26798	,,
PP-LDF	30571	,,		PP-LDV	30549	,,
PP-LDG	26869	,,		PP-LDX*	30288	,,
PP-LDH	30350	,,		PP-LDY	30260	,,
PP-LDI*	30343	,,		PP-LDZ	30217	,,
PP-LDJ	30224	,,		PP-LEA	246	,,
PP-LDK	26535	,,		PP-LEB	26886	,,
PP-LDL*	33467	C-46D		PP-LEC	33304	,,
PP-LDM*	26397	C-46A		PP-LEC(2)	26944	,,
PP-LDN	33457	C-46D		PP-LEF	26750	,,
PP-LDO	26919	C-46A		PP-LEG	30309	,,
PP-LDP	27046	,,		PP-LEJ	226	,,
PP-LDQ*	30343	,,				

Douglas DC-4 (1957)

PP-LEL	18383	*Pará*
PP-LEM*	18336	
PP-LEQ*	10544	
PP-LER	27251	*Ceará*
PP-LES	10487	*Bahia*
PP-LET*	18393	*Guanabara*
PP-LEW*	10348	*Maranhão*
PP-LEY	18338	*Goiás*
PP-LEZ	27250	*Rio Grande do Norte*

Douglas DC-6A (1959)*

PP-LFA	45527	*Amazonas*
PP-LFB	45528	*São Paulo*
PP-LFC	45529	*Rio Grande do Sul*
PP-LFD	45530	*Pernambuco*

*These four aircraft were purchased new, but never went into service with Lóide. Aircraft leased to Panair do Brasil 1959–1961.

Transportes Aéreos Salvador (TAS) 1950–1956
Beech Bonanza A.35 (1950)

PP-SLA*	D-2132	PP-SLC*	D-2138	PP-SLE	D-1813
PP-SLB	D-2130	PP-SLD	D-1581		

De Havilland D.H.114 Heron 1 (1952)

PP-SLF	14003	PP-SLG*	14004

Beech AT-11 (1955)

PP-SLI	3530	Leased from Nacional

Douglas DC-3 (1955)

PP-AND	9004	Ex-Nacional	PP-SLL	1500	Ex-REAL
PP-ANE	34299	Ex-Nacional			

Curtiss C-46A (1959)

PP-ITE	439	PP-SLJ*	26535	PT-AXV	26919
PP-ITI	30498	PP-SLK	430	PT-AYA	30309

TAS was acquired by Nacional in 1956, incorporated into the REAL Consortium, but later came under the control of Sadia when VARIG took over REAL.

Aeronorte 1950–1960
Percival Prince (1950)

PP-NBA*	50/2	PP-NBF	50/11	PP-NBG	50/15

Junkers-Ju 52/3m (1950)

PP-DZY	6510	Leased from H. Martins and B. Lacerda

Lockheed 10-A Electra (1950)

PP-NBB	1029	Ex-VARIG	PP-NBD*	1074	Ex-VARIG
PP-NBC*	1073	Ex-VARIG			

Beech A.35 Bonanza (1951)

PP-NBE	D-2146

Lockheed 12-A (1952)

PP-NBI*	1202	Ex-Aerovias Brasil

Douglas DC-3 (1953)

PP-ANV		PP-YPC (V)	20719	PP-YPY (V)	11670
PP-NBJ	4957	PP-YPI (V)	4361	PP-YQN*	1919
PP-NBK	4419	PP-YPK (V)	20181	PP-YQS*	4914
PP-NBL	20244				

Curtiss C-46A (1957)

PP-NBM	83	PP-NBO	30217	
PP-NBN	26750	PP-NBP	226	

Nord 1203 Norécrin (1953)

PT-AAZ	213	PT-ABE	—	PT-ABI	209
PT-ABA	214	PT-ABH	208	PT-ABQ	221

Aeronorte was purchased by Aerovias Brasil in 1953 but continued its separate existence, including a period as part of the REAL Consortium, until the latter was itself purchased by VARIG in 1961.

(V) Absorbed into VARIG's fleet.

Paraense 1952–1970

Consolidated PBY-5A Catalina (1952)

PP-BTC	417	Initially operated as PT-ASX. Purchased from Venezuela
PP-BTD	87	,, ,, ,, PT-ANU. Ex-Aero Geral
PT-AMR	1995	Ex-Aero Geral

Curtiss C-46 (1957)

PT-AYA	30309	C-46A		PP-BTN	33248	C-46D
PP-BTA*	26901	,,		PP-BTO	33021	,,
PP-BTB*	33304	C-46D		PP-BTP*	33015	,,
PP-BTE*	30260	C-46A		PP-BTZ	26919	C-46A
PP-BTF*	26944	,,		PP-BUA	86	,,
PP-BTG*	30350	,,		PP-BUB	33294	C-46D
PP-BTH*	30571	,,		PP-BUC	26687	C-46A
PP-BTI*	30549	,,		PP-BUD	30225	,,
PP-BTJ*	27021	,,		PP-BUE	30394	,,
PP-BTL	33397	C-46D		PT-BEE*	27051	,,
PP-BTM	33369	,,				

PP-BTE was named *Brasilia*.

Douglas C-54 (1962)

PP-BTQ*	10506	PP-BTS	36040	PP-BTV	10474
PP-BTR	27237	PP-BTT	10478		

Douglas C-47 (1963)

PP-BTU*	25235	PP-BTX	9203

Fairchild FH-227B (1967)

PP-BUF*	556	*Rio Negro*	PP-BUI	568	*Rio Tocantins*
PP-BUG	565	*Rio Paranaiba*	PP-BUJ	569	*Rio Amazonas*
PP-BUH	567	*Rio Tapajós*	PP-BUK	505	

Sadia 1955-1969

Douglas DC-3/C-47 (1955)

PP-AND	9004	PP-ASO	32785	PP-ASS*	12985
PP-ASJ	4103	PP-ASP	4306	PP-AST	9659
PP-ASK	20182	PP-ASQ	9203	PP-AVY	13632
PP-ASN	27198	PP-ASR	19176	PP-SLL	1500

Curtiss C-46A (1956)

PP-ASL	26886	PP-SLJ	26535
PP-ASM	30456	PP-SLK	430

Handley Page Dart Herald (1963)

PP-ASU	161	PP-SDH	186	PP-SDL	191
PP-ASV	149	PP-SDI	177	PP-SDM	149
PP-ASW	169	PP-SDJ*	190	PP-SDN	194
PP-SDG	185				

Short Skyvan (1969)

PP-SDO   SH.1852   *Patinho Feio*   Leased from Shorts

Sadia introduced BAC One-Elevens in 1970, changed its name to Transbrasil in 1972, and subsequently standardized on jet aircraft — BAC One-Elevens and Boeing 727s — and Embraer 110C Bandeirantes.

Special Note on Brazilian Airlines

The individual fleet lists contained in this section include those of the dozen or so largest Brazilian airlines, only four of which survive today. In this book, there are references to other airlines in the text and in the genealogical chart in Chapter 23 (Page 470). Almost without exception, these companies were short-lived and had little influence on the course of development of the air transport industry of Brazil. However, in the interests of presenting the complete picture, the following notes on the minor airlines may be of interest to the specialist researcher. (For full airline names, see text and index).

Airlines existing before 1945

1929   **E.T.A.** One Klemm L 20 (P-BBAA) and two L 25s (P-BBAC and D).

1930   **Companhia Aeropostal Brasileira.** (Brazilian subsidiary of the French Aéropostale) Two Latécoère 25s registered in Brazil: P-BEAA and P-BEAB (later PP-AAA and PP-AAB).

1933–1939   **Aerolloyd Iguassú.** Two Klemm Kl 31As (PP-IAA and B) and three Stinson Reliants (PP-IAC, D, E). Company purchased by VASP in 1939.

1944–1949   **Aerovías S.A. (Minas Gerais).** Stinson SM-8 Junior (PP-LAF); Stinson SR-8 Reliant (PP-LAG); Fiat G.2 (PP-LAM) ex-VARIG; two DC-2s (PP-AVG, H); two C-39s (PP-MGA, MGB).

Airlines acquired by Cruzeiro du Sul

1947–1966   **SAVAG.** Three Lockheed 18 Lodestars (PP-SAA, B, C) ex-Panair do Brasil; two DC-3s (PP-SAD, E) ex-Cruzeiro do Sul.
1947–1966   **TAL/TAC.** Six DC-3s (PP-AJA—E, PP-CDG), the last four ex-Cruzeiro do Sul.

Airline acquired by VARIG

1947–1952   **Aero Geral.** Five Consolidated PBY-5A Catalinas (PP-AGA—D and H); Curtiss C-46 (PP-AGE); two DC-3s (PP-AGF, G).

Airline acquired by Aerovias Brasil

1946–1949   **TAB.** Four DC-3s (PP-ACA—D).

Airlines acquired by REAL

1944—1952   **VASD.** Two Consolidated PBY-5A Catalinas (PP-SDA, B); Budd Conestoga (PP-SDC); three DC-3s (PP-SDD, E and PP-ANL).
1945–1951   **LATB** (Trans-Continental). Five Avro Anson IIs (PP-ATA—E); five DC-3s (PP-ATF, G, H, J, and PP-NAL); Beech D-18S (PP-ATK); and Curtiss C-46D (PP-ATI).
1946–1950   **Natal.** Four DC-3s (PP-JAA — D).
1947–1950   **Wright.** Two Lockheed 18 Lodestars (PP-WAA, B).

Airlines acquired by Nacional

1947–1950   **VIABRAS.** Six DC-3s (PP-KAA — D, PP-ANJ and PP-ANR).
1948–1956   **Itaú.** Ten Curtiss C-46s (PP-ITA — J). PP-ITA, B, C, E and J passed from Nacional to VARIG.
1948–1950   **Central.** Four DC-3s (PP-IBA — C and PP-ANB).

Airlines forming part of the Lóide Consortium

1945–1951   **LAP.** Lockheed Hudson (PP-LPA); five DC-3s (PP-LPB — E and G); Curtiss C-46 (PP-LPH) ex-LAB, Bolivia.
1948–1962   **TABA.** Two Consolidated PBY-5A Catalinas (PP-BLA, B) ex-VASD; DC-3 (PP-BLC); four Curtiss C-46s (PP-BLD, E, F and PP-LDV); DC-4 (PP-BLG) ex-Capital Airlines.

Independent postwar airlines not acquired by any group

1945–1946   **Meridional.** Three Avro Anson IIs (PP-MTA — C).
1945–1948   **Bahiana.** Two Lockheed 18 Lodestars (PP-BHA, B) ex-Panair; Boeing 247D (PP-BHC) ex-AVIANCA; three DC-3s (PP-BHD — F) ex-AVIANCA.
1946–1948   **Arco-Iris.** Seven de Havilland D.H. 89A Dragon Rapides (PP-AIA — G).
1946–1948   **LAB.** Seven DC-3s (PP-BRA — E and PP-AJA, B) ex-TAC.
1948   **Universal.** Two Lockheed 18 Lodestars (PP-BBA, B); and C-46 (PP-BBC).
1955   **Aero Transportes Vitória.** Lockheed 12-A (PP-VTA); Cessna UC-78 (PT-DAE); Beech 18 (PP-VTE).

Chile

LAN-Chile 1929–1965

Information about the fleet of Línea Aeropostal Santiago-Arica (until 1932) is sparse, as are the details of Línea Aérea Nacional, its successor, until the 1940s. Complete fleet lists are not possible, therefore, until the introduction of the Lockheed 10-A Electras in 1941. Limited data are as follows (first service date in brackets).

De Havilland D.H.60 Cirrus and Gipsy Moth (1929). Eight in fleet, one still in service in 1937.

Ford Tri-Motor (1930). Three were acquired. One crashed on 22 December, 1930, and another on 10 May, 1938.

Fairchild FC-2 (1931). Up to six were probably acquired from the Chilean Air Force and modified for commercial use. Four crashed: 27 February, 1932; 24 May, 1933; 14 March, 1936; 9 March, 1939.

Curtiss Condor T-32C (1935). Three, c/ns 33, 38 and 39, acquired from American Airlines. C/n 38 crashed 29 July, 1936.

Potez 56 (1936). Nine acquired 1936–37. Known accidents — 27 March, 1937; 13 October, 1937; 18 January, 1943; 29 March, 1943.

Sikorsky S-43 (1936). Two acquired, c/ns 4318 and 4319. The second crashed 2 June, 1937.

Junkers-Ju 52/3m (1938). One leased from Syndicato Condor.

Junkers-Ju 86 (1938). Two Jumo-engined examples acquired. One crashed 14 March, 1939.

At some time LAN used the three Air Force Junkers-G 24s. Two bore the serials J4 and J5.

Lockheed 10-A Electra (1941)

CC-224*	1141	LAN 505	Later CC-LEN and CC-CLE. Crashed 4 Aug., 1947
CC-225	1142	,, 506	,, CC-LFN ,, CC-CLF
CC-226	1145	,, 507	,, CC-LGN, CC-CLG and CC-CLEA
CC-227	1146	,, 508	,, CC-LHN and CC-CLH
CC-228	1147	,, 509	,, CC-LIN ,, CC-CLI
CC-229	1148	,, 510	,, CC-LJN, CC-CLJ and CC-CLEB

Lockheed 18 Lodestar (1943)

CC-CLA	2400	LAN 501	CC-CLD*	2617	LAN 504
CC-CLB	2467	,, 502	—	2482	,, 503
CC-CLC*	2602	,, 503			

Douglas DC-3 (1946)

CC-CBG*	9716	LAN 210	Later CC-CLDP	Crashed 3 April, 1961	
CC-CBH	26906	,, 212	,, CC-CLDR and CC-CBV		
CC-CBI	26704	,, 213	,, CC-CLDS ,, CC-CBW		
CC-CBJ	13296	,, 214	,, CC-CLDT ,, CC-CBX		
CC-CLH*	11883	,, 209	,, CC-CLDO	Crashed 29 May, 1954	
CC-CLI	7395	,, 211	,, CC-CLDQ and CC-CBU		
CC-CLK	—	,, 201	,, CC-CLDG ,, CC-CBM		
CC-CLL	34255	,, 202	,, CC-CLDH ,, CC-CBN		
CC-CLM	34260	,, 203	,, CC-CLDI		
CC-CLO	13872	,, 205	,, CC-CLDK and CC-CBQ		
CC-CLP	9742	,, 206	,, CC-CLDL ,, CC-CBR		
CC-CLQ	19383	,, 207	,, CC-CLDM		
CC-CLDJ	19218	,, 204	,, CC-CBP		
CC-CLDN	13727	,, 208	,, CC-CBS		
CC-CLDU*	9783	,, 215	,, CC-CBY	Crashed 5 Dec., 1969	
CC-CLDV	9927	,, 216	,, CC-CBZ		
CC-CPF	6190	,, 356	,, CC-CAL and CC-CBO		

Martin 2-0-2 (1947)

CC-CLR	9125	LAN 261	Later CC-CLMA and CC-CCK
CC-CLS	9126	,, 262	,, CC-CLMB ,, CC-CCL
CC-CLT	9127	,, 263	,, CC-CLMC ,, CC-CCM
CC-CLU	9129	,, 264	,, CC-CLMD ,, CC-CCN

De Havilland D.H.104 Dove (1949)

CC-CAA	04280	LAN 301		CC-CLE	04268	,, 307
CC-CAB	04282	,, 302		CC-CLN	04272	,, 308
CC-CAC	04283	,, 303		CC-CLW	04273	,, 309
CC-CAD	04284	,, 304		CC-CLX	04274	,, 310
CC-CAE	04285	,, 305		CC-CLY	04275	,, 311
CC-CAF	04286	,, 306		CC-CLZ	04276	,, 312

Douglas DC-6B (1955)

CC-CLDA	44690	LAN 401	New	Later CC-CCD	
CC-CLDB	44691	,, 402	,,	,, CC-CCE	
CC-CLDC	44692	,, 403	,,	,, CC-CCF	
CC-CLDD*	45513	,, 404	,,	,, CC-CCG	Crashed 6 Feb., 1965
CC-CLDE	45514	,, 405	,,	,, CC-CCH	
CC-CLDF	45515	,, 406	,,	,, CC-CCI	
CC-CLDG	45516	,, 407	,,	,, CC-CCJ	
CC-CCG	45063		Ex-Braniff		
CC-CDM	45534		Ex-Western Airlines		
CC-CDN	45535		,, ,, ,,		
CC-CDO	45536		,, ,, ,,		

Convair CV-340 (1961)

CC-CLCA	136	LAN 301	Ex-Allegheny Airlines	Later CC-CBG	
CC-CLCB	137	,, 302	,, ,, ,,	,, CC-CBH	
CC-CLCC	58	,, 303	,, ,, ,,	,, CC-CBI	
CC-CLCD	116	,, 304	,, ,, ,,	,, CC-CBJ	

Sud-Aviation Caravelle VIR (1964)

CC-CCO	140	LAN 501	CC-CCQ	160	LAN 503
CC-CCP	164	,, 502			

Chilean Independent Airlines 1950–1975

Lyon Air Ltda 1950–1954

Curtiss C-46 (1950)

CC-CAH	33544 C-46D	CC-CAT	33236 C-46D	CC-CYA*	26445 C-46A

Air Chile 1952–1954

Consolidated B-24 Liberator (1952)

CC-CAN   Passed to ALA with merger. Damaged beyond repair 21 Feb., 1955

CINTA 1953–1961

Lockheed 10-A Electra (1953)

CC-CBC	1146 Ex-LAN	CC-CBD	1147 Ex-LAN

Lockheed 18 Lodestar (1954)

CC-CBK	2400	CC-CBM	2467	CC-CBT	2482

Douglas DC-3 (1956)

CC-CBK	11664	CC-CBM	6330

Douglas DC-4 (1957)

CC-CAJ	10511	CC-CBO	18379	CC-CBP	10356	N90405	10489

ALA (Merger of Lyon Air and Air Chile) 1954–1957

Curtiss C-46 (1954)

CC-CAB	22474	C-46F	CC-CAH*	33544	C-46D
CC-CAG	167	C-46A	CC-CAT	33236	,,

Lockheed 049 Constellation (1957)

CU-T547   2036   Leased from Cubana

Douglas DC-4 (1957)

CC-CAJ	10511	CC-CAK	10502

627

LADECO 1958–1976

Douglas DC-3 (1958)

CC-CAO	4219	CC-CBM*	6330	CC-CBZ*	9927
CC-CBK	11664				

Douglas DC-6B (1966)

CC-CAX	45135		CC-CEV	44891	
CC-CCH	45514		CC-CFH	45110	
CC-CDJ	43544	El Salvador	HI-146*	43270	Leased
CC-CDK	43545	El Chuquicamata			

Colombia

SCADTA 1920–1939

(Because of its great historic importance, this fleet (although not complete) is shown in more detail than some others)

Junkers-F 13 (1920)

A-2*	557	Colombia	Delivered by a Dutch ship 20 July, 1920. SCADTA records show Colombia as being lost in 1923, with one crew fatality.
A-4*	554	Bogotá	Delivered by a Dutch ship 20 July, 1920. Ex-D-29. Crashed 1927
A-6	543	Huila	Delivered 23 July, 1921. Ex-D-152 of Lloyd Ost-flug and Dz 152 of Danziger Luftpost
A-8	602	Magdalena	Delivered 1921. Returned to Junkers in 1929 for study after 3,200 hr and 600,000 km
A-9*	618	Cauca	Delivered 1921. Crashed 5 June, 1927, on trial flight at Barranquilla
A-10*	615	Caldas	Delivered 1921. Crashed at La Victoria 3 Sept. 1926
A12*	573	Santander	Delivered 1923. Burned out refuelling at El Banco, 2 Sept, 1930
A-16*		Tolima	Delivered 1924. Crashed at Barranquilla, 8 June, 1924, killing Hellmuth von Krohn (SCADTA's chief pilot), Wilhelm Fischer (pilot) and Ernesto Cortissoz (one of SCADTA's founders and first president)
A-18		Cúcuta	Delivered 1925. Allocated to COSADA when its Dornier Komet II proved unsatisfactory
A-21		Bucaramanga	Delivered 1925. Allocated to COSADA periodically. Later C-21
A-22		Huila (No.2)	Delivered 1927. Later C-22
C-24		Antioquia	

A-25		Boyacá	Delivered 1927. Later C-25

A-25   *Boyacá*   Delivered 1927. Later C-25
Operated first international schedule to Guayaquil, 29 July, 1928. Used on 1929 Peru survey. To Military Aviation Service 1932

A-26   *Nariño*   Delivered 1928. Later C-26. Out of service by 1935

C-29   *Atlántico* (No.2)   Delivered 1928.

C-30*   *Chocó*   ,,   ,,   ,,   Crashed 1929

C-31*   *Valle*   Delivered 1928. Crashed 1929

A-32*   *Pacífico* (No.2)   Delivered 1928. Later C-32. Crashed 1934

C-35   *Darien*   Delivered 1929. Had Pratt & Whitney Wasp. Crashed 13 May, 1938

A-36*   *Garcia Rovira*   Delivered 1929. Later C-36. Crashed 1933

C-40*   *Córdoba*   Delivered 1929. Had Pratt & Whitney Hornet. Total loss at Chocó 6 August, 1936

C-41*   *Santa Fé*   Delivered 1929. Total loss at Girardot

SCADTA is known to have had the F 13s c/ns 2023, 2048, 2061. Three F 13, reregistered C-77, C-78, C-79, were still in service in 1939.

CMASA-built Dornier Wal (1925)

A-19   34   *Atlántico*   Owned by Condor Syndikat, leased to SCADTA 1925. To Germany as D-1012, then to Brazil

A-20*   *Pacífico*   Ex-I-DOOR. Owned Condor Syndikat, leased to SCADTA 1925. Crashed near Paraguaná Peninsula, Venezuela, 1926

C-28   *Colombia* (No.2)   Delivered 1928. Second or third use of name. Inaugurated service to Panamá 1929. To Colombian Govt. 1932.

Dornier Merkur (1927)

A-23   124   *Simón Bolívar*   Later C-23. Retired 1931–32

C-27   167   *Pedro nel Ospina*

Junkers-W 33 (1928)

C-33   *Cundinamarca*   To Colombian Govt. 1932

Junkers-W 34 (1929)

Cundinamarca (No.2)		*Huila* (No.3)	C-71 or 74
Boyacá	C-53*	*Magdalena* (No.2)	

The list of W 34s is incomplete. Six were reregistered C-80 — C-85. C-84 was sold to the Andian National Corp and later returned to AVIANCA. C-84 and C-85 were still in service in 1943.

De Havilland D.H.60 Gipsy Moth (1929)

C-34*   *Gaviota*   Used for mail and photography. Crashed 1930

C-37   *Gavilan*   ,,   ,,   ,,

C-39*   *Garza*   ,,   ,,   ,,   Crashed at Cali 15 Feb, 1930

C-42   *Halcon*   ,,   ,,   ,,

C-43*   *Halieto*   ,,   ,,   ,,   Crashed 1931

Sikorsky S-38B (1929)

C-45*		*Ernesto Cortissoz*	Crashed 1932
C-46*	114-6	*Von Krohn*	Ex-PAA NC9107. Crashed 10 March, 1934
C-47		*Olaya Herrera*	
C-49*		*Guillermo Restrepo*	Wrecked 1940
C-50		*Vasquez Cobo*	
C-52*		*Guillermo Valencia*	Crashed 6 August, 1936

All from PAA sources but precise identity only known for C-46

Fokker Super Universal (1931)

C-44*	828	*Medellín*	Crashed at La Mesa 15 Dec, 1932
C-48*	880	*Bogotá* (No.2)	Crashed 1934

Sikorsky S-41 (1934)

Alfonso López*   Crashed at Barranquilla 14 Feb, 1936

Ford 5-AT (1932)

Barranquilla	C-60*	114	Had Edo floats. Wrecked near Quibdo 1938
Cartagena	C-66		Had Edo floats
*Leticia**	—		Crashed 14 March, 1939
Manizales (No.2)*	—		Crashed†
Tarapaca	C-62		

Fleet included C-44, C-47, C-67, C-69, C-111, C-202, C-203, C-204 (c/n 54), C-210 and C-270. Other aircraft names included *Cali*, *Cartago* and *Santa Marta*. It has proved impossible to match names and c/ns.

†This was the accident at Medellín on 24 June, 1934, when a Ford Tri-Motor of SACO went out of control on take off and collided with the SCADTA aircraft, killing all the occupants of both aircraft. Details appear in the Colombian section of the book.

Clark GΛ 43J (1934)

C-90	2205	*Bolívar*	Floatplane. Used on Barranquilla–Santa Marta route. Passed to AVIANCA

Boeing 247D (1937)

C-71		*Belalcazar*	Ex-United Air Lines
C-79*		*Quesada*	,, ,, ,, Crashed 29 Feb, 1940
C-138			Destroyed by fire 1943
C-139			
C-140			
C-141	1720		Ex-United Air Lines
C-142			
C-143	1716		Ex-United Air Lines
C-144	1949	*Rodrigo de Bastidas*	Ex-USAAF
C-145	1692		Ex-Wyoming Air Service
C-146*	1708		Ex-United Air Lines. Crashed 27 Feb, 1944
C-147	1687	*Pascual de Andagoya*	,, ,, ,,
C-148	1948		Ex-Western Airlines
C-149*		*Antonio de Olalla*	Crashed 15 March, 1939
C-150			

Other known names and c/ns are — *Nicholas de Federmann*, *Pedro de Heredia*, c/ns 1731, 1950 and 1954, but it has proved impossible to relate these to particular registrations. There were two C-144s and C-145s and the first C-144 crashed on 24 October, 1942. Surviving 247Ds passed to AVIANCA in 1940.

SCADTA also operated two Fokker C.II biplanes — *Cali* and *Manizales*. These were owned by LIADCA and both crashed during 1924.

SACO 1934–1939

Curtiss Kingbird D-2 (1934)

K-1	2001	K-2	2002	K-3
		All ex-Eastern Air Lines		

Ford 5-AT-B (1935)

F-31*   6   Ex-TWA   F-32   16   Ex-TWA

*Collided with SCADTA Ford Tri-Motor at Medellín on 24 June, 1934

Curtiss Condor T-32C (1937)

C-35   21   Later C-100   C-36   31   Later C-101
Both ex-Eastern Air Lines

Lockheed 10-E Electra (1939)

C-110   1133   New   C-111   1134   New

The SACO Condors and Electras passed to AVIANCA in 1940

ARCO 1939–1940

Beech 17 (1939)

C-48   271   C-17D   C-49   135   C-17B

Ford 5-AT-C (1939)

C-204   54   *Bolívar*

Ford 8-AT (1940)

C-210   1   *General Santander*

One Beech 17 was named *General Paez*. Surviving ARCO aircraft passed to AVIANCA in 1940.

AVIANCA 1940–1959
(excluding aircraft taken over from ARCO, SCADTA and SACO)

Douglas DC-3 (1940)

(H after the c/n indicates conversion to Hi-Per DC-3, * indicates crashed or written off)

Reg	c/n	Notes		
C-100	2012	Ex-PAA		
C-101		,,		
C-102		,,		
C-102	4231H	Later HK-102		
C-104	1992	Ex-PAA		
C-105	1989	,,		
C-107*	11723H	Ex-USAAF	Later HK-107	
C-108*	4829	,,	,,	
C-109*	4753H	,,	Later HK-109	
C-110*	4181	,,		
C-111*	4105H	,,	Later HK-111	
C-116*	4786	,,	,,	HK-116
C-117	9139	,,	,,	HK-117
C-118*	6182H	,,	,,	HK-118
C-119*	6217	,,		
C-120*	4314	,,	,,	HK-120
C-121	4370H	,,	,,	HK-121
C-122	4688H	,,	,,	C-101 and HK-101
C-122	4414H	,,	,,	HK-122
C-123*	6160	,,	,,	HK-123
C-124	4349H	,,	,,	HK-124
C-125	4410	Ex-TACA de Colombia.Later HK-125		
C-126*	4290	,, ,, ,,	,,	HK-126
C-127	4332	,, ,, ,,	,,	HK-127
C-131	12953	,, ,, ,,	,,	HK-131
C-140	6354H	Ex-SCOLTA	,,	HK-140
C-142*	1957	,, PAA	,,	HK-142
C-143*	10088		,,	HK-143
C-149	4593H	Ex-USAAF	,,	HK-149
C-150	4697	,,	,,	HK-150
C-153*	4711H	,,	,,	HK-153
C-154	6215H	,,	,,	HK-154
C-155*	4338	Ex-TACA	,,	HK-155
C-159	6068H	Ex-USAAF	,,	HK-159
C-160*	19540	Ex-American Airmotive	,,	HK-160
C-161*	19630	,, ,,	,,	HK-161
C-166	12560		,,	HK-166
C-167*	4272	Ex-Transair Inc	,,	HK-167
HK-303*	10032	Ex-LANSA		
HK-308*	19758	,, ,,		
HK-312	4757	,, ,,		
HK-314	4436	,, ,,		
HK-316	6253	,, ,,		
HK-317	9091	,, ,,		
HK-318	6173	,, ,,		
HK-319*	19680	,, ,,		
HK-324	4351	,, ,,		
HK-325	19654	,, ,,		
HK-326*	4631	,, ,,		
HK-327	19513	,, ,,		

Douglas DC-3 contd.

HK-328*	20224	,,	,,	
HK-329	4404	,,	,,	
HK-500	19637	Ex-SAM		
HK-502*	19653	,,	,,	
HK-508*	4527H	,,	,,	
HK-1201	4479	Ex-SAETA/LANSA		
HK-1202	4402	,,	,,	,,
HK-1203	9970	,,	,,	,,
HK-1204	13746	,,	,,	,,
HK-1315	4307	Ex-VARIG		
HK-1316	9714	,,	,,	
HK-1340	11704	Ex-PAA		
HK-1341*	11706	,,	,,	

Douglas C-39 (1944)

C-103   2058   Ex-PAA   C-106   2079   Ex-PAA

Consolidated PBY-5A Catalina (1946)

C-131	CV-409		C-134	
C-133	21998		C-135	1551

Douglas DC-4 (1946)

C-112	18377	Ex-PAA	Later HK-112
C-113*	10469	,,	,, C-130 and HK-130
C-114*	10439	,,	
C-115	10500	,,	Later HK-115
C-135*	10418	,,	,, HK-135
C-136	10407	,,	,, HK-136
C-172	10280	,,	,, HK-172
HK-170	10436	Ex-American Airlines	
HK-171	7461	,, ,, ,,	
HK-173	42905	Ex-SAS	
HK-174*	42929	,,	
HK-178	10362	Ex-PAA	
HK-180	10383	,,	
HK-186	18335	Ex-AVENSA	
HK-654	18391	Ex-PANAGRA	
HK-728	10507	Ex-CMA	
HK-729	10532	,,	
HK-730*	18325	,,	
HK-731	10367	,,	
HK-1027*	18392	Ex-Taxader	
HK-1028	3071	,, ,,	
HK-1309	10403	Ex-Greyhound Leasing	

Curtiss C-46A (1950)

HK-156	30428		HK-164	26814
HK-157	30462		HK-165	30364
HK-158	30573		HK-332	—

Lockheed 749A Constellation (1951)

HK-162	2663	HK-650	2544	HK-652	2564
HK-163*	2664	HK-651	2557	HK-653	2645

Lockheed 1049 Super Constellation (1954)

HK-175	4554	New 1049E, converted to 1049G
HK-176	4555	,, ,, ,, ,,
HK-177*	4556	*Colombia*. Crashed 21 January, 1960. 1049E
HK-184	4628	*Santa Fé de Bogotá*. New 1049G

During the 1940s AVIANCA owned Rearwin 8135-T C-33

SAM 1946–1976

(R) = Operated by Rutas Aéreas SAM (later Rutas Aéreas de Colombia — RAS).

Douglas DC-3 (1946)

C-500	19637	Ex-USAAF	Later	HK-500
C-501	18986	,,	,,	,, HK-501
C-502	19653	,,	,,	,, HK-502
C-503	10171	,,	,,	,, HK-503
C-504*	10062	,,	,,	,, HK-504
C-505	9380	,,	,,	,, HK-505
C-506	6061	Ex-VIARCO	,,	HK-506
C-507*	4725	,,	,,	,, HK-507
C-508	4527	,,	,,	,, HK-508
C-509	4763	,,	,,	,, HK-509
C-510	6152	,,	,,	,, HK-510
HK-521	12953	Ex-KLM (Caribbean Div.)		
HK-522	11994	,,	,,	,,
HK-523	42965	,,	,,	,, (R)
HK-524	12075	,,	,,	,, (R)
HK-525	9904	,,	,,	,, (R)
HK-526	11831	,,	,,	,,

Curtiss C-46 (1950)

HK-510	—		HK-516*	384	C-46A
HK-512	26784	C-46A	HK-517	—	
HK-513*	33210	C-46D	HK-520	26714	C-46A
HK-514*	30363	C-46A	HK-527	33215	C-46D
HK-515*	26941	,,			

Douglas DC-4 (1955)

HK-180	10383			HK-753	3120
HK-521	10432	(R)		HK-755	3061
HK-522	10488	(R)		HK-757	10404
HK-526	7455	(R)		HK-767	35993
HK-528	10449			HK-1028	3071
HK-529	10748			HK-1065	35943
HK-558	10468				

Douglas DC-6B (1960)

| HK-534 | 43555 | (R) | | HK-535 | 43552 | (R) |

Lockheed 188A Electra (1969)

HK-553	1013	*Jupiter*		HK-691	1043	*Apollo*
HK-554	1005	*Mercurio*		HK-692	1053	*Saturno*
HK-555	1029	*Neptuno*		HK-1274	1010	*Venus*
HK-557	1014	*Marte*		HK-1275	1030	*Pluton*

Cuba

Cía Nacional de Aviación Curtiss/Cubana 1930–1971

Curtiss Robin C-1 (1930)

| NM-1 | 436 | Bought new | | NM-2 | 658 | Bought new |

Curtiss Thrush (1930)

| NM-3 | 1002 | Bought new |

Ford 4-AT-E (1930)

| NM-4 | 69 | | NM-5 | 70 | | NM-7 | 63 |

All ex-Eastern Air Transport

Sikorsky S-38B (1931)

| NM-10 | 114-15 | Ex-PAA | | NM-11 | 214-5 | Ex-PAA |

Ford 5-AT (1932)

| NM-1 | | NM-14 | | NM-24 |
| NM-2 | | NM-22 | 11 | NM-25 |

All ex-PAA

Lockheed 10 Electra (1934)

NM-11	1005	Ex-PAA	Later NM-16 and CU-T11
NM-12	1019	,,	,, NM-26 ,, CU-T12
NM-15	1009	,,	
NM-17	1004	,,	
NM-24†	1061		

†Previously IM-24 (I = Internacional, N = Nacional)

Lockheed 12 (C-40A) (1940)

| NM-18 | 1264 | Ex-PAA |

635

Douglas DC-3 (1945)

NM-39	11646	Later CU-T7*	CU-T172	11671
NM-40	11744	,, CU-T8	CU-T266	11684
NM-43	—	,, CU-T9	CU-T586	4927
CU-T38	4100		CU-T808	4397
CU-T128*	4104		CU-T810	32723
CU-T138	2229		CU-T826	20186

Douglas DC-4 (1948)

CU-T188*	10368	*Estrella de Cuba* Ex-PAA
CU-T397*	10319	*Ruta de Colon* ,, ,,
CU-T641	10370	Ex-Aerovías 'Q'
CU-T710	10282	Ex-Cuban Air Force
CU-T785	10318	Ex-Canadian civil

Lockheed 049 Constellation (1953)

CU-T532	2061	Ex-PAA	CU-T547	2036	Ex-PAA

Curtiss C-46 (1954)

CU-C145	174	C-46A	CU-T557	—	
CU-C202	33209	C-46D	CU-T558	22453	C-46F
CU-C343	32841	C-46D	CU-T583	—	
CU-C385	—		CU-T607*	—	
CU-C555	26560	C-46A	CU-C787	—	
CU-C556*	264	C-46A	CU-C807	26979	C-46A

Lockheed 1049 Super Constellation (1954)

CU-P573	4557	1049E	Leased
CU-T601	4632	1049G	Bought new
CU-T602	4633	,,	,, ,,
CU-T631	4675	,,	,, ,,

Vickers-Armstrongs Viscount V.755 (1956)

CU-T603*	91	CU-T604	92	CU-T605	93

Vickers-Armstrongs Viscount V.818 (1958)

CU-T621	317	CU-T622	318	CU-T623	319

Bristol Britannia 318 (1958)

CU-T668	13432	*Libertad*	
CU-T669	13433		Ex CU-P669
CU-T670	13437		
CU-T671	13515		

Ilyushin Il-14 (1961)

CU-T814	CU-T817	CU-T820	CU-T823
CU-T815	CU-T818	CU-T821	CU-T824
CU-T816	CU-T819	CU-T822	CU-T825

Antonov An-12 (1966)

CU-T827*

Ilyushin Il-18 (1966)

CU-T830*	182004905	Il-18V	Ex-Aeroflot
CU-T831	182005202	,,	,,
CU-T832	182005501	,,	,,
CU-T899	11102	Il-18D	Bought new
CU-T900	11104	,,	,, ,,

CU-T831 was named *Capt Fernando Alvarez*

Antonov An-24 (1967)

CU-T875	—	An-24V	CU-T880	—	An-24V
CU-T876	—	,,	CU-T881	—	,,
CU-T877	—	,,	CU-T882	02602	,,
CU-T878	67302410	,,	CU-T923	09404	An-24RV
CU-T879*	—	,,	CU-T924	09405	,,

Ecuador

SEDTA 1938–1941

Junkers-W 34 (1938)

HC-SAA* 2608 Ex-DLH Crashed 11 Sept, 1939, repaired and transferred to Syndicato Condor as PP-CBO, 14 January, 1941

A second ex-DLH W 34 crashed on 5 March, 1938, killing Fritz Hammer.

Junkers-Ju 52/3m (1938)

HC-SAB*		*Ecuador*	Ex-DLH. Crashed 10 Dec, 1938
HC-SAC	5053	*Guayas*	Ex-DLH. To Syndicato Condor 10 July, 1941. Became PP-CBR
HC-SAD			Ex-DLH
HC-SAE	5109	*Azuay*	From Syndicato Condor 20 Nov, 1939. Requisitioned by Air Force
PP-CBA	5283	*Aconcagua*	Chartered from Syndicato Condor 25 April, 1941. Requisitioned by Air Force
PP-CBG	4075		Chartered from Syndicato Condor 10 Feb, 1941. Returned

SEDTA is also believed to have acquired a Messerschmitt Me 108.

Aerovías Ecuatorianas (AREA) 1951–1968

Curtiss C-46 (1951)

HC-SJA*

Douglas DC-3 (1951)

HC-ACL*	19779	HC-SJE	4425	HC-SJI	34394
HC-SJB	12374				

Boeing 307 Stratoliner (1952)

HC-SJC	2002	HC-SJD	1995	*Quito*

Avro Anson V (1953)

HC-SJJ	MDF- 295	HC-SJL	MDF- 294	HC-SJN*	MDF- 182
HC-SJK	,, 1083	HC-SJM	,, 117	HC-SJO*	,, 117

Fairchild F-27A (1959)

HC-ADV*   1A   US production prototype

Douglas DC-4 (1961)

HC-AGB	27244	*Ciudad de San Juan*
HC-AHJ*	18355	

Douglas DC-7B (1964)

HC-AIP*	45194	*Guayas*	HC-AIR	45196	*Azuay*
HC-AIQ	45195	*Pichincha*			

De Havilland Comet 4 (1966)

HC-ALT   06428

Douglas DC-7C (1968)

HC-AOR   45091

Ecuatoriana 1957–1973

Curtiss C-46 (1957)

HC-ABQ	26480	C-46A	HC-AMD	22491	C-46F

Douglas DC-6 (1958)

HC-ADJ	36326	HC-AMF	43037	HC-AQA	42859
HC-ADU	42887	HC-AMZ	42858	HC-AVF	43049
HC-AIT	42900				

Douglas DC-6B (1964)

HC-AIO   44082

Lockheed 188 Electra (1967)

HC-AMS	1002	Model A	HC-AYL	1031	,, A
HC-ANQ	1004	,, A	HC-AZJ	2004	,, C
HC-AQF	1042	,, A	N278AC	1050	,, A
HC-AVX	2002	,, C	N7138C	1087	,, A

Douglas DC-4 (1967)

HC-ANP	—	
HC-AON*	10608	Crashed at Miami 14 April, 1970. Two crew killed.*
HC-ARG	10405	
HC-ASC	36036	

*The only Ecuatoriana fatal accident.

Douglas B-23 (1968)

HC-APV   2717

Douglas DC-6A (1970)

HC-ATR   43817   HC-AVB   —

Mexico

CMA/Mexicana 1921–1965

Lincoln Standard (1921)

M-SCAE	M-SCAK	M-SCOC	M-SCOL
M-SCAI	M-SCOA	M-SCOD	M-SCOQ

The first three were probably inherited from CMTA

Fairchild FC-2 (1927)

M-SCOE	9	M-SCOY		Ciudad de Veracruz
M-SCOH		M-SCOZ		Ciudad de Mérida
M-SCOI		X-ABCM	30	
M-SCOR		X-ABCN	41	
M-SCOS		X-ABCO	143	

First seven acquired through Fairchild, last three through PAA

Travel Air (1928)

M-SCOT   M-SCOV   M-SCOW   M-SCOX

Ford 4-AT (1928)

M-SCAL   M-SCAM   M-SCAO

Stearman C-3B (1929)

X-ABCX	—
X-ABDA	147
X-ABDC	204
NC9068	209	Later X-ABDD
NC9069	213
NC8817	231

All acquired via PAA

Ford 5-AT (1929)

M-SCAN*	12	*México* Later X-ABCO, X-ABCB, XA-BCB
X-ABCA	22	
X-ABCC	11	Later XA-BCC
X-ABCD	27	X-ABCU, XA-BCU
X-ABCE	31	,, X-ABCV, XA-BCV
X-ABCF	40	,, XA-BCF
XA-BCW*	45	
XA-BCX		
XA-BKS	74	

All but the last aircraft, a 5-AT-C, were 5-AT-Bs acquired via PAA

Fairchild 71 (1929)

X-ABCG	606	X-ABCI	603
X-ABCH	618	X-ABCK	601

New, via PAA

Fokker F.VIIb/3m (1929)

X-ABCL	612	X-ABCP*	614

Both ex-PAA

Fokker F-10A (1930)

X-ABCR	1050	X-ABCS*	1053	X-ABCT	1052

All ex-PAA

Curtiss Robin (1930)

X-ABDB 300

Consolidated 20-2 Fleetster (1934)

XA-BEK 4   Transferred from Aerovías Centrales

Lockheed 10 Electra (1934)

XA-BAS*	1043	Model E		XA-BEM	1004	Model C
XA-BAU*	1041	,,	,,	XA-BEO*	1007	,, ,,
XA-BCJ	1042	,,	,,	XA-BEQ*	1022	,, ,,

All except XA-BCJ transferred from Aerovías Centrales

Lockheed 9 Orion (1936)

XA-BAY* 169 From Aerovías Centrales   XA-BDH* 174 From PAA

Boeing 247D (1936)

XA-BEY	1684	Ex-UAL	XA-BFK	1738	Ex-PCA
XA-BEZ	1713	Ex-NAT			

Douglas DC-2 (1937)

XA-BJG	1367	XA-BJL(2)	1368	XA-BKQ	1408
XA-BJI	1304	XA-BJM	1249	XA-BKV	1599
XA-BJL	1255	XA-BKO	—	XA-BKY	1371

All ex-PAA

Douglas DC-3 (1939)

XA-BLN	1989	XA-DUH*	11725	XA-HIY	20472
XA-BLO	—	XA-DUK*	11721	XA-HUS*	7388
XA-BLW	—	XA-DUM	—	XA-JAE	4961
XA-CAB	2128	XA-FEG	4180	XA-JAG	4814
XA-CAG	2228	XA-FIL	11748	XA-JAM	6043
XA-CAM	2230	XA-GAM*	4350	XA-JAN	9088
XA-CAO	2231	XA-GEU	4281	XA-JAO	13818
XA-CAY	—	XA-GEV	7339	XA-JAT	4905
XA-DEE*	2196	XA-GEW	4088	XA-JAX	—
XA-DIH	—	XA-GIB	9000	XA-JER	4889
XA-DIK*	3292	XA-GIN	—	XA-JID	4588
XA-DIN	7359	XA-GUJ	25354	XA-JIP	4301
XA-DUG	11713	XA-HAO	2193	XA-LEX	19201

Cessna T-50 (1941)

XA-BLU 1000 Ex-PAA Later XA-DOF

Douglas C-39 (1944)

XA-DOB	2088	XA-DOJ	2080	XA-DOT	2075
XA-DOH	2064	XA-DOQ	2077		
XA-DOI	2069	XA-DOS	2091		

Avro Anson V (1944)

XA-DUC   XA-DUD   XA-DUE

Douglas DC-4 (1946)

XA-FIP	10468	XA-GEC	—	XA-GUT	10394
XA-FIT	10507	XA-GIK	10367	XA-JEF	10527
XA-FIU	10532	XA-GIX	10374	XA-MIL	18325
XA-FOW*	10493				

Douglas DC-6 (1950)

XA-JOR*	43211	XA-LAV	42903	XA-MUK	43121
XA-JOS	43212	XA-MOM	43141	XA-MUV	43103
XA-JOT	43213	XA-MON	43104	XA-PON	42857
XA-LAU*	43059	XA-MOO*	42877	XA-SAN	42859

Douglas DC-6B (1953)

XA-KIQ 43836   XA-KIR 43837

Fairchild C-82A (1956)

XA-LIZ	10095	XA-LOK	10126	XB-PEX	10177
XA-LOJ	10110	XA-LOL	10136		

Douglas DC-7C (1957)

XA-LOB	45127	Bought new	XA-LOD	45129	Bought new
XA-LOC	45128	,,	XA-LOE	45130	Ex-PAA

De Havilland Comet 4C (1960)

XA-NAR 06424   XA-NAS 06425   XA-NAT 06443

De Havilland Comet 4 (1965)

XA-NAZ	06418	Ex-BOAC	Later XA-NAP	
XA-POW	06420	,,	,,	XA-NAB

CAT 1929–1932

Lockheed Vega (1929)

X-ABHA	62	Model 5B	X-ABHJ	61	Model 5B
X-ABHB	59	,, 5	X-ABHK	100	,, ,,
X-ABHC	90	,, 5B	X-ABHL	71	,, 5
X-ABHH	97	,, 5	X-ABHM	88	,, 5A
X-ABHI	103	,, 5B	X-ABHN	84	,, 5

Ryan B-1 Brougham (1929)

X-ABHD 56	X-ABHE 174	X-ABHF 175	X-ABHG 176

Bellanca P-200 Airbus (1931)

X-ABHO 701

CAT also operated Bach 3-CT-6 Air Yacht c/n 8

Aerovías Centrales 1932–1935

Fokker F-10A (1932)

X-ABEA	1014	Ex-PAA	X-ABEC	1018	Ex-PAA
X-ABEB	1016	,,	X-ABED	1022	,,

Fairchild 71 (1932)

X-ABEE 601 Ex-CMA   X-ABEF 603 Ex-CMA

Northrop Delta 1B (1933)

X-ABED* 4   Blew up on delivery flight

Lockheed Orion 9 (1934)

XA-BEI	169	via PAA	XA-BEL	174	via PAA
XA-BEJ*	173	via PAA			

Consolidated 20-2 Fleetster (1934)

XA-BEK 4 Ex-PAA

Lockheed 10-C Electra (1934)

XA-BEM	1004	Acquired via PAA
XA-BEN	1005	Ex-Cubana (via PAA)
XA-BEO	1007	Acquired new via PAA
XA-BEP	1008	,, ,, ,,
XA-BEQ	1022	,, ,, ,,

Aeronaves de México 1934-1965

Verville 104C (1934)

X-BAEW 4

Ryan B-1 Brougham (1934)

X-BAHE   174   Ex-CAT

Fokker Super Universal (1934)

X-BAHS

Bellanca CH-300 Pacemaker (1934)

| XA-BAC | XA-BAT | XA-DAF | XB-AAI |

Stinson Reliant (1935)

| XA-CAW | XB-AJI |

Beech B.17R (1938)

XA-BEV   52

Boeing 247D (1941)

XA-KAJ   1702

Waco cabin biplanes (1942)

| XA-CIH   3894 | XB-BEX   5061 | XB-KON   5062 |

Avro Anson IV and V (1944)

XA-DUD	—	XA-FUG*	96349	XA-GAK	73034
XA-DUE	—	XA-FUN	39030	XA-GAP	37263
XA-FOS	90929	XA-FUU	9686		

Douglas C-39 (1946)

XA-DOI   2069   Ex-CMA

Douglas DC-3 (1947)

XA-FEW	—		
XA-FIY	6102		Ex-Reforma
XA-FUA	3259	*Topiltzin*	Ex-LAMSA
XA-FUJ	3262	*Axayacatl*	,, ,,
XA-FUM	3255	*Ahnizotl*	,, ,,
XA-FUV	3261	*Xicotencatl*	,, ,,
XA-FUW	3260		,, ,,
XA-GAU	4085		Ex-PAA
XA-GAV	9927		Ex-Reforma
XA-GAW	9783		,, ,,
XA-GAX	10160		,, ,,
XA-GEW	4088		Ex-PAA

Douglas DC-3 contd.

XA-GII	3293	*Techotlata*	Ex-PAA
XA-GOC*	4101		,, ,,
XA-GUF	1931	*Ciudad de Durango*	,, ,,
XA-GUN*	7358		,, ,,
XA-GUQ	2149	*Hopaltzin*	Ex-Aerovías Latinas Americanas
XA-GUS	4491	*Tayoltita*	Ex-CMA
XA-GUX	4383		Ex-LAMSA
XA-HEP	7361		Ex-PAA
XA-HIP	4926		Ex-Reforma
XA-HIQ	4891		Ex-Panini
XA-HIR	3290	*Quinatzin*	,, ,,
XA-HUE	12891		Ex-Reforma
XA-HUF	19802		,, ,,
XA-HUG	19242		,, ,,
XA-HUH	20554		,, ,,
XA-HUI	18978		,, ,,
XA-JUT	3257	*Tizoc*	Ex-LAMSA
XA-KAD	4240		

*XA-GUF was at some time named *Ciudad de Nogales*

Douglas DC-4 (1949)

XA-JAV	10470	*Ciudad de Juarez/Torreón*	Ex-LAMSA
XA-KOK	10467	*Ciudad de Chihuahua*	Ex-PANAGRA
XA-LIA	10282	*Ciudad de Torreón*	Ex-Los Angeles Air Service

Convair CV-340 (1954)

XA-KIL	142	*Ciudad de México*
XA-KIM	146	*Ciudad de Puerto de Acapulco*
XA-KIN	156	*Ciudad de Guadalajara*
XA-KOU	158	*Ciudad de Tijuana*

Lockheed 049 Constellation (1957)

XA-MAG	2052		XA-MAH	2059

Bristol Britannia 302 (1957)

XA-MEC*	12918	*Tenochtitlán/Acapulco†*
XA-MED	12919	*Tzintzuntzan*

†Sometime named *Moctezuma*

Lockheed 749A Constellation (1958)

XA-MEU	2620		XA-MEW	2619	*Acapulco*
XA-MEV*	2665		XA-MOA	2534	

Douglas DC-6 (1959)

XA-JIF	43107	
XA-NAH*	43133	*Huizilihuitl*
XA-NAI	43123	*Izcoatl*
XA-NAJ	43120	*Netzahualcoyotl*

Douglas DC-6 contd.

XA-NAK	43135	*Cosijoeza/Ixtlixochtzin*
XA-NAL	43122	*Tariacuri*
XA-NAM	43132	*Moctezuma/Acampichtli*
XA-NOU	42854	*Cuitlahuac*
XA-NOY	42860	*Chimalpopoca*
XA-NOZ	42861	*Coanacochtzin*
XA-PIO	42889	*Tetlepanquetzal*
XA-PIT	42892	

Douglas DC-8-21 (1960)

XA-XAX*   45432   *20 de Noviembre*   Crashed 19 January, 1961

Douglas DC-8-51 (1962)

XA-DOD	45641	
XA-NUS*	45633	*Chapultepec*
XA-PEI*	45652	*Tenochtitlán*
XA-PIK	45685	*Chapultepec/Veracruz*
XA-SIA	45878	*Puebla*
XA-SIB	45855	*Jalisco*
XA-SID	45935	*Guanajuato*

Note: During the 1930s the airline operated a Travel Air S.6000B and a Stinson U trimotor.

Líneas Aéreas Mineras S.A. (LAMSA) 1935–1952

Sikorsky S-38B (1935)

XA-BAX   314-5   Ex-US civil

Lockheed 9 Orion (1936)

XB-AHQ   172   Ex-San Luis Mining Co

Lockheed Vega (1937)

XA-BFR*	124	Model 5B	Ex-Bowen Air Lines
XA-BFT*	50	,, 5	Ex-Braniff Airways
XA-BFU	23	,, 5	,, ,, ,,
XA-BKF	121	,, 5B	Ex-North American Aviation
XA-BLZ*	109	,, 5B	From US sources
XA-DAH*	125	,, 5B	,, ,, ,,
XA-DAI*	102	Special	,, ,, ,,
XA-DAM	127	Model 5B	,, ,, ,,
XA-DAY*	157	DL-1	,, ,, ,,
XA-DEB*	133	Model 5B	Ex-Mid-Continent Airlines
XA-DEC	60	,, 2	,, ,, ,, ,,

All except XA-DAH, XA-DAY and XA-DEB converted to Model 5C

Bach 3-CT-9K (1938)

XA-BJW

Two other aircraft of this type were operated.

Boeing 40B-4 (1941)

XA-BLY

Boeing 247D (1944)

XA-DIY	1693	XA-DON	1686	XA-DUY*	1723
XA-DIZ	1688	XA-DUX	1690		

All obtained from USA when United Air Lines bought LAMSA, changing the name Mineras to Mexicanas. XA-DIY was named *Estado de Chihuahua*.

Douglas DC-3 (1946)

XA-FUA	3259	*Ciudad de Torreón*	Ex-United Air Lines		
XA-FUJ	3262	*Ciudad de Juarez*	,,	,,	,,
XA-FUM	3255	*Ciudad de México*	,,	,,	,,
XA-FUV	3261	*Ciudad de Chihuahua*	,,	,,	,,
XA-FUW	3260	*Ciudad de Mazatlán*	,,	,,	,,
XA-GAJ	3258	(leased)	,,	,,	,,
XA-GUX	4383	*Ciudad de Durango*	,,	,,	,,
XA-JUT	3257	*Ciudad de Nueva Casas Grandes*	,,	,,	,,

Douglas DC-4 (1949)

XA-JAV   10470   *Ciudad de Juarez/Terreón*   Ex-PAA

Note: One Curtiss Robin was introduced in 1942.

Servicio Aéreo Panini 1936–1947

Travel Air S.6000B (1937)

XA-BKB

Four other examples were used.

Douglas DC-2 (1940)

XA-BKY   1371   Ex-CMA   XA-GEE*

Verville Air Coach (1941)

XA-BLX

Boeing 247D (1944)

XA-BEZ	1713	Ex-CMA	XA-FEL	1947
XA-DOM	1951	Ex-USAAF		

Douglas DC-3 (1946)

XA-FUX	XA-HIQ	4891	Ex-Aerovías Braniff
XA-FUZ	XA-HIR	3290	Ex-PAA

Lockheed Vega 5C (1947)

XA-FAF   121   Leased

Avro Anson 12 (1947)

XA-GOX   Ex-Reforma

Note: Panini had two Buhl CA-6s in 1936; a Curtiss Robin from 1937 until the early 1940s; and a Luscombe 8 in 1941. The Luscombe was written off.

Aerovías Reforma 1946–1953

Douglas DC-3 (1946)

XA-CAY*	—	XA-GAX	10160	XA-HUF	19802
XA-FIX	19217	XA-HIP	4926	XA-HUG	19242
XA-FIY	6102	XA-HIY	20472	XA-HUH	20554
XA-GAV	9927	XA-HUE	12891	XA-HUI	18978
XA-GAW	9783				

Avro Anson 12 (1947)

XA-GOX   Ex-RAF

Avro Anson IV (1948)

XA-FOU*   52450   Ex Golfo y Pacífico

Aerovías Guest 1948–1962

Douglas DC-4 (1948)

XA-GUO	—		XA-HEG*	10324	
XA-GUP	10397		XA-HEN	3110	
XA-GUT*	10394	*Asterias*	XA-HIZ	10511	
XA-GUU*	10390	*México*	XA-HOA	27243	*Llanes*
XA-HAN	—		XA-MAA	27249	

Lockheed 749 Constellation (1948)

XA-GOQ	2503	*Veracruz*	XA-LIO	2572	
XA-GOS	—		XA-LIP	2573	

Fairchild C-82A (1955)

XA-LIK   10128   Ex-USAF   XA-LIL   10117   Ex-USAF

Douglas DC-6 (1959)

XA-MUB	43129	XA-MUK	43121	XA-MUM	43134

Lockheed 1049G Super Constellation (1959)

XA-NAC	4672	XA-NAD	4677	XA-NAF	4678

De Havilland Comet 4C (1961)

XA-NAT   06443   Leased, with one other, from Mexicana

Trans Mar de Cortes 1948–1962

Douglas DC-3 (1948)

XA-FIR	13702	XA-HUE	12891	XA-JEL	12990

Fokker F.27 Friendship (1959)

XA-MOT   2   New. Owned by Aeronaves de México, operated by Trans Mar de Cortes

Aerolíneas Mexicanas 1956–1960

Douglas DC-3 (1956)

XA-FEV	—	XA-FUW	3260	XA-HUF	19802
XA-FEW	—	XA-GUX	4383		

Douglas DC-4 (1959)

XA-JAV	10470	XA-KOK	10467

Both ex-Aeronaves de México

Paraguay

Líneas Aéreas Paraguayas 1962–1977

Convair CV-240 (1962)

ZP-CDN	50	*Carlos Antonio López*
ZP-CDO	62	*General Bernardino Caballero*
ZP-CDP*	72	*José Gaspar Rodriguez de France*

All ex-ZONDA/Aerolíneas Argentinas

Lockheed 188 Electra (1969)

ZP-CBX	1032	ZP-CBY	1078	ZP-CBZ	1080

All ex-Eastern Air Lines

Douglas R4D-1 (DC-3) (1972)

ZP-CCG*   4362   Ex-Airflite

Peru

Faucett 1928–1967

Stinson Detroiter (1928)

OA-BBB*	OA-BBF
OA-BBC	OA-BBG
OA-BBD*	OA-BBI
OA-BBE	

Travel Air

OA-BBH

Stinson-Faucett F.19 (SM-6B) (1934)

OA-BBJ*	1	
OA-BBK*	2	
OA-BBL*	3	
OA-BBM	4	
OA-BBN*	5	
OA-BBO*	6	
OA-BBP*	7	Later OB-PAA-104
OA-BBQ*	8	,, OB-PAB-105
OA-BBR*	9	
OA-BBS*	10	
OA-BBT	11	Later OB-PAC-111
OA-BBU*	12	
OA-BBW*	14	Later OB-PAD-120
OA-BBX*	15	
OA-BBY*	16	
OA-BBZ*	18	Later OB-PAE-132
OA-BCA*	19	,, OB-PAF-133
OA-BCB*	24	,, OB-PAG-139
OB-PAH-140	25	,, OB-R-140
OB-PAI-141	26	,, OB-R-141
OB-PAJ-143	27	,, OB-R-143
OB-PAK-144*	28	
OB-PAO-147	29	Later OB-R-147
OB-PAR-148*	30	

Notes: The last Stinson Detroiter was used as the experimental model for the Stinson-Faucett F.19.
No.29 (OB-PAO-147, later OB-R-147) has been preserved as OA-BBQ at Jorge Chávez Airport at Lima. On 27 March, 1937, the original OA-BBQ (No.8) flew nonstop from Lima to Buenos Aires in 13 hr 38 min; piloted by Commander Armando Revoredo Iglesias.

Douglas DC-3 (1946)

OB-PAL-145*	34362	
OB-PAM-146*	34206	
OB-PAQ-167	34328	Later OB-R-167
OB-PAS-199	32729	,, OB-R-199
OB-PAT-200	32737	,, OB-R-200
OB-PAU-201*	32740	
OB-PAV-223*	26819	
OB-PAX-224*	25882	
OB-PAY-226*	25819	
OB-PBA-246	9980	Later OB-R-246
OB-PBD-456*	34356	
OB-PBF-473	7384	Later OB-R-473
OB-PBG-500	20225	,, OB-R-500
OB-PBH-530*	7331	
OB-PBJ-544	13177	Later OB-R-544
OB-PBK-551	4801	Later OB-R-551
OB-PBN-659*	25839	
OB-PBO-676	26360	,, OB-R-676
OB-PHI-516	26184	,, OB-R-516

Douglas DC-4 (1946)

OB-PAP-148*	10284	Later OB-R-148
OB-PAZ-228*	10277	
OB-PBB-247*	7462	Later OB-R-247
OB-PBC-248	10285	,, OB-R-248
OB-PBE-463	18328	,, OB-R-463
OB-PBM-625	10511	,, OB-R-625
OB-R-776*	10591	
OB-R-847	27253	

Douglas DC-6B (1960)

OB-PBL-552†	44256		OB-R-827	44433
OB-R-746	43838		OB-R-846	44432
OB-R-750	45505		OB-R-920	45176

†Later OB-R-552

Cóndor Peruana 1937–1941

Curtiss Condor BT-32 (1937)

OA-FFA-272	59	*Iquitos*	New	Later	OA-IIA-310
OA-FFB-273	60	*Cuzco*	,,	,,	OA-IIB-311
OA-FFC-274	61	*Madre de Dios*	,,	,,	OA-IIC-312
OA-FFD-275	62		,,	,,	OA-IID-313

When the Cóndor fleet received their second registrations, in 1939, the airline had been renamed Línea de Aviación Cóndor. All aircraft were taken over by the Peruvian Government and used by the Fuerza Aérea del Perú for several years.

Deutsche Lufthansa Sucursal en Perú 1938–1941

Junkers-Ju 52/3m (1938)

OA-HHA-294	5272	Taken over by Peruvian Govt
OA-HHB	5261	
OA-HHC-304	5060	Taken over by Peruvian Govt
OA-HHD	—	

Peruvian International Airways 1947–1949

Douglas DC-4 (1947)

OB-SAA-170	10277	OB-SAC-172	10341	OB-SAE-174	10393
OB-SAB-171	10343	OB-SAD-173	10290	OB-SAF-175*	10286

Trinidad and Tobago

British West Indian Airways (BWIA) 1940–1964

Lockheed 18 Lodestar (1940)

VP-TAE	1954	Ex-TACA
VP-TAN	2330	Ex-USAAF C-60A
VP-TAO	2442	,, ,, ,,
VP-TAP	2319	,, ,, ,,
VP-TAQ	2543	,, ,, ,,

Lockheed 14-H (1942)

VP-TAF	1439A	Ex-TACA		VP-TAH*	1406	Ex-TACA

Lockheed 12-A (1942)

VP-TAI 1203 Ex-Aero Research & Sales

Lockheed Hudson IIIA (1944)

VP-TAJ	7452	VP-TAK*	7569	VP-TAL	7560
		All ex-RAF (Canada)			

Vickers-Armstrongs Viking (1948)

VP-TAT	119	*Trinidad*	Ex-BEA/BSAA
VP-TAU	122	*Antigua*	,, ,, ,,
VP-TAV	110	*Jamaica*	,, ,, ,,
VP-TAW	111	*Grenada*	,, ,, ,,
VP-TAX	112	*Barbados*	,, ,, ,,
VP-TAZ	129	*British Honduras*	Ex-BEA
VP-TBB	137	*Bahamas*	,, ,,
VP-TBC	138	*British Guiana*	,, ,,

Short S.A.6 Sealand 1 (1949)

VP-TBA	SH.1565	*St Vincent*	Not put into regular service
VP-TBB	SH.1566		Not delivered
VP-TBC	SH.1567		,, ,,

Douglas DC-3 (1952)

VP-TBE	9885	*St Kitts*	Ex-Bahamas Airways		
VP-TBF	13114		,, ,, ,,	Later	9Y-TBF
VP-TBJ	33189	*Tobago*	Ex-RAF	,,	9Y-TBJ
VP-TBW	13173		Ex-DLH/Skyways	,,	9Y-TBW
9Y-TCR	13114		Ex-LIAT		

Vickers-Armstrongs Viscount (1955)

VP-TBK	71	V.702	New, via BOACAC	
VP-TBL	72	,,	,, ,, ,,	
VP-TBM	73	,,	,, ,, ,,	
VP-TBN	81	,,	,, ,, ,,	Later 9Y-TBN
VP-TBS	235	V.772	,, ,, ,,	,, 9Y-TBS
VP-TBT	236	,,	,, ,, ,,	,, 9Y-TBT
VP-TBU	237	,,	,, ,, ,,	,, 9Y-TBU
VP-TBX	238	,,	,, ,, ,,	,, 9Y-TBX
VP-TBY	78	V.736	Leased from Fred Olsen	

Uruguay

PLUNA 1936–1969

De Havilland D.H.90 Dragonfly (1936)

CX-AAR	7532	*Churrinche*	CX-AAS	7534	*San Alberto*

De Havilland D.H.86 (1938)

CX-AAH	2325	*Santa Rosa de Lima*	D.H.86	Ex-British Airways
CX-ABG	2346	*San Felipe y Santiago*	D.H.86A	,, ,, ,,

Potez 621 (1942)

CX-ADH	64027	Ex-Air France

Douglas DC-2 (1944)

CX-AEF	1351	*Espiritu de las Americas*	Ex-PAA
CX-AEG	1324		,, ,,

Douglas C-47/DC-3 (1945)

CX-AFE	32551	CX-AJZ	2266	CX-BDF	4400
CX-AGD	13306	CX-AQC	9226	CX-BDG	19212
CX-AGE*	12113	CX-BDA	12083	CX-BDH	12863
CX-AIJ	4471†	CX-BDB	33392		

*Crashed on test flight 9 October, 1962. This was PLUNA's only fatal accident and did not involve passengers.
†*Paysandu*

De Havilland D.H.114 Heron 1B (1953)

CX-AOR	14019	CX-AOU	14045	CX-AOV	14046
CX-AOS	14025				

Vickers-Armstrongs Viscount V.769D (1958)

CX-AQN	321	
CX-AQO	322	*Libertador General José de San Martin*
CX-AQP	323	*General José Artigas*

Vickers-Armstrongs Viscount V.745D (1967)

CX-BHA	130	*Presidente Gestido*	Ex-Alitalia
CX-BHB	131		,, ,,

CAUSA 1938–1967

Junkers-Ju 52/3m (1938)

CX-ABA	5877	*El Uruguayo*	CX-ABB	5886	*El Argentino*

Short S.25 Sunderland (1946)

CX-AFA*	SH.5C	*General Artigas*	Mk.3	Ex-RAF
CX-AKF	SH.6C		Mk.3	Ex-ALFA
CX-AKR	SH.60C	*Capitan Bosio Lanza*	Mk.5	Ex-RAF

*Written off 11 September, 1956.

Short S.25 Sandringham 7 (1950)

CX-ANA*	SH.59C	Ex-BOAC	CX-ANI	SH.58C	Ex-BOAC

*Written off 22 October, 1955

Curtiss C-46 (1961)

CX-AYR	22403	C-46F	CX-BAH	22531	C-46F
CX-AZS	30393	C-46A	CX-BAM	22392	C-46F

Lockheed 749A Constellation (1963)

CX-BBM 2661   CX-BBN 2641   CX-BCS 2640

ARCO 1964–1981

Curtiss C-46 (1964)

CX-AYR	22403	C-46F		CX-BAH	22531	C-46F
CX-AZS	30393	C-46A		CX-BAM	22392	C-46F

Convair CV-240 (1970)

CX-BHC 18   CX-BHS 20   CX-BHT 33

Convair CV-600 (1976)

CX-BJL 92 Ex-US civil   CX-BOJ 13 Ex-Bar Harbor Airlines (USA)

TAMU 1970–1980

Douglas DC-3 (1970)

CX-AFE	32551	CX-BHO/509	—	CX-BJD/508	13744
CX-AGD/525	13306	CX-BHP/516	25608	CX-BJG/510	19021
CX-AIJ/524	4471	CX-BHQ/519	33431	CX-BJH/511	34881
CX-AQC/523	9226	CX-BHR/521	19231	CX-BKH/514	20604

Fokker F.27 Friendship (1970)

CX-BHV/T-560 10199   CX-BHW/T-561 10202

Fairchild FH-227D (1971)

CX-BHX/T-570 571   CX-BHY/T-571* 572   CX-BIM/T-572 574

*Crashed in the Andes 13 October, 1972, and found ten weeks later.

Embraer EMB-110C (1975)

CX-BJB/T-582	081	CX-BJE/T-584*	083	CX-BJK/T-581	079
CX-BJC/T-583	082	CX-BJJ/T-580	076	CX-BKF/T-585	187†

*EMB-110P1

Venezuela

Aéropostale 1930–1934

Latécoère 28 (1930)

YV-ABA	961	*Mariscal Sucre*	New aircraft
YV-ABE	962	*General Paez*	,, ,,
YV-ABI	963	*General Urdaneta*	,, ,,
YV-ABO	911	*General Marino*	From Aéropostale (France)
YV-ABU	913	*General Bermudez*	,, ,, ,,

LAV (Aeropostal Venezolana) 1936–1964

Fairchild 82B (1936)

YV-ABO 46	YV-ABU 47	YV-ACA 49

Lockheed 10 Electra (1937)

YV-ACE*	1078	YV-ACU	1111	YV-ADU	1143
YV-ACI	1079	YV-ADA*	1126	YV-AFA	1144
YV-ACO	1110	YV-ADE	1132		

Bought new. C/n 1111 was Model 10-E, others were Model 10-A.

Lockheed 14 (1939)

YV-ADI* 1509	YV-ADO* 1510

Lockheed 18 Lodestar (1942)

YV-AFI	2166	Ex-Defense Supply Corp
YV ΛFO	2218	
YV-AGA	2504	Ex-USAAF C-60A
YV-AGE	2389	,, ,, ,,
YV-AGI	2390	,, ,, ,,

Douglas DC-3 (1945)

YV-C-ACO	19241	YV-C-AKO	9174	YV-C-AMO	13656
YV-C-AFA*	4525	YV-C-AKU*	4581	YV-C-AMP*	19292
YV-C-AFE*	26798	YV-C-ALA	9750	YV-C-AMQ	19053
YV-C-AFO	13699	YV-C-ALE	4537	YV-C-AMU*	9512
YV-C-AGI	10111	YV-C-ALI	6210	YV-C-ANA	12932
YV-C-AGU*	4205	YV-C-ALO*	—	YV-C-ANG	—
YV-C-AHA	—	YV-C-ALU*	4791	YV-C-ANH	20595
YV-C-AHI*	34254	YV-C-AMD	20037	YV-C-ANI	42960
YV-C-AHO*	—	YV-C-AMF	6115	YV-C-ANL	—
YV-C-AKA	4449	YV-C-AMG	4458	YV-C-ANQ	25264
YV-C-AKE*	4705	YV-C-AMH	19783	YV-C-ANR	11687

Most of LAV's 33 DC-3s were ex-USAAF, as war surplus equipment through the Reconstruction Finance Corporation. Thirteen C-47/DC-3s also acquired from TACA de Venezuela—making a total of 46.

Lockheed 049 Constellation (1946)

YV-C-AME   2081   *Simón Bolívar*
YV-C-AMI   2082   *Francisca de Miranda*

Lockheed 749 Constellation (1947)

YV-C-AMA*   2560   *José Marti*
YV-C-AMU   2561   *Antonio José de Sucre*

Martin 2-0-2 (1947)

YV-C-AMB   9130   *Rafael Urdaneta*   YV-C-AMC   9131   *Andres Bello*

Curtiss C-46 (1951)

YV-C-AMK*   254   C-46A   YV-C-AMN   30318   C-46A
YV-C-AML   32836   C-46D   YV-C-AMR   415   ,,

Lockheed 1049E Super Constellation (1954)

YV-C-AMS*   4561   *Rafael Urdaneta*   YV-C-AMT*   4562   *Simón Bolívar*

Lockheed 1049G Super Constellation (1956)

YV-C-AME   4636   YV-C-ANC*   4575   YV-C-ANE   4577
YV-C-AMI   4674   YV-C-AND   4576   YV-C-ANF†   4562
YV-C-ANB   4572

†YV-C-AMT rebuilt.

Vickers-Armstrongs Viscount (1956)

YV-C-AMB   24   V.701, ex-BEA
YV-C-AMT   81   V.702, ex-BWIA
YV-C-AMU   235   V.772   ,,   ,,
YV-C-AMV*   94   V.749   *Arichuna*   Bought new
YV-C-AMX*   95   ,,   *Marca*   ,,
YV-C-AMZ*   96   ,,   ,,

Fairchild C-123 (1972)*

YV-C-ANI   Cargo aircraft leased from Air Force

LAV purchased its first Hawker Siddeley HS.748 in 1965 and then standardized on HS.748s and Douglas DC-9s.
*Although not delivered until 1972 the C-123 is included because it is believed to be the only example used by an airline.

AVENSA 1943–1970

Ford 5-AT (1943)

No registrations known, c/ns 22, 54 and 61

Douglas C-39 (1944)

YV-AVG	2057	YV-AVK	2083
YV-AVJ	2060	YV-AVL	2085

— 2074

All ex-USAAF

Douglas DC-3 (1945)

YV-C-AVA	20225	YV-C-AVJ	11649	YV-C-AVS	4372
YV-C-AVB	11620	YV-C-AVK	9049	YV-C-AVU*	4432
YV-C-AVC	4958	YV-C-AVL	4269	YV-C-AVV	—
YV-C-AVD	4955	YV-C-AVM	4086	YV-C-AVX*	7391
YV-C-AVE	4179	YV-C-AVN*	19984	YV-C-AVY	4785
YV-C-AVF	6321	YV-C-AVO	4863	YV-C-AVY	11772
YV-C-AVG*	4762	YV-C-AVP	3291	YV-C-AVZ	4551
YV-C-AVI	2195	YV-C-AVQ	2232	YV-C-EVM	13372
YV-C-AVJ	2194	YV-C-AVR	20558	YV-C-EVO	4240
YV-C-AVJ	4202				

Mostly acquired from USAAF or PAA. The last DC-3s (c/ns 11649 and 11772) were acquired in 1969.

Douglas DC-4 (1952)

YV-C-AVH	7480	YV-C-AVT	18335	YV-C-EVB	10408

Convair CV-340 (1953)

YV-C-AVC	122	Ex-KLM		
YV-C-AVD	143	,,		
YV-C-AVH	236	Bought new	Later YV-55C	
YV-C-AVT	237	,,	,,	
YV-C-EVA	139	,,	,,	Later YV-60C
YV-C-EVE	149	,,	,,	
YV-C-EVI	164	,,	,,	Later YV-62C

Curtiss C-46 (1955)

YV-C-AVB	30573	C-46A	YV-C-EVF*	22577	C-46F
YV-C-AVF			YV-C-EVL*		
YV-C-AVK	26465	C-46A			

Convair CV-440 (1957)

YV-C-AVZ	445	YV-C-EVD	485	YV-C-EVJ	446

Converted to CV-580

Douglas DC-6B (1958)

YV-C-EVG	44111	Ex-PAA	YV-C-EVR	44109	Ex-PAA

Fairchild F-27 (1958)

YV-C-EVH*	12	YV-C-EVP	25		YV-C-EVS	24
YV-C-EVK	13	YV-C-EVQ	26			

Convair CV-580 (1964)

YV-C-AVA	161	Later YV-53C	YV-C-EVD	485	Later YV-61C
YV-C-AVG	157	,, YV-54C	YV-C-EVJ	446	,, YV-63C
YV-C-AVP	454	,, YV-56C	YV-C-EVS	15	,, YV-64C
YV-C-AVZ	445	,, YV-59C			

Sud-Aviation Caravelle III (1964)

YV-C-AVI* 20 Ex-VARIG

TACA de Venezuela 1944-1952

Beech 18 (1944)

YV-AZB 177 Ex-Prairie Airways (Canada)

A second Beech 18 was used but its identity has not been traced.

Douglas C-39 (1944)

YV-AZF 2068   YV-AZI 1509

These, plus c/n 2070, were ex-USAAF.

Douglas DC-3 (1945)

YV-C-AZA†	43079		YV-C-AZN	9661
YV-C-AZC†	25278		YV-C-AZO†	19385
YV-C-AZD	11653		YV-C-AZP	20750
YV-C-AZF†	43078		YV-C-AZQ†	19986
YV-C-AZH	26267		YV-C-AZR†	9882
YV-C-AZI	34368		YV-C-AZS†	4773
YV-C-AZJ†	19193		YV-C-AZT†	19141
YV-C-AZK†	19121		YV-C-AZV†	13449
YV-C-AZL	19122		YV-C-AZX†	19411
YV-C-AZM	19189		YV-C-AZY†	43077

†Transferred to LAV (Aeropostal) when TACA assets were acquired.
The first four and last four DC-3s listed except YV-C-ACX were transferred from TACA associated companies in Colombia, Costa Rica and Salvador. All others ex-USAAF.
Venezuelan registrations were often repeated when aircraft were replaced.

Transportes Aéreos Centro-Americanos, S.A. (TACA) 1931–1981

This airline's multi-national base during its early period under the direction of Lowell Yerex makes the compilation of a registration list, by country, almost impossible. Complete Yerex records—if they ever existed—are beyond recall. Before 1942, almost every aircraft flew under two registrations, one of which was normally Honduran. After 1942, El Salvador replaced Honduras as the common denominator. In many cases, three registrations are known for the same aircraft. For the period of Yerex control, therefore, the tabular arrangement in this appendix has been modified. It has also been extended to include the period under Waterman control.

| | 1931–1956 | | |
Type	Introduced	Number Operated	Known c/ns
Stinson Junior	1931	5	10001, 10002, 10003
Stinson Model U	1932	2	9023
Stearman	1933	1	
Ford 4-AT	1933	2	39, 64
Bellanca CH-300 Pacemaker	1933	2	153, 156
Fokker Universal	1934	2	443
Bellanca CH-400 Skyrocket	1934	3	601, 615, 627
Waco C	1934	1	
Ford 5-AT	1935	24	4, 7, 8, 11, 13, 14, 16, 18, 26, 28, 30, 31, 35, 36, 39, 43, 52, 64, 71, 73, 75, 89, 90, 103
Kreutzer K-5	1935	2	104, 113
Hodkinson Trimotor	1935	1	
Fleet	1935	1	
Curtiss Kingbird	1935	3	
Ryan B-1 Brougham	1935	1	
Bellanca 300W Pacemaker	1937	1	147
Flamingo G.2	1937	5	2, 3, 4, 18, 19
Bellanca 31.50 SR Skyrocket	1937	2	804, 815
Lockheed Vega 5A	1938	1	96
Lockheed 14-H	1938	6	1401, 1403, 1405, 1406, 1432, 1439A
Lockheed 10-A Electra	1939	4	1084, 1104, 1133, 1134
Travel Air 6000	1940	7	892
Stinson SR-8 Reliant	1940	1	9825
Hamilton	1940	1	
Pilgrim 100A	1940	3	6000 (Model 100), 6602, 6608
Stinson Model A	1940	1	
Lockheed 18 Lodestar	1940	16	1954, 2232, 2274, 2291, 2292, 2299, 2301, 2302, 2374, 2450, 2476, 2493, 2547, 2561, 2566, 2568

Curtiss Condor T-32C	1942	3	21, 31, 39
Beech 18	1942	4	171, 178, 221, 365
Lockheed 12	1943	1	1202
Vultee V-1A	1943	1	45
Burnelli UB-14B	1943	1	
Grumman G-21A Goose	1944	1	1175
Douglas C-39	1944	1	2086
Douglas DC-3	1945	39	2210, 4290, 4332, 4338, 4410, 4773, 4825, 4889, 4910, 6138, 6350, 7333, 9090, 9884, 11653, 11724, 12061, 12062, 12204, 13372, 13449, 13819, 19046, 19141, 19214, 19242, 19725, 19779, 25227, 25245, 25246, 25278, 25452, 25481, 26078, 34406, 43077, 43078, 43079
Lockheed Hudson	1945	6	6082, 6116, 6130, 6306, 6330, 6337
Douglas DC-4	1946	4	10468, 10474, 42904, 42915
Curtiss C-46A	1946	2	261, 432
Junkers-Ju 52/3m	1947	1	5283
Avro Anson V	1947	3	1151, BRU-1456

1957–1977

Vickers-Armstrongs Viscount (1957)

YS-06C	324	V.784D	Leased from Philippine Air Lines
YS-07C	286	V.798D	Ex-Hawaiian Airlines
YS-08C	332	V.786D	*El Centroamericano*. New, built for LAC Colombia
YS-09C*	82	V.763D	New, built for Howard Hughes
YS-11C	333	V.786D	Ex-LANICA
YS-28C	212	V.745D	Ex-United Air Lines

BAC One-Eleven 400 (1966)

YS-01C	108	*El Izalco*	Ex-LACSA
YS-17C	093	*El Centroamericano*	New
YS-18C	106	*El Salvador*	,,

Douglas DC-6A (1971)

YS-35C	45323	YS-38C	44260	Leased
YS-37C	44255	YS-39C	45217	

Canadair CL-44 (1974)

YS-04C   1   Ex-RCAF

Lockheed 188AF Electra (1976)

YS-06C   1147   YS-07C*   1069   *Pangeran Diponegoro*

NYRBA 1929–1930

Sikorsky S-38A (1929)

NC5933   14-A   *Washington*

Sikorsky S-38B (1929)

NC8044	14-10	*Montevideo*
NC9107	114-6	
NC9775	114-2	
NC73K	214-4	*Montevideo*[2]
NC75K	214-6	
NC113M	214-10	*Porto Alegre* (also named *Pernambuco*)
NC146M	214-17	
NC943M	314-1	*Haiti*
NC944M	314-2	*San Juan*
NC946M	314-4	*Port of Spain*
NC301N	214-19	*Bahia*
NC302N	214-20	*Tampa* (also named *São Luis*)
NC304N	414-2	
NC308N	414-6	*Porto Alegre*[2]

Ford 4-AT-A (1929)

NC1780   11   *Río de la Plata*

Sikorsky S-37 (1929)

NC1283   1   *Southern Star*   NC942M   2   Not delivered

Ford 5-AT-C (1929)

NC8417	55	*Santiago* (also named *Mendoza*)
NC402H	61	*Santiago*[2]
NC404H	63	*Salta*

Consolidated 16 Commodore (1929)

NC658M	2	*Rio de Janeiro*
NC659M	3	*Havana*
NC660M	4	*Cuba*
NC661M	5	*New York* (also named *Santos*)
NC662M	6	*Uruguay* (also named *São Paulo*)
NC663M	7	*Porto Rico*
NC664M	8	*Port-au-Prince*
NC665M	9	*Argentina*
NC666M	10	*Miami*
NC855M	1	*Buenos Aires*

NYRBA ordered 14 Commodores but only 10 were delivered before the Pan American Airways takeover.

Fleet 2 (1929)

NC632M   202   NC633M   203   NC634M   204

Consolidated 17 Fleetster (1929)

NC657M   1   NC671M   2   NC672M   4

Lockheed 3 Air Express (1930)

NC514E   65   *Maracá*   NC307H   77   *Marajó*

Consolidated 20 Fleetster (1930)

NC673M   1   NC674M   2   NC675M   4

Some aircraft were registered to NYRBA, some to Tri-Motor Safety Airways Corporation and others to New York Safety Airways Corp.
All the aircraft in this fleet list are shown with US registrations but some carried Argentine and Brazilian markings.

PANAGRA 1928–1967

Fairchild FC-2 (1928)

NC6853   139   P.1   NC8023   168

Fairchild FC-2W2 (1928)

NC8026   519   NC9715   532
NC8039   529   P.4   NC9723*   527   P.3

Fairchild 71 (1929)

NC9798   619   P.6

Loening Air Yacht (1929)

NC9717*   215   P.7

Curtiss Kingbird (1929)

NC310N   G-2

Ford 5-AT (1929)

NC8416	54	P.8	*Santa Rosa*	NC400H	59	P.9	*Santa Mariana*
NC8417*	55	P.18	*San Pedro*	NC402H	61	P.19	*San Pablo*
NC8418*	56	P.10	*San Cristobal*	NC403H*	62		*San José*
NC9639	17	P.27	*San Fernando*	NC407H*	66	P.24	
NC9672	22		*San Antonio*	NC433H*	100	P.22	*San Felipe*

From 1934–35 some Fords were operated by PANAGRA subsidiary Aerovías Peruanas. These were: OA-AAA (c/n 17), OA-AAB (c/n 61), OA-AAC (c/n 54) and OA-AAD (c/n 59).

Sikorsky S-38B (1929)

NC144M	214-15	P.17		NC18V	414-9
NC945M	314-3	P.13	*San Juan*	NC19V	414-10
NC300N	214-18			NC22V	414-13

Lockheed Vega 5B (1930)

NC9424 78 P.14   NC397H 82 P.15

Acquired from US sources.

Fleet 2 (1930)

R 146   Ex-NYRBA   R 147   Ex-NYRBA

Curtiss Falcon (1930)

NC7455 3 P.16 Ex-Charles Lindbergh

Douglas DC-2 (1934)

NC13729	1255	P.35		NC14273*	1306		
NC14268	1301	P.28	*Santa Ana*	NC14292*	1352	P.31	*Santa Silvia*
NC14270	1303	P.29	*San Martin*	NC14298*	1370	P.32	*Santa Elena*
NC14272*	1305	P.30	*Santa Lucia*				

Sikorsky S-43 (1936)

NC15065* 4305 P.33 *Santa Maria*   NC16928* 4317

Boeing B-1E (1936)

NC5270 1028

Consolidated 16 Commodore (1937)

NC668M 12

Douglas DC-3 (1937)

NC14967	2190	NC21718	2134	NC30092	11775
NC14996	2191	NC25652	2192	NC33645*	4124
NC15583	4867	NC28334	4800	NC39334	7331
NC18118	1994	NC28335	4801	NC49550	11771
NC18119	1995	NC28380	3284	NC54213	4432
NC18936	2011	NC30008	4177	NC54311	4830
NC19364	12570	NC30009	4178	NC86564	4415
NC19470*	11680	NC30014	4183	NC86565	4516
NC19912	11716	NC30031	6333	NC88726	13056
NC19913	11718	NC30091	11774	NC88754	34356

DC-3s with c/ns 4801, 4830 and 11771, were re-equipped with Pratt & Whitney R-2000s especially for operation at Quito (elevation more than 9,000 ft).

Stinson SR-10F Reliant (1942)

NC26215   7-5940   P.40

Almost all PANAGRA aircraft before 1942 were from PAA sources including NYRBA. The last DC-2 and the S-43s were new, and Ford 5-AT c/n 17 was from TWA.

Douglas DC-4 (1946)

NC15568	10374	NC88817	18328	NC88934	10366
NC60114	18335	NC88904	18391	NC88937	18391
NC60115	10467	NC88925	10368	NC91067	10295
NC79012	10274	NC88929	10407		

Douglas DC-6 (1947)

N90876	42876	N90878	42878	N8103H	43103
N90877	42877	N6141C	43141	N8104H	43104

Douglas DC-6B (1952)

N6255C	44255	N6536C	43536	N6537C	43537
N6256C	44256				

Douglas DC-7B (1955)

N51244	45244	N51701	44701	N51703	44703
N51700	44700	N51702*	44702	N51704	44704

Douglas DC-6A (1959)

N7822C   45520   Leased from PAA

Douglas DC-8-31 (1960)

N8274H   45274   N8276H   45726   N8277H   45277
N8275H   45275

Douglas DC-8-55F (1966)

N1509U   45858   Leased from Douglas

The last two DC-7Bs and all the DC-8s were transferred to Braniff at the merger. Five DC-8-62s on order for PANAGRA were delivered to Braniff.

Index

All entries are contained in one single index. References to items other than in the main text are dealt with by suffixes, as follows: A = Appendix, C = Chart, E = Exhibit, G = Chart (genealogical), M = Map, P = Photograph, T = Table.

Entries are according to the significant name. Thus, Líneas Aéreas de Nicaragua is under Nicaragua, as there could be uncertainty as to whether the prefix is Líneas, Aerolíneas, Cía, or Transportes. The entry is also repeated by the acronym, and is only cross-referenced (with the acronym taking precedence) if there are several secondary references under the same name. The prefixes or suffixes S.A. or Ltda, etc are omitted, except when their omission could be misleading. Major airline or aircraft references are shown in bold type. Abbreviations are freely employed, e.g.: Arg = Argentina, Bol = Bolivia, Braz = Brazil, Col = Colombia, C.R. = Costa Rica, D.R. = Dominican Republic, Ec = Ecuador, El S = El Salvador, Hon = Honduras, Mex = Mexico, Nic = Nicaragua, Par = Paraguay, Uru = Uruguay, Ven = Venezuela, V.I. = Virgin Islands, W.I. = West Indies.

Commonly-used phrases such as Líneas Aéreas de. . . are shown as L.A. de. . . Aero-related words such as Aéreo, Aerovías, Aerolíneas, Aeronaves, Acrotransportes, etc are sometimes abbreviated to A.

Aircraft are normally listed by manufacturer and type only, and referenced under an operating airline only to draw attention to a special aircraft-related event. This also applies to photographs.

667

670

671

672

674

675

677

681

683

684

685

692

693

694

697

698